KEATING

KEATING

KERRY O'BRIEN

ALLEN&UNWIN
SYDNEY·MELBOURNE·AUCKLAND·LONDON

First published in 2015

Allen & Unwin
83 Alexander Street
Crows Nest NSW 2065
Australia
Phone: (61 2) 8425 0100
Email: info@allenandunwin.com
Web: www.allenandunwin.com

Cataloguing-in-Publication details are available
from the National Library of Australia
www.trove.nla.gov.au

ISBN 978 1 76011 162 5
ISBN 978 1 76029 2195 (special edition)

Set in 11.5/17 pt Minion Pro by Midland Typesetters, Australia

Printed and bound in Australia by Griffin Press

10 9 8 7 6 5 4 3 2 1

MIX
Paper from
responsible sources
FSC® C009448
www.fsc.org

The paper in this book is FSC certified.
FSC promotes environmentally responsible,
socially beneficial and economically viable
management of the world's forests.

CONTENTS

INTRODUCTION

I have known Paul Keating for 40 years. I was first introduced to him in the non-members' bar of the old Parliament House when he was a hungry young backbencher in the Whitlam Opposition in 1975, and I suppose I was a hungry young journalist working for an ABC program called *This Day Tonight*. I met him again the day he became Gough Whitlam's youngest and last ministerial appointment, three weeks before the Dismissal. He already had the swagger and an eye for a good suit, and he had future leader written all over him.

I saw Keating at work inside the political system when I was press secretary to Whitlam in his final stint as Opposition leader in 1977, and to deputy leader Lionel Bowen until 1980. Keating was constantly in and out of both offices, his influence and stature growing by the month. I watched him cut his teeth as a brash young parliamentarian. I was also exposed as much to the views of his enemies as his friends, and heard all the criticisms as well as the accolades.

Over the decades of watching politics closely and after countless television interviews with Paul Keating, many of them tense, we have developed what might be described as a relaxed professional relationship rather than a friendship, within which he's never stopped being a political animal and I've never stopped being a journalist.

It's a lonely business, politics. Friendships between politicians aren't impossible and can be deep, but most seem to have a limited life. Very few endure. Journalists, on the other hand, are so endlessly fascinated by power that they wouldn't know whether a relationship with a politician is friendship, or just a reflection of that fascination mixed with varying degrees of respect and mutual self-interest.

When we were negotiating the ABC television series, apart from a request for minimal intrusion on his family life, Keating's only caveat was that the conversations be more discursive than the combative style of the usual *7.30* political interviews, which was what I'd intended anyway.

You can still be the tiger, he said, and I'll be the tamer.

When we recorded the conversations for the series, my focus was so centred on the challenge at hand that I dismissed all thought of extending the material into a book. Besides, there were already three biographies, Don Watson's prime ministerial portrait, and various other credible accounts of Keating's time as Treasurer and Prime Minister.

What ultimately drew me to this exercise, apart from the overwhelming response the series created, was that our sixteen hours of conversation left me with as many questions as they gave me answers. Powerful medium though it is, the limitations of television and the tyranny of the ticking clock meant that after the extensive edit, many topics were touched on but not exhausted, and others were not even raised. For instance, media policy has always been one of the great Labor obsessions, and no one was more obsessed than Paul Keating, but I felt if we didn't have the time to tackle that topic properly then we shouldn't waste precious time on it at all.

I was particularly frustrated, and I know Keating was too, by the impossible task of doing justice to the policy and politics of four-and-a-quarter years of the prime ministership in one hour. Looking back twenty years after it all ended, I was surprised how much ground there was to cover, and how much was left unanalysed.

We are never going to get an autobiography from Paul Keating, which is pretty extraordinary given his impact on modern Australia. He's been consistent in saying that for many years. Yet it's clear he cares about his place in history, which was his incentive in cooperating with the television series and now the book. At the same time I could see as we travelled through the years that reliving the times is surprisingly painful for him, a tacit acknowledgement that even the most successful political lives do come at a cost. Probably the more successful, the bigger the cost.

Keating's regret and frustration over the relationship with Bob Hawke is particularly palpable, that such a productive partnership could end so bitterly, and he and Hawke will never agree now on why it failed. On the one hand, Keating wants the strength of the relationship and its legacy to be properly understood. On the other, you get the sense he'll never come to terms with his own bitterness over its ultimate collapse.

In the same way, he still seethes at his recollections of the schism between he and his office and the Labor Party's campaign office during the 1996 election campaign. He will never accept that party officials might be smarter on campaign strategy than a leader who had been making sharp political judgements daily for thirteen years, and is particularly angry that they didn't give him even a sliver of a chance of beating John Howard. It says something about the intensity and complexity of the man that he still can't let go all these years later.

I have read a lot of biographies over many years, some of which have been superb. But often you emerge with a sense that the authentic voice of the subject is leached out to varying degrees in the filtering process. David Marr's biography of Patrick White was one wonderful exception, not least because Marr had the great good sense to let White's own voice come through from his copious letters.

With a political autobiography you might get the authentic voice of the politician but the self-serving side of the enterprise will not be tempered by the challenge of an honest broker that you will hopefully get from a biographer.

I am neither Paul Keating's biographer nor his ghostwriter, and I'm not aware there's been an exercise quite like this before. What I think and hope has emerged with this book is an amalgam of the two; that, along with the Keating's authentic voice in a series of free-wheeling conversations, are some robust challenges to his account of the political history he lived through and his part in it; and that readers get enough of both to make up their own minds about what this notable political life represents.

In shaping those conversations I have drawn on many thousands of pages of Keating biographies and other excellent accounts of the political times in which he lived, including biographies of other politicians, autobiographies, memoirs, political diaries and other works of political history including Paul Kelly's seminal work; on thousands of newspaper articles collected week by week through Keating's career, many unflattering to him; hundreds of pages of interviews recorded with all the key Hawke Cabinet ministers for the ABC's groundbreaking *Labor in Power* series; Cabinet documents and Keating's own extensive notes of milestone meetings such as the Mabo negotiations, providing further intimate insights to history.

I found Keating's digitised newspaper archive fascinating to flick through because, even allowing for imperfections within stories, the patterns that emerged from issue to issue, from event to event as recounted or analysed by five or six different reporters or commentators, were often very revealing of the times. And then there were the insights from his comments in the margins.

As well as the sixteen hours of conversations for the ABC series, I recorded a further sixteen hours in a series of sessions in Keating's Potts Point, Sydney office over eighteen months. Many of the questions were less about the detail of policies than about getting a true sense of how he functioned, how he related to others, how he won his big reform battles, how he regrouped after the losses, and his methods as he came to dominate both his party and the Parliament. But within the framework of Keating's account of those times, what I really wanted to do was provide an intimate study of leadership wrapped in a powerful and complex personality, including, as Patrick White so nicely put it, the flaws in the glass.

Keating said to me at one point that this exercise had justified his determination not to write an autobiography, that this process had forced him to think about and deal with many questions that would never have occurred to him to reflect on—and that it was therefore more complete than anything he might have written himself.

The book is peppered with remembered conversations in quotes. It goes without saying these are paraphrased from memory and should be judged in that light, but very often the sense of them is substantiated by the record, or by the accounts of others.

My one concession to Paul Keating through this process was to allow him to read back through the edited material, not to change the sense of anything he'd said or to take anything back, but occasionally to improve the flow of his words for the page. I felt he had a point: that we were recording the whole conversation orally, but it was to be published in book form. He was true to his word. No attempt at censorship, no changes of heart, but a definite improvement at times in the way it read.

I wasn't interested in being drawn into direct comparisons between Keating and other post-war political leaders. Too many complications, too many what ifs. It's the sort of pontificating that's better left to dinner parties and university lecture halls. It is enough for me to see this man, flaws and all, as one of the standout figures since Federation.

Keating was surrounded by talent, particularly in the Hawke Cabinets and happily acknowledges that the Australian public's extraordinary love affair with Bob Hawke made a huge task of reform easier, but no one had a more ambitious agenda than he did in those years, and no one who was there doubted his influence, and often the stamp of his authority on the outcomes. That's why he wears the second worst recession in Australian history more than anyone else engaged in public policy at the time. His response is classic Keating: I'll take responsibility for the recession if you'll also give me credit for the 20-plus years of continuous growth and low inflation that have followed.

There is never one complete picture of any phase of political history. There are too many prisms. I hope this adds to the mosaic, and to the understanding of how one man came to power, and used it.

THE
FORMATIVE
YEARS,
1944–75

THE LAND OF THE FIBRO HOUSE

In the immediate aftermath of World War II, it was understandable that Australians would stick with the government that had got them through the war, just as it was understandable that the soothing, persuasive presence of Robert Menzies and a promise of steady-as-she-goes stability would be irresistible to many of those same voters three years later in the Cold War environment that was escalating on the other side of the world. But not even Menzies' most ardent fan would have dreamt for a moment that he would lay the ground for conservative rule for the next 23 years.

That was the world Paul Keating grew up in—albeit in a Catholic, working-class, Labor household—but it only goes part of the way when seeking to understand one of the most fascinating, colourful and dominating characters to walk Australia's political stage.

Sydney's western suburbs in those days were epitomised by Bankstown, the population solidly working class, and almost exclusively white, but in Keating's memory it had a greater sense of community than adjoining suburbs. The young Keating was not the only boy who had learned to dismantle a car by his teens, but not many in Keating's place and in his time would have been driven by such burning curiosity to so voraciously soak up his eclectic range of cultural pursuits. It was one thing to be inspired by classical music, first heard by chance, at the age of twelve, or to be drawn to the perfection of an antique watch at fifteen, even though these things were exotic in his own home, let alone the neighbourhood. It was quite another to pursue them so passionately, so early, in the same way he would come to absorb and pursue politics and his place at the tables of power.

There's a moment in the Keating interviews that didn't make it to air, where he recalls meeting a young Leo Schofield browsing through catalogues in a central Sydney antique shop—the beginning of a lifelong friendship—and musing over what on earth had spawned these two unlikely characters, the boy from Bankstown and the escapee from outback Brewarrina. Keating attributes it to the search for perfection, but why?

In seeking to peel back the layers of any complex personality, you'd start by looking to the parents and the home environment. It's easy to assume that having learned his politics at his father's knee—a father steeped in Labor history and Catholic social values who had parlayed his boiler-making trade into a successful engineering business— that Matthew Keating was the driving force. That might explain the politics, but it doesn't explain the driving ambition or hunger that got Keating to within one caucus vote of joining the first Whitlam Ministry in 1972 at 28 after only one term in Parliament, which to this day would have enshrined him as the youngest minister in Australian history; or that saw him seize the prime ministership at forty-seven. For that, as he acknowledges, look to the women of the family—his mother and grandmother.

Paul Keating grew up in the long shadow cast by the devastation of World War II. In January 1944, as he was tasting life for the first time in the cocoon of his parents' classically humble fibro house, the Allied forces had begun their drive up through Europe's underbelly in Italy in preparation for the Normandy invasion. On the Eastern Front the

Red Army had entered Poland and was also advancing on the Baltic countries. In the Pacific, there was much bloody conflict to come, but the writing was on the wall for Japan.

Two of Keating's great wartime heroes, Franklin Roosevelt and Winston Churchill, were already making postwar plans for Asia and Europe. His other hero, John Curtin, was in the process of driving a historic shift in Australia's primary postwar alliance from England to America.

By the time Matthew and Min Keating's first-born started processing his first conscious memories, the war was over, but the family photograph of his Uncle Bill, a casualty at the hands of the Japanese, sat in the living room as a constant reminder right through his childhood. That small icon, the family conversation it sparked, and what it came to represent to young Keating, would have a big impact on Australia's future foreign policy.

One of the things people came to associate most with the Keating persona was the air of swaggering confidence, of a man dancing very definitely to his own drumbeat, something not many political leaders can easily lay claim to these days. Where did the inner confidence in the rightness of his judgements, the strength of conviction spring from?

Leaving school and going off to work at such a young age may have been normal enough for the times, even joining his trade union. But when I thought back on what I was doing at fourteen and fifteen, joining a political party would have been one of the furthest things from my mind. I'd only barely begun to notice girls.

PJK: I was caught up in the Labor Party from a very early age, and there was a tribal quality to it. Your typical local branch allocates a grid of streets to members, which they letterbox, and also a polling booth to man on election day, so I used to join my father, running round with a bag, letterboxing, and in the polling booths. I was doing this from about ten. And we would always lose—you'd pick up the Sunday paper, and you'd lost again. My father held Menzies in contempt and could never see why a moderate Labor Party, appealing to the great body of the community, couldn't get elected. But I was intrigued by politics and public life.

I was very conscious of the black cloud of the Second World War and for my twelfth birthday my father bought me a book called the *Last Days of Hitler* by Hugh Trevor-Roper. He was a British intelligence agent who had the job of piecing together Hitler's final days in the bunker in Berlin in 1945, and confirming his death. My father's brother had died in the death marches in Sandakan in Borneo in March 1945 and his picture sat on the piano at the family house, so I was very conscious of that.

What I could never quite understand was why good people failed to stop Hitler when he was at his weakest, when he made the incursions into the Rhineland and the Sudetenland. The person who stopped him was Churchill, and I came to a view early in life that in the great business of enlargement—small movement here, big movement there—the profession with the greatest leverage was public life, and the archetypal leader was the big-brained, heroic Churchill, the one person who wouldn't trade with the criminal, Hitler. I was drawn to that great moral clarity. I thought, if this is the business this guy is in, then this is the business to be in. And of course there was Roosevelt in the Pacific war.

When I started work in Sydney at fourteen I used to go to the book dealers Berkelouws, who were then in King Street, and I'd pick up back copies of the *Strand* magazine because Churchill used to write for *Strand* every month in the 1930s. These were the bad years for him politically. He'd mostly be writing about the European scene or about himself or about English history, but I had this interest in him.

Bankstown, where I was born and raised, had a great clannishness about it, and it was as if it had a sort of border around it. The next suburb, Punchbowl, was completely different. It didn't have the same sort of cohesion.

In those days people used to attend church, Sunday Mass, and kids you were at school with would turn up with their parents. They'd come out of mass at nine, and still be there at twenty to ten, still chatting out the front. So there was that tribal sense of the place, and the Labor Party used to meet in the band hall on Bankstown Oval, in a little timber hall. Those things together gave it a sort of cohesion. You belonged to something. So when I first started turning up to meetings I already knew some of the people in the room, but I was the youngest person there by a lot of years.

It was the land of the fibro house. It was square kilometres of fibro houses and old cars in the late 1940s and 1950s. We started out with an Austin 7 and then later moved to a Morris Oxford. The guy next to us had a Vauxhall Wyvern. Everyone repaired their own vehicles and there was a local traffic in spare parts. There was in these communities a great sodality—it's an old word now, sodality. But there was a great sodality, and because everyone had modest incomes—they were not poor, they were not poverty stricken, but they had very modest incomes—the standard of living was only moving up ever so slightly.

KOB: I can remember being shocked as a journalist when I researched a story on Queensland and discovered that in the era I was born into, immediately postwar, only 13 per cent of secondary school-aged children actually stayed in school. The others did what you did, left school at fourteen or fifteen. Most of the boys went into trades or semi-skilled work, or maybe clerical jobs like you, while most of the girls had jobs without much career orientation because they assumed they'd be leaving work when they got married and start a family. What sort of a student were you at De La Salle College?

PJK: I was an impatient learner. I always wanted to pick up stuff that I was interested in. If I wasn't interested, then I dropped off. In a class of 30, I'd always come about eighth, ninth or tenth. And every year at the bottom of the report card it would say, could do better. Going to university wasn't anything like the priority for most families it is today. You wouldn't even think about it today because kids go to Year 12 at eighteen years of age and then go to university. That was not true of my class—four or five went on to do the higher school certificate, then called the leaving certificate, and then only maybe one or two of them went to university. Maybe only one.

I think I picked up a Catholic sense of social justice, that is, we all arrive equally and we go out equally. Also the poison of racism— I think I took that from it. I don't know that they teach you too much at the De La Salle Brothers that is unique, but they certainly drilled that into you.

I was also into a bit of behavioural science in the classroom. I used to score the teachers for their ability to teach and pass across ideas. When they'd chew a kid out I'd think, I wouldn't have quite done that. Maybe I'd have done this, but not that. I was always—always— looking at behaviour and I think preparing for something bigger, but I didn't know what that was.

I particularly remember one teacher, Brother Bernard Hawkins. He quit the monks later, but he used to bring in one of those big spool tape recorders with Question Time from Parliament on it. In those days, Labor people like Eddie Ward and Doc Evatt and Clyde Cameron and people like that would stand out. He used to do that every week when Parliament was in session, and we'd hear the cacophony of Question Time.

We'd all have to be quiet and he'd stop and decipher what the debate was about.

I can't recall now whether I was riveted to each thing, but you got the sense of it, and there were certain people we liked and enjoyed.

Ward was one. Les Haylen was another and there were people around like Arthur Calwell who people focused on.

I don't think I was necessarily ambitious by nature, but I was always trying to find the sense of things. What did it all mean? I was a bit like the pigeon doing the rounds before it decides which way is home. I was trying to work out where things were in life, what made sense. I was keeping my interest in politics alive but living an adolescent life, like most people did.

In the middle of my last year at school, my mother took me to a school careers night, where they looked at your mark, your aptitudes and discussed this with you and your parents. The careers advisor, who was quite a skilful sort of guy, said he thought I should try architecture or panel-beating, of all things. Now, the panel-beating could have come from my interest in the shape of things. It's not as silly as it sounds, and also the architecture, and my mother said, 'Oh well, you know, he does have an interest in public life and I think if he's thinking about anything in his life, it's the prime ministership of Australia rather than doing other sorts of work.'

My mother had great ambitions for me. She didn't quite know what they were, but she knew I was not going to be put in a slot. She used to say, 'I told Dad to get out of the railways, that he'd go nowhere there. He had to get out of there and start his own business.' Dad was a sweet-hearted guy. He didn't believe in conflict at all—he wanted everything more or less smooth and resolutely nice, whereas Mum would be into the conflict.

She was like a lot of women of her time: born in the 1920s, suffered the Depression, then the Second World War. They never really got their shot at life. So, in a frustrated kind of way, they would try to direct their husbands and then their children. That was certainly the case with my mother. I think my mother in a modern world was a killer, an absolute killer!

My grandmother and my mother invested a ton of love in me, especially my grandmother in the early years. She thought I was the bee's knees. My mother used to say later that if Dad said anything harsh to me, my grandmother simply wouldn't eat. She'd just get up from the table and walk away. That was her protest against Dad correcting me. I walked around with grandmotherly and motherly love, and I think it radiates for you and gives you that kind of inner confidence. It's almost like wearing the asbestos suit—you go through the fire but you're not going to be burned because someone loves you. You are complete, you are together.

I remember a survey years ago of members of Parliament. About 68 per cent of members were the first child of the family, and that was probably because of the same investment that parents put into the first child. It's true of my father as well as my mother in a different way if someone puts you on a pedestal. The first big pedestal-builder was my grandmother. It's something that sticks with you all your life. It has always stuck with me. I always think about her. In fact I went to her grave very recently because I thought again, there is the person who most believed in me. You have to go through life with someone thinking you're special, giving you the love quotient when you have to get the sword out in real combat.

I was twelve when my grandmother died. Her death was the most harrowing thing that had happened to me. She thought I was the most special person on the face of the earth. It wasn't just some sidebar affection from a happy grandmother: it was a very focused affection, and you think, well, whatever else happens to me I've got that—I've got that completeness and I do think that that completeness does carry you through the hellfire. You need other bits and pieces to help you. In my case, often the music and things like that and friends, but what sticks to you is that investment, that huge affection and emotional investment.

KOB: In the era you started work, Bob Menzies was coming to the end of his first decade as Liberal Prime Minister. Australia was still riding on the back of the wool boom, the Labor Party was riven with deep ideological differences, but trade union membership was strong, and the unemployment rate rarely strayed over 2 per cent. You would have been very impressionable, starting work at the Sydney County Council at such a young age. Your biographer Edna Carew wrote that even as a young clerk you left home dressed like the chairman of the board.

PJK: That was from my mother. She always had me dressed up. I was always well dressed. They used to call the clerks the shiny bums. But at work I had to wear a dustcoat, otherwise you got sprayed with transformer oil, a mineral oil that's not good to be around.

I was at the Sydney County Council transformer-handling depot where they used to bring transformers in and recondition them. They were attended to by electrical fitters and labourers. The labourers did the bullocking and all the dirty jobs while the electrical fitters did the trade work. There were about 60 of them there and you saw it all—the language, the profanity; you could have cut the language with a knife, and there was an art form to it. And they had the kinds of jokes, humour of a kind that has gone from Australian life now. All the time, the jokes.

And you'd hear how someone's run off with someone else's missus and someone else has done this and someone else has done that and then someone's got caught for stealing and so on. The whole grab bag of things that made up Australian life—it gave me great respect for these people, for people who had nothing to sell but their time, who had developed a set of focal skills and who were dedicated sorts of people, but wild. Wild. It was a snapshot of working-class Sydney.

Dad started as a tradesman, got himself a diploma in engineering, then was an inspector on the railways. And then with two other chaps started a business making ready-mix concrete machines, the ones you see on the back of the trucks. His was really the first firm to make these in Australia, and the batching plants that went with them. So it became a successful small- to middle-sized business in our area.

He had a great latitude about his attitude to business He was loyal to Labor to a fault, but at the same time he knew that the days of robber-baron capitalism were over with the Depression. You just mostly had people with modest amounts of capital trying to turn them into businesses and employ people. He had a lot of reasonableness in his view, and I think I picked that up from him.

Dad was very kind by nature. There was a chap who was a labourer, and Dad had trained him to be a welder and then paid him tradesman's rates. Anyway, we were standing on a polling booth, my father and me. It was a by-election, and this fellow, Joe, I forget his surname, came down and I handed him the Labor how-to-vote card. Or Dad might have. He said, no, Mattie, I'm not taking that one. And this is a guy my father had lifted up to a tradesman's wage, and Dad said, 'Poor, silly bugger. You know, you try to help these people but some are beyond help.'

KOB: What was his influence on you politically?

PJK: Well, it was the whole view about the Menzian era, right? If you think of the country as a kind of rock, you had the social strata, the Cambrian, the Permian, the Jurassic, but there was no energy coming through it. There was no oil and gas. No sparks. There was a block. A block. Uncompetitive, presided over by the court of a political dandy, the master of the glib phrase, and yet there were people trying to assemble capital and make it work.

What was apparent to my father and apparent to me through him was that it was so difficult to corporately save, so difficult to garner capital, so difficult to borrow money to invest, and there was a great struggle in building businesses. Therefore one of the primary influences he had on me was that the Liberals couldn't do capital.

It wasn't beyond the wit of man to do capital but the Liberals couldn't do it. He didn't see Labor in one camp and capital in another because his very life was about spanning the two, and principally through him I picked up that same notion.

KOB: Your father died very young—he was 60—and I think you were the last person in the family to see him alive.

PJK: Yes, he was walking round to put a bet on a horse at the TAB and he died sitting on the side of the road. I was washing the car nearby and someone came by and said 'where is number eight?' And I said, 'Oh, that's my parents' place. He said, oh, well look, it must be your father. I don't think he's well.'

So I then went up the hill. There he was, stretched back across the footpath, but dead. It took me a decade to get over it—a decade to even talk about it, and it is always with me. I mean, it's a great thing, parental love and love of parents. Losing a parent is a hell of a loss, and if the parents are close to you, you never get over it. But you don't want to get over it, you know? There is a place for sadness and melancholy. There is a place. You don't want to be sparkling and happy all the time. You need the inner life, the inner sadness. It's what rounds you out.

BLEAK TIMES FOR LABOR

Looking at today's Labor Party, where lines are more likely to be drawn around personalities and factional loyalties than ideology, it's hard to imagine the depth of emotion and ideological difference that led to the great Labor Split of 1955 and fanned deep enmities for decades, presenting successive Liberal governments with the gift that kept on giving, particularly at the federal level.

The great Labor character Fred Daly, who was in Parliament from 1943 under Curtin, to 1975 under Whitlam, captured the mood within the Labor caucus at the time of the Split like no one else I've heard or read. Describing a brawl between the Labor leader Doc Evatt and his supporters, and a group of anti-communist, largely Catholic MPs from Victoria, over a motion to spill the leadership positions, Daly wrote:

> I will never forget the scene when Eddie Ward, a real hater, called for a division. To everyone's amazement Evatt leaped onto the table, pencil and paper in hand, red-faced and excited, and triumphantly called out, 'Get their names, get their names!' It was Evatt and Ward at their hating best.

Some of his supporters stood on chairs around the room repeating the call 'Take down their names' as members crossed the floor to vote. It was a degrading and disgusting spectacle— twenty-eight members lined up like Japanese war criminals by colleagues with hate, vindictiveness and triumph written all over their faces.

Paul Keating was eleven at the time, but his father, whose Catholic anti-communism was almost as ardent as his loyalty to Labor, would have relived his pain around the kitchen table over the massive damage caused by the Split. And as a mover and shaker within the local branches, Matt would have readily reflected the air of bitter intrigue that was dogging his party. The worst of the Split was concentrated in Victoria and Queensland. To some degree the NSW branch of the Labor Party managed to quarantine itself from the damage, but the depth of searing bitterness permeated the whole party. The Split was more deeply cemented with the formation of the breakaway Democratic Labor Party (DLP) in 1957, and Labor supporters grew weary watching election after election until 1972, when Liberal governments were returned with DLP preferences.

The environment inside both the industrial and political arms of the labour movement was little better by the time young Keating began to impose his presence on the branch and state structures of the party in his late teens to early twenties. It was fascinating to watch him close his eyes tight in concentration at 69 and take himself back 50 years to the hate-filled days of those branch and conference battles—even for the fledgling warriors in Young Labor. The one great constant for the Right in NSW in its battles with the Left was that it was backed by largely Right-controlled Labor state governments from 1947 to 1965.

PJK: It was virtually a shooting war in my early years. People wouldn't talk to one another. The factionalism was bad and it was also still sectarian. Many people in the Left belonged to the Masonic Lodge, while the ruling group in New South Wales was heavily but not exclusively Catholic. This was an important undercurrent of the whole thing. In our branch we were all like-minded characters, but if you went to the branch next door you'd find a different view of the world altogether, and those ideological differences would all collide at the state and federal electorate councils.

NSW was the state that didn't really split, so the Right largely held together in NSW. Federally the party was dominated by the Left, and while the contest between Right and Left in NSW was great, the Right was assisted by the fact that we held government through that period, which gave the party legitimacy, and gave the moderates in the party the upper hand the Left was never able to strike down.

But the contest at branch level was severe. So you had this bitter intellectual tug of war, and overlaying it was the Cold War. It's gone now, thank goodness, but the Split left an intolerance to moderate Catholic Labor members, and threaded through it all was the contest between Masons and Catholics that also permeated society.

When I started work you would see job ads in a Sydney newspaper that said 'Catholics need not apply'. It was still around in a big way. It always amused me why these roaring lions of the Left would end up in the Masonic Lodge, with all of its ceremony. I never quite got that, but they were mostly in the Lodge in those days, so there was a sense that they were coming at you socially and politically.

KOB: But there was also this very strong view on the Left of Labor that the Catholic Church had far too much influence inside the Labor Party and that people like B.A. Santamaria and Archbishop Mannix were pulling too many strings.

PJK: They were, and that was the cause of the Split in Victoria, but in New South Wales the hierarchy of the Catholic Church decided that Catholic Labor people should stay in the party, that it shouldn't split off, and that was perhaps their great gift to the place.

The church took the view that it should remove itself from the daily battle. So while there were these Catholic-influenced industrial groups in the 1950s, in which my father was involved, trying to wrest control of the unions from the Left or the Communist Party of Australia, after the Split the church dropped back. Laypeople on the Right of the Labor Party in NSW then stepped up to the plate—people like Charlie Oliver, John Ducker and Geoff Cahill. They weren't necessarily Catholics, but some people like Barrie Unsworth later became Catholic.

The Left fundamentally controlled the National Executive of the party in those years, and NSW was like an island in the middle of it all, maintaining its legitimacy through its moderate state government. At the branch level you still had a real cross-section of people. You had labourers, people who worked on the garbage service at the council. You had fitters and turners. You had people who were clerks in the taxation office.

It was a broad cross-section, but it had a very parochial drumbeat. We'd be discussing whether we were going to have a new street crossing over the railway line, whether it ought to have lights on it, and then the state member of Parliament who was a Labor member would come and give the state government report every month. Then someone would get up either attacking or supporting the federal Labor leader, Arthur Calwell, or supporting Gough Whitlam against Calwell, or earlier Evatt, so you would get a bit of spice that way.

But our branch, Central Bankstown, was mostly seeing things the one way. It was when you got to the Federal Electorate Council [FEC] level that you'd start to see the contests. That's where it was just a deadly battle to keep control of the party in NSW, which was in the hands of the Left federally.

The hatreds were visceral. In our FEC, we had one chap who was the secretary of the Left-controlled branch next door, and my co-delegate used to accuse him of not washing. He'd call him Pongo, so the first thing he'd do at a meeting was to sit down, open a bottle of Airwick and pull up the wick and put it on the floor beside him just to make the point. That's how vicious it was. It was so vicious. It was a kind of civil war, in a way. A Cold War inside the Labor Party in those days.

When I was a preselection candidate for the federal seat of Blaxland, which took in the Bankstown district, I'd go to some branches, which were dominated by the Left, to muster support. There was one branch in particular, one of the large ones, where the chairman would say, 'We'll hear from the candidates' and of course they'd hear from their guy and there'd be plenty of questions and answers.

Then I'd get up to speak, and not a soul would ask a question, and when it was over you would sit there like you had rabies. Then, as they locked up, they'd stand around out the front and have a bit of a chat, and not a soul would say a word to you. You'd just walk away . . . just walk away as if you'd had no part in it whatsoever.

The political dividing line was stark. The Revesby Workers' Club was called the Kremlin because in the vernacular of those days it was run by the Coms. This was one of the big issues. Some people in those days used to say it was all a fantasy to think the Communist Party was actually active in the Labor Party. Well, after the Soviet military occupation of Hungary in 1956 and then particularly after the invasion of Czechoslovakia in 1968, the Communist Party splintered in Australia, and many of those people decided to join the Labor Party as the only effective vehicle available to pursue their political commitment. So then you had people on the Left who would not speak publicly against the mixed economy but who would have preferred to nationalise everything. On the one hand there was this old Left dogma about government ownership of the high points of the economy, and on the other hand you had the internationalism of the Communist Party worldwide in the Cold War construct. This affected the Labor Party deeply, so I spent most of my young years fighting to keep moderate Labor people in control of the party in New South Wales.

KOB: You've never held back on your antipathy to Bob Menzies during those long years when Labor was in the wilderness federally, but the truth is that whatever you thought of Menzies, he was well and truly helped by your party, which kept finding new ways to beat itself.

PJK: Absolutely. Menzies was a specialist in symbols—the Queen, the monarchy, the empire, the Cold War, a fetish about communism, a divided Labor Party—and had an absolute ton of luck. That was Menzies, and we just kept handing it to him on a plate. You had to basically explode the myth that somehow this sort of glib conservative orthodoxy that he spoke of was shown for what it was.

When the salad days of postwar growth ran out as they did about the time he retired, and Australia started to fall behind, you saw with Menzies' successors—Holt and Gorton and McMahon—the country went nowhere because it had nowhere to go, and yet, here was the Labor Party, unable to put labour and capital together.

KOB: You were very much the young man in a hurry through the 1960s, working your way up through the party structure. How quickly do you think you were switching on to what politics really was about, and how quickly did you decide that you wanted to make a career of it?

PJK: I became president of the New South Wales ALP Youth Council at 21, and that's when I started to meet the party hierarchy. I met the State President who was then Charlie Oliver, the State Secretary Bill Colbourne, the Assistant Secretary, John Armitage; so I was in the know. You knew who was on the disputes committee, you knew who was on the various policy committees. In those days there was a great contest between Calwell and Whitlam at the federal level, and we were in favour of Whitlam. And that was a big point of discussion, particularly at the Youth Council.

I had people like the late Frank Walker opposing me from the Left, god love him, and we'd have these really, really snarly battles, and there'd be big fights over credentialing; whether their credentials were in order, so that would go off to the credentials committee. Every delegate was fought over, every credentialing was fought over, every little bit of policy expression was fought over, and while that was happening there were these big battalions fighting for control of the trade unions. In my years the battle was led by John Ducker in New South Wales and Barrie Unsworth. So there was an industrial fight going on and there was the party branch and organisational fight also going on and the battle was around the future of the Labor Party. Would we ever see Labor back in government? Would we ever see a moderate federal Labor Party again, an electable moderate federal Labor Party?

KOB: Were you each as ruthless as each other, the Right and the Left?

PJK: Oh yeah, oh yeah. But the Left were shockers. They were always cheating.

KOB: But there would've been cheating on both sides, I'm sure.

PJK: There was. Everything was fought over, but it did one thing for you. It trained you in combat, particularly at those big conferences. The NSW conference had met every year at the Town Hall, since 1893, a thousand people every year, and you stood up there surrounded by your peers for three days. Everything you said was noted for or against you, and if half of them didn't like you they would be stamping their feet, so you'd have this massive drumroll. So you got this training.

'YOU HAVEN'T GOT A SECOND TO LOSE'

Paul Keating stands as an interesting contradiction to the time-worn adage that you can't put an old head on young shoulders. Whether it was by instinct or sheer curiosity, he was drawn from an early age to seek out the tribal elders who could help soften an otherwise steep learning curve. It is a well-documented pattern in his career, starting long before he entered Parliament. The first significant mentor in this vein, outside the family, was Jack Lang, one of the most fascinating and contentious figures in Labor history.

For most Australians in the 1960s, Lang was a remnant of the past, all but forgotten. On the one hand he had been one of Labor's great early reformers as NSW Premier in two stints totalling four years in the 1920s and early 1930s, but on the other hand he came to be seen as a divisive and destructive force within his party, hated by the supporters of federal leaders such as John Curtin and Ben Chifley, and ultimately expelled.

Physically large and bold in personality, Lang dominated the parliaments of his day, converting Labor hopes into law in areas such as widows' pensions, child endowment and workers' compensation, abolishing public high-school fees, reforming the arbitration system, legislating for fair rents and establishing a government insurance office.

But as a sworn enemy of the conservative establishment, including that in Britain, particularly as the Great Depression took hold, Jack Lang sealed his political fate with his determination to defy the British banks with his refusal to pay hundreds of thousands of pounds in interest to British bond-holders, while dividing the Scullin Labor Government in Canberra. He was dismissed by the State Governor, Sir Philip Game, in May 1932. In 1943, after public attacks on the Labor Premier in NSW, Bill McKell, and Labor Prime Minister John Curtin, Lang was expelled from the party, but turned up in the federal Parliament three years later with his own party, the Australian Labor (Non-Communist) Party.

By the time the eighteen-year-old Paul Keating came knocking at the door of his Sydney city office in 1962, Jack Lang cut a lonely figure from the desk where he still put out a weekly political newspaper he'd started in the late 1930s. But Lang could still dominate a room. His father's influence would obviously have been an element behind the visits because Matthew Keating had been a Langite in those contentious years, but the young Keating wanted to tap the history Lang carried in his head. My interest in pursuing this connection was not just to get a sense of what influence the old political warrior might have wrought on him, but also to explore what it said about his single-minded pursuit of power, even at that young age.

PJK: Lang's role in the Depression interested me. He had led the fight against the economic orthodoxy during the Depression and he was just a huge figure. In a small place like Sydney was in those days, for someone like Lang to emerge was remarkable in itself. He'd eat the people around him. He seemed to have a political energy and radicalism that the sort of vanilla state Labor Government of my day didn't have. So I went down to his office in Nithsdale Street, just off Hyde Park, and introduced myself.

Lang was at Henry Parkes's Federation rallies. He was Henry Lawson's brother-in-law, but he never volunteered to speak about the past. I had to push him, but he'd give you pen sketches of Labor leaders like Bill Holman, Billy Hughes and Doc Evatt, other significant figures like the Chief Justice Sir John Latham or the conservative leaders like Stanley Bruce and Earl Page. He'd fill me in on their little foibles, and the issues of his times, particularly the First World War, the Second World War and the Depression. It was like an intimate condensation of Australian political history from Federation in 1901 through to when I was talking to him in the 1960s. His focus was on the future of the world. He was always interested in things like the common market, how Europe was changing, how the world would change. It was a big brain, and what you got in distilled form was a view of the country's history through to the third quarter of the twentieth century.

I used to see him twice a week for about seven years. Strangely he used to call me Mr Keating and I was only eighteen in those days. He was very formal. I used to address him as Mr Lang. Among other things, I asked him whether I should go on and do a university degree, and he thought for a while before saying, 'Mr Keating, you have too much to learn for a university degree, about the getting of power and the using of it. There are no courses in this.'

Sometimes when he was working on his newspaper I would help him with what they call the pull, the lead run for the front page. He used to write in an exercise book and he would write a big essay for the front—no changes, no arrows, no crossing out, it just all flowed out, and sometimes I'd read the handwritten exercise book or other times I'd read the pull. But he had this ability to write with great clarity of mind and do an essay of maybe 2000 words front to back with not a correction, all essentially written in his head. Amazing ability.

He and I disagreed on a lot of policy fronts like protection and tariffs, and I'd say on much of the world debate I would probably have been on the other side to him. I didn't want that from him. I was okay on the contemporary stuff. I wanted the dynamics, and how the game was played.

What I particularly picked up from Lang was his use of language, the force of his language. He had hugely long arms, as if they were concertinaed. They'd come out at you as he talked. He had the celluloid collar and the gold chain, and that big jaw, and he'd say, 'Mr Keating, I'm telling you this', and he'd lean across the table with a look that would bore a hole in you. He was then 87 or 88. There was no one like him then.

He used to say to me, 'Always put your money on self-interest, son. He's the best horse in the race; always a trier.'

KOB: I did an interview with you in 1986 where you described how you learned from Lang to be hard in your judgements. What did you mean by that?

PJK: Lang once said to me, 'One of your problems, Mr Keating, is you take people at their word. This is a business where duplicity is the order of the day. Look for the best in people by all means, but keep a sceptical eye peeled for what they are saying to you and what they really mean. What you should look for is the support of the earnest people. There will be a lot whose support you will never have. But you'll never be anyone until you have a reasonable stock of enemies.' It's the issues that sort people out. It's just so true, because having enemies worries some people. For me, it's a badge of honour. It's never worried me that a group of people would have not a bar of me. And that's the way Lang conducted his life.

Even so, I never really took that kind of almost morbid cynicism on board as an operating principle. I always found better in people in public life, and if you go through a caucus like I did for nearly 30 years, you've got to build coalitions and friendships with people. So there are people you trust. I never subscribed to the solitary school, that you're on your own and only on your own, but I did subscribe to the fact that you've got to look at what is said to you and look behind it. You have to end up being a good judge of character and a good judge of what is really being said to you, as well as a good listener.

People may be members of a political party, but they get to Parliament in their own right. It's like a team with a captain but the members of the team earn their place independently, so to stitch together majorities in Parliament continually, you've got to look at people to see what their interests are, what things they have in common, what natural point of agreement you have with them, or points of disagreement.

KOB: In an interview with journalist Jennifer Hewitt back in 1981, you said that Lang once told you he'd met a person who admired you greatly and that person in the end would be the only one you could trust. Can you remember that story?

PJK: I can, now you remind me, and he was talking about me. He was saying the only one you can rely upon is yourself, and that no one would think better of you than you. Another thing he said to me one day, he said, 'Mr Keating, you're a young man and people will tell you you have plenty of time but the truth is you haven't got a second to lose.'

And he was right. Because it's a bit like you see in these great tennis matches, the great Grand Slams—you can see where they get lost when someone loses a point, just one point somewhere in the match, and that's the turning point.

A political life is like that, and it's played with enormous dexterity and professionalism. A lot of people think it's all haphazard. There's nothing haphazard about it. It's hugely professional, and therefore you can't miss too many points. You've got to keep going all the time. In truth you don't have a second to lose. That is the truth.

KOB: What about Lang's reputation for divisiveness?

PJK: He had a reputation for divisiveness, but he never had a divisive bent in the years I met with him. In 1970, when he was 93, I moved a motion to have him readmitted to the Labor Party, which was defeated principally by the State Secretary Bill Colbourne. There were no mobiles in those days, so when that happened I ran down to Town Hall railway station to find a public phone, and rang him up at home.

He said, 'How did we go?'

I said, 'Well, we got beaten. Not by much but we got beaten essentially by Bill Colbourne's speech'—because Colbourne was with the federal Labor Party in the 1930s, you see, and still carried the bitterness.

And Lang said, 'Oh well, old Bill. He's always been a good Labor man.'

He didn't have a nasty word to say about him. You would have thought he would have had a bit of invective. Lang was finally readmitted the following year. I don't doubt that he was a source of division in the 1930s, but it was never evident in our conversations.

KOB: Why were you looking to learn those things from people like Jack Lang at the age of eighteen?

PJK: Because he was an indefatigable warrior, Lang. Indefatigable.

Remember that guy, Bob Haldeman, from the Nixon days? He wrote a book called *The Ends of Power*. This phrase, 'the ends of power'—you put the words around your fingers, like strings, and you make them work for you. You've got to know where the bits are and how it all works. So when I became a member of the House of Representatives I made a point of seeking out people in the motor industry, the mining industry, the steel industry, some of the older people who'd built these industries. I was essentially sucking experience from them. Experience that was central to building a composite picture of the economy and the power equation.

KOB: But why were you interested in learning about power at eighteen?

PJK: Because that was the business I had by then determined I wished to be in. It wasn't that I wanted power for power's sake. You have to understand that the obsession in our household was opposition to Menzies. The Split had already happened, so my interest wasn't primarily an obsession about the Left, it was Menzies. He'd collapsed as Prime Minister when the game turned nasty going into the Second World War, but came back after Chifley had set up the postwar economy. My father thought Menzies was a well-dressed conman. My interest in learning about power was because I shared my father's belief in Labor as the natural party of government, and I saw the possibility of great and truly good works and deeds; that there was a better formula, that you could cut through the conservative ortho- doxy in Australia and arrive at something much better.

But the arraignment of power requires organisation. That's why I spent all that time with Jack Lang and others soaking up the history. That's why I spent a lot of time collecting and reading the *Labor Daily Year Book*. *Labor Daily* was the party's paper through the 1930s, through the Depression, and they used to have a year book that would have every little detail about the labour movement. For example, it would have the East Sydney Federal Electorate Council with all the delegates listed. Further down you'd have the Glebe North Branch, with the president's name, the secretary and the postal addresses.

Then there'd be the Rubber Workers' Union or the Railways' Union, so the whole labour movement was there. And there would be articles written by the various movers and shakers.

It took me a lot of years to assemble them; my archive started at about 1928 and covered more than a decade. It was the minutiae of labour history, a chronicle of things like the first pension legislation, with a story on how that came about, or workers' compensation. So when I walked into those Labor conferences as a young man of eighteen or nineteen, I pretty well had the whole background— as much as you can get it—the protocols, all the familial connections, the ethos of the movement, both the unions and the parliamentary party, the histories of the splits, the Lang Labor Party and the federal party, the personalities.

The best guide to the future is the past, so I used to have a look back. How did the Labor Party develop? Where is the jump from Deakin? What energises the first Labor Government? What distinguishes them? Andrew Fisher's first government. There'd be an article written by King O'Malley for instance, about the Commonwealth Bank in 1912, and you'd file it away in your head.

REBUILDING THE SOUL

Superficially, by the time he'd become Treasurer and Australians were becoming more informed about his back story, it wasn't too difficult for Paul Keating's political enemies within his party and without to paint him as the elitist who wore Zegna suits, collected French antique clocks, restored a vintage Mercedes and, horror, listened to classical music. He even once gave the Queen a tongue-in-cheek lecture about the history of a silver gift collection of antique English dinnerware on the dinner table at the Lodge when Bob Hawke was Prime Minister.

But it wasn't elitism that drove Keating to start immersing himself in the world of classical music when he was barely in his teens, or plunging into the world of 1790s neoclassicism at fifteen, spending several months' salary on an antique watch, or building his philosophy in life from the aftermath of the French Revolution. It certainly wasn't elitism that excited him about a Sydney blues and soul band called the Ramrods, which drew him into a different world of music, with queues of girls around the corner at the venues. It took him no time at all to establish relationships with the entrepreneurs and record companies.

It would be wrong to suggest that a working-class kid from Bankstown couldn't be passionate about the high-end arts, but it certainly wasn't the norm in his day, and it was still exotic by the time he became Bob Hawke's right-hand man through eight years of a crowded reform agenda, and when he replaced Hawke as Prime Minister. With family and politics, these things were and are Paul Keating's lifeblood. The replenishment of the soul. They are the things, he says, that kept him sane. When the going was tough in those early years slogging through the parish-pump politics and bitter ideological disputes in the back channels of his party, building his career block by block, the arts sustained him.

PJK: I can actually remember the first time I noticed classical music. I was out riding a bicycle with a friend of mine from school and we went back to his parents' place, a fibro house in Bass Hill. We parked the bikes, and his father was sitting in his shorts and singlet on the wooden veranda that had a sort of rolled-up canvas blind, and he had a piece of music running. It was a short piano concerto and the rhythms of it and the colour of it got my attention.

I said to my friend, 'Would you mind asking your father if he could put it on again?'

It was a piano concerto written for an English film in 1941 called the *Warsaw Concerto* by a British composer, Richard Addinsell, who composed in the manner of Rachmaninoff. And it went for about eight or nine minutes. It was a mini-concerto, but very colourful. It had great tonal qualities, tonal poetry I had not heard before. I was hugely thrilled by this piece of music. It was on the second side of the LP. The first side was Rachmaninoff's second piano concerto, and that's really where I began with classical music, at about twelve or thirteen. It's become one of the most important things in my life.

All of our minds are wired; the DNA is wired for music. You'll even see it in little infants. They'll dance to a tune, or they'll tap their feet. We're wired for it, and the great composers know how to play with us.

They write the compositions to pull you in if you are prepared to go with them, and I found that music, particularly classical music, opens up an enormous vista of an altogether different place, a big promotion to your imagination—a big, big energetic hit to the imagination like electricity to the electric motor, the music energises your brain. It used to give me such a lift and still does.

When I was learning the repertoire, I'd bring something home from EMI like Otto Klemperer doing Beethoven's *Fifth Symphony*, that great granite conducting, and you'd think, 'God, this is fantastic.' I'd play them until the records were scratchy. I've always found with classical music that it puts the normal things of life into a clear context.

KOB: I wonder how important the music was to you when you were running that gauntlet of hostility you talked about in the Left-controlled branches when you were campaigning for preselection. Those meetings where you were left standing alone outside, feeling humiliated. You must have felt absolutely drained emotionally by the time you got home late at night to an empty bedroom with a head full of negative thoughts.

PJK: I used mostly to put on one piece of music when I'd get in the door. It was Chopin's *Barcarolle*. It's a nice lilting thing. Peaceful. You'd pick up the resonances and you'd be out of it, out of the horror stretch and back into the comfort zone, and then I'd work up to something else. If it was late at night it wouldn't be loud. If it was at the weekend, it'd be louder. On the weekends I'd have on the Wagner overtures, *Rienzi* or *Tannhäuser*, rebuilding the soul, and then I'd go out to do battle again.

For the toughness of the battle you had to have a system of replenishment, and for me it was always the music, both classical and popular. It was also histories—reading history. I was very keen about histories.

I wasn't so absorbed by politics that I had no social life. I used to go out to places to hear music and meet up with people and have a drink. I ran across a group of musicians at a hotel in Ashfield in Sydney, and this was the Ramrods. They were fantastic. Of their time, and I'm talking about the early 1960s, they were doing the sort of music you couldn't hear played live in Sydney, what I suppose people would identify today with a Tamla Motown sound or soul. Sam Cooke, Otis Redding, Ben E. King, Memphis Slim, plus covers of new stuff that was turning up. Something like 'Please Please Me' from the Beatles was a bit too popular for them. It wasn't quite pure enough.

They were doing Chuck Berry on 'Route 66' or 'Johnny B. Goode'. The Rolling Stones and the Beatles, and the so-called skiffle groups, were doing the same things in Liverpool and in London, but very few people were doing this in Sydney. We used to get the music from the United States by mail order. I used to go to the rehearsals, and if we got hold of a new record, I'd get the words down while they were picking up the music, and we'd have another song for the repertoire.

I was fascinated with these guys. They were well able to earn money moonlighting at night but some organisational focus and better venues did help. That is where I had a role. We were encamped in certain hotels for years. They were making much more money at night than they were making in their day jobs, so they became quite well off. It was a scream, really. There'd be two or three hundred metres of people round the corner, girls everywhere of course—girls everywhere—and we'd hoon around. I had the Austin Healey 100/6, and it was a good time.

One of the guest groups appearing with the Ramrods was the Bee Gees. We had them on two occasions, and on both occasions they were booed off. Their high falsetto voices attracted a few expletives across the stage, and finally they walked out. They came back for a second go, and the same thing happened again. Because the people were there for that black music, that soul music from America in the

1960s, and the Ramrods used to really belt it out, whereas the Bee Gees by comparison were testing a new idiom.

The Ramrods started recording with EMI on Parlophone. After 1962 Parlophone was the Beatles' label, and it was very hard to crack. I made a point of getting to know the people at EMI, and through them I'd meet other groups coming through. I used to meet all the rock-n-rollers.

Through EMI, I met Tom Jones. I was very friendly with him. I used to go to his shows at the Silver Spade in the old Chevron Hotel. He was like a black cat on stage—he had all the moves and he had the big, bluesy, black voice. When he did that first song 'It's Not Unusual' it succeeded because black America went and bought it, thinking he was one of them.

I always loved star power. It gives you that charge, whether it's in a very great tennis player or a great singer. I saw Jones at the Silver Spade when I was 21, that's 48 years ago, and he's still singing around 200 nights a year 48 years later. He's an amazingly gifted performer, and full of fun. I saw a film clip of Tina Turner one day, and someone asked her where she got her moves from, and she said, 'Where we all got them from, Tom Jones.'

Tom used to carry round this little card from Frank Sinatra, because they used to do the Sands each year in Las Vegas, and Frank used to say, 'You give the suckers too much Tom, give the suckers too much.'

Frank would turn up for his show, they'd start their acts at the same time, and Frank would finish, get dressed again and then turn up at Tom's performance and he'd still be singing. He told Jones he was the greatest singer of Frank's lifetime, so Tom carried this little plastic case with a card from Sinatra. It said, 'Remember Tom, you are the great one.' So I'd turn up, see him perform, then we'd go and have a dinner in Chinatown or somewhere afterwards.

KOB: And you got to know the entrepreneur Robert Stigwood. I get the sense you burrowed into that whole scene, pursued it almost like you were pursuing politics?

PJK: I knew Stigwood. I wanted the Ramrods to actually write their own material and try their luck in Britain but they were not up for that. They were very talented musicians but I don't think they really wanted to make that kind of investment. A couple of them had just been married and didn't want to give work up and take the big gamble.

KOB: Would that have been a turning point for you? Would you have been prepared to walk away from politics at that stage and gone with them to Europe?

PJK: I don't know the answer to that. I could have. It's possible, but I would have liked to have seen how I went with the politics, I think, because this was something I knew and this was where the serious side of my head was. But I could just as easily have failed on that front. I could have lost the preselection for the seat of Blaxland and then what would I have done at 24? I would have had to think well, do I try again or do I do something else? What do I do? Do I take music or go back to the family business, which I could also have done.

One of the other great things I was able to do in those days was to get entry to the EMI classical library. This was in the days of Walter Legge, the great producer at EMI in Britain. So what they now call the EMI back catalogue was largely produced by him. He was married to the soprano, Elisabeth Schwarzkopf, and he recorded Callas and Nathan Milstein, the violinist, and the great German conductor, Otto Klemperer. These recordings would come to EMI in Australia with 'factory sample, not for sale' stamped on them, so a gentleman at EMI, Kevin Ritchie, said to me, 'Paul, you're welcome to have any of these you like'. These were the great days of classical music in Europe, and these were the great recordings. So I was pursuing this dual interest in popular music on the one hand and classical music on the other.

KOB: The other great personal interest in your life that started in those early years was your passion for antiques. You seem always to have been a collector, almost by instinct, particularly drawn by the neoclassical period, and kind of hand in hand with that, the philosophical thinking of the Age of Enlightenment or the Age of Reason. I wonder what that tells us about you.

PJK: It's instinctive. The first antique that caught my eye as a young man was a watch. It was the most simple elegant pocket watch, and it had engraved on it 'Eleve de Breguet', student of Breguet, and it turned out that Breguet was the greatest watch-maker of all history. This was made in about 1795 and it cost me about three or four months' salary. I was fifteen and I remember bringing it home. And Dad said, 'What have I raised? And you paid three months' salary for it? They could sell you the town hall clock.' He couldn't believe it, but there it was. I had that compulsion to have it because what's common in all this, and I don't want this to sound trite but it is true, it's a search for what approaches perfect.

KOB: How did you know at fifteen that there was any perfection about that watch?

PJK: I used to go round to Stanley Lipscombe's shop in Bathurst Street, around the corner from the Queen Victoria Building in Sydney where I worked, and Stanley would give me *Connoisseur* magazine, and I'd go back and read the stuff and get into it. But I'd always look for what was pure, what was clean—clean to the eye, but resolved. That period, the 1790s particularly, was the period I thought had the greatest resolution.

The Victorian ones there were mostly gold, but this was gold with a silvered dial with a single minute hand, while the hours were in a little box that came up in numerals. And it was flat like an oyster. A wonderful thing. It was just the sheer cleanliness of it, the purity of its design.

I've maintained that interest all my life. I brought my mother home a clock in my first year at work. It was a German thing. It was of an elegant woman with the pendulum swinging on her outstretched finger. Mum loved that clock. Leo Schofield said to me not long ago, 'You know, I don't know where you and I came from. I came from Brewarrina, you came from Bankstown but we end up in Stanley's shop, we end up searching for the same things all our lives.' Do you know that by Leo's late twenties he and his wife Anne had put together one of the great collections of period clothing. The sophistication. And they bequeathed it to the National Gallery of Victoria.

There's something about your eyes and ears, and I don't know what it is. But it's like my experience with the *Warsaw Concerto*, a bell rings in your head. A bell in your head or your eyes pick out something that is great. And what you can't see you go looking for in museums or catalogues. All of these interests of mine had a common link, whether it was architecture, decoration, music or people in public life or political thoughts. When you get on the gold seam, when you start going down those pathways, the revelations are huge. You are forever searching for the ideal or what is near ideal.

KOB: What was it philosophically that drew you to that brief period in history from the French Revolution, and how did you apply that in your working life?

PJK: It's the beginning of the modern political age, when the French National Convention decided to abolish the privileges for the First and Second Estates, to give greater freedom to the Third Estate—the people. Letting any French citizen hold the highest positions in the land. This essentially underwrote modern Europe, the decline of the monarchies, that of absolutism, feudalism and the power of the church. It was also a driving force of the American Revolution. The French Revolution came down like Damocles's sword on the contemporary world, sheering off all that was ancient and expendable, exalting all that was modern. But it was all powered by the Enlightenment.

The Enlightenment brought with it one commanding idea—that we all arrive in this world with an equal capacity to reason. This may not seem remarkable today but in feudal Europe a person's place and capacity was viewed as a product of their culture and standing— the old historicist idea that one's reasoning was a product of one's background.

So, it didn't take long before the Enlightenment precept that each of us has an equal capacity to reason turned into a demand for equal rights. And these rights brought further demands for natural laws, the things that Rousseau, Voltaire and Montesquieu proselytised over.

A little historic standback helps here. It should be remembered that the Renaissance with its great flowering of art was conducted within the aegis and philosophy of the Catholic Church. Alberti, Michelangelo and Bernini were all deeply religious. But two centuries later the privileges of the aristocracy and the corruption of the church worked to bring the whole order into disrepute. By the second half of the eighteenth century the social task was to establish a new moral order, a secular one, governed by natural laws—laws of utility that also gave individuals inalienable rights, not the old ones conferred by privilege.

One needn't have been a social philosopher to pick the outcome. From this combustible vapour the French Revolution exploded, invoking on its path all the virtues and stoic classicism of republican Rome.

The combustion really brought on two revolutions: the American Revolution and the French Revolution, both of which underwrite the modern political age, the one we live in today.

This is primarily where my long interest in the Enlightenment and neoclassicism comes from and why I have always been interested in it.

The art of revolutionary France gave expression to the new secular morality by symbolic reference to the art of ancient Rome, Greece and Egypt. It rejected what it saw as the frivolity of the Rococo, the trappings of the aristocracy, pictures by the likes of Boucher and Fragonard or interiors of the kind promoted by Madame Pompadour.

It's not understood today but in the days before newspapers and public media, political and philosophical ideas were in very large measure transmitted by art. This is why the moralising history pictures by the likes of Jacques-Louis David, such as his *Oath of the Horatii*, were so powerful as an inspiration in the lead-up to the Revolution. The father drawing an oath from the three centurion sons to do their civic duty while the mother and sisters wept.

This decorative and moral grandeur went hand in hand with purity of form, with the sobriety of line and rigour of thought. And, in my own way, I sought to apply this kind of thinking to the big public issues of my time—clean, long lines of logic with minimal decoration. That's what I always hoped for. So, the core of my interest was in the revolutionary and republican years of France and not of Bonaparte's empire period that followed a decade later, notwithstanding that some cartoonists liked to dress me up as Bonaparte.

But, if ever there was an Arcadian period, where Arcadian nostrums ruled, where public sodality was uppermost, it was probably just after the Revolution, after Robespierre but before the Empire. Those ten years, 1794 to 1804, marked the beginning of the modern world. It has certainly had my attention and informed much of my outlook.

KOB: Yet you were dealing yourself into the game of democracy, and democracy is the practice of the deeply imperfect. The concept of democracy might be great but the practice of democracy isn't, so you spent your life searching for perfection as a politician in what is a fundamentally imperfect art.

PJK: To make significant change, you have to have a revolutionary phase, and the reconstruction of the Australian economy was a revolutionary idea. You have to have an anchor, a notion of what an ideal might resemble. With the ideal in mind, we approach the problems of change but along revolutionary pathways.

I love the straight line of logic, Kerry. Love the long, straight lines. I used to say to the Cabinet, 'We do not cut corners. We're always going to try to get the best we can. Keep the logic with us.' There is no such thing as the ideal, and you would be foolish to try to replicate it, whatever you think it is, but it's a reasonable guide to what you should be doing.

KOB: Do you think looking back that some of the manifestations of your interest in neoclassicism were used against you, or seen as a negative for you politically, that there were people out there who might never accept that these were the interests of a working-class Labor politician?

PJK: There's no doubt quite a few people may have thought that, but there's another way of looking at it. I have always thought the arts were central to a country, central to a society, holding up a mirror to itself, celebrating itself, and anyone who's had an emotional experience with the arts has that connection. If you haven't had that emotional experience you never quite understand that.

So I had that, but at the same time I had the working-class mind, the working-class vernacular. In politics, I could tell you what was in the opinion polls before they turned up. I worked in the Sydney County Council for the first six years of my working life among fitters and turners and labourers, and the life was so raw and ribald. Believe me, you wouldn't hear any of that in a university. I carried that with me for life.

Bob Hawke used to often say to me, 'Oh, you know you should get out and meet the public.' Bob went from university to Oxford and then was shoehorned into the ACTU. And I'm down here, starting at fifteen, as raw as it can possibly be, and spending a very large part of my time there, and then later as a trade union official to my mid-twenties. I had the whole mindset of working Australia pretty much off pat. Once you are inoculated with the real world there is no antidote. It's always in your bloodstream.

THE BATTLE FOR BLAXLAND

Human nature may be the same across any field of endeavour, but there are some fundamentals that set politics apart from other careers. One of them is that for the individual pursuing his or her hopes and ambitions, politics is a long-term investment that has to be carefully planned but that can unravel in a minute. You can recover from a few bad games on the football field, a few ordinary concerts as a performer, or even a few howlers climbing the business ladder, but one serious error of judgement as a politician can bring years of painstaking work undone. It could be something completely outside your own control like an electoral redistribution that suddenly robs you of a seat, and a place in the parliament. In that regard, it's a tough and unpredictable gig.

Paul Keating learned that lesson early. In 1965, at the wise old age of 21, with a flying squad of supporters on the Right within the ranks of Labor's Youth Council like Laurie Brereton and Leo McLeay, and practical support from his father Matt and old Labor stalwarts in the local branches, Keating began his push for Canberra. His target was the safe Labor seat of Banks, the family heartland. It was Right-dominated and the long-term member, Eric Costa, was quietly planning to retire after the 1966 election—an election, incidentally, in which Menzies' successor as Liberal leader, Harold Holt, had a landslide win. It was also Arthur Calwell's third election loss as Labor leader, and Gough Whitlam stepped into his shoes soon after.

This was the period where the young Keating was working to cement his place as a front-runner for preselection in Banks, not just relying on old branch loyalties to his father, but building a new base of younger members, and keeping them coming to meetings—the crucial ones at least. Then came the redistribution in 1968 that nearly brought his whole plan undone. He could have kept his push for Banks going but the heart of his power base, the Central Bankstown branch, was now in the seat of Blaxland, and he'd have to knock over a veteran sitting member in Eli Harrison, and, more formidably, a number of Left-dominated branches that had been moved into Blaxland from the neighbouring electorate of Reid. In fact the new Blaxland was an amalgam of branches from four seats, and Keating's political career could have been stillborn. It's how he went about meeting that challenge, to the extent of building his own secure ballot boxes for the preselection vote, and then borrowing from John F. Kennedy on the other side of the world to shape his campaign in 1969, that I was interested in, for the glimpses it showed of the man to come.

PJK: The Blaxland I inherited in 1968 was an equal construct of four earlier electorates: a little piece of old Reid, a little piece of Grayndler, a piece of old Blaxland and a piece of Banks. So the happy hunting ground I had in Banks suddenly changed, and I pick up these branches on the Left who, in the main, hated the sight of me. It nearly did me in because I was from the Right of the party. The Left was building up branches, packing in new members to beat me, and I was doing the same. In the end I had this huge retinue of people. I would have to bring them to branch meetings, feed them cups of tea and scones or make sure other people came and picked them up. This was the way preselection ballots were fought in those days.

That's the period I used to do fourteen or fifteen meetings a month. Every month, I'd go to the lot. The car would almost run without directions. You'd go from one meeting to the other, and if you were then going to a State Electorate Council or Federal Electorate Council, you'd pick up the other right-wing delegates in case they didn't turn up. There was always a big effort going on between the Right and the Left to get the numbers in the SEC and the FEC to appoint delegates to the State Conference. People would fight over getting one place at the State Conference.

KOB: You had an E-type Jaguar during this period. Did you actually drive the E-type to branch meetings?

PJK: Yes, I used to. In fact it met a very sticky end outside a Labor Party State Conference in the Sydney Town Hall. One of my opponents had come out during the conference and poured brake fluid all over it. Brake fluid was a mineral oil and it went straight through paint into metal, and when you touched it, the paint came off on your fingers. That was the last time I ever took a car to a State Conference. The very last time.

KOB: When you were battling the Left in the preselection process, it's always intrigued me how you define the difference between legitimate recruitment and questionable branch-stacking.

PJK: It's a matter of whether the people have an interest in being in the party, and staying. The test of branch-stacking versus people who are coming as legitimate members is whether they stay, and most of the people who joined the party in my day stayed through their lives.

Before the preselection I had the seat of Banks by the throat, but all of a sudden I'm in a new electorate and, and the Left were absolutely determined to knock me off. As it turned out I not only won Blaxland but with my organisation, the Right won the seat of Banks with Vince Martin, who was working in the tax office at the time. So he became the member for Banks in 1969 and I became the member for Blaxland. The Left hated it. The top area of my seat was called the red belt. You don't need any knowledge of geography to work out what that was about.

KOB: It was certainly a very heated battle, and the Left had selected quite a well-credentialed candidate, a young academic economist named Bill Junor. When it came to the vote, there was a dispute about whether a branch where the votes were crucial to you should actually have been counted in a different electorate.

PJK: Yes, they were crucial. In fact it was Rafferty's rules. The Returning Officer was an old leftie called Murt O'Brien, and they used to vote in shoeboxes, a piece of Sellotape around them, and a slit in the top. And I'm thinking, 'There's five years of my life in these boxes,' so I had thirteen or fourteen wooden boxes made, with locks. This became a big dispute, that I was implying that they were dishonest.

In the end, on the night I won my preselection, Murt O'Brien wouldn't count the last branch, so we had to get the State Returning Officer Lindsay North out of bed to intervene. He lived in Haberfield and he came over with his trousers pulled on over his pyjamas. You could see the pyjamas underneath. Laurie Brereton was with me standing guard. Laurie rang Gough Whitlam, and it was Gough who got Lindsay out of bed.

Lindsay walks in and says, 'What's going on here, Murt? I'll take those boxes.' So he picks up the thirteen locked boxes and puts them in his car and drives off. They were later opened at head office, where all of the ballots were counted—including the ones Murt O'Brien wouldn't include. Without that trip, I wouldn't have had the seat of Blaxland.

This was all part of the battle for control of the party between Left and Right. The national fight was running perpetually. The Left had control of the party machine federally, and Whitlam had only a few votes up his sleeve as federal parliamentary leader over his rival Jim Cairns who was on the Left. So Gough was keen to see Vince Martin and me preselected because we would represent another two votes for him.

I had a majority of votes in those boxes, including the branch that was in dispute. The Left had run this phoney appeal, and even though the appeal had been heard and knocked over by the State Executive, Murt O'Brien as Returning Office was going to take action on the night to leave the votes out of the count in order to declare Bill Junor from the Left the provisional winner.

The Left-controlled National Executive would then have been called upon, manipulated to confirm Junor as winner. The Left was completely unscrupulous.

KOB: So you're 24 and you've won preselection for one of the safest seats in the country and Gough Whitlam is the new leader of the Labor Party. In many ways it seems to me you two were chalk and cheese—he was highly educated, had an upper middle-class background and was in his fifties—but he must have been impressed with what you'd pulled off.

PJK: I'd like to think that but I don't think he was terribly. Gough was a guy with a legal background who saw public life in certain protocols. His father was Solicitor-General of the Commonwealth. By that stage more people were coming into the party with university degrees, and

I think he thought that I was just another factional warrior from New South Wales who'd busted through. I was going to vote for him, so that was a tick, but I was part of the Catholic Right like Frank Stewart in the neighbouring electorate who was another of his supporters, whom Gough liked but did not regard as a thinker.

KOB: So you saw him as something of a silvertail, and maybe he saw you as somebody he had to suffer on the way through.

PJK: Yes, I saw him as something of a silvertail, and although he saved the Labor Party with the internal reforms he forced through, I belonged to a wholly different school of politics. I was arriving at a point in time where I wanted to see the Labor Party bridge the gap between capital and Labor, something I thought the Whitlam school of leadership would never do.

KOB: If I can reprise your early political life up to this point: you've essentially studied life at your father's knee as he transformed himself from boilermaker to running his own quite successful small- to medium-sized business. You're seeing men who are to become future captains of industry like Sir Tristan Antico passing through his kitchen, you're hearing the conversations.

At the same time, you're exposed to Labor history from the indefatigable warrior, Jack Lang. So, is the young Paul Keating putting the first pieces of the economic puzzle, the political and economic puzzle together, that were to become your future guiding principles?

PJK: That's what I was doing. I thought that the so-called socialisation objective, that is, the government managing the highpoints of the economy like, for instance, the Chifley attempt at the nationalisation of banks, the idea that we could have a sort of a quasi-centrally planned economy run in part by a group of state-owned enterprises, was just old thinking—old, old thinking. The future belonged to a new breed of Australians who had the ability to use capital and employ people, with the primary growth in the economy coming from the private economy, not the public economy.

KOB: Even you must find it fascinating to contemplate the story of two parallel lives, Paul Keating and John Howard. Two boys growing up not far from each other, both from fairly humble origins, both inspired by Churchill as kids, both becoming Prime Minister one after the other, but political enemies, polar opposites.

PJK: Well, I have always said Churchill would have disowned Howard. He would have regarded him as a rank conservative, too safe and too timid. I mean, Churchill was an adventurer and, when it mattered, a lion.

KOB: Howard was inspired by Menzies and you didn't like Menzies as Howard mightn't have liked your Labor heroes either, but the fact is you both came from similar backgrounds but you went in different political directions. That I find interesting.

PJK: I think this gets down to the question of enlargement. To enlarge a country like Australia, you have to bring together the motor forces and in my view, that had to be markets, not business.

The Liberals were always interested in business bodies, cabals, monopolies, duopolies. I wasn't. I was interested in markets, not business. I had faith in markets, in competition. But I wanted that faith in markets to have the movement of markets carry labour in its locomotion. L-A-B-O-U-R, labour.

In other words, putting together an entirely new amalgam, a sort of consensus. It turned out many years later in 1983 Bob Hawke was trying to do that with his Economic Summit, but I was thinking of it in a much more primal way: robust markets, open banking competition, open financial markets, open product markets, and ultimately a flexible labour market.

KOB: John Howard recalls in his autobiography how you once derided him as the bowser boy from Canterbury because his dad ran a suburban petrol station. He said that was a badge of honour for him.

PJK: I was making the point in response to something that was said from the other side in the Parliament.

I said, 'Look, we employed a hundred people or more in my family business.' I said, 'I could have been in the Junior Chamber of Commerce, I could have been over there with you. But you think you are there to run the rest of us because you were in small business; alone as the bowser boy in Earlwood.'

I said, 'Doesn't it strike you there's something strange about this?'

KOB: And yet, Howard saw that as one of the things that worked against you in the eyes of many Australians. He painted that as you deriding small business, and the people who constituted small business, like his father.

PJK: Well, my point was referring to the presumption that the Liberal Party believes it's the born-to-rule squad, born to run the rest of us. In his case, from the bowser at Earlwood. I was simply making the point my family was employing up to a hundred people. We could just as easily have made a stronger claim to run the country.

KOB: I'm interested that you took a leaf out of John F. Kennedy's book in your first campaign in 1969, because, again, it's an insight into how you did things in those days. You didn't go to the Labor Party head office for instruction—you looked instead at how Kennedy had run his presidential campaign in America in 1960.

PJK: I stole all his graphics. I took all the campaign paraphernalia straight from the Democratic Party in 1960 and used it in 1969. The old way was to do what we called 'snipes'. A snipe is an advertisement you glued to a telegraph pole. I thought that was second-rate, and a bad look. After it was all over, no one ever took them down, and they became counterproductive.

So I did the first storyboard-sized advertising in Australia, a metre-and-a-half by two-thirds of a metre, on waterproof masonite that we silkscreen-printed. I was the first to do the silkscreen printing of my photograph with iridescent green lettering on a blue background. 'Kennedy for President' became 'Keating for Blaxland'. We put 300 of them up in the electorate so you couldn't go anywhere in Blaxland without seeing one.

Then I bought a school bus from the town of Merriwa, north-west of Newcastle, because one of my great worries was that the Left would go on strike and not work in the campaign. So I bought this bus and spray-painted it white. I had to get a truck driver's licence for the bus and an audio system. I then attached signs: 'Keating for Blaxland.'

In fact, when I'd won the seat of Blaxland, I switched the signs over and a few weeks later I was driving around Randwick for Laurie Brereton. It had 'Brereton for Randwick' on the same bus, and I'm driving around as the new federal member for Blaxland with the microphone, going around the streets of Randwick proselytising for Brereton in the NSW election. This was the election where I think John Howard was handing out Liberal leaflets at Randwick Middle School.

THE BOY FROM BANKSTOWN GOES TO CANBERRA

In the same way that the 1949 election was a dramatic turning point in postwar Australian politics, so was 1969. In the same way that a new generation of Liberals arrived in Canberra under the rejuvenated leadership of Bob Menzies in his sweeping victory of 1949, so twenty years later it was a new generation of Labor politicians under their charismatic new leader, Edward Gough Whitlam.

Menzies had retired after sixteen years as Prime Minister, Harold Holt had drowned, and the internal instability that had developed under John Gorton's leadership proved to be very costly for the Liberals at the ballot box. Labor recorded a massive 7.1 per cent swing, picking up seventeen new seats, and Whitlam came within four of claiming government. By far his youngest new backbencher was Paul John Keating. In that same year Bob Hawke became President of the trade union movement's supreme council, the ACTU. He was forty.

Where the party had been hopelessly divided in terms of both personality and ideology for most of its twenty years in the political wilderness, Whitlam's near victory fanned a new hunger for government in Labor ranks that brought with it a chance of a somewhat more united parliamentary party, in the fervent hope that 1972 would be their time. The 1969 result was all the more remarkable given that every state at the time had either Liberal or Country Party governments.

Even so, the old hatreds within Labor weren't about to die overnight. When Keating arrived for the first parliamentary sitting of 1970, that fact was soon made obvious to him, and the presence of four DLP senators in the upper house—five after the 1970 half-Senate election—was a constant reminder of the price Labor was still paying for the Split.

Apart from the negatives of incumbency for the Liberals, there were two keys to Labor's claims to office. One was its charismatic leader's determination to drag his party into the modern world with policy relevance across a broad front, and the other was that to gain that relevance he had to reform its hopelessly strangled internal processes, in which a virtual handful of unelected party officials could dictate policy to its elected members, including the would-be Prime Minister—the so-called 'faceless men' syndrome.

Those reforms were to continue through Paul Keating's first term, and although Labor's improved façade of unity was to develop a few cracks as Whitlam continued to push his more contentious policies through, like support for state aid in education, those cracks were overshadowed by ongoing dissent in the Liberal ranks. In March 1971, after his Defence Minister Malcolm Fraser resigned, accusing him of disloyalty, Gorton effectively ended his own prime ministership when a party-room motion of confidence in his leadership was split 33–all. Gorton then took the extraordinary step of using a casting vote against himself, and although it transpired that Liberal Party rules didn't recognise such a vote, there was no coming back. The new Liberal Prime Minister, Billy McMahon, was to prove a disaster.

To this day Keating remains somewhat reserved in his embrace of Whitlam's place in the pantheon of Labor heroes, but the old bull and the young bull weren't entirely chalk and cheese. Whitlam's crash-through-or-crash mentality was not that far removed from Keating's own instincts for toughness in the face of opposition, and the boy from Bankstown was also later to dominate Parliament with the same irreverent humour but abrasive style as Whitlam did right through his leadership. And both were driven by policy reform. The fundamental difference lay in economic policy, where Old Labor was still steeped in its centralist traditions and the New Labor market economy of Hawke and Keating was yet to emerge, but gestating in young Keating's mind.

The setting was the old Parliament House, built originally as a temporary dwelling while its early residents argued interminably over where to locate the permanent building. By 1969 it was hopelessly overcrowded, and the more junior MPs had to share offices. Keating shared with another new member, Lionel Bowen, who was new to Canberra but not to politics. Bowen had cut his teeth in both local and state government on Labor's Catholic Right, and his charming affability hid a wily political brain. Just eight years later Bowen was to come within four votes of winning the Labor leadership against Bill Hayden, and later end up as Deputy Prime Minister to Hawke. He was just one of the figures the young Keating assiduously courted on both sides of Labor's ideological divide, but an important one.

This was all taking place against a background of great national division over Australia's participation in the Vietnam War. In one moratorium against the war in May 1970, an estimated 200,000 people turned out across Australia to march in protest. In Melbourne alone, as many as 100,000 took to the streets. Labor policy was to withdraw Australian troops from Vietnam, but its association with the protest movement, including its more vehement members, was a tricky one for Whitlam to manage, and although he appeared at rallies he didn't align himself as passionately as some of his colleagues on Labor's Left, like Jim Cairns. Whitlam took the view that they would only win withdrawal from the war and overturn conscription through the ballot box.

Keating put it more succinctly. When Jim Cairns once chastised him for not wearing a moratorium badge, he told his much more senior colleague, 'I'm not here to protest, Jim. I'm here to be in charge.' We can probably glean from that, that it didn't take Keating long to find his feet in the new environment. In a single decade and not yet 30, he'd come from a clerical job at the Sydney County Council as a young teenager, to an organiser's job in a small trade union representing garbage men, to the nation's capital representing one of the safest seats in the country.

PJK: My first impression walking into the Labor caucus of 1969 was that it was hugely divided between the factions, between the Left and the Right, but there was a coming together of the old guard. People like Kim Beazley Senior and Frank Stewart on the Right and Clyde Cameron, Jim Cairns and Tom Uren on the Left, and Frank Crean, who was sort of non-aligned, were coming together to try to capitalise on Whitlam's success in the election and win government next time round. But it was still tribal.

The day after the swearing-in, I was standing in Kings Hall talking with Kim Beazley Senior. We were leaning over a glass case displaying a copy of the Constitution signed by Queen Victoria, when a fat guy who walked like the comic strip character, the little king, came up to me. He had to sort of tip himself backwards to stay upright, and he said, 'You're the young guy from NSW, aren't you?'

I said yes. He said: 'D'ya want a bit of advice?' and I said, 'Oh yeah ...' and he said, 'If you want a career in the Labor Party get yourself a tin suit.'

It was Vince Gair, the DLP leader in the Senate. Beazley chuckled in his own lofty way. This was really code for Gair saying that, in another time, he would have been with us, yet he's looked across at this madcap Labor Party and he thought he'd offer some sage advice. You picked up friends, but it was so institutional, the whole thing.

The big federal intervention into the Left-dominated state branch of Victoria over state aid happened in 1970, so that was also fought out inside caucus. You would go to the Members' Bar and one group would stand at one end and one group at the other. Some people on the Right were more likely to talk to Liberals before they would talk to people on the Left. They'd sit in the caucus in their particular corner and their cabal and that was it.

It was an interesting mix. There were a lot of clever new members who came in in 1969, but with the depth of experience in the older guard, some of whom had been there since before 1949. Fred Daly had been a backbencher under Curtin and Chifley. The frustration among these guys was profound after sitting on the Opposition benches for twenty years—some of them had come to believe that they would never win.

But I think the 1969 result and Gough's reconstruction of the Labor Party in 1970 and 1971 gave the whole party a sense of excitement and anticipation, so by that stage he had all the old players from the various factions supporting him. You could see the factionalism dying down in the interests of winning, but the underlying antipathy was ever present.

KOB: Having scored one of the party's safest seats at such a young age you must have attracted attention from the old hands. You already had a reputation for toughness and clearly you're sending out signals that you are a young man in a hurry, right?

PJK: You had to be tricky about it, though. You could not be overtly ambitious, seemingly ambitious. What you do is learn to play the game, get to know people, get to judge them, see what they are really made of, what they really think, and try to put coalitions together inside the place. Coming from New South Wales, I was familiar with all the people on the Right of the party from New South Wales and many from the other states.

But then there were other people I came to like, like Clyde Cameron. Clyde was on the Left, but he was such a character. I liked Clyde, and you know what? When you like someone they know it, and if you like them they generally like you. So I got on well with Clyde.

I got on reasonably well with Jim Cairns, who was a more distant fellow than Clyde. I got on well with Frank Crean. I used to sit on the table in the parliamentary dining room. They used to call themselves the LOGS—Labor's Old Guard Socialists—and Frank was called father. He would sit up the end of the table and order the wine, and you'd say, 'What have we got tonight, Frank?' and he'd say, 'Well, I've got a very nice wine from the Yarra Valley,' and they'd all put their money in.

I'll leave names out but some people were so mean that they wouldn't order a meal because a cup of tea with a bread roll was available for ten cents, so they would just have a cup of tea and the roll. One guy used to say, 'Paul, you don't need that tea, do you? All the pot?' So he wouldn't even pay the ten cents. He was famous for it.

We had another table where Kim Beazley Senior sat at the head. His nickname was the Student Prince because he used to do degrees without actually attending the courses. He used to get the lectures and sit the exams. He'd sit up there, thinking, and you would be in the middle of lunch, and he'd suddenly say, 'George III in 1762 . . .' and he'd go on with a monologue about George III or some other matter.

It'd be so interesting, and at the end we'd say, 'Well, thanks for that, Kim.'

He'd say that's okay. Kim Senior used to say to me, 'You should do what I do. Don't do the courses, just get the books and sit the exams.'

I could have done that, but I had many things to learn. I think if I had my time over I would have probably done a degree in philosophy, the history of human thought. But I was already reading widely, doing my own degree to my own curriculum.

I shared a room with Lionel Bowen. I was 25 and he was 48, an experienced bloke who had been in state and local government. He was a solicitor and a person marked out for the ministry who knew a lot. He was a complete loner but very canny. I used to listen to him talk and think, 'God, there's a lot I don't know.'

Then you'd run into other clever people like Joe Berinson, who came from Western Australia in 1969, or even people you'd simply call foot soldiers in the game, like Len Keogh or Manfred Cross from Queensland. They just knew a lot, and I thought, 'God, I thought I knew a bit but now I don't know what I know.'

You'd go to caucus committee meetings and they'd be full of specialists on foreign affairs, specialists on Aboriginal affairs, and everyone went to the economics committee. This was a much higher level of debate than I'd seen in the branch or State Conference structure. For instance, I used to go to the Aboriginal Affairs Committee, chaired by Les Johnston, another chap from the Left who knew a lot, and also attended by Kim Beazley, who was regarded as the intellectual there. There was Gordon Bryant and a whole lot of other people, and they'd all have stories and positions. At that stage, I didn't have the stories or the positions.

I spent a lot of time reading on economics and the fact that we'd been in a long period of postwar growth, which I thought was probably going to change. I was already interested in what they call Kondratiev waves, the long waves of economic growth. I'd picked that up along the way. There was a Russian economist called Nikolai Kondratiev, who believed that economic growth is run by innovation. First you get the innovation, then the infrastructure. For instance, electric light brings the power station, the substation, the cable reticulations. Then it brings heating, radios, air-conditioning. In other words, economic growth is fostered by the innovations of the era and these long innovative waves mostly lasted for 25 years. This wave had begun in 1947 so by 1972 or thereabouts, it was prone to end, particularly if the economy was inflation-prone.

I always regarded inflation as the monkey on everybody's back— the most corrosive thing in the economy. It reduced people's savings, mostly the working class. It reduced the value of their savings and put enormous mortgages on their backs. People with assets did well from inflation but people without them did very badly. What it mainly did was to tear away at the country's competitiveness. I always regarded inflation as something that, as a party, we had to be able to fix and control.

KOB: The veteran press gallery journalist Alan Ramsey once compared you in your early years in Parliament to a fictional Hollywood character named Sammy Glick, full of raw intelligence and hungry ambition. And Ramsey wrote that you had 'a hide as thick as an elephant, that you weren't in the place five minutes before you were running in caucus ballots, twisting arms, organising numbers, and generally operating like a political Sammy Glick who'd pick your pockets while he wheedled your vote'.

PJK: Well, that's probably a fair enough description of what I was up to in those days. Politeness gets you everywhere, and a bit of charm has its place, and recognising the value in other people. They may not be your people but they all brought something. I had friends on the Left whom I regarded well; people who mattered, so after a while I used to try and break down the divisions. After a while you start to develop a group of unlikely friends who might one day support you in an argument or vote for you in a ballot. You might get two or three here, two there, one there. But all the time I was always trying to soak stuff up. Whitlam said to me one day, 'You seem to have a fascination for all these old men like Connor,' and I said, 'That's because I'm trying to suck experience from them—congealed wisdom.'

KOB: Rex Connor was something of a stubborn old loner like Jack Lang. Tell me what it was about Connor that appealed to you.

PJK: He was interested in the wealth machinery of the country. Rex and I didn't share a common view about government ownership of what I would otherwise regard as private assets like national pipelines, but he saw the future for Australia as a big exporter of natural gas and iron ore and coking coal—in other words, the very staples we rely on today. This was 40 years ago. When you went to that caucus, people were interested in things like the Vietnam War, they were interested in Aboriginal affairs, social security, but you wouldn't find anyone interested in minerals and energy, hardly anyone. So he was interested in those kinds of industries and he was also interested in the economic debate. So he was a very good thinker and a good interlocutor for me. Compared to most of the people fighting out the ideological party positions, he always seemed to me to have a larger vision of the place. He was also a great interpreter of the mid-century Labor Party mood in New South Wales, from the 1950s to the 1970s. He'd been a member of the State Parliament. So he and I really got on well.

I also used to arrange meetings with people outside Parliament who offered what I'd call distilled wisdom. For instance, I arranged to meet Sir Laurence Hartnett, who was the founding managing director of General Motors Holden, to give me real insights about the car industry. He built the first Holden. He was a chairman of the State Library of Victoria so I met him there a couple of times. He was also involved with the Commonwealth Aircraft Corporation, which built the Wirraway military training plane at Fishermen's Bend in Victoria in the Second World War, so I went to the Commonwealth Aircraft

Corporation to learn about the production of aircraft. And also to Hawker de Havilland in Bankstown, where a famous aviator from the Second World War with a famous name, Rollo Kingsford-Smith, was the managing director.

I always felt that Australia had to have a defence capacity. We could never be left like we were in 1942, trying to bring in at the last minute some Hawker Hurricanes or Spitfires from somewhere because we had nothing. You had to have capacity to build these things, so I wanted to learn about the aircraft industry, about defence procurement, about motor cars, about the manufacturing industry generally.

I got to know Ian McLennan, the Chief Executive at BHP. I was very interested in the development of Bass Strait, East Gippsland oil and gas, and his decision to go offshore. What I was doing was hearing it from the masters. If you want to learn something, go to the masters. The thing about people at the end of their careers, mostly they will give you an honest summation of what they found and encapsulate it for you. You're getting really distilled ideas from them, so I used to try and then make sense of it all. Are the tariffs too high? Are we just killing the place by ring-fencing it? I was trying to work out the codes, and trying to reach the people I thought could teach me things.

I also had general histories running in my head. I was fascinated by two things: the French Revolution, as I have said, and the lead-up to the First World War. I was reading the American historian Barbara Tuchman's *The Proud Tower*, and later in life, books by people like Robert Massie, *Dreadnought*, the history of the developing antipathy between Germany and Britain in the last decade of the nineteenth century. I was especially interested in the fall of the Weimar Republic, of how a Labour Government could not hold power and grasp the massive change wrought by the Depression, including the impact of the US financial markets on Europe—reflecting itself in German inflation and unemployment. The decline of Chancellor Bruning's government and then the rise of Hitler. So I had these interests: the

French Revolution, the First World War, Second World War, Berlin in the 1920s and 1930s and finally Hitler.

KOB: Through those early years, I know you were also tapping into the senior levels of the bureaucracy, and the senior ranks of the press gallery. Was that all part of the same process, just like you were picking the brains of older Labor people like Rex Connor?

PJK: I was always trying to work out where the balance of power lay in the bureaucracy. Fundamentally, I think I had a kind of executive mind. I was working out how to grab hold of the thing and make it work for you. I was working out the relationship between the Treasury and the other departments, how the Cabinet worked, who was good and who wasn't. I also got friendly with Sir John Bunting, who was Secretary to the Prime Minister's Department. I met him at the Commonwealth Club, of all places. He used to meet there every Friday with a small group of the most senior public servants, and I used to stay at the Commonwealth Club occasionally. So I tried to piece together this wide network of people, working out how the place all knitted together. I think Bunting took it as a compliment. He said to me one day, 'You're one of the very few backbench people who ever sought me out.'

KOB: I'm surprised he gave you the time of day.

PJK: He used to tell me interesting things. He said to me once, 'Poor Harold Holt. When he was Treasurer, he used to die a thousand deaths every day at Question Time. He'd go in, he'd hang onto his files like a safety jacket, and he'd be in a lather of sweat just getting across the issues.'

This was the kind of stuff that would inform you. In the days of the Liberals, the bureaucracy ran the government. I mean, the ministers had the white cars—actually in those days they were black cars—they had their nominal positions, and there was an operative Cabinet, but nothing like changing the policy as in the Hawke years or my years, nothing like it.

What I learned from Sir John Bunting was that what was *de rigueur* was incrementalism: millimetre movements at a time because there was no political authority, so the bureaucracy could only pinch little movement at a time. When the senior officers met at the Commonwealth Club every Friday night—that's the Head of Treasury, Prime Minister's, Defence and so on—they were swapping yarns but it was really about how they moved the system along. There was no active political authority in the long years of the Menzies torpor. No political authority for change.

I'll tell you a little story. Jim Cairns came up to me once at the men's urinal in the old Parliament House and he said, 'Paul, I'm very disappointed you're not wearing your moratorium badge'. This is the moratorium on the Vietnam War.

I said, 'Well, look Jim, that's the difference between you and me. I'm not here to protest, I'm here to be in charge. I want to run the place. I'm not going to protest to this government. This government is not worthy enough to be called a government.' And if you want to run the place you've got to work out how all the organs function. I did this particularly in the period of the Whitlam Government, I made myself busy going around the bureaucracy working out where all the bits were.

KOB: So why were you picking the brains of journalists in the press gallery? What was that about?

PJK: Well, I used to go up to the *Financial Review* bureau and chat with Max Walsh and Fred Brenchley in the days when you had to walk over the old Parliament House roof to get to their offices. They were relatively young people, but they had the ear of Treasury and the rest of the bureaucracy, and often the Cabinet. They would generally have the drumbeat on what was happening inside the Coalition, and when we won government they were covering the Whitlam Government. So they were getting stuff from inside the government and I was tapping into their sources and their views.

KOB: You were using Max Walsh in particular, and Brenchley, to take you through the minutiae of how the budget papers came together.

PJK: Yes, Budget Statement Two—what to look for, how to read it, what it was really saying, comparing it with the previous year, see what the Treasury was saying, see the movements. That was 1969 to 1972. Gough, of course, had the squeeze on the Coalition for most of that term.

There are things I'll never forget. I remember John Gorton voting against himself in his party room and handing the prime minister-ship to Billy McMahon, then coming into the Parliament to announce it, though taking the deputy prime ministership and the Defence Ministry, thereby guaranteeing ongoing instability. In that period I was conscious that the Coalition was going down, that the likelihood of Whitlam winning was rising, and that my chance of becoming a minister was a prospect, though slim. I had to muster all the skills I could, get around the caucus and establish a base for whenever I could put my hand up. That was the drift up to 1972.

THRILLS AND SPILLS

American-style political campaigning came to Australia in 1972. It was this country's first presidential campaign, which was exactly the way Labor strategists wanted it. It was also the first time the power of television was fully exploited to win an election. The contrast couldn't have been greater: the little bald guy with big ears and quavering voice, and the tall, silver-haired, good-looking guy with charisma to burn. Gough Whitlam was probably the first political leader in Australia to use a blow-wave to help get him across the line.

Everything that could go wrong for Billy McMahon did go wrong, right down to the portable autocue that kept breaking down at town hall meetings, with dreadful consequences. It fed perfectly into Labor's 'It's Time' slogan and the sense of a government in terminal decline. At one point Party Secretary Mick Young warned Whitlam of the risk that half the electorate had started to feel sorry for McMahon.

Even so, it underscores the innate conservatism of the Australian electorate that even with a Prime Minister who had become a laughing stock, a Coalition majority that was paper-thin, and a media in which even Rupert Murdoch's papers had backed Whitlam, Labor still went into government with a cushion of only nine seats and a hostile

Senate. There wasn't much room for trial and error, particularly given the ambitious size of Whitlam's policy program. Up to that point, Labor had only governed the nation for seventeen of the 71 years since Federation.

There are three keys to understanding what went wrong in the three short years before Labor was back in opposition. One was the 1974 global oil crisis that pushed much of the world into recession. Another was that Labor faced one of the most obstructive Senates in history. The third and most important element was the legacy of 23 years in opposition—that is, the volatile mixture of frustration and bitterness, excitement and expectation, and dangerous inexperience. This might not have mattered quite so much if the Whitlam policy program hadn't been so all encompassing, but for Gough Whitlam, it was a program written in blood, from which he would not take a backward step, no matter the political or economic circumstances. Paul Keating would identify a fourth element to their downfall: the serious lack of economic competence around the Cabinet table, except for Bill Hayden and a handful of others.

As it turned out, the first two weeks were a powerful portent of what was to come, and of the force of Whitlam's personality on his government. After advice from the Chief Electoral Officer that while Labor had clearly won, the outcome in a number of closely contested seats might not be known until 15 December, Whitlam was so impatient to get 'The Program' going that he persuaded the Governor-General Sir Paul Hasluck to swear in Whitlam and his loyal deputy, Lance Barnard, as a two-man government. On the Tuesday after election day Whitlam gave himself thirteen of the 27 portfolios, and over the next two weeks until the full ministry was announced, implemented a whirlwind array of policy decisions, ranging from the repeal of conscription, the recognition of China, reducing fares on the government's domestic airline TAA, taking the first steps to grant Aboriginal land rights down to the release of the previously censored film *Portnoy's Complaint* and initiating moves to scrap the honours list.

The serious pursuit of representative politics is undoubtedly one of the toughest games around. Put yourself in the shoes of one of Whitlam's senior shadow ministers, say, Frank Crean or Kim Beazley Senior, who had earned their stripes through all of Labor's trials and tribulations for more than twenty years, all the exhausting and debilitating internal dogfights and the humiliating election defeats. Just as the big payoff and their time in the sun arrives—their chance to pursue their policy dreams—along comes a young upstart called Paul Keating, promising but still an upstart, barely three years in Parliament and no doubt still a kid in their eyes, and he dares to put his hand up for the first Whitlam Ministry.

Not only that, he actually runs in the first ballot for the unofficial inner Cabinet, in essence saying that he regards himself as better than at least one of them. That's certainly how he thought some of those senior shadow ministers might regard it. In the end, the 28-year-old came very close to serving in that first ministry. The writing was clearly on the wall that he would figure large in Labor's future, but there were some sharp political lessons to be learned along the way.

PJK: I'll never forget the 1972 election. I went to the big policy launch in Blacktown. There were nearly 2000 people there. We had the momentum rolling our way by that stage. McMahon attacked his own ministry in the middle of the campaign, so we thought we were going to be over the line and, as it turned out, we were. The return of Labor after 23 years was very exciting in the country and in the party. It submerged a lot of the Left–Right dichotomy that had prevailed earlier. Frank Crean was Treasurer, Clyde Cameron was Labour Minister and Bill Hayden had Social Security charged with bringing in Medibank as a universal health scheme.

Looking back, Gough's great legacy is that he saved the Labor Party being marginalised electorally. The destruction of the Socialist Left in Victoria, the Hartley faction, opened up the party to the light of day in a policy sense, and brought people like John Button, John Cain, Michael Duffy and Barry Jones into the mainstream of the Victorian branch. Gough saved the party electorally—a renewal of the kind Tony Blair did for the Labour Party in Britain.

In policy terms, there were the big foreign policy initiatives: the recognition of China, withdrawal from Vietnam. In domestic policy, Medibank, multiculturalism, greater equality in education, divorce law reform, urban planning and electoral reform. They became big turning points in this country's history.

What Gough or his ministry didn't have was knowledge of the wealth management machinery, how the economy operated. It was only later when it became apparent that there was really no link to the business community, that no one had any real idea about how the economy functioned, apart from Hayden, who only became Treasurer in the latter period of the government.

Gough only had a shadow ministry of thirteen but there was going to be a full ministry of 27 in government. Gough decided the election would take place in two caucus ballots, the inner thirteen in the morning and the remaining fourteen in the afternoon. I couldn't decide whether to declare my hand and run against the established front-runners from the shadow ministry in the first ballot, because by doing so I was saying to one of the thirteen, I should be there instead.

I asked Rex Connor what he thought, and he said, 'Well, it's a simple rule. If you want to get into the ministry, you run.'

I thought, 'Well, let's go back to first principles here. Do you want to be a minister in this government? Yes. Do you have the courage of your convictions? I hope so.' So I threw my hat in the ring for the first thirteen, and I came sixteenth in the field.

I've kept a record of the vote—I have the file here. I have how I voted and how everyone else voted. Ratting is hard to do in the Labor Party.

Lionel Bowen also decided to run even though he wasn't in the old shadow ministry either. He got 24 votes and I got 23. Had it been a total vote for the full ministry I would have been the sixteenth elected out of 27. What happened then, before the second ballot after lunch, was that the rats in the ranks—people from the Right in NSW— attacked me. Some in my own faction closed ranks against me, and fundamentally did me in. People like Bill Morrison and Al Grassby ran the risk of being eliminated if I got up, as was the case with Doug McClelland, a senior senator from the NSW Right. They got onto the party machine in Sussex Street and the message was clear.

'That bloody Keating—unless we shift votes from him, one of us won't get up.'

I remember saying to Lionel Bowen that I'd made a bad decision tipping my hand. I would have been better off running quietly for what was effectively the outer ministry in the second ballot. As it turned out, Lionel got into the ministry and I came twenty-eighth. That is, I was the last person eliminated. I came fifteenth in the ballot for the second fourteen.

I remember John Ducker, the State President of the party, was on a Russian cruise ship at the time, and his sidekick Geoff Cahill had done what the others had asked of him. I sent Ducker a telegram saying, 'John, I wanted to thank you for your efforts on my behalf in the ballot. You and Geoff stuck to me like a limpet mine.'

They caught up with me on that occasion, but they never caught up with me again. Factionally I was becoming much more powerful in New South Wales so from then on, I pretty much ruled the roost.

KOB: I assume you kept building alliances with the party machine that was very much a part of your future?

PJK: I certainly stayed in touch with the machine. Some of my colleagues like the Grassbys and the Morrisons would not know what the machine was, but I knew that conference floor like the back of my hand. I knew most delegates on it. I knew where all the battalions came from, and where they were going.

Public life is about delivering change, and if you don't know how to work the machinery you can't get the job done. Execution is the key. A lot of people in public life have got ideas about doing things, but if people look at my public record, policies were executed because I was able to make the organisms of the Labor Party work for me. You have to have the political and industrial movement working for and with you.

KOB: For those who supported Labor in the 1972 election, the Whitlam Government began with high excitement: the drama of the Whitlam–Barnard two-man government, and then the sense of doors being opened, of change. You were inside that process through all the tumult of those three years. What was your view from the inside as things started to change?

PJK: Well, it was thrills and spills, with a big emphasis on the thrills because it was a very reforming government. It really did change the direction of the country, in social policy, in foreign policy, in education—in a whole range of things. But then came the closing down of economic growth worldwide, and with it the incapacity to manage the budget—the tearaway levels of government spending. I think Commonwealth outlays grew 23 or 24 per cent in one year alone, whereas in the years that I was Treasurer in the Hawke Government, sometimes we had outlays growing at less than the inflation rate. Or plus 1 per cent. Under Frank Crean and then Jim Cairns as Treasurer, the budget just tore away, which had implications for demand, for interest rates and inflation.

KOB: I can remember Clyde Cameron as Minister for Labour deciding quite early on that he was going to use public-service salaries as the pacesetter for wage increases around the country, the end result of which was a wages explosion.

PJK: It was. This is how mad it was. I think wages rose 16 per cent within a year, as the Commonwealth salaries underwrote a national wage round. This was completely destructive, firstly, of the profit share in the economy, and then private investment. It was basically the old Labor Party again, the old confusion of ends and means: trying to run wages policy off the public service, trying to grow the economy off the back of the budget, off government spending, rather than private investment. They regarded as nonsense any concern that the attendant bond-selling program and the interest rates that followed would crowd out private investment.

But let me say one thing in their defence. It's very important to say this about all of them. In economic history, people now refer to the postwar long wave of economic growth as between 1947 and 1974. The oil price spikes associated with OPEC, the Middle East oil cartel, one in 1972 and a second in 1974, and the beginning of tearaway inflation, declining commodity prices, the general decline in investment from about 1965 onwards, meant that you could almost plot, across the world, the end of the postwar cycle of growth. Nobody in Australia could really have known after this long period of growth, that virtually from the day Whitlam was sworn in as Prime Minister the world economy began turning down, and with it the Australian economy.

It was this unfathomable problem that led them, for instance, into the Cairns budget of 1974, which had outlays growing at 23 per cent that year. In other words, they thought you could get growth off the back of the government sector simply by pumping up the economy. Gough, who had no real idea about any of this, could never have fathomed that just as he arrived, the party was over.

Up to the point when I became Treasurer in 1983, the press gallery mainly responded to four matters only—election speculation, leadership changes, tax cuts and maybe inflation, but certainly nothing about the country's competiveness, savings, productivity, not any of that. If you ask any of the people who were in political journalism then, they would tell you they did not have these matters on the radar screen. Most people in the political debate, including the journalists, assumed the growth would keep going, and the Whitlam Government had only to focus on its distribution.

KOB: In the early tumult of the Whitlam years, you're 30, you've never left home. You meet Annita. Can you describe that moment in your life?

PJK: This is where my relationship with John Bunting paid off. John Bunting rang me one day and he said, 'Paul, there's a Commonwealth Ministers' Conference on in Zambia and the Prime Minister doesn't think any of the new ministers should leave. As you were the last backbencher eliminated in the ministerial election would you represent Australia? You would go with the status of minister.'

I agreed to go and I met Annita on that flight. So, you see, getting beaten for the ministry actually did me a lot of good.

Some months later Annita came to Australia with her mother and looked me up at Parliament House. I was attending a dinner for the Duke of Edinburgh and I get this note from somebody whose name I didn't recognise staying in a motel, so I rang up. It was Annita and her mother. So I saw them the next day. The next time I saw her was in the Netherlands about six months later, and so it went.

KOB: But by the time you marry at 31 you're already well into your political career. You're living and breathing it really, consumed by it. Do you think either of you had the faintest

idea how hard it would be to make a marriage and a family fit
with that?

PJK: The great mistake in the federal system of Australia was to place
the capital in Canberra. The idea that we all fly off from homes around
Australia on a Tuesday morning and stay in motel rooms for three
or four days and join the boys' club, as it was in those days, in the
Parliamentary Dining Room, and then back home at the end of the
week, is a pretty crazy way to conduct life. And when I became Party
President in NSW in 1979 I used to get back to Sydney on Friday
morning and go straight to the Administrative Committee of the
Labor Party in Sussex Street. So I would leave Tuesday morning and
return home Friday night. Long days, long weeks.

KOB: Annita is a beautiful, sophisticated, globetrotting woman
from Europe. Suddenly she's in suburban Bankstown, alone a
lot of the time, with the children when they come along. That
must have been incredibly tough. Do you think you realised
what you were asking of her?

PJK: Well, it was tough and probably, no, I didn't realise quite what it
would be like. Nevertheless we did take the opportunity of moving to
Canberra when I became Treasurer. This made a big difference.

KOB: Were you impressed by Whitlam in Parliament?

PJK: He was impressive and he dominated it, but I was a very different
political type to Gough. I learned one thing from him. That we shared
a common cause on one matter: both of us believed we should be in
charge. Now, that may sound trite, but somewhere in your head you
have to have that view before you can climb the mountain. Because if
you don't have that view, you never make it.

Now, where do we get that belief or instinct? In my case I probably owe it primarily to my grandmother and to my mother, who always thought I was special. So I had that inner confidence. I'm sure something similar happened to Gough. The same thing certainly happened to Bob Hawke.

But Gough had a parliamentary view of the world that I really did not share. He did hold the contemporary Liberal Party in contempt yet he did not understand their venality or know what to do with it when it became apparent. In the end he wasn't tribal, where I was tribal working-class Labor. In true combat, that matters.

The other thing I wanted was to be in charge of that big business community out there. I don't think he felt that. I felt once you were in charge of that you were in charge of the whole game—you could have all your social policies sorted.

I think I pretty well had that worked out by the time I came into the Parliament in 1969. It comes back to my father in the Menzies years. We could never work out why a country of working-class people kept electing elitist Tory governments who were not part of them socially and had no capacity to innovate the place.

KOB: But you would have seen business leaders as being hand in glove with those same Tories in the same way the unions were hand in glove with Labor. That being the case, you would have seen the business community as being part of the enemy?

PJK: I did. But I also knew unless you could operate with business and operate business, it would in the end defeat you. You had to operate it to stay on top while producing the wealth. You had to be in charge of it. In other words, you had to have a framework in which they had a seat at the table, and in the end I believed the framework where they could sit had to be an open market economy.

The one thing most of these industries shied away from was competition. They all relied on a managed exchange rate, a government licence to operate in the case of the banks, and in television, the Frank Packer two-station rule. All these businesses existed on monopolies or oligopolies.

One of my first meetings as Treasurer was with the Chairman of the National Australia Bank, Sir Robert Law Smith, who had a property in the western districts of Victoria. He said to me with a plum in his mouth—he could have been from any Tory club—he said, 'Of course, Treasurer, we're in the free enterprise business, we prefer competition,' and I said, 'Well, Sir Robert, so do I. The only difference is, I'm going to give you some.'

He said, 'Oh, what do you mean by that?'

I said, 'Well, you guys have been featherbedded for years. You have effectively had no competition, we have no real entrepreneurship in the four banks.'

He said, 'Oh, you think that, do you?'

I wanted to take them on at their own game. One of the things I often used to say about the Liberal Party and about the Labor Party I led, is that the Liberal Party believes in business, companies and cabals, but it doesn't believe in markets. Whereas the new Labor Party believed in markets, not being a captive of business.

That was a view I wish Gough had brought. If you grew up in the Menzies era you had to take charge of Menzies' constituency, and I don't think there was anything in the Whitlam template—either with him or his government—that displaced the Menzian view of how the place was run.

I used to meet some of the business leaders of their day through my father. You knew people in business, but Australia was a country intermediated by banks. It never had a capital market like the United States. Companies like my father's could not go to a capital market and raise capital. They had to go to a bank. Our bank was the ES&A

Bank (the English, Scottish & Australian Bank), a shocking outfit in terms of competitiveness.

So I cottoned on to what Rex Connor was onto, in terms of the business of the place, the mineral wealth, the fact that we could harness it and grow it, spreading this into the Labor constituency. I cottoned on to that, but I didn't believe in the kind of state socialism that Rex had faith in. I embraced the minerals and the wealth on the basis of a competitive framework where you set up the marketplace, where Labor constructs a new economy, where the government steers the boat, not rows the boat.

One of the reasons I became Shadow Minister for Minerals and Resources from 1976 onwards was because I was the only one in the show who wanted to deal with these big industries. It was the default job: 'Give it to him, because he wants to do it and we don't.'

KOB: If it was a big challenge for Labor to adjust to government after 23 years in opposition, then the same had to be true in reverse for the Coalition. What do you remember of the Liberals in opposition under Billy Snedden's leadership?

PJK: I think a substantial part of the Liberal Party had come to believe that their time was well and truly up, and that it was a good time for them to think about their place in public life and to regroup. I know that because in the days before the Whitlam dismissal in 1975 there was quite a degree of social intercourse between the opposing parties during the parliamentary sessions. At night back at the Kurrajong Hotel where a lot of us stayed, Coalition MPs used to speak quite freely. So from that I thought a substantial number of Coalition members believed it was their time to be on the grass.

On the other hand there was a group of them who didn't think that, who could never accept that they'd been rejected by the elector-ate. Frankly, I don't believe Snedden had any revolutionary zeal about him. I don't think he was affronted personally or ideologically by the Whitlam Government or its agenda, or felt the need to try to bring the government to an election at a time of the Opposition's choosing, which was the tactic they came to employ in the Senate.

These were people who supported democracy as long as they were in power. They'd had that power for 23 years, but apparently that wasn't enough, so the Senate became a place of obstruction virtually from the outset, where traditionally it had been little more than a rubber stamp for government legislation. So their tactic was to create a mood of volatility about the government's program, and when the government's popularity suffered, to try to push it to an election and beat it.

It was people like Reg Withers, and there a number of them, who were more affronted ideologically by the Whitlam agenda, and I think they boxed Snedden in, and forced him to pursue a more aggressive and disruptive approach. You must remember that the Senate was nowheresville for much of our federal history. The irony for Labor is that it was Lionel Murphy who, when we were in opposition, showed everyone how to give the Senate teeth by strengthening the committee system as a means of attacking the government. Before that it was a bit like old home week in the upper house and they more or less rubber-stamped the legislation of the day. The Liberals learned a lesson from Murphy. Suddenly they could see the Senate's power. It fed their propensity for a fight.

There was also the savagery of the then Country Party before it became the Nationals. I remember the viciousness with which 'Black Jack' McEwen, Doug Anthony and Peter Nixon in particular, attacked Jim Cairns over his leadership of the anti-Vietnam moratorium campaign when we were still in opposition—running a two-day debate in the House of Representatives, sitting the Parliament until three in the morning, people having their evening meal at midnight so they could move a censure motion quite viciously against Cairns.

This was a pretty mean crowd. I would say that combinations on the Coalition side of people like Anthony and Nixon—not so much Ian Sinclair—with disparate elements in the Senate like Reg Withers, came to command the strategy inside the Coalition that pushed Snedden along.

There was also an anger and contempt for Whitlam on their side. They regarded him as a kind of social traitor who they believed had switched camps and was employing 'high brow' tactics, if you like, against them. Gough had come from a background that they would have regarded as being owned by the conservatives. His father was Solicitor-General under Menzies. It was a classically arrogant attitude on their part, that if you came from the elite then you must be one of them. They really had a hatred for Whitlam and all the things he came to stand for. They never accepted Labor's right to govern for three years, even after 23 years in opposition. They did think they were the born-to-rule squad. They thought Gough was a traitor and they had come to understand that if they used the power they had in the Senate, they might be able to push Labor to an election at a time of their choosing.

KOB: In the Hawke–Keating years you came to command the Parliament. I wonder what you learned from Whitlam's parliamentary style?

PJK: He definitely commanded the debate and he had ministers who had been in the Parliament a long time in opposition who were both competent and confident in that sense—people like Clyde Cameron, Fred Daly and Frank Crean, and even newer ministers like Lionel Bowen. They had the skills. The government in the House of Representatives had good form about it. That's not to provide a commentary on how the government was doing in the media or in the public's eye, but in the Parliament it dominated the debate, and looked like it was in charge.

After the soporific nature of the Menzies years, the excitement and action around the Whitlam Government was like a moth to a flame for the press gallery, with new policy announcements rolling out almost by the day. For ministers to suddenly go from very small offices in the shadow ministry to a lot more staff and a lot more policy action, with press secretaries who'd been working journalists all their lives who had to learn discipline and discretion about the inside information they suddenly had at their disposal, was a big ask. It was a difficult public relations exercise. Not a disaster, but difficult. For the first time ever, a lot of active journalists were suddenly on the inside, sitting in the box seat in the ministers' offices at a time of immense change, having to remove themselves in their heads from the game they had just left.

It didn't help that the place was set up as it was with the non-Members' Bar on the ground floor off one of the parliamentary quadrangles as a meeting place for journalists and staffers, and even Labor backbenchers every night of the week. It was a great marketplace for stories. The conversations and the information flowed freely. It was a journalist's dream. It was also very hard to maintain any sort of discretion in the internal policy debate within the government with the press gallery just one floor above, in what was essentially a small building.

There was a set of stairs directly outside the double doors of Labor's caucus room leading up and across to the press gallery, and as a caucus meeting broke up, the journalists would be waiting on those stairs to get their stories. Discretion was impossible. MPs would be standing around in that small space, trying to talk discreetly to each other without success. I can remember coming out one day and a young bearded Paul Kelly coming down the stairs and sidling up to me and asking what had happened on this or that issue. That was the way it was. You just had to glance around Kings Hall to see who was talking to whom. Another section of the press gallery was also directly above the Prime Minister's office and the Cabinet room, so the comings and goings within the government were easily observed.

KOB: As the Whitlam years unfolded the impression was created that the government was something of a roller-coaster ride with a certain lack of cohesion. What do you remember of that?

PJK: The government had a great factional unity of purpose most of the time, and while at other times there would have been high factionalism in the party and in the caucus through that long period in the wilderness, you did have factional leaders from the Right and the Left with a desire to see a united front in government. So that even though some ministers might not have been at the front of the game, the fact that they were in the game at all was enough to keep the show together.

The backbenchers who made up the other half of the caucus had to tread very warily in a caucus discussion, to be careful what they said because they'd wear the admonition of the leaders of their own factions. The first caucus chairman was Senator Bill Brown from Victoria and he'd been part of the Socialist Left in his home state, so if one of the 'bad guys' in the Right's terms was actually chairman of caucus, it meant that their adherence to the system had overtaken their former unruliness.

I remember on one occasion I moved a motion in caucus to set up a royal commission into the public service. I didn't think the service was working for us because it had been used to having conservative masters for 23 years and because of the culture of incrementalism, making changes one small step at a time. This motion was really frowned upon because it hadn't come up in the normal way as part of the government's internal conversation. The ministerial presence inside the caucus was quite powerful in providing an equilibrium.

Gough's beloved program that he was so obsessive about had
very important elements to it, like access and equity in health and in
education, particularly higher education, or the big changes in foreign
policy that you could fashion a good story about, but we were not that
good at actually telling the stories. For all the interest we had from
the press gallery, our run rate on storylines and actually telling those
stories was low.

Gough's speeches were first-rate. The speeches he wrote himself
or with Graham Freudenberg were great. But in terms of the general
'shooting star' nature of the program, the storyline in the newspapers
lacked an overarching coherence, notwithstanding the virtues of
any individual policy story. Each in their own right had important
implications for the country but there wasn't in that ministry a sense
of internal coherence and discipline, despite the fact that the Prime
Minister had a great capacity for storytelling and for the evocation
of issues.

KOB: Whitlam was obviously very impatient about
implementing 'The Program', and you made a speech to the
Whitlam Conference of Labor Historians in 1985, the third year
of the Hawke–Keating Government, in which you referred to
'the undisciplined dash to implement a decade's worth of
reform'. That was one fundamental problem with the Whitlam
Government, wasn't it, trying to do too much too soon from
a base of relative inexperience? By comparison, although
you didn't start government with a program as specific as
his, across such a wide policy spectrum as his, nonetheless
as your agenda developed you gave yourselves the time to
implement it.

PJK: Put it this way, if we were reviewing the Hawke–Keating years,
the chapters would have a sequence and a coherence about them,

whereas, without diminishing any one chapter in the Whitlam book, the last chapter might come second and the third chapter might come eighth. In other words the Whitlam Government didn't have a rolling discipline and coherence about it.

The caucus in general had picked up on the inchoate quality that the 27-member Cabinet had. When the caucus gets wind that there's strife in the Cabinet on this issue and that issue, it lowers the standing of the Cabinet within the caucus. What happened within those three years was that as the caucus respect for the Cabinet diminished, caucus members were more prepared to chance their arm with their own opinions. So by mid-1974, the faction leaders were becoming less effective and caucus members were more inclined to deal themselves into the policy debates. A lot more independence of mind was being seen within the caucus on particular resolutions that wouldn't necessarily have helped maintain a sense that there was a unity of purpose in the government.

I can remember Gough having to lay down the law to caucus a number of times, sometimes ferociously. But the mere fact that he had to do it was a bad look. Gough was assiduous at attending electorate functions or party events for his backbench colleagues, and he remained that way all his life, but there was no interleaving of the prime ministerial authority with the casual encounter, no real common touch. When I was Prime Minister, members knew they could walk up to me and raise something without getting their head bitten off. If a member came up to me after Question Time to raise something with me, I'd never dismiss them, whereas with Gough you got the message he was in a hurry to get on with his day.

KOB: To come back to the Opposition's aggressive strategy in the Senate: they essentially forced Whitlam's hand, calling a double dissolution election in May 1974 after only eighteen months in office, with the threat to block supply hanging over

Labor's head, how did all that impact on your side of the
Parliament?

PJK: We were affronted by the tactic to threaten supply. There was
no sense of crisis in the government apart from the fact that key
legislation like Medibank was not getting through, but that was
our problem. We should not have been obliged to go to an early poll
just because the Liberals didn't like being in opposition. It was the
Opposition that created the feeling of instability. It was redeemed
somewhat by the fact that, although we lost seats, voters put us back
into office, which allowed Gough to call a special joint meeting of
both houses of Parliament in order to pass the big backlog of legislation that had previously been rejected twice by the Coalition in the
Senate. But we should not have had to go to that election, and within
twelve months we had a similar threat hanging over our heads again,
courtesy of the new Opposition Leader Malcolm Fraser.

But the joint sitting of Parliament did have something of a salutary
effect on us, the feeling that the Constitution was seen to have worked,
that a joint sitting was an avenue by which an impasse could be
resolved. For instance, I had a big interest with Rex Connor in the *Seas
and Submerged Lands Act*, which the states-centred Opposition had
refused to agree to. The High Court had held that the Commonwealth
had jurisdiction from the low-water mark where the water laps the
beach to the edge of the continental shelf. Connor wanted to put this
into law under the *Seas and Submerged Lands Act*. It was resisted by
Coalition people like John Ellicott who was running the states' rights.
I remember how good we felt when we saw that go through. The joint
sitting was quite a historic moment to see all that previously rejected
legislation go through.

Having jumped that hurdle we felt we were back in open territory
to get on with pursuing the agenda of a Labor Government but

the Coalition attitude in the Senate didn't change. The common man in all this was Reg Withers, combined with the general sense among Snedden's colleagues that he wasn't really up to it. I can remember Snedden saying immediately after the 1974 election, 'We didn't win but we didn't lose.' He used to say things like 'My members would follow me through the valley of death over hot coals,' which really just drew everyone's attention to the fact that his hold on the leadership was precarious. Snedden was more or less a traditionalist and the tactics leading to the 1974 election were his undoing.

When Malcolm Fraser arrived in the leadership with that upper-class conceit, and apparent disregard for the norms of parliamentary behaviour, and our mob were becoming something of a ragtag show, you could see Fraser wasn't going to be good for us.

The one bright spot was when Gough removed Jim Cairns as Treasurer and replaced him with Bill Hayden. Jim McClelland replaced Clyde Cameron as Labour Minister and introduced a much more disciplined wages policy. Hayden brought some discipline to the budget in August 1975, and the economic management was looking better. Gough was still a force to be reckoned with, and some solid new ministers were coming in like Joe Riordan and Joe Berinson. There was some hope in the place, but against that, Cameron was angered by his demotion to the Science Ministry and was starting to destabilise the show, and Connor was in strife over the Loans Affair. It was the sacking of Connor and Jim Cairns over the Loans Affair that dragged the show down and robbed the Cabinet of its credibility.

KOB: It was in the second half of 1975 that Rex Connor really went off the rails in pursuit of his dream to build big national infrastructure projects and develop Australia's mineral wealth—chasing shonky money men on the other side of the world to borrow money, basically because he couldn't get Treasury's endorsement to raise the kind of money he wanted.

PJK: We got into this crazy stuff with Rex and the Loans Affair. He had the Treasury running around trying to stop him raising money in the Middle East to pay for infrastructure in Australia. It was nonsense.

I used to say to him, 'Rex this is crazy, you've got to give this up.' But he wouldn't.

He would just sit there all night with his ticker tape machine waiting for this Khemlani fellow to produce verification for the loans he was supposed to be arranging. It became an obsession. A big obsession. Gough had a misplaced loyalty in Rex. He should have forced him to stop this earlier than he did. In the end, he sought to fire him rather than correct him.

Rex was well meaning and imaginative. He believed in the place, he could see the future, but he never had the right modus operandi to get the industry on his side. Again, the confusion of means with ends.

KOB: It gradually became a scandal and the sad irony for you, I imagine, was that when you finally did get to take your place in the ministry it was at Rex Connor's expense because the scandal had consumed him and he had to resign.

PJK: Indeed, and I urged him not to resign. I suggested he tell Gough's emissary to go to buggery, and he initially did. Again, as a last word in his defence, he understood the importance of minerals and energy to Australia, and in this day and age a large part of our national income is coming from it. But Rex had the old Labor model in his head, that assets like the pipeline authority had to be owned by the government. Could only do an economic job if owned by the government.

When I did get to the ministry I didn't realise I'd only be there for three weeks before Sir John Kerr dismissed the government. But I must say it was a bag of fun. The first full ministry meeting I went to was unbelievably chaotic. Joe Berinson, who hadn't been in the ministry long, said to me, 'When you come in you won't believe how mad it is.'

He said, 'You think I'm exaggerating, don't you?'

And I said, 'Well, I'll wait and see.'

So when I walked in, not one person says, 'Welcome, it's nice to have you here.'

It was back to square one, bottom of the class. I knew where Connor sat, so I went to sit in his vacant chair. Immediately, Gough said, 'Don't sit there! You don't sit there!'

I said, 'So where do I sit?'

He said, 'Bowen, you sit here. Riordan, you take Bowen's seat, Keating, you take Riordan's seat.'

I said, 'I don't care which seat I have, Gough, as long as I have one.' This is in the Cabinet room!

The constitutional crisis was beginning to appear, and there was a long dissertation from Kep Enderby, who was Attorney-General. He used to speak very rapidly and went on and on, and I saw Gough grimacing and showing his annoyance and then finally it got the better of him.

He said, 'Enderby you garrulous so-and-so, when will you shut up?'

And Enderby says, 'Who, me?'

He said, 'Yes, you.'

And Gordon Bryant, another minister, says to Gough, 'You shouldn't speak to him like that.'

And Gough says to Bryant, 'You shut up!'

To which Bryant replied straight back at him, 'And don't speak to me like that either.' At this point Joe Berinson sent me a note down the table: 'Told you so.'

By this time the discipline in the Cabinet was badly shaken. The only hope in all this was that Bill Hayden, who had finally become Treasurer had begun dragging the budget back to something approximating what it should always have been. If you look at the Hawke years, and my years as Prime Minister, the solemnity with which the Cabinet process was conducted, the disciplined way people considered Cabinet submissions, where there was a corporate discussion with each minister taking responsibility for their matter— there were light years of difference.

THE DISMISSAL

The seeds for the way in which the Whitlam Government fell in November 1975 were planted in the lead-up to the previous year's double dissolution election. By April 1974, just sixteen months after the election, the Opposition in the Senate had rejected nineteen government bills, ten of them twice. Six of the ten rejected bills qualified as triggers for a double dissolution.

The Opposition Leader Billy Snedden initially resisted the urging of his Senate leader Reg Withers to delay the introduction of money bills into the Senate, but when he did move to embrace the Withers strategy, Whitlam replied with his own—a double dissolution.

It was politics played on the cliff edge by both sides. Snedden wanted to force Labor to a lower house election with only half the Senate up for judgement. The threat to the Liberals posed by a double dissolution was twofold. With the full Senate in play, not only might Whitlam win a fresh term in the lower house, but also conceivably gain control of the Senate, which was every conservative's worst nightmare. Even without Senate control, a subsequent joint sitting of both houses would see Labor's major reforms like Medibank passed into law.

If ever there were grounds for a double dissolution, Whitlam had them, and Sir John Kerr as Governor-General formally agreed. Billy Snedden lost the election in May 1974 by just four seats, but in the process his leadership was fatally damaged. The game changed dramatically from the moment Malcolm Fraser replaced Snedden early the following year, and it wasn't long, with the Whitlam Government barely through the first year of its second term, having only served seventeen months of its first, before Withers was pushing the same advice to Fraser that had proved disastrous for Snedden— blocking supply.

There have been few more volatile years in Australian politics than 1975. The economy had turned sour with a vengeance, unemployment and inflation were up, and wages had exploded. By the August budget, Labor was into its third Treasurer and its third Deputy Prime Minister since the 1972 election. The government's relationships with some of its most senior public servants were just short of openly hostile.

Then came the Loans Affair scandal involving Rex Connor, who had been closely supported by Whitlam in his bid to fund big infrastructure projects to unlock Australian mineral wealth, which eventually engulfed the government and provided Fraser with his 'exceptional circumstance' to block supply and force an election.

I'm not going to trawl through the massive volume of material written about the events leading up to the Dismissal, because none of the key players have changed their justification for their part in the drama, and never will. For those who want more detail, they can reference Malcolm Fraser's memoirs and Gough Whitlam's book, *The Whitlam Government*. There are countless other books, including one from Sir John Kerr, but if you read Whitlam and Fraser, you've got both sides from the protagonists. There is one startling postscript to the Dismissal that bears a mention in terms of Keating's comments in the interviews. Not long before we sat down to record them, the academic and author, Professor Jenny Hocking, published the second volume of her Whitlam biography in which she revealed from Sir John Kerr's own previously unpublished archive that the Governor-General had been in secret talks with the then High Court Judge Sir Anthony Mason going back months before 11 November. It was known that Kerr had sought last-minute advice from the Chief Justice, Sir Garfield Barwick. Kerr's notes for his archive revealed much more extensive consultations with Mason over many weeks, and quite a deal of strategising on Kerr's part well before Fraser had decided to block supply.

There was even an impromptu conversation with Prince Charles in September at the Papua New Guinea independence celebrations, where Kerr flagged the possibility that he might have to dismiss the government or even that Whitlam might ask the Queen to dismiss him. A presumably startled Prince Charles dropped a few reassuring remarks, but he clearly did pass the message back to the Palace. From Hocking's archival research, Kerr subsequently received a letter from the Queen's Private Secretary, Sir Martin Charteris, referring to Kerr's fears of dismissal at the Prime Minister's hands if he tried to sack Whitlam. Charteris said the Queen 'would try to delay things', but in the end would have to take the advice of the Prime Minister—the very opposite of what her representative in Australia would come to do on her behalf.

To bring Paul Keating back in, he had just become a minister, he could see Bill Hayden's first budget as Treasurer had brought a discipline and some credibility to Labor's economic management that had been sorely lacking, and although the realist in him knew the next election would inevitably see a conservative government back in power, he thought that might still leave him up to eighteen months to build his own credibility and experience, and climb another rung or two within the Cabinet before the electoral axe descended.

As coincidence would have it, Keating had two brief Zelig-like moments in the dismissal tableau. He just happened to be present at

Whitlam's last meeting with Kerr before 11 November. On the day itself, he was on the Parliament House steps, looking impossibly young as he warmed up an angry crowd that needed no encouragement, before Gough strode through the big double doors, took the megaphone from his most junior minister, and uttered those words that are now sandblasted into history. For a few unforgettable moments they stood side by side, the old bull and the young bull, one's painfully long journey to the top crashing down around him, the other having barely established his base camp.

PJK: When I look back at the Dismissal, I think of what Jack Lang had to say about how much you are able to trust people. You've got to look carefully at who is in front of you. Look at their motivations for what they say and do. Look at their background and their ambitions, even thwarted ones, and then make a judgement about whether you can rely on them.

I never got to know Kerr personally before he became Governor-General, but I had heard about him representing various unions on the Right, and in disputes involving the industrial groups. But I had never thought he was one of us. He didn't necessarily need to be one of us, but you would expect a person you're appointing to a position like Governor-General needing to have the balances right. Gough appointed Kerr, I appointed Bill Deane. There was a world of difference in the assessments brought to those two appointments.

It is absolutely clear that Kerr deceived Whitlam over his intention to sack him. I was with Gough on the last day he saw Kerr before the Dismissal, on the Thursday before. I was there as Minister for Northern Australia appointing the former Labor Lord Mayor of Brisbane, Clem Jones, to be Chairman of the Darwin Reconstruction Commission.

We had an Executive Council meeting of three—Gough, Kerr and me—but initially I waited outside with Kerr's secretary, David Smith, while Gough and Kerr had a meeting about the state of play over supply. When I was invited in to sign off on the Executive Council minutes, Gough and Kerr were in a huge state of laughter about Lionel Murphy arguing with the Chief Justice Garfield Barwick over a uniform for his female tipstaff. It was all very friendly and relaxed.

It only took us a few minutes to sign the documents, and as we walked down the long corridor to the car Gough said, 'Look at that leonine mane', referring to Kerr's bouffant head of white hair.

We get in the car, he sits in the front and turns on the music, and I say, 'Well, he seems all right Gough,' and he says, 'Oh, he'll be okay, he's completely proper.'

I remember that clearly: 'He'll be okay, he's completely proper.'

So as they sat there laughing together in Government House, Kerr was in the course of deceiving his Prime Minister whose advice he was obliged to take but intended to ignore.

The Parliamentary Liberal Party was on the point of collapse as it got closer and closer to the brink. Fraser was barely holding his troops together. Kerr saved Fraser by his precipitate action.

On the morning of the Dismissal, I was despatched as the most junior minister to formally welcome a German government minister at Sydney Airport. On the flight back to Canberra, I sat next to Bob Cotton, one of Fraser's senior senators from NSW, and he said to me, 'Fraser's gone mad, Paul. This can't work and it can't last. I just hope this week will sort itself out.'

There were a handful of Liberal senators preparing to bail out and I have no doubt, in the end, supply would have been passed. In fact Gough was about to act to solve the political stalemate by calling a half-Senate election, which Kerr knew.

When it happened, when the blade came down, a lot of ministers seemed to take it in their stride. I was outraged by it. I said to Fred Daly and to Frank Crean and Frank Stewart that we ought to arrest Kerr, and they thought this was outrageous. They thought I was nuts.

If I had been Prime Minister I would have been very tempted to have had Kerr arrested. I don't think Gough and the people around him were capable of that kind of thinking. Gough was a legal constitutionalist kind of guy who believed in the institutions. But the institutions were being put asunder.

What had happened to us was a coup. As clear as day, a coup. The exercise of the reserve powers is not a matter for the High Court or its judges. It was a matter for the Prime Minister and the Head of State who should take advice from the Prime Minister. And, of course, the Queen, and the protocols of the country. I knew the blade had been lowered, that this was a coup.

Yet when I just briefly raised the idea that we should arrest Kerr, it was met with derision. Here was Kerr secretly consulting with the Chief Justice, Sir Garfield Barwick, a former Liberal Attorney-General under Menzies, and another High Court judge Sir Anthony Mason, working out how to sack an unsuspecting, democratically elected Prime Minister who still enjoyed the confidence of the House of Representatives.

Looking back, I can only speculate on what I would have done if I had been Prime Minister.

I would have at least called a Cabinet meeting to determine a strategy. I've no doubt that one effect of that would have been not to present the Supply Bill back into the Senate. Malcolm Fraser had undertaken to Kerr that he could guarantee the passing of supply. Fraser had no means of forcing the Supply Bill back to the Senate and he didn't have the numbers in the House of Representatives. The effect of that would have been that Fraser could not have met Kerr's principal condition, the one which he had appointed Fraser as interim Prime Minister to deliver—the guarantee that supply would pass.

At that point Whitlam and the Cabinet had the option of recommending Kerr's removal to the Queen. Not only had Kerr exercised royal and let us say queenly powers under the powers reserved to the monarch—yet never used—but he did it in a way where he had improperly and secretly invited two High Court judges and other people into the process. All the while refusing to let his Prime Minister know what he was intending. He clearly breached the conventions, if not the law. In which case it would have been completely within Whitlam's remit to recommend to the Queen that she act quickly to remove him. Gough didn't take that path. The Cabinet never met and supply was passed. The rest is history.

I couldn't bear to do nothing, so I was out there on the front steps of Parliament House, on the megaphone warming up the crowd. In fact, if you see the film footage, you will see me handing the megaphone across to Gough as he comes through the door to speak to the crowd.

There's another thing to say about this period. Before the dismissal of the Whitlam Government, although possibly the mood had changed even earlier when Billy Snedden moved to delay supply in 1974, there was a much greater leavening between the parties.

There was a civility of sorts that has disappeared since. It all vanished and never returned after 1975.

THE
ROAD TO
REFORM,
1976–86

TWO LOST YEARS

It would be difficult to exaggerate the depths of despair that gripped the Labor Party in the wake of the Whitlam Government's dismissal, and the devastating election result that followed.

The cocktail of emotions felt throughout Labor's support base and what was left of the parliamentary party was profound. Shattered hopes and dreams combined with anger at the nature of Whitlam's departure, but the wild ride of the previous three years was just too much for too many voters. For them, the great wave of change that had seemed so exciting and so right at the beginning had been overwhelmed by the political volatility, the economic roller-coaster ride and the scandals.

In a 6.5 per cent swing to Malcolm Fraser's Liberal–Country Party coalition, Labor lost 29 seats in the House of Representatives. The new government had 91 seats to Labor's 36, a huge cushion of safety for Fraser of 55 seats. Six ministers lost their seats.

Labor was back in the wilderness in the most debilitating way. The worst aspect of all for the party's hopes of recovery was that the now terminally wounded Gough Whitlam continued to lead through the next term in opposition. Whitlam's first instinct in the immediate aftermath of such an unprecedented bloodbath was to seek a successor and bow out, although others suggest it was a somewhat lukewarm effort. He approached Bill Hayden, who had been far and away the most consistent performer in Whitlam's ministry, first as the champion of Australia's first universal health insurance scheme, and then as the last and easily most credible of the three Whitlam treasurers.

When Hayden took the call from Whitlam at his Ipswich home in Queensland the night after the election, he was both angry and shell-shocked at the scale of the disaster, having barely held on to his once safe seat by 122 votes to emerge as the only federal Labor MP left in the state. Hayden declined the offer, partly because he knew the leadership wasn't Whitlam's to give, but the jealously guarded prerogative of the party caucus. He was so battle-weary that when Parliament returned he took himself off the Opposition front bench, and started a law degree at the Australian National University as a somewhat disengaged backbencher.

Whitlam's next approach was to Bob Hawke, the nakedly ambitious and charismatic ACTU and Labor Party President. Hawke wasn't even in Parliament, and declined, opting to keep his powder dry for a more auspicious debut.

In the end the Labor caucus locked in behind Whitlam, but with the unprecedented proviso that the leadership would be revisited mid-term. Clearly there was a significant body within the party wanting to put Whitlam on notice. Paul Keating was one of them: he would have preferred to see Labor's fallen hero deal himself out of the game.

Traditionally only lower house MPs were eligible for the party's deputy leadership, and it says a great deal about the fractured nature of the party in the immediate post-election period that eight people— nearly one in four—nominated for the position. Not only did Keating nominate, he came within three votes of becoming Whitlam's deputy, losing in the final count to Labor veteran and lion of the Left, Tom Uren.

At 31 years of age, the writing was on the wall. As Gough Whitlam and his rump of a caucus limped on through Malcolm Fraser's first term, Paul Keating emerged as one of his party's two or three most effective parliamentary performers.

KOB: After the devastation of the 1975 election, notwithstanding the residual loyalty Labor people felt for Gough Whitlam after the way he'd been removed from office, you believed that his time had come and gone. Can you explain why?

PJK: Most of us thought Bill Hayden would put his hand up to contest the Labor leadership after the 1975 election. We thought Gough would step aside, and it came as a surprise that Bill had decided not to run and was going to go back to university. My impression was that Gough had no intention of giving up the leadership after 1975, notwithstanding anything he might have said to Hayden. Bill's decision not to contest the leadership made Gough's re-election a foregone conclusion, even though there were a couple of challengers.

The deputy leadership was a different issue. I didn't want to run, partly because I didn't want to tie myself to Gough as his deputy, but I had just beaten Mick Young for the last appointment to Gough's ministry only a few weeks before the Dismissal and I didn't want to surrender that advantage to him.

So I rang Mick and said to him, 'Please don't nominate, because if you do then I'll have to nominate too, and I don't want to. I don't think it's going to advantage either of us much being Gough's deputy. Any longer term decision about either of the leadership positions shouldn't be made now. Would you think about it and let me know?'

When I came back to my Bankstown electoral office after lunch Mick had left a message: 'Get your running shoes on.'

It was psychologically bad, organisationally bad and, in career terms, bad. Tom Uren from the Left was mostly likely to win, and he did win by three votes from me. I was so pleased he won, because it would have been a poisoned chalice for me.

There was also a sting in the tail for Gough. Because of the mayhem leading up to the Dismissal, which reflected on his leadership, caucus decided for the first time in the party's history to introduce a mid-term parliamentary election for the leaders. In other words, all leadership positions would be declared vacant mid-term, which was a terrible slap in the face for Gough. This meant there was an eighteen-month interregnum after which people thought the real leadership discussion would begin.

Given the ferment of it all and the massive ups and downs with the Dismissal, the election defeat and the upsurge of Fraser, there was a view that maybe we needed the eighteen months to get our equilibrium back, to find what our coordinates were. Gough had not long settled back into the leadership when the story emerged that he and the party's national secretary David Combe had secretly tried to raise money from Iraq's ruling Ba'athist Party to help fund the 1975 election with the help of Bill Hartley from the Socialist Left in the Victorian branch.

This showed terrible judgement on Gough's part, because it was utterly compromising, taking foreign money from any source, let alone a despotic regime. I spoke against him in the caucus about it. I thought, 'I am not going to overlook this. This is B-A-D bad.' I said, in the light of it, that Gough should consider his position.

He must have stewed on this. That evening, almost at the end of the adjournment debate, I was sitting with Lionel Bowen on the Opposition front bench when the doors of the House swung open and Gough strode down the stairs, silver locks flowing in the breeze.

He came over to me and hit me with a flood of invective: 'How dare you call my position into question in the caucus, you and your mates from NSW.'

He was referring to the group that had supported him always, as I had.

I was roundly ticked off, and climbed right back into him. Everyone else in the chamber was watching this, and as Gough left Lionel said, 'Christ, that was really bad.'

Sadly, what the Iraqi incident did was to rob Gough of whatever ballast and credibility he had left. None of us wanted to see him torn down, particularly by a media campaign that Murdoch's papers were conducting. But there had to be some rebuke because of the tawdry way we were being portrayed in the wider public debate.

KOB: How do you remember the mid-term leadership contest of May 1977?

PJK: Bill Hayden was back on the front bench by then and in the lead-up to the leadership ballot he told me he was thinking of running for the deputy leadership. He'd had lunch with two senior Labor senators, Jim McClelland and John Wheeldon, to talk it over and they advised him to talk with me, 'because he runs the numbers for the NSW Right in caucus, and because he ran for the deputy leadership himself last time, and you should know what he's thinking about the ballot this time'. They knew Hayden and I didn't have that much of a relationship at that stage.

Hayden asked me if I would defer to him in the ballot for deputy leader rather than run myself. I said I would defer to him, but that he would end up being 'Deputy Death'—and was there any point in becoming Deputy Death at that time in his career when he was the heir apparent?

I think it was in his head that by becoming deputy leader he was staking his claim to the leadership down the track but I told him it was not wise for a man who aspired to be leader and Prime Minister to stand as deputy to a leader who was in such a weakened position. I said if he wanted to run for anything, it should be for the leadership. He asked if I thought he could win, and I said I thought he could.

In the end he did run against Whitlam and was only narrowly defeated. There were only two votes in it. I voted for Bill, although I don't think he ever quite believed that I had. I still have the record of who voted for whom in all those ballots. The late Peter Bowers wrote in the *Sydney Morning Herald* at the time that those supporting Gough to stay leader could be called either romantics or traditionalists.

In the mid-term ballot, again I didn't want to run for the deputy leadership for the same reasons, but I felt forced to run because Mick Young again decided to run and I did not want to give him an edge in the pecking order. It was a similar outcome, with Tom Uren getting the deputy leadership again, which suited me.

KOB: Having come so close to winning the deputy leadership at such a young age, after having only been in Parliament for six years, what impact did that have on your standing within the parliamentary party?

PJK: The electoral defeat of one's opponents and peers inside the caucus certainly helps. Nevertheless many of the people I nominated against and out-voted were senior to me in the caucus—so this did cement my position.

KOB: What role did you perform in Parliament under Whitlam through that first term in opposition from 1975 to 1977?

PJK: I had a much bigger role in the day-to-day battles against Malcolm Fraser than I'd previously had in Parliament, as did Mick Young. Mick and I supported Gough in the chamber along with

Lionel Bowen. Initially I was Shadow Minister for Agriculture and moved up to Minerals and Energy around the end of 1976.

I think at that stage Gough still saw me as a NSW hustler, although he used to say to me, 'You will at least fight. The others just want to lie down, but you will at least fight.' From Gough, that was a compliment.

Fraser was a pretty aloof kind of fellow as Prime Minister, much as he probably was throughout his life. Nevertheless the nature of how he came to power, the way he presented himself, his style of speaking, his dismissal of the people around him, most obviously the Opposition, meant that he was a prime target for parliamentary attacks.

I didn't think a great deal of Malcolm as a debater, because he would debate issues in a declaratory way, from on high, with a display of contempt rather than with real discussion or debate. I don't think that worked very effectively in Parliament, but because of the weakened state of the Opposition he had the game by the throat.

Labor actually came back in the polls coming up to the 1977 election, partly because Fraser had had strife with some of his ministers, and he actually relieved Phillip Lynch of the Treasury and gave it to John Howard because Lynch was getting bad headlines over a land deal he was somehow supposed to be involved in. But we were never going to win that election.

To Whitlam's credit he opened up the party to a whole new generation of talented politicians. Great victory though it was, the 1972 election delivered a pretty tough outcome for Gough in terms of the ministry because he inherited frontbenchers who'd been in Parliament since the 1940s. Fred Daly was elected in 1943, Kim Beazley Senior won Curtin's seat after his death in 1945, and Frank Crean, Clyde Cameron and others entered Parliament in 1949.

By the time we finally won government in 1972 these people had undeniable ministerial and policy ambitions but they lacked freshness, dexterity and a contemporary link to the community.

It was ironic because Whitlam himself presented a dynamic leadership and sense of vision, but he was always battling to make that ministry work. It's also true that after Whitlam intervened in Victoria to force reforms and open up the party, there was an influx of fresh talent into the Parliament, which Bill Hayden, and then Bob Hawke, inherited.

THE HAYDEN YEARS

The Fraser Government's first term represented two lost years for Labor. Short of being handed victory by a deeply incompetent government, Gough Whitlam was never going to win again. As a young press secretary to Whitlam in 1977, I can remember attending a pre-election campaign meeting in Melbourne where Labor pollster Rod Cameron briefed party secretaries and the leader's office that Gough was no longer electable. Whitlam wasn't present, and wasn't informed. To be presented with the political facts of life so clinically would have been a killer blow to his confidence in the shadow of an election, but he knew he couldn't win.

Given the authority delivered to it through the sheer weight of numbers, the Fraser Government didn't exactly cover itself with glory in its first term. But under Whitlam's leadership, Labor was caught short on new policy or any sense of rejuvenation when Malcolm Fraser went back to the polls a year early in December 1977. The net gain to Labor was just two seats. That night, the man who had led Labor out of the wilderness and back again resigned the leadership.

In the shadow of Christmas that year I was waiting in Gough's office when he returned from the caucus meeting where he formally tendered his resignation. Bill Hayden was elected to replace him after a close contest with Lionel Bowen. Caucus also chose a new shadow ministry. When I asked him how it went, Gough replied, 'Comrade, if only they'd given me a ministry like this one.' As well he might have, because that shadow ministry was to become, with little change, the first Hawke Ministry that was to deliver by far Labor's longest uninterrupted hold on federal power in its history, thirteen years. One of the key figures on Hayden's front bench was Paul Keating.

There was a small nucleus of survivors from the Whitlam ministries—Hayden, Bowen, Keating, Ken Wriedt and Tom Uren. But substantially thanks to the internal reforms Whitlam had forced on his party in his earlier years as leader, there was a whole generation of educated, talented and fresh recruits ripe for the picking, including people like John Button, John Dawkins, Ralph Willis, Gareth Evans, Peter Walsh, Susan Ryan, Neal Blewett and Don Grimes.

Compared to his predecessor, Whitlam, and his successors, Hawke and Keating, Bill Hayden was an unlikely Prime Minister in waiting. Diffidence was his stock in trade. In politics confidence might not be everything, but you don't travel all that well without it. Hayden's confidence tended to ebb and flow, and perhaps because he learned from a tough Brisbane childhood not to trust easily, he could be deeply suspicious of the motives of those around him. Paul Keating was later to identify this as the cause of his downfall.

Ask yourself if the following pen picture, taken from Hayden's autobiography, is the self-perception of a successful leader in such a gladiatorial arena:

> I knew only too well my shortcomings for the task. Media analysts put them forward cogently enough once I was elected to this position: a natural diffidence of character some described as an inferiority complex, caution about others, a tendency to

personal remoteness . . . all very much products of a disturbed childhood, or so I was informed by the commentators.

There was also my voice, thin, high-pitched, reedy, even whining, or so I was informed after my election. I took to reading randomly selected tracts from the Bible, alone each morning at Canberra, before my burnt muesli and skim milk, in the interests of putting a bit more timbre in my voice . . .

Certainly I was the best equipped on ability to be leader of those making themselves available, but that does not say much in favour of any of us who were available.

You'd think anyone expressing that kind of self-deprecation or ambivalence could not expect to be a successful political leader in such a 'take no prisoners' environment, but working off an extremely low base in his first election as leader in 1980, Hayden claimed a substantial swing back to Labor. If not for a significant campaign setback on capital gains tax, he would have come very close to beating Fraser and becoming Prime Minister.

One of his new backbenchers from that election was Bob Hawke, a bird of prey by nature as well as by name. Even before he got into Parliament, Hawke had already sounded out Keating to support him in a leadership takeover bid.

By his fifth year as leader, before he succumbed to the remorseless stalking by Hawke and his influential band of supporters, Hayden had pushed through further internal party reforms, built a highly function-ing front-bench team with a new set of policies and a sense of maturity, and must have felt the prime ministership was tantalisingly close.

In March 1982 Hayden won a by-election in the Liberal-held seat of Lowe in Sydney with a swing of 9 per cent against the government. At a general election a uniform swing of only 1.4 per cent would deliver power to Labor. One of Hayden's supporters up to that time, Keating also had a vested interest in seeing him succeed.

Even though Hawke had not shone in Parliament in his first two years, he had managed to build pivotal help in his leadership quest not only from trade union backers, but from Labor-machine powerbrokers in three key states: Victoria, Queensland and New South Wales. It probably still rankles with Keating that Hawke almost certainly would not have been able to force Hayden out and become Prime Minister without support from the heart of Keating's own NSW right-wing tribe. Chief among them was Graham Richardson, who ran the state party machine and, with Keating, the NSW right-wing parliamentary faction in Canberra.

Keating's own ambitions were clear. He'd come to Parliament from one of the country's most prized Labor seats at 25, barely missed the first Whitlam Ministry at 28, and the deputy leadership of his party by a whisker at 31. He could see his path to the leadership through the late 1970s and early 1980s.

But Hawke had a fourteen-year head start in life and was launching his bid from a much broader base, and had a higher and more popular public profile. He had much of the industrial movement and a significant bank of rank-and-file support, as well as the fascination of the media and popularity in opinion polls.

As a Rhodes scholar to Oxford with an economic literacy honed by his years fighting wage cases for the ACTU, Hawke carried an easy and abrasive confidence into any public debate. In these years, the polls were his bible, and in Australian political history, no one else had connected to the broad populace the way he had. He was made for the television age.

Keating could only beat Hawke to the parliamentary leadership if Hayden was able to hold Hawke at bay for long enough to defeat Fraser at an election. Had Hayden done so, Keating would have been in a position to enhance his credentials for succession as the reforming treasurer he became, and as a superior parliamentary performer to Bob Hawke. In those circumstances it would have been a real contest. But the quest for power in politics is littered with 'if onlys' and 'what ifs'.

KOB: I know you felt Bill Hayden was the natural successor to Gough Whitlam after 1975, but compared to Whitlam, Hawke or you, or Fraser and Howard on the Liberal side, he had a marked diffidence about his own leadership abilities. Can diffidence or even humility really be a virtue in leadership?

PJK: I think the whole idea that the job should be yours, which comes from either an earned confidence or an instinctive confidence, is a necessary attribute for the prosecution of the big prizes of public life: general elections, the articulation of ideas, ascendancies in the ideas market. It's very difficult to do these things without that inner belief. Now, many people would say a lot of people haven't earned these views about themselves and that's true of a lot of us, but Bill's self-doubt was probably more evident in his demeanour than it might have been in other people.

Let me go from either side of that ledger. Bob Hawke, for instance, had the confidence all the time that the job should be his and he was ready to have it, and wanted to take it. That extra energy gives a leader enormous turbo-boosting. Bill Hayden didn't have the inner turbo-charge he might have needed, but his self-reflections are also reflections on his own honesty of character, which, ironically, was a great attribute.

With Fraser's prime ministership diminished, and if he had had a reasonable level of self-confidence, Bill would have been in a position to turn the numbers he had into the prime ministership. He said when he stood down for Hawke that even a drover's dog could have won the election. Bill was much better than a drover's dog. If he'd had a lot keener inner belief, and with the good team he'd drawn around him, and just the killer instinct to keep Hawke off, he would have got there.

KOB: I can remember Hayden saying to me once, having just come out of the parliamentary chamber where John Howard was speaking from the government despatch box, 'That guy in there is our biggest problem in the government.' At that stage Howard was Treasurer, and Hayden said, 'He should be our prime target, but the trouble is everyone on our side likes him.' I would imagine if you were leader at that point, you might have liked or respected Howard, but that wouldn't have stopped you going after him.

PJK: No. The bifurcation of politics means that those sorts of considerations have to be put to one side. In the end there's got to be that raw energy to capture the job. Bill had enough of it to get eight-tenths along the way. He just didn't have enough of it to blast through and take the prize.

I was pretty certain he would have won in 1983. He had put together the primary team that essentially became the ministry of the Hawke years, and he spent time with people, checked people out and made judgements about them. He nurtured the collective effort, so you had to give him high marks as Opposition leader. Having done an economics degree, he knew that at the fork in the road of national income, the greater proportion of it should go to the private economy, not to the public economy. Other people didn't accept that, but he did. Unfortunately, as a leader, doubt probably got the better of him.

KOB: While Hayden was establishing his leadership and the team around him in his first term from 1977 to 1980, Bob Hawke was circling outside. Everyone knew that you also nursed your ambitions for future leadership. Can you describe the dynamic among the three of you?

PJK: By 1979 I was president of the NSW branch of the Labor Party and leader of the NSW Right in the federal parliamentary caucus. I was very much in the Hayden camp, trying to reshape the party policies around the person whose public credibility was strong. It's worth remembering of Bill that when he became Treasurer in the Whitlam Ministry in mid-1975 with an unholy mess to clean up, he had fashioned a very credible budget that, for all his talk of economic calamity, Fraser kept intact for the next nine months after the Dismissal.

Hawke had built his credentials through the trade union movement and had a lot of barrackers from within it. I was barracking for Hayden. I was not necessarily barracking against Bob, but I was not sure whether he was going to make the jump into parliamentary politics or what sort of parliamentarian he would be. Subsequently he did get elected for the seat of Wills in Melbourne, and then he was on a different battlefield.

KOB: The longer Hayden stayed, the more it suited your ambitions, didn't it? It meant you had longer to develop a bit more gravitas, get a bit more experience, build your reputation a little more, which meant the stronger your credentials would be in a leadership contest against Hawke.

PJK: Indeed. I would have been completely happy to see Hayden as Prime Minister. He would have made his mark in the job and I don't think he would have worn out his welcome. In fact he intimated to me a number of times he wouldn't stay all that long. In other words he might gift the job to me, and he knew as I knew that the interstate Left had already approached me in 1979, 1980 and 1981 to back me for leadership after Hayden to stop Hawke. In those years they were absolutely opposed to Hawke becoming leader.

Tom Uren arranged a meeting for me in his Canberra home in 1979 with Arthur Gietzelt and Bruce Childs from NSW, and Bill

Hartley and George Crawford from the Left in Victoria, pushing me as the guy to stop Hawke if Hayden fell over as leader.

When I agreed to become NSW Party President in 1979 after John Ducker retired unexpectedly and under pressure from Barrie Unsworth, I knew I was putting the Left support for me in Parliament in jeopardy because I was put into the presidency to hold the line for the Right in NSW. The Left had a stronghold in Victoria, and they were threatening to take control in NSW. That would have been a disaster for the party in policy terms and potentially kept us out of government with the old centralised economic approach the Left still passionately believed in.

In the late 1970s—it might have been around 1980—I can remember Arthur Gietzelt, as a Left faction leader in the caucus and a junior member of Hayden's shadow ministry, arguing on the front page of the *Nation Review* against the West German social democratic model and supporting the centrally planned Eastern European model run out of the Soviet Union. That gives you an idea of the confused policy agenda inside the party at the time.

Hayden and I, among others, were regarded with suspicion by Gietzelt and others on the Left because we were breaking new policy ground, moving away from the old central planning, using market-based policies to grow the private economy.

John Faulkner, who was then part of the new generation from the Left, tells a story of Arthur trying to knock him out of the Assistant Secretary's job in the NSW party machine because he wasn't a Marxist.

The Left's views on the economy were diametrically opposed to mine and yet they were prepared to back me for the leadership after Hayden, which tells you how strongly they felt about Bob taking the leadership, although they changed their minds later.

KOB: In 1980 the NSW Labor power broker and future Premier, Barrie Unsworth, arranged a meeting between you and Bob

Hawke in Sydney. Why did he call that meeting, and what was the essence of what was said between you?

PJK: Barrie said to me, 'You know I've got to hold our forces together in NSW and at the ACTU, and you know we now barrack for Hawke, and you don't seem to know him very well or have anything to do with him. How about we catch up and have a talk?'

I said I didn't really want to meet Hawke, to be honest. I was happy for him to stay in the industrial sphere, with me in the political sphere. I'd run into him a few times socially, not with great pleasure. Bob used to belt the bottle a bit and all the rest of it. He was always rude, not to me, but to the groups, so I thought, 'I don't really need to meet Hawke.' Barrie said, 'Come on, we want you to meet him.'

What Bob wanted to talk about was getting support for the leadership. He said that if he got to the federal Parliament, he would want the NSW Right faction in Parliament, led by me, to support him against Bill Hayden. He said that in the event he became leader and then Prime Minister, there'd be a place for me in that government, and a place for me succeeding him as leader. In that conversation he said he'd only want to stay a couple of terms.

KOB: Why would the two of you have been talking about his leadership versus yours at that time? Hayden was performing well as leader, he hadn't yet faced an election and when he did later in 1980, he very nearly beat Malcolm Fraser. This was a period when loyalty to the leader in the Labor Party was still held in very high regard.

PJK: I didn't want the conversation. What Bob had in those days was popular appeal with the public measured through opinion polls, but he didn't have the breadth of performance that comes with the hard policy work in Parliament. I didn't think the President's job at the

ACTU in the 1970s was sufficient qualification alone to become party leader and Prime Minister. Hayden, on the other hand, had fought a very tough battle as parliamentary leader, cleared out a lot of the 1960s and 1970s policy baggage, and nearly won the 1980 election.

KOB: What agenda did you set for yourself through the Hayden years?

PJK: By that stage I was the Shadow Minister for Minerals and Energy. I'd been in every mine and every corporate head office in the country umpteen times, so I knew that section of Australian business very well. I also used to participate in the economic debates, but what I was really doing was trying to work out the real story behind the Australian economy. Why was it performing so badly? Why were we condemned to such low growth?

I was trying to find the codes and work out what a Labor approach should be, bearing in mind that it was not beyond the wit of us to make the link between labour and capital—that is, to have the right arraignment of capital and to pull labour in its stead. That's what I always thought we should have, the right arraignment with capital, using labour in its locomotion with an equitable spread of the benefits.

The shadow cabinet used to meet every Tuesday morning about 9.30 when Parliament was sitting and there weren't enough seats at the table, so some people had to sit around the walls. It was always a coherent discussion because there was an intensity of focus on having a solid policy core to take us into government, and there was an acknowledgement that people had specialisations like Don Grimes on social welfare or Neal Blewett on Medicare.

It was coherent and cooperative, and never descended into bickering and had a good-naturedness about it. Everyone was aware of the battle to rebuild Labor's fortunes after 1975 and 1977.

That mood didn't really change when Bob Hawke came into Parliament at the 1980 election, although there might have been a bit of wariness initially in the Hayden camp. People were curious to see how Bob would adapt to the challenges of the new environment, and it's now well recorded that he had difficulty in those early days handling Parliament. It was not a natural forum for him, which was a surprise and disappointment to some of his followers.

You have to work within the rules of the parliamentary chamber, to know them and be comfortable with them. Bob had difficulty drafting questions which were in order and which were politically effective. He would either be making a preamble or semi-speech in lieu of a question. The rules of the game were not natural to him, so there wasn't too much concern about Bob in the Hayden camp when he arrived, although his purpose was clear.

He used to sit on the front bench sometimes at night during the adjournment debate and someone would sit down beside him and Bob would pull out the latest *Bulletin* poll or some other opinion poll and say, 'I don't know whether you've seen this . . .'

He had a permanent promotional campaign running, but not rudely. Never disruptive or intrusive.

KOB: As a key performer in Hayden's parliamentary team, how consciously were you shaping your debating style and your broad strategic approach to parliamentary engagement?

PJK: One has to be an amateur psychiatrist in the game, so one is permanently assessing the colleagues as well as the Opposition. The people on the other side who drew my attention were very descriptive types—people like Doug Anthony, Peter Nixon and Ian Sinclair in the National Party or Phillip Lynch or Malcolm Fraser himself. You could identify the particular views they held and the particular ways they went about proselytising them.

The game is really quite sophisticated. Many viewers of public life don't quite understand the true level of sophistication that a parliamentary player must have to be effective. The most effective players in the Fraser Government were the nucleus of the National Party. Sinclair was probably the most charming, and Nixon would have been the most effective. The one who most objected to us was Doug Anthony.

I suppose sometimes I was consciously looking for ways to get under their skin, but I was much more intent on injecting real content into debates. In the second reading debates on legislation, if your contributions were reasonable they were covered in the media, and there was a necessary focus on getting your words noticed.

So, often, if it was a debate, I would be talking around the subjects more than I would be attacking the government. I think the game has descended somewhat now from the level of parliamentary debate I grew up in. In those days there was a lot more trafficking in ideas and information than you might find now. And people were more inclined to sit and listen.

In debates on matters of public importance, which was one of the devices available to oppositions during which critical issues were raised, you'd be more likely to use those forums to attack the government rather than to be informative, although you'd try to be both.

I don't want to sound absurd here, but the whole parliamentary discussion was more learned then. For instance, if Bill Wentworth, who had been John Gorton's Minister for Aboriginal Affairs, would appear to talk about an Aboriginal issue I'd go and listen to what he'd have to say, because he was genuine and knowledgeable on the subject.

We all have strengths, and my long suit was that I always made a point of replying to the issues raised, rather than simply gratuitously attacking them. That's why I think I did better than most in Question Time when I was in government because I always took the question seriously and always answered it—but it didn't stop me having a little bit of fun along the way at the other side's expense.

In opposition, if I were in a debate and Doug Anthony was talking about, let's say, the states' former rights to minerals in the territorial sea before the Whitlam Government had legislated to give the Commonwealth power, and they were trying to bifurcate those powers, I would listen to their reasoning and their arguments, and then address them quite specifically.

I started writing with a fountain pen in the 1970s, and I still do every day, because with a pen you can write faster, while a biro is slower and puts more strain on your wrist. A fountain pen slides over the paper without wrist wear, and if you are listening to someone speaking and you're trying to cover that longhand, then you can write more quickly and get the points down. Once you've done that you have a framework for the reply. Replies to each of the points is as powerful as it is disarming.

In the first instance you have to be a good listener. Secondly, you should give the person speaking the credit for some intelligence and for having a position. I employed this technique in all my Cabinet years when colleagues would speak in a Cabinet debate.

So in those early debates from opposition I'd get up in reply and say, 'Mr Speaker, the minister said ten minutes ago . . .' and I'd be able to quote him precisely.

You could also use a bit of humour and, where appropriate, a bit of mischief. When little gems came along you stored them in your head, but they have to have genuineness to be gems. They can't be confected. They've got to be real.

For instance, in the 1977 election campaign I was in the Cooktown Hotel talking with an old drover at the bar and watching the news on a television set on the wall in a corner. An election story came on and Malcolm Fraser's head suddenly filled the screen. In a classic bush drawl, the drover said, 'You know, if I had a dog with eyes as close together as that I'd shoot it.' I filed it away and it came in very handy one day when Malcolm was in full patrician flight in Parliament. It took the wind out of his sails and got a good laugh, so it was effective.

Mick Young and I ran the primary opposition against the government in Parliament behind Bill Hayden from 1977 to 1983. On matters of public importance, which were the primary vehicle for the daily assault on the government, mostly the leader wouldn't do them, and the relevant shadow ministers would run each debate.

It was a good and effective team behind Bill and we enjoyed ourselves, and I was still learning things. You went there thinking you knew some things and then you'd discover you didn't know very much at all. You've got to be able to keep putting the pieces together. It's a bit like the way an MRI works today, a magnetic resonance image of your body or torso. It comes in slices, but when it shows up on a computer screen it presents a complete internal picture, and this is pretty true of public policy and public life. You pick up bits of wisdom in slices, but then you've got to make it whole and give it life.

That is what I used to try to do: make sense of it all. What does this really mean?

Most of the information people needed in order to have authority in what they had to say was available if they knew where to look. Statement Number Two of the budget papers each year would have a reasonably good picture of the economy, and the explanatory memorandums attached to legislation would give you a reasonable handle on any bills you had to debate, so if you were energetic enough to digest the material and wise enough to analyse it and identify both its policy and political relevance, then you could continue to grow.

KOB: You had another meeting with Bob Hawke about the leadership in 1982, by which time he was established in Parliament and pushing Hayden strongly. What prompted that meeting?

PJK: The second meeting was about whether the NSW Right would support Bob in his poorly arranged challenge to Hayden in the middle of 1982. Having declared his hand, Bob was marooned with not enough votes. He'd called on a challenge that he couldn't complete.

The headlines at the time said it all: 'Hawke's target twenty defectors by Friday.' 'Keating is now Hawke's last hope.' 'NSW switches to give Hawke his chance.' And here's the final one: 'How Hawke was dragged back from oblivion.'

In the end Hayden won 42 to 37. Without our seventeen votes it would have been Hawke twenty, Hayden 59. It would have just about knocked him out of the contest. He might have been able to come back, but it would have been much harder.

Why Bob had chosen to challenge with so little solid support was a mystery to all of us, particularly me. He'd been encouraged by, of all people, Tom Uren, who had previously been strongly opposed to him. Tom later denied this—and Tom and I did get on well, I thought the world of him—but Bob had been given some Dutch courage and he had such confidence about his own standing that he believed there would be momentum for him.

But what happened was that this ill-conceived challenge was announced but the votes that materialised for him were actually quite modest. Bill could have crushed him completely if the NSW Right had not swung in behind Hawke. I was the NSW Party President, a senior member of Bill's front bench and, in all manner of things, a Hayden loyalist. But I had lost part of the Right in NSW over one now seemingly unimportant matter.

Labor in opposition had four leadership positions in Parliament: leader and deputy leader in each house of Parliament, and each one of those four became members of the party's National Executive. As party leader, Bill had supported Don Grimes on the Left over Doug McClelland on the Right to the deputy opposition leadership in the Senate, which meant that the Right lost a critical vote on the National Executive.

McClelland was deeply wounded by Bill's actions and made his displeasure obvious for months thereafter. People in the NSW party machine like Graham Richardson, who felt they had a promise of Bill's support for McClelland, said to me, 'Well, that shows you about your mate Hayden. When you sorely need him for something he runs out on you.'

Bill's reason for that action was so ephemeral I've since forgotten it, but it was a mad thing to do. If not for that I believe he would have beaten Hawke off and become Prime Minister.

I had told him that if he stopped worrying about factional machinations, as NSW Party President I could keep his support solid from the Right. I said, let me worry about the Right. But after that move against McClelland, I couldn't hold them all together.

What was on display for my colleagues on the Right was Hawke's completely confident view about himself and his ability to displace Fraser, compared with Bill's self-doubt, which was an issue in their minds. They just didn't quite know, notwithstanding how close Bill had come to winning in 1980, whether he would actually lunge over the line in 1983, whereas with Hawke they were pretty sure they'd win.

Hawke had a lot of support from the Victorian Right from people like Gareth Evans and Robert Ray, but had I kept my support with Bill it would have split the NSW Right. So the judgement had to be made, and in many respects I had to make it, as to whether we could afford to let the leadership instability continue or whether we'd come to the point of having to make up our minds.

As much as I had misgivings about Bob's capacity and experience to lead the party through another year of Parliament if Fraser ran full term, because Bob hadn't been handling Parliament all that well, I made the call to go with him as the leader we knew we would win with, as opposed to Hayden, the leader we *might* win with.

KOB: Bob Hawke suggested in the *Labor in Power* interviews that you basically succumbed to factional pressure in supporting him, to which you rejoined that you were the hitter not the hittee, and Hawke was the beggar, not the chooser. What exactly did you mean by that?

PJK: In a sense I saved Bob from himself. I wasn't forced to support him because I still had huge influence in the show and had I chosen to stay with Bill I would have taken a body of our factional members in Parliament with me. By the same token I had been in public life at that point for thirteen years and effectively had never been a minister, other than for a brief few weeks in the Whitlam Government before the Dismissal. There was a risk that the show would run out of puff if we didn't win the next election.

I was having great trouble holding the faction to Hayden. I had great trouble rounding them up. I could have split them. I desperately wanted to see Hayden get his shot at the prime ministership, but with Bob we were certain we would beat Fraser and with Bill we were uncertain, so our bloc of votes went over to Bob. He still lost to Hayden, but only narrowly. And that was really the big stepping stone to the leadership for him.

The great ongoing issue between Bob and me is that I don't think he ever quite understood that he saw me as just another rung in his ladder to the top, another stepping stone in his career. He'd always had people to smooth the way for him, people in the trade union movement like Charlie Fitzgibbon from the Waterside Workers and Bill Landeryou at the Storemen and Packers, or John Ducker at the New South Wales Labour Council. In his terms I think I was just another one along the way, which was a fundamental error, because it came to affect his judgement about a sensible leadership transition to me down the track.

Bob was very magnanimous to Bill immediately after the challenge was resolved in Bill's favour, but it didn't last, because he soon started taking the polls out of his sleeve again to show people. After we lost the Flinders by-election late in 1982, which Labor should have won with a significant swing against the government, things deteriorated around Bill, and it was in that period that he made me Shadow Treasurer to try to strengthen his own position.

I had asked Bill for the Shadow Treasury portfolio after the election in 1980, but he decided then to stay with Ralph Willis. In those days I believed I had a much better model developing in my head for the economy and was in a better position to sell that model than anybody else, including Ralph, but Bill decided to stick with Ralph. By January 1983 he was in all sorts of strife over the leadership and he gave me the Shadow Treasury to help shore himself up against another Hawke challenge.

By that time I felt I didn't want it. I was running my own race but Bill insisted I take it. I would have preferred the Hawke thing to be settled other than through some surrogate move to make me Shadow Treasurer.

Bob was outraged. He said to me, 'He's buggered the lot of us.' He intimated, without asking me outright, that I should reject it.

I said to him, 'Bill's the leader, Bob, and the leader's got the right to change the front bench. It means I've got to go up the big learning curve but what else can I do?'

KOB: Hayden's leadership collapsed within weeks of you taking the Shadow Treasury. He stepped down and Bob Hawke became leader. On that same day Malcolm Fraser called an election, thinking he was going to lock Hayden in. Suddenly he was faced with Hawke, who was really in the box seat going into that election campaign. All the impetus seemed to be with him. You must have had mixed feelings watching him step up to realise his ambition, because it was a key fork in the road in terms of your future.

PJK: The mixed feelings I had at the time were for Hayden. Politics is actually a very sentimental business as much as anything else. By that stage Hayden and I had been together in the parliamentary party for more than a decade—not personally close, but in a close working relationship. So that day I wasn't thinking about my leadership ambitions, I was thinking about Bill losing his great shot at history.

It would have been a good time for Hayden to lead. In the Fraser years going into 1983, economic growth under the Liberals was a derisory 1.8 per cent. We more than doubled that. There was the big wages explosion in the Whitlam years, declining levels of competitiveness and the long secular decline in the terms of trade. The value of the things we were buying on the world market in those days, such as colour televisions, videos and motor vehicles were expensive, and the things we were selling like iron ore, coal, copper, lead, zinc were becoming cheaper. In other words Australia was caught in an income vice and the Liberal Government under Fraser had just trotted along.

It would be no news to anyone the utter contempt with which I hold the Liberal Party because of their incapacity to run the economy, their complete lack of imagination and lack of faith in the Australian people. I'm talking about having the fundamental belief that we can hack it with the best in the world.

The country went into an industrial museum in the Menzies years and simply faded into the sand.

I was watching all this in the 1970s with the fundamental conviction that this structure was all wrong. I was trying to put the pieces together.

Treasury didn't have the answers either. It could identify the problems, but didn't have the answers. We simply weren't able to get labour and capital together. We had a completely sclerotic financial market, product markets protected by tariffs and quotas, and arbitrarily set wages with inflation locked in through wage indexation. The poison of inflation kept running through the veins of the economy because it was indexed. So we had no chance of being competitive.

KOB: But when you talk about your contempt for the Liberals, the fact is that for the bulk of Australia's history after Federation, Australian voters had opted for conservative governments. Either you're saying that the Australian people had a great capacity to get things wrong or the conservatives were getting something right.

PJK: Well, voters might have had a capacity to get it right while the salad days of postwar growth carried Menzies and his governments along, but they got it wrong when they returned the Liberal governments of Holt, Gorton and McMahon in those very important years when the long wave of postwar economic growth was coming to an end. My complaint against the Liberal Party was their dumbness, their incapacity to actually structurally change the place. The country was just rolling along, and rolling into the sand.

Politically they had a divided Labor Party to exploit, particularly in Victoria and Queensland. Menzies had a 10 per cent head start with the DLP, and he had incompetent opponents in the inept Bert Evatt and Arthur Calwell, who just didn't connect with the community at all, despite the fact that Labor under Calwell nearly won the 1961 election. I'll acknowledge that we did this to ourselves. We chose the leaders and we kept them there. With a less divisive leader than Evatt the party would probably never have split.

Time after time the Liberals proved that they weren't broadly up to the job of setting the country up for a prosperous postwar future, and it was very telling at Menzies' final press conference, how little he was able to say about his policy achievements after sixteen years. I mean, you'd hang your head in shame if you'd set the bar that low. The bar was so low that Menzies only had to lift his quasi-royal foot over it to get a pass mark.

KOB: One undeniable achievement of the Menzies years was his substantial boost to tertiary education in Australia, which would have come at an extremely important time in Australia's postwar social and economic development. At the beginning of his sixteen years there were something like 12,000 students going to universities across Australia, and by the time his reign had come to an end, it was very close to 100,000. One of the keys to that growth was the Commonwealth scholarships he introduced. I think you'd have to say it was Menzies who began to break the mould where university was the preserve of the elite or the sons of the elite, to a somewhat broader representation at least.

PJK: I'm not saying that in sixteen years the Menzies Government achieved nothing. I'm saying the bar was set painfully low. When Hawke and I started our run in 1983, three kids in ten completed Year Twelve at school. When I finished as Prime Minister it was nine in ten, a trebling of Year Twelve retentions.

A great part of that bulk was made up of girls, young women who for the first time completed Year Twelve. And to follow that growth through, we had to treble university places. We took university places from 200,000 to 600,000. This happened with the Dawkins reforms.

We went from being a country with just a basic primary education and a trickle of kids completing high school and going to university, to one where nearly half the student base was going on to a tertiary education.

KOB: When you suddenly had to face an election campaign in 1983 so soon after becoming Shadow Treasurer and a very seasoned opponent in John Howard, who'd been Treasurer for five years, what problems did that pose for you?

PJK: It was a very presidential campaign. There was Fraser as Prime Minister with a big personality, and the larger than life Bob Hawke, both surrounded by big campaign teams. There were debates between Howard and me but you'd have to say the preponderance of coverage of that election campaign fell to the two leaders.

KOB: Did that let you off the hook somewhat, that so much of the attention fell elsewhere, that you were less likely to have journalists trying to catch you out on some esoteric economic technicality?

PJK: I knew enough about the general economic debate to pull myself through that sort of minefield, but my big problem was that we didn't have the kind of credible remedial policies I believed we needed and that we should have had. I was stuck with an economic framework we'd had through the balance of 1981 and 1982 that I didn't particularly believe in but I had to sell.

The Accord with wages policy as its centrepiece was a key part of Bob's campaign. Ralph Willis was a primary architect of the Accord, and I went with Ralph to meet the key trade union leaders of the Left at the Miscellaneous Workers' headquarters in Sydney. What became apparent to me in that meeting was that beyond broad principles, there was no agreement whatsoever at that stage about how wage restraint would be maintained or how as a group we would exit Fraser's so-called wage freeze.

The essence of the Accord was that if we could take a softer approach to monetary policy and get a little more growth there could be a trade-off with the unions in return for their restraint on wage claims. But even as late as three weeks before the election there was still no practical agreement under the so-called Accord that Bob had nominally put together with Ralph.

KOB: How does it feel to have to do the dance endorsing policy you don't believe in or have doubts about? For instance, you had personally supported the entry of foreign banks into Australia for years, but in the election campaign you had to speak against that in line with your party policy while John Howard was endorsing it.

PJK: It doesn't feel good because you're not arguing with any veracity. I was on the record in Parliament six years before, arguing for greater competition in the banking sector, probably through the introduction of foreign banks, and within weeks of the election I announced that we would be revisiting the Campbell Report that recommended foreign banks. Then in the campaign itself I had to oppose such a move. I didn't feel particularly comfortable doing that but the Accord represented a bigger problem for me because, for all the preening that had gone on about us having developed a new way on wages policy— the third instrument of economic policy in tandem with budget policy and monetary policy—in reality there was no wages policy.

THE REINS OF POWER

On election night 5 March 1983, I co-anchored the Seven network's coverage from the Canberra tally room with the veteran political journalist Ken Begg. Tally rooms are now a thing of the past, but those who were there that night will never forget the electric moment in the huge barn-like room packed with expectant Labor supporters when Bob Hawke appeared at the entrance to claim victory with Hazel on his arm, his wave definitely regal in style.

Another moment I'll never forget that night is Hawke, sandwiched between Begg and me on our election set, when Malcolm Fraser appeared at Melbourne's Southern Cross Hotel to concede defeat. Hawke didn't move or say a word, his gaze locked on the monitor, radiating a fierce concentration as he soaked up the sight of Fraser forcing the words of concession past a quivering lower lip.

It's a reasonable assumption that two things were driving Hawke's intensity. It was no secret he had been nursing his ambition to lead the country for decades, and this moment was the culmination of that journey. Secondly, as the head of the trade union movement and Labor Party President at the time of the Whitlam Dismissal, there was a personal sweetness to his victory, that he was the Labor hero leading his party back from the wilderness.

In Hawke's eyes, this was his destiny. Whatever momentary flickers of uncertainty he might have privately felt about the job ahead in the odd quiet moment on the campaign trail, there was no room for any self-doubt that night. Hawke was super-charged with adrenaline and anticipation, believing he could set up Labor for a long run in power.

Celebrating the night with his supporters back in Sydney before flying to Canberra, Paul Keating would have had a somewhat different set of reflections. Yes, there was the sense of triumph in beating Labor's arch-enemy Malcolm Fraser after three terms on the Opposition benches, and the obvious excitement of forging new Labor policy for government, but also a measure of apprehension.

Although he had participated regularly in economic debate as Shadow Minister for Resources and Energy for seven years, Keating had only been Shadow Treasurer for weeks, with little time to build important new relationships and establish his credentials with the broad economic and financial community or wrap his head around the language, culture and form of economics and finance. There would be nowhere to hide as he faced an incredibly sharp learning curve in the first months of government.

Labor was inheriting a daunting economic trifecta—double-digit inflation, double-digit unemployment and high wages, with a serious terms-of-trade decline in the pipeline and a 50 per cent larger than expected budget deficit. Interest rates were also in double figures.

Hand in hand with this, Keating had a set of predetermined Labor policies developed by his predecessor Ralph Willis with which he had privately disagreed substantially while promoting them in the election campaign. He had also inherited Willis's economic advisors who had helped shape and still firmly believed in those policies.

He also had a potentially hostile head of Treasury in John Stone, who had not endeared himself to Labor in the Whitlam years, who had been a thorn in the side of the Fraser Government as well, and who would have had his own doubts about Labor's economic credentials, based on what he'd seen in the early 1970s. Stone by reputation was a man who firmly believed that the Treasury way—his way—was the only way. Treasury was notorious for putting up briefing papers to governments that only had one point of view.

There was a desire in senior Labor ranks to see Stone shown the door, and even Stone may have expected to be given his marching orders. On election day, in a speech to students graduating from Sydney University, he appeared to throw caution to the winds, when referring to the campaign: 'All of us must have been reminded of Dr Johnson's famous remark that the appeal of patriotism is the last resort of the scoundrel. There may also have occurred to us another aphorism, that empty vessels make the most sound.'

It's an unusual senior bureaucrat who would so openly express such scorn for politicians, particularly in the circumstances.

Coupled with the challenge of a fledgling Treasurer being expected to sack his head of department virtually as he walked through the door, Keating had a new leader with whom he had no special relation-ship, who knew he nursed his own leadership ambitions, and who had already made known his preference to give the Treasury portfolio back to his old ACTU colleague Ralph Willis—a preference Keating headed off at the pass with support from his factional comrade Graham Richardson.

What Hawke and Keating did have in common was a determina-tion that the lessons of the Whitlam years would not be forgotten, that this time Labor would be disciplined and economically credible from the outset.

Ironically, in his very first briefing paper to Hawke and Keating, which revealed a far higher deficit than expected from the final Fraser–Howard budget, John Stone handed them a powerful excuse to dampen the spending expectations of their caucus and

Cabinet, and change the whole economic direction of the new government.

What was to come, in arguably the most sustained period of economic reform post-Federation, was a catalogue of change that fundamentally transformed the nation, and in the process, the Labor Party as well. Not all of the outcomes were anticipated, like the huge speculative spending splurge through the late 1980s after big changes to the banking system, but the extent of that broad sweep of reform would have been far more problematic without the dynamism and unanimity of purpose of the Hawke–Keating partnership.

PJK: It was a great victory over Malcolm Fraser. He had ripped up the rulebook in 1975 and then they ran the economy into the ground. Contrary to the popular view that the Liberals were supposed to be better economic managers, just look at the record. The deepest recession to that point was the one presided over by Malcolm Fraser and John Howard, the biggest declines in GDP in 1981 and 1982, and a second wages explosion—so it was good riddance to them. I was hugely buoyed by the result, and by that stage I was Shadow Treasurer. I believed I would be Treasurer and I was thinking that the whole framework of economic policy had to change. I couldn't run with the old Labor orthodoxy.

The party had to make the choice of facing a different policy future at this point in its history after nearly a hundred years of socialist-style objectives: management of the economy by government institutions and boosting economic growth by making the budget deficit bigger. And yes, I had some apprehension at that moment. I had only been Shadow Treasurer for a matter of weeks, but anyone who walks on stage, whether a thespian or a politician, has certain nerves in the belly. If you don't have those you'll never be any good.

So at the same time as I was celebrating a great victory, I also felt a heavy sense of responsibility falling on me. Recovery from recession was the immediate problem. But here was an economy where Australia's terms of trade had been dropping since about the time Menzies retired in 1966. We had double-digit inflation and double-digit unemployment. We had a budget deficit around 5 per cent of GDP under Howard's last budget. Government spending had gone from 23 to 30 per cent of GDP through the Whitlam and Fraser years. Wages were massively higher than they should have been, the so-called real wage overhang. The profit share was smashed to pieces, and investment had fallen through the floor.

But as Treasurer, when you get the job, you get the job. You can't suddenly say it's the guy next to you.

KOB: It came out much later that Bob Hawke considered going back to Ralph Willis as Treasurer after the election, but you found out at the time. I know Graham Richardson told Hawke it wasn't on but how did you deal with that personally?

PJK: Ralph had worked with Bob at the ACTU before he became a parliamentarian, and broadly Bob was comfortable with Ralph as a personality. Ralph was also a trained economist. But Bob was smart enough to know that the models were all wrong. In his heart of hearts he knew that the general framework was way out of date for Australia.

He'd inherited me as the Shadow Treasurer and all of a sudden he seemed to be having second thoughts. I don't know how seriously he was thinking about it, but it was enough for me to say to him, 'Bob, you try and touch me as the Treasurer and I'm going to invoke the Harry Truman doctrine of massive retaliation, and I mean massive.'

His response was along the lines of, 'No, no, we're right mate.'

KOB: What can you remember of the atmospherics of that first dramatic meeting you and Bob Hawke had with John Stone and other Treasury officials at the Lakeside Hotel the morning after the election, and the revelation that the deficit was far higher than you expected?

PJK: It was a very surreal day. We'd won the election, the bureaucrats turned up with the normal sort of brief they prepare for the incoming government, and we were meeting in an atmosphere of urgency because of the run against the currency that had been going on over the fifteen or so days up to polling day. The Reserve Bank Governor Bob Johnston was there as a consequence.

The Treasury document had a great deal of hyperbole in it about the deterioration of the budget being greater than at any time since the Second World War and so on. What it really meant was that the budget deficit in prospect was nearly 5 per cent of GDP, which would be about $75 billion in today's dollars, outlays were touching 30 per cent of GDP when they'd been 23 per cent a decade earlier, and there was a great deal of pressure on the dollar in the foreign exchange market to boot.

I recall having the discussion at a table sitting in front of the dark and empty downstairs bar at the Lakeside, where Bob and I were staying. There was a pervasive smell of stale beer, which didn't help the mood.

It's interesting looking back on it now that we were sitting there only hours after winning government, getting a whole new picture on the state of the economy and at the same time having to decide on a quite significant devaluation of the dollar. At least the decision to devalue was more or less cut and dried. It was just pretty obvious that the rate had to go down, but the decision to move in a discrete and large way by ten percentage points meant that the old authority of the calibrated crawling peg system was largely blown away. We were acceding to market pressure, and a consequence of that accession was the destruction of the crawling peg adjustment system we'd been regulating and relying upon for years.

KOB: You were new to the job, you knew Bob Hawke had thought about bringing Ralph Willis back as Treasurer, you had a head of Treasury in John Stone who many of your Labor colleagues regarded with hostility and suspicion from the Whitlam years, and you wanted to change the economic canvas. As you prepared to establish yourself with your bureaucrats from Treasury, knowing you were going to have to win their respect and there was a fair chance they'd be looking at this young guy as something of a novice, did you have a clear view about how you were going to approach the job?

PJK: No, I didn't, but I did understand one thing—power. I knew how to put the electricity into the cables. When I went to Treasury for my first meeting, John Langmore, who I'd inherited as a senior adviser from Ralph Willis, stood at my office door with his manilla folder full of papers, and I told him, 'John, I'm going to go myself.'

He said, 'What do you mean you're going yourself?'

I said, 'I'm going on my own. I'm not going to go on the presumption that we have a whole view counter to Treasury, or that they would think is counter to them, particularly through your presence.'

He said, 'Well, I've waited twenty years of my life to be a senior private secretary to a Labor Treasurer for that trip to Treasury.'

I said, 'Well, John, you're going to have to wait a bit longer,' and I went over by myself.

Stone didn't know what to do with me. I walk in without a briefing paper, just a pen, to see the whole Treasury leadership and say, 'I'm working on the presumption that you will serve the government and serve me, but you will have to earn your spurs with me. And you can begin by telling me how you might do that.'

KOB: How did John Stone react to that?

PJK: He obviously thought this was quite unusual. I think his view was, we give them papers, they take notice of them and then they sign up. Suddenly they had just an inkling that the government might actually start running the policy.

KOB: But isn't it true at the same time you were very aware that no minister survives who is not able to carry his ministry with him, who is not able to work with his senior public servants?

PJK: If you have any talent you will always find the best talent to have around you, and never fear having talent around you. I was always looking for the best instincts and I had reasonably presumed that John Stone was a loyal Commonwealth public servant and a competent one, and that he would serve the government of the day.

But as well as sending them a message that the government was here to govern, I needed to win their trust. I always believed in institutions and structures. It's very hard to put new institutions and structures into place, and when you already have them there but they are deteriorating or have been marginalised, then you can probably assume there's something fundamentally wrong.

In the case of Treasury, they had fallen out with Malcolm Fraser in particular, and as a consequence he had split off the disbursements function into a new Department of Finance.

There was an independent revenue function with the Taxation Office, which had a set of statutory powers, but at the same time taxation policy belonged with Treasury along with disbursements or outlays—the transfer payments, health, defence—belonged with Treasury too. Fraser split that off to a new Department of Finance, and he'd also built an economic advisory body within his own Department of Prime Minister and Cabinet. So Treasury was in the doghouse.

All this reeked of immaturity. Something was wrong. If Treasury wasn't serving the government properly or the government wasn't requiring the things of Treasury that Treasury was capable of doing, then everything in me said this is not the kind of structure I want to inherit and without question.

I said to them, 'I accept at face value that Treasury should be the primary economic adviser to the government of the day. To the extent this position has been diminished by the events of recent years, let's try to re-establish that, and Treasury's views and the imperatives of Australian economic policy at least will be put at first hand and in a primary way, in any Cabinet I belong to.'

I did think it was important that I went there alone, not being managed or protected by staff. You hear what they say in undistilled form, and they hear your thinking. I thought if I couldn't win their confidence, I could not succeed. Besides, John Langmore possessed old Labor Party views about economic planning and state controls of a kind I thought were entirely inconsistent with the needs of a modern mixed economy, certainly the kind of market-oriented economy I had in mind. His presence would have confirmed in Treasury that his naïve views would have an influence on policy.

Notwithstanding, there was a great deal of pressure on me from within the party to dump Stone because of the bad blood between Treasury and the Whitlam Government. I remember Mick Young in particular being vociferous about it, but I had to resist. You've got to remember Australia was a managed economy with a managed exchange rate—the government set interest rates, with a centralised wage-fixing system in which the government had a heavy role.

As the wider financial world saw Australia, we were running current-account deficits they were funding, and as far as London and New York were concerned, Stone was 'Our Man in Havana', 'Our

Man' with Morgan Stanley, JP Morgan and Salomon Brothers in New York, and Barclays in London.

The last thing we needed to look like was the Beverly Hillbillies arriving again after the economic instability of the Whitlam Government and the further big expenditure blowouts by Fraser and Howard. Guess what, the hillbillies are back in town and they've decapitated the one guy we know.

I thought the sentiment to get rid of John was both a misjudgement and unfair to him because we were not yet in a position to know what he really thought or would do, but even more than that, the country being wrong-footed in these big global marketplaces would seriously impact on us. What people thought of us really did matter.

I said to Bob, 'You and I are smart enough to be able to make judgements about Treasury and its progress under Stone, so we should reappoint him but keep him under review.'

From memory, Bob always supported my view that Stone should stay.

Coming into government in the circumstances we did, you get no time to settle in. After the devaluation, the first big challenge for me was the Economic Summit, which Bob had scheduled to bring business and the unions together. The place was in such a ruin. It was a horror stretch. The business community were happy to be consulted but they couldn't offer much. Their profits had been shot to pieces and the country was massively uncompetitive.

At the same time we felt the economy may turn the corner after the savage recession, with the stimulus of the last Howard budget coming through the pipeline, and we were still coming to terms with the big deficit we'd been left. In my speech to the Summit I had to find my way past Treasury, who wanted to pull the deficit way down, and the Left, who wanted to pump everything up. I wrote the Summit speech in Sydney with David Morgan from Treasury.

One of my economic advisers, Barry Hughes, wrote a version, which I thought I could not live with. I didn't think it had the understanding of the stimulus already in the Fraser–Howard budget and also the psychological shift I was looking for to move away from the big bang stimulus stuff that Labor had formerly supported.

At the Summit, we were looking for the right balance between stimulus and restraint. Until then I had these competing factions and views. Technically I still had Langmore on my staff and the influence of others in the big bang camp in the mix. On the other hand we had Treasury saying no, we have to pull everything way down.

The other big Summit agenda item was the wage distortion in the economy. Wages had blown out under both Whitlam and Fraser. We'd inherited a wage freeze that Fraser put into place before the election, so we had to set the timing to come out of the wage freeze. This was where the Social Accord between the Labor Government and the trade union movement came in. It had been largely authored between Ralph Willis as Shadow Treasurer and ACTU figures like Laurie Carmichael, Charlie Fitzgibbon and Bill Kelty, and sponsored by Bob Hawke before he became Labor leader.

The Accord was to be a third arm of Labor policy to go with fiscal and monetary policy—that is, with the budget and interest rate settings—and that was a wages policy through the Accord, trading off wage increases for job creation. In the prevailing orthodoxy Treasury regarded the notion of voluntary restraint on wages as a complete nonsense. Nevertheless that was a central policy of the government and we were going to give the Accord a reasonable shot. I wanted only Treasury's compliance in doing what the government reasonably asked of them. This was central to Hawke's campaign, and Bill Kelty's contribution to the Summit, promising wage restraint in return for job creation and a reduction in unemployment.

After the Summit I felt I was off and running. We went from there to preparing our first major economic statement in May, reflecting the new financial realities, recasting our election commitments and making cuts to existing programs. I then had to get these proposals through the caucus committees and Cabinet. I spent a lot of time and effort in consultation but in the end, I got the changes through.

I delivered the statement on 19 May 1983, three months after Bob's policy speech. And instead of increasing the deficit by $1.5 billion as the policy speech had proposed, we reduced it by $400 million— a $2 billion shift in the prospective budget balance, which is a ton of money in today's dollars.

But to come back to the Economic Summit, that was really Bob's forum, Bob's stage, and it was a big success. The central idea he sold in the campaign was reconciliation, reconstruction and recovery. Reconciliation was a big part of the Summit and it set a mood for a new relationship with the unions and also with business.

KOB: You've said that you'd made it your business in your early years in Parliament to learn how to cut through the intricacies of budgets and the various budget documents, but I assume that as the new kid on the block, in facing the challenges of your first mini-budget or May Statement, that you would have had to rely heavily on Treasury to show you around the nooks and crannies of the budget process.

PJK: The May Statement brought forward measures that would otherwise have sat in the August budget, but the real debate was how big the budget deficit should be. The budget deficit we were led to expect by John Howard was around $6 billion. That had grown by more than 50 per cent by the day we took office to $9.6 billion. But in the modelling from the more expansionary forces in the Labor Party, they were looking at deficit options of between ten and fifteen billion dollars. I regarded this as lunacy. These would be huge numbers in today's dollars.

Deciding on the appropriate deficit was basically what put Bob and me into harness. It was his intuitive view and my own that we had to pull the budget deficit in prospect down, not up. If Ralph Willis had been Treasurer it would have gone up; with me as Treasurer it was going to go down, at least partly on the basis that the stimulus already underway in Howard's last budget was about to pull the economy from recession anyway.

At that stage, to use the corporate analogy, Bob was chairman of the board and managing director and I was chief financial officer. Later I would become the undeclared managing director under his chairmanship but in that first year he and I were as thick as thieves. He'd press the button on his intercom and say, 'What are you doing mate?'

I'd come up and have a coffee or tea, and he'd offer me a cigar. I'm not a cigar smoker but occasionally I'd have one with him. It was happening all the time. You can't imagine what pals we were. I would spend half of my evenings up there in his office and often at the Lodge for dinners.

We were on such a roll in that first year and the economic changes we wanted were coming through. Bob luxuriated in all that and so did I. It was a genuine friendship, not just one born out of pragmatism.

When Bob invited me to accompany him on his first overseas trip as Prime Minister when he went to America to meet Ronald Reagan, it was a generous act on his part. The Treasurer had no reason to be seeing the American President. I was there basically because Bob liked having me around.

At this stage of his career Bob was prepared to go on the magic carpet ride. He was getting less cautious and more prepared to do the big deregulatory changes, and I loved that because it fitted my own philosophy and my reason for being around. I wanted to make good policy central to political strategy.

In my early years in Parliament, the media would mostly get excited by election speculation, tax cuts, leadership changes and budget leaks. And politically there was all this imagery from Menzies such as Reds under beds and tensions with Indonesia. With Harold Holt in 1966 it was the fear of the Vietnamese coming to get us in their *sampans*. There were cartoons with big red arrows coming down to Australia from Asia.

Nowhere was there a premium on real quality or good policy. Good policy was regarded as some sort of foolish thing you might try, but get burnt for your trouble. But I always believed political strategy should be built around good policy for which I believed there would be a public reward. In other words I took the view that an informed Australian community would be conscientious and that if a government did good and hard things to reinforce the public good, and explained them properly, the public would give you a mark for it. This was a complete change from the old approach to political leadership.

Bob's economic instincts were good and he was delighted to find his Treasurer had a commensurate set of similar instincts. The penny dropped for Bob that had he gone with Ralph and the Left of the party, it would have been a different story. Ralph was a great minister and later a great Treasurer in his own right, and a great member of Cabinet, contributing for years, but at that point he would have supported an expansionary budget with the effect of high interest rates crowding out private investment. My key point was that you could not bring the Australian economy back to growth off the back of public investment and public employment. The primary driver had to be private investment and private employment.

In those first few months of Cabinet meetings my critics would say, 'Oh you've been taken over by Treasury.'

I said, 'No I haven't, but in these respects Treasury is right.'

KOB: So, in the early days, who led whom in your relationship with Treasury?

PJK: To do the job well as Treasurer you've got to have a model in your head. You've got to stand up in Parliament and argue the economic issues credibly, you've got to stand up in the caucus committees and have the arguments in your head. You can't survive on a handful of briefing notes from Treasury. You can't proselytise someone else's policy.

One of Australia's biggest problems was that too many treasurers had lived off their briefing notes, using them in Question Time like a security blanket. I was apprehensive in those early Question Times because while I might have the model clear in my head, I wasn't necessarily familiar with finer detail. The questions could come from any angle such as payments to the states, or interest rates, or the budget balance, or it could be about the tax system, so I was somewhat apprehensive. At the same time I was divining a new model that wasn't Treasury's forlorn model and wasn't the big bang model of the Labor Party.

I was very conscious of the high wire I was walking, with everyone watching for a slip. So there was a substantial level of discomfort in those early months, but I built a lot of confidence from the Economic Summit and then the May Statement.

In the end I was the guy who had inherited the long secular decline in Australia's terms of trade from the middle 1960s. It got to the bottom in 1986, the banana republic year, but it was already there in substance when I arrived. The place had become more closed and more rigid with each year, so you either went along with the orthodoxy and watched it decline further, or you decided to blow the game up and say we're taking a new path.

THE FLOAT

The arrival of the Hawke Government coincided with substantial and irrevocable changes in the global financial sector. The internet and the capacity it delivered to financial traders to move massive amounts of money in the blink of an eye was still more than a decade away, but the borderless world of finance was already well and truly underway.

In that context, with a fixed exchange rate against the world's other significant currencies, the only way the Australian dollar could be maintained at or close to the rate the government wanted was for the Reserve Bank to buy and sell dollars in the marketplace. If big speculators decided to target the Australian dollar, there was a limit to how far the Reserve could go to resist that pressure. The more the dollar was targeted by investors and speculators, the more unstable it became.

The arguments for and against the level to set the dollar against foreign currencies were political as well as economic. In principle Treasury was inclined to support a stronger dollar because it tended to help keep inflation lower through cheaper imports. Farmers and miners tended to support a weaker dollar because they could sell their products more competitively to their overseas markets.

In the decades of Coalition governments, the Liberal Prime Ministers were inclined to take the Treasury line and their frequently politically tougher Country Party (later National Party) partners always argued for a weaker dollar. The effect of the government's decision either way was economically significant in terms of both money supply and interest rates. To put the fate of the dollar more in the hands of a free-flowing market than under the regulatory thumb of government would inevitably open the rest of the Australian financial system to competitive pressures. Once the dollar was floated it would only be a matter of time before pressure would also be felt to adjust wages or to deregulate the labour market.

The Fraser Government with John Howard as Treasurer had commissioned a sweeping review of Australia's financial system by a well-respected corporate leader, Sir Keith Campbell, whose report in 1981 recommended a complete overhaul of the financial system underpinning the Australian economy. It challenged the Fraser Government to move from a fixed exchange rate for the dollar to a market or quantity-based rate, and to allow commercial banks to set their own interest rates—which were both currently the responsibility of Treasury, in tandem with the Reserve Bank acting as its agent in the market.

Fraser and Howard will never agree on which of them was primarily responsible for shelving the recommendation to float the dollar, but Campbell's biggest single opponent was John Stone. He hadn't changed his views by the time Paul Keating came along.

Although Keating quickly established his own independent review of the Campbell recommendations, run by former banker Vic Martin, that exercise really seems to have been designed primarily to put a Labor stamp on a failed Liberal initiative to help pave the way for financial deregulation through a suspicious caucus. In any event, Campbell and Martin between them supplied the blueprint for unprecedented financial market deregulation in Keating's first years as Treasurer. In the process he was changing his own party irrevocably.

In the same way Fraser and Howard have disputed responsibility for their failure to implement Campbell, so too, as part of the bitter legacy of their later battle for the prime ministership, Hawke and Keating now argue over the credit for the float, and the mantle of chief financial market reformer.

At the time the two seemed to be as thick as thieves. From a distant and competitive relationship at first, the two grew close in their first year in office. It was a turbulent year with myriad challenges for a new Labor Government wanting to modernise itself and the country. Having given up on his desire to replace Keating with Willis, Hawke went out of his way to extend the hand of friendship and Keating responded.

In that first year, Keating also went looking beyond John Stone for other talented brains to pick in Treasury and the Reserve Bank as well as reshaping the bank of advice in his own office.

KOB: The first big reform test for you was the float of the dollar. Thirty years on, it probably doesn't sound like such a big deal, but it was the big landmark moment signalling the start of your whole financial reform agenda. Why was it necessary?

PJK: It was necessary because the Australian economy was locked up and uncompetitive and the dollar was too high in value, so it was killing miners and farmers particularly. Forget the tariff-supported industries, it was hitting the internationally competitive ones. The ones that dug up copper, lead and zinc, coal and iron ore were barely competitive because wages were too high and the exchange rate was also too high.

Secondly, you couldn't run an effective monetary policy with a fixed exchange rate where the Reserve Bank opened its shop every

Monday morning at nine o'clock and bought all the foreign exchange and then issued Australian dollars. Those dollars then pumped up the money supply, adding kerosene to inflation. You were burning your own inflation rate with the Reserve Bank continuing to add each day to primary liquidity.

The other thing was that Treasury—Mr Stone *et al.*—had the exchange rate too high in order to make imports cheaper, which they thought would put downward pressure on local prices and thereby hold wages down. So the whole structure was wrong.

I'd begun to crystallise my thinking on the exchange rate when I was the spokesman on minerals and energy after 1975, and doing the rounds of every major mine in the country. I remember in 1977 talking in Mount Isa with Jim Foots, who was the chief executive of Mount Isa Mines, and asking him why, with middling commodity prices, MIM was making no money. He said it was partly that the wage share of the economy was too high, and he said the other big contributing factor was the exchange rate.

That was when I first started to notice the exchange rate reinforcing uncompetitiveness, being used by the Treasury as an anti-inflationary tool, making imports cheaper to keep downward pressure on local prices—but murdering agriculture and mining in the bargain. So it was no surprise to me as Treasurer that John Stone would be strongly opposed to a float where Treasury would have to relinquish control over the dollar.

The key influence for me was the Reserve Bank Governor Bob Johnston. The exchange rate was set every Monday morning by four officials: the Treasury Secretary, the Reserve Bank Governor, the Finance Secretary and the Secretary of the Department of Prime Minister and Cabinet. It was called the crawling peg system and they used to move the rate in discrete adjustments. But once the big players in the financial markets decide they're going to make money off you, you're kidding yourself you can sit every Monday morning doing small adjustments. So Bob Johnston said to me the day after we did the big devaluation in our first week in office, 'Of course, Treasurer, you know the crawling peg system has had it. They've got our number.'

Because that was so obviously true, all the arguments John Stone and other Treasury officers later made against the float simply seemed hollow to me.

The only issue therefore was timing, and after presiding over such a big depreciation in the week we formed government, it goes without saying that I had a natural interest in following the dollar's fluctuations over the weeks and months that followed.

KOB: How did you go about managing the deep disagreement between the Reserve Bank and your own department, between Bob Johnston and John Stone? That must have been very tricky.

PJK: You've got to remember in those days the Reserve Bank was simply a bond-selling agent of the Treasury. It had no great policy standing because the exchange rate was determined by officials and interest rates were fixed in a band decided around the Cabinet table on recommendations from the Treasurer and Treasury. That left the Reserve Bank more or less subordinate, and Treasury looked down its nose at it.

I used to notice in meetings whenever the Governor or the Deputy Governor turned up, they were always very circumspect about what they'd say while the Treasury Secretary and Deputy Secretaries were present, because Treasury was the one calling the policy shots. We had a situation where the leadership at the Reserve Bank believed the system had to change. They had a Treasurer who was listening to them, but they didn't have the bureaucratic standing or the confidence to knock Treasury over.

Bob Johnston was an impressive character. He had represented the Reserve Bank at the Campbell Inquiry established by the Fraser

Government to review the whole financial system, so he had the entire framework in his head. He had a kind of world-weary composure and he'd often say, 'You know, we've all seen this before, Treasurer.'

His storyline always had integrity to it, and I bought his view that the existing exchange rate system was finished. But after the devaluation in March we had some six to eight months before the markets came back to attack us again, so we had some time to pave the way to a float. As it happened, the markets gave us the time to prepare, and we needed every bit of it because it was uncharted territory for Australia, and there was a great deal to think through.

About May or June at our regular monthly debrief Bob Johnston raised with me the need for an articulated plan to prepare for it.

He said, 'There's no literature on this, Treasurer, so let's try and get a bit of literature in place.'

I said, 'What we need is a kind of *Gregory's*,' which is a set of Sydney road maps, and Bob said, 'You mean a War Book.'

That was an arrangement agreed between Bob Johnston and me, not with Treasury, though Treasury was always kept informed. Whatever document I had from Bob for the debrief, Treasury also saw, but I never invited John Stone into the conversation I had with Bob Johnston around the monthly board debrief.

Under the *Reserve Bank Act*, the Treasurer and the Bank board were charged to agree or endeavour to agree on matters before them, so there had to be that regular debrief from the Bank. But I wanted to be on top of the economic heap, not below it, so I kept Stone over at the Treasury building, away from my discussions with Bob around the prospects of a float. At the same time I knew that Stone was emphatically opposed to a float.

It's clear from the record that I supported a float, because there's a document written by Johnston to me in July talking about the movement to a quantity-based system, and he mentions the War Book. Bob Johnston and his deputies Don Sanders and John Phillips and I continued to talk through those months. It was never a question of whether to float but when.

My position on this was pretty clear as early as April 1983. On 4 April, four weeks after I became Treasurer, I did an interview with Ross Gittins in the *Sydney Morning Herald* where I said I was going to set up a new committee to revise the Campbell recommendations around financial deregulation. This was the Martin Committee. Since you can't have flexible financial markets alongside a rigid exchange rate, I was really telling Gittins we were heading for an open financial economy and, by implication, a market-determined exchange rate. You couldn't be explicit, but there it was, four weeks after I became Treasurer.

KOB: The broader public probably couldn't care two hoots about who pushed harder for the float or who said what first, but it is now a source of deep disagreement between you and Bob Hawke.

PJK: That might be the case now but it wasn't at the time, nor right up to the point when I defeated Bob for the leadership. Before I took the prime ministership, you never heard any debate about the float. This debate first came to light in the so-called history Bob wrote, *The Hawke Years,* where he dresses himself as the progenitor of the float. It took him a long time to get around to those claims—a decade, in fact.

I kept Bob completely in the loop through May, June, July. Around May I told him I thought a float was not only inevitable but desirable. This is what I wrote about that discussion in an appendix to John Edwards' book on my time as Treasurer and Prime Minister, published in 1996:

> I was completely open with him [Hawke], frank with him. There was no note or minute; the kind of relationship we had and the quality of our close discussions on something as significant as

this was such that any written advice would have seemed very strange to him ... At any rate he was pleased by my analysis and the conclusion. We had had a weighty conversation, and he believed he was across the main parameters. As often was the case with him after I had sold him on something, he became an enthusiast for it. I would go in with all the argument, weight, passion and persuasion I could muster, and if I could get him interested or committed he would often subsequently be an enthusiast for it. This was very much the case with the float. He had a broad predilection towards it and, upon hearing cogent argument for it, he became committed. But a lot of the engrained difficulties would remain uppermost in my consciousness, but not his. His enthusiasm sometimes turned into impatience while I actually had the task of making a decision work ...

The question was rather when to float and how to float and how to bring the system with us. How we would do it with authority and be able to maintain the authority if it went wrong.

The discussion in the ensuing months involved watching how the system was performing and how it might perform in a quantity-based environment.

We were watching, assessing and refining our thoughts. I say 'we', I mean 'me', Johnston, Sanders, Phillips and, by August or so onwards, Tony Cole. This was a big leap for the Reserve Bank. It hadn't done anything like this before. It was convinced, but wary. The markets gave us time but we needed time. And I think we used it well. Getting their measure, sizing the scene up, learning how we would actually do it.

We were essentially getting ready for the big wave (of market speculation on the dollar) to come as we were convinced it would, having devalued in a big way once before.

By around September the Hawke office, in its general early government exuberance, regarded the decision to float as a foregone conclusion. By September, watching and waiting and looking at questions of execution it had gone way beyond the limits of its sophistication. A discussion about the future of exchange controls had, I think, barely registered with them.

When the next wave came in October we decided at a meeting we had at the RBA building in Canberra to float the forward rate to get the market focussed and to get it thinking and us thinking about how we would manage the spot rate. This meeting was attended by Johnston and some colleagues from the Reserve Bank, Stone and a number of Treasury officials, myself and the relevant people from my office, and Ross Garnaut from Hawke's office. Hawke was not in attendance. In a sense, it was an officials' discussion presided over by me.

At this meeting Stone said the RBA and the bureaucracy were on the whole ill-prepared for a wholesale change to a full market-based system. He said the RBA was asking the government to commit to it as an act of faith. He said while the managed system had its limitations, it had insulated Australia from the volatility in currency movements and that, by throwing the system open, we as a small economy would be thrown about like a cork in the ocean. He said he believed the exchange rate would also be appreciated, compounding our problems of competitiveness. He said we couldn't be sure that interest rates would be more stable, either. But he said he could agree to free up the exchange market somewhat by the RBA withdrawing from the forward market. This would develop some more depth of experience in the markets in setting the forward rate.

While I did not support Stone's view about insulating us from volatility or the 'cork in the ocean' line, or even the appreciation of the rate, the move to a more open forward market would give us a better handle on the system when we eventually threw it open.

I did not condone Stone's histrionics or some of his more extravagant arguments, but a move to a more open forward rate would give the whole system more experience—including the bank. It would also give us more time. I was not entirely persuaded that the bank had faced up to all the exigencies of what an immediate throw to an open system would entail . . .

The in-principle decision, by then having well and truly been taken, I believed my job—the Treasurer's job—was to see that when we threw the ball we walked away with a kewpie doll.

I told Stone that I saw the float as inevitable, and notwithstanding some of the more weighty arguments he put against it, the next time we faced a run against us, we would float. And we would do it with or without him.

When the big wave came in December, Johnston, Sanders and I discussed the problem all afternoon on the advice we were getting from overseas markets, judging how strong the run might be and whether we felt we should let the rate go.

As the day wore on and the evidence mounted, our view hardened. I discussed this with Hawke in his office through the late afternoon and evening and talked to a few key colleagues about it. Parliament was breaking up that night for the year, and of course many were not in the mood or of a mind to face such a matter.

By late evening, we had decided to close the exchange on the Friday or otherwise wear a poultice of funds, and I phoned Johnston at home to tell him. He said, 'You know Treasurer, with the exchanges being closed we will have to have a large discretionary adjustment or a float.' I said to him, 'Get yourself down here tomorrow morning Bob, because we will be doing it. We will be floating. You can deal with Stone's arguments.'

The group of us—Hawke, I and our advisers, both office and departmental—met in the Cabinet Room and then later on argued the case to the Economic Committee of Cabinet. And that was that.

KOB: Bob Hawke told the ABC series *Labor in Power* that the initiative for the float of the dollar came from within his office. 'Paul Keating had to be brought along,' he said.

PJK: That is a complete lie. On Sunday 23 October, Ted Evans, the Head of General Financial Policy in Treasury, wrote to John Stone, saying, 'The Treasurer rang me at home noting his concern with the way monetary growth had been proceeding and referring to discussions the Treasurer had had with the Reserve Bank about the float. When we met with the Treasurer that night he asked for the views of each of us present (Treasury officials) on the proposal to float the dollar, to which he was inclined.' (That is, to which I, the Treasurer, was inclined.)

This was on 23 October. The float came in December. From March when we devalued the dollar by 10 per cent to September while preparations to float were being developed, the markets basically left us alone. They didn't start to put pressure back on until September.

I introduced a memorandum to Cabinet on 2 November where it is as clear as day I am putting the Cabinet on notice that a float was in the offing. This was formal advice by me to the Cabinet, not a note for file or an off-hand comment.

KOB: The Bob Hawke view is reinforced by his economic advisor Ross Garnaut, and by one of your own economic advisers Barry Hughes, who also told *Labor in Power* that while you were in front of the reform cart on other issues like banking reform, you weren't in the vanguard on the float.

PJK: Bob and I were so matey and as one at the time, it is inconceivable that we would have had different positions on so central a matter and one that had been so comprehensively discussed, and over such a long period. The key staffer in my office at the time was my private secretary Tony Cole, who later became Head of Treasury after being Chairman of the Industry Commission. He wrote in 1990, 'I think it's fair to say that both the Treasurer and the Prime Minister had decided a float was on prior to the 28th of October. From then on it was only a matter of when circumstances were right.' Tony Cole was the official person in the office and the one most aware of my thinking. Barry Hughes was a valuable econometrician but he always lived in the shadow of Garnaut's influence.

KOB: Bob Hawke said there was a sense that you wanted to float, but that John Stone was holding you by the feet.

PJK: That's nonsense. Bob and I had agreed on the float months earlier. The markets had not come back to pressure us until September. In the end we floated on 8 December. So any debate is about the timing within those eight weeks only.

It's worth making the point that I conducted the press conference for the float. If Bob Hawke had been the true progenitor of the float, as he has later alleged, and it was the most important decision since sliced bread, he would have presided over the press conference himself. But I did the press conference with Bob Johnston. And the reason I did was because Bob Johnston was RBA Governor and the bureaucratic progenitor of the float as I was the political progenitor.

John Stone said to me, 'Do I come, Treasurer?'

I said, 'No, John, I can't have you there. You're opposed to it. You'll get asked about it and you will accurately reflect your views, views that have been overridden by the decision of Cabinet. So I can't have you there.'

Bob Johnston was a bit embarrassed that he was sitting with the Treasurer, without the Treasury Secretary. This is the first time ever that the Reserve Bank began to look like what we now recognise as an independent central bank. This was hugely significant.

KOB: David Morgan remembers that when you had the press conference to announce the float, you were asked whether Stone had been excluded because he disagreed with the float. You responded, 'Well, there's more than one view within Treasury.' He says that sparked a witch hunt by Stone during which Morgan confessed to him that he had in fact expressed his support for the float to you.

PJK: David did support the float but was not the only Treasury official to support the float, effectively in defiance of Stone. On the day, it was like riding the tiger's back in part because of Stone's warning that we'd be thrown around like a cork in the ocean. I had said in response to that warning, 'I've got more respect for markets than you have, John.'

In the end, people will not sell their foreign exchange if it's too cheap and people will not buy someone else's dollar if it's too expensive. In the end, sense and balance matter. The idea that all of a sudden we'd end up with a thirty-cent dollar could only be true if someone were prepared to sell an Australian dollar for thirty cents American. Discerning people don't do things like that.

THE ACCORD COMES OF AGE

Whatever doubts Bob Hawke harboured about having Paul Keating as his Treasurer going into government in March 1983 must have been well and truly dispelled by the time 1984 rolled around. With two budget statements and the float of the dollar behind him, Keating's early hesitancy in the job was long gone, and a quick glance at the economic headlines dominating the newspapers in the early months reflected that.

On 2 January 1984, the *Sydney Morning Herald* reported that the Australian stockmarket was the best performer in the world. The All Ordinaries Index for 1983 recorded a 59 per cent increase compared to 22 per cent for Wall Street, 29 per cent for London, 23 per cent for Tokyo and 14 per cent for Hong Kong.

The *Financial Review* front page for 13 January carried three good news stories for the economy. One reported an increase in employment of 80,000 jobs for December. A second recorded consumer confidence at its highest level for a decade, and a third described Australia's trade performance as improving significantly over the previous six months, including a 20 per cent increase in manufacturing exports.

In March 1984, just one year after Bob Hawke and Paul Keating arrived in office on the tail of the worst recession since the Great Depression and a nasty deficit surprise, the *Sydney Morning Herald* carried the lead front-page headline: 'Keating: growth best in 25 years.' Inflation in the year to March 1984 was also down from 11.5 per cent the year before to 7.6 per cent. After one year, the double-digit inflation and unemployment of the Fraser years had gone, and although the final Howard budget and the end of a crippling drought had contributed to some of those improved figures, they still represented an economic and political triumph for the new government and its Treasurer.

At the same time the radical direction Keating had taken his party away from its old philosophical comfort zone was hardly being welcomed by all across the labour movement. He and Hawke were in lockstep on Labor's enthusiastic embrace of financial markets and a less interventionist approach in its broad economic strategies. In February 1984, Vic Martin delivered his report on financial deregulation, broadly endorsing the Fraser Government's Campbell Report, including the recommendation to allow foreign bank entry into Australia.

In March Keating had begun circulating the new draft economic policy platform he intended to take to the party's national conference in July. These days the carefully stage-managed and pre-ordained ALP conferences are utterly anodyne. That was not the case in 1984, when the Left decided to fight the Keating agenda.

One sharp reaction from the Left came from Lindsay Tanner, a fiery young industrial lawyer in Melbourne, who wrote, 'One by one the major distinctions between the ALP and the Liberal Party are being jettisoned, no more so than in the economic sphere. Labor policy and practice are becoming increasingly and more uncritically pro-capitalist . . . In the longer term Labor cannot sustain a substantial base of business support and remain the political party of the trade unions.'

Tanner accused Keating of sanitising Labor's platform to remove anything that might be offensive to business.

Keating's response in an interview with Alan Ramsey in the now defunct *National Times* on 9 March was typically dismissive: 'I think if I'd had a couple of years in opposition as our economic spokesman I would have ended up having a bit of a stink inside the party about my views. Now if they want to have a stink they have to pull me out of the job.'

Politics is full of ironies, and Tanner's political journey was one of them. On Labor's Opposition front bench during the Howard years before becoming Kevin Rudd's Finance Minister, Tanner had come to describe himself as a social radical and an economic conservative, the precise opposite of Howard's self-description. Tanner's warning that Labor would not be able to sustain its claim to be the political party of the unions has been neatly turned on its head in contemporary times, when the real issue is how the party extricates itself from disproportionate trade union control.

Another irony in 1984 was that while Keating was taking on his party's Left over the economic platform, he was forging a whole new working relationship with some of the trade union movement's old firebrands of the Left through the Social Accord. The Accord was the brainchild of Keating's predecessor as Shadow Treasurer, Ralph Willis, drawing on his days as an ACTU researcher, and he ran it as Industrial Relations Minister in tandem with Bob Hawke in the first year or so of government. But having been sceptical of the Accord at first, by 1984 Keating had come to embrace it to the extent that he ultimately became its leading exponent in the government.

KOB: Why weren't you enthusiastic about the Accord initially?

PJK: Variations of the Accord had broken down in every other place in the world they'd been tried. We'd had two big wage explosions in 1973–74 and 1981–82, one of which Bob had presided over as ACTU president. So we'd had two big bangs that had destroyed our competitiveness. They were classic pyrotechnic displays. Therefore I thought the idea of trying to trawl around in the trade union movement for some commitment to accept national responsibility for restraining wages was a reasonably forlorn prospect, but I was prepared to give it a go.

It was also pretty much unformed as a policy beyond the principles underpinning it, as I said earlier in this conversation. All the key union leaders had agreed an incomes policy was a good idea but no one had agreed on any numbers. So we had actually gone into the election with an Accord that had no meat to the agreement. The only specific element was the proposition Bill Kelty put together at the Economic Summit to agree to a wage discount for the Medicare levy. That was the first material agreement under the Accord.

KOB: The Accord was Ralph Willis's brainchild when he was Shadow Treasurer. Once you were in government, how long did it take to crank it up to the point where it was seriously in gear?

PJK: As long as it took me to get Bill Kelty's trust, which took a while. But in the end you've got to be awfully dumb not to spot value, and Bill was value-plus. Conscientious and real, and in the end he thought the same of me, and you know what? When you like someone they generally like you and on that relationship we built the Accord that served the government and the economy right through the Labor years.

The first thing that really sparked our connection was superannuation. That was because we'd had a disagreement on super in the May Statement of 1983 when I'd changed the tax treatment on lump sums in superannuation, removing the concessional 3 per cent tax on lump sums. The unions were opposed to it, but I said,

'Look, if we don't bring some sort of equanimity to the taxation of superannuation, we can't extend it to the whole workforce,' and Bill said to me, 'Are you thinking you can extend this to the whole workforce?'

I said, 'Well, that's a possibility. Why should superannuation be the preserve of public servants and managers in business but not for the bulk of the workforce?'

And that issue started a cooperative discussion between Bill and me. By the latter part of 1983 or early 1984 it had reached the point where, if the ACTU wanted something, they would see Bob, but they would talk to me first.

The cooperative model under the Accord was framed so that working people would be cut in on the action. They got a piece of the capital growth of superannuation assets, they got real wages growth, they got access and equity in health, they got access and equity in education, with a trebling of the retention rates in Year Twelve at school, and then later there was enterprise bargaining with a safety net; a national wage case for people who couldn't bargain and a set of formal minimum award rates under that.

Once the ACTU and the guys on the Left like the Tas Bulls and the Laurie Carmichaels, and some guys on the Right like Joe De Bruyn from the Shop Assistants Union, saw I was their man in government, then the whole Accord process began to work for Bill and for me. Bill was powerful because he was creative and had my ear and we had real, cooperative, creative discussions all the time.

The wages committee would come to Canberra. There'd be Carmichael and John Halfpenny and others. They'd see Bob in his office directly above mine in the old Parliament House. I remember one occasion he had his dinner delivered on a tray and they sat in a line in the office while he had dinner in front of them.

I remember Laurie Carmichael saying afterwards, 'Christ, mate, we've come back down here to get a feed.' So I would often send

Jimmy Warner, my driver, over to Civic for hamburgers, and the real nuts and bolts discussions would go on while the members of the ACTU wages committee would be sitting around the table chomping through big boxes of hamburgers. These meetings would sometimes go past midnight, often with another round of food, with taxis back to their hotels at the end of the night. So there was a good feeling about it towards me and the Treasury.

By the time Bernie Fraser became Treasury head, he regarded the Accord as an extra dimension to the two traditional arms of policy, fiscal and monetary policy, where John Stone simply wasn't broad enough to learn how fruitful the Accord might be.

From the trade union side they came to trust Treasury, which they interfaced through Greg Smith and Ken Henry in my office, with Dr Don (Russell) above them, so the whole model was trusted. The formal Accord structure, freely entered and earnestly complied with, became an effective arm of policy. The relationship became so close that if an ACTU wages committee bloke came to Canberra for something, he'd more than likely leave his bag and operate from our office while attending other meetings around the place.

By mid-1984 the Accord was intertwined with our whole economic strategy. It had become a partnership in which both sides could see the value in accepting tax cuts as substitutes for wage increases—that costs would drop and inflation would therefore drop, easing pressure on families' costs of living.

With a different hat on now from his old ACTU days, Bob realised that having this kind of collective power with the ACTU freed up the market to do its best. What it really meant was restraining the top end of the ACTU constituency to make a commitment to the employment of the weaker end of the ACTU constituency; in other words, the strong people in the labour market not cannibalising the interests of the weaker members in areas that couldn't bear the load of generalised wage increases across the board.

It was driven by a powerful logic. We had the depreciation of the exchange rate causing the landed costs of imports to rise, which promoted inflation. We had the real wage overhang coming out of the 1981 wage explosion under Fraser, Howard and Hawke. Therefore there was an intellectual case for the unions to restrain their top-end power by not exploiting a growing economy that could otherwise deliver more jobs, which was central to everybody's interests, no matter where you stood in the economic debate.

Before that, managing wages was about managing demand, and traditionally you managed demand by fiscal policy and by monetary policy via interest rates. But in the Fraser years the management of demand had become a game of 'flattening the economy' in an endeavour to curtail wages growth and inflation.

After that policy failed it was not a revolutionary idea to get agreements from those representing the top end of the ACTU power structure to accept that the government might endeavour to run a higher growth policy, which would of itself produce more employment. But wage restraint had to be delivered and observed by the ACTU in the broad, delivered on a basis of maturity.

Tax cuts were important in this, because they were a cash addition to household disposable income rather than that coming from some inflationary wage round.

Growth in our first year came from one-off influences like the end of the drought, the fiscal stimulus from the Fraser Government's final budget and a spurt in housing growth. We needed to encourage a pick-up in business investment to encourage a more sustained economic recovery with private spending and investment taking over from the fiscal stimulus. Tax cuts became an important tool in compensating for a real wage cut, which in turn acted to pull inflation back.

In that regard, the new Cabinet, no matter how generally enlightened it was, never saw great virtue in the Treasurer trading away otherwise expendable income for their programs by way of tax cuts, notwithstanding their broad commitment to employment and to economic growth. The economic ministers embraced the argument that the tax cuts were accepted as a mechanism for dampening wages in the name of lower inflation. But the spending ministers in the Cabinet were always cognisant of the tax cut debate because every dollar spent in tax cuts was money they could not call upon. So you always had to sing for your supper with tax cuts because it took so much bread from the spending departments.

The spending ministers had to be persuaded to accept the notion of a more reasonable economic equation where top-end union power was restrained to produce more moderate wage outcomes in the face of a growing economy, to try to break the dismal legacy that Australia had always had—that in any economic pick-up, benefits were frittered away in senseless price and wage rounds. Fortunately there was enough interest, commitment and maturity in Cabinet to join with a similarly conscientious ACTU executive in giving this kind of agreed policy framework a go.

One of the big pay offs for the unions under the Accord came in September 1985 when we clinched the deal for superannuation cover for all workers over the next two years. Bill Kelty told the ACTU Congress it had brought their superannuation strategy forward by twenty years.

KOB: In May 1984 you had to persuade the full ministry not only to accept significant tax cuts but also to maintain spending constraints in the budget which, over time, would reduce the government sector. Was that a particularly tough statement to sell?

PJK: I certainly had Bob behind me, because he wanted to translate the idea of an agreed policy framework that the Accord typified, and give it expression. He wanted to be seen to be getting on with the ACTU and Bill Kelty, with whom he'd had a long relationship. But in those days it wasn't just Bill Kelty. Cliff Dolan was the ACTU President and he wasn't as cooperative to deal with as Bill. Nor was he as cerebral. But the fact that I was getting along with Bill and that as Treasurer I would put my hand up for an Accord-type framework and I would argue for tax cuts in policy unison with the ACTU meant that in any Cabinet discussion I had Bob's full support.

KOB: John Edwards has written that in the specific Accord agreement you and Bill Kelty reached for the 1984 budget, you were the primary player for the government. In other words, from 1983 where you and Ralph Willis were sharing the responsibility for the Accord, by 1984 you had become the principal player. He said you worked out in general terms how much would be available for tax cuts and the ACTU would then put forward a proposal on how they would be distributed. Was that how it worked?

PJK: It was actually interpreted by the media as the ACTU's $1.3 billion tax-cut package rather than the government's, and that Bill Kelty was the architect of how it should be delivered, but the whole thing was a cooperative venture. When I sat down with the ACTU wages committee in Melbourne in late July 1984, I had Bernie Fraser with me, the new head of Treasury, as well as Tony Cole and Greg Smith, and they were able to run through tax scales and models on the spot.

You could imagine the general goodwill obtained around the ACTU table when the head of Treasury and the person running its taxation policy are sitting down with the Treasurer with an amount of money on the table and then calculating the scales to see where you could best deliver the money.

For a start, the unions had never experienced such goodwill or consultation like this in their lives. Treasury had never been actively in a position where it could garner this kind of wage restraint other than by some crushing interest rate burden.

Because everyone knew what we were doing was revolutionary for Australia—restraining wages growth in a structured way by agreement—then I was always happy to represent it as it was, a cooperative discussion within a cooperative framework.

Sometimes I would leave Canberra at night in one of those little Mystere jets, say nine-thirty or ten, arrive in Melbourne about half-past ten, get to Treasury Place around eleven, and we'd start negotiations with the ACTU wages committee from eleven until three or so in the morning. We did that often. Sometimes we'd fly back into Canberra just as day was breaking.

There was a sort of jollity that pervaded the atmosphere in those rounds of ACTU talks. I had a good guy driving me in Melbourne and I'd send him down to some late-night place to get the usual box of hamburgers at 2 a.m. But it all produced a good spirit around the table.

The fact that nobody 'split', that nothing was said indiscreetly, that it didn't make it into the papers, was indicative of the support everyone gave it and the importance they saw in it, and it meant that the agreement had the full weight of the ACTU wages committee behind it.

It underlines the point as to how consultation pays off. And trust. Include people in the problem, and they'll mostly come to the same conclusion.

KOB: Bob Hawke has had a few things to say after leaving politics, suggesting that your stamina sometimes let you down. Did you find it hard to sustain that kind of pace?

PJK: You couldn't have worked harder. I certainly couldn't have through those years. My GP used to say, 'Paul you've got a constitution like a horse but you just can't keep giving yourself a belting. Something will give.' But I was able to maintain that kind of pressure for years and years, although I hit a rough spot leading up to the 1988 budget that was to give me a health problem I still live with today.

KOB: Could you honestly say you took the same approach with business as you did with the union movement?

PJK: Where it mattered, I did. Where it mattered. But business interests are spread more thinly. They're not as centralised as the unions were through the ACTU. We would have discussions with people like Bert Evans at the Metal Trades Industry Association (now the Australian Industry Group) with the same degree of trust and confidence we did with the ACTU but not with all business groups. The Chamber of Commerce and Industry were pretty much all carrying the Liberal Party ticket in their pockets, but Bob and I had a good set of relationships with most of the corporations that made up the Business Council of Australia. Not so much with the BCA itself, but certainly with the bulk of their member companies. This was a period of genuine consultation, with the movement forward of economic policy by agreement and consensus.

KOB: What can you remember of how the personalities played out around the table with the unions, interacting with those old-style warriors of the Left like Laurie Carmichael, who you would once have counted as your ideological enemies within the labour movement?

PJK: Laurie had a great commitment to classical music, as I did. He had a very deep knowledge of repertoire. We'd be sitting in some wages committee and I'd send a note to him across the table, 'Just picked up a recording of Klemperer doing Bruckner's *Fifth Symphony* live in Budapest in 1952—phenomenal.'

He'd send a note back, 'What label is it?'

I can remember at a number of meetings he'd bring me two or three discs and I did the same with him.

Tom McDonald from the Building Workers, another old warrior of the Left, would come up and see if you could solve a problem with the way some element of the *Tax Act* worked and suggesting a more sensible way it could work. I'd take a note and see if it could be fixed. So the process had that kind of personal interplay going for it as well as the central discussions.

KOB: You must have thought back on how those relationships turned from foes in the old days to friends.

PJK: Without Bill Kelty, I wouldn't have had those relationships. He was the one who spanned the old industrial Left, the old CPA (Communist Party of Australia) who, it must be said, were both reliable and constructive. I think they recognised in him his earnestness and conscientiousness and his commitment to them and their workers. He was never really on the Right, more an industrial centrist.

I'm not saying it wouldn't have been possible to have a good working relationship with the ACTU wages committee if someone else had been ACTU Secretary, but I would never have had one with such intelligence operating, because Bill would have worked all the issues through with his people before we turned up, and to the extent that there were issues he couldn't get an agreement about before we all sat down, he would let them negotiate directly with us. It was a very real process, but the glue that held it together was that centrist element in the ACTU, the group that Bill led.

KOB: The sense I have of the way you were expanding into your role, is that inside Labor you were increasingly becoming your own man, and increasingly drifting away from your old factional base in NSW.

PJK: The Labor Council in NSW, then led by Barrie Unsworth and later by John McBean, lacked what I thought was an appreciation for the wider picture. They could never quite see a system built on low inflation, and how much easier it would be to keep it in place, but getting there was the objective. The fact is, Bill Kelty simply had a superior industrial outlook and strategy.

By the same token it wasn't just the Left sitting around in those wages committee meetings. The NSW industrial Right would have had its representatives there as well. Bill had good relationships with the Right too, because they all recognised his genuineness and honesty in dealing with them. But from the middle of 1984 onwards, I was more or less running my own race.

At the same time Bob and I had a pact, and the pact was that the Treasurer could run the policy but would be consultative and wise and would not blow the show up. So when I was delivering those May Statements and budgets, the understanding was that the policy changes would be considered, they'd be tested, and they'd be discussed. And for a very large number of these discussions Bob was there himself as Chairman of the Expenditure Review Committee.

But in the general negotiation of wages or the broad economic aggregates, I was more or less able to run the show from 1984 onwards, enjoying Bob's confidence as to my ability to do it.

The 1984 Budget was the first real point of consolidation I was able to present to the public since taking office in March 1993. In that Budget I was able to report that the economy had grown by more than 10 per cent, year on year—the best performance in the 25 years for which quarterly national accounts had been compiled. Over the course of the same year, 230,000 Australians found jobs, compared with the 240,000 who had lost them a year earlier.

Inflation had fallen to 6 per cent but during the last six months up to the Budget, was running at an annual rate of around 5 per cent. A big change from the double-digit inflation left to me by John Howard.

In fiscal terms I was able to bring in a budget deficit for 1984–85 of $6.7 billion, a reduction of $1.2 billion over the previous year. As a proportion of GDP it was even more impressive, reducing the budget deficit to 3.3 per cent of GDP, down from 4.3 per cent a year earlier.

This quite dramatic consolidation had proved the 1983 Budget strategy right. This is what Bob got, having me appointed as Treasurer, rather than Ralph who, along with big-spending merchants like Langmore, would have blasted the deficit into the low stratosphere.

But the budget was more than about economic growth and fiscal consolidation. It also had a number of goodies for business; for instance, for the first time, group taxation, where companies with common ownership could account in tax terms as a group, being able to offset losses against the income of other companies otherwise separate though commonly owned. The Labor traditionalists would never have done these things.

This budget set up the 1984 election for Bob, announced in October. But, as we know, he conducted that disastrous seven-week campaign, frittering away large chunks of the goodwill. I had the ball on the tee for him—he only had to hit it. As it turned out, we hung on against Peacock, but with a 1.7 per cent swing against us, costing us four seats.

During the campaign I had inflation at its lowest level in eleven years, housing interest rates falling and the opening of the financial system to foreign banks—everything that opens and shuts. I even opened the first shots on national superannuation. We should have absolutely buried Peacock. Instead, Bob allowed him to climb out of the grave.

THE BANKS

At the time Paul Keating entered Parliament, there were many faces of capitalism that Labor traditionalists loved to hate, but probably their symbolic public enemy number one was the banks.

Jack Lang had declared war on them in the Great Depression, and in that same period the Federal Treasurer 'Red Ted' Theodore in the Scullin Government was also at loggerheads with them. As Prime Minister in the late 1940s, Ben Chifley had tried and failed to nationalise them. The Commonwealth Bank—the People's Bank—founded under the Fisher Labor Government in 1912, was as close as they would ever get.

In 1975, facing the Fraser Opposition's blocking of supply in the Senate and at risk of running out of money to pay public servants, among other things, Gough Whitlam had his own contretemps with the banks. He was still trying to force them to underwrite the Commonwealth's bills while he stared down a defiant Senate when Sir John Kerr sacked the government.

A lot of that residual feeling remained within the caucus when Keating embarked on a process of bank reform including the deregulation of interest rates, and the introduction of foreign banks to increase competition but in the process hand the existing Australian banks a bigger share of the market at the expense of non-bank institutions such as building societies and credit unions.

It's much easier to see the big economic picture when the canvas has been filled than in the painting of it, but it must have dawned on caucus by 1984 that its leaders were determinately forging a path for the party away from the old cornerstones. Fiscal rectitude, wage restraint and financial-market deregulation from the currency to the banks were becoming the order of the day.

KOB: After the float, banking reform was squarely on your agenda, and you had always had a bee in your bonnet about a lack of competition in the Australian banking system.

PJK: They were deadbeats. Something I first learned from the way the oligopoly of the so-called free enterprise banks treated businesses like my father's. So I always believed in a need for competition, but no one could ever engender any competition. In 1977, six years before I became Treasurer and six years before Bob became leader, I made a speech in the House of Representatives saying we should open Australia up to foreign bank competition. The Managing Director of the Commercial Banking Company of Sydney wrote a letter to all members of staff, pointing to my speech, saying it would destroy the banks' principal lines of business and the sweet spots in the market would be taken by foreign banks. The banks didn't like me and I didn't like them, so there should have been no surprises to them when I became Treasurer.

The first banker I saw as Treasurer was a fellow named Sir Robert Law-Smith, the Chairman of the National Australia Bank with his Managing Director Jack Booth. They came to see me in my office in old Parliament House around April 1983.

Sir Robert, with a plum in his mouth, said, 'Of course, Treasurer, you know we believe in competition.'

I said, 'And do you know what, Sir Robert, I'm going to give you some.'

And he said, 'Oh are you? And how might that be done?'

I said, 'I'm going to give you more freedom to take deposits.'

He said, 'That sounds good.'

And I said, 'But I'm going to let in an array of foreign banks to compete for them.'

'Oh,' he said. This was my first discussion with anyone from the banks and that conversation went around the banking world like wildfire.

What I gave the banks, in the end, was the gift of a lifetime when I lifted deposit maturity and lending controls. For instance, at that time a savings bank couldn't accept deposits under 30 days. Funds went to things like cash management trusts. We had the haphazard development of permanent building societies, all trying to get around the regulations, as the banks' control of credit continued to shrink.

How mature is a financial system where the institutions prudentially controlled by the Reserve Bank have a declining share of national credit? So I had to stop the growth of the permanent building societies, credit unions and the cash management trusts and bring the banks back to a position of primacy. At the same time, in their new-found freedom, to address their lack of competitiveness, I wanted the foreign banks to step in. So I gave the banks more freedom but within a new competitive structure.

KOB: Banking reform was also an important part of the Campbell Report into financial deregulation that John Howard had commissioned at Malcolm Fraser's behest, and in the shadow of the 1983 election Howard supported the entry of ten foreign banks in line with Campbell's recommendations.

You were in your first weeks as Shadow Treasurer and you opposed it. Given your own long-standing support for competition through foreign banks, why did you oppose it just before the election?

PJK: I gave Howard credit for articulating a view that the government was inclined to open the banking system to foreign banks. At that time the Labor Party had the head-in-the-sand view that we shouldn't have foreign banks. In a four-week election campaign there was no way I was going to get the shadow cabinet back together to overturn the party's foreign bank policy so, for the period, I was stuck with it.

When I first walked into the Treasurer's office after we won the election, there was a copy of the Campbell Report on a shelf, and it had faded in the western sun. The back of the Treasurer's office faced due west, and I said to one of my advisors, Barry Hughes, who had walked in with me, 'This tells you something.' It was a sort of a metaphor for the fact that the Fraser–Howard regime had let the Campbell recommendations lapse.

KOB: If, as you say now, you had always supported financial deregulation and knew the float would potentially open the floodgates to other financial market reforms, why did you bother setting up your own expert group, the Martin Inquiry, to review the Campbell Report?

PJK: The problem was that the Campbell Report recommendations had not just faded, they had died. There's an orthodoxy about these days which suits Howard and the Liberals to say, 'Oh, we set up Campbell and there was an inevitability about these changes.'

There was no inevitability. None at all. The Campbell Report had died a quick death. I might add that only Bob Hawke and I supported the Campbell recommendations during the caucus discussions when the report was released, and Ralph Willis was Shadow Treasurer in 1981. I was asking questions of Frank Crean when he was Treasurer in 1974 about the legitimacy of cash management trusts and permanent building societies using regulations to get around the banking system. And I was making speeches supporting foreign bank entry three years after that.

But let's return to the key point. If you have a core document that is recommending the opening of the financial markets including a floating exchange rate, if you believe in it, you would get it through. It's not good enough for Howard to say he couldn't get it past Country Party ministers like Doug Anthony and Peter Nixon, or he couldn't get it past Fraser.

The fact is Howard died on the job and the Campbell Report was dead on arrival. Politically I now had to push these ideas through the caucus, which eventually I did. I wanted a new approach that also had some idea about the complexion of the Labor Party. The Martin Report was a political exercise, a new branding.

A lot of Labor members of Parliament were members of their own local permanent building societies and credit unions and they didn't want to see these flows of funds return to the banks.

But I said, 'You can't have an economy which is capital-adequate with the banking system only controlling 46 or 47 per cent of the credit. Do you believe in the prudentially managed institutions? You tell me you believe in a Reserve Bank.'

They said, 'Oh yeah, we all believe in that.'

So I said, 'You believe in the prudentially managed institutions, the big four, being supervised by the Reserve Bank?'

'Yes,' they said.

And adequate capital ratios?

'Yes.'

Career structures?

'Yes.'

I said, 'But you don't believe they should have primacy in deposits, is that what you're telling me? You want these itsy-bitsy credit unions and permanent building societies to grow but you want to hold the banks back. This is not a tenable situation.'

They had two sets of standards: one for the banks and another for the institutions they liked. So the banks were sitting with a declining share of credit. How can you build a country with a structure like that?

The caucus was reluctant but I always started with the caucus committees. And almost everyone in the caucus would come to the economics committee. After two or two-and-a-half days running through the arguments, the last six or so MPs who were left would go to get the three o'clock plane to Melbourne or Sydney. And when they drifted off I knew I had the thing in the bag. So, as a technique, I would always run through the arguments for each set of policy changes.

It was yet another case of the old Labor Party confusion over ends and means. This was about the ability to run a mature banking system funding debt requirements as necessary for the development of housing, for the right to buy a house, for the ability of a developer to build a building or an estate, for the ability of banks to fund small businesses.

None of that was possible on a grand scale while we had the old regulations. But the Labor Party ends were to see open financing for housing and open financing for business but they never quite understood how to get there. In practice, regulation was largely a set of rules for the rich, while deregulation meant a set of arrangements for the clever—and the clever people had been locked out of Australian business by the regulations.

I used to say, 'We get a choice. Are we with the rich guys or the clever guys?' and the caucus would put their hands up for the clever guys.

'In that case,' I said, 'we have to make these changes.'

Now, this was all a Labor end, but it was not by the traditional Labor means. The traditional means was control. Or what they believed was control.

I said, 'Look, I'll put my arm around the permanent building societies and I'll turn them into banks.'

So what became the St George Bank was created from the St George Building Society. From the Melbourne Permanent Building Society I created the Bank of Melbourne, which now belongs to Westpac. In fact, both now belong to Westpac.

I said, 'I'll put my arm around the credit unions, making it easier for them to specialise in small loans and personal finance, but we must have a mature structure. Banks must be at the centre of it. But they have to be competitive. Currently, they're slothful and uncompetitive and that's where the foreigners will sharpen them up.'

Cabinet had to be convinced of the principles of an argument, but it was easier to persuade in the Cabinet room if there was a groundswell of support coming from caucus. In the end I'd consulted my head off on the banking reforms. I'd sat in those meetings for days.

KOB: When you announced the government's approvals of sixteen new trading banks, and you said 'and they said it couldn't be done', who were you addressing?

PJK: The system in general, and the Labor Party in particular. In other words, that the Labor constituency in the broad and the banks themselves would together unite to stop the foreign reforms. One classic example was Jack Ferguson, who was Deputy Premier of New South Wales and leader of the Left, standing up at the Labor Party Conference in 1984 saying, 'If I get a choice with these banks I will take our banks rather than these foreign banks,' which was exactly the wrong choice. Right through the grain of the Labor Party, the four banks were confident they could stop the foreign banks.

KOB: Looking at the way powerful interests, whether driven by self-interest or by genuine concerns, can align against big reforms with potentially big impacts, is there a formula for changing minds, for winning opponents over, for bringing people along?

PJK: As I said earlier, you make the political strategy around good policy rather than around trickery and imagery. In the end if a conscientious community can go to a bank and borrow for a house or an apartment and get the money they need and be able to afford it, they'll give the government of the day a tick. This was not true before 1984, 1985 and 1986, when finally I deregulated housing interest rates. If you have the framework right—and my framework was the internationalisation of the economy and a financial system that got blood to the muscle of the economy—then a conscientious community will give a government a tick for that.

This is a very important point. Whether it was in the House of Representatives or in those long press conferences I did at Parliament House with the press gallery or on radio, I always talked up to the community. I always assumed they had the sense to know what I was saying and to include them in the conversation as I would a caucus member. If you have that policy of engagement around a big story, then basically you pick up adherents.

KOB: By the same token wasn't it a kind of love–hate relationship that the Australian public had with you through those days? You were a very effective storyteller but with a streak of unpopularity.

PJK: Yes, but the model won us four elections in a row from 1984 to my own win as Prime Minister in 1993. It won us four elections on the trot. We built the new political structure and the new policy structure around good policy. We were burning up political capital each time, but the idea that governments have political capital yet not spend it, which many governments do, means that in the end you pay a price anyway but for not much result.

In our case, Bob delivered much of the political capital while I fashioned and spent it. But let me say this in Bob's favour. Prime Ministers need reforming Treasurers like they need a dose of rabies. You say, have I got an idea for you, and with it comes a political horror stretch, like removing tariffs, opening up all the financial system, changing the tax system, introducing capital gains and all the other reforms. Most Prime Ministers would say, go away, go away. Bob could see the value of the ideas I brought him and I could see the value his support brought me, and that was the essence of the team we had.

Bob and I had a truly cooperative relationship through these times. We had our issues. We had a fight over tax in 1985. We had a fight over the banana republic in 1986. We had a battle over the date and calling of the election in 1987. We had a battle over tariffs in 1988. But nevertheless we always kept the main chance in mind, winning and moving the country forward.

KOB: John Howard has said more than once after he became Prime Minister and was dealing with Labor Oppositions that tried to block his attempts at reform that you had a broadly supportive Liberal Opposition in the Parliament in those years of your big push for economic reform. The political battle would have been much harder, wouldn't it, if there hadn't been some reasonable measure of bipartisanship with the other side?

PJK: I always appreciated any support the Coalition gave but they egg the pudding. They opposed superannuation cheek by jowl. They opposed every wage increase that arose under the Accord. And you have to remember these contributed to restoring our competitiveness and breaking the back of inflation. They were central. They opposed capital gains taxation and fringe benefits. They were fine about bank deregulation and tariff cuts until John Hewson tried to upbraid me later and boast that he could do it better. But then again, I did not need the Liberals on bank deregulation any more than I did on floating the exchange rate or the move to enterprise bargaining. I carried the heat on all these changes. And you might remember the Liberals opposed native title outright as they cavilled at any plan for an Australian republic.

I love the Road Runner analogy, and used to call Hewson Wile E. Coyote because he was always trying to blow me up. I used to say to caucus, 'The reason I love the Road Runner is because he runs so fast he burns up the road behind him. There's no road left for the others.'

And basically that's the policy I pursued. If the Coalition supported me on something, well and good, but I was going so fast anyway it really didn't matter. It fundamentally didn't matter. It was a momentum play. I'm happy to acknowledge their support on some things, but not on the broad scope of changes. Not on wages, not on superannuation, not on a lot of the social policy changes, and not on the tax reforms like capital gains tax. In the end I had to rely on Don Chipp and the Democrats in the Senate to get the changes through. In fact, Don Chipp did more to facilitate many policy changes in my years than any of the Liberals did. But Howard was always a better rewriter of history than Don Chipp was ever likely to be. Chipp was really a first-class individual, a very conscientious and responsible guy.

KOB: When you look at the banking sector today what do you see, apart from the big four banks making incredible record profits and becoming ever more dominant? Where is the competition today?

PJK: The real competition died in the crisis in 2007 and 2008. I would not have allowed the Commonwealth Bank to buy BankWest. I wouldn't have allowed Westpac to buy St George. I wouldn't have allowed it any more than I allowed them in my day to buy each other. I put the four pillars policy into place to stop them cannibalising each other, and had they done the cannibalisation we would have had a lot of the problems that the American financial system had. We avoided that because the four pillars policy saved us. Saved us from the banks' silly behaviour of trying to get big quickly. When companies try to get big quickly by acquisition, by taking indigestible meals, you end up with problems. Competition in banking took a big step backwards when St George Bank went, BankWest went and the mortgage lenders such as RAMS went.

My concept of strong competition between banks has in large measure been derailed. Before my reforms the banks had a three-percentage point margin on a housing loan. Three hundred basis points. After the reforms and before the crisis in 2007–08 that margin was reduced to 75 basis points; that is, from 300 points to 75 above the official rate. The bank's margin was three-quarters of a percentage point instead of three percentage points. This was all delivered into the mortgagees' pocket, into ordinary householders' pockets. Now they've expanded that margin again, although in fairness to them, nothing like the old days when the banks had that whopping 3 per cent margin.

OUT WITH THE OLD

The ALP National Conference in July 1984 now stands as another milestone on the way from old to new for the Labor Party and its economic policies, becoming, as it turned out, a party that many voters today say they have trouble differentiating from its traditional political enemy, the Liberals.

Paul Keating's new economic policy platform was accepted pretty much as he wanted it. Banking deregulation was just part of the story. The old socialist agenda of the radical workers' party that emerged from the bitter shearers' strike of the late 1800s—the socialisation of production, distribution and exchange—the party Whitlam had called a democratic socialist party, was now being called a social democratic party.

The shift was less than subtle. In some ways the party platform was belatedly giving legitimacy to policies already in train, such as the float of the dollar, bank deregulation and the broad Keating drive to shift economic focus more from government to market. The 1984 conference adopted a formalised review of tax policy and although the Left's desire for a politically troublesome wealth tax had been thwarted, the review opened up other possibilities, including a broad-based consumption tax and a capital gains tax.

Keating by now had the ball very firmly in his court. Although his critics still argued that he was too much under Treasury's doctrinaire influence, he had become much more the master of his universe. By comparison, John Stone, despite his impressive intellect and, by bureaucratic standards, flamboyant personality, must have felt increasingly isolated in his large Treasury office as he watched his influence and authority wane. He had disagreed with the float of the dollar, he disliked the nature of the Accord and wages policy, and could see his stamp on the budget slipping away. He was particularly discomfited by the way his minister would lift the phone to various specialists within Treasury to get their advice directly rather than having it filtered through what they saw as the often dogmatic prism of their boss. No one had run a tighter bureaucratic ship than Stone.

The ultimate clash between the bureaucrat and the politician was played out around the 1984–85 Budget and there could only be one winner. Before the year was out, Stone would take himself out of the game but Keating saw his departure as an opportunity rather than a setback. The learning curve had been conquered.

Firmly backed by his Prime Minister, and increasingly blazing his own trail, by mid-1984 Keating was unchallenged as the second most important member of a formidable Cabinet. As a combination, Hawke and Keating were essentially irresistible on all the big economic reforms. They just had to stay in step.

KOB: You were about to present your second budget in August 1984. It was a tricky budget because you had to offer reasonable tax cuts to keep the Accord intact, you had to keep the deficit's credibility intact in the eyes of business and the markets, and you were under pressure to increase welfare payments. Six days before the budget's release John

Stone resigned. The timing suggests something must have happened between you.

PJK: I think it simply dawned on John that I wouldn't take any more of his nonsense. Statement Two of the budget had come to be recognised as Treasury's work in the budget presentation. The Statement Two draft for 1984 was counter to the government's incomes policy, its fiscal policy and a whole range of other things.

In the old days the Treasurer, say John Howard, wouldn't write Statement Two or have a role in its writing. It would be written by Treasury and presented to the Treasurer. But in the end it has your name on the front cover and it is published as the government's document. Yet here was a whole litany of stuff written by Stone and his senior officers like Des Moore and Dick Rye, which was counter to the government's policy. So I told John we could not abide their draft.

'Treasurer?' he said. 'Don't you realise this statement is regarded as the Treasury's statement? It's seen by the outside world as Treasury's own statement, yet you're going to direct me to change it or change parts of it?'

I said, 'Yes, John, I'm going to direct you to change it. I present these papers as an official set of documents to the nation with my name on them and they at least should represent the combined or consensus view of the government and the department.'

I said, 'Let me go to some of the sentences.'

As I went through the text I said, intermittently, 'We just can't agree to that.'

He said, 'What do you mean we can't agree?'

I said, 'Well, it's got to be struck out, John.'

'Well, that will be a first,' he said. 'No Treasurer to my knowledge has ever said they wanted to alter even a single line in Statement Two.'

I remember Tony Cole from Treasury, who'd come to work in my office, saying to Stone about one of his assertions in Statement Two, 'Well, John, you can't argue with this one . . .' and Stone said, 'Tony, we don't need some low-brow discussion. If you're giving us instruction to take it out, we'll note it.'

So Dick Rye, who was Deputy Secretary, took notes as I outlined the objectionable bits. He said at particular points, 'What do you want to do with this, Treasurer?'

I said, 'Delete it all—the whole paragraph.'

What Stone had given me was intolerable in the end. Basically he was shoving it up the Government's nose. So in the end I stood him up and knocked it all out.

KOB: By this stage John Stone must have felt his power and influence had become seriously diminished within the government, and perhaps even within Treasury. Tell me about the battle that went on over the forecasting responsibilities that had traditionally sat with Treasury alone and on which you wanted wider input.

PJK: The forecasts in many respects give dimension to the picture. It is on the forecasts that most of the budget projections of revenues and outlays are built. So the budget deficit or surplus in prospect in very large measure is shaped by the forecast. I had a stake in the forecasts being both plausible and reasonable, because my name as Treasurer was attached to them.

The economic adviser in my office through this period, Barry Hughes, was first and foremost an econometrician, so he ate, slept and drank forecasts. It didn't mean that just because he was an econometrician he should be a part of the forecasting team, but there was every reason for the Treasurer's office to be a part of the forecasting process, and I was also trying to broaden the base of expertise available to me.

I wanted to open the forecasting up to other departments, and from memory we also included the Prime Minister's Department. We created a new body called the Joint Economic Forecasting Group, the JEFG. Stone fought that very strongly, saying it was a vote of no confidence in Treasury and that the whole sanctity of the budget forecasts would be farmed out to what he used to call 'meretricious players'—staffers and what he called ancillary departments. Rather than seeing it as a virtuous thing to do he believed it would diminish the quality of the inputs into the forecasting process, and remove it from Treasury's exclusive domain. We had a very big disagreement about this.

KOB: Much later, after he'd left the job, John Stone released parts of his resignation letter and described the 1984 Budget as a lost opportunity to head off future problems, that is, the banana republic, because he said there was a phenomenal revenue surge that gave you a chance to cut into the deficit much deeper than you did.

PJK: Treasury were always like a mangling machine. They always wanted to cut things. But the point was that in Statement Two, Stone was actually being directly critical of our whole incomes policy. We couldn't tolerate that, so once I directed the changes in Statement Two, John knew the game was up. After overruling him on the float and the dismantling of exchange controls, the forecasting system and then Statement Two, the jig was up.

Nevertheless, I had had a very civil relationship with him, and had treated him very kindly. It was John who elected not to go with the government's policies. He rang me to say he was going to resign and he wanted to present me with a letter, so I said I'd come to him. In his office he handed me the letter with a brandy and dry, and poured himself a whiskey. It was a very surreal occasion.

John Stone's big mistake was to misjudge the opportunity of the first postwar reforming government. From Treasury, he was in the box seat to participate across the financial markets as never before: across the exchange rate, across microeconomic reform including tariffs, privatisation, bank reform, telecommunications and all the other things that followed.

There was a sense of honour and of public service in John but he was a deeply conservative guy. He could have been the Secretary of Treasury who commanded the great reform years yet he passed it up to become a senator for Queensland in the National Party. When someone once asked Billy Hughes if he was going to join the National Party, he said, 'Son, you've got to draw the line somewhere.'

Stone always regarded himself as a toff, an economic toff, and if he'd left the public service and gone to the Liberal Party as a leading contributor and thinker on the conservative orthodoxy that the Liberal Party was supposed to specialise in, one could have understood that. But to have gone to the National Party—and more than that, to the National Party in Queensland which was then a fiefdom run by Joh Bjelke-Petersen—was beyond my capacity to understand.

I do think that a lot of John's objection to the government was to Bob himself. I treated him very respectfully, and he wrote me a very nice note at the end of it, which I still have. The evidence of my treatment of John is clear in the notes he sent me. But I suspect in the end he could not accept the fact that he was working for Bob, because they had both gone to a selective school in Perth called the Perth Modern School, and he saw himself as an intellectual cut above Bob.

As well as that he had this nuisance Treasurer who wanted to do things that he regarded as ill-advised at best, and at worst risky. We were doing an incomes policy with the ACTU and moving beyond the orthodoxy and, worse still, encouraging more blasphemous elements within Treasury itself, who were going around him to talk to me. He hated the fact that I would deal directly with people like Ted Evans, who was running general finance and economic policy, and with David Morgan.

Stone would tear his hair out when he found I'd been speaking to 'his people' without him. His view was that the Treasurer would deal with Treasury through him and him only. All of Treasury's views were to be distilled by him. Instead the Treasurer possessed the unruly habit of talking to subordinate officers.

KOB: Stone's departure eighteen months into your first term allowed you to hand-pick his successor, Bernie Fraser. Some of his career choices after formally retiring from public service years later suggest that Fraser didn't quite fit the classic bureaucrat mould. He was to become something of a cult figure, promoting industry superannuation on television, as the tough-looking guy with the broken nose that contrasted with the slow, understated drawl, and he also trained thoroughbred racehorses. What were you looking for in Bernie Fraser and what had your partnership with Treasury become by this point?

PJK: I was looking for someone who would serve the government conscientiously, point one; who was imaginative, point two; and who had faith in the model, which included a wages policy, point three. And Bernie fitted all of those categories. Previously it was in Treasury's DNA not to believe in a wages policy. In contrast to Stone, Bernie became a great supporter of an incomes policy, both as Treasury Secretary and later as Governor of the Reserve Bank. But more than that, he just had a can-do attitude. He knew we were on the gold seam, on the biggest economic changes since Federation. He knew he was on the big conveyor belt of change and he was not going to miss a second of it.

By this stage I was talking freely with various Treasury people as different issues arose, which Bernie thought was a good thing. If, for example, we were going through Statement Two I'd ring up the guy looking at the balance of payments and exports and say, 'What have you got in for grains or what have you got in for wool because I don't want to gild the lily,' and he'd give me a note on it. When I was putting the budget together I'd move over to the Treasury building and relate consistently with relevant officers.

KOB: How would you describe your relationship with Cabinet by then, eighteen months in, because they were a pretty strong bunch of ministers, a pretty strong collection of personalities, some of them quite intimidating intellectually? How had their relationship with you and with each other evolved through that first eighteen months?

PJK: I think a Cabinet minister has to earn his or her place perpetually. You've got to keep doing the tricks. You've got to have their conscientious support and you should always be seeking to have the group discussion, the corporate mindset, such that the Cabinet is coming with you on the big directions, and that you could never presume that. You can never take the Cabinet cheaply and any minister or Prime Minister who takes the Cabinet cheaply is very foolish, so I tried hard all the time, with every one of them.

You couldn't rely just on airing arguments in the Cabinet room, but having conversations in advance of a meeting, and discussing the issues further when we came out. If a relevant minister was worried, you'd go and talk things through with him or her in their own rooms.

In Cabinet you have corporate responsibility, so you're not just considering your own matters but everyone else's as well. The sum total of a proper working Cabinet is greater than the parts. A proper Cabinet produces better results. A proper Cabinet debate, a perpetual debate around central issues, produces a bigger outcome than the sum bits of individual inputs.

KOB: On that point I can remember reading in Bill Hayden's autobiography an observation he made about Rex Connor as a minister in the Whitlam Cabinet. According to Hayden, Connor would arrive at the Cabinet table to prosecute his brief, and when he'd finished he'd get up and leave. It didn't matter to him, according to Hayden, what his fellow ministers had on the table.

PJK: Yes, tragic. Completely the wrong approach. I'd sit through every Cabinet subcommittee, every Cabinet discussion. In fact I would stay so late that when the note-takers wrote the decisions I would stay back until they were written accurately. Sometimes I'd stay until one or two in the morning to make certain we actually got the decisions we'd agreed. So I would spend inordinate amounts of time on the Cabinet, on individual ministers and on the process.

The other thing I came to believe was that people are gratified by being taught things. If you want to take people through a process of education they will appreciate it, and we can all go through this process of education all the time. We all love learning things. If you don't take the process cheaply and set the framework and the context well, and make it completely clear, then it's highly likely that their conclusions and your conclusions will be the same. If you follow that process conscientiously you'll mostly get a good result.

KOB: Do you honestly believe that the bulk of your colleagues around that Cabinet table would feel that you showed them the same respect that you expected from them to you?

PJK: Yes. If you read Neal Blewett's diary published after he left public life, he talks about how self-deprecating I could be. I'd often provide the jokes and the fun as well, something was needed to lighten the moment. I always assumed that to stay in front you needed to keep the colleagues with you.

That certainly didn't stop me arguing a case. I had a big fight against Kim Beazley's telecommunications reform because I thought it was a second-best model by a long way. That was a really big fight in the Cabinet room, and maybe I pushed it too far, but a big fight is okay provided your track record is truly consultative.

KOB: Speaking of consultative, over that period even Hawke's traditional enemies, his old rivals from years past, had a great deal of respect for his consensus style. I think that was pretty much a universal view around that Cabinet table, was it not?

PJK: That's true. I had respect for Bob Hawke's consensus style as chairman of the Cabinet, and the trust and autonomy he gave to ministers. It was an important part of the government's success and engineering a decent debate and letting it run so it comes to its natural conclusion doesn't need too much shaping from the leadership.

This was all in the shadow of the Whitlam years. We all remembered the lessons of those years as well as the triumphs. Gough's ministry and ours were three light years apart. The Hawke Cabinet and my own were the epitome of process and clarity with regard to broad objectives and the consideration of functional departmental roles within those objectives.

The disciplines we generally had in the Expenditure Review Committee or the full Cabinet bore no comparison with the Whitlam years, although you have to remember that Gough was saddled with a full ministry and no inner Cabinet. Our whole focus on discipline, on high-value discussion, knowing as we did that the sum of the whole was bigger than the inputs in a well-documented and argued case was the hallmark of government—Hawke's and mine—from 1983 to 1996. With few exceptions, that applied to the whole thirteen years. That approach governed the lot—clarity about objectives, clarity as to means and rigour in process.

KOB: I'd like to get a sense from you of what some of those other Cabinet personalities were like, and the kind of dynamics they brought to the table. Who were the colleagues you had particular respect for?

PJK: Bill Hayden had naturally good instincts on economic issues, and he supported me on the float, on financial deregulation and on many other things. He sat next to me in Cabinet, and I really enjoyed his company and his input. So, too, with Susan Ryan, who was the Education Minister. In the big brouhaha over the 1985 tax package and the consumption tax, she supported me.

Neal Blewett was always a sceptic about rationalist instincts within Treasury but had a good mind and was able to discern value and organise his own portfolio of Health within that framework. Blewett was a very savvy guy and a valuable contributor.

Gareth Evans was Attorney-General before he fell foul of a few issues and became Minister for Minerals and Energy, where he was very successful. Through that portfolio he took more of an interest in economic issues and joined the Expenditure Review Committee (ERC). He was on the ERC for a very long time. Gareth was also outstanding in Foreign Affairs when he took over from Bill.

Brian Howe was one of the great learners of the show and he was also brought into the ERC. In his early days under the influence of the old-school Left, he was always bristling with contempt for the Right of the party and the prevailing economic orthodoxy. He also had the biggest spending department, Social Security. But once he joined the ERC and got comfortable in the power structure, he was able to see how, within the limits of the economic aggregates, the avenues for new and better policy could be developed, paid for by other policy adjustments.

Howe was always an enlightened fellow, but being inside that ERC process enlarged his view of the world. In the end I relied a lot on him for many of the big decisions we made through the ERC, policies that you wouldn't otherwise have expected a member of the Left to support.

At the same time, I did things with him that were important to him. He and I set up the Child Support Agency, which was a big social advance. We got the Tax Office to collect maintenance for children of separated couples through the garnisheeing of wages.

I remember when I first called Trevor Boucher, who ran the Tax Office, to open this up with him, he said, 'Oh surely, Treasurer, you're not going to have us chasing maintenance dodgers along with all the other people we're already chasing?'

He was a very progressive person, Trevor Boucher, and you could always reason with him. I said, 'You've got to look at what we're going to get out of this, Trevor. I've done a bargain here with Brian Howe, and a part of the bargain will deliver things on the revenue side which will be good for the overall picture. You can strike this down, Trevor, because you're the ones who'll have to make it work, but it will be costly inside the place.'

He said, 'Of course we'd never strike it down, Treasurer. We'll make it work.'

The bottom line is this. How many women with children today rely on the Child Support Agency for their core sustenance? This was one measure I can think of at the moment, but one of many that came out of the goodwill that developed between Brian Howe and me.

John Dawkins was a very intense kind of person: conscientious, collegiate, committed to the broad philosophy of the government— the internationalisation of the economy—to opening up the then financial and product markets. But in these other areas, and in the shockingly laborious ERC rounds John Dawkins sat there, month in, month out, year in, year out, through all those areas of detailed discussion across every department's spending. Dawkins not only singlehandedly reformed the whole tertiary education sector, he was the most consistent supporter I had.

In the end these ministers knew more about the government's program delivery than a lot of people in the departments because they'd become completely familiar with the programs, having gone through them line by line for years, whereas a lot of the public servants were moving on, circulating through the departments.

The core force in the ERC in the early days, with Bob as chairman and me as Treasurer—Peter Walsh, John Dawkins and Ralph Willis as well as, by stature John Button, and later Brian Howe and Gareth Evans—was a pretty formidable and disciplined group.

KOB: Describe John Button's personality. Journalists loved him for his sense of humour and impishness, and a great streak of unpredictable candour that produced quite a lot of stories for the gallery.

PJK: To say that John Button was mercurial is an understatement. You'd be searching through the superlatives to find the right one, but mercurial is probably the only thing the English language offers us. But that said, it was all to a higher aim, although the higher aim was not always rationally framed. He wanted to move with the government on the internationalisation of the economy and the general positions we were taking, but reserved the right to duck and weave as it might have suited him.

KOB: The journalist Peter Bowers once wrote that Button had the ability to dance through a rain shower and not get wet.

PJK: Well, that's a very apposite thing to say of him. But you could approach him on a big matter and get a considered and conscientious view. I'd go around to his office to discuss something we hadn't been able to agree on, and he would at least give you the credit of having a rational position, and within that position have a real discussion with you. He wasn't a lush. He wouldn't cheat on you, say one thing and mean another. He wouldn't fob you off with some easy or convenient concession and then rat on you later.

KOB: Describe Peter Walsh.

PJK: Funny guy, Peter. He was a series of contradictions. We used to call it Doodlakine economics. He came from a wheatbelt town in Western Australia called Doodlakine, which reflected a kind of cockie philosophy in which you capitalise gains and socialise losses, and somehow Peter had got to the point where he found all this deeply offensive and pursued an ultra-rationalist approach to things.

In doing so he made a very important contribution, always drawing out the contradiction in positions ministers and others would often hold, and he would make a spirited and rational case for particular policies, and he'd often lose his temper on something and throw a few expletives into the equation.

The thing that characterised his public life was the way he dispensed with cant and humbug when it came to the budgetary process, and although the numbers would often present their own tyranny, he would embrace them and try to fit his philosophy within that framework.

Often I would have disputes with Peter because he never knew when to let up. He lacked judgement. We used to call him Sid Vicious. Sometimes it might take me all afternoon to get a minister to sign off on a savings option—I'd get $60 million out of a program which was a big deal because in those days people would fight over $5 or $10 million—and it would be someone really canny like Neal Blewett, who really knew how to play the system to the advantage of his portfolio when we were on the hunt for serious spending cuts.

Neal was like a fisherman playing a trout on a line. We'd be at it and at it for two or three hours and it would be getting near to the dinner break. It would be twenty to six and I'd have $63 million in savings from a Blewett program within my grasp, and Peter would throw his pencil down and say, 'Neal, we are not agreeing to three new staff positions in this new little sub-agency of yours. We've got to stop this creeping growth in Commonwealth employment.'

And Neal would play him along in an argument until Bob would say, 'Well, I think we'll break for dinner,' and up we'd get, with Peter saving three staff positions worth a couple of hundred thousand dollars, but my $63 million had just fallen off the table.

We'd come back at eight-fifteen, and Neal would have a new piece of paper ready, offering $31 million instead of $63 million, and we'd have to start all over again. And I'd say to Peter, 'Peter, for Christ's sake mate, you have to be better with the judgements. When we've got a big saving on the block you've got to bring the blade down while you have the chance, rather than keep the blade up while we have a navel-gazing argument about three staff places.'

Those sometime fruitless hunts of his down the rabbit warrens were often the cause of falling-outs I had with Peter over the years. Regular disputes which often would be about support for people on lower incomes. I remember having a real go at him one day when I said, 'The only point in us being in here, Peter, is to help poor buggers like these. Yes, we have to keep trying to garner all these savings, but not chopping off people who really need support.'

I'd gradually move him around, or Bob would overrule him. That said, he was an important contributor to the general task.

As ERC chairman Bob would most often just let the arguments play themselves out, and would take the opportunity to catch up on other matters. Gareth Evans has written his impressions of Bob as the helmsman and chairman. And he described how Bob would let debates go on interminably, and people would be looking for just a little expression of opinion from him, a little bit of authority and he wouldn't provide it, so the sessions just went on and on. This became de rigueur through the second half of the 1980s.

KOB: How had your relationship with Bob Hawke developed by mid-1984 leading up to the budget, with an election not far away?

PJK: Absolutely tip-top. Bob and I were hardly out of each other's company, in the business of government or socially. We were a kind of tag team. By the end of 1985, the Tax Summit year, Bob and I were joint managing directors, but through the first term, Bob was chairman and managing director and I was chief financial officer.

Bob brought a big bank of public goodwill to the table, which we could draw down and use politically for good policy, and what I brought was a new model for the economy which instinctively Bob supported, whether it was financial deregulation, foreign banks or, later, tariffs.

The great pity with the ABC's *Labor in Power* series was that it focused too much on the last six months and our falling out over the leadership at the end, after eight-and-a-half years; years that included something like fifteen budgets and May statements. But for most of those years, Bob and I ran a cooperative regime for the benefit of Australia.

KOB: There were some pretty wild moments apart from the last six months.

PJK: And I'm happy to talk about the wild moments, but in the end Bob and I got our kicks on Route 66 by seeing the country do better. In the end we were both policy snobs.

KOB: How robust was the relationship through some of the tougher policy moments because that would have been a true test of the friendship? Could you in those early years have a serious disagreement without anger?

PJK: We occasionally allowed ourselves the luxury of talking badly about each other to our own staff, but that was the end of it. I used to say to him I know what you've said about me, and he'd say the same, but he always supported me when it mattered and I always covered his back when it mattered.

KOB: Can you shed light on how such a dynamic relationship was affected by the knowledge that one of you was the Prime Minister and the other one wanted to be? Was it something left unsaid but that nonetheless sat on the table between you?

PJK: In the first term there was no issue about me leading the party. I was happy with Bob as Prime Minister. I used to say, 'You know the scene here, Bob, there are two leaders in the one party.'

He didn't like that so much. That was dirty talk for him, but fundamentally I was not after Bob's job until one serious discussion in 1988, but even then I carried on for three more years.

KOB: Can I liken it to say a cricket or a football team that's performing well? The captain's enjoying a long run at the head of the team and there's an heir apparent waiting his turn. But if the heir apparent is ambitious, I imagine even if he's giving complete loyalty to the skipper, with every year that passes he gradually becomes more and more conscious that he has to stay on the top of his game, he has to keep adding to his score, knowing that one serious mistake on his part could knock him out of the calculations for succession.

PJK: Absolutely. In my case, I collectively did fifteen budgets and May statements. More than anyone ever in the history of the place. And I'd throw the balls up and say, 'Do I get a clap for that?' and I'd get a clap out of the press gallery and the polls. Then I wouldn't get claps and I'd say, 'Well, what about this one?' and I'd do a new trick. In the end I was doing so many tricks, for so many years, that Bob finally misunderstood the nature of our relationship. It defied reality that he could stay forever, but he tried in the end nevertheless.

TAXING THE RELATIONSHIP

If the first two years of government for Paul Keating were about bedding himself in as Treasurer, establishing the budget principles for new Labor, putting the foundations under financial deregulation and gradually becoming more involved in and committed to the social Accord with trade unions, 1985 was dominated by tax. But the reforms that were achieved that year came painfully and messily, played out in a very public way. Perhaps for such far-reaching reform on such sensitive political ground that was always going to be the case, but there was nothing well oiled or carefully planned about the way the debate unfolded, either in Cabinet, caucus or the media.

The tax landscape that Labor had inherited more than 80 years after Federation included a top rate of income tax set at 60 cents in the dollar and company tax at 46 cents. Tax avoidance and evasion had become so rife that the Fraser Government and its Treasurer John Howard had made themselves deeply unpopular with their own constituency by introducing legislation retrospectively to try to stamp out one of the most blatant tax-avoidance mechanisms contrived by tax lawyers, known as the bottom-of-the-harbour scheme. There was no tax on wealth accumulation such as a capital gains tax or death duties, and corporate fringe benefits large and small escaped the tax net.

The broad issue of taxation had always been a contentious one for Labor, internally as well as externally. An undisciplined thought bubble from Peter Walsh during the 1980 election about the possible merits of a capital gains tax allowed a somewhat embattled Fraser to unleash a scare campaign about the threat such a tax would pose to the family home, which effectively killed off the very real chance of a Hayden Labor Government. And at the 1984 National Conference, Labor's Left had tried unsuccessfully to have a wealth tax included in the tax policy review approved by conference delegates. Indirect taxation had become over the years an untidy potpourri of revenue-raising.

A prickly internal party debate about tax policy in the shadow of an election was the last thing either Hawke or Keating would have wanted, and 1984 was shaping as an election year, at least in Hawke's mind and at the urging of some of his advisors. At the same time tax reform was increasingly occupying Keating. His discussions within his own office and with Treasury were ongoing, and he and Hawke had both begun to contemplate the idea of a consumption tax.

When Hawke finally announced on 8 October an election on 1 December—eighteen months early—he was motivated by several factors. First, a half-Senate election was due anyway. Second, given his unshakable faith in the magic of his magnetic connection to the people and his view that the Coalition leader Andrew Peacock was a weak and easy target, why not go early and expose Peacock to a long, seven-week campaign.

But a number of unforeseen events seriously affected the political landscape. Hawke had fallen into a bigger emotional hole than people had realised over the news in September of his daughter Rosslyn's heroin addiction.

Peacock turned out to be a far more effective campaigner than Hawke and Labor strategists had given him credit for, and Hawke had gone against advice and agreed to give Peacock a formally structured election debate. The campaign was so tediously long it became a curse for Labor. Hawke has also talked since about the painful injury he carried through the campaign after being struck in the eye at a cricket match.

Unfortunately for the government, Peacock remembered how effectively Fraser had damaged Hayden's campaign in 1980 on speculation of a capital gains tax, and on the basis of the tax review Labor was now committed to, cranked up his own scare campaign on tax. In what was apparently a spur of the moment decision by Hawke to try to neutralise tax as a campaign issue, he committed the second Hawke Government to a Tax Summit with all stakeholders involved. Keating hadn't been consulted and certainly didn't see it coming. He had argued strongly against an early election, and to him the idea of trying to develop effective tax reforms in full public gaze was anathema, but he was stuck with it.

Hawke has since swallowed his pride and acknowledged that he did indeed run a bad campaign, which, instead of setting Labor up for longevity, saw a considerably reduced majority and, it would seem, significant damage to his own standing with voters.

Labor's pollster at the time, Rod Cameron, later told *Labor in Power* the 1984 election, 'based on pure naked pragmatism', was Hawke's greatest mistake. Cameron's polling showed that the electorate resented the early election, the length of the campaign left Hawke overexposed, and the more the electorate saw of him, the more his appeal suffered and the more they came to believe he was just a politician like all the others, and not above the fray.

Cameron described the decision to have a debate as stupid, 'based on nothing more than a desire to prove to the electorate that he could beat Peacock', which Hawke then failed to do. The end result, Cameron said, was that despite coming into the election in an enormously strong position, Labor lost 2 per cent of its primary vote.

Importantly, the veteran pollster of countless state and federal elections believed that, based on subsequent polling, in 1984 Hawke damaged his brand for the elections to come. It tarnished his love affair with the nation, and while his popularity remained high in opinion polls, that could no longer be counted on to translate into votes. Not surprisingly, it also had the effect of unsettling his colleagues.

KOB: To come back specifically to the period around the 1984 budget, Labor was flying high with Hawke looking likely to exercise his option of an early election. Out of the blue Bob and Hazel Hawke are confronted with the discovery by doctors while their daughter Rosslyn is undergoing a caesarean operation to deliver her first child that her heroin addiction poses a serious health risk to mother and child. You were one of the first people Hawke told. In the intensity of that moment, how did you identify with his emotional upheaval?

PJK: Hugely, because that day Bob had to meet with Dr Mahathir Mohamad, the Malaysian Prime Minister. I was with him for the meeting and he broke into tears. Dropping your guard in front of someone like Mahathir would only happen if you were in real emotional turmoil. So the news had obviously knocked him around very badly. Bob fell into a very big hole at that point, and I did everything imaginable to share it, to warm him up and metaphorically rub him down, and keep the show going. He had a lot of support from other colleagues and friends like Peter Abeles, but it was a very bad moment for him.

I felt for Bob and Hazel through that period, but the work had to go on, and what happened over the months that followed is that Bob stopped nourishing the government. I'm not saying his whole leadership ended there, but the leader has to nourish his party and his Cabinet, and the nourishment stopped at that point. If you look at

Hawke in the first eighteen months of government, the way he brought the Cabinet together, the way he used the theme of reconciliation so effectively through the Economic Summit, the sort of energy he brought to his support for the big economic reforms of 1983–84, you'll see a stark difference compared to what followed.

Bob never recovered the leadership and energy he showed in those early days. Through the years 1985 to 1990, it became the case that the Cabinet supported and nourished Bob way more than the other way around.

I had to provide the energy and the leadership to the government in those years on the dominant matters of the day. Bob disputes this, but the events speak for themselves. And so does the record. In 1985 it was the Tax Summit and the final massive tax package in September that dominated the politics of that year. In 1986 it was the terms of trade collapse, my banana republic statement and the budget response to that statement. In 1987 it was the $4 billion of budget cuts in my May Statement that set up the politics of the 1987 election, the date of which I was central in choosing, including the destruction of John Howard's tax package, which I undertook single-handedly. All while bringing the budget back to surplus for the first time.

In 1988 the year was dominated by the huge May Statement, which included the seminal change in the tariff structure driven by me and bringing forth an August budget with a record $5.5 billion surplus. While in 1989 the agenda was dominated by a bursting economy, rising interest rates, a May Statement with tax cuts to prevent a major wage breakout and a budget surplus of $1.9 billion.

The newspaper record of the major dailies covering all of those events makes clear that I was the progenitor of the policy responses to those major issues throughout the five years.

And not just progenitor but chief salesman. It was unfortunate for Bob personally and for the party that the 1984 election followed so soon after his initial setback. We went into that election flying high as a government. The economy was performing extremely well, jobs were being created at a tremendous rate, the Accord was holding well and we had a handy lead in the polls against a weak opponent in Andrew Peacock. Those of us who were close to the campaign hadn't fully realised how much Bob was still affected until the campaign began to gather momentum.

Bob has himself acknowledged that it was not one of his better performances, so what should have been one of Labor's great election victories, adding even more seats to the landslide against Fraser in 1983—and setting us up for other victories down the track—ended up with us giving both votes and seats to Peacock. Over the course of the campaign we lost ground to the extent of about 3 per cent. Instead of being in a great position for the next three years and beyond, we were on notice that we could take nothing for granted and would have to be on our game to win again. It really should have set us up for two terms. Instead, from that point on, we were looking over our shoulder.

There was one odd moment in the 1984 election when the campaign team had proposed Bob and I both speak at a business lunch at the Regent Hotel in Sydney. I suggested to his staff that it didn't seem a good idea to have both the Prime Minister and Treasurer on the same stage. It seemed like overkill. But they felt it was a good idea for Bob to give a broad overview of the government's virtues and I'd talk specifically about the economy. They were also worried about his performance on the road, and so I was there to bolster him.

Bob spoke first from a prepared text and seemed a bit flat. I spoke off the cuff about the economic picture because it was a good story to tell, with growth rocketing along and unemployment and inflation coming down, as well as our financial reforms like the float. It got a good response.

As we were leaving I said to Bob that I thought it seemed to go down well and he replied, 'My friend, you can have this job when I'm ready to give it to you, and that won't be before 1990 at the earliest.'

This came right out of the blue. He was a jealous little bugger, Bob. And this comment was a case in point. I had done too well. After that, in sharing a platform with him I always put myself on a handicap. Dropping the presentation down a notch—more often, a couple of notches.

KOB: One issue that left Labor somewhat exposed in the 1984 election was the party's commitment at its National Conference to a broad tax review which put things like a consumption tax and capital gains tax potentially on the table, a particularly sensitive issue at any election. Is that why Hawke suddenly announced in a radio interview in Perth in the middle of the campaign that the next Hawke Government would call a Tax Summit to consult widely on any proposed tax changes?

PJK: Bob's announcement took me by surprise because I'd spoken to him by phone earlier that morning in his Perth hotel room. We'd talked about the economic issues likely to come up that day and I'd said we could expect the capital gains tax to run as a big issue that day. We'd made no decisions about tax reform but the Liberals were trying to put it onto us, as they had in 1980 when Peter Walsh had made references to a capital gains tax during Hayden's campaign, and it was very detrimental to the Labor Party at that time. So I told Bob to be wary on that front, and ran him back through the points of a statement we'd put out about tax principles. But then the Tax Summit just appeared from nowhere.

A radio presenter named Bob Maumill on 6PR said to Bob something like, What would you say, Prime Minister, to some sort of public event like a Tax Summit or some sort of public discussion about taxation, and Bob agreed that we could have a public process to debate tax reform.

KOB: Bob Maumill has since revealed that the Hawke camp suggested he should ask that question. Did you know that?

PJK: If that's true it was a complete curve ball. No one in Cabinet had heard of it, and I certainly hadn't heard of it. I wasn't happy with it because it represented a very different proposition to the Economic Summit. The Economic Summit was specifically designed to build a spirit of reconciliation between business and the unions and to lock the unions into the Social Accord.

But I couldn't imagine a worse way of making good tax policy than by doing it in public. We wanted to make changes of substance after years of neglect, marry good policy with good politics, but that was not the way to do it. The problem with a public process of formulating that sort of complex policy is that a great deal of it was highly technical in nature and extremely sensitive politically. But Bob locked the Summit in that day on radio and we were stuck with it.

KOB: Among the thousands of articles in your personal newspaper archive collected through those years, there's a comment piece written by Laurie Oakes during the campaign which noted that some in Labor were asking why the government was being forced to deal with awkward tax questions in a campaign, and you wrote across the article, 'because Bob is all over the shop'.

PJK: Well, he was all over the shop. He was in a terrible mental state. Notwithstanding the personal angst and sorrow he had, which was real, when you're in an election campaign, particularly a long one, you have to have discipline and consistency, and we just couldn't get that from Bob.

After the election I had to plunge into preparations for the Tax Summit with a team of Treasury officers, to produce a template for significant tax reform. It was a very intense process. From a cold start it was a massive amount of work. For instance, the downstairs cafeteria of Treasury was emptied out, and a team of people was installed there to work on the White Paper. We brought Ken Henry back from New Zealand to head up one of the divisions of the White Paper group and there were a stack of other Treasury officers involved, all overseen by Ted Evans and David Morgan.

It was an enormous effort. Officers sometimes had to have their children with them, sleeping on mattresses under their desks. The effort the department put in was phenomenal. It was essentially rewriting the tax system in five months, starting with proposals for Cabinet discussion and finally a White Paper for the Tax Summit.

Bob and I together decided to proceed with a consumption tax early in the White Paper process after his office and mine met with departmental people from Treasury and Prime Minister and Cabinet. As a bureaucratic group they produced a formula for the tax. But over the period leading up to our Cabinet deliberations, Bob ran hot and cold because some people in his office didn't want it for political reasons. My first substantial discussion with Bob on the consumption tax and other reform aspects was at the Lodge one Sunday in January 1985. Bob was cautious but he was in favour of the consumption tax.

The argument from Treasury was compelling. Commonwealth government spending had risen from 23.5 per cent of GDP before Whitlam took office to 30.5 per cent as Howard and Fraser finished. Outlays had risen by 7 per cent of GDP, and because the so-called budget razor gang of the Fraser years had failed so dismally to curtail outlays, Treasury had no confidence that we would ever be able to cut government spending sufficiently. So to deal with the budget deficit, which was around 5 per cent of GDP, they believed we had to find extra tax revenue. The personal tax rates were already too high, so Treasury believed it had to come from consumption.

We also wanted to cut personal tax rates, so we came to the conclusion that Treasury was probably right—we couldn't deal with the legacy of the spending in the 1970s and early 1980s without some new base in taxation, and the obvious one was in consumption.

The top personal rate that Howard had presided over and bequeathed to me was way too high at 60 per cent. People were avoiding it. It wasn't an effective rate of tax. The company tax rate was too high at 46 per cent, and we were taxing dividends twice. If you were a single trader you were taxed once, if you were a partnership you were taxed once, but if you were incorporated, you were taxed twice.

I could never see the sense of this.

We also couldn't go on tolerating massive tax avoidance with a major loophole like the absence of a capital gains tax. We had to broaden the tax base, cut corporate concessions and tax fringe benefits where they were untaxed, like motor cars, free meals, credit cards and the like and we could then lower tax rates.

In the end, we had three options going into the Tax Summit, famously options A, B and C. Option C included the consumption tax, but first we had to debate the whole framework in Cabinet, and that was the biggest debate I'd had to that point. I put my back into it because there were so many elements to consider, and because we knew a lot of them would be contentious within the ministry and the caucus, we scheduled Cabinet discussions in one long run to avoid the risk of leaks.

The consumption tax wasn't a value-added tax like the GST, it was a once-levied tax at the retail level. And for which I was offering massive overcompensation for people on lower incomes. The ACTU knew that and the welfare lobby knew that, and if they'd had sense they would have taken it. So, the Summit came at the end of a very intense and exhausting process.

In the build-up to Cabinet's consideration of the draft White Paper in May, I'd have Bob in the tax cart and then he'd get out of the cart and then he'd be back in the cart and then he'd be out of it again. This was partly a hangover of the psychological problems he'd experienced in 1984. But this was now over a year later.

KOB: Hawke strongly contests the view that he continued to be affected by his family problems beyond a few weeks. He would argue that the political concerns he had over a consumption tax were real.

PJK: Bob can say what he likes, but in the end his staffer, Ross Garnaut, sat in his place in the Cabinet room arguing the case against the consumption tax. In Bob's place. Do I have to say more?

KOB: With regard to the intensity of that Cabinet meeting, David Morgan had this to say to *Labor in Power* as one of the Treasury officials who sat through it: 'Contrary to the taxi driver's view of Paul Keating, he's a remarkably broad, interested and interesting multi-talented man. And I think we saw all of those qualities in his performance over 48 hours-plus. He used rationality, he used his intellect, he used his charm, he used his humour, he used his anger, he used his theatrics, he used his spleen, he used his withering language, all of them turn and turn about, and it was the most remarkable performance I've ever seen in my years inside a Cabinet room.'

PJK: We were attempting the grand rewrite of the tax system. There's been nothing like it before nor since, and the department had gone to extraordinary lengths to facilitate a Cabinet discussion around these matters. The country is always beset with the leaden nature of the legacy systems, of legacy policies, and the taxation system was one of the worst.

You might recall that in the Howard years people were abusing the tax system, largely using capital gains, by the tax-free nature of capital profits, but there was also criminal evasion. Tax avoiders had been supported by Garfield Barwick as Chief Justice of the High Court. Tax administrators like Bill O'Reilly and Trevor Boucher were bewildered as to how they were expected to run a revenue system that leaked like a colander. There was no rationality to it. Capital gains not taxed at all, company income taxed twice, personal individuals taxed at a top rate of 60 per cent, and for private companies, Division Seven tax obliged them to distribute profits to their shareholders, taxed at the full marginal rate. They couldn't retain any earnings—no corporate saving.

So a company today like Linfox in transport or Visy in paper products could only retain minimal profits to reinvest and expand the business. Because they had to pay 60 cents at the margin on distributions. It was hugely avoided and induced massive distortions.

So, Treasury and others thought the only way of changing this was not to cut spending in the budget because they had no faith that any government would have the grit to do it in a meaningful way. They believed the only way to fund the extra outlays of the Whitlam–Fraser years and avoid an ever-expanding deficit was to create another base of taxation. This was a 12.5 per cent tax on consumption, so this was included in Option C in the White Paper.

You've got to see the tax debate in two elements. One, changes to the structure in lowering the top income tax rate from 60 to 49 per cent, of lowering the corporate rate from 46 per cent to 33 per cent, and second, the introduction of dividend imputation; the taxation of capital gains at full marginal rates, and then dealing with a plethora of middle-class welfare such as untaxed fringe benefits.

You can park that on one side of the 1985 tax debate under the various options A, B and C for the Tax Summit. On the other side you had the consumption tax, which induced no behavioural effects on the economy, but had one virtue only: to pay for the tearaway outlays that the Commonwealth had between 1972 and 1983.

Most taxes do change behaviour. A capital gains tax changes behaviour, a lower company tax rate changes behaviour, dividend imputation changes behaviour in respect of the payment of dividends. The abolition of fringe benefits as a deduction changed behaviour. A consumption tax didn't change behaviour, it was simply a tax. People still bought the things they usually needed.

Going into the Cabinet debate, I thought to myself that every time the country gets near one of these really big behavioural changes it fails. Every single time. We've had so many tax reviews over the years. Each time the documents are presented, they're left to gather dust. I was determined that this was not going to happen on this occasion. I was completely across all the technical and theoretical aspects and had Bernie Fraser, Ted Evans, David Morgan and Greg Smith for back-up at the Cabinet table. But this was a vast undertaking and I had to sell it to a tough audience around the Cabinet table. I had to give it context and I had to deal with the politics of it.

I had not asked for this debate, it sprang from Bob's radio interview in the heat of an election campaign. But we had to have it. The department rose to the challenge, and we tried to make Cabinet jump to the tune. I was charged up and ready to go, but conscious that Bob was still in the mental trough he had been in since 1984.

KOB: But what you were also contending with was the long-held Labor view that taxation should be progressive to protect the limited resources of people on lower incomes, and many of your colleagues would have seen a consumption tax not only as regressive, but also as a political millstone around the government's neck, simply by virtue of being a new tax that would hit every consumer in the country.

PJK: The Cabinet went into this reform program aware it was a big change, not simply in Australian terms, but in world terms. You wouldn't find any government in the OECD proposing a change of this breadth. So Cabinet knew it was on the cusp of something big, and knew it had to be a high-grade discussion—high-grade inputs and contributions, the sort of stuff most Cabinets would never be presented with or become party to.

I can recall other ministers saying to me as we'd walk out for a break, how good it was to be part of a discussion running at this level of integrity and creativity. People were saying this. It's been an exhausting day, but what a great conversation we've had. I can remember Susan Ryan saying that to me, I can remember Gareth Evans saying that. But there was resistance. Hayden was worried about it, and so was my old rationalist mate from the ERC, Peter Walsh.

Peter brought his head of Finance, Ian Castles, with him to present alternative scales for income tax, and alternative tax proposals. In the give and take of a big Cabinet with big ideas it's probably reasonable for the Treasurer to believe that the Minister for Finance can introduce tax tables and alternative tax proposals to his colleagues rather than this being done by the head of his department. Personally as Prime Minister I would never have allowed this to happen, but Bob allowed it. So all of a sudden I'm arguing with Ian Castles, a bureaucrat. Peter would introduce a submission but then take a back seat and allow Castles to run the discussion. Here I was, a politician, a Cabinet minister, in a political forum, being obliged to argue with a public servant.

Peter Walsh eventually said in exasperation at the proposed 49 per cent top rate for income tax, 'I thought I joined a party that believed in a progressive tax system.'

I said, 'Well, Peter you did. But it has to be effectively progressive, and one that's complied with rather than abused. So only a PAYE middle-level public servant pays the 60 per cent marginal rate, not anyone else, because they're all into the full range of minimisation opportunities. The current system is replete with tax dodges. What are we seeking to do here? We're seeking to broaden the base of the system and cut the rates. You make more people pay, and you lower the rate they pay at.'

And Peter said, 'Okay, that's rational enough. I don't agree with it but it's rational enough. But tell me, why did you nominate 49 per cent as the top income tax rate?'

And this is where governments and countries make choices.

And I said, 'Peter, I'll give you the answer. To make the philosophical point that the state gets less than half of your income.'

And he said, 'That's what I thought,' and he chucked his papers down and put on a real stink.

I said to them, 'Look, I believe in rendering to Caesar the things that are Caesar's, but if you let Caesar confiscate the revenue of the country in his dictate, then you'll always have an economy limping along that doesn't have great increments to wealth, where people can't save, where the incentive to work and grow is diminished. These are philosophical matters. Broadly the Labor Party has never believed this, but the Labor Party has been wrong about this for at least the postwar years.'

David Morgan refers to my anger in the Cabinet, and I can remember being very snaky when Ross Garnaut, came in. Bob was sitting in Cabinet like he'd been hit with a formalin dart, and he delegated Garnaut to speak on his behalf. So Ross was in there arguing with me against the consumption tax. He wasn't just testing the points I was making, he was making the full broadside against it. I'm dealing with the economics and the politics of the consumption tax and explaining why we had to have it to bridge the gap between government revenue and spending if we were to have any chance of bringing the budget into surplus. I had David Morgan and Ted Evans from Treasury beside me, and in those days they regarded Garnaut as a way less economic mortal than themselves, but they had to restrain themselves because he was the Prime Minister's economic advisor.

In the dinner break, Bernie, Ted, David and I went to a restaurant and I asked Ted if he thought enough of Garnaut to give him a job in Treasury. Ted ruminated for a while and said, 'Oh yeah, I'd give him a job.'

I asked him what sort of job, and he said, 'I'd think about him for something at AS Level.' An Assistant Secretary is about the fourth level below Secretary. It was not a derogatory comment against Ross but Ted was making clear he was questioning the legitimacy and depth of Garnaut's role in that Cabinet discussion.

So, with my most senior Treasury advisers looking on, I was fighting Ross, somewhat muzzled. But I had to do it with some restraint because I didn't want to lose Bob altogether. As you know I had him in and out of the cart through the whole process in formulating the reform package. Butchering his advisor was not the best policy but it did take a lot of restraint.

Overall it was a very high-grade debate, with a number of contributions coming from other ministers. The Centre–Left ministers like Hayden and Walsh broadly threw their lot in with the Left, although Susan Ryan stuck with me. Towards the end of a marathon Cabinet debate, Gareth Evans observed that he had now listened for about 48 hours to all the attempts to punch holes in the proposals and that as far as he was concerned all these attempts had failed. This was an important contribution at the time.

Finally it all shaped up as Options A, B and C, which we were to present to the Tax Summit.

After three days in Cabinet, Stewart West plucked up the courage to say, 'Paul, I don't think you have a majority here for your package.'

And I said, 'Stewart, but do you have a majority to stop me walking out the door with a decision?'

KOB: Meaning what?

PJK: Meaning that Bob didn't want to put it to a vote, and I was claiming Cabinet had agreed to it. And when I walked out with the Treasury officers—Bernie Fraser, Ted Evans, David Morgan, Greg Smith and Ken Henry—Ted said, 'Christ, that was the toughest meeting I've ever been in! The toughest I've ever been in!'

When you look at how hard it was to convince Cabinet, consider then what chance the reforms had in a public forum like the Tax Summit. It was bound to fail. The process was flawed from the start.

KOB: The journalist and political historian Paul Kelly has written in his book *The End of Certainty* that you prevailed in Cabinet because you put your position as Treasurer on the line, and that Hawke wasn't prepared to cut the ground from under you.

PJK: Basically Bob was for the consumption tax. His instincts were to have it. The same as mine. Bob and I were both trying to move the country forward on these big aggregates, these big changes, but we had different views of what the traffic would bear. It was a very tough debate and in the end at the Tax Summit, Bob died on me. He did the deal with the ACTU overnight without telling me. He dumped me without informing me.

KOB: Paul Kelly also said, referring to your ultimatum at the end of the Cabinet debate on Option C: 'The result was a dramatic omen. It signified the decline of Cabinet and government during the Hawke era and the rise of the führer principle, the capacity of the man of power to impose unilateral decisions.' I assume he's saying that you were the man of power imposing the unilateral decision on Cabinet?

PJK: We met over three days. We started on the Saturday and finished at about three or four on the Monday morning. I'd say Cabinet was probably more or less evenly divided about the consumption tax, but not the rest of the package I had in mind. The other changes were actually more sophisticated than the consumption tax. A tax on consumption represents a big revenue change, but it's not a really big idea. There's no sophistication in taxing consumption, but changing the way capital is formed, taxing capital profits, re-skewing the whole financial and corporate system in favour of the production of income is a sophisticated idea, and that all ended up in the final package in September 1985.

KOB: So why did you allow yourself to become so passionately caught up with the consumption tax? You all but staked your career on it.

PJK: At that stage I thought the chances of getting Cabinet to cut 5 or 6 per cent of GDP from outlays was pretty low. We either had to increase tax revenue significantly or save the equivalent in spending cuts, the longhand route. Having lost the consumption tax I then embarked on spending cuts but it took me five years.

KOB: But when the consumption tax fell at its first hurdle, you just abandoned it?

PJK: After the terms of trade collapsed in 1986 I embarked with the ERC on a five-year program to bring outlays back from 30 per cent of GDP after the Whitlam and Fraser years to 24 per cent of GDP. After that we didn't need the consumption tax.

In some respects it was again the old Labor Party arguing with the new Labor Party. It was the old view about the role of taxation in society against the view I was advocating. I thought there was a clear logic to my position.

Once you understood that all the tax avoidance schemes were built on the fact that capital profits weren't taxed and that a whole category of individuals took their income from cars, fringe benefits, superannuation and all sorts of other payments, adding to stacks of corporate welfare, we knew that if we broadened the base we could substantially cut the income tax rates. This therefore seemed to me to tick all boxes. We got more equity in broadening the tax base and we got more opportunity in cutting the tax rates.

We also built in big compensations to cushion people on lower incomes against the initial hit of the consumption tax. Not supporting Option C at the Tax Summit, which included the consumption tax, was the welfare lobby's great mistake. We had massive over-compensation for people at the bottom end. We took the household expenditure survey numbers for 1983–84, and where there was very little income to people in the bottom two or three deciles, we imputed a much higher level of income to them than they could ever have had, and gave them compensation for it. But the welfare lobby ran out on me, aided and abetted by the Business Council. Together they shot Option C down.

But in Cabinet they all said at the end of it, what a fantastic debate it had been at every level. And that's food and drink for a government. That mood permeates to the staff level and goes to the outer ministry and the caucus. And they feel they belong to an organisation that has probity, resourcefulness and ambition.

KOB: David Morgan told *Labor in Power* a small handful of Treasury officials went back to your office at about three or four on the Monday morning after the Cabinet decision to open a bottle of champagne, feeling euphoric because they believed you'd all just played the ultimate grand final, that you had just seen a significant moment in the economic history of the Federation. Their expectation, and I suppose yours, was that with Cabinet support, you'd get full ministry support and caucus support, and that with the work you had done on the ACTU and the welfare groups you were well on the way to getting Option C as official government policy. Can you remember the celebration?

PJK: We knew we had slid the thing through, huge as it was, over the heads of the doubting Thomases, although we knew that probably a majority of Cabinet thought it was a great political risk, and maybe one not worth taking. Nevertheless with the scale of the project and force and quality of the debate, we were able to leave with a Cabinet decision. My Treasury guys knew they'd been involved in an unbelievable decision of government that no Treasury would otherwise expect to be part of, and secure. They'd walked in with a monster proposal and walked out with a Cabinet document reflecting it. So yes, they wanted to celebrate. They were over the moon about it.

KOB: Is it true, as Paul Kelly wrote, that you called Bob Hawke 'jellyback' for his lack of nerve in that period?

PJK: No, that was Peter Walsh. I have never called Bob 'jellyback'. I've called him plenty of things since, but 'jellyback' was not one of them. It was too deprecatory of Bob's values and positions. I never ever used that term.

KOB: Kelly again: 'Keating was unable to conceal his patronising attitude towards Hawke, made manifest in repeated private references to having to get Hawke back into the tax cart.'

PJK: That's true. But you have to know about power, Kerry. Leave a void and someone will fill it. Bob left a massive void in the power equation through 1985 to 1990, and in a very large measure I filled it. He was off the game for such a long period and that's not just my contention.

On 13 April 1985 Michelle Grattan wrote in *The Age*: 'Hawke struggles to counter a creeping lack of confidence.' Paul Kelly wrote in *The Australian* in May 1985: 'Is the job becoming too much for Hawke?' And there was more of the same in 1986, 1987 and 1988.

It wasn't just me, it was just obvious. You know the old saying, give a dog a bone and he'll bury it. You leave a hole, someone will fill it. In the end I don't blame Bob for skipping out on the consumption tax. It was a tough ask. But I do blame him for not telling me before he decided to go to the ACTU, in the middle of the night during the Summit, and kill it.

KOB: Let me put an alternative proposition as to why Hawke pulled the rug. He was reflecting broad based and genuine fears inside the labour movement, including among a number of your Cabinet colleagues that the risks of losing the next election were too great, and in the end he exercised his prerogative as leader based on that judgement.

PJK: I think his nerves went. I worked on the Road Runner principle: running fast and hard; a momentum play. If you run hard enough and fast enough for a great change, you will get it. Look over your shoulder once, and you're dead meat. Belief and advocacy are the keys. Believe in things and advocate them, and bring the public with you by talking up, not down, to them. The political system these days mostly talks down to the community. But if you talk up to people, pay them the respect and the courtesy that they're intelligent enough to understand the central issues, then they will mostly come with you.

KOB: But in this instance, the bottom line was that even your mate Bill Kelty at the ACTU and your other trade union allies on the Accord wouldn't support you on Option C. Wasn't that what really killed the package?

PJK: What really killed the package was the Business Council of Australia. When Bob White got up and said we won't support options A, B or C, Bill Kelty said to me, 'Well, mate, if the most likely supporters and some of the principal beneficiaries of this consumption tax and this cast of policy won't support it, how can we?'

KOB: The unions campaigned against you on the consumption tax at the Summit, but you went for drinks with them after they'd helped roll you, and Bill Kelty presented you with Norman Lindsay's *The Magic Pudding*, signed by the entire ACTU executive. They'd beaten you, but in the process, as was inscribed in the book, you had won their respect and their trust. How did you interpret that?

PJK: They knew that in terms of the big reforms and sticking to the labour movement, they had more access to power through my portfolio as Treasurer than they'd ever had in the entire twentieth century. And while they'd had a disagreement with me on the consumption tax, they weren't going to down me, because downing me was costly. More than that, they liked me and liked dealing with me. But when Bob White and the Business Council dumped us I couldn't really take a whip to Bill Kelty or Simon Crean. By the same token, Bob should not have sold me down the drain overnight at some motel without telling me, but he did. Even so, I pretty well forgave him and kept working cooperatively with him.

We were trying to do what politicians over the postwar years had largely failed to do. They wouldn't tell the public what should really happen and wouldn't put their neck on the line to make it happen. I wanted a new kind of political leadership built around good public policy, something with uprightness about it. I used to say to Bob, we might last three years, we might last six. However long we last, let's go for broke all the time, let's do the best we can.

I won't pretend the Tax Summit wasn't a setback. But Cabinet knew after the long and detailed debate it had gone through that there was no going back on significant tax reform. It was in the ether.

The great mistake people made for a number of years after, was that they thought without the consumption tax, the reform package we came up with a couple of months later was a squib. But the final package accepted in September had substantial behaviour-changing characteristics about it and without the consumption tax. This package represented change on a world scale. But because the consumption tax had become a *cause célèbre*, by the time it eventually disappeared, everyone thought the reforms would be a damp squib without it. They were wrong, but that did not make it easier at the time.

KOB: Eating humble pie in public is not something most people would associate with you, but you ate humble pie when you fronted up at the end of the Tax Summit and acknowledged that a wheel had come off the cart. You are clearly a very proud man. How hard was it to pick yourself up from that defeat and throw yourself back into the task of framing a credible alternative tax reform package that you and your colleagues could live with?

PJK: It was very tough indeed, but I did it. I had to begin with a Cabinet subcommittee, about three weeks later, and then from June to September 1985 I worked on the final package, again with Treasury officials and people from my own office. A package of changes that still hold up today. That is, the top margin rate went from 60 per cent to 49 per cent, then 47 per cent, the corporate rate within two years went from 49 per cent to 39 per cent.

Today governments are flat out cutting one percentage point from the corporate rate. I took it from 49 per cent to 39 per cent and, with it, full dividend imputation. In other words, removing the classical taxation treatment of company tax by taxing company income only once. And that's why investors today like self-funded retirees invest for those franked dividends. The franked dividend came from that 1985 tax package. There was also a fringe benefits tax and the capital gains tax. It was a revolution, and the crucial people in helping to get that package through were John Dawkins, Gareth Evans, Neal Blewett, Peter Walsh, John Button and Susan Ryan.

KOB: How easily were you and Bob Hawke able to mend the fracture in your partnership through the rest of 1985, because Edna Carew has written that the Summit was indisputably a new low point in the relationship?

PJK: No, the lowest point was the full tax package, because come September Bob didn't want to hear about tax reform at all. He'd had a gutful of it. So basically he'd decided to do the package in. So he set me an enormous hurdle to get it through the full ministry. It's hard enough to get a massive tax change through an informed Cabinet of thirteen or fourteen people. Imagine if you've got to spend three days with 27 ministers, thirteen of whom have never in their lives had to grapple at close quarters with complex economic policy—people like Tom Uren, Arthur Gietzelt, Barry Jones and the like, yet they were all there. The full ministry.

In one conversation Arthur said to me, 'Well, Paul, we agree with you about capital gains, but we don't agree with you about cutting the top personal rate and we don't agree with you about dividend imputation.'

And I said, 'In which case, Arthur, you'll be getting nothing.'

And he said, 'What is this, a dictatorship?'

'No,' I said, 'it's a package. We introduce a new tax on capital but on the other hand we lower the tax on income. If you don't want to lower the rates we are not able to broaden the base.' At one stage I told Arthur and Tom they couldn't sell ice cream in the Gobi Desert.

It went on for three days.

The low point in my whole relationship with Bob was that he went to Papua New Guinea that weekend and left me alone with the whole reform package. In fact, Gareth Evans had a real go at him. I've got the report quoting Gareth with the headline, 'Tax go-slow rebounds on PM':

> At one stage there was a sharp exchange between Mr Hawke and the Resources Minister, Senator Evans, who complained about the slow pace at which the meeting was proceeding. Senator Evans, a factional ally of Mr Hawke, was worried that the real purpose behind his deliberations was to ensure that no tax package was ever finalised.

And that was completely true. That's when the game really got savage. I didn't forget that. It was the only one I can say I never forgave Bob for.

When Bob landed at Fairburn Airbase back in Canberra from Papua New Guinea in the evening, he rang me on the car phone and said, 'Paul, Bob here. How did you go?'

I said, 'I got it all through.'

He said, surprised, 'Got it all through? What, to cut the top rate? And the imputation?'

I said, 'I got the lot through.'

That was not the way the plan was supposed to go. I'm sure Bob thought the full ministry would basically jam me and throw me back into another ill-defined process.

Bob is reported to have said he wanted a meeting of the full ministry to widen the base of support within the party for the final package.

This of course is untrue. A case of after-the-event rationalisation to excuse his shabby and unforgivable behaviour.

KOB: Another biographer, John Edwards, who worked as your adviser when you were Prime Minister, wrote of the Tax Summit's impact on your relationship with Bob Hawke that: 'It snapped the collegial bond of trust between you and put in its place a harder, more enduring, but wholly mercenary relationship of mutual advantage.'

PJK: That's not right. It wasn't mercenary. It's important to understand when you refer to the moments when Bob and I were at odds, that Bob stuck to me and I stuck to him on almost every other thing. The low point is the September 1985 tax package meeting—a meeting around issues of such weight with no Prime Minister present. But that reform is still the core of the Australian tax system with Howard's GST added on.

But for all that, the show had to go on. The show had to go on. And there was always a point of affection between Bob and me, and I mean that. In the end I was a soft touch for him and he was a soft touch for me. We left it that way for national progress. You've got to elbow your way through the system to get the changes. Public life is only about getting the changes. The system otherwise runs itself.

KOB: But what does it say about what real friendship was left when there you were in the middle of putting that final tax package together, and you were in your office writing angry comments about Bob Hawke on your own personal archive of newspaper files like 'The envious little bastard did everything to destroy it'.

PJK: He did do everything to destroy that package. Bob got to shockingly low points of bad behaviour. But I could always engineer a better moment with him, and keep the show rolling. The public will never understand the value they got from Hawke and me. Eight-and-a-half years we were together, and the changes were revolutionary. I would kick and shove and gouge, and he would do the same but nevertheless both of us kept our eye on the main chance—the greater good of the place.

KOB: How happy were you with the final tax outcome in 1985 as the man whose overarching philosophy was to strive for perfection?

PJK: I thought it was phenomenal, and that's why its architecture still forms so much of the tax system today. I took the top rate from 60 to 47. After twelve years of the Liberals, Peter Costello was only able to take it from 47 to 45. Big deal. And in my package, the corporate rate came down from 49 to 39, plus full dividend imputation. I'm quite sure one of the reasons the business community turned to Bob and to me through the 1980s was that massive tax change. It was so pro-capital and so pro-entrepreneurship.

KOB: Where were the workers in all this?

PJK: The workers got huge benefits. The bottom tax rate went down from 31 to 21, and the tax-free threshold rose. It was the fairest tax change ever. And we clamped down on rorts and tax avoidance with the fringe benefits tax and the capital gains tax. It made us so different from the Liberal Party. Here they were, the men of business in the pin-striped suits. They had run the show for most of the post-war years yet they still had a 60 per cent top marginal rate, taxed dividends twice and let capital profits go free. God help us!

KOB: For a man who'd spent his life soaking up lessons from others, what did you learn from that process? How painful were the lessons of necessary compromise to get a result?

PJK: I had to take a lot of stick for my trouble through the Tax Summit process. And the Treasury team who had put their backs into it felt the rejection. If ever a department of state worked for a government, Treasury worked for the Hawke Government throughout 1985. It was an excruciating effort on their part. So delivering that massive package in September that year was, in large measure, justification for them, as it was for me.

KOB: What evidence was there that the public embraced that package?

PJK: It completely changed the way the business community, including small business and the professions, looked at us. In a private company under John Howard's tax system you retained $21 out of $100 of income. After my changes, in that same company you could retain $67 out of $100 of income. If you taxed it at Howard's old corporate rate, and then taxed the distribution at the top personal rate under Division Seven tax, you could keep $21 only. So I trebled the retention of after tax capital in private companies. It revolutionised capital formation in private companies. The Liberals never understood capital or capital impulses.

KOB: On the one hand you were driven by this philosophy of the need to create wealth in Australia, with the necessary second strand that a fair share of that wealth reached the greatest number of people. And yet the 1980s also became the decade of conspicuous consumption among the very wealthy, many of whom had done particularly well through your policies. Did that bother you?

PJK: Most of the wealth was shared through employment growth, and then through real wages. We had created 1.6 million new jobs.

The high flyers were conspicuous but they were a tiny portion of the community. Anyone can lift the top half a per cent up, but who can lift the other 99?

The business I was in with Bill Kelty was lifting the 99 per cent up with a structure of minimal award rates—best in the world—strong real wages growth after inflation, lower prices through competition, and superannuation. But none of that would have been possible in a low-growth economy. We doubled the Australian economy's capacity to grow. This is a huge claim to be making. It used to grow at 1.6 or 1.7 per cent in the years under Fraser. In our first seven years it averaged 3.5 per cent. That's what produced the huge increment to wealth and brought the equity.

KOB: So after nearly three years in the job, with one election behind you, how were the stresses and the strains of the job hitting you?

PJK: Getting the policy right was one thing but you still had to do the sales task. You still had to account to Parliament, Question Time and all the rest. These events were always exhausting. It's a big pump-up to do Question Time. To do that highly sophisticated, subtle act every day is a big demand. Done well, it is hugely sophisticated. Often high and complex policy blended with politics.

As a shadow minister stands for a question, the thoughts are already running through your mind. Who is it? Is it an organised question or a spontaneous one? It's a National Party MP from Gwydir, so as he's walking, you are slicing down through the possible topics he would be likely to ask about. As he gets to the despatch box, you know it might be about wool, or about water, but it will definitely be to do with agriculture.

The thing for somebody like me was long questions. Because once you get a long question the mental computer has had time to go right through the file. And then at the end of the question you say to yourself, which bat do I select to knock this one into the stand? In other words, you experience the balls coming in slow motion. If you get very good at this, the balls roll up to you in slow motion whereas if you're not across the brief, everything is coming rapidly, and when they come rapidly, generally you're in trouble.

KOB: What about the language that you used, and indeed revelled in, that became very much a hallmark of Paul Keating, some of it just one step back from the bar room?

PJK: It's an art form. You're on the stage. You must maintain the psychological control. Someone like Alexander Downer would step up to ask me a question and I'd turn to my crowd and say, 'His mother loves him!' I used to call Peter Costello the talking knee and when he'd ask a question I would always turn to my colleagues and tap my knee. They'd all laugh. But those laughs are so off-putting and confidence-destroying. You must be winning in Parliament; you must keep the psychological hegemony, and that means when they come to ask you the questions, you have to have the answers and be psychologically in charge.

KOB: Do you accept that while your parliamentary style was a very big part of the government's weapons arsenal, it was also very much a part of why a very sizable block of people didn't like you, they didn't like that aggressive side of you, the arrogance that they perceived from the way you performed?

PJK: Yes, but what about all the ones who did like it? God, there were millions of them. They still walk up to me in the street, saying, God, we miss those Question Times. Not a week goes by that that is not said to me. Sometimes it would have cost me, but I've always believed in the power of the political metaphor, and not just the power but the legitimacy of the political metaphor, because to speak metaphorically to a community about change is really to educate them in a way that they can absorb and internalise. You're not talking down to them, you're talking up to them. You're giving them a picture around which they can encapsulate the argument.

The arguments have to be digestible but must also be put with flair and panache in delivery. There also has to be a bit of fun in it. I never took it deadly earnestly. It's a job that has to be done and done to secure public policy changes. I can say that I left public life with feelings of enmity to no one on the Opposition benches.

KOB: I'm assuming your music was still incredibly important to you, just as it had been all those years ago in Bankstown when you used your music to reinvigorate yourself.

PJK: It did two things for me: it expanded my mind to the possibilities open to me, and I used to get ideas when the music came. I'd always have a pad and a pen to take ideas down. Music for the brain is like electricity to an electric motor. Once the current starts the locomotion begins. Music stimulates you, so I'd be absorbing the music and thinking I could do this or I could do that. But at the same time as exciting me, it would also humble me, and I mean really humble me.

KOB: A lot of people would be surprised that you saw yourself as a humble person.

PJK: I think I'm actually a very humble person. You can take pride in your work but also have humility. If you are allowing yourself to ride with, say, a Wagner opera or a great work like Bruckner's *Symphony No. 5* or something like that, the scale of the genius, the scale of the whole thing just tells you, sorry, I'm not in that league. You say to yourself, these people are immortals whereas I am merely mortal. These people, the great composers, are supernatural while I'm down here doing very mundane stuff. It is a great leveller.

I used to listen to orchestral and symphonic works before budgets because they'd pump me up as to the scale of possibilities, but at the same time remind me how ordinary it was; what I was doing. You could do jobs of the kind I was given as best you could and make as big a difference as possible. But in the great scheme of things you are a bit player on a very large stage.

FROM TREASURY TO THE LODGE, 1986–91

THE BANANA REPUBLIC: NO TURNING BACK

1986 was a pivotal year for the Hawke Government and for Paul Keating. He later told one of his biographers, John Edwards, 'Up to 1986 we controlled the agenda, and then we did not.'

Twelve months into their second term, and two years after the float of the dollar, Bob Hawke and Paul Keating were discovering that the more they moved to free up the economy, the less predictable it became. Call it the unintended consequences of reform, or maybe just a fact of life in the more volatile environment of a freer financial marketplace.

By late 1985, with the scars fading from a tax debate that had taken up nearly the whole year, Paul Keating was grappling with headlines such as 'Aust dollar hits record low', 'Interest rates soaring as dollar keeps falling' and 'Aust trade problems worsen'.

Keating's banana republic moment in the face of a perceived crisis over Australia's current account deficit was still months away, but the portent was becoming clear. As early as April 1985 the emerging picture was one where imports were far outstripping exports: the Australian economy was substantially reliant on a small handful of

233

commodities to maintain its export base, and manufactured exports were stagnating, heavily exposing the country to the vagaries of world commodity markets. Ironically, the growth the government was presiding over had become part of the perceived problem. Australia's increasing demand for sophisticated manufactured goods was being fed from overseas rather than domestically.

Also feeding into the current account problem was the traditional imbalance between investment capital coming into the country and the money Australians invested abroad. Because of our size we'd always had to rely on overseas investment. We simply didn't generate enough capital to fund the nation's development. This has been true since the First Fleet weighed anchor in Port Jackson.

Its impact would have been smaller if overseas investment flowing in was used productively to expand the Australian economy. As it turned out through this period, some was and some wasn't. In April 1985, however, the trade picture was deteriorating: the current account deficit stood at $7.57 billion, foreign debt was building and the global markets treated the Australian dollar accordingly. The shrinking dollar would in turn fan inflation because the prices of imports were rising.

The balance of payments and current account deficit statistics were released monthly, and the irony for Keating in the headlines they were attracting was that he was becoming a victim of his own success. He had set out to educate the parliamentary press gallery to a higher degree of economic literacy than they could ever have boasted in the past, but the more literate they became, the more they understood the problems, including their political significance. Journalists relish political problems because they create news.

Bob Hawke in Canberra and Paul Keating, who was in New York, were moved by the April figures to issue simultaneous warnings that Australia was essentially living beyond its means and had to do more to 'earn its way in the world'. In the process they flagged spending cuts in the next month's mini-budget.

It was then that Cabinet was first put on notice that the government faced a significant structural rather than cyclical problem that could cast an ominous shadow on the economy, affecting budget strategy, broader economic and social policy and ultimately the government's own fate.

The economy was slowing slightly but still historically strong. New jobs were popping up all over the place and inflation was still trending down, but come November the current account deficit was still being described as horrendous and the dollar was down to around 65 cents against the US currency, a depreciation of 30 per cent across the year.

The Reserve Bank felt compelled to keep monetary policy tight with high interest rates to coax foreign investors back into the dollar, while the government was locked into the Keating strategy of ongoing budget restraint, with a pledge that Commonwealth expenditure and the budget deficit would not increase as a percentage of GDP.

Housing interest rates had not yet been deregulated and were held at a ceiling of 13.5 per cent, but 'quality bank borrowers' were paying as high as 19.5 per cent—unsustainable in terms of the economy and the politics.

At a personal level the pivotal relationship between Hawke and Keating had settled back into one of (apparent) cordiality and mutual support within Cabinet, but looking back years later, Keating maintains that in spirit Hawke had still not recovered from his family crisis of the previous year and that the drive, the confidence, the massaging of personalities and issues that he had brought to the Cabinet table as leader in the first eighteen months were now largely absent.

Not surprisingly Hawke vigorously contests the Keating view, and their Cabinet colleagues also vary in their opinions. But there is evidence in the news commentary through this period that senior journalists sensed something was amiss with the Hawke leadership. The question of whether the Prime Minister had lost his mojo remained as ambient noise.

Even though Hawke's popularity was still relatively high in 1986, and John Howard's low by comparison and trending into the teens, the Hawke magic with voters in 1983 had been weakened through the 1984 election. There was no room for complacency. Even Hawke's biographer, former lover and future wife Blanche d'Alpuget publicly described him in March 1986 as depleted.

Here's the thing about leadership and the power that goes with it, and the relationships between those who have it and those who desire it: it can erode and corrode even the strongest of friendships or partnerships, and while the story of Hawke and Keating had a long way to run, it didn't seem to take much after the 1985 tax reform tensions for them to resurface, and back they came with a vengeance after the April 1986 balance of payments figures were released on Tuesday, 13 May, showing another unexpectedly sharp rise.

On the day Keating chose to say nothing, as if girding his loins for battle. The next day, with Hawke in the air on his way to Japan and China, his Treasurer went on talkback radio with John Laws from a kitchen phone at a Labor fund-raising lunch on the outskirts of Melbourne.

Keating had been talking about trade deficit issues for months now, but not quite as bluntly as this. He even invoked the D word.

'I get the clear feeling,' he told Laws, 'that we must let Australians know truthfully, honestly, earnestly just what sort of international hole Australia is in. It's the price of our commodities. They're as bad in real terms as they were in the Depression. That's a fact of Australian life now. It's got nothing to do with the government. It's the price of commodities on world markets but it means an internal economic adjustment, and if we don't make it now we never will make it. If the government cannot get the adjustment, get manufacturing going again and keep moderate wage outcomes and a sensible economic policy, then Australia is basically done for. We will just end up being a third-rate economy.'

Under further questioning Keating eventually said Australia risked becoming a banana republic. The comments may have been off the cuff but they reflected Keating's view that caucus, and indeed many ministers in the traditional spending portfolios such as welfare, were still resisting his arguments to tighten the budget and recognise a new economic reality.

The next morning the *Australian Financial Review* observed, 'The dealing screens that dominate the working lives of foreign exchange traders flashed quotes from Keating's talkback conversation almost as he finished speaking.' As one of the press gallery journalists travelling with Hawke subsequently pointed out, in the nine hours it took them to fly to Tokyo the dollar lost four cents, the biggest single drop since the float. The markets went berserk, almost as if the Order of the Banana had been delivered on the nation that day. It was pretty dramatic, not helped by the fact that in stark contrast to Keating's somewhat alarming message, Hawke was briefing journalists on the plane in far less pessimistic terms, with no idea of what Keating had said.

Sparks flew across two hemispheres over the next few days. While the travelling press peppered Hawke and his staff in Japan the following day, Keating was not backing away in his speech to chartered accountants: 'All Australians must appreciate that the decline in the terms of trade means a reduction in our national income.'

The next day, without Hawke's prior knowledge, and in tandem with Industrial Relations Minister Ralph Willis, Keating announced that a meeting of employers, unions and the states would be convened to discuss 'the greatest challenge facing Australia'. In the prevailing mood it was quickly labelled by the media as a crisis meeting. On the table would be a deferral of tax cuts due in September as part of the Accord trade-off with unions in return for wage restraint. The historic first round of compulsory superannuation might also be affected. Even before the April balance of payments figures, Keating had won endorsement from the full ministry for severe expenditure restraint in the 1986–87 Budget and 'control of borrowings at both the Commonwealth and State levels'. Now they were being told there was another layer of pressure to absorb.

For three years the Hawke Government had delivered strong growth, significant reductions in unemployment and inflation, wage restraint and reduced deficits, as well as the reintroduction of Medicare, big tax reforms and a deal to deliver national superannuation across the workforce. So why the sudden sense of crisis? How had it come to this?

It certainly wasn't a crisis Hawke was easily able to handle well from a distance. In an age when Prime Ministers travel abroad frequently, it's an unwritten rule that it's unreasonable to expect the PM to answer detailed questions about domestic issues while overseas. To try to tackle problems long distance without all the facts or a feel for the nuances is too risky.

In this instance the story back home was running so hot and strong that neither the journalists nor Hawke could ignore it. Hawke's advisers—later dubbed disparagingly by Keating as the Manchu Court—felt journalists were starting to conclude that Hawke was becoming irrelevant and Keating looked like he was running the country. One Hawke political advisor, Bob Hogg, told the ABC's *Labor in Power* series eight years later that at least three press gallery bureau chiefs were making plans to leave the Prime Minister's party in Beijing and head back to Australia.

Hawke was persuaded to be seen to reclaim control of the government by instructing the acting Prime Minister Lionel Bowen to take charge of Keating's economic conference and leak the fact that Hawke was 'dealing' with Keating. That in turn resulted in headlines such as 'PM pulls Keating into line', 'Angry Hawke rebuffs Keating' and 'PM gets tough with Keating'. Hawke also let it be known that weekend that he'd ordered a phone conference from Beijing for Monday morning with senior ministers in Canberra, including

Keating, who presumably would come away feeling suitably chastened in front of his colleagues.

Instead, according to others present for the phone hook-up, Keating sat there as Hawke spoke from Beijing, ticking off each point Hawke made against those Keating had already read in that morning's newspaper stories filed by the journalists travelling with Hawke, and let fly. That, too, was leaked. One unnamed minister who was present wouldn't recount exactly what Keating had said to Hawke, but added, 'I can say he didn't miss his target.'

In his newspaper archive collected contemporaneously, Keating wrote in the margin of one story from Beijing published in the Tasmanian *Mercury* headlined: 'Treasurer gets rap from PM' that the story had been backgrounded by Hawke and his senior advisor Peter Barron. Keating noted, 'Hawke is still in his mental fog.' In the margins of a similar story in the *Financial Review* Keating wrote that the hostility from Beijing was 'all Barron's doing', that Barron had 'told Hawke he looked piss weak'.

With a less effective, less stable Cabinet and a more effective Opposition, the story of these two dominant figures could have been dramatically different. It might have come to tears much sooner than it eventually did five years later. Even so, for several months the close interest from gallery journalists guaranteed ongoing coverage that distracted from the government's attempts to regain some sense of control over the economy and reassure Australians the problem was in hand. If Keating's warning that the country was headed for third-world status was to be taken seriously and that the country did face a crisis, then the ongoing headlines—'Hawke, Keating: The rift widens', 'A collision of super egos'—were needed like the proverbial hole in the head.

A quite important side-play was also going on. It had begun to be noticed that Keating was no longer as close to his factional power base in New South Wales as he had been. The Right-wing machine in

New South Wales, headquartered in Sussex Street on the edge of Sydney's Chinatown, had developed over decades. Its highly disciplined unity at branch and conference level as well as in the state parliamentary caucus was the key to Labor's power base and dominance in the state for decades. Factional leaders such as John Ducker, Barrie Unsworth, John McBean, Graham Richardson and Paul Keating himself when he became State President in 1979, ruled with an iron hand, not always in a velvet glove.

But the more Keating was driven by the desire to reform, and by 'the long straight lines of logic' as he saw them, the more he found himself in conflict with Sussex Street, although he says he was always able to rely on the loyalty of his factional mates within the parliamentary party. The drift, as he saw it, was from the Sussex Street mob. At one point a senior political correspondent, Mike Steketee, wrote that Keating and Graham Richardson hadn't had a real conversation for six months.

In 1986 there were two such moments of conflict, one involving Keating's desire to deregulate housing interest rates on which a ceiling of 13.5 per cent had sat for some years. In Keating's view you couldn't open up banking to market forces on some fronts but not on others. Those opposing the move were concerned by the political impact of housing interest rates rising sharply to the market levels of other unregulated rates. Under pressure from factional heavyweights in NSW including Richardson and Neville Wran, Hawke blocked Keating in Cabinet on 20 March. 'Only temporarily', was Keating's written comment in the margin of the following day's newspaper story—accurately, as it turned out.

Another issue that annoyed Sussex Street was the bold bid by controversial Western Australian entrepreneur Robert Holmes à Court to take over the mining giant BHP. Again, Keating chose to go it alone, opposing calls from within Labor, and most particularly from the NSW Labor Council boss John McBean, the man who inherited the state party presidency from Keating, to intervene and head off a takeover on the grounds that Holmes à Court would break up the mining empire, hitting jobs in the process. Keating argued that BHP did not warrant government protection and that market forces should prevail.

Ultimately Holmes à Court went away, and business went on pretty much as usual for BHP and its workers. But it was another breakaway moment for Paul Keating with his traditional NSW allies. He was increasingly running his own race, dancing to his own drumbeat. Sometimes that worked against him, but more often, for him.

KOB: When we look now at your banana republic warning, we can see a clear example of how dramatically differently people can react, depending on a choice of words or imagery. You'd been warning about the trade imbalance for a year, but suddenly that one phrase made all the difference in how the problem was perceived.

PJK: To contextualise it, the terms of trade started falling in what became a secular decline about the time Bob Menzies retired in 1966, and that decline started to accelerate through the 1970s. The terms of trade compare the value of the things you sell to the value of the things you buy. The things we were selling—wheat, wool, grains, iron ore, coke and coal, copper, lead, zinc—were going down in value, while the things we imported were rising in value, such as colour TVs, VHS recorders, computers. So we were getting poorer. Every Treasurer had ignored it—too hard, under the carpet.

By the time we got to the mid-1980s we were starting to see a rapid deterioration in the terms of trade. On a graph you can see it very markedly. So by March 1986 our terms of trade were at a record low. They were last at that level in the Depression, from 1931 to 1933. So our national income had been quite dramatically cut. The prevailing economic orthodoxy demanded more remedial changes through the budget process.

KOB: Do you remember your closing comments to Parliament in your May Statement of 1985 to justify unpopular cuts: 'If there is a short-term political price in these measures we are prepared to live with it.' This was all about dealing with the terms of trade a year before your banana republic comments. Why did you have to use such a dramatic way to reissue the same warning a year later?

PJK: I used to say these things in Parliament rather more guardedly so as not to unduly alarm the community, but making the point that we were in a long secular decline and the decline was accelerating. I couldn't really get any traction on the problem in Cabinet.

In each of the economic reviews through that period these current account figures were just getting worse and our terms of trade were continuing to go down, but the problems were so big and so difficult to face, Cabinet colleagues would say, 'Well, thank you for that, we've noted that', but there wasn't much appetite for a big structural adjustment of the kind that was necessary.

We'd been through the issue over many months, but now it was coming to a head. Bob Hawke was in Japan and China, and I blurted out the comment to John Laws from a telephone in the kitchen of a reception centre just outside Melbourne. With the clatter of pots and pans behind me I warned that if we didn't address the fundamental problems, we risked becoming a banana republic. It was not at all pre-meditated, I simply couldn't keep the truth of it in.

KOB: The Reserve Bank Governor, Bob Johnston, told the ABC's *Labor in Power* series that your comment was 'one of the most statesman-like remarks that had ever been made in Australia. It certainly was a jolt to the community in that they felt at last someone was being candid and frank about the problems'. Johnston recalled that at times you would look pensively out of his window of the bank building at the top of Martin Place in Sydney, wondering whether that was the greatest or most stupid remark you'd ever made.

PJK: In the end, you can't be what you are not. You can't bottle up stuff like this. I couldn't, on the one hand, say I was forging a new political relationship with the Australian people, giving them something better than the dross they'd been fed for 40 years, but by the way, we're not going to tell them about the massive decline in our national income. In the end you've got to spit it out. Now, it might have been embarrassing for the government and put a monkey on my back, but it was a monkey I was prepared to wear.

KOB: Bob Hawke later wrote in his autobiography that your remarks 'traumatised both the public and the markets, a form of shock treatment gone wrong. Paul had created a disaster for the government'.

PJK: That's a post-event re-evaluation. It turned out not to be a disaster, but the turning point in the Australian reconstruction to deal with this big secular decline in the terms of trade that had begun in the 1960s. I've got a copy of the *Age* here from more than two months before that point. On the front page, 21 March 1986: 'Terms of trade at record low' was the headline. 'Australia's terms of trade were at their worst level since the Depression, the Treasurer, Mr. Keating, said yesterday.' Now the Cabinet knew this was the case, and so too did the economic journalists.

KOB: But surely by the same token you can sympathise with how Hawke must have felt, caught on the other side of the world reading reports that his Treasurer was saying the country could become a banana republic, and then seeing the market's panicked reaction. He must have thought, what on earth is Paul up to?

PJK: But I had used the phrase 'banana republic' before in a speech overseas. It had been reported, just not the big splash the later reference got. But the way these things happen is not always understood. Issues play on your mind, and you get policy-bilious. All of a sudden you're in a phone conversation in a noisy kitchen to John Laws and out it shoots.

I didn't make the banana republic remark to shanghai Cabinet, though in fact Cabinet was forced to then respond to those remarks all through 1986 and then 1987. Had it not been in a casual, more unguarded conversation in a restaurant kitchen in Victoria, it might not have come out quite that way.

KOB: One obvious thing that struck me in reading back through the dramas between you and Hawke over your comments to John Laws was that if he hadn't been flying to the other side of the world as you made them—if he'd been sitting at his desk in Canberra—the blue between the two of you, the sense of crisis, might never have eventuated.

PJK: I'm certain that's right. Because Bob would always take notice of what I'd say, he'd always give it serious thought. If he were concerned about something I'd said, the two of us would sort it out in a sensible way. The fact that he was on the other side of the world made that much more difficult, but the timing was completely accidental.

KOB: But because the terms of trade figures that triggered your comments had been released a couple of days before and you hadn't yet responded to them by the time he'd got on the plane for Japan, he gave a more guarded response on the figures to journalists on the plane. By the time he arrived in Tokyo the dollar had dropped four cents. The markets were going berserk.

PJK: That sense of drama back home caught him unawares, and the gallery journalists were putting him under pressure. I wasn't trying to embarrass him, I was just trying to keep the show going and get some real focus on the fact that we had a very real problem we had to deal with.

KOB: The day after your comments to Laws you told a conference of chartered accountants that 'all Australians must appreciate that the decline in the terms of trade means a reduction in our national income'. These were more considered comments but you'd obviously decided to ram the message home. That's almost exactly what you had said a year before, but this time the banana republic context suddenly made them so much more explosive.

PJK: The impetus for all this had come from that terms of trade quarterly release in May. The current account deficit rose more sharply, the terms of trade fell much more forcefully than we'd expected. I was recorded at the time by Ross Gittins in the *Sydney Morning Herald* as saying that they'd dropped by two percentage points in the past three months, and I'd belled the cat on the Laws program.

KOB: You and Ralph Willis as the Minister for Employment and Industrial Relations then called a meeting of employers, unions and the states to discuss the issue, which was immediately dubbed by the media as a crisis summit, even though you were using an established forum to have it.

PJK: It was a routine meeting; we used to meet regularly. There was nothing extraordinary about the meeting or its timing. The Advisory Committee on Prices and Incomes, the ACPI process, was set up under the Accord with regular meetings, and this was scheduled. It was the media that played it up and beat it up.

KOB: But this time you gave it some urgency. You said it was to address 'the greatest challenge facing Australia'. Hawke's advisors obviously became concerned that you were looking more like the PM than Hawke and told him as much. That's when things got testy, wasn't it?

PJK: Peter Barron was saying to him, 'You're the Prime Minister and you've got to look like the Prime Minister.'

You're correct in saying if Bob had been in the country Ralph Willis and I would have just gone upstairs and had a chat with him and said, 'Bob, we can put this on the agenda for the next ACPI meeting' and he would have said, 'Okay, fine'. But the fact that he was abroad looking isolated, with the sense that I was dealing with a crisis back in Australia and Barron saying to him 'you need to look like you're in charge' pushed him into these background briefings against me from Beijing. That was when Hawke said he'd put Lionel Bowen in charge of the meeting to put me in my place.

KOB: Another Hawke advisor, Bob Hogg, told *Labor in Power* years later that at least three gallery bureau chiefs were making plans to leave the PM's party and head back home to where the story was. You can understand why Barron and Hogg were getting anxious, can't you?

PJK: I can. They worked for the Prime Minister, not for me.

KOB: What can you remember of the phone hook-up Hawke ordered with you and other senior Cabinet colleagues back in Canberra, ostensibly to pull you back into line, which was also leaked in advance, generating headlines like 'Angry Hawke rebuffs Keating' and 'PM gets tough with Keating'?

PJK: I ticked Bob off on the phone. I said, 'What are you doing over there, Bob? You're like a chook with its head cut off. What are you up to? You know what I'm doing here. The same things we've been speaking about for months. What's all this about?'

I got right into him. I said it's like a *kabuki* show. What is this *kabuki* show you're running? I'm only repeating what I've said to you and have already been saying. The fact that it got picked up on the Laws program is completely incidental to you being abroad, and the meeting Ralph and I talked about was the scheduled meeting of ACPI.

Ralph was on the phone hook-up and agreed with the substance of what I said, so before the conversation was over Bob had climbed down.

It's one thing having this responsibility tipped onto me by virtue of Bob's condition after 1984, but it's another thing to have him objecting to me doing the work. It may have been inconvenient for him to be out of the country, and it may have been true that it looked bad for him, but it certainly wasn't true that I was doing something that was in any way different to what we had broadly already been saying.

KOB: But perhaps it revealed an underlying anxiety on his part that you were beginning to represent a real and genuine threat to the future of his leadership, that he could see your influence in the Cabinet room and the media perceptions that inevitably flowed from it.

PJK: That may be so but there was also a plaintive helplessness, a sense that Bob didn't know what to do. On the one hand he knew we needed to make remedial changes, and on the other he didn't have the stomach for pushing the framework. He needed me to put the new framework into place and, more than that, he was happy to see the framework put into place. He just didn't want all the pain of it.

This is where people think they can make a case about Bob Hawke and me being leadership rivals as early as 1985 and 1986. Intellectually it may be true, but in a positional sense it's completely untrue because I was not at all trying to push Bob from the leadership. Not at all. Even more than that, Bob, in a very dependent way, wanted me to keep pushing the changes through, which was to his credit.

There's no doubt that for a brief period it did strain the relationship with Bob, but it's worthwhile getting this whole period into context. We'd just gone through 1985 with the Tax Summit, the tax reforms later in the year, we'd had the spending restraints through the May Statement and the budget, and now in 1986 we were facing a major decline in the terms of trade, a volatile Australian dollar and, with all that, adjustments to real wages through the adjustment of the exchange rate.

In the end Bob and most of the Cabinet didn't have the heart for the remedial shift needed to deal with the terms of trade. It was too hard. By May, when I made the banana republic comment, this was the context. Paul Kelly wrote in the *Australian*, 'Leader with a leadership problem', and he said, 'The profound paradox of Bob Hawke as Prime Minister is that he knows what needs to be done, yet lacks the drive to lead his government to the Rubicon. He is paralysed by inertia at the big decisions.'

But perhaps the most revealing piece published in that period was written by Bob Hawke's now wife, Blanche d'Alpuget, in March 1986, in a two-part series for the *Herald* and the *Age*. It was headlined: 'Bob Hawke, a stunning change.'

It was a two-hour interview, and she wrote: 'The atmosphere felt like lead ... observing a man so withdrawn into himself that he apparently did not care whether I listened to him or not. There was a tremendous change to be seen that day, but it was more subtle than dullness. My overwhelming impression was of a lack of vitality; that he was vanishing. I thought Hawke seemed chronically fatigued.' And then she went on to say: 'Going to talk to him for the first time in three years I expected the old zing, and was taken aback by its absence, an absence that seemed poignant and shocking.'

Blanche d'Alpuget knew him well and these were her considered observations. That's really how Bob was.

I'm not blaming Bob for his condition. How could I? I used to help him through all of these policy things when he was in that general state. But we had a collapsing terms of trade, we had a collapsing balance of payments problem. I had talked about it in March, I had talked about it at other times. But with the exception of the economic ministers no one wanted to do anything about it.

KOB: By the same token, regardless of what you saw as a general malaise in Bob Hawke, you yourself told *Labor in Power* about your banana republic comment some years later: 'It wasn't designed to be shattering to the government but in the end it was.' You yourself are saying that your comment was shattering to the government. How so?

PJK: It meant that once you let the public in on the secret that you've got a big, big drop in national income, and soon there'll be a change in competitiveness via the exchange rate, then there's going to be a reaction to that, but at least it prepared the public and the markets for a whole lot of remedial policy that subsequently went into place.

KOB: But you've said yourself in the past that you're a grenade-thrower and occasionally you blow off a foot. And you also once painted a picture of yourself as the political version of the skier going down a black run with one ski and no poles. In other words, the risk-taker.

PJK: I know. I am a risk-taker. But the country had had its leg pulled for 30 or 40 years. For 30 or 40 years. The place was massively uncompetitive, with declining terms of trade. Who else was going to blow the whistle and take this basket case on? But let me say, on his account, when Bob returned from China and we got back to the policies at hand, he very quickly adopted not just my policy framework, but said he and I were on the one page and went out of his way to do that.

This goes back to the kind of relationship we had, which was so conducive to large public changes. I could show you another newspaper article where it says, 'Hawke swings onside'. So he would have liked me, in some respects, not to do the bomb-throwing, but he also liked the policy space I garnered. He also liked the fact that I wore a lot of the flak.

KOB: Can we reflect for a minute about the relationships between ministers and their advisers? You obviously valued your staff, as Bob Hawke valued his. They're important relationships, but they can be complicated, can't they? You're the elected politicians, they, in the end, are the hired guns. Did you ever have to remind your staff of that line in the sand?

PJK: I never had to do that with any of my staff. My office was fundamentally managed by public servants: Tony Cole in the first instance, then Don Russell. And other policy advisers in my office also came from the department. My press secretary Tom Mockridge wasn't departmental. He came from the Fairfax group, but my office mostly had a governmental culture. I had a different view from Bob on how governments should best run. Bob had quite influential inputs from people like Bob Hogg and Peter Barron, who were good people but were political advisors. Bob Hogg, Peter Barron and Ross Garnaut were not public servants.

I always believed if you want to run a government on a big policy reform front, as I was doing, you need the departments—in this case, Treasury and Finance—locked in and engaged, and the way for the engagement was through the ministerial office with the department well represented in the office. So my office was too public-service oriented to get involved in political games against Bob's office.

KOB: You were clearly hot under the collar when you publicly called Hawke's advisors, particularly Peter Barron and Bob Hogg, and his economic advisor Ross Garnaut, the Manchu Court around that time. What were you saying with that reference?

PJK: All this gets back to Bob's mental state. I remember Peter Barron saying on one occasion, 'Bob, I don't fucking care what decision you make as long as you fucking well make one.' This was a staffer talking to his Prime Minister, addressing him like a schoolboy. This was as a consequence of Bob's state of mind.

KOB: What did you mean by 'Manchu Court'?

PJK: They would sit like courtiers around him, and I would come to Bob's office and he'd be hunched at his desk, and he'd be saying 'Ross says . . .' or 'Peter says . . .' and he'd never finish a sentence and they'd pipe up. And on one occasion I spun on them and said, 'You speak when you're spoken to.'

One of them said to Hawke, 'Are you going to let him speak to us like that?' and Bob says, 'Oh, don't be like that. Don't be like that.'

I'm brought before them knowing they'd be passing an opinion to Bob after I'd left, and they'd intersperse my comments with their own. They always sat in the same position in that narrow office of Bob's in the old Parliament House. I'd be sitting in front of his desk, and their three chairs would be set a little off the wall. You were appearing before the court and the courtiers would say what they thought of you, usually after you'd left.

KOB: Your Cabinet colleagues must have also been bemused by the sudden sense of crisis. They were broadly aware of the economic challenge, but suddenly it was critical. What was the mood around the Cabinet table as you told them they had to saddle up again for tough medicine in the 1986 Budget?

PJK: For all the ups and downs it was a very conscientious Cabinet, and the economic ministers knew we were up against it. Our national income had been cut and we were running this big and growing current account deficit. So we embarked on another round of cuts in expenditure to reduce the call by the government sector on Australian savings. The advice to us was that this would then, in a mathematical way, reduce the call by Australia on overseas savings and therefore overseas debt. This would be reflected in the 1986 Budget and then in the current account deficit.

KOB: In the intensity of the governing process, as Cabinet ministers have less and less time to stay in touch with their caucus colleagues and even fellow ministers, is there a risk of becoming closer to staff than to your political colleagues and the party rank and file? Were you always able to stay adequately in touch with your various constituencies in the government and the party?

PJK: I hope I had the skilling. I'd been party president in NSW and I'd been steeped in this stuff from a very early age. I could hear the ants change step in the NSW Labor Party and the Right. All the time I'd have these guys on the phone or coming to my office. It's like trying to conduct the orchestra with the woodwinds doing one thing and the violins doing another. I'd have the woodwinds working nicely for me, that is, my people in the caucus, and with the Cabinet I'd have the violins working down the front, getting the tonal harmonies right. This game for me was always and only about getting the changes through. The political game is only about public policy changes.

Don Argus, who was BHP Chairman at the time, said to me not too many years ago, 'When I speak at meetings of staff about leadership I often mention you, Paul, because you often not only conceived the changes, but you also executed them—put them into place. And that's the key thing I tell these people, that it's not simply a matter of telling the board what they think the policies should be, but executing them and getting them done.'

KOB: The caucus did have a very important and legitimate part in that policy process as the elected representatives of electorates all around the country. When you would start the process of selling one of your policy reforms and you knew it was going to be a politically tough sell—either because it challenged a Labor tradition or because there might be some political pain or both, and that push–pull game was going on at the various levels of government—did you always have an end point in mind that factored in the inevitability that you would have to give some ground?

PJK: This is a very important point in the whole equation, and you could see it in contemporary politics with the Abbott Government. I made an artform of consultation. I'd have those members of the Economics

Committee of caucus around to my office, and we'd throw stuff around for a few hours and I'd get food in when necessary. I would always take them through the issues. You can't always win, but for earnest people— and most of them were earnest—provided they think the guy at the top has a strategy that will work and that you've brought them genuinely into the process, 90 per cent of the time, they'll go with you. But what you can never do is just announce this stuff in a budget or some other forum without that kind of close-in consultation.

KOB: There was a lot of talk about the J Curve through this period, when you were grappling with the terms of trade crisis. What was the J Curve and its significance in the economic debate at the time?

PJK: The point of the J Curve was that you'd put the changes in place but things would get worse before they'd get better. The graph would measure a downward curve before things got better and the turn up would result in the J.

KOB: Did Treasury sell the J Curve to you, and how much faith did you invest in it?

PJK: It was really a tool to paint a story with some economic respectability at a time when the economy was sending out distress signals—namely, that remedial measures take time, but when they do kick in, you get a response from them. It was a shorthand way of saying you may not see immediate results from taking the budget medicine. There will always be a lag before it kicks in. It was a piece of poetry that was presented in the media like a piece of poetry.

Here's the *Financial Review* of August 1986—and you know the *Financial Review* was always a critic of mine—'Mr Keating's remarkable budget' the headline says. They say:

The Treasurer Mr Keating has produced a remarkable budget. He has met the most optimistic of market expectations, maintained the high levels of welfare spending, confounded many of the criticisms which the Opposition had signalled in advance, and taken a political gamble that his measures might not be fully effective in time to save Labor at the next election.

The point is that the strategy I got Bob and the Cabinet into paid off for us politically, and within a month we were getting stories on opinion polls like this one on 22 July 1986 headlined 'The Hawke Government defies political gravity: The Labor Party was up two percentage points to 48 per cent, while 43 per cent supported the Coalition'.

In the circumstances that was remarkable. We've had the upheaval over the banana republic, and not only have I not led them into a dry gulch, I've led them into the Promised Land. The 1986 Budget and the 1987 May Statement set up our election win in 1987.

KOB: Then came the day in July when the Australian dollar plunged to 57 cents, an all-time low. According to John Edwards in *Keating: The Inside Story*, you sought the advice of the Reserve Bank Governor, Bob Johnston, that day, and he said, 'Frankly, Treasurer, I don't know what to do!'

PJK: That's true, but in the end we did a lot of very urgent things, like turning our foreign investment policy inside out. I changed the tax treatment of repatriated dividends and earnings, and I said to Johnston, 'Bob, I'll make this announcement and you throw a ton of money at the rate.' That got us past the immediate problem.

He had another saying that has always amused me. He said, 'Of course we've got the bottom drawer policy, Treasurer.'

And I said, 'What's that, Bob?'

He said, 'Something will turn up!'

And you know, there's a lot of wisdom in that sort of world-weary view of life. Conditions do change and things do turn up.

KOB: What was your formal relationship with the Reserve Bank Governor at this point? In personal terms it sounds like you had a very close rapport and a very good working relationship.

PJK: We did work closely together but the formal relationship was one where the *Reserve Bank Act* stipulated that the management of monetary policy should be such that the Board and the Treasurer seek to agree. So there was a statutory requirement on the Governor and his Board, and a statutory requirement on the Treasurer to endeavour to find agreement on the issues that arose. Not that this was always on our minds, but we were always trying to agree with one another, because that's what sensible, good people do.

KOB: How serious a crisis was the plunging dollar and what risks did you face if you chose to just sit on your hands, brazen it out and let the market take its course?

PJK: The markets would have pounded us into the ground if we hadn't acted decisively. We would have had a very low dollar, another burst of inflation, the wages system probably would have broken down again, so it really meant that when you float you're riding the tiger's back. There's no sentiment in the market. And if you're riding the tiger's back you don't have the luxury of being able to slow down and look backwards. You've just got to keep on going.

KOB: Did you have any worries about the ways in which markets can be manipulated, of Australia becoming a target of the serious market players like George Soros, who's been blamed for all sorts of things? If the players are big enough and clever enough, can they actually distort the market?

PJK: Already, the Australian dollar was about the fourth or fifth most traded currency in the world. You needed a lot of volume to change that. I had faith in the markets, and I still do. A Soros could take on the UK pound because the fundamentals were on his side. He would never have won against us with the fundamentals against him. If you know how to shift the markets—which I learned—and take the remedial action, you'll stay in front of the game.

Our particular challenge with the 1986 Budget was to go back to the budget that we'd already locked away for printing with the deficit down to $5 billion. But I thought the foreign exchange markets would be looking for more and would still judge us harshly, even though we'd already made significant cuts.

So, in one big effort, we cut another $1.5 billion and brought the deficit down to $3.5 billion, heading towards surplus. Essentially we did that in one meeting involving Bob and me and our advisers. We wanted ultimately to reach the point where the government's call on Australian savings was zero at worst, or better still, in surplus.

No government in Australia had ever taken a program-by-program approach to outlay reductions at Cabinet level as conscientiously as the Hawke Government did. That had happened in each of these budgets and May Statements, and as the task got bigger it became that much harder. So we were doing line-by-line items which Peter Walsh would bring along as a savings option from the Department of Finance, and which I'd then barrack for as Treasurer.

It only worked because these decisions to cut were made at Cabinet level with the authority of the Prime Minister and Treasurer, with the direct involvement of every minister. In the Whitlam and Fraser years they had various interdepartmental committees, but when Treasury officials would ask for cuts from the Health Department, for instance, the health bureaucrats would say, 'We're not going to agree to that.'

So they never got anywhere. That's why the outlays had grown so inordinately in those earlier years. You needed the political authority at the Cabinet table to say, 'Look, we'll do this with the pharmaceutical scheme, or we'll do that with family allowance benefits.'

By the end of 1986 we were getting stories like this one in December, 'Dollar soars as interest rates drop'. Not only had the budget been well received, but the dollar had surged back to a six-month high of 67 US cents.

KOB: But because of the ground rules you set for yourself you had to keep proving yourself to the markets year after year, so you were constantly jumping through your own hoops.

PJK: Two budgets a year for five years. It wore us out. We made a monkey for our own backs, but the country needed the break. Not only was Australia a closed economy, but our inflation had been out of line with our trading partners and the major economies for a decade. You can't hope to exchange your dollar for their dollar if you've had inflation at double their rate for a decade. There's got to be a reckoning, an adjustment to our competitiveness.

In the end, whether we liked it or not, we lined up for seven to ten weeks a year, ten hours a day, to cut Commonwealth Government spending. And that's why, when Howard and Costello took over in the second half of the 1990s, the structural changes we'd made to the budget allowed things to move back to surplus as growth returned after the recession. Spending programs like the assets test on the pension were structural changes that, once made, sat there for the future.

By the time we got to August 1986 and finished the budget round we were paralytically tired. But when I announced that we'd got the deficit down to $3.5 billion, it attracted huge support in the marketplace. The dear old *Financial Review* felt compelled to call it 'Keating's remarkable budget', and the dollar surged to 67 cents on the back of it.

This was a case of uncharted waters among the OECD countries. Nobody in the western world was doing this. No one would have a Cabinet and a Prime Minister sitting there for ten weeks a year, going through the budget line by line. I remember talking to one of the ministers in the Blair Government about this, and he said Tony Blair wouldn't sit for one hour in such a meeting, much less ten hours a day for ten weeks a year.

KOB: Around this time, while you were dealing with the dollar and revising the budget, I was working on a Keating profile for *Four Corners* with your cooperation, and we filmed a sequence with Bob and Hazel Hawke hosting a Sunday lunch for you, Annita and the kids. It was certainly all sweetness and light between you that day. We even talked about the leadership with the two of you sitting at the table as if butter wouldn't melt in your mouths. Now, pardon the hint of cynicism, but was that mood genuine or was it staged for our benefit?

PJK: This is the point: I never took a hard view in those days about the fact that the effervescence and energy and direction that Bob gave the government through 1983 and 1984 had started to dissipate through 1985 and 1986. He'd had a big personal shock and this had gone on, and rather than sit in judgement, I helped him. And when we had one of these discussions about things once, I said, 'Bob, at the end of the year when you're at Kirribilli reading novels over Christmas, you might ask yourself, who's done the right thing by you, sticking to you on the policy, you know?'

And he said, 'Oh mate, look, I know', and that's why when you saw Bob and me at the Lodge with Hazel and Annita, it was a genuinely good thing, notwithstanding the fact he didn't like the way the banana republic comment came out.

But Bob in his conscientiousness knew that we needed these remedial shifts in fiscal policy. Getting there was messy, but then he

tacked in behind me and we went on and got it done. Happy days are
here again, you see? That was how we worked.

KOB: Also in 1986 you moved to deregulate housing interest
rates, which were stuck at a ceiling of 13.5 per cent imposed
by the previous government. Why did you want to remove
that ceiling? To do so was inviting the banks to raise their rates
which, if you were a Labor backbencher in a marginal seat,
you wouldn't have thought was great politics. I think you even
predicted that housing interest rates would rise by 2 per cent
as a result.

PJK: The rate was fixed at 13.5 per cent for a housing loan up to
$30,000, but many people simply couldn't get loans. The $30,000
wasn't enough to buy a property so they'd have to have cocktail loans:
the primary loan at 13.5 per cent, then they'd have a secondary loan
at a higher rate, and then maybe family money. In other words we had
an immature structure and we never had a housing industry that
had consistency. It was always boom and bust, boom and bust.

Financial deregulation turned banks from rationers of credit to
creators of credit. In the system, before I turned up, banks were given
quantitative restrictions by the Reserve Bank on what they could
lend and they would dole that out to the customers they preferred.
They were not creators of credit. Once we removed all the deposit and
lending controls, including for housing, the banks could then decide
the risk profile of their customer in the context of those freedoms.
They could decide if they wanted to lend more than $30,000, and
whether or not that person's income and the quality of the assets they
were lending against were such that the banks could become creators
of credit.

The deal I did with the party was that I would grandfather any
existing loan at 13.5 per cent. What I knew and they didn't, was that

the average length of an Australian housing mortgage at that point was five-and-a-half years. With inflation coming down it was a reasonable bet that within five years most homeowners would have turned over their mortgage, and that was fine by me. I didn't want to cold-turkey the system with borrowers getting it in the neck and pushing people into variable rate mortgages at higher rates because they had based their calculations of what they could afford at 13.5 per cent.

This was a huge structural change. The whole housing industry since—the apartment towers you see in Sydney and Melbourne and Brisbane—could never have happened without it. Today the fundamentals a developer takes to the lending institutions are that they own the site and have the 10 per cent deposits from pre-sales. That's their capital as they raise their debt to fund the development. People couldn't pay the 10 per cent deposit before housing deregulation because they wouldn't know if they could get the other 90 per cent to settle. There were no pre-sales before 1986.

That's why you had a whole lot of small developers and very few big ones, building only individual quarter-acre houses. You couldn't get anyone to build a 200-unit building because they couldn't get the money—they could not get the banks to lend the development finance.

KOB: When Hawke yielded to those opposing your policy to end the 13.5 per cent ceiling, mostly from your own faction in NSW, including the Premier Neville Wran, and blocked you in Cabinet on 20 March, you wrote 'only temporarily' in the margin of one story reporting your defeat the next day. How long did it take you to shift Hawke?

PJK: Here are some of the headlines: 'Wran attacks the PM on housing'. It says, 'The ceiling on new home loan rates should have been raised, not abolished, says the NSW premier'.

Peter Barron would have been orchestrating that. Neville never said anything on federal matters without talking to Peter Barron. They would have had a discussion about it. In those days Peter was the best friend in the world with Graham Richardson, who was then the NSW Party Secretary, and they would lunch together. The whole opposition to lifting the interest rate ceiling was orchestrated by Richardson and NSW backbencher Gary Punch, and you could add Wran. And Barron had Hawke's ear.

KOB: It still didn't take you long to win back Hawke's support. On 2 April, you had a victory in Cabinet to remove the ceiling on new home mortgages. The *Financial Review* described the Cabinet meeting as tense and volatile, with a remarkable political backflip by Hawke and a very public victory for you. You were quoted as predicting home interest rates would rise from 13.5 to 15.5 per cent, which sounded almost like a boast. How did you read the politics in all that because some of your colleagues must have thought you were off your rocker to be predicting a 2 per cent interest rate rise as a virtue.

PJK: I knew that, but housing is a very big part of investment in Australia and you might recall the radio interview where I criticised the quarter-acre block and the Hills hoist, which drew a lot of flak. I said Australians were being robbed of housing choice and that cities would increasingly become massive suburban areas because we couldn't increase the density. Developers couldn't get the investment money to provide alternatives.

It followed that having lifted lending maturity controls from banks in 1984 after the float of the exchange rate in 1983, we should not have been stuck in that firmament, with housing mortgages of a fixed rate and ceilings. It simply couldn't stay that way, because the cost of staying that way was that we'd never have a housing industry capable of providing its share of national investment or, with it, housing choice.

It was the last important piece of financial deregulation, and it was too important to be lost in a factional battle.

KOB: You talked earlier about being able to hear the ants change step when your factional colleagues might be getting restless. It didn't take much to hear them change step on this, but you defied that.

PJK: I came into a meeting in front of Hawke in 1986—Bob was sitting there in his semi-slumped posture—with Richardson and Gary Punch. Richardson said to me, 'We're not copping this.' I said, 'You'll cop what I give you. When I became Party President I had to hock my reputation to drag you out of trouble and you're telling me you're not going to cop this? Really?'

Bob said, 'I don't know why you've got to be so aggressive, I don't know why you've got to go on like that.'

I said, 'Bob, I've got to go on like this because these two are standing in the way of a very important change.'

I left, and Bob sided with them and knocked me over. Days later I came back with the compromise: locking in all existing loans at 13.5 per cent but allowing banks to fix their own rates on new loans. I always knew I was going to have to compromise somewhere. But Australia got an entirely new housing industry from that day on—adequately funded, no more credit squeezes, no more booms and busts.

KOB: Did you pay any short-term personal price with the factional mates?

PJK: Yes, but I was in the slaying business. I gave recalcitrants trouble, not the other way round. You've got to remember that many other factional supporters like the Leo McLeays and the Stephen Martins were on my side. Not unreasonably, Richardson had influence over them, but I always knew that I would have a receptive audience for a good change. Again, if the author of the changes doesn't have the self-confidence and doesn't keep pressing, the system will prop. They will stop you. You've got to have a strategy; you've got to believe in the strategy and you have to transmit the belief.

KOB: You seemed to be well and truly running your own race by now because again in the first half of 1986 there was drama around attempts by the Western Australian business entrepreneur and corporate raider Robert Holmes à Court to take over BHP. For many people this was an attack on Australia's corporate icon and unions feared there could be massive job losses in the shake-out, but you said 'let the market prevail'. Once again that put you well and truly at odds with your own Sussex Street power base, didn't it?

PJK: This time they lined up with the BHP board, which was an odd alliance.

KOB: How hard was it to resist that pressure and why was it important to you to do so?

PJK: On what basis does a federal government decide to forbid a market purchase, in this case 30 per cent of BHP stock? Because we like the company, or we like the board or we like the existing management? It was all capricious. The best thing was to stand back and let the Melbourne establishment deal with Holmes à Court, which they finally did with John Elliott. The BHP board engaged Elliott and together they fought Holmes à Court to a standstill and got him to sign a non-compete agreement where he wouldn't go over 30 per cent of the stock. That's how it stayed until the 1987 stockmarket crash.

KOB: Would it have mattered if Holmes à Court had taken it over, broken it up and sold it off?

PJK: I don't think he was ever likely to break up BHP. I have a view about Robert. He was somebody who went into the bush determined to grab a tiger by the tail. And when he did grab one by the tail he didn't quite know what to do with it but he couldn't let the tail go.

Robert was a speculator who became not just an activist investor but owned a third of the stock. It was an extraordinary achievement. BHP today is a $200 billion company; a third of that is $65 billion. This is Warren Buffet levels of wealth. The remarkable thing was, Holmes à Court had the confidence to persuade the markets to fund his $10 billion investment. When it came to the crunch I don't think Robert had a strategy. That was something the market should have sorted out, not the Cabinet. In the end that was the way it went. Sanity prevailed inside the party.

THE MEDIA: POLICY AND PAYBACK

Over more than a century of history, it has become a part of Labor's DNA to regard the media in Australia with suspicion. The traditional Labor view, spawned from its earliest days, was that newspaper proprietors were almost automatically a part of the ruling class, and therefore the natural enemy of organised labour.

By the time Gough Whitlam came to power in 1972 the party platform included the goal that a federal Labor Government would establish an Australian newspaper commission—essentially a print version of the Australian Broadcasting Commission. It wasn't that the ABC had come to be seen as a Labor ally, but that in Labor's view it was the closest thing Australia had to a genuinely independent media organisation and the least biased.

Notwithstanding the fact that Whitlam had been assisted into office by editorial support from Rupert Murdoch through the *Australian*, the Sydney *Daily Mirror* and his recently acquired *Daily Telegraph* (bought from Sir Frank Packer in the shadow of the election), Whitlam was keen to see an ABC of print. Years later he was still asserting that there was no reason in theory 'why such a newspaper should not become as valuable, respected and authoritative' as the ABC had become as an alternative to the commercial broadcasters.

Ironically, in the age of media convergence 40 years later, the ABC of necessity is now competing directly with newspapers on various digital platforms, but at the time newspapers thought the idea of a publicly funded print opponent was outrageous. With bigger policy fish to fry, Whitlam surrendered that dream.

He did, however, pursue reforms in broadcasting, essentially repainting the commercial radio landscape, and forcing commercial television networks to broadcast a prescribed amount of local content. The Whitlam view of radio was that successive conservative governments acting in the interests of a few large commercial radio proprietors had resisted the introduction of frequency-modulation broadcasting, FM, a vastly superior high-fidelity sound with, as he put it, 'a signal virtually impervious to interference'. His introduction of FM licences as well as extra licences on the old AM band, plus additional FM networks at the ABC, changed the face of radio in Australia. But the structure and nature of print and commercial television ownership in Australia remained the same.

By the time Hawke and Keating came to power any idea of a public newspaper was well and truly out the window, but both men still had a clear personal interest in pushing media reform. Hawke had been an enthusiastic and successful litigator against media outlets in his ACTU days, but in office, according to John Button, had developed an obsession with trying to have media proprietors on side.

Button, who also had a natural interest in media matters and had been Shadow Minister for Communications under Bill Hayden, later wrote in his memoir *As It Happened* that 'Hawke had a courageous and capable Minister for Communications in Michael Duffy but his own prime concern seemed to be accommodating the media tycoons [Kerry] Packer and [Rupert] Murdoch'. It was no secret in those years that the Right-dominated ALP machine in New South Wales was close to Packer in the Wran era and beyond.

Keating, on the other hand, had been on the record for fifteen years raising questions about the feasibility of restructuring media ownership so that a proprietor could control either print or television outlets but not both, an idea he'd drawn from American practice. By 1976 Keating cared strongly enough about what he saw as an intolerable concentration of media ownership in Australia that he introduced a private member's bill into Parliament to stop newspaper proprietors buying into radio and television. It was defeated.

When the Hawke Government came to power, Australia's significant media owners with both print and broadcasting interests included Rupert Murdoch's News Corporation, the Fairfax family empire, the Herald & Weekly Times Group and Kerry Packer's Consolidated Press. Newspapers weren't regulated but no individual or company could own or control more than two television stations and eight radio stations.

The laws didn't discriminate on where the television stations were, and so ignored the fact that to own stations in Sydney and Melbourne, as Packer did, was to command a big slice of the national population. Throw into the mix a bunch of radio stations and a stable of newspapers and magazines, and you had a great deal of concentrated power.

The Fraser Government was persuaded by Packer in 1979 to commission a domestic satellite that allowed far greater broadcasting penetration into regional Australia, putting almost irresistible pressure on a future government to facilitate genuinely national television networks.

In mid-1984 the Australian Broadcasting Tribunal urged a complete restructuring of the broadcasting system. The subsequent policy debate within Cabinet through much of 1985 and into 1986 ended with a months-long impasse between Hawke and his Communications Minister Michael Duffy over how much audience reach each television owner should be allowed.

Murdoch (Channel Ten) and Packer (Channel Nine) each had stations in Sydney and Melbourne, which were calculated to deliver a potential audience reach of 43 per cent. Duffy wanted to establish 43 per cent audience reach as the upper limit for ownership for new players, and Packer and Murdoch would have to be content with what they already had.

Hawke wanted to restrict newcomers to 35 per cent reach, while allowing Murdoch and Packer to 'grandfather' their existing ownership. Blind Freddy could see the Hawke option blatantly favoured the two media giants, and Duffy wouldn't yield. Gareth Evans, who later replaced Duffy as Communications Minister, has since confirmed in his diary of the time that relations between Hawke and Duffy were poisonous, and that Hawke had become isolated on the issue.

Having been included in a committee with Hawke, Duffy and Senate Leader Button to resolve what had become an embarrassing stand-off for Hawke, Keating seized the opportunity to widen the debate to include all media ownership. With bitter memories still fresh in his mind of how badly he felt Labor had been treated by newspapers in the 1984 election, particularly the Melbourne-based Herald & Weekly Times Group with its powerful readership through much of Australia, Keating was happy to churn up the entire system. He embarked on a campaign to persuade both Cabinet and caucus to embrace what he sold as a solution to the Hawke–Duffy stalemate: removing audience limits on television ownership, but prohibiting any single proprietor from having significant ownership across both print and television.

In November 1986 Duffy announced a reform that was to change the face of Australian media, based substantially on the Keating model, the so-called cross-media rules. As Keating himself put it, you could be 'a prince of print or a queen of the screen' but you couldn't be both. By the time the reform became law television proprietors couldn't take their station holdings beyond a 75 per cent audience reach, but that still allowed anyone with the cash and the chutzpah to put together a genuinely national television network.

The Keating reform was seen as less blatantly supporting Packer and Murdoch, but both still emerged as massive winners. Packer consolidated his Nine Network before selling it to Alan Bond for more than a billion dollars, which Packer famously described as a once-in-a-lifetime deal. Before the media reforms Nine had been valued at less than half that amount. The sale catapulted Packer from merely rich to the richest person in Australia. According to Paul Barry in his biography *The Rise and Rise of Kerry Packer*, the newly arrived billionaire privately predicted he'd be buying the network back within three years for half the price. He subsequently got it for a fifth of the price.

Murdoch sold his two Ten Network stations to the retail landlord Frank Lowy for $840 million and a huge profit, but in walking away from television, he added the powerful Herald & Weekly Times newspaper group to his stable, with extensive holdings around much of the country. Murdoch ended up with just short of 70 per cent of Australia's entire print output: capital city, suburban and regional.

As far as Keating and many other Labor figures were concerned, the Herald & Weekly Times, and the Fairfax Group, which published the *Sydney Morning Herald* and *Age*, were Labor's traditional ideological enemies. By the time the dust had settled on these reforms, the Herald & Weekly Times had disappeared, and Fairfax had been greatly weakened, although the latter had at least as much to do with the inept response of the Fairfax board, and particularly young Warwick Fairfax, as it did with the reforms themselves. Keating was perfectly happy with the result, but Packer and Murdoch were both to bite the hand that had fed them just a few years later.

KOB: Thinking back to your early years in the Labor Party, did you tend to nurse the same broad view as most in your party about the commercial media in Australia that, by and large, the media proprietors were traditionally pro-conservative and anti-Labor?

PJK: I did basically subscribe to that view.

KOB: When you first started getting engaged in media policy, when you put up your private member's bill back in 1976, what was your motivation?

PJK: I thought the only relief for Labor in the broad media commentary in Australia was that a multiplicity of voices, competition in news and comment, would produce more sympathetic treatment of the Labor Party's position.

KOB: Why?

PJK: I believed that having many more organisations reporting the same news events and bidding for the same pool of readership or audience would encourage more edge and diversity in the way the news was covered. In the process they would be more attracted to proselytising the Opposition party's views. In other words, while ever the Herald & Weekly Times owned the great bulk of newspapers, much of the rural press and Channel Seven in Melbourne and Brisbane as well as radio, the chances of Labor getting fair and reasonable coverage from those sources were very low.

Ditto for John Fairfax & Sons with the *Sydney Morning Herald*, the Melbourne *Age* and the *Australian Financial Review*. Rupert Murdoch's influence was growing but still small compared to the others. He'd parlayed his ownership of an afternoon tabloid newspaper in Adelaide into starting the *Australian* from scratch and buying the Sydney *Daily Mirror* and then Frank Packer's *Daily Telegraph*, but he still didn't have the power or the influence of the others.

The real bar against Labor through those years came from the Herald & Weekly Times, the business Murdoch's father had run, and from John Fairfax & Sons.

I was always impressed by American media legislation at a national level, the FCC (Federal Communications Commission) legislation that decreed a structural separation between newspapers and television. An early attempt by the Labor Party to establish its own newspaper, the *Labor Daily*, failed because despite the valiant attempt and no matter how much effort was poured into it, there was no way a Labor paper would succeed in the market.

What Labor was forever going to face in print, radio and television, with the exception of the ABC, was commercially managed organisations, so in my view the only hope we had for reasonable media exposure was competition. That's why splitting them up made such sense to me. That's what led me to the private member's bill in the 1970s and I used to say to our people, 'You've got to be a bit smarter. You've got to pit them against each other, otherwise we'll never win.'

KOB: That suggests that you were always seeing media policy through the prism of what was good for Labor. What about what was good for the country?

PJK: I used to think, first, what was good for Labor because Labor was the mass party, it was the one that had the broader national interests. Certainly that's what I always believed. But in the prevailing media circumstance it was never able to proselytise its case on anything like an equal basis with the other side of politics. Until 1961 the *Sydney Morning Herald* never supported the re-election of a Labor Government, and we all know the speculation about the personal reasons why Sir Warwick Fairfax backed Labor in the traditional election-day editorial that year. By the next election he'd switched back to supporting the conservatives.

In my view we had to break up the owners and put them into boxes, and that's what I sought to do in 1976.

KOB: Whitlam had come to government with a media policy that included establishing an Australian newspaper commission similar to the ABC. Were you attracted to Whitlam's idea at the time?

PJK: I wasn't unattracted to it, but I didn't really think the big media forces—the Herald & Weekly Times, Fairfax and the rest—would accept an ABC as a direct competitor in print. The ABC was already broadcasting in radio when television arrived so it would have been impossible for the commercial media proprietors to stop the public broadcaster from having its own television network. But can you imagine the campaign those vested interests would have run against a government that tried to create a publicly funded competitor in print and threaten their power and their profits? They'd have slaughtered us.

Everything pointed to going back to a commercial remedy and that had to be about media diversity and competition, not a small handful of large media blocks.

KOB: Going into government in 1983, what was your view of Rupert Murdoch, who wasn't always as predictable in his editorial line as the others may have been?

PJK: I had a rather more sympathetic view of Murdoch than most of my colleagues did because he was so dynamic. From a relatively small base in Australia he elbowed his way into the British and American markets. He was head and shoulders above any other Australian entrepreneur, and so pre-1983 I viewed him as a fundamentally commercial figure rather than an ideological one, which he is these days. In those days he might sometimes oppose us but he might also support us.

The Herald & Weekly Times absolutely never supported us and nearly defeated us in 1984 with a strident anti-Labor campaign, particularly against our policy to introduce an assets test for the aged pension. The Melbourne *Herald* and the Melbourne *Sun*, the Adelaide *Advertiser*, the *West Australian*, the Brisbane *Courier Mail*, the Hobart *Mercury* together ran a huge campaign, and the combination of Hawke's poor campaign against Andrew Peacock combined with the Herald & Weekly Times campaign very nearly put us back in opposition after a term of less than two years.

Shortly after the election I was in the old Ansett private lounge at Melbourne Airport, and a guy came up and introduced himself as John D'arcy, the Chief Executive of the Herald & Weekly Times.

He said, 'We should sit down and talk about where we go from here,' and I said, 'Where we go from here is you go. That's where we go from here.'

'I'm sorry to hear those sorts of sentiments come from you,' he said. 'Surely reasonable people can sit down and discuss these things.'

I said, 'You guys have all been injected with the Coalition needle. You'll never be any different.'

I brushed him off but I let him know we wouldn't be involved in any conversation with him.

KOB: Did you differentiate in your mind between the general reporting of a campaign and editorial comment? Presumably you weren't too fussed if a newspaper wrote an editorial against Labor.

PJK: In the case of the Herald & Weekly Times I was concerned about the impact on editorial content of a management decision to try to nail the government over the assets test. A newspaper's proprietor can determine the content and direction of an actual editorial, but not the right to distort the process of fair and accurate news coverage in accordance with accepted journalistic standards, in order to change the outcome of an election. I regarded that as an abuse of their market power.

Essentially when a newspaper management decides to arrange the news presentation for the length of a whole election campaign and vehemently opposes the government over one of the most rational changes ever—putting an assets test as well as an income test on the pension—it can hardly expect to sit down with the government afterwards as if nothing had happened.

You would expect a conservative organisation to support such a change, not oppose it. You would think they would approve of a conscientious federal government putting an assets test as well as an income test on the pension.

The further we got into that seven-week campaign against Peacock we became more vulnerable than we should have been, and the Herald & Weekly Times obviously thought they could knock us out as a one-term government.

KOB: Media policy came into focus for the Hawke Government with the advent of a domestic satellite in 1984 that delivered a far greater broadcasting reach into regional and rural Australia than had previously been possible. Duffy was the Communications Minister and I'm sure you remember the long and bitter debate he had with Hawke about how to restructure commercial television ownership. It ran through much of 1985, and then ground on through 1986. What can you remember about that debate before you were invited to become a participant to try to resolve the Hawke–Duffy stalemate with a new formula?

PJK: People think this policy change was all about nailing major newspaper groups but it actually stemmed from aggregation and multi-channel licences.

KOB: All of which was sparked by the introduction of a domestic satellite that Kerry Packer had persuaded Malcolm Fraser back in 1979 that Australia needed. It was no coincidence that it also suited his plans to establish a more powerful television network for himself.

PJK: Most people in rural Australia only had two television choices up to that point: their local ABC and one commercial station. And what Duffy's department wanted to do was give those commercial station owners two extra multi-channel licences. These were mostly National Party people and we were going to gift to each of them two licences for free.

Hawke and I were on a unity ticket on this. We both thought it was exceptionally dumb. Gareth Evans says in his published diary of those years, 'It became apparent that neither the Hawke nor the Duffy positions had a great deal going for them. Towards the end Keating made a suggestion permitting aggregation but not requiring it, letting the markets produce the results.'

Gareth quotes me as saying to Cabinet that the fundamental point at issue had been missed in the whole debate. It was not simply about regional TV but the larger question of media concentration—cross-ownership versus the print media—and it was crucial to look at the Herald & Weekly Times and Fairfax. Gareth wrote that down as I said it in the Cabinet room.

KOB: Now up to the point where you interposed that idea Hawke's position had come to be identified very much as pro-Packer and to some degree pro-Murdoch because Murdoch had the Ten Network stations in Sydney and Melbourne.

PJK: As always, Bob had no framework.

KOB: John Button, who took a close interest in media policy, wrote in his memoir that in the Cabinet discussions Packer and Murdoch were 'like Banquo's ghost loitering behind the Prime Minister's chair'. Fair comment?

PJK: That was true. I think that's fair comment. And Gareth writes again on 21 October 1986 about a discussion he had with Hawke and me where we briefed him on 'basically a scheme which set no limits on television station ownership'—in other words, you could network 100 per cent of the country—'other than no acquisition should be in a city or town where the proprietor had control of a print organ'—in other words, you would grandfather existing ownership, but where they wished to buy further television reach they couldn't buy it where they currently owned a newspaper.

So we were saying to the Herald & Weekly Times, 'You can keep your print and you can keep HSV7 in Melbourne.' We were saying to John Fairfax & Sons, 'You can keep the Melbourne *Age* and the *Sydney Morning Herald* and you keep ATN7 in Sydney, but you can't go buying new television stations where you have print.'

KOB: And that evolved into the 'princes of print and the queens of the screen'?

PJK: That's right.

KOB: The only change from that blueprint was that you had to compromise by dropping television ownership from 100 per cent audience reach to 75 per cent.

PJK: Bob said, 'Should we accept the Senate amendment?' and I said, 'We'll accept the amendment, Bob, because 75 per cent lets you network all the mainland capital cities. I think that's a goer.'

It's worth remembering that I had first proposed the principle of limiting cross-media ownership in a private member's bill to the Parliament from opposition in 1976.

KOB: Coming back to Button's comment about Banquo's ghost, it was no secret that Sussex Street was very close to Packer, as was the Wran Government. Barron came from Sussex Street to his job as Hawke's senior adviser with that close Packer connection. Hawke's approach was very favourable to Packer, wasn't it?

PJK: That's true.

KOB: Were you conscious of Barron and Richardson at work there?

PJK: I was conscious of their closeness to Packer through Wran. But what I did was give them intellectual structure. Before this reform the Seven Network consisted of HSV7 in Melbourne and BTQ7 in Brisbane, both owned by the Herald & Weekly Times, ATN7 in Sydney owned by Fairfax, and the other capital city stations in the network.

I said, 'Does it really matter to us who owns the Seven network? News presentation is not going to change just because it's owned by one proprietor rather than several. It will still function as a network in the same way it does now, so why not let them own the lot?'

But they can't go buying a new station like Perth if they own the *West Australian* newspaper. They can't buy a new station in Adelaide if they continue to own the *Advertiser*.

KOB: How intense was the lobbying from proprietors through that whole process?

PJK: Huge, particularly by Fairfax. Fairfax always prided itself on being so upstanding, but I had this very, very bolshie lunch arranged by Max Suich, with Greg Gardiner and Fred Brenchley at Suntory, the Japanese restaurant in Kent Street.

Suich opened by saying, 'We think we can beat your cross-media rule in the Senate.'

I said, 'Well, you can do your best.'

He said, 'We are intent on buying HSV7 against what you propose.'

I said, 'Well, I'll tell you this, Max. I'll get the rule through so you'll be buying it counter to the rule. So what you have got me here to tell me is that you're basically going to try and abort the government's legislation, and will slip under the wire and buy HSV7 before we get the legislation through.'

At that point Brenchley got up and said, 'This is a lunch I don't think I wish to stay at any longer,' and walked out, leaving Gardiner and Suich.

At that point Gardiner began to get a little less resolute, leaving Suich somewhat isolated. As you now know, they did go and buy HSV7, for a little less than $400 million, and the cross-media rule did come in and they had to sell it. They suffered a significant loss on that purchase and it was that event that brought Mary Fairfax and Warwick Junior in to make a bid to buy the company. They believed the Suich–Gardiner management was dragging the company down and their investment in it.

What happened then is that young Warwick fell under the influence of Laurie Connell and Brian Burke. Strange but true, and that was the end of the Fairfax dynasty until John Fairfax Junior got control of it again years later. But the event that triggered the action of Mary and Warwick was the absolute determination of the Fairfax management, Suich and Gardiner, to pick up HSV7 against the intent of the government's legislation.

KOB: Just explain your antipathy to Fairfax.

PJK: It was to do with the way Brian Toohey and the *National Times* were arraigned against me and others connected with NSW Labor for a couple of years. Their whole belief was that the NSW Right was corrupt, and therefore anyone of the Right must be corrupt too. I remember being called by someone well placed within Fairfax one day and told that Toohey and his team were working on a story that when it came out would end my career. After the *National Times* finally published their big piece on me in 1986, which was a damp squib, Max Suich came to see me in my office in the old Parliament House, walked in as bold as brass and said, 'Well, you've been given a clean bill of health.' I said, 'But Max, I always had a clean bill of health. I didn't need Fairfax to scarify me on the way through.' I said, 'In policy terms I stand for everything the *Sydney Morning Herald* editorialises for these days, a new economy and all that entails. And what have I got for my trouble? I've been lumped in typically with the NSW Right and I've come in for this treatment with the *National Times*. So you can't expect to have any good relationship with me.' That's what happened.

KOB: Max Suich wrote a minute to the Fairfax board after one meeting with you which he said went for five hours. It's not clear exactly when it was but it was before your Suntory lunch. Maybe it was the meeting in your office that you've referred to. Part of the Suich board minute is published in Colleen Ryan's book *Corporate Cannibals* in which he says: 'The Treasurer is a product of the NSW right wing of the ALP and his conversation is littered with threats, references to getting even, doing deals and assisting "our crowd" in business, the press and within the ALP . . . He also has a very strong feeling about what he calls old money or establishment money, which he describes as dead money stultifying the economy, and he sees great advantages in new money—in which he includes Murdoch and Packer—being given opportunities to knock off old money.' Would you say that has a ring of authenticity?

PJK: I only ever had three meetings with Suich. But never one of five hours. There was the one in my office while Treasurer, the infamous one at the Suntory restaurant, and one I had with Suich and Gardiner, the company CFO.

The Suich/Gardiner meeting was about Fairfax's ongoing attempts to destroy the Wran Government with the aim of nobbling Wran himself and, in so doing, nobbling the NSW base of federal Labor. I can't recall exactly when that meeting was but I certainly remember the sense of what I said. I told them that Hawke and I regarded the relentless attacks by Fairfax journalists on Wran personally and on the Labor base as attacks ultimately designed to pull the NSW rug from under federal Labor. And that Hawke and I would respond accordingly, with a completely open, public assault on Fairfax. I told them all we wanted was fair and balanced coverage. Nothing more.

And I reminded them that Hawke and I were not Doc Evatt or Arthur Calwell, waiting to be kicked around like some immobile or passive target. That we would bite back. Possibly the core of Suich's note came from that conversation. But, of course, the note never carried the nuances or the sophistication of it. Suich was like a lot of journalists nominally on the left: happy to do the bidding of their conservative managers and proprietors.

KOB: What about Murdoch? He wouldn't have been inactive through that period.

PJK: No, he was up to no good as well. Everyone was consulted about the legislation: Murdoch, Fairfax, the Herald & Weekly Times, Packer, everyone was consulted. I was in Bankstown, attending a function in the electorate on a Sunday, and I was driving past the old Skyline drive-in at Chullora when I got a phone call.

'Is that you Paul? Rupert here.'

Because I didn't hear the beep-beep signalling an overseas call, I thought he must be calling from within Australia.

He said, 'Now, look, I want to get this straight. We could bid for the Herald & Weekly Times group but we couldn't keep HSV7 because we have Ten in Melbourne, is that right?'

I said, 'That's right', and explained again what I'd previously told him.

His great interest was really Queensland Newspapers, which was part of the Herald & Weekly Times stable.

I thought, 'This is very strange.' That is, he might use the opportunity of the open consultation, of the knowledge, to make a bid for the Herald & Weekly Times before the various proscriptions contained in the prospective legislation took effect.

I didn't ask him if he was in Australia but I suspected he was, and stopped the car at the top of the hill at Bankstown and rang Michael Duffy.

I told Duffy, 'We should put a statement out today saying that these rules apply as of a certain time,' and dictated the statement to Duffy's daughter Alana. She typed it down and Duffy released it, I think on AAP.

I got another call the next morning from Rupert, and he said, 'I saw what you guys said. I thought there might be space to consolidate before it goes ahead.'

That event remained in my memory, that notwithstanding the openness and the consultation, News might have moved to make a bid for the Herald & Weekly Times or the *Courier Mail* before the prescriptive legislation was either formally announced, enacted or proclaimed.

There's a word for media proprietors that no one uses these days. Brigands, and if you don't know they're brigands you can't deal with them. You can never make any progress with them because you can never assuage their fundamental brigandry.

KOB: What was your relationship with Packer at that point?

PJK: In those days, pretty good. He was a blunt character but exceptionally bright. This was his patch. He said to me a couple of times, 'Look, you can't compare me to Rupert. Rupert's run way past me. What Rupert does, I don't do. Rupert's taken on the world. I'm not. I'm staying here.'

He was interested in the licences here and the way the system ran here. The cross-media rules suited him because he owned no newspapers. But the ability to network the country, buy up Channel 9 Perth and Channel 9 Brisbane because he already owned Sydney and Melbourne meant that he was a net winner from the change. It was his approach to Alan Bond to buy Nine in Perth which Bond owned that led Bond to make the offer Packer couldn't refuse—to buy Packer's holdings in the network for a billion dollars.

KOB: How ruthless was Packer at prosecuting his case?

PJK: I'd say interested, but not ruthless. For Packer the difference in economic terms between running the Nine Network and getting rental out of Nine Perth, Nine Brisbane and Nine Adelaide and owning them all was not a whole lot different.

KOB: How hard was it to get all that through the caucus? They'd become pretty bolshie themselves when you put the cross-media proposition on the table.

PJK: The Right of the party—Richardson *et al.*—were very much in favour of the proposals I'd put together. My real problem was Don Chipp and the Democrats in the Senate. But the thing about Chipp was that he was a very reasonable person and he did have the national interest uppermost in his mind. You could sell him a reasonable policy. We cut a trade with him by dropping the television audience reach from 100 per cent to 75 per cent and he fundamentally accepted that media diversity was an important element in the equation.

KOB: You would have worked out very early in the piece where each existing proprietor's interests lay. The whole world knew Murdoch's interest in having the Herald & Weekly Times, particularly with his father's connection to it.

PJK: Rupert had already made a bid two years earlier, which they'd rejected.

KOB: I assume it didn't bother you seeing the Melbourne establishment shaken up by Murdoch.

PJK: The Melbourne establishment and the Fairfax view was, 'We decide who runs the government and the country, and yes, the Labor Party got past us in 1972 but it didn't take us long to put them away, and they got past us again in 1983, but in 1984 we'll put them away again.'

KOB: I thought James Fairfax, the Chairman of the Fairfax Group, was different from what you describe.

PJK: James was, but I don't think James Fairfax was dictating policy. In the end the sentiment within Fairfax had earlier come from Rags Henderson, who was the power behind the throne, and this power passed across to Suich and Gardiner.

KOB: When the dust finally settled on what had become your policy, what did you think of the outcome: Herald & Weekly Times gone to Murdoch, Fairfax weakened and ultimately controlled by the Canadian conservative and Thatcher confidant Conrad Black, Murdoch with close to 70 per cent of all Australian print outlets, plus a new generation of television proprietors who didn't last very long—Bond, Skase and Lowy, who all paid too much and were in and out in the blink of an eye?

PJK: In the end it was actually a good outcome because what we began with was the Herald & Weekly Times owning television stations plus the *West Australian*, the Adelaide *Advertiser*, the Melbourne *Sun*, the Melbourne *Herald*, the Hobart *Mercury* and the *Courier Mail* in Brisbane, but they also owned every other significant Queensland regional newspaper.

They also owned the Victorian regional papers, plus agricultural news magazines, and the radio stations. Between Fairfax and the Herald & Weekly Times they just about had the game locked up.

What we ended up with was a much more diverse scene. Fairfax, the Herald & Weekly Times and Murdoch all sold off their television interests. The three commercial television networks have all since changed hands.

While it is true that we had the bare transfer of the Herald & Weekly Times capital city mastheads to Murdoch, it's also true that the block of assets the Herald & Weekly Times had was broken up. Apart from broadcast assets, the *West Australian* newspaper was spun off and is now run by Kerry Stokes and the Seven group.

In Queensland, the most decentralised state in the country, all the city newspapers outside Brisbane, which were owned by the Herald & Weekly Times, ended up with the APN Group, the former O'Reilly chain that bought them as part of the Herald & Weekly Times break-up. I think the diversity became significantly greater than it had ever been.

KOB: The one big argument against that is Murdoch and his 70 per cent ownership of print throughout Australia.

PJK: From the Labor Party's point of view the Herald & Weekly Times control of print outlets was not only greater than everything Murdoch has now but historically much worse for us.

KOB: I would suggest to you that the role the Murdoch papers eventually played against the Rudd and Gillard Governments and for Tony Abbott is arguably worse than what the Herald & Weekly Times tried to do against you in 1984.

PJK: I think you can argue that, and that is largely true. But it was also true the Herald & Weekly Times had played its ugly hand for the better part of a century. When you hear people say today that Murdoch has 70 per cent of print, you never used to hear the same people say in yesteryear that the Herald & Weekly Times had over 70 per cent of the newspapers *plus* television and radio, and always felt it had the right to kick the Labor Party to death. It was a situation that had existed for so long that people just accepted it as the norm. That was okay providing you didn't inhabit the Labor Party.

KOB: Can you understand how the anger and frustration you've described, which clearly was a big motivation for you pushing the media reforms, can be easily seen as an abuse of your own power to punish your media enemies and shape a more benign media landscape for a Labor Government?

PJK: But here was the complete abuse by the Herald & Weekly Times of their mastheads. And we're supposed to say, 'Oh that's okay, that's democracy, Australian-press style?' Good policy should be put aside while these thugs continue their conservative thuggery?

Getting done by the Herald & Weekly Times offended my sense of political smartness. Having a couple of bovver boys from Brisbane and Melbourne nearly knock us over in a national election, grossly distorting fair reporting in the process. Then they talk about the need for a free media. Give us a break!

KOB: The term 'bovver boy' was also applied to you in those days.

PJK: Well, let's say a couple of bovver boys ran into a sharper bovver boy.

KOB: Nonetheless you put enough store in the newspapers through your political life to build a massive personal archive of many thousands of articles covering Australia's political history as it happened, from 1977 through to the present day, often with your own personal annotations on the side. What drove such a time-consuming exercise for so many years?

PJK: In a busy public life you don't really have time to keep a detailed diary. If you went home tired at night and tried to record the Treasurer's day or the Prime Minister's day, you'd spend two hours writing up the first hour. You couldn't keep a note that covered such complex events, changing so quickly day by day. I knew I was presiding over nation-changing events and I wanted some sort of record. The sequence at least.

All you can do is have a recollection of the period, so what I used to do on a Saturday morning for about an hour was go back to the previous Sunday and cut out a cross-section of all the major newspapers' reports for the week. It might be a piece by Ross Gittins announcing the government was abandoning monetary targeting, or a comment piece by Michelle Grattan, or something by Paul Kelly, Alan Ramsey, Geoff Kitney or Michael Stutchbury. I'd occasionally write a note in the margin and put them away as a kind of *aide-mémoire*. It required discipline because you can imagine at times it was the last thing I felt like doing on a Saturday.

KOB: How selective was your record? How many stories did you keep that were critical of you?

PJK: All my enemies are there. If you're on top of the game you have to stay in touch with your enemies. You can see them as you go through the archive. People like Peter Smark and Paddy McGuinness. Paddy hated the sight of me. I was happy to keep a record of their rantings.

I now have a digitised record of all those articles and it works as a storyline of the reconstruction of Australia through that period. You've seen those books where if you flick the pages, the margin image comes alive like an animation. That's the impression you get by scanning through the archive on a computer. As you press the mouse the stories flick across the screen like a long continuous ribbon showing the national story as it is being told.

THE 1987 ELECTION

It's a fact of life that some political leaders are luckier than others. Of course they still have to be smart enough to capitalise on it. Bob Hawke's arrival in office coincided with the breaking of a drought that had helped cripple the Australian economy and contributed to Malcolm Fraser's defeat. The rains became a part of the nation's economic recovery.

You could also argue he was blessed with the luck of having Andrew Peacock as his first Opposition Leader. Peacock had seemed born to rule the Liberal Party, was given a dream run into politics, backed by the powerful Victorian Liberal establishment, and was a glamorous and effective Foreign Minister for his time. But tested by a strongly performing government and lacking the drive or killer instinct to match his ambition, he struggled to convince Australians that he had what it took to lead the country. He also allowed himself to be spooked by his party deputy, John Howard, a distraction you can't afford if you're trying to make gains on a formidable government.

At one point Peacock's popularity sank to 14 per cent, and notwithstanding a strong performance in the 1984 election campaign, he still failed to put the stamp of authority on his leadership, even in the eyes of many of his own colleagues. He had decisively beaten Howard for the job when Fraser stood down in 1983, but Howard had not gone away. As Shadow Treasurer and deputy Liberal leader he was guaranteed a high profile, seemed impervious to the political odium from the recession and big budget deficit that had settled more on Fraser than his Treasurer, and he was still popular in Liberal ranks.

More than that, Howard had essentially outmanoeuvred Peacock in the battle for ideas. He had become the leader of a powerful group of economic rationalists within the opposition—the so-called Dries—and increasingly they dominated the policy debate in their party room, to the extent that Peacock ended up with a foot in two camps, the rationalist Dries and his own philosophical supporters, the Wets.

It was no secret that Howard still harboured leadership ambitions, and by mid-1985 Peacock was feeling the heat. Howard has said since that he was doing nothing to stir the situation, and it was hardly his fault that he was outperforming his leader, but there were many observers at the time who would regard that description as more than a little bit disingenuous.

Even after Peacock successfully outperformed the front-running Hawke in the 1984 campaign, Howard inadvertently revealed a scathing condemnation of Peacock's leadership in a phone conversation that was only revealed a year or so later, after Howard had finally replaced him. Melbourne *Sun* journalist Peter Rees had rung Howard at his home the day after the election for comment. Unfortunately for Howard, he thought he was talking to fellow Liberal, Peter Reith, and proceeded to lambast Peacock as a man who stood for nothing and who had had his chance.

'I don't think Andrew is ever going to be Prime Minister ... we have been directionless for eighteen months,' he told the somewhat bemused journalist. 'I'm not certain he won't fall over next year.'

When Howard realised his mistake he persuaded Rees not to publish the comments until some future time. Rees subsequently told the story after Howard fulfilled his own prophecy and replaced Peacock in September 1985. In effect Howard was handed the leadership on a platter after an act of woeful strategic misjudgement by Peacock, who allowed himself to be panicked into bringing on a leadership crisis, which he then managed to lose despite having the party numbers.

In the year that followed Howard had a great deal of trouble settling his party down. It wasn't just about personalities and bruised egos but about ideology, and much of the instability was played out through leaks in the newspapers. Where Hawke and Keating seemed able to recover fairly quickly from their differences, no matter how torrid they might have been in the moment, the Howard–Peacock conflict was both raw and stark.

Even so, perhaps reflecting the uncertainty and crisis created through 1986 by the banana republic comments, the plunge of the dollar and some harsh budget medicine, by late that year the Morgan poll had the Coalition several points ahead of Labor. And although Hawke regularly outpolled Howard as preferred Prime Minister, his 1984 campaign performance had taken the shine off his shield of apparent impregnability.

Then along came Sir Joh Bjelke-Petersen, Australia's second-longest serving premier, with delusions to grandeur. After a record election win in Queensland in November 1986—his eighteenth year as premier— Sir Joh decided that his own brand of folksy but tough conservative populism could be rebranded sufficiently to take him all the way to Canberra and the Lodge. The fact that his National Party was a rural rump everywhere but Queensland, and very much the junior partner of the Liberal–Nationals Coalition federally, didn't deter him.

Sir Joh's populism might have worked in Queensland, where he once reduced the Labor Opposition to the size of a cricket team in Parliament, but the idea of him running foreign and defence policy, let alone the economy, lacked credibility then and seems positively ridiculous now. This was a man whose response to protest against a plan to demolish the historic Bellevue Hotel next to the equally historic Parliament on the Brisbane River was to bring in the wreckers in the dead of night. It had disappeared by morning.

With good reason, history now judges the Bjelke-Petersen reign as one that produced institutionalised corruption, yet at the time some smart people were reported to be flirting with his 'Joh for Canberra' push. One was the former Treasury head, John Stone; another was the prominent South Australian farmer and former cricketer Ian McLachlan. The big surprise when it was reported at the time, although never confirmed by him, was Andrew Peacock.

Before Joh's campaign ended, he had split the Coalition asunder in Canberra. In February 1987, the *Australian* commissioned a special Newspoll which reported that 33 per cent of Australians preferred Sir Joh as the 'best leader of conservative politics' in Australia, with Peacock next on 30 per cent and Howard on 17 per cent.

This was manna from heaven for the Hawke Government. Even so, there was much indecision in the Labor camp about election timing: go early and capitalise on Coalition disunity with the risk that too many voters might still judge them harshly on their recent economic performance, or bank on the economy improving and go later in the year?

It was a debate that once again put Hawke in conflict with Keating. Not only did Keating want to go early, risking a winter election, but he also wanted to deliver another tough mini-budget in advance. Keating could never be accused of being risk-averse.

The polls in early May had Labor in its best position since the 1984 election, but Keating was prepared to test the strength of that voter support with even more budget constraint in order to keep the financial markets on side.

Howard was to acknowledge of that period in his autobiography twenty-three years later that in direct contrast to his own side, 'Hawke continued to govern decisively. On May 13 the Treasurer delivered a major economic statement outlining a reduction of $4 billion in the prospective budget deficit. It gave the appearance of a government dealing directly with the economic challenges then facing Australia.' That's not what Howard said at the time, describing the May Statement on the day as 'a con job done by mirrors'.

The newspaper coverage of the May Statement was peppered with stories of blood-on-the-floor program cuts. A Moir cartoon in the *Sydney Morning Herald* was indicative: a voter chained to the wall with Keating wielding a whip across his chest, saying, 'Cheer up. Think how good it'll feel when I stop.' Standing in the wings, holding a couple of spare whips at the ready, was the much smaller figure of Bob Hawke.

The markets loved the May Statement and economics commentator Ross Gittins wrote, 'While no one is likely to thank Paul Keating for zapping the voter's hip pocket, it's probably also true that the government will suffer public disapproval if it's been judged not to have been tough enough.'

Exactly two weeks later Hawke announced a double-dissolution election on the pretext that the government's legislation to introduce an Australia Card had been rejected twice in the Senate. That was the one and only point in the campaign at which the unpopular Australia Card had any relevance, as a trigger to get the Governor-General's approval for an election six months early.

Despite a four-seat gain for Labor in the election, the Australia Card then disappeared without trace. But what did re-emerge quite soon after the jubilation of a third straight election victory, something federal Labor had never achieved before, was another round of tension between the two bulls in the political paddock.

KOB: Your 1987 May mini-budget delivered the biggest public-sector spending cutback in 30 years, much of it from areas like health, education, welfare and jobs programs. How hard was it to win support for those cuts inside Labor on top of what you'd slashed already?

PJK: It was a shockingly difficult task. Because I believed we should go to an election in the middle of 1987, I cancelled an overseas trip to the International Monetary Fund, sat the budget Expenditure Review Committee down for another six or eight weeks and brought the budget forward. In the May Statement we cut $4 billion from outlays. That would be like $15 to $20 billion today. We also foreshadowed tax cuts. That was an absolutely huge change, all designed to strengthen the exchange rate, to put another down payment on fiscal policy, to continue to regain the confidence of the markets and have a stable scene where Bob and I could win another poll.

Let me give you another indication of the relationship I largely had with Bob, and the trust between us. I chaired the Expenditure Review Committee for the 1987 May Statement, where Bob had chaired the previous ERCs. If you think the banana republic comment put a stick of dynamite under the government, just imagine how explosive it was potentially to change entitlements and taxes like we did in that May budgetary round.

Yet Bob had complete faith in me doing it. I remember going up to see him at the Lodge and saying, 'Look, mate, there are four or five issues I want your judgement about.'

He said, 'What are they?'

And I'd go through them.

He said, 'Oh, I think we can live with this one, and I think we can live with that.' And because they were tailored well and crafted well and were fair, there wasn't really a problem getting them through caucus. We didn't have to do the strong-arm stuff to get them through.

KOB: Through a process like that, did you personally seek in your own mind to measure the social impact that this was going to be having on households around the country? Did you take a look for yourself to get a sense of how it was actually going to affect people out there?

PJK: That's what Labor Treasurers do. We're mostly worried about the 90-odd per cent of people who live on the ebb and flow of the economy and whose fortunes are really set by the big parameters. That's why during my terms, programs like the Family Allowance Supplement, or the huge funding for education to lift Year Twelve retention rates for kids, changes to the Pharmaceutical Benefits Scheme—which drugs went on the free list and which didn't—all those micro-decisions were very carefully thought through.

KOB: Did you, from time to time, take yourself out there around the suburbs, the towns, the communities of Australia to actually remind yourself what the real world was like?

PJK: Kerry, I didn't leave Bankstown until I was thirty-nine. I lived in a working-class western suburban community in Australia's biggest city, really lived with them for virtually all of my first forty years. After that length of time it comes intuitively to you. You know when people are living in the ebb and flow of the economy, you know how they rely upon government payments, you know how they rely upon the health system, upon education funding for their kids. I also used to do my Federal Electorate Council about every two months.

I'd go back to Bankstown and the branch members would run through their issues, or I'd attend local events. And I'd always get a lecture or two when I turned up at the ACTU. They wanted to be consulted and have things explained to them, but they were pretty much always happy with the explanation.

The truth is, if you are a conscientious member of the federal parliamentary Labor Party, it's part of your DNA to worry about the people on the bottom. And I'd say that was true of all the ministers who were material to the ERC processes. They were all seriously concerned about the tough budgetary stuff, not just the politics of it all but the personal impact.

KOB: The journalist and political historian Paul Kelly wrote of the 1987 mini-budget that it marked a decisive shift at the centre of the country's political gravity to the Right, and the economics commentator Des Keegan, who himself was on the economic Right, wrote that you'd 'won your spurs with the first significant rollback in government spending since World War II, that modern Labor had come of age'. How did you feel, as a Labor Treasurer, to be seen to be leading that shift to the Right, and being lauded by the Right?

PJK: In a way, that had to happen. After all the old Labor Party confusion over means and ends, for the first time a federal Labor Cabinet wanted to see the national accounts and the budgetary accounts of the Commonwealth in good shape to deal with the contemporary problems we were facing. So the discipline of running four or five years of outlays at no more than the inflation rate, and often less than population growth, was really quite remarkable.

It was no surprise in a way that the Des Keegans of the world recognised and gave the government credit for that. But we did it with such a Labor heart that we always protected the most vulnerable people from the hardest impacts. A lot of business welfare went, a lot of middle-class welfare went, but we always tried to stay true to the people at the middle to lower end.

KOB: We discussed earlier how so much of your philosophical base came from your father, whose influence was very important to you but who'd died at quite a young age. Did you ever use him as a mental check on yourself as Treasurer—how would Dad have reacted to this?

PJK: It's interesting you say that, Kerry, because I often used to say to Don Russell and Tom Mockridge in my office, 'What would the troops at Bankstown think we did for them this week? Are we lifting them up? Behind all the numerology and all the rest of it, in the end, underneath it all, is there value for them?'

KOB: Without labouring the point, Labor under Hawke and Keating was not just the moderate Labor Government that you and your father used to talk about all those years ago, building a bridge between labour and business but with a strong working-class backbone. This was a right-wing Labor Government steeped in dry rational economics that was also making a lot of wealthy people wealthier.

PJK: But in the old locked-down economy where you had a rigid exchange rate and a sclerotic financial market, a lot of businesses had diminished values. The All Ordinaries stockmarket index was about 450 when I became Treasurer and when I left it was 2600. So the stockmarket had gone up about five times in value. This didn't just reflect wealth for a few but a shift in national wealth and in the creation of growth and jobs.

KOB: Another senior political journalist, Geoff Kitney, wrote just before that 1987 mini-budget, 'Keating is dog tired, not just because of the huge workload he's had to carry in the past few weeks, but because of the accumulated fatigue of working at high physical and mental pressure levels for more than four years.' Kitney said everyone else around you was the same, 'People sitting at the Cabinet table like stunned mullets.' How vividly do you still remember those atmospherics?

PJK: The discipline of it was shocking: running through line items in social security and education, in science, in trade, in foreign affairs, discussing whether or not we could open a new embassy or a consulate somewhere. It got down to that sort of detail for seven to ten weeks a year for the May Statement, and then several more weeks in the budget round. So yes, by 1987 we were like stunned mullets. And then you still had to do the sales task, you still had to go through the process of parliamentary accountability, the Question Times and the rest of it. In the straitened national circumstances of the kind we found, you had a choice. Either you rose to the challenge or you joined those governments of the past who had swept it all under the carpet. What sustained me, and I'm sure others in that ERC process, was that we were doing what was right fundamentally, trying to give the country a break of a kind it hadn't had for most of the twentieth century.

KOB: On the same theme but going back a year, John Edwards wrote in his biography that he met you ten days after the 1986 Budget and found you unexpectedly relaxed, funny and obliging, but suffering a strange sort of mid-life crisis indicating that your 'whole pleasure in the exercise of power had diminished with familiarity'. Had the pleasure of the exercise of power diminished for you by 1986?

PJK: The truth is that it is a very long, hard job. There is a time in everyone's political life where political success and political promotion are really central and important to you in a very personal kind of way. But you get to the switch-over point where the real value is the value you add to the country, and that's really what you then think about most of the time. You can't divorce it from your own desire to succeed, but by and large these bigger impulses take over.

Now after floggings of the kind I took doing those sixteen budgetary rounds, May Statements and budgets, lofty ideas about how important you are and how you're enjoying the power tend to evaporate. You become the absolute servant of the show and you take on the headspace of a servant.

KOB: I wonder whether by that point you'd come to really understand the essence of power. What was the essence of power for you?

PJK: I think you have to be born with an instinct for power. I'm not sure you can learn about the exercise of power. I think you've got to be born with it, grabbing the naked flame and hanging on, surviving the experience, drawing the inclinations of a community into a concentrate, one that you can use to effect change. That's the kind of power I'm talking about, and not being afraid to use it to the best of your ability, and not wasting its power to change.

KOB: John Edwards recounts how in that same conversation you talked about the 'arid' nature of politics, and that the longer you continued as Treasurer the more you pondered a remark from an old friend and mentor, the former *Financial Review* Editor, Max Walsh, who told you, 'You are a conscript of history, and when the rest of us are enjoying our lives you will be chained here doing history's bidding.' Is that what public life had become for you?

PJK: That's what it had become for me. That remark was true. I was a conscript of history and I knew it. I was there for thirteen of the hardest years you could imagine. But look at the shift, look at the country now. With 22 years of compound growth, we lead the western world, fundamentally as a result of those changes.

KOB: Feeling that aridness of the politics as you had come to see it, what remained of those early passions and dreams, the early inspiration from Churchill that the only game you wanted to be in was public life? Was that still resonating with you?

PJK: It was. Basically I'm a public person. I think in public terms. I can't help it. I always do, because public life provides the great leverage. You get into a parliamentary structure where you have a majority in Parliament controlling the executive government and in close personal terms you can move something by a micron. But out there in the big world that small movement on the bridge shifts the country by a mile. In other words, the leverage is profound. Wearying, but at the same time exhilarating.

As distinct from monetary income, the psychic income from public life is a complete aphrodisiac, a completely different thing. This is why all these people who have done well in the professions and corporations as CEOs and bankers are all bored stiff in their sixties. I see them around Sydney and Melbourne. They're about to join this and they're about to do that. They discover good social works as their social conscience finally pricks them, and sometimes they try to engage me in their social works.

I'm thinking, 'Hang on, I've done my 40 years before the mast, I don't have a need to feel fulfilled! You might, I don't!'

KOB: Tired or not, chained down or not, while grappling with the May Statement in 1987, you were also throwing your two bob's worth into the discussions about an early election. You'd opposed the idea when it was first raised in February to go to the electorate in April, but then you changed your mind and felt that you could actually turn a hack-and-slash mini-budget into a political virtue and win an election. You proposed a winter campaign, but some of your colleagues thought you were nuts.

PJK: They did. There was a piece by Geoff Kitney, which said as much. He reported a meeting in Hawke's office where we talked about it and they thought I'd lost my marbles. This is what Kitney wrote:

> Fatigue is how some are accounting for the strange view from Keating's corner of Parliament House about the timing of the election, that it should be called in July. What purpose he had for supporting this view is difficult to fathom, a mid-winter election. It is said that Keating believes the July tax cuts would turn the electorate's mood in the government's favour. To those who understandably cannot accept any of these rationalisations for the Treasurer's snap election talk, the most sensible alternative explanation is foolishness induced by tiredness.

In fact what I'd said to Bob was this: 'Look, if we have an April poll with the dollar just hovering and the foreign exchange markets ready to dump on us at any moment, we're taking a big risk.'

I said Howard would come out with unfunded tax cuts as the Liberals always did, the markets would say the country, Labor and Liberal, had no real fiscal rectitude, and we'd have the dollar sliding on us in the middle of an election and that would be the end of us.

I said, 'This is my view. Bring the Budget forward, make a much bigger down payment on fiscal policy, consolidate the markets, and off the back of that have a winter election.'

And they all burst into laughter.

But I said, 'If you try an April poll, with absolutely skittish markets, we've got a reasonable chance of crashing and burning.'

At any rate, because I possessed the horsepower and took responsibility for my suggestions, Bob and the advisors went for it. We cut $4 billion out of outlays and the polls responded really well. The *Australian* then wrote, 'Springboard for an election! Hawke says early poll hint'. The next thing we were off to 'Hawke's winter battle'.

KOB: When Bob Hawke did call an early election for July the veteran journalist Alan Ramsey wrote a very detailed piece about how you had earlier suggested a July election and been ridiculed by Hawke and others. All these years later, reading that, it does read very much as if that analysis had come directly from you, or someone very close to you.

PJK: Ramsey liked me at the time. There were moments when he didn't like me, but not at that time, and that article may simply reflect the people he spoke to who knew about my earlier input. But Ramsey was on to Bob. He knew he was just hanging in the job and that the really big directional decisions were being taken or influenced by me. And if not by me alone, by the core of us—Walshie, Dawkins and me.

KOB: But looking back now at the reporting of those years, you can see patterns at times suggesting you and Hawke were leaking against each other.

PJK: I was never in the leaking business. I was never in the business of wilfully telling journalists stuff. I had no need of encouraging journalists. I ran the show; that gave me the kind of deference I had earned from the gallery.

KOB: But there's a difference between wilfully feeding journalists and targeted leaking.

PJK: The Kitney piece definitely came from Hawke's staff.

KOB: But what about the Ramsey piece?

PJK: I don't think and can't remember whether it came from my office but nevertheless, what is the central point? The central point is

I picked the propitious moment for the government's third election, set up the May Statement to win it, bolted up the markets and then personally destroyed Howard's tax package. I made Howard wait nine more years for the prime ministership. He had that sleazy tax package, and I made him pay a huge price for it.

KOB: There was also the happy fact for Labor that Howard as Opposition Leader was struggling with a divided party and Joh Bjelke-Petersen's destructive push to enter national politics.

PJK: That's an accurate reflection of the situation earlier in that year, but our task was to go to the election with credibility, which we did.

KOB: Tell me how you went about finding the accounting error in the Howard tax package that created such damaging headlines for the Opposition in the middle of an election campaign. Can you take me through the detective work that pinpointed where the hole was?

PJK: In trying to construct a new template for Australia where political strategy was built around good policy, I had subjected the government to enormous personal and corporate pressures in that Cabinet room over all those years doing those budgets and May Statements. I also sought to establish a regime where the same rules applied to the Opposition.

Before 1987 the Coalition would never have had a set of spending and revenue promises out there before an election. They would never have had a set of costed spending, savings and tax plans for examination, but under the new disciplines I had created—a new notion of Australia's political culture—Howard would have to comply.

But to do that the Liberals would have had to have the same set of disciplines Labor was applying to itself. That is, if you're going to have tax cuts you have to cost them, you have to account for them, whether you are in government or opposition.

In 1977 Malcolm Fraser had famously offered voters a fistful of dollars in tax cuts reflected in a crudely illustrated advertising campaign, a promise he then had to renege on. And in 1980 he and Howard beat Hayden with another promised tax cut, where voters could ring a number and find out how much their tax cut would be. So I knew Howard would go back to tax cuts in 1987. He couldn't help himself. Unfunded, unaffordable tax cuts.

So I put the Department of Finance and Treasury onto costing Howard's tax policy, and did the same in my own office. I said, 'Look, there's no way these numbers will stand up. If he was able to afford tax cuts like these, so would we. There's a hole in there somewhere and I want it found.'

KOB: Your senior advisor, Don Russell, says in *Labor in Power* that it was the Department of Finance that finally located the hole.

PJK: I knew we just had to look long enough to find it, and we did. It was billions. I explained it all in a press conference and although Howard played mum for a couple of days he had to acknowledge the error in the end and then it was all over.

I still have the newspaper coverage of that day. It is one of my favourite front pages from thirteen years of public life. 'Howard: My sums wrong.' I nailed him and that destroyed his 1987 election. Now, Howard beat me for the prime ministership in 1996 but I beat him in 1987.

KOB: And I imagine he has a favourite poster from the 1996 election.

PJK: He'd have one, but I made him wait for the prime ministership for nine years. I dogged him.

KOB: So Labor won its third election in a row, and Hawke addressed the Labor caucus after the win and thanked everyone for their contribution. Is it true, as he has since written in his book, that you sulked because he didn't credit the particular parts you played in the victory? In other words, he didn't single you out for praise?

PJK: I didn't sulk at all, but I had set up the May Statement and the savings believing they would be popular, a massive set of tax and fiscal changes and secured the support of the markets while convincing Bob to have the July election. I then blew Howard's tax package to pieces. What more had I to do? Bob stood up in the caucus and thanked every minister except me, and Kim Beazley, who was a great pal of Bob's, who shared the office next to me in the old Parliament House, came in and he said, 'Mate, that was the meanest thing I've ever seen Bob do.'

KOB: But given what had gone between the two of you before, and given the job ahead, wouldn't the greater wisdom have been for you to roll with it, even if you took offence?

PJK: I did roll with it but I'd given Bob his third win and everyone in caucus knew it.

KOB: You're essentially saying you gave him that victory, but does that mean he brought nothing to that election campaign? Surely his base popularity always delivered a block of votes to Labor as a starting point, certainly in those days?

PJK: Yes, he had to lead the campaign, but the popularity this time came not from Bob's reservoir of goodwill but off the back of the government program and the massive savings package. Without this Bob would never have otherwise considered going into that election at that time.

KOB: What Hawke does say in his autobiography is that the 1987 election marked the watershed in your relationship, that in your mind, 'the time had come for Labor's most successful leader ever to begin clearing the way for his successor, and the sooner the better.'

PJK: I didn't necessarily want Bob to hand the leadership over to me at that point and what's more, I wasn't insisting upon it. But I wanted him to acknowledge that part of our arrangement of two leaders in the one party, was that at some point, in an organised way, he would hand the leadership over to me. And I wanted him to acknowledge that in some way, which he did a year later with the Kirribilli Agreement following the 1988 Budget.

KOB: But Hawke said you had a sense of urgency about succession at that time—this is mid-1987—because you believed Labor's time was running out. There was truth in that, wasn't there?

PJK: Not then about the succession. But there was some truth that this could have been our third and last Parliament, that we'd never won four before, and that winning the fourth in a row was going to be difficult in 1990. At least I wanted Bob to acknowledge that and have a real conversation about it. Bob remained a popular figure but nevertheless our primary vote dropped from 1983 onwards and was down to 39 per cent by 1990.

Even the Liberal Party put the 1987 result down to me. The reason the Liberals are always so snaky about me is that they put 1987, 1990 and 1993 down to my account. They believe they should have won those elections, which was why they were so vicious to me after 1996—they thought I'd done them more harm than anybody else on our side. And they were right.

I took that as a high compliment by the way, but doing the Liberal Party harm was the business I was in. That was what made me tick.

KOB: Hawke said that your focus on becoming leader from then on distorted your analysis of the historical record, and this is what he said in his book: 'Before long, the version according to Paul was that single-handedly he had floated the dollar, deregulated the financial sector, run the Expenditure Review Committee, powered the Government and won the elections. He was the prime mover and in all but name, the Prime Minister.' Is that all that far from what you did come to believe?

PJK: In a very large measure much of that was true but I never at any stage set out to diminish Bob's popularity nor his contribution to winning four elections in a row. But it's clear from any reading of the public record who was driving the government from the end of 1984, clear as day.

KOB: And these things were playing on you?

PJK: Kerry, if you're doing ten weeks a year in an ERC meeting and you're sitting there with a sunshade and a pair of sunglasses to soften the reflected light from the white paper as your health's deteriorating, yes, they start playing on you, believe me. You sit there for eight and ten hours a day, day in and day out, reading through endless stacks of submissions, and after a while it starts to really affect you. You go balmy. In fact we had a formal discussion about changing the colour of the cabinet paper from white to green so we wouldn't get the harsh reflections off it from the fluorescent downlights.

Combine that with the cigar smoke and you can just imagine what it was like. Bob was a massive smoker through a lot of that time. And Peter Walsh and Kim Beazley used to join him. You could feel yourself being worn down, and that happened to me. I was happy to do it for the public and for finding policy solutions and for our victories over the Liberal Party but by that stage the idea that it was all Bob was a fantasy that only Bob would entertain.

By the same token, the idea that I would have sulked over Bob's failure to acknowledge my efforts in the 1987 campaign to caucus is a nonsense. I had a whole new reform agenda I wanted to introduce and basically I got on with it immediately.

INDUSTRY: A NEW WORLD FOR SURE

Australia's first two Prime Ministers, Edmund Barton and Alfred
Deakin, were protectionists. The fourth, George Reid, was a free trader.
Sandwiched between them was a Labor Government whose members
were split between protection and free trade. Changing governments
was like changing socks in the first decade of Federation, but few issues
aroused passions more than the debate on tariffs. In those days, the
word carried two meanings: protecting fledgling industries in a new
nation and a developing economy, but also by implication protecting
a white Anglo culture in an alien Asian world.

For most of the twentieth century, the protectionists prevailed,
and by the time Gough Whitlam came to power, the walls sheltering
Australia's manufacturers and farmers had grown very high indeed,
at least as high as anywhere else in the industrialised world. Farmers
who might otherwise have resented the higher internal cost structure
that inevitably followed protectionism had long since been bought off
with their own forms of protection, thanks to the Country Party.

You can argue until the cows come home over how strong or
durable an industrial base Australia would have been able to build
without heavy protection and the foreign investment it attracted,

but the bottom line was that by the early 1970s there were many complacent and inefficient factory owners with obsolete machinery and more than a few well-fed trade union officials for whom the tariff wall worked just fine. A powerful combine of bosses and workers had taken shape to fight any government that dared to try to tamper with the system.

At the same time the import of cheap clothes and other products from the huge pool of cheap labour in Asia was set to explode. Although the bad old days of the White Australia policy were fading, Chinese or Filipino factory workers in so-called 'Free Trade Zones' threatening Australian jobs was an emotive issue.

Whitlam arrived in the job a free trade man. He argued that tariffs had failed to secure employment in protected industries. He said the most heavily protected industries were the least efficient and therefore the least able to adapt to a new industrial world, and that most protected industries were constrained by a small domestic base and not export-oriented.

As an early priority, the Whitlam Government hand-picked a committee to review tariffs and then in July 1973, Whitlam himself announced a 25 per cent tariff cut across all industries. He later wrote:

> I took a cautious attitude to protection because it seemed to me that companies, very often foreign companies, were setting up industries in Australia in the confidence that, no matter how uneconomic the industry turned out to be, governments would always ensure sufficient protection to keep the industries afloat.
>
> Secondly I saw the burden which protection for some industries imposed on other industries which did not receive or need protection. Industries which would never be able to provide products for Australian consumers as cheaply as they could get the products from overseas were compelling other industries to charge unnecessarily high prices to their Australian customers

and to charge prices which put their products beyond the reach of export markets.

Whitlam's logic might have been right, and his announcement without warning might have headed off stiff resistance from trade unions and employers in the affected industries, but his crystal ball hadn't identified the global oil price shocks of 1973 and 1974 whose recessionary impact was yet to be felt. Nor was his 'cautious attitude' cautious enough to anticipate the impact on employment of such a big cut across the board in the manufacturing states.

Lionel Bowen, who became Manufacturing Industry Minister in 1974, inherited the unenviable job of trying to placate angry retrenched workers at factory gates in Victoria and Tasmania with offers of financial support and retraining. The irony of Bowen's position wasn't lost on him—he was an ardent protectionist.

Notwithstanding the mixed outcome from Whitlam's assault on tariffs in 1973, there was a strong nucleus of powerful senior ministers in the Hawke Cabinet who were convinced of the need to pick up where Whitlam had left off, and Paul Keating was chief among them.

But the writing was on the wall very soon after Labor came to power in 1983, partly due to the recession which was just starting to taper off as Bob Hawke took office, but also because of fundamental inefficiencies. Two of Australia's biggest manufacturing industries, cars and steel, were in crisis.

BHP Steel had just incurred its first losses in 60 years, and responded with shutdowns and sackings. In October 1982, a horde of angry steelworkers from Australia's three steel cities—Newcastle, Port Kembla and Whyalla—marched on Parliament House and broke down the doors. There was talk inside BHP of shedding its steel arm altogether and focusing entirely on minerals, oil and gas.

In the heat of the 1983 election campaign Hawke had promised that he would produce a long-term plan within a hundred days of his government to save the industry. It was a tall order because the industry had a poor record of productivity, an abysmal industrial relations record and obsolete technology, and was increasingly vulnerable to cheaper and higher quality steel from Korea.

But if BHP, which had an effective monopoly on domestic steel production, thought it could order up substantial protection without promising a complete overhaul of its operations, it was to be disappointed, as were trade union officials if they were expecting to give nothing from their side.

Hawke was lucky to have John Button as his Industry Minister. Button was an affable but very bright and shrewd industrial lawyer from Melbourne. The veteran journalist Alan Ramsey, who covered eight prime ministerial reigns, once described Button as the best Prime Minister Australia never had.

After countless hours of negotiation dealing in equal measure with anger, arrogance, suspicion and entrenched attitudes, Button eventually came up with a five-year plan that provided generous assistance to the industry but with a range of strings attached, including a promise of significant investment in new technology from BHP, workforce reductions through voluntary retirement, industrial dispute settlements adhered to, and a genuine drive for greater productivity.

The car industry was an even bigger challenge. In protection terms it had become Australia's sacred cow. The Holden leather-and-saddle business had begun in Melbourne in 1856, become a carriage builder in 1885 and begun trimming motor vehicles in 1910. By 1924 it was making more than 20,000 car bodies a year, half of them for General Motors, which bought them out at the height of the Great Depression in 1931. By the time the humble Holden first rolled off the assembly line in late 1948 as Australia's first home-grown car, the company had survived two world wars and a Depression. The Holden sold for £733, two years' salary for a worker on average income.

By 1983 the heavily protected industry had now grown to five manufacturers producing thirteen car models from plants spread across five states, which Button later described in his memoir as 'a monument to the stupid side of Australian federalism'. In terms of quality, the words 'lemon' and 'car' became synonymous in the vernacular for various models. Yet imported cars were restricted to 20 per cent of the market, with a tariff protection around 120 per cent, which gave the local industry a huge leg up.

There were too many unions covering the industry, often with their own distracting ideological and factional disputes, and a fragmented car component sector that was also often in dispute with the car-makers. Ironically, in the context of Button's problems with the steel industry, local car manufacturers had to import steel for their body panels because the quality of BHP's steel was too poor for their needs.

Within three months of the Hawke Government taking office, GMH sacked 3000 workers and signalled its intention to retrench another 3500, which was indicative of an industry-wide problem.

In his memoir Button told a very funny story which was as good an insight as any to where the industry was at in 1983:

In Melbourne a young GMH executive came to see me. In the course of our discussions I said, 'I don't know why you keep on manufacturing the Camira. I don't think it's a very good car. It doesn't sell well. What are you going to do about it?'

He thought for a moment. 'Well,' he replied, 'we are going to have a new advertising campaign for the Camira.' I expressed some surprise, which he didn't fully seem to understand. Then he left.

A few minutes later there was a knock on my door. 'Come in,' I said.

My GMH visitor put his head round the door. 'Sorry to interrupt,' he said. 'I just wanted to say Minister, that you're right. The Camira is a shithouse motor car. I know, my wife's got one.' Then he closed the door and left.

A year later Button produced a seven-year plan for the car industry that squeezed protection, phased out quota tariffs and would inevitably lead to a reduction in manufacturers from five to three within a decade, and halve the number of factories. Car models would also be slashed from thirteen to six, encouraging bigger and more efficient production runs of the remaining models. The components industry was also rationalised.

Button later remembered the fiery left-wing metal workers' union heavyweight Laurie Carmichael coming up to him in Kings Hall in the old Parliament House, briefcase in hand, his eyes darting left and right, his long overcoat trailing behind him like a cloak, looking like a courier from the court of Medici. He hissed at Button with a fierce stare, 'You bastard, you bastard. But I'll say this for you. Someone had to bite the bullet, and you've done it.'

The head of Nissan Motors in Japan reminded Button of a samurai in a Japanese film. 'I thought, if this man had a sword, he would run me through with it.'

The steel and car plans were both broadly hailed as a significant step away from easy assumptions that struggling manufacturers had an automatic entitlement to suck on the public teat without a substantial quid pro quo for taxpayers as well as consumers and the workforce.

As a postscript, Nissan closed its Australian manufacturing operations in 1992. Ford is slated to shut down its Australian operations in 2016, and Toyota and GMH in 2017. BHP shut its iconic Newcastle steelworks in 1999 and said goodbye to its steel business altogether in 2002.

But these were just two of the heavily protected, inefficient industries that ringed the capital cities, particularly Sydney and Melbourne.

By mid-1987, with the steel and car plans firmly in place, on the Monday after the election, I interviewed Paul Keating for *Four Corners* on Labor's third-term agenda. A full-frontal assault on the whole protection culture of Australian manufacturing was squarely at the centre of his plans. With the big-ticket macro items like financial deregulation and tax reform behind him, he nominated microeconomic reform as his priority, starting with tariffs. Lurking unacknowledged in the background was the privatisation of the government-owned domestic airline TAA (with Qantas a logical next step) and the people's bank, the Commonwealth.

KOB: Why were tariff reforms so important to you in 1987?

PJK: The whole internationalisation of Australia would have stopped stone dead if we'd achieved flexible financial markets but still had rigid product markets. For me there were three big reform areas that went hand in hand: we had to open up the financial, the product and the labour markets. This was the big opening of the product markets.

KOB: John Button was Industry Minister, and he was definitely in the tariff-cutting cart, but immediately after the election you sought to take the Industries Assistance Commission from his portfolio and make it part of Treasury. What was that about?

PJK: It wasn't just tariffs I was concerned about, it was the whole structure of industry assistance and the areas of productivity left languishing in the Australian economy. I felt that the Industry Department, as the public-sector partner of industry, shouldn't also be responsible for the Industries Assistance Commission, which had a role to investigate inefficiencies in industry and promote productivity. Treasury, on the other hand, was completely independent of industry and was focused on the need for productivity.

I had a very good relationship with John. There wasn't much he and I didn't talk about and most times on very friendly terms. For a long time I'd said to John, you can't be poacher and gamekeeper at the same time, not when we've still got the tariff mountain to deal with. Apart from Button as Industry Minister, other key ministers like John Dawkins, Peter Walsh, Bill Hayden, Gareth Evans and others were in broad support, and Bob Hawke himself was on board.

The key point is this. I did an interview with Michael Stuchbury in the *Financial Review* on 29 May 1987, just weeks before the election. Stuchbury wrote:

Efficiency measures are priorities for Paul Keating. Keating has set his sights for a third-term Labor government on micro-economic efficiency issues.

In an interview yesterday Mr Keating said the Government had been so overwhelmed by the immediacy of its problems in 1983 repairing the fractured balance between wages and profits, dealing with competitiveness, the terms of trade collapse, rapid adjustments to fiscal and wages policies, that some of the delicate issues in micro policy have been left to be dealt with at another time.

'That's our story. We have intellectually chosen the route of internationalisation. If you're going to internationalise it must be about being efficient in world terms and that's our only place in the future.'

In other words I was letting him and his readership know that there was some chance of me getting the Industries Assistance Commission after the election. As it turned out Hawke agreed to take the IAC away from Button and his Industry Department and to give it to me.

KOB: Did Button try very hard to fight that?

PJK: He did, but I think he knew it was a losing battle.

KOB: Before your general assault on tariffs, there were the various industry plans that John Button had introduced in the first two terms—the steel and car plans in particular. Would you describe them as curtain-raisers to the main game?

PJK: When I became Treasurer, the level of protection for the Australian motor vehicle industry was an effective rate of more than 80 per cent. It was so outrageously high that Button, notwithstanding the car plan, was trying to bring it down from outrageously high to only moderately high.

It wasn't just about making cuts in tariffs from industry to industry. It was all about the quality and scale of it and what I wanted was a tops-down cut, not an across-the-board cut. With an across-the-board cut, say you cut everything by 20 per cent. That would mean that if an industry enjoyed an 80 per cent tariff, it would only be cut to 60 per cent.

What I wanted was all tariffs over 15 per cent to come down to 15 and everything between 15 and 10 to come to 10. So it was a huge qualitative difference, which meant that no matter how high a tariff was, it would come down to 15 per cent, and everything else would come down to 10. It was called a tops-down change and it took me a long time to get John Button into that, and Bob didn't want to knock him over. This is in 1987 and Bob is still in the warp. He didn't want blues or arguments.

I said, 'Bob, if we do it John's way we're still going to be left with high tariffs even if we have a 25 per cent tariff cut.'

The great bulk of tariffs were really pitched at about 20 and 25 per cent. What I was proposing was a far bigger change than a flat 25 per cent cut across the board.

KOB: What was the IAC's role in all that?

PJK: Its role was to point out what the structural impacts would be, and then our role was to put adjustment packages in place to cushion the process. A lot of my negotiations with Button were really about the adjustment packages.

The IAC facilitated the shift by Treasury and the Treasurer away from macro policy—from fiscal and monetary policy—to microeconomic policy, the ability to review any particular sector of the economy.

KOB: So essentially you had a broad vision of where you wanted to end up, but putting the building blocks of that vision in place was a gradual process through the late 1980s and into the 1990s once you took over responsibility for the IAC.

PJK: For the first time ever, the principal economic department of state, the Treasury, had responsibility for industry assistance and industry review.

KOB: How conscious were you of what had happened under Whitlam, when he cut tariffs by 25 per cent in one hit in 1973 and by 1974 all those factories were closing?

PJK: It was a different economy by 1987. We now had a floating exchange rate and we'd had wage restraint. Our competitiveness had been restored. Movements in the Australian dollar were greater than the actual impact of the tariffs cuts in some cases. In any event the whole internationalisation of Australia would have stopped stone dead if we'd had flexible financial markets but rigid product markets. We had to open Australia up to competition because the landscape was littered with a potpourri of protection from tax preference to tariffs and quotas to bounty preferences. We had to reallocate what were scarce national resources.

Essentially the deal John and I came to in the end was that he would go for the tops-down formula on the basis that I funded significant adjustment packages, and I negotiated those packages with Bill Kelty in the ACTU.

KOB: How crucial was your relationship with the unions through the Accord and your friendship with Bill Kelty in terms of getting union cooperation and support for the tariff cuts?

PJK: It was always a great pressure for Bill, but he knew they had to change. The days of highly protected manufacturing industries were over and for Bill it was about getting the right adjustment packages for his various sectors.

KOB: Could you have got that agenda through without the Accord relationship you'd forged in the early years?

PJK: The tariff cuts had to come, Kerry. You can't have an open economy and a set of industries which are uncompetitive. I wouldn't do any of this stuff without talking to Bill, but you asked me the question would the tariffs have remained because of ACTU opposition, and the answer is, no they wouldn't have remained. The tariffs would have gone. Now, it might have been more bloody, more skin off the nose on the way through, but they would have gone because they had to go.

After the relationship between Bob Hawke and me, the next most important relationship over the lifetime of those governments was my relationship with Bill Kelty. I trusted him. He trusted me. His judgement was first rate, and he had a first-class economic mind. He knew what he could sell to his constituency and what he couldn't. I had a reasonable idea of what he could sell and what he couldn't. When he used to say to me he couldn't, I knew he couldn't. I knew he wasn't negotiating. Bill was never into phoney negotiations, never. He was never into that sort of stuff.

KOB: Looking at the state of manufacturing today, the rust belts around the major cities, industries like cars and steel in a world of trouble, so many skills lost, jobs exported to Asia. Are you still sure it was the right thing to do it the way you did it?

PJK: Absolutely. It advanced us donkeys' years. When I became Treasurer the average rate of protection on a motor car was about 80 per cent. Do you know how poor the quality of Australian cars was? Ordinary working men and women were being asked to pay twice the price to buy a car of very moderate quality, and that was also true of shoes, shirts, underwear, clothing, textiles and footwear.

KOB: But many of those factory workers are now staring back at jobs that were wiped out forever. Skilled, semi-skilled, unskilled alike—gone forever.

PJK: Yes, gone. And do you know what they found? A better job a week later, in a growing economy with big employment growth. We got them off the factory floor. The aim was not to leave them doing repetitive jobs on a factory floor but to get them off the factory floor doing better professional jobs out in the big service economy we were becoming. All these people got picked up.

KOB: You make it sound so simple. A week later they had another job. Do you really think that's how it always worked out?

PJK: The labour market in Australia had grown by 25 per cent. We'd created 1.7 million jobs, and with adjustment packages to help their transition those people found better jobs.

KOB: A lot of those jobs were in the service sector.

PJK: Where would you want to be? Line up at seven-thirty in a blue-collar job on a cold factory floor or work in the service sector, and people said 'Thank you, I'll take the service sector'. But again they didn't lose their job overnight. It took a while. The tariff cuts were made between 1988 and 1991 and then we brought in the second round in the 1991 to 2000 package. So there were thirteen years of change—gradual enough, predictable enough, funded with assistance packages and jobs to take people up as they left. It was absolutely the right thing to do.

KOB: Did you ever meet any of these people on the old assembly lines?

PJK: Of course I did. I remember talking to one woman at Gloweave and she had glasses like the bottom of Coca-Cola bottles. I said, 'How are you, love?' and she said 'Oh, I've been here thirty years Mr Keating. My eyes are gone and of course sniffing up the lint off the cotton—every time the needle goes up and down there's a little bit of fine lint released—and it's ended up in my chest, so I've got real chest problems and real eyesight problems.'

This is what slave labour was all about under tariffs and quotas.

KOB: But what about the army of long-term unemployed that emerged during your prime ministership? Mostly older men in their forties and fifties who'd lost their attraction in the eyes of employers? I'm not arguing against the tariff reforms, but there were some workers who inevitably paid a heavy price, weren't there?

PJK: I don't doubt that's true, but what is also true is that the employment growth in the economy picked up most people who were displaced through the tariff cuts. It may not have taken them all up into permanent or full-time employment, but certainly the great bulk of them had either permanent or casual employment. For many people the part-time employment would not have been the panacea they'd have expected upon losing jobs they'd grown up with. But in an economy which had to go through a transition of the kind Australia simply had to go through, what mattered was to try to retrain as many as possible and to set up new economic opportunities for the businesses which otherwise would have closed.

You might remember as Prime Minister I also set up the Working Nation policy, which was about case-managing up to 25 people individually under one case manager for a job subsidy, which gave people work for six months. This made very rapid changes to long-term unemployment.

I don't doubt that a body of the workforce suffered, particularly in Victoria, from the structural changes after the tariff cuts but those cuts were also very gradual. We announced them in 1988, and again in 1991, so that most of these major tariffs were reduced to 10 per cent or under by 2001. It basically happened over thirteen years and often the exchange rate fluctuations had a bigger impact than the tariff cuts themselves. The tariff cuts each year were modest.

I don't think there was any easy way to do it, other than a policy which took effectively a decade and a half to implement—where business knew what the likely level of protection was going to be, and where people in jobs knew that the job was not likely to be there into the future and that they should start looking somewhere else.

But in a peppy economy which just had more and more growth, and more and more jobs, that was the moment, and really the only moment you could implement a policy like this. Because you had some reasonable expectation that the great bulk of them would either get a new permanent full-time job or at least a part-time one.

KOB: Privatisation also emerged after the 1987 election as part of the government's agenda, but it seemed that Bob Hawke was the prime mover there initially. There were headlines like 'Hawke bays for blood in the privatisation stakes' and 'Hawke puts asset sales on the ALP agenda'.

PJK: The privatisations that mattered were the sale of the Commonwealth Bank, which occurred in the latter part of 1990, and the sale of Qantas during the Keating Government.

KOB: Where were you on Labor's privatisation agenda? What did you want to achieve on privatisation?

PJK: The point was, having moved the macroeconomy and got to the point where we were starting to produce budget surpluses and then the first round of tariff cuts, it was the microeconomy where we had this stultifying resistance to economic change. There were parts of the microeconomy like tariffs and the tax system where we could make policy changes, and there were the enterprises we owned which should otherwise have been commercial entities, not government institutions.

Most of the instrumentalities were owned by the states, but we owned a couple of the big ones. One was the Commonwealth Bank, which was poorly capitalised. Its only capital injection ever came from me in about 1985 or 1986. It couldn't be a gutsy competitor to the big commercial banks because it simply didn't have the capital, and it had outlived the time it should have remained in the government's ownership.

That was a natural thing to do. It had the biggest deposit base in the country but it didn't have a deposit base in Victoria and yet it gained that when I bought the State Bank of Victoria and folded it into the CBA.

KOB: You might regard the argument against having sold the Commonwealth as a sentimental argument, but many people are angry at what they perceive as a lack of real competition among four dominant commercial banks including the Commonwealth, and say things might have been different; that if only you hadn't sold the Commonwealth it could have acted as a foil to the others.

PJK: But it just didn't have the capacity to act in that way. Basically it was a post office bank with the deposits of pensioners, and it had the cast of mind of a post office bank.

KOB: Are you saying it would have taken a massive injection of capital by the government for the Commonwealth to build and function as a genuine competitor against the other banks?

PJK: In the end you had to develop a private board to, in turn, create a whole new and private ethos in the bank for it to be competitive. The proof of the pudding is in the eating. We floated it at $5.60 a share and it has been higher than $90 a share. In economic value it's now in the top twenty banks in the world and the premier bank in Australia. Its service to the country and to Australian society is now far greater than anything it could have done or did do as a government-owned bank.

KOB: Notwithstanding the sentiment the public had for it as a government-owned bank?

PJK: The sentiment is just misplaced and, at its core, ill-informed. If the Commonwealth Bank didn't have the economic value to the economy that it does today its shares would not be $90. That's a reflection of real economic value and public utility. It's the utility that matters, not who owns the stock.

KOB: Are you saying that if it was still in public hands today governments would never have been able to provide the capital to allow it to grow as big as it has, or able to act as a genuinely competitive but more socially oriented pace-setter for the rest of the banking industry?

PJK: It would have looked like a large version of the Bank of Queensland. It would never have been a go-to commercial bank, it wouldn't have had the big housing book it has today with the loans it has provided to people to buy their homes, it just wouldn't have been able to make the contribution to the nation's economy that it now does as a sophisticated commercial bank with everything from commercial loans through foreign exchange to stockbroking to personal finance.

Because it is now unshackled from the capital constraints of a government and its culture has changed, it has done a service to the economy it could never otherwise have done.

I appointed a private board after the first tranche of privatisation. I asked Tim Besley to become Chairman and David Murray to become Chief Executive and, after that, John Ralph became Chairman, so the whole culture of the bank changed. It was capitalised properly on the market and after it got momentum it never looked back.

KOB: How tough a challenge was it to sell privatisation to caucus and the broader Labor movement? Of all your reforms this was the one that opponents could link emotionally to Thatcherite-type ideology. How did you deal with that?

PJK: The Commonwealth Bank was the hardest to get through caucus, but in the end what allowed it to happen was that the State Bank of Victoria was failing, and it had the biggest deposit base in Victoria. I don't know whether you recall the Pyramid and Geelong Permanent Building Society and the enormous cost to the city of Geelong and to taxpayers when it failed in 1990 with debts of $2 billion. Imagine then the State Bank of Victoria, a bank the equivalent of the former State Bank of NSW.

Imagine if the biggest deposit base in the state had been allowed to fail. So, to rescue it as it began to topple, I had the Commonwealth Bank bid for it, and support from the Victorian Premier Joan Kirner, who was also a leader of the Left in that state. I went to the caucus and said, 'If you allow me to sell a quarter of the Commonwealth Bank I will fund what would otherwise be the collapse of the State Bank and the decimation of the Victorian economy.'

I also said that as we got the bank's value up and it improved as an attractive asset we'd sell the next quarter. So we wouldn't be just giving it away. Of course the second quarter then became much more valuable than the first quarter and so on.

KOB: Why didn't you sell Telstra, or Telecom, as it was then? Was the Howard Government right to sell Telstra?

PJK: It was not right to sell Telstra the way it did—with the backbone. Howard and Fahey should have taken the backbone out of it, the local loop as it was called, and let it stand alone as a public service provider where BT or AT&T or Optus or anyone else could access the network.

The Rudd Government had to develop the National Broadband Network because the old backbone was sold into the market by Howard along with the rest of Telstra.

If the backbone had been retained in public ownership Telstra would have become a business that was about running brands and marketing, so it would have transitioned from an engineering business to a brand and marketing business. So Telstra's brand and marketing would have been attached to that backbone in the same way as Optus, say, would have been similarly attached.

It turned out John Howard as Prime Minister and John Fahey as Finance Minister did the worst possible thing in Australian telecommunications. It was simply the bare transfer of a monopoly from government to private ownership, which included the network exchange and loop backbone. When the investment banks wanted the backbone separated, believing in public policy terms it should have been separated, Fahey rejected that advice.

That rejection meant that we had no real competition in telecommunications for nearly two decades, and we are only getting that now with the NBN.

KOB: Going back to when you were Treasurer, what was it in your mind that said it made sense to sell the Commonwealth, to sell Qantas, but not to sell Telstra?

PJK: I believed Telstra should stay in public hands until we had decided on the terms of structural separation. I would have kept the backbone company in separate public ownership as NBN is today, and the rest of Telstra's business would have become a private business. All telcos would have been using a public switch, one that would have remained within a Commonwealth Government structure.

OF BUDGETS AND BACON

Going into their third term after the 1987 election, Bob Hawke and Paul Keating had navigated their way through just four of what was to become thirteen years of Labor rule. But even allowing for the natural self-confidence in both men, they were not to know how many years they had ahead of them. Labor had actually gained seats at the election but its national vote had gone down, and it was already playing on Keating's mind that Labor federally had never won four elections in a row, that it had been a gruelling journey of hard-won reforms and economic and political ups and downs to get this far, and that the road ahead looked equally tough.

It proved to be much tougher.

Keating had by now already privately expressed the concern that Labor's best years would be behind it by the time he could reasonably expect to take the reins from Hawke, and he couldn't abide the thought that he would continue expending a great deal of blood, sweat and tears on the reform process, only to see his time as Prime Minister cut short. Worse still in his eyes was the thought of a future Liberal Government reaping the economic and political benefits of Labor's efforts—efforts that he considered were largely driven by him.

Leadership transitions in politics are rarely handled smoothly. The headiness of the power and privilege that come with prime ministership is deeply seductive. Bob Menzies is the most recent Prime Minister to retire on his own terms. That was just shy of 50 years ago.

There was a sense that Hawke had always seen the job as his destiny. He was well on the way to becoming Labor's longest-serving Prime Minister, clearly enjoying the adulation he received whenever he ventured into the electorate, clearly believing he was the best person to lead his party, and was never going to find it easy just to walk away, no matter how many elections he won.

By now it was clear that Keating was Hawke's heir apparent. The two personalities being the kind of natural headline material they were, the leadership issue was never out of the media spotlight for long. For Hawke it must have felt at times like a slow drip, and even if, as Keating maintains, he had no hand in stringing the press gallery along, the stories were going to be written anyway.

But the headlines cut both ways.

One month Keating was profiled as the Prime Minister-in-waiting, and the next, his aspirations were fading. One month Hawke would be said to be preparing the way for succession, the next he would be reported as digging in for the long haul. One month Hawke would be hailing Keating his successor; the next, he'd be throwing in names like Kim Beazley and Mick Young. Sometimes these stories were well sourced and sometimes not, but few were helpful either to Hawke or to Keating, or more particularly to their Cabinet and caucus colleagues.

There was a period soon after the 1987 election when the tide of sentiment swung against Hawke within the parliamentary party. His move post-election to reshape the ministry into a series of super-ministries was seen as designed to increase his influence in the bureaucracy and move closer to a US-style presidential system. That meant some ministers' and departmental heads' power declining.

At the same time Hawke was pushing aggressively to reclaim his share of the economic reform mantle, pinning his name to a privatisation agenda that didn't immediately go down too well with the troops. Even some of his close supporters began to actively consider a succession plan before the next election. So up bobbed the leadership stories again, such as the Paul Kelly feature on Keating in the *Weekend Australian Magazine*, 'Our Prime Minister in Waiting'.

Such was political life for Labor after 1987 until Keating finally took over more than four years later; whenever he was seen to do well, leadership speculation was never far away.

The 1987 Budget was a classic case in point. Because the election was in mid-July, the Budget was delivered in September rather than August. There were two particularly notable things about it: one, it delivered a deficit of just $27 million, in effect a balanced budget, the best budget outcome in seventeen years. Two, rather than the traditional post-election budget designed to get all the bad political hits out of the road as far away from the next election as possible, this one read more as if there was an election around the corner.

'Keating's Brilliant Budget' was the bold tabloid headline in Sydney's *Daily Mirror* (since merged with the *Daily Telegraph*). The Melbourne *Sun* blazed away with 'Budget Bonanza', and in the *Financial Review*, 'Bulls roar, rates fall as markets cheer Budget'. The Melbourne *Herald* (since merged with the *Sun*) had 'Keating—in full command', headlining a story speculating that he might now be poised to take over the reins from Hawke.

Other stories recorded an immediate voluntary cut in the housing interest rate by the big commercial banks from 15.25 per cent to 14.5, with predictions of a further drop to 14 per cent by Christmas.

'INTEREST DOWN—DOLLAR UP' was the *Australian*'s headline.

Keating's budget cuts represented the biggest real decline in spending after inflation for 30 years, down 2.4 per cent in real terms, most of this result reflecting the work already done in the May

Statement. Never one to hide his light under a bushel, Keating told one television interviewer this was a 24-carat budget in a golden age of economic change.

But he still had his critics, including economic journalist and author John Edwards, later his staffer and biographer. Edwards described the budget as too smart by half. He pointed out that the books were all but balanced by counting a billion dollars worth of asset sales as a savings measure rather than a one-off windfall. Others said it had only been achieved through a tax bonanza delivered by income-tax bracket creep as more and more workers moved into the highest tax bracket.

The *Sydney Morning Herald*'s Ross Gittins wrote that behind the apparent good housekeeping 'lies a complacency borne of fatigue'. He acknowledged it was a budget that kept faith with Hawke's election promise that there'd be no new taxes or no big spending cuts, but identified a risk that the economy might grow too quickly over the coming year as a result.

Indeed the head of steam in the Australian economy that ultimately led to a recession was already building, but it was masked by a world stockmarket collapse just one month after the budget. On Black Monday, 19 October 1987, Wall Street plunged more than 20 per cent, the biggest one-day crash in history. Half a trillion dollars was wiped off share values.

It had a domino effect around the world. By the end of October, 41 per cent had been knocked off the value of the Australian market. Heavily indebted business entrepreneurs who were relying on corporate expansion to drive their share value must have been quaking in their boots. In a single week, the share value of Robert Holmes à Court's companies, Bell Group and Bell Resources, plummeted 60 per cent.

Market analysts later were inclined to write the crash off as merely a correction, albeit a dramatic one, for a speculative boom combined with the introduction of computer trading, which had driven a

44 per cent surge on Wall Street over the first half of 1987. But in the immediate aftermath there were inevitable comparisons with the 1929 crash and the Great Depression that followed.

This was to sway Australia's central bank Governor Bob Johnston against moving interest rates up early in the new year when he might otherwise have done so, as it became clear going into 1988 that the economy was at serious risk of overheating.

Just to accentuate the picture of confusing economic duality, with the shock waves from the plummeting markets still reverberating through the economy, and just six weeks after delivering the budget, Keating and Finance Minister Peter Walsh revised the $27 million deficit forecast to a surplus of $580 million, built off a fresh revenue surge from growth in the economy.

Keating was soon preparing the ground for another May mini-budget and another round of spending cuts, a special premiers' conference to clamp down on state government borrowing, and more wage restraint.

But the wild horses that had taken hold of the Australian economy driven by unlimited credit from the banks in a newly deregulated environment would not be easily tamed. Recovery on the markets didn't take long, and in Australia it very quickly became business as usual.

In his regular economic lectures to the gallery, Keating often talked about pulling levers and keeping various balls in the air as he painted the big reform canvas. The Coalition in those years came to see the press gallery as sitting comfortably in Keating's pocket. Senior members of the gallery at least—people like Laurie Oakes, Alan Ramsey and the like—weren't easily gulled, but there was undoubtedly a beguiling quality to the way Keating wove his words with both confidence and conviction, the way he wanted to bring everyone along for the ride, that resonated within the gallery as it did within Cabinet and caucus. Even the Opposition had a grudging admiration, along with a deep frustration that came from so often being outplayed in Parliament, particularly when they should have had the ascendancy.

But what was looming for Keating and the other economic ministers and the 'official family' on monetary policy—the Reserve Bank and Treasury—over the next two years was a particularly complex juggling act where the levers would be pulled and the engine wouldn't respond.

By 1987–88 Keating and Treasury were talking less and less about the J Curve as their favourite illustration for the message that there had to be a lag between action on the economy and results. But the Twin Deficits Theory, that lower government spending and tight budgets would automatically reduce the current account deficit, was still driving much of the government's strategic thinking through the second half of the 1980s. Unfortunately the reality was not matching the theory.

Despite the good election result in 1987, there was clearly a brittleness in the electorate as evidenced in the by-election for Trade Minister Chris Hurford's seat of Adelaide after he left the Parliament to become Consul-General in New York in February 1988. The seat went to the Liberals with an 8 per cent swing.

The next month the Unsworth Labor Government in New South Wales was swept from office with a massive swing to the Liberal–National Coalition led by Nick Greiner. Partly it reflected an inevitable reaction to a twelve-year incumbency and Neville Wran's retirement, but this was Labor's traditional stronghold state, and the brand was clearly tarnished.

Nonetheless Keating was more concerned with policy than politics when two months later he produced his May mini-budget in 1988, foreshadowing a big surplus.

The May Statement reflected just how tricky the government's balancing act had become between policy and politics, between the ongoing push for growth and jobs and minimising the risk of over-heating, of managing inflation, the dollar and the current account deficit while ramping up the next round of micro-reform. At the same time the Reserve Bank, with strong backing from Keating, was at last acting with some conviction on interest rates in what became a steady and sustained upward movement that was to last for about twenty months.

The 1988 May Statement included the first big round of tariff cuts, while cutting company tax by 20 per cent from 49 to 39 cents in the dollar. It foreshadowed further cuts in spending of 1.5 per cent in real terms for 1988–89, and forecast a surplus of more than $3 billion, with a promise of income tax cuts the following year in yet another trade-off under the Accord to keep wages in check.

P.P. McGuinness in the *Financial Review* described it as 'an impressive affair', but again the *Sydney Morning Herald*'s Ross Gittins saw it as 'lots of shuffling, but not much action', pointing out that bracket creep had underwritten the surplus by $1.5 billion.

Their coverage was dwarfed for impact by a five-page cover story in Kerry Packer's *Bulletin* magazine boldly headed 'The Next Prime Minister', declaring that Keating had started his run for the top job, and citing a new poll to back its claim that Keating was successfully softening his image in preparation for leadership.

The poll put him alongside Hawke and well ahead of Howard for intelligence, said he was much more inclined to keep his promises than either Hawke or Howard, but was less likable than either of the others. Notably, his approval rating as Treasurer had gone up from 33 per cent to 51 per cent in two years. The figures were interesting enough, but the nature of the *Bulletin*'s splash, with Keating's cooperation, was provocative.

Hawke would not have been amused. Shortly afterwards, the story emerged that he had held discussions with senior colleagues on the possibility of moving Keating from the Treasury in a ministerial reshuffle later in the year. If the speculation had been encouraged from the Prime Minister's office, it backfired. On 17 June, the *Sydney Morning Herald* ran a front-page story headed 'Hawke forced to deny doubts on Keating'. But within two days a *Sun-Herald* front page banner set the hares running again: 'HAWKE PICKS NEXT PM. It's not Keating!'

The story said Hawke had been sounding out 'his closest colleagues' on an early retirement and had also discussed it with his wife, Hazel. It claimed he favoured Kim Beazley and wanted to give him a major domestic portfolio.

In August 1988, with the current account still misbehaving, although slightly reduced compared to the previous year, and the economy still surging on the back of a massive asset boom, Keating delivered his 'bringing home the bacon' budget.

His opening words that night made full use of a special occasion. It was the first sitting day in the grand new Parliament House on Capitol Hill, and the historic first day of parliamentary broadcasting for television. Ironically the decision to televise came against the strenuous objections of one P.J. Keating. This was what he had to say:

> Madam Speaker, tonight I can report to the people of Australia that the nation is emerging from its most severe economic crisis in a generation. Unquestionably a dramatically better state of affairs now exists than when I warned in 1986 of the threat of Australia degenerating to the status of a banana republic. The Australian people can be proud that they have responded to economic adversity in a manner which the critics claimed was impossible.

He went on to reveal a forecast that the surplus would hit $5.5 billion, a record surplus up to that point.

In his traditional press conference recorded inside the press gallery lock-up a couple of hours earlier, the theme was similarly sweeping. His opening lines: 'This is the one that brings home the bacon. This is the budget that pulls the whole game together from 1983 onwards.' One of his most trusted advisers at the time, Seumas Dawes, was to reveal in *Labor in Power* that the 1988 Budget was particularly important to Keating because he thought it might be his last budget in politics, 'almost as a last will and testament'.

But the warm inner glow of positive headlines, and whatever sense of goodwill remained in the Hawke–Keating relationship had evaporated within a mere 24 hours. The budget was important politically in rebuilding Labor's stocks towards the next election within the next eighteen months. No seasoned politician would want to squander the goodwill it was generating. But inexplicably to those watching from the outside that's exactly what Hawke did.

In an ABC *7.30 Report* interview with Paul Lyneham, Hawke signalled that his Treasurer was expendable and that there was plenty of talent in the wings to replace him if he decided to go. At a *Financial Review* budget dinner that same night Hawke said he hoped to continue as Prime Minister for years to come. No amount of spin could hide the heavy and provocative message fired directly at his erstwhile friend, and the single biggest driving force within his government. The media had a field day, and the selling process went out the window.

Within the next 24 hours, Hawke was forced into damage control after a private lashing from Graham Richardson and some straight talking from other senior colleagues. So out he trotted for his next television interview—this time with Ray Martin on *A Current Affair*. Suddenly Keating was the best Treasurer in the world, the best ever in Australia, who'd done a magnificent job for the nation.

Nobody was fooled. It descended further into farce after it emerged that in response to a phone call from Richardson, Keating had unloaded all his frustrations, describing Hawke and his actions in the most blistering terms. The conversation came to a sudden end when Keating discovered Richardson was using a car phone—this, in an era when security on car phones was notoriously unreliable. That in turn gave Hawke the excuse to unload on Keating, also by phone, but this time a landline.

What had been the government's key strength for five years was now in danger of becoming its greatest weakness.

On the Monday after the budget, the *Financial Review* reported Labor's Senate Leader, John Button, saying that Hawke should set a timetable for an orderly leadership transition to Keating, possibly before the next election. It also quoted another senior minister that the best that could now be hoped for between Hawke and Keating was 'an orderly relationship without friendship'.

Even acknowledging the major contributions to social and economic policy by other members of the Hawke Cabinet, and Hawke's own remarkable connection to the public at large that had helped Labor's stocks immeasurably, it was Hawke and Keating together who had spearheaded Labor's longest uninterrupted run in office—and, in the process, changed the whole dynamic of Australia's economy.

KOB: I want to come back to the 1987 and 1988 budgets against the background of constraint forced on you by the ongoing trade deficit problems. In the post-1987 Budget you virtually balanced the books with a projected $27 million deficit. When framing that budget and striving to get into surplus, did you start with a set goal to balance the books and then work backwards to find the savings, or was it just your usual hunt for whatever savings you could achieve and then see how close that got you to a balanced budget?

PJK: I started with the goals pretty much as they turned out. This was my point, that the 1986 Budget was just a down payment on the national structural adjustment on the lower terms of trade. Had we even contemplated going to an election in 1987 without a further down payment on the budget which came in the May Statement that year, I don't believe Hawke and I would have got through that election without a currency collapse, particularly as Howard was offering those unfunded tax cuts of his.

If you look at Australia from abroad the government would have been seen to shirk the fiscal challenge while the alternative government was actually offering unfunded tax cuts. What was the point of the budget being back in surplus? So Australia could say there was no call on Australian savings by the government sector. And the markets couldn't find fault with whatever call the private sector made on Australian savings for investment in business growth because theoretically that investment would drive growth in the economy.

That's why I was heading to budget balance as quickly as I could, and after $4 billion of government spending cuts in the 1987 May Statement I had to go through the process again in the September Budget to bring the budget to balance.

KOB: You're clearly proud of the fact that the government won the 1987 election off the back of that tough May Statement, but then the post-election budget in September sounded almost the opposite.

Normally in the first budget of a parliamentary cycle the government takes the opportunity to get its more unpopular measures out of the road so public memories of the medicine have faded by the time the next election comes around. But if you look at the headlines, the 1987 Budget sounded more like a pre-election budget: 'Budget Bonanza', 'Home Rates Slashed', 'Tax Cuts Hint', 'Keating's Brilliant Budget'. You might remember calling it a '24-carat budget in a golden age of economic change'.

PJK: Did I? There's some hyperbole in that. The explanation is simple enough. The bulk of the cuts were done in the May Statement. What I wanted to do was get Australia out of the cold while we had the opportunity. With these big headaches with the terms of trade it could not be apparent then that we would ever see anything like we've seen with the commodity boom post-2000, thanks largely to China.

We were forced to confront the notion that, as a commodity exporter and as an importer of high-technology goods, we'd be running structural current account deficits. The only way we could ask the world to provide international savings and therefore international debt to fund our national lifestyle was if we could say that the Commonwealth budget made no claim on Australian savings.

But to get out of the cold as quickly as we could I had to take the next step to getting the budget into surplus, which involved some further cuts in spending. But it was also helped by rising tax revenue in the context of continuing economic growth. That's why there was a minimum of political pain in the 1987 Budget and positive headlines. Growth and revenue were strong, and the cuts had been made earlier in the May Statement.

KOB: The budget cuts represented the biggest real decline in spending for 30 years, most of which, as you say, had been achieved in the May Statement, but not all the commentary was flattering. Economist John Edwards, for instance, described your efforts as too smart by half. He criticised you for counting one billion dollars of asset sales as a savings measure rather than a one-off windfall—I think you sold the Japanese Embassy real estate for a fat sum—and I can remember the Opposition picking up on that at the time.

PJK: John's commentary improved as he gathered experience. In the end money off the budget is money off the budget regardless of where the cuts or windfalls fall. But let me focus on the 2.4 per cent real reduction in spending—that was a 2.4 per cent *real* reduction in spending below the inflation rate. Budgets have never produced anything like this since. GDP growth was at 2.75 per cent: not remarkable, but not bad, a modest increase in the terms of trade of 2 per cent, yet we achieved a budget deficit of only $27 million, which we were able very soon after to revise to a surplus of $500-odd million.

KOB: Ross Gittins and others wrote that it was at least partly achieved through the tax windfall from a booming economy and bracket creep. Gittins also wrote that: 'Mr Keating runs the risk that the economy will grow more quickly than he expects with consumer spending spilling into imports and limiting the improvement in the current account deficit.' Isn't that exactly what eventually happened, which ultimately led to a recession?

PJK: Ross had good and bad moments with me. He used to like trying to prod us to get a reaction and to get more done. I kind of spoiled these guys. He and others were hard taskmasters. That was why I remarked about the complimentary *Financial Review* front page. That was the only front page I ever had of that kind in all those years. As I've said, you'd put all the balls in the air and do your tricks but the best they would give you was mild applause and ask for the next trick. But nowhere else in the world was there anything like a 2.4 per cent real reduction in national budget outlays being undertaken.

What happens is that you get confidence effects. All of a sudden you've got a government that's actually bringing outlays back to where they were 25 years earlier. You've got a government that's bringing the budget into surplus. You've got a government with a competitive exchange rate. You've got a government with a falling wage share and a rising profit share. Hardly surprising that it lit up an investment boom.

KOB: But at the same time you were supposed to be trying to limit the boom so it didn't get out of hand, which it eventually did.

PJK: Yes, but what was Gittins arguing? That the big cuts of 1987 should have been even larger, or that the surplus should have been even bigger? The $380 million in new expenditure cuts in the budget on top of the $4 billion we'd identified in the May Statement was only a modest sum but in line with Bob's election commitment. But as a commentator Ross had already put the earlier $4 billion in his pocket and then said, 'Now what are you going to do?' I spoiled these fellows—they kept on expecting trick after trick.

KOB: You called it an achievement of historic proportions but within a week it was revealed that Peter Walsh had said in a private briefing in Perth that the budget had been oversold. He was quoted as saying the government lacked the political courage to tackle some 200 welfare programs. How did you react to that?

PJK: In public life you're surrounded by people who are not up to the task of getting and managing power. Peter was a great finance minister but was not up to getting and holding power. We had a big run of positive headlines from that budget. Peter never understood that you needed that kind of political approbation to draw down the power necessary to continue making the big changes, and that if you were trying to run an unfashionable budget that had no public support for a clutch of hair-shirt changes, you came unstuck.

KOB: Walsh was always about the blunt unadulterated truth, wasn't he?

PJK: No, it wasn't an unadulterated truth—or even plain truth. Complaint is not necessarily truth. Without the political skilling to get the things through, it is to no avail. Blunt truth has a place but political skilling is an altogether higher order matter.

So-called truth without political facilitation—well, you may as well whistle dixie.

Can I just say something about senators, particularly senators involved in the financial management of the country? They are, of their essence, a more modest form of political life. They don't work on the big canvas, they generally don't have the political skills, they don't have a well-defined electorate to answer to, they can't sell the material, they can't draw down the power and they can't get the changes done. They don't have the same compulsion or frame of reference as a treasurer in the House of Representatives.

But a treasurer can't do everything. You do need finance ministers and other ministers helping. Some ministers from the Senate are more politically attuned than others, more capable of drawing down political authority from the community and exercising it, but often they don't. As much as Peter Walsh contributed to that gruelling line-by-line budget process over all those years, he was not politically adroit. I still had to set the economic parameters and do the packaging. And when push came to shove, ramrod the budget savings through the ERC (Expenditure Review Committee).

KOB: Paul Kelly wrote the day after the revelations about Walsh's budget criticism that there was a split between the two of you over the pace of change. What defined the split?

PJK: Peter had this obsession with what he thought were 'leftie' policies that underpinned the social wage and social security system and he wanted to hop into a lot of social security programs. Some of what he wanted to cut you could justify, but in terms of the macro changes the country had been through and our response to them, there was no basis for any real complaint on his part. There was no basis for rational objection to what the government had chosen to do, including the programs it had chosen to protect rather than to cut.

Being maudlin about some program he thought touchable because the Left had supported it was really wearying.

KOB: For all his eccentricities did you miss Walsh when he went?

PJK: I did, and I talked him into staying the first time he wanted to resign. He was a great hand, but he got to the point where the negativity and moods became counter-productive. You have to pull caucus colleagues onto the task and sign them up, not confront and alienate them. Peter made a great contribution but the political job of shaping change and then selling it was not one of his strengths.

KOB: In October 1987 you suddenly had to deal with a major global sharemarket crash. How hard was it to read how that was going to affect the Australian economy? Were you getting conflicting advice on its impact or were your various different arms of advice in agreement?

PJK: Important question. In the wake of the crash Bob Johnston attended the Bank for International Settlements, the central bankers' club in Basel in Switzerland. The BIS believed that the crash portended another 1930s-type Depression; that this was the first shock in what was going to be a large slide in equities across the world.

Johnston returned to Australia with a clear message to keep monetary conditions accommodating and I emphasise the word 'accommodating'—softly, softly. He was particularly worried about the big exposure that the Australian commercial banks faced. They had $10 or $12 billion in debt out to Robert Holmes à Court. They had billions out to Murdoch. They had billions more out to Alan Bond and these would have massive effects on their capital base in the event of collapses. So Bob Johnston was keen to look at financial market conditions and policy and he advised me that he should keep monetary conditions more accommodating when otherwise I should have liked interest rates to rise to keep the boom in check.

KOB: What was Treasury saying?

PJK: They would have liked to have increased the rates but probably didn't have the courage to say so. I think they went along with the Johnston view, which was a very informed view. This was the consensus in the BIS, that the stockmarket crash was the first instalment of a 1930s Depression phase.

KOB: But did you argue the toss with him? When he said 'keep a soft approach on interest rates' did you say to him 'I think they should be higher'?

PJK: I did, but I didn't know with certainty what the effects would be either. The markets went down 27 per cent in one hit. It was huge. But when I went to Noosa with the family for a holiday in January and saw cranes everywhere across the skyline, I rang Bob Johnston and said, 'Bob, there's a bear transfer going on up here from stocks to property and we should be rethinking interest rates.'

He said, 'Oh, I wouldn't let cranes from last year influence you too much, Treasurer.'

I said, 'Well, intuitively I'm telling you, Bob, I think the economy hasn't missed a beat and it's jumped over the stockmarket crash and it's basically still off and running. There's so much pent-up demand that I don't think we can leave monetary conditions soft into 1988.'

He said, 'Well, let's wait and see.'

As it turned out, I was right. There was no particular pleasure in being right because it just meant we were storing up problems down the road, but the Reserve Bank did keep monetary conditions soft, with lower interest rates into 1988 against my otherwise firm judgement. By April and May I was telling Bob Johnston and the Board, 'In my opinion we should be putting rates up now because if we don't, we'll just cop a hiding from demand later this year or next.' At this point Treasury was more or less with me.

KOB: At the same time as all this was happening, there was a kind of Roaring Twenties mentality going on in the banks. The country was awash with easy money, free-spending entrepreneurs littered the landscape, developers were running amok, and the banks were lending like crazy.

PJK: That's right. The banks were trying to protect their base against the foreign banks so they were bankrolling second- and third-rate business propositions just so the foreigners didn't get any share of it in the first flush of deregulation.

KOB: And some of the people lining up for money were complete spivs, not to put too fine a point on it.

PJK: Well, there was a lot of spivery at the time.

KOB: But these were your reforms and this goes to the dilemma of significant reform throwing up unintended consequences. Could you reasonably have been expected to foresee that this was going to happen, or does that let you off the hook too easily?

PJK: A whole lot of things came together at once. The real wage overhang had dropped so the profit share had risen, the budget had moved into surplus, confidence had come back to the exchange rate, monetary conditions were more accommodating—all of this turned into a heady mix bringing on a massive boom in investment—investment which the nation had needed for years.

KOB: Except that a significant amount of that investment was not productive. A lot of it was speculative and added little to the economy.

PJK: But a lot of it was productive, and the fact is we'd had low investment to GDP for donkeys' years in Australia and all of a sudden we have our dream investments happening in a big way, but it was just too big.

KOB: Paul Kelly has written that you went through 1988 wanting the best of both worlds. You wanted to tighten monetary policy but you wanted to deny responsibility, misjudging the clout that was needed to halt the boom. In his view you were saying to the Reserve Bank 'I think we should be putting interest rates up' but you didn't want the risk of electoral odium for being the one fronting the public and explaining why. Kelly says Bob Johnston said subsequently that perhaps he should take responsibility for that because he was saying 'softly, softly'.

PJK: I didn't want 'softly, softly'. I wanted to get the impact of an announcement that interest rates were going up substantially. I wanted to put rates up by one percentage point, for a start, and other steps of 1 per cent to tell all the people out there in the marketplace, 'You need to understand that the party has to cool down. The Bank is putting rates up and we're announcing it.' And that's what I was saying to the Reserve. But again, the Bank was new to the business of managing monetary policy under a floating exchange rate.

They had the problem of the 1987 crash and these big open positions with the banks, with entrepreneurs like Bond and Holmes à Court and Murdoch. They were now prepared to tighten but they had this expression in the bank called 'snugging', which meant they could put the actual official interest rate up or down slightly without people noticing, and I used to say, 'But we want them to notice because we want them to change their behaviour. Having a tighter monetary policy without the impact of an announcement just denies us the effect we're after. It means we're going to end up having interest rates higher for longer.' These days the Reserve Bank publishes a statement after each meeting.

KOB: I realise I'm saying this with the great wisdom of hindsight, but did it occur to you then to suggest a system of statements by the Reserve Bank with each interest-rate movement?

PJK: These were the first building blocks of an independent Reserve Bank evolving from the bond-selling age before the float and I had to go with the Governor at the pace he and the board thought the Bank, as an institution, should go. I couldn't run the Bank from Canberra and I didn't try. This was the world post-float. In the end the Reserve Bank had to grow up and we all had to grow with it.

KOB: But even though the Reserve Bank was now more independent of government than in the past, if you felt so strongly that they weren't moving quickly enough in early 1988 to signal their intent to use interest rates quite toughly to take the heat out of a booming economy, why couldn't you have found a politically acceptable way to start your own jawboning process with strong public warnings that interest rates were well and truly in play if the investment splurge continued, that there were big risks ahead for investors and the working community?

PJK: This all gets back to the global stockmarket collapse of October 1987 and the judgement made by the Bank for International Settlements about this. The Australian Reserve Bank was part of the BIS structure and couldn't ignore their advice. No point the Treasurer saying one thing and the Bank not following through.

KOB: With a Reserve Bank now more independent of government, did you feel that you had the right to express the concerns publicly that you were expressing privately, about the need for a tougher interest-rate regime to bring growth back under control? Not to imply any disagreement between you and the Bank, but at least telling the investment and business community what was in store if they didn't start reining in the madness?

PJK: The *Reserve Bank Act* had a clause which said the Board and the Treasurer should endeavour to agree. I knew that a very open-minded and courageous fellow like Bob Johnston would take this cautious view about monetary policy in the face of the growing buoyancy in the economy only if he felt he had to. The thing I had to do was convince him that that judgement was in the end wrong: that there wasn't going to be another big collapse and the economy had just gone over the stockmarket crash like a wheel over a pothole; that we'd seen a big growth in non-residential construction and residential construction; that the cities were booming; that the banks were lending like fury to stop the foreign banks encroaching on their traditional customer base; and that the right thing to do was to change the stance of monetary policy.

I took the view that it was not possible to move them publicly without disrupting altogether the relationship I had established in the early development of an independent central bank. This was five years after the float and the move to genuine independence for the Bank, so you can't at the same time wilfully undermine the notion of independence by being seen to be in open conflict with the Bank, or have the markets interpret that you're trying to instruct them on what to do.

We had to jawbone the Bank privately rather than engage in the risky strategy of trying to publicly jawbone the lenders and the borrowers into understanding that the boom was unsustainable and hope that they'd see sense.

That's why Don Russell from my office would talk each week to the Deputy Governor John Phillips about monetary conditions and policy, with the recurring question, 'How much more buoyancy do you want to see before you are convinced that your concerns over the 1987 crash are no longer valid?'

Just to give you an idea of what the economy was doing at that time, the growth forecast by the Joint Economic Forecasting Group would periodically revise the previous budget's growth forecast, and in January 1988 they revised it to 3 per cent. By April they'd revised it up to 4.25 per cent.

KOB: By May 1988 you'd had another mini-budget, introducing tariff cuts and a 20 per cent cut to corporate tax. Broadly it was supposed to keep the lid on growth again while paying down debt and foreshadowing tax cuts as a payoff for wage restraint, but coming up to the August budget the economy was still running too strongly again, wasn't it?

PJK: It was. The budget went into surplus by $5.5 billion, the first massive surplus of its kind, around 1 per cent of GDP or a little under. An Australian first. So again it was tight government spending. And we were picking up the revenue from growth.

All this produced a very substantial surplus and at the same time we had these big changes in the air after the May Statement, like the cuts in the company rate from 49 to 39 cents in the dollar. Contemporary governments have been flat out cutting 1 per cent in the dollar from the corporate tax rate. In the May Statement of 1988 we cut it by ten percentage points, not 10 per cent, but ten percentage points. It was about a 20 per cent cut in the actual rate. The dollar hit 80 cents. This was really a very, very good period for us.

KOB: But, once again, in both mini-budget and the budget proper, you and your colleagues were back in the parliamentary dungeon of the ERC process, the queues of ministers lining up to argue against cuts in their spending programs, the forensic line-by-line hunt to locate more money. More fatigue again?

PJK: Same atmosphere, again more fatigue. Tightening Australia's fiscal policy, pulling down the structural level of outlays was a killing task that took the better part of the decade to do. That was when Peter Walsh came to see me.

He said, 'I'm resigning. I've had it. I honestly don't know how you go on and you've got a finger in every pie. I've had it. I'm brain dead.'

I said, 'Oh Walshie, don't give up. We can get a bit more mileage out of you.'

He said, 'No, no, not this time. This time I'm going.'

KOB: After that 1988 May Statement, in which you announced the first big tariff cuts since Whitlam fifteen years before, you floated for the first time that labour-market reform was the last great area of change to be tackled. You'd had all the other macro reforms, you had the tariff cuts in play. Can you remember how this clear signal from you that you had yet another big reform idea, which threatened nearly a century-old tradition for the whole labour movement, impacted on Bob Hawke, on Cabinet, on caucus and on the unions?

PJK: That *Financial Review* article also reported on my briefing to caucus immediately after the May Statement, which it described as 'a message of hope and a warning':

> As he dropped the document on the table in front of him, he [Keating] said, 'Well here it is folks, all you people who thought you were going to lose your seats at the next election, this'll save you, this'll get us back into government.
>
> 'A Labor Government has got to have an ongoing reform agenda. If you don't then you'll be like a dead cat in the middle of the road, being run over by a steamroller.
>
> 'By moving to declare labour market flexibility as the next great challenge Mr Keating advanced on to almost the last area of policy ground the federal government has tried to stake out for itself, and into which there may be the trickiest challenge. But whereas on most other issues the government has stolen the Opposition's silver, on this issue voters have a clear choice.'
>
> The May Statement was negotiated bit by bit with the trade union leadership; the tax strategy, the predictive costs, the removal of restrictions on the operations of government businesses; the personal tax cuts etc. Mr Keating's way to reform is the cooperative, consultative way. Howard's way to labour market reform is reducing union power. These are the hostile lines of difference.

You've got to understand that the *Financial Review*, in saying that, understood that Bob Hawke loved the centralised industrial relations system, he loved the Arbitration Commission where he'd built his reputation and credibility, that he would never move to a system of enterprise decentralisation.

Bill Kelty and I at that stage had agreed on award restructuring. This was the first step down the road of labour-market deregulation. It had to come. You've got to remember that with award restructuring there were a huge number of awards governing wages and conditions between employers and employees, and there were many layers within awards as well.

Award restructuring and the rationalisation of unions together represented a big challenge in their own right. That was independent of the need to move away from a centralised wage-fixing system. This was the start of that particular reform process but I had to wait until I became Prime Minister to move away from the centralised process to a system of collective bargaining. Bob simply wouldn't have a bar of it.

KOB: While all this was going on it seemed, at least according to media coverage, that leadership tensions continued to bubble away. It's notable looking back through your newspaper archive how the speculation continued to swirl around through 1987 and the first half of 1988 for no apparent reason. One minute it's being reported that a succession plan is being put in place to smooth your path, the next minute Hawke has strengthened his position. One minute he's nominating you as his successor, the next he's talking about Beazley or Mick Young. A lot of these things seemed to come out of a clear blue sky but the leadership issue was never quite off the boil, was it?

PJK: Yes, because this was all a product of the psychological state Bob was in, which these days he and the Hawke forces wish to deny. But when you talk about all the fluctuating leadership speculation, here's another banner, 'PM's judgement worries the ALP'. This is 14 March 1988: 'Senior members of the Labor Party are seriously concerned about the political judgement of the Prime Minister. The recent upheaval shows alarming signs of turning into a fundamental loss of direction.'

You see, there was no spiritual nourishment of the Cabinet by Bob from 1984 at least until 1990. And there are repeats of these stories in every year—1985, 1986, 1987, 1988, 1989 and 1990.

KOB: It was always a sexy story for the media, and an easy story in a way, but are you saying that fundamentally there was no structured push for the leadership from you or others on your behalf through those years, but that broadly it was just reflecting an underlying restlessness within caucus?

PJK: No, there was no push. Here's another piece by Geoff Kitney in 1988:

> Of greatest concern to some senior Labor Party figures in the government and the party organisation are signs Mr Hawke seems to be unaware and unconcerned about the seriousness of the problems his government is now experiencing.
>
> Hawke's contact with the Labor backbench and particularly caucus members in marginal seats has been almost non-existent since the election. He has not met once since the election with the marginal seat holders, and there has not been a full ministerial meeting to discuss political strategy.
>
> In fact there has not even been any real opportunity for the Cabinet to discuss political strategy, and the Treasurer Mr Keating, the sharpest political operator of all in the Cabinet, has been preoccupied with the demands of his portfolio and the problems in the NSW state Labor Party.

KOB: Almost immediately after the May Statement Kerry Packer's *Bulletin* devoted a huge amount of space to you with a cover headline that read in bold print: 'The Next Prime Minister.' The opening sentence simply said: 'Paul Keating has started his run for the top job.' Can you remember what prompted such a big, flattering spread?

PJK: Well, these things were popping up. In March 1988, for instance, there's a story headed, 'Hayden anoints Keating as future prime minister'. Then there's 'PM's judgement worries the ALP', that's also March. Then a piece from Warwick Costin in the *Sunday Telegraph* on 20 March, 'Labor looking to life after Hawke'. Another one, 'Bob Hawke's imperial delusions' from Paul Kelly in the *Australian*.

There was all this disquiet about Hawke and his leadership, and that was the primary generator of those stories. They did not reflect my ambitions or my restlessness. They reflected Bob. Bob as he had become.

We then come to the 1988 Budget, where Hawke says the day after the Budget that I was expendable; he didn't need me any more after I'd been keeping 90 per cent of the economic balls in the air for five consecutive years.

Unlike having the Parliament in London or Paris, in an isolated place like Canberra where MPs live in the place morning, noon and night, where every bit of corridor gossip is transmitted through the gallery, you cannot have the Prime Minister in a hole for four or five years, and not have it as the currency of discussion.

KOB: But it must have been like Chinese water torture for him, the long, slow drip.

PJK: It was, but he couldn't do anything to get himself out of it. Intellectually he didn't seem able to summon the energy to pull himself out of it. I think he understood I wasn't behind the stories because I think he knew that he was the cause of them himself but he didn't know how to remedy it. There was a kind of resignation about it. Bob was in daily contact with me through much of that time. You get a feeling when you're in that kind of intense daily contact whether another person is after you, is seeking to dislodge you, and Bob knew I wasn't after him.

KOB: Yet this speculation continued.

PJK: But you must remember that a lot of the Centre Left ministers talked regularly and unguardedly to the *National Times*, the *Financial Review* and others, and so often they would put commentary around. Peter Walsh was at it perpetually. Some people might have assumed it was me, but it was not me—definitely not me.

KOB: Shortly after the *Bulletin* splash another story emerged that Hawke had held discussions with senior colleagues on the possibility of moving you from Treasury in a ministerial reshuffle. Do you remember that?

PJK: I do recall that, and I said to Bob, 'There's no way I'm going to Foreign Affairs or somewhere like that. I'm not giving up the key job to go somewhere else.'

KOB: Do you think Hawke was serious?

PJK: He didn't have the courage to force it on me.

KOB: Is it true, as Paul Kelly has written, that you went into the 1988 Budget hoping it would be your last as Treasurer and trying to make it your best, your 'bringing home the bacon' budget?

PJK: That was a possible scenario. You've got to remember that the party had no inclination to change the leadership at that point and Bob had shown no inclination to leave. I was always first and foremost a realist. So I did the May Statement and I did the budget three months later and it nearly killed me doing both but I didn't expect to end up leader of the party as a consequence.

At the same time I was hoping in 1988 Bob might say something firmly to me about his intentions in the longer run, that it wouldn't just drift on year after year. I couldn't keep doing this indefinitely.

It was too debilitating, and I thought we'd reached a point where he might say to me, 'Look I'll go around again for one more election in 1990 and after that I'll take off.'

KOB: If, as Kelly wrote, you saw the 1988 Budget as the centre-piece of your ultimate case for the Lodge, might it have been a different budget if you weren't also seeing it in the context of leadership? The underlying point he was making was that the budget papers revealed a level of economic growth that would strain Australia's external deficit again.

PJK: The fact is, I had no realistic—and could never have had any realistic—expectation that I would become leader of the party after the 1988 Budget. The caucus wanted to keep Bob and me. Even in my own broad faction on the Right, I wouldn't have had a majority of their votes, and there was no way Bob was going to move.

KOB: So you weren't taking soundings, month by month, or even every six months?

PJK: No. There was a lot of press criticism of Bob coming through in 1988, but that had had nothing to do with me. Paul Kelly may have written that I thought the 1988 Budget would have been my last, but I can't see how it could have been my last without Bob's acquiescence. That is, his agreement to leave.

KOB: Can I just clear up any confusion in what you've said about Bob Hawke as Prime Minister through this whole period? On the one hand you contend that he didn't have the zing of his early years, but on the other hand you don't argue that he was still responsible for 27 ministers, putting in long hours and getting across the briefs with oversight of every piece of policy development in each of those ministries, that he carried a significant part of the foreign policy load, the big international relationships, and he was ultimately responsible for making sure that every political brush fire that flared up across every ministry was put out.

PJK: I would confirm that description with not a problem. Of course he was. But rote toil could never amount to inspiration or perspicacity. There was a sense of absence by Bob within the real meaning and purpose of Cabinet leadership.

KOB: You certainly scored some triumphant headlines from Budget night 1988, but Bob Hawke made comments in two forums the day after. One was a television interview with Paul Lyneham on the *7.30 Report* in which he said you weren't indispensable as Treasurer, and that if you chose to leave there were a number of other talented ministers who could do the job well. The other was a post-budget dinner in which he dropped another provocative line that he'd like to be back as Prime Minister for another six such dinners. It's an understatement to say you took exception.

PJK: Of course I took exception. In saying he'd stay six more years, Bob was completely failing to understand the nature of his relationship with me and the government, or to even acknowledge it.

Secondly he knew that I had done a superhuman task of getting that big May Statement and the tariff cuts and the rest of it into place, and lining up for another August Budget. There was no hint of acknowledgement of these things from him, no hint of appreciation. The message I took from that was that the partnership was over. I had done too well and that jealousy in Bob got the better of him.

I'm not sure how he expected me to react, but I told him I wasn't prepared to be another one of the handmaidens he'd had for most of his career. I repeated to him what I'd said before, that there were two leaders within the government, and I wasn't going to be treated in this way.

His timing was a wilful act of vandalism because it completely distracted the public from all the good news we were enjoying from the budget with that massive surplus of $5.5 billion. It had been extremely well received, and the dollar shot up to 80 cents off the back of it. Yet the Prime Minister was happy to punch a hole in it. A hole in the absolute best effort of his own government.

KOB: But Hawke and others from his office have said since that what drove his comments at that point was that he was sick of you denigrating him behind his back to colleagues and journalists.

PJK: I was too busy with the May Statement and the budget to denigrate anyone. I hadn't had time to scratch. Both had almost consigned me to the sick bed. Imagine in all that me talking to press gallery journalists about Bob—of all things. This is post-event rationalisation by Hawke's rusted-on advisory staff. I never denigrated Bob to a journalist, ever. In my own office I might give Bob a bagging if he did something badly in some ERC round or something of that ilk, but that was it. I never ever took the discussion outside of my office.

KOB: Not even to other close colleagues, other MPs?

PJK: It was a very professional place. You couldn't go around knocking the Prime Minister among Cabinet colleagues and at the same time maintain equilibrium within Cabinet. You couldn't do that. It doesn't work.

KOB: But you know how Canberra operates. You know that indiscretion rules at least as strongly as discretion, gossip rules as much as secrecy, and if the noise were there, then one way or another it was coming from you or your camp followers.

PJK: The fact is, I was doing for Bob and the government things no treasurer had ever done before. I had set up and won the previous election in the main, so what we needed was some acknowledgement by Bob that a transition had to come at some point, and to sit down and talk about it, which he patently refused to do. That said, I was so busy doing the May Statement and then the budget out of policy ambition and professional pride. The idea that, at the same time, I was swanning around the press gallery talking about Bob is just a complete nonsense.

KOB: But put yourself in his shoes. There had been ongoing speculation in the media about the leadership, then came the 1988 Budget with all the adulatory headlines it attracted for you. Can you understand how unsettled he must have been by them, to make that rather drastic comment about you being expendable?

PJK: Of course he was unsettled—he had been outclassed. He was not nourishing the government, he was not providing the leadership, he was not driving the remedial changes to our collapsing terms of trade and the need of the budget to move back into surplus. And with all the structural changes into the bargain. In the end he was sitting there like a bunny in the headlights. And a bunny in the headlights is a very uncomfortable place to be.

KOB: I just want to get the chronology right after Hawke's comments to Paul Lyneham on *7.30 Report* and then the *Financial Review* budget dinner. Richardson reportedly read Hawke the riot act on your behalf and that prompted Hawke to go back on television to sing your praises to an embarrassing degree. Had you talked to Bob Hawke before Richardson did?

PJK: No, I hadn't. But you've got to remember that two budgets a year, in May and August through all those years, were so debilitating intellectually, psychologically and in health terms, to be told after we're back into surplus and the government is back on top, that he doesn't need me anymore was the height of indecency. It was shocking. Low.

So of course I reacted to it. The point was, he only had to say to me, 'Let's try to get through the next poll and after that I'll hang my gloves up.'

That's all he had to say. He wouldn't have had to even nominate a time. There didn't need to be any formality. It only had to be genuine. The narcissist in him simply wouldn't allow him to contemplate it.

KOB: You've also said you took a hit to your health in the final days leading up to the 1988 Budget. In what way?

PJK: It was such a shocking workload, and in the Canberra winter I'd picked up some sort of throat infection. In the five days after Cabinet signed off on the budget and it was being printed, I agreed to visit the electorates of two of my colleagues in Western Sydney. Fundamentally I had the flu, and a throat infection. After spending time in the electorates I did a dinner in the evening—I could barely talk and was sopping wet with sweat by the end of the night. When I went back to Richmond RAAF Base to fly to Canberra I was so weak I could barely get up the stairs of the plane. The next day I saw my doctor and he diagnosed a badly inflamed throat and a chest infection. I had to deliver the budget within a couple of days and he gave me a wide-spectrum antibiotic called Vibramycin, one of the tetracycline family of drugs.

Reading the newspapers at 6.30 the next morning in the quiet of Canberra I suddenly heard a buzz in my ear. The drug had given me tinnitus, a whistle in the ear. It turned out subsequently that these drugs were known to attack the hair cells in the inner ear. I'd run myself into such poor health doing the May Statement and then the budget preparations, and struggled to get through budget night to find the very next night, Bob goes out and says, 'I can do without him.'

Instead of us all going out there to sell a high-octane budget, I'm dealing with headlines about how Hawke signals he can live without Keating. The utter villainy of it was manifest.

KOB: Are you saying that the state of your health contributed to the strength of your reaction?

PJK: No. It was such a wilful, catty statement, so I ticked him off well and truly. And I didn't miss, I can tell you.

KOB: At some point in that upheaval after the budget Graham Richardson rang you on his car phone to talk about Hawke's comments, and you dumped on Hawke without realising it was not a secure line. Can you describe that conversation?

PJK: I can't remember exactly what I said but I do remember that I was hot with rage about it. I was so disappointed. It was so crude of Bob, made worse by the fact that it was coming from someone who was so vulnerable, and who had surrendered so much of the drive that is fundamental to leadership. I get into you right upfront and when I spoke to Bob I got into him right upfront. I could never be accused of saying anything about Bob that I hadn't said to him face to face.

KOB: Was it in the car phone conversation with Richardson that you said the relationship with Hawke was dead in the water?

PJK: Something like that. Richardson was angry. He knew Bob had blundered and was worried that I might walk. I can't remember exactly what I said in the heat of the moment but I did call Hawke an envious little so-and-so. But Hawke then went back on television to say what a good Treasurer I was. It was all pretty phoney but nevertheless it took some of the heat out of the public spectacle.

KOB: And well into the conversation you suddenly realised Richardson was on his car phone.

PJK: I said, 'You're not on a car phone, are you?' And he said, 'Yeah,' and I said, 'You're a bloody fool, Graham,' and I hung up.

KOB: Hawke then heard about you sounding off against him on the car phone and not surprisingly took the opportunity to dump back on you.

PJK: But the central point about all this is, leave a political void, and someone will fill it. I was simply doing my job for the government as best I could, and the more I filled the void, the more Bob resented it. And he resented it notwithstanding the fact that he knew I was not trying to take him down or bring on a leadership challenge. My mere presence and my style doing the stuff annoyed the hell out of him.

The economic task was so overwhelmingly large and it was so obvious that I was in charge of it, that while ever I was Treasurer in a big reform phase I surpassed him in the public stakes.

I was due to go to Washington to an IMF meeting the following week, and two of my closest staff said that I should think about my future while I was away. One said I should think very hard about whether I should bother to stay. The other very strongly urged me to resign and leave Parliament. He said, 'Don't think about it, just leave.'

When I did think it through I came to the view that if I walked away, Hawke would probably lose the 1990 election and we'd be handing the fruits of all our sweat and toil to the Liberals. Why hand them a completely remodelled economy after they'd sat on their hands for a half-century?

Bob and I subsequently had a discussion about the leadership at the Lodge when I got back.

I said, 'Bob I've never asked you for any guarantees about when you would go but the idea that you stay indefinitely and that I stay here doing one handstand after another, one trick after another with all this laborious work, year in and year out, is just not acceptable. I've got to have some acknowledgement from you that you see there's an endgame here.'

I pointed out that the electoral clock was ticking for us, and that our next election was our fourth, that we'd never won four in a row before and that if we did win, we would be on borrowed time. Great companies and great businesses all have succession planning. This was the longest period in government the Labor Party had ever had, and the party deserved a succession plan, and I think I deserved a succession plan.

But Bob thought he could just continue winning. The ego was never touched.

He did win in 1990, but with a ton of help from me. I set up the 1990 election and the budget before it, just as I had in 1987. It was the old Stiffy and Mo routine. Without me, the 1987 and 1990 election wins wouldn't have happened.

KOB: The postscript to that whole contretemps was the Kirribilli Agreement, the secret meeting at the Prime Minister's Sydney residence where you each had a witness as you signed a deal in which he promised to retire from the job at a sensible time after the 1990 election. Whose idea was it to have a formal agreement?

PJK: Hawke proposed the Kirribilli Agreement. I told him I wanted to know what he was doing, and how long he was intending to stay, but the whole idea about his business friend Peter Abeles being there, the formality of it all, was his idea. I then asked to have Bill Kelty there as well but the idea for Kirribilli came from him.

KOB: That must have been one of the most surreal moments in your political life, because when it eventually became public it certainly seemed bizarre to the rest of us.

PJK: It was kind of bizarre. At that Lodge meeting in 1988, after I'd returned from the United States, he said to me—and I'll never forget this—'Of course, you don't appreciate the significance of my work in foreign affairs, like apartheid, for instance.'

I said, 'Well, Treasury helped you set up the financial sanctions on South Africa. I'm well aware of that, Bob.'

He said, 'Well, I'm going to be handed the keys to the City of London as an acknowledgement by Britain of my role in the Commonwealth, and I want to stay as Prime Minister at least long enough to have those keys handed to me.'

I didn't know whether to burst out laughing or crying. Here he is, telling me that the reason he wants to stay Prime Minister is to be presented with the keys to the City of London, and he meant it.

When he suggested he bring Peter Abeles along as a kind of witness I said, 'Bob, if we're going to do this, you can bring Peter and I'll bring Bill Kelty.'

Peter was a lovely guy and a friend to both of us but he would always be Bob's friend before he'd be my friend in a squeeze, and I couldn't expect Peter to come out in the full glare of the public eye bearing witness to the events, whereas I felt that if Bill Kelty was there as a much more robust public figure, it would put a seal on the deal if there was any dispute later. At least then everyone would know what had happened.

KOB: What took place at that meeting?

PJK: It was all very polite. We sat in the main drawing room at Kirribilli and after a bit of chit-chat Bob came to the point and said, 'Everyone here is familiar with the purpose of the meeting. I'm prepared to think about leaving the job voluntarily, and according to discussions I've had with Paul, that would be sometime after the 1990 election.'

I said the only thing I needed was at least a year as Prime Minister to garner a larger and different public profile than the one I had as Treasurer before I had to face the electorate in my own right. Since I'd had the tough and sometimes unpopular job of economic reconstruction, I thought it was reasonable to expect some time to establish myself in the leadership role. But given Bob's sensitivities and since he'd made the gesture of having the meeting, I didn't want to press the point about having a more precise timetable for his departure.

The one really odd moment in the conversation was when Bob decided to give me a bit of a lecture about being more respectful of the colleagues by being on time for Cabinet meetings. If I was late for Cabinet meetings it wasn't long, and usually it would be because I was trying to finesse submissions beforehand about which there was some disagreement, so we didn't have to confront them in the actual Cabinet meeting.

As Bill Kelty and I were leaving Kirribilli, he had a chuckle over this new prerequisite for being Prime Minister—never being late for Cabinet. The fact is, I could never have got the big changes through Cabinet over those years from 1983 if I had shown my colleagues the contempt Bob seemed to be suggesting.

Bob kept insisting on one condition. After we'd shaken hands on the deal, just as we walked out the door, he said again, 'Remember the one condition: any public utterances about this and the bargain's off.'

So we all walked away with the assumption that the agreement would never see the light of day because there would be an orderly transition at some point.

I think the important thing is that in Blanche d'Alpuget's book, *Hawke: The Prime Minister*, she said, 'Bob was very happy about the Kirribilli Agreement.'

I believe the reason he was happy was that he never intended to keep the commitment in the first place. I'm completely convinced of that. It became apparent to me by 1989 and into 1990 that Bob had no intention of keeping the Kirribilli Agreement, that he had offered it to me in 1988 to pacify any inclinations I might have had of pursuing the leadership through 1989 and into 1990.

The key point is that Bob never accepted that there were two leaders in the one government and that, at some point, he had to make space for the other. His vanity led him to believe he was the one and only one. In the end he was prepared to deploy a lie, a deception, to stay on unchallenged for three years—the Kirribilli Agreement.

THE WINDS OF RECESSION

In the modern global economy recession seems to be a recurring fact of life decade by decade. Australia's first postwar recession was in 1952 after a spectacular wool boom and the Korean War. The next was 1961, then 1974–75, then 1982, and 1991–92.

In almost all cases, the Australian economic slowdowns coincided with international recessions. The only one we avoided where America and Europe succumbed was in 2008–09, when the Rudd Government threw everything but the kitchen sink at the economy by way of fiscal stimulus to keep it growing.

In his Boyer Lectures in 2006, the former Reserve Bank Governor Ian Macfarlane exhaustively analysed Australia's 1991 recession and pointed out that of the eighteen biggest OECD countries, seventeen experienced a recession in the early 1990s. This wasn't exclusively an Australian slowdown.

What seemed different about 1991 compared to other recessions in Australia was that so much of the odium attached very personally to Paul Keating. In previous slowdowns the political blame seemed to lie much more with the Prime Minister than his Treasurer.

Menzies wore the 1952 and 1961 recessions. Politically, Whitlam copped the flak from 1974 rather than Frank Crean, and Malcolm

Fraser rather than his Treasurer, John Howard, wore 1982. Menzies nearly lost in 1961, Whitlam and Fraser did lose in 1975 and 1983 respectively, and in all three cases recession was a primary factor.

But for many Australians who had begun to feel the brunt of the 1991 recession long before it was formally confirmed, this was Keating's recession, not Hawke's.

Looking back, the reasons seem obvious. Keating was the person most associated with the eight years of economic reform preceding it. He was the super salesman who had educated the press gallery and the wider community to a higher level of economic literacy over those years. He was the politician whose air of confidence was often separated from arrogance by a very thin line, whose dominance of the Parliament was of huge strategic importance to the government but didn't always go down well with the public, particularly after television broadcasting was introduced.

And finally, when he had to stare down the nation and acknowledge that Australia was officially in recession, he chose defiance over commiseration. This was 'the recession we had to have'.

I remember the press conference. It was one of those moments you instinctively knew at the time was going to become a part of history. The parliamentary committee room was packed to the gunnels, standing room only. We all knew Keating wasn't going to take a backward step. He never did. His press conferences often went for close to an hour and this was no exception.

As he often did, he painted word pictures and conjured up imagery that caught the attention of even those with a bare working knowledge of economics. At one earlier press conference he had likened the economy to the champagne glass that was so effervescent it was bubbling over the sides. He probably walked back to his office thinking this one had gone all right, and in the sense that he commanded the room, it had.

As it turned out, the politics were all wrong.

How had it come to this?

It is interesting to reflect more than twenty years later on the way Hawke and Keating managed their reform agenda, and how, the further they sailed into uncharted waters, the harder it got.

The first seven of the Hawke–Keating years yielded average annual GDP growth of 4.5 per cent and annual growth in employment of nearly 3.5 per cent, which was pretty remarkable coming out of the turbulence of the 1970s and the 1982 recession.

Unemployment came down in that period from 10.2 per cent to 5.6 per cent, inflation from 11.5 to 7.5 per cent, and notwithstanding the problems with the current account deficit and at times the wildly fluctuating dollar, the economy was going like the clappers. But even though inflation was down, it was defying all attempts to bring it right down to the historically acceptable level of around 3 per cent. Every time the dollar came down, it undercut other anti-inflationary measures like the wage controls through the Accord.

The fact that the country was increasingly awash with money didn't help. The entry of foreign banks and the spirited response of domestic banks led local investors and entrepreneurs to throw caution to the winds and embark on what could only be described as a wild lending spree. Paper fortunes were being made as the value of assets soared. Spivs were thick on the ground.

In his Boyer Lectures Ian Macfarlane, who was a senior Reserve Bank official through the build-up to recession, offers some vivid memories of the madness that prevailed then. He quotes the journalist and economic historian Trevor Sykes: 'Never before in Australian history had so much money been channelled by so many people incompetent to lend it, into the hands of so many incompetent to manage it.'

Macfarlane observed that the more entrepreneurial borrowers had:

seen prices rising quickly for more than a decade, and concluded that the way to increase wealth was to acquire assets whose prices would rise. The best way of doing so was to maximise the use of debt, the interest on which was tax deductible ... and the biggest risk takers were the biggest winners for most of the second half of the eighties.

As a result, credit extended to the corporate sector grew by an average of 25 per cent per annum in the five years to 1989, and the gearing ratio doubled. Share prices rose by eighteen per cent per annum in this period despite the sharp fall in October 1987.

This was the period when the South African-born upstart Robert Holmes à Court had tried to buy BHP, and the television and tourism entrepreneur Christopher Skase tried to buy MGM in Hollywood.

The madness extended to a housing boom, particularly after Keating in the 1987 Budget reintroduced negative gearing for investment in residential properties that he had sought to kill off in 1985. By 1989, the Accord was also under heavy strain because the jobs market, too, was caught in the boom mentality and the pressure on wages was enormous.

As Macfarlane saw it:

> The more borrowing increased, the more asset prices rose; the higher asset prices were then used as collateral for further borrowing. The corporate sector became dangerously over-geared and the banks' loan books were filled with loans to corporations holding over-valued assets. The economy was clearly vulnerable to any contractionary shock.

According to Keating, this latter point weighed heavily on Reserve Governor Bob Johnston after the October 1987 stockmarket crash, and explains his reluctance to lift interest rates to put a break on the madness earlier than he did.

It's interesting that although much of Australia's lending and spending spree was clearly connected to Labor's financial market reforms like the float of the dollar and banking deregulation, many other countries were going through similar asset booms which also ended in tears in the early 1990s.

But trying to read the Australian economy and calculating if or when to put a brake on became a nightmare for the 'official family' on monetary policy: the Reserve Bank, the Treasury and the Treasurer. Keating's refrain in the years since has been that Bob Johnston was too slow putting interest rates up to cool down the overheated economy, and his successor Bernie Fraser was too slow pulling them down again as recession loomed.

Even if you accept his account that he had urged both governors to act sooner—and there is evidence to suggest that he did—the truth is, they were all flying blind.

The bittersweet pill for Keating in all this is that by floating the dollar he reduced his own influence over an increasingly more independent Reserve Bank, and in deregulating the banks he inadvertently gave them the means to open the floodgates for at times grossly irresponsible lending, which was inevitably followed by soaring interest rates as the Reserve eventually tried to bring the boom under control.

When rates did start moving up from around April–May 1988, they climbed dramatically over the next twenty months; the cash rate rose from a monthly average of a little over 10 per cent to nearly 18 per cent in November 1989. Housing loans went from the fixed 13.5 per cent rate to 17 per cent. You don't need interest rates at those levels for long before the squeeze starts to take effect. But trying to measure how quickly that impact is coming down the pipeline is another matter.

Macfarlane again:

The issue of how monetary policy could have been better conducted in the 1980s will probably never be resolved. I think we can conclude, however, that to the extent that there was a failure of monetary policy, it was not due to the traditional problem of the government and the central bank being unwilling to take tough measures, but was instead due to a failure to understand the implications of a sudden financial deregulation.

It was not that there was something fundamentally wrong with a deregulated financial system, or that we should have gone back to the old regulated one, the problem was that we did not understand the transition phase between the regulated and a deregulated system. We had not seen this before in our working lives.

Incidentally, John Edwards notes in his biography of Keating that in the first half of 1989, Macfarlane was 'the most prescient of the forecasters at this point in the cycle' when he warned that a slowdown was on the way and that it would be longer and deeper than Treasury was expecting. Edwards describes a confusing swirl of contradictions within and between the Reserve Bank and Treasury, while Keating was also necessarily taking the political cycle into account with an election likely within a year.

You could argue that, apart from the inherent problem of calculating how quickly interest rate hikes were impacting on the economy, the government's ultimate failure to read the signs was a cultural one. There has always been rivalry between departments in the battle for policy influence in Cabinet and the power dividend it delivers. This was certainly true between Treasury and John Button's Industry Department through the late 1980s and into the 1990s over tariff reforms. Button's department didn't take kindly to the loss of the Industries Assistance Commission to Treasury after the 1987 election, and there was a perception held by Button and his senior bureaucrats that both Treasury and the Treasurer regarded them as lesser players in the big economic game.

But while Treasury dealt mostly with the big-picture statistics to keep its finger on the economic pulse, Industry was positioned much closer to the coalface, and dealt regularly with business leaders and factory operators. Button himself spent a great deal of his time going in and out of manufacturing and service sector enterprises across the country. In his memoir published in 1998, Button wrote that:

> in the heady days of deregulation euphoria, the [Industry] Department was generally ignored. Among the priesthood [Treasury] my department's views were always suspect, because it had in the past, under different governments, supported industry protection. I thought protection was a mistake from a time of short-sighted policy making. The high priests thought it was heresy, a sin not to be forgiven. But my department knew a fair bit about manufacturing and service industries. For Treasury these areas were 'terra incognita'.

Button's view of the prevailing mood within the government and its senior advisors in 1988 was that nobody seemed to have much idea how quickly interest rate increases would work to slow the economy or what the extent of the increases should be.

'They crept up,' he said, 'seemingly with little effect on the boom. Cabinet had no say in interest rate changes. It was an art form administered by experts. We could merely draw attention to the effects of the changes on business and employment.'

Button said that as Industry Minister he received most of the complaints from business, which he sometimes passed on to Hawke, who thought he was exaggerating. He wrote:

> On November 27 1989 I went to the opening of the Zionist Federation headquarters in Canberra. There were a number of prominent businessmen at the function. I talked to some of them briefly but at length with Richard Pratt of Visyboard. He said, 'I can't see anybody here who will vote Labor at the next election.' He pointed out various businessmen around the room saying things like, 'He's in trouble, that one over

there will be broke by Christmas, that one is talking about selling his house.'

Button says he had one of his staffers pass the sentiment on to Keating's principal adviser, Don Russell, who listened carefully and then replied petulantly, 'Why doesn't anyone tell us these things?'

Button recalled how towards the end of 1990 'misery and despair descended on the country like a yellow fog', by which time he was seriously pissed off with both Hawke and Keating. He said, 'Bob Hawke seemed incapable of believing that a recession was about to happen and incapable of believing it when it finally came.'

Button described one Cabinet meeting on 5 November 1990 where they had 'a rare opportunity to discuss the government's overall performance'. Button talked about a high level of business failures and was dismissed by Hawke as the 'resident Jonah', but was supported by Graham Richardson and Michael Duffy, who 'added some depressing stories based on his own electorate which embraced the Melbourne industrial suburb of Dandenong'.

The next day's *Financial Review* carried a front-page headline, 'Keating offers touch of steel', with a story from economics correspondent Steve Burrell outlining how Keating had told his Cabinet colleagues to hold their nerve. By that stage interest rates had already been cut five times.

Of Keating, Button said:

I had some sympathy for him. The levers he pulled didn't always start the right engines. He was getting consistently bad advice couched in theoretical jargon. He relied on fatigued models unable to take account of the deregulated economy which he largely had brought about. It was too often provided by a comfortable elite resentful of criticism and intolerant of different ideas ... in Cabinet Keating was troubled but continued to speak in Treasury tongues.

At the end of November 1990, the quarterly accounts confirmed that Australia was in a technical recession—the one we had to have. Inflation was dropping, but at what price? By that point, the enforced slowdown had cost some 250,000 jobs.

KOB: So while your relationship with Bob Hawke was again going through its ups and downs in the late 1980s, what was the economy doing?

PJK: After the low commodity prices that helped inflict the terms of trade crisis in 1986, commodity prices lifted rapidly in 1988. The Reserve Bank commodity chart shows a big loss of national income in 1987 and then a big surge of income in 1988. Any government would be battling to hold things together. We had had the biggest investment surge in 30 years.

It was an explosive cocktail of demand. Gross National Expenditure (GNE) rose by 11 per cent that year: there was an enormous income surge coming from exports, an enormous investment surge and a housing and construction boom as well—all happening at once.

What I was trying to keep in mind was the dismal legacy of the economic history of Australia. With every boom, we had a wage explosion and with every wage explosion we had high inflation, so after all the pain of constraint reform through the 1980s, I didn't want to just go back to the sorry past with our tails between our legs as wages exploded yet again, as they had leading into 1981–82. We had to beat that dismal legacy, I hoped, once and for all.

KOB: We know now that a nasty recession was slowly moving on Australia like a malevolent stormfront through this whole period while the Labor gods fought out their personal ambitions. Looking back now, had you only been concerned about your day job, not angsting about leadership or personality conflicts, might you have seen that recession coming with a little more clarity?

PJK: Leadership and who was leading did not change the policy workload or the policy settings. Not one iota. It's a matter of written record that I wanted interest rates to rise early in 1988 much faster than the Reserve Bank moved them up. By the time they did, the demand boom was off and running. By the end of 1988 it was a house on fire.

KOB: But while on the one hand you've said you supported the idea of the Reserve Bank becoming more independent post-float and therefore couldn't pressure them to raise interest rates earlier than they wanted to, didn't you also say about the Bank in 1989, 'They do as I say,' which clearly implied the absolute opposite.

PJK: People misunderstood that. What I was trying to say was that in economic terms we could affect fiscal policy through the budget, interest rate movements through the Reserve Bank and wages through the Accord. I said I have the Reserve Bank on side . . . or I forget the expression. In other words we're an economy equipped with tools to manage it, that's what I was really trying to say.

KOB: Paul Kelly says that Bob Johnston, with whom you had such a close relationship, was appalled by that comment 'they do as I say,' and didn't know whether to correct you publicly or resign. Did you two ever have a conversation about that?

PJK: Bob Johnston said, 'I know what you were trying to say, that you have all the arms of policy ready and working,' and I said, 'Well, I could have chosen the words better.' I think he regarded that as a kind of an apology and he was happy to carry on, but that's what I did mean.

In the actual operation of monetary policy under me, relations between us were entirely proper. In fact this is an expression Bob Johnston used in his last speech as Governor. He said, 'I must say that relations between the Labor Government and myself and the Bank and its board over the period have been entirely proper,' and they were.

I liked Bob Johnston and he liked me. We were great friends and I would never have done anything to embarrass him.

KOB: Can you take me inside that process? It was quite an intimate group really, a handful of people in your office advising you, a handful of senior people at Treasury and a handful of senior people in the Reserve Bank, essentially a very tight little group but not all in sweet agreement with each other. I'm sure you would have been conversing with Hawke too, but Cabinet essentially was locked out of monetary policy at that stage, as the figures bounced around. How frank were the conversations?

PJK: The *Reserve Bank Act* instructs the parties—the Treasurer and the Governor and the board—to endeavour to agree. When the *Reserve Bank Act* was set up we had an old managed exchange rate system and we were now in a floating system, but nevertheless the Act hadn't changed, so civility and commonsense demanded that we try to run the place cooperatively and we did. So when we would have a policy meeting we'd have the Governor, the Deputy Governor, the Assistant Governor, and we would have the Treasury Secretary often and the person in Treasury running general financial policy and myself and my Principal Private Secretary Don Russell. Maybe six or seven people. They tended to be monthly meetings generally built around each Reserve Bank board meeting.

KOB: And in that context you would all have your say with one degree of candour or another, but in the end the Bank Governor and his officers would make their own interest rate decisions. So early in 1988, while you and the Treasury were urging a blunderbuss approach in terms of impact, the Reserve Bank was still fundamentally in disagreement.

PJK: In the end the Bank had its way and interest rates didn't rise until May 1988. They should have risen in February, it should have been up 2 per cent in short order, and we should have announced it.

KOB: So in the new system you found yourself unable to persuade the Reserve. But John Phillips, the Deputy Governor of the Reserve Bank who was part of all of those discussions, has subsequently said that he remembers no difference of view among you at that time.

PJK: There certainly was. In the end Don Russell, my Principal Private Secretary, was ringing Phillips each week saying, 'John, when are you going to move the rates up? You know we've agreed at the last two board meetings to put them up, yet they're not up.' I finally got to the point where I told David Morgan at Treasury, 'If Johnston and Phillips don't put the rates up soon I will actually give them a parliamentary instruction under the Act to do it.'

KOB: Can you remember what he said?

PJK: Yes, he said, 'I don't think we have to get to that, Treasurer.'

I said, 'Look, I can't take this obfuscation any longer, David. All this stuff John's going on about snugging and keeping the rates down—the place is on fire.'

KOB: I assume Bob Johnston was in agreement with John Phillips in all this?

PJK: Bob was a paid-up member of the Bank for International Settlements, the Reserve Bankers' club, and he was saying, 'Treasurer, we've still got Holmes à Court with $10 billion in debt, we've got Bond with billions and we've got Murdoch for billions, and the banks' balance sheets may not be able to suffer losses of this kind.' Bob did believe the 1987 crash was but an early tremor to a larger earthquake.

I kept expressing my view that we'd skipped over the stockmarket crash as if it were no more than a pothole.

Now, the Reserve Bank has learned its lessons. These days not only does it announce its intentions but it actually publishes the minutes of the meeting showing why the decisions were made. But at the time we paid a price for the Reserve Bank's growing independence and the development of its own protocols. It's ironic because I understood the virtue in the Reserve becoming independent, and I've got the scars down my back to prove it. I should have the words Independent Central Bank tattooed on me.

Turning what was a bond-selling agency of the Treasury into an independent central bank was a good and worthwhile thing, but I couldn't do that and at the same time command monetary policy when it suited me.

Nation-building is a tough caper. And building institutions like the RBA helped build the nation. There are prices to be paid in these constructions.

KOB: In early 1989 you said in a television interview that interest rates should have been lifted more sharply during 1988 to dampen down strong activity. I take it that wasn't a self-critique, but letting the public know it was the Reserve Bank that hadn't been tough enough, early enough, with interest rates?

PJK: The economics commentator Paddy McGuinness used to call them the Reverse Bank because they were always going the wrong way. That was a bit harsh, but in this instance they were too slow on the way up and too slow on the way down. In fact, in 1990 Bernie Fraser as the new Governor announced a monetary holiday on rate reductions, and the markets just pumped a ton of dollars into Australia when they heard that. These were all good intentions, but the fact is the Bank simply didn't pick the massive growth and demand in 1988, from the terms of trade, from investment, from housing, from wages, from profits.

KOB: When interest rates really did start moving up they jumped by 6 per cent over about fifteen months. You must all have been stumped, watching interest rates go up at that rate but still not seeming to have an effect.

PJK: The demand was so strong nothing seemed to slow it. The other big story was the issue we had with the current account deficit and the balance of payments. The Treasury and the Bank were strong believers in the twin deficit theory, which basically argued that if a country had a significant current account deficit as well as a fiscal deficit—which Australia did—that it could leave us exposed to a sharp and deep depreciation of the currency.

So in theory if you cut government spending by 2.5 per cent of GDP, you would effectively be cutting the current account deficit by 2.5 per cent of GDP. I had at that stage reduced the budget balance from a deficit of 4.7 per cent of GDP to a surplus of 2.5 per cent; a 7 per cent swing in the balance. According to that theory we had every right to expect that if the government had effected a 7 per cent plus reduction in the call by the government sector on Australian savings, the current account would drop by at least 2.5 per cent. But it simply didn't.

KOB: It's worth pondering Ian Macfarlane's reflections in the Boyer Lectures nearly twenty years later, because you respected him as maybe the sharpest of either the Reserve or Treasury officials on how exposed the economy was to a contractionary shock. He said in the Lectures that the failure of monetary policy wasn't due to a reluctance by either the government or the Reserve to take tough measures, but was due to a failure to understand the implications of a sudden financial deregulation.

PJK: Dead right. And add to that the Governor's and the Deputy Governor's concern about us rolling back into a 1930s-type Depression. So in other words, we're not even applying the usual monetary restraint that such deregulation might otherwise have brought on, for fear of slumping into a structural depression.

That's why Macfarlane says we'll never resolve the question of whether monetary policy could have been better exploited to manage the boom, because as the Chief Research Officer at the bank he knew that in accepting the view of the Bank for International Settlements in Switzerland, the Australian Reserve Bank couldn't apply interest rate policy as it might have otherwise or would have.

I'm sure Ian Macfarlane would agree that without the stockmarket crash and the subsequent advice from the BIS, we would have been able to move sooner to slow the boom and with a less harsh outcome than the recession we had.

KOB: Do you agree with Trevor Sykes, the financial commentator and author, that: 'Never before in Australian history had so much money been channelled by so many people incompetent to lend it, into the hands of so many incompetent to manage it.'

PJK: I would endorse that. What they don't say, and you have to keep in mind, is that the Australian banks were lending at an unprecedented rate because they were trying to burn off the foreign banks to stop them gaining a foothold in the market. They wanted to take everything off the table so the foreign banks couldn't get a look-in. In the process they picked up a lot of rubbish in their lending portfolios, a lot of ill-advised risk.

KOB: You're saying it was a somewhat panicked reaction by the Australian banks?

PJK: It was, to try to keep Citibank, HSBC and others from building a base. Stewart Fowler from Westpac said to me at the time, 'Paul, I'm not going to give them an inch. We'll even take the marginal stuff from them.' They were not going to let the plant take root.

KOB: By the late 1980s those banks were carrying bad debts like millstones around their necks.

PJK: Absolutely.

KOB: Do you remember Ian Macfarlane warning in the first half of 1989 that a slowdown was on the way and that it would be longer and deeper than Treasury was expecting?

PJK: I remember the Bank taking that view and Ian was their Chief Research Officer at the time.

KOB: And what did you think about that?

PJK: I thought it was basically right but the settings were already in place and we just had to wait and see what came of it. The Bank at that time was still putting rates up. The one thing the Reserve didn't believe then but believes now—and this is true for the American Central Bank as well—is the public benefit to be gained from public statements revealing the Bank's expectations about the economy and likely interest rate policy.

In those days, particularly in the John Phillips school of monetary policy, it was like a mysterious black box that should be known only to the Reserve Bank. They never saw the value of the real economic effects flowing from a more open process by the Bank, by public announcements of its intentions on monetary policy.

These days Glenn Stevens as Governor makes regular announcements and speeches, and even does interviews encouraging the public to pay attention to where policy is going. That has its own beneficial impact.

But back in those days, while I didn't mind doing brave things when I thought they had to be done, it would have been very brave of a Treasurer to publicly contradict the Reserve Bank Governor when the Governor conscientiously believes there's a very real risk of a deep international recession in the offing.

KOB: Through this critical period there was another debate going on inside the government, and this was on the difference between the anecdotal evidence coming from John Button and his Industry Department who were in regular contact with the world of business, including but not exclusive to manufacturing, and the traditionalist economic theory coming from Treasury and the Reserve. What he was saying was that he and his department were not given proper attention when they were feeding back the anecdotal evidence that business was doing it tough. He said he felt very lonely at the time.

PJK: I think that was fundamentally true. And when John would say these things to me I would acknowledge I thought they were true. The problem was that I couldn't radically alter the settings. I couldn't more rapidly change the fiscal policy settings, and I had to leave the monetary settings to the Reserve Bank and wait upon the evidence that they were working.

When the party gets overheated, it's hard to take the punchbowl away and that's what we were doing. The rates were rising, the cash rate was at 17 per cent because the economy was still running hot. Because the Reserve had been slow getting the rates up, they simply had to stay higher for longer.

KOB: Button's view of the prevailing mood within the government and among its senior advisors in 1988 was that nobody seemed to have much idea how quickly interest rate increases would work to slow the economy or what the extent of the increases should be. Cabinet had no say in interest rate changes. He said Treasury saw it as an artform best left to them. Looking back reflectively, was that a weakness in the system, a sense from Treasury that it knew best?

PJK: You've got to remember this: at this point in the debate even Treasury's hands were tied.

KOB: In the context of what John Button was saying, in May 1989 you were still arguing that the prevailing high interest rates wouldn't push the country into recession.

PJK: At that point the Treasury thought there would be a much softer landing. This was not the Bank's view, by the way. Ian McFarlane took a view that we'd have a harder landing than Treasury thought, and it turned out to be the case.

KOB: But where were you on whether it would be a soft landing or a hard landing?

PJK: I didn't know, really. It was very hard to pick it. It was like the cowboy with the bucking bronco, you wouldn't and couldn't know how high and when you might be thrown.

KOB: In June 1989 you received a report from your Joint Economic Forecast Group telling you that the next year's current account was going to be worse, and they couldn't identify the timing of the slowdown. These were your forecasters and you wrote on that forecasting report, 'Noted with thanks. It makes the twin deficit theory look like bullshit.' But this was the theory you'd come to rely on in setting policy to control the boom and avoid the bust.

PJK: Exactly. But this wasn't just the prevailing orthodoxy in Australia. This was the international orthodoxy. All the officers who served me had worked in the OECD and the IMF. All believed in the twin identities—between savings and investment.

KOB: Button said he had some sympathy for you, that 'the levers he [Keating] pulled didn't always start the right engines. He was getting consistently bad advice couched in theoretical jargon. I suppose in a way you would agree with Button now. You did come to believe Treasury had sold you a pup with the twin deficits theory.

PJK: I did. Treasury's argument to me was this: 'We used to run a current account deficit at around 2.5 per cent of GDP for most of the postwar years. We're now running one at 4.5 per cent. So, Treasurer, if you reduce the government's call on savings by 2 per cent of GDP the current account will return to its norm: 2.5 per cent.'

Through all those years of running tight budgets, I reduced the Commonwealth's call on savings by more than 6 per cent of GDP yet the current account deficit simply didn't behave as Treasury predicted it would. I trebled the task, the response that they had asked and required of me, yet it still didn't change the current account balance the way they suggested it would.

KOB: So you became captive to a theory that fundamentally turned out to be wrong?

PJK: That's right.

KOB: But you're the instinctive politician who, while on holidays in Noosa, sees a multitude of cranes on the skyline, and rings up Bob Johnston and says, put interest rates up.

PJK: I know, I picked it at the beginning of 1988. At that stage I was thinking that not only did we have the budget in balance, but it was actually significantly in surplus, so no longer a drain on Australia's savings, but actually adding to savings by running a government surplus. So why then should we be worrying about the private demand by private investors on overseas debt? If it's a deal between consenting adults, and some company in Australia wants to borrow from some financial institution abroad, why don't we let them? Why are we taking that on as our responsibility? As it turns out I was right. My instincts here were right. Ken Henry as Secretary of the Treasury only disavowed the twin deficits theory in 2002, fifteen years later.

Once I'd moved the budget heavily into surplus there was no way you could hold the government sector responsible for adding to the current account deficit.

So who was producing it? The private sector was producing it, borrowing to invest and to spend, so what business was that of ours? None, in my view then.

I can remember reading a paper by Professor John Pitchford from the Australian National University arguing this at the time and he was right: I said so at the time to Treasury colleagues. Treasury hated the analysis but it was essentially right. The Pitchford argument struck a chord with me but if you raised it inside Treasury they would come at you vociferously with loads of international precedents. They would say it's mathematically unarguable that these are twin identities. If you reduce your call on savings you'll reduce your call on overseas debt and with it the current account deficit.

KOB: So was the Treasury culture too rigid?

PJK: Disappointingly rigid. Just not smart.

KOB: But this was the culture you'd worked with and sought to change over eight years as Treasurer, which you had decided was too rigid under John Stone's influence.

PJK: They didn't quite understand the forces of deregulation and also at the same time globalisation.

At that stage I had already performed half a dozen miracles, opening up the financial markets and the product markets and balancing the budgets. You get to the point where you reach the limit of what the Treasurer as a person can do within an independent permanent bureaucratic system of the Westminster model.

KOB: The irony for me, and for every political journalist from those times, and many members of the public, is that one of the abiding images of Paul Keating through those years as Treasurer was the man who loved painting on the big canvas, the man who loved pulling the policy levers. This was very much part of your act. As it turned out, you were pulling levers but they weren't working.

PJK: I pulled a lot of levers that worked. The big structural ones worked. Otherwise we would not have the economy we have today. But the fact is, I was very proper with the bureaucracy. It was true of my relationship with the Reserve Bank and it was true of my relationship with Treasury.

KOB: That may be the reality, but I'm thinking more about the kind of image you struck with the broader electorate, that you were in command of the economy and all you had to do was manipulate the levers. Maybe that's why an awful lot of people marked you down as arrogant because when the recession hit it turned out you certainly weren't in command of everything.

PJK: No one could be in command of a big boom in commodity prices or of a big boom in investment. And happening concurrently. That said, I had structurally changed the place from the ground up.

KOB: Was that the price you paid for the image you painted of yourself with the electorate?

PJK: People can confuse pride in one's craft with arrogance. You must have pride in craft and be conscientious in the task, in my case moving these big national aggregates; ones that had never moved for all those years. Nobody in government ever took this stuff on. I did.

But after the stockmarket crash in 1987 then the boom in 1988 and arguments in the official family as to whether we ought to keep conditions soft or not, it's very hard for the Treasurer to say, I have all the answers. I had a few, a lot of big ones actually, but I couldn't say I had them all.

KOB: John Edwards wrote in his Keating biography:

This was the point at which Keating began to be, as he would later remark, hoisted on his own petard. He was appalled by the long string of bad current account deficits which were now the single most important piece of economic and political news.

His colleagues, especially Dawkins and Walsh, were depressed and bewildered. In 1985 and 1986 they had counted on the J Curve. It had not worked, or at least not in the way they had expected. Now the twin deficits theory was apparently not working. A six percentage point increase in interest rates over 15 months was apparently not working.

KOB: So Edwards was saying at that point you'd become disillusioned with and sceptical of Treasury advice.

PJK: I was sceptical that interest rates should be used as a demand management tool for the purpose of dealing with current account objectives. You see, Australia is a large continent operating as a single country. We require a great deal of capital: long railways, multiple ports around a vast coastline, along with mining infrastructure.

If you take another country with an equivalent population to Australia, like the Netherlands, you can drive across the Netherlands in three hours. The capital requirements of a large continental country like Australia will always be greater than the country's savings, so we would always be running a current account deficit. But the world recognises this and is prepared to fund and bank it because they believe they're banking the continent. That it represents a good bet.

So therefore this sort of no-no-ville of 'don't run current account deficits because we can never repay them' represented a very poor judgement of our economy's innate strength of being able to offer good investments with good returns on capital.

Therefore my own instincts about this were fundamentally right, but I was told by every person in the economic debate—the Reserve Bank, Treasury, Prime Minister and Cabinet, everybody—that if you change the budget balance by two or three percentage points of GDP then the current account problem will go away because of what they described as the 'twin identities' linkage. It was said with such certitude from all quarters. All quarters.

KOB: Have you wondered since if they hadn't been so glued to the twin deficit theory, how different the approach might have been?

PJK: Except that the breaking of inflation remained the primary objective. In 1988 to 1990 you had the overlay of monetary policy breaking the back of inflation. Ten years late, no doubt, but done nevertheless. A huge accomplishment.

KOB: You had described the current account deficit as public enemy number one, but inflation was right up there. What do you say now, looking back?

PJK: Inflation was always the central core virus. Therefore even though we were using monetary policy to manage the current account deficit as a demand management tool, it was also doing the other task of pulling inflation down in tandem with the wages system and the Accord.

KOB: Edwards makes a point about Chris Higgins, who became Treasury head after you appointed Bernie Fraser to replace Bob Johnston as Reserve Bank Governor, that he was deeply focused on inflation. How much did that influence your own hawkishness on interest rates at that time?

PJK: The anti-inflationary constituency in Australia was very small. This is a very important point. You would assume that the anti-inflation constituency would include the major business organisations, the retailers and so on, but no. They all benefited from inflation. And even the welfare industry had the indexation of pensions. The core anti-inflation constituency ended up being me, Bill Kelty, Bernie Fraser at the Reserve Bank, and Chris Higgins in Treasury. It was a constituency of four, and if you added Don Russell from my office to that, it was a constituency of five. So we were a decade late in doing for Australia what Paul Volcker did in America as Central Bank Governor. A decade late in what I called snapping the inflation stick. Hearing it actually break. We were a decade late in breaking those inflationary expectations. But we did break them.

KOB: Was killing inflation part of your judgement when Bernie Fraser as Reserve Bank Governor had said to you he was against another increase in interest rates and you went to Bob Hawke with Don Russell to argue the opposite, that there should be one last increase by a full percentage point?

PJK: Yes, inflation had to be drenched with antibodies. But you have to remember that what the tearaway economy did was put the wages system completely at risk. All the gains under the Accord were then put at risk. Kelty was trying under heavy pressure to limit the wage increases but this was in an environment where employers were offering 13 and 14 per cent. The place was on fire with activity.

So we were about to go back to the dismal legacy of double-digit inflation every time there was a pick-up in the economy. To save the wages system and to save the gains and to break inflation, I felt the strategy of using sharp interest rates needed to apply. A bit like Volcker, really.

KOB: Were you making that plain when you were giving those long Keating press conferences?

PJK: No, but I used to say inside the place, 'Even if the twin deficits theory is actually wrong, and I think it is, I'd still be employing these rates to break inflation and to protect the wages system.'

KOB: Looking back at that recession, the depth to which it bit and the misery it caused, are you sure it was worth the pain to break the inflation cycle?

PJK: The proof of the pudding is in the eating. We've had 23 years of compound low inflationary growth. The country is just so much wealthier now. Real wages are up 45 per cent over the period. Countries never look back from a milestone like that. I know I'm repeating myself here, but it's important to stress that if we had not lost those months of earlier interest-rate adjustments owing to the 1987 stockmarket crash, we would have had a much smoother, much more calibrated, less harsh management of the slowdown. We would have let the boom down more gently and still broken inflation.

KOB: So how hard was it in that climate to frame the 1989 Budget for August of that year?

PJK: I had to introduce significant tax cuts to prevent another wage explosion. The whole system was so overheated with demand, wages were under enormous pressure to blow again, just as they had done in 1981–82. We would have lost the whole battle with inflation and nearly a decade of work around the budget, and the Accord would have been lost. It would have been appalling. There was a sense that wages were simply going to explode. In fact Bert Evans at the Metal Trades Industry Association, the voice of manufacturing in Australia, said, 'There she blows.' He thought it was going to all blow away.

Bill Kelty was trying to hold the dam wall back at the ACTU and he needed me to help him. I can remember Bill calling me to say that the Shell Company had offered its refinery workers in Melbourne wage increases of 15 per cent that year. Just imagine what that would have done to the inflation rate. It would have flowed right through the whole economy. We needed the ACTU to hold the line, and keep wages within reason against the backdrop of a boom that was threatening to run right away on us.

So I included tax cuts of $30 a week in the 1989 Budget paid from the surplus, and Bill held the wage increases to 7 per cent rather than 14 or 15 per cent. He did an utterly magnificent job.

KOB: One of the criticisms subsequently of your handling of the recession was that the tax cut fanned the flames.

PJK: That is a trash argument. Had I not given Bill Kelty the means and some tools to hold back the dam wall and avoid a wages breakout, we would have been back to 1981–82 all over again. Essentially the 1989 Budget was about holding and pinning the game that Bob and I had put together from 1983.

KOB: In the end you and Bob Hawke sold the 1989 Budget as a double act, a far cry from the previous year. With another election around the corner and the Kirribilli Agreement locked away, was the leadership able to stay in calmer waters through 1989?

PJK: I'd given Bob my word I would help him win the 1990 election after the Kirribilli Agreement and I put my absolute back into it. In fact I wrote in the margins of one of the newspaper stories around budget time that this was the hardest three months I'd done in six years as Treasurer. That was, trying to keep Humpty Dumpty together in the face of the big demand explosion of 1988–89, putting another Accord together, plugging the dam wall on wages and persuading the ACTU wages committee to accept a $30 tax cut in return for halving their otherwise market-based wage deals.

The militant unions wanted to go out and get 12 and 13 per cent. They weren't going to take 7. They were telling Kelty to go to hell so we had to assuage these people, which meant another budgetary round of savings to pay for the tax cuts. It was that budget that was the straw that broke the camel's back for some ministers, it was just so tough. The work was debilitating.

You've got to understand it's in the DNA of trade union officials to drive the best deal they can for their workers. If the Shell Company's offering you 14 or 15 per cent you take it, particularly after six years of wage restraint. I was dragging myself through the budget process, but Bill Kelty was also stretched right out.

Imagine, Bill had been preaching wage restraint since the 1983 Summit, and in 1988 and 1989 the unions thought the jackpot had arrived with the companies making huge wage offers. There's poor Bill, his back to the wall, saying, 'We've got to halve these wage rises and that nice Mr Keating's going to give you a $30 tax cut, and they're saying, "Come on Bill, tell it to the marines".' He had a huge job holding the wages system together across nearly two years, as I did with the Cabinet. They were all well-intentioned people but they were also tired after six or seven years of this massive juggling to get the structural aggregates right and to get the inflation rate into some sort of low and consistent order. By 1990 the economy had been growing strongly for most of the previous five years, where it had previously been growing at an average of 1.7 per cent.

KOB: John Edwards wrote just before the 1989 Budget that support for your policies of high interest rates and deep budget cuts was vanishing within a caucus that was facing an election within a year. Among economic commentators in the business community, he said, the discord within the government was interpreted as a sign that Keating was losing control over economic policy.

PJK: Yes, but there was support for me too. I remember Alan Wood, who was a conservative economic commentator and no policy friend of mine, saying, 'if someone had told us in 1983 that by 1990 we would have the budget in surplus for three years, that we'd have a 15 per cent reduction in real wages, we'd have the highest profits era in the economy, a 39 per cent corporate tax rate and dividend imputation, we would have said they were dreaming, but Keating has delivered all these things.' Wood also said that the Treasury owed me a better analysis than the twin deficits linkage because it was the twin deficit linkage on the current account that had kept monetary conditions so tight. There was only so much you could have expected me to do by that time.

KOB: Can you remember the speech you gave in Sydney where you sent a public message to the Labor caucus saying you wouldn't be distracted by tricks and baubles or spooked by economic ratbaggery? You weren't bothered by the nervous nellies of the backbench. You were in charge. Did that have the deserved effect?

PJK: Well, they had all started to wet their pants. That's what happened. Some people who should have known better were starting to panic. There was one headline, 'Keating resists push for mortgage relief'. Graham Richardson and people like him were telling Bob, 'We've got to make housing mortgages deductible like the Americans do.'

You know how tax-preferred Australian housing is. It's not capital gains taxed, so imagine the sort of society we'd have if interest payments on the family home were deductible as well. But this was a big push at the time and I had to knock it down.

Then in July 1989, after I made the so-called Menzies Hotel speech saying ratbaggery is out, the headlines said, 'Government to stick with Keating's policies'. Basically I acknowledged that things were testy, interest rates were high, the boom wasn't yet subsiding but the government had a strong rational policy in place and that we were not going to wet our pants and go for ratty policies. So the caucus, and then Bob when he came back from Paris, adopted the same line. In other words, 'Richardson, goodbye'. Then the headlines read 'Despairing Labor looks to Keating for a burst of morale'. That was 10 July 1989.

KOB: You were facing an election in March 1990 and by the end of 1989 the Reserve Bank and you were finally in agreement that the boom was effectively over. That must have been an enormous relief for you, although the new Governor Bernie Fraser was still holding back on dropping interest rates.

PJK: Having taken over from Bob Johnston, Bernie Fraser was ready to start moving rates down, but he wanted to keep the board together and there was one recalcitrant member of the board, a guy called Gordon Jackson, who was the former CSR managing director. He used to always get around in a black three-pieced suit and I used to say to Bernie, 'He looks like a bad priest. This guy will never agree to reduce interest rates, so just knock him over.'

'Treasurer,' he'd say, 'I've got to keep the board together. That's part of the job.'

I said, 'What, we'll have the economy burning to keep Gordon Jackson happy?'

I said, 'Bernie, cut it out. This bloke's a menace.'

At any rate Bernie got the better of Jackson but it was not until January 1990 that the interest rate reductions first started. I've got that headline too: 'Keating Eases the Screws', 24 January 1990. Then another one in February: 'Hawke's Poll Chances Soar.' That's 2 February, off the back of that interest rate reduction.

KOB: It's interesting to see that headline 'Keating eases the screws' because it suggests the media had missed the

Reserve's transition to independence and thought you were running interest rate policy. Your reaction?

PJK: The media, of course, had not yet picked up that Keating alone was not 'easing the screws' as Keating was concomitantly trying to develop an 'independent' central bank. Keating was asking the new Governor to tease out a policy of monetary easing. Doing it cooperatively with the 'new' RBA, shoehorning them into independence.

KOB: With a March election looming and housing interest rates at 17 per cent, your desire to see that cut must have been as much a political consideration as an economic one.

PJK: There was a bit of that, but I could not have the economy burning—this is the killer point reflected in a *Financial Review* story at the time, 'Business Falls in With Labor's Wages Strategy'. In other words, business is saying thank you Mr Kelty and Mr Keating, we agree with you, we don't want a wage explosion and we don't want to go back to 1981. So when you've got both labour and business together, you win. Andrew Peacock had grabbed the Liberal leadership back from John Howard, so we had to beat Peacock again. My job was to assemble the forces of labour and business, which I did.

KOB: So on 24 March 1990 Labor and Bob Hawke won their fourth straight election which made Bob Hawke an absolute Labor hero, but you must have been feeling pretty good too. How seriously did you believe at that point that within the next eighteen months, possibly two years, you were going to be Prime Minister in accordance with the Kirribilli Agreement?

PJK: Pretty seriously, because I had more than fulfilled my side of the Kirribilli Agreement. Bob was cock-a-hoop at winning in 1990. But I did influence the timing and frame of that election also. When others were talking about not going before July or possibly even as late as August, I told Bob I was more inclined to Ian Macfarlane's view that there was going to be a harder landing than the Treasury view that it would be soft. I counselled Bob to have the election in March just as I had the winter election in 1987. In other words, slip under the wire in case the landing was likely to be tougher.

The scars from our disagreement in 1988 might not have completely healed but we were going well. There's actually a picture of us in August on the front page of the inaugural *Sunday Age*, 'And They Said It Wouldn't Last'. After 1988 Bob and I got on really well. Partly because I regarded his commitment as a conscientious one but mainly, and I stress mainly, because I wanted to see the government actually break inflation, yet be rewarded for it.

KOB: Interest rates tumbled through 1990 and in the budget that year you declared a $9 billion surplus and said governments can only do so much. It almost sounded like an admission of defeat.

PJK: A surplus of $9 billion was 2.5 per cent of GDP. That today is a surplus of $40 billion. This was not because we had a poultice of money coming from the commodity prices because they were nothing like commodity prices during Peter Costello and John Howard's time or Kevin Rudd and Wayne Swan's time. These prices were 40 per cent lower than the Howard–Rudd years. They were better than after the 1987 crash but they were still low commodity prices. This surplus came fundamentally from real cuts in government spending representing structural change for future budgets. This came from six laborious years of sitting through the ERC. Having got outlays down, as we tightened our belts, any pick-up in revenue went straight to the surplus.

KOB: As I say, interest rates tumbled through 1990 but it was too late. In November of that year you fronted the press gallery with the declaration 'This is the recession Australia had to have.' You've lived with it ever since, haven't you?

PJK: I have, but let me also live with the unprecedented 23 years of growth and low inflation that followed. I'll live with responsibility for the recession, but give me the credit for the 23 years of low inflation and the flexible wages system thereafter. For setting up the economy for nearly a quarter of a century. A nation-changing event.

KOB: It seems to me that your comment 'the recession Australia had to have' was not driven by the instincts of a Bankstown boy in touch with the public mood, was it? Perhaps more the wordsmith with the love of the metaphor and the clever turn of phrase than the canny Bankstown boy?

PJK: I never used this phrase without checking it first with Bob. I went round to see him with Don Russell, and Don has a clear note of Bob saying, 'Well, Paul if you think that explains where we are I'll leave that to you.' He didn't say, 'Oh no, don't use a phrase of that kind.'

In his book he says, 'Oh no, this was all Keating's doing.'

Let me be clear about this. I'm not blaming Bob for it and I'm not putting it onto Bob. It was my phrase, but he was agreeable to my using it. And the reason was that it was the recession Australia had to have, because had we not had it, wages would have been back to 1981 levels again and inflation would have been back in double digits.

Now, would I have liked a softer landing? Yes, of course.

Would I have liked the Reserve Bank to have put the rates up earlier in 1988 and got them down more quickly in 1989? Yes. But once I was stuck with the RBA's monetary settings I was determined to stuff the inflation genie back in the bottle.

KOB: Strictly speaking, it wasn't the recession you had to have if the levers had been pulled correctly, if you, the Reserve and the Treasury had acted together to raise rates earlier and bring them down earlier. I say that with great hindsight, but technically it wasn't the recession you had to have. It was avoidable.

PJK: It may have been avoidable but those are big ifs. And again you don't quite know, because Gross National Expenditure was running at 11 per cent all through 1989 with commodity prices rising, a monster investment boom, house prices in Sydney and Melbourne going up 20 to 25 per cent and banks lending like fury. I don't think you can get the Vernier dial with its fine calibration, and the Treasurer and the Reserve Bank saying, 'Oh don't worry, we'll just dial up this nice slow landing for you.' It's not that easy.

If it were that easy, no country in the world would have recessions.

KOB: But you see in your education of the great Australian public about how economies work, you'd led us to believe that all you had to do was precisely that—just pull the odd lever and tweak the calibration.

PJK: That's called salesmanship.

KOB: Perhaps too good in this instance.

PJK: Maybe. But you don't get much time to finesse what you're going to say when a set of figures is released by the statistician and it's bad news. In this instance when the six-monthly national accounts came out, the press conference had already been scheduled for an hour later. You run things through quickly with your office staff, you get a note across from the Treasury almost straightaway. You then bolt around to see Bob and walk into the press conference to explain it as best you can. The frustrating thing about all this was that when the national accounts were revised six months later, there wasn't even a negative number in the second quarter; so technically it wasn't a recession, as it turned out. We only slipped into it by a very slender statistical number. According to the revised figures I would never have had to face that press conference saga and the politics involved.

KOB: But, in reality, in terms of its impact on people, it was a recession, wasn't it?

PJK: It was a recession, yes.

KOB: So in the end what were the lessons learned from that whole thing?

PJK: That monetary policy is as much an art as a science. That all this hocus-pocus the Reserve Bank used to pull out about cash conditions this week and cash conditions that week and looking at demand and GNE—none of it was scientific.

In the end, road feel is more important. I think what a Treasurer does get over time is a feel for the road. Good instincts. If there were any lessons in all this for me, it would be to trust your instincts once you've had time to develop a feel for things. Consider all the data, but where there's confusion or disagreement, in the end, trust your instincts.

In all the years since I was Treasurer I've invariably picked, pretty accurately, where the economy was headed. Even as a private citizen, you never lose the road feel. Looking back, I can say with all truth that I had a better idea of the big deregulated and open market economy than either the Reserve Bank or Treasury had. I'm certain of this.

KOB: After all those long debates with policy advisers within your party, various stakeholders around the place in the years leading up to and including the recession, in the end the buck stopped at your desk. What responsibility ultimately do you take for that recession?

PJK: You have to take responsibility for the outcomes. I do take responsibility even though there was a nominally independent Reserve Bank. This is just the hand you're dealt, and if you're the Treasurer you have to take responsibility for it.

KOB: Your last big tilt on the reform front as Treasurer was the second round of tariff cuts. There, nearing the height of the recession in March 1991, with jobs evaporating and businesses struggling, you are pushing through a new round of tariff cuts. The climate could not possibly have been worse. There must have been pressure on you inside the party and out on the street not to do that. You must have had a big tussle even inside your own head, some serious soul-searching?

PJK: God, yes. I was alone in the end, apart from John Button and John Dawkins. Broadly alone. Nonetheless the Cabinet and caucus accepted my view that, if by 1991, in the second round of tariff cuts, we were not to go to a 5 per cent tariff and smash the tariff wall down, in the end the impetus for the internationalisation of Australia would wilt. You can't conscientiously open up the financial markets and not genuinely open up the product markets. Bear in mind that the shifts we were getting in the exchange rate then were greater than the shifts in the annual tariff reductions. So if you look at the period from 1991 to 2001 when tariffs came down to 5 per cent from 15 and 10, they were really only about 1 per cent a year and 1 per cent a year was often far less than the movements in the exchange rate. The *Australian*

Financial Review front page on 30 January 1991 said it all: 'Keating: "no retreat".'

KOB: But there was a psychology at work and the psychology of hearing about another round of tariff cuts that were going to affect jobs in one way or another would have been like having the proverbial dead cat in the middle of a party.

PJK: Nations get made the hard way. Nation-building is a hard caper and I had to make sure this slothful, locked-up place finally became an open competitive economy. I would have broken my back to get those tariff cuts through, and I did.

OPERA, LEADERSHIP AND THE HOLY GRAIL

The Kirribilli Agreement had brought peace and stability back to the Hawke–Keating relationship through 1989 and most of 1990, though the leadership issue did not entirely go away. Remarkably, no word had leaked about the existence of the agreement. Cabinet and caucus sailed on through the 1990 election and beyond in blissful ignorance that, on paper at least, an orderly leadership transition was in the works.

News of its existence would have been immensely damaging for Labor. Hawke would have become a lame duck Prime Minister overnight in the eyes of the electorate. Caucus would have been angered at the implicit assumption that the Labor leadership and the prime ministership were Hawke's to give.

But what about the electorate? Hawke had promised at the 1990 election that he would serve a full term, yet here was a formal agreement he'd signed back in 1988, confirming his plan to step down in favour of Keating within a reasonable time frame in the next term. This was no small matter of credibility.

Keating, on the other hand, was the unpopular treasurer with the threat, if not the reality, of recession on his hands. Unemployment was surging, interest rates were extremely high and only just starting to come down. The faith of Labor's supporters, like the caucus itself, was being sorely tested. Undoubtedly some potential swingers voted for the Hawke brand, believing his vow to stay the full three years if he won, and arguably may have switched to the Liberals if they'd known that a vote for Hawke was a vote for Keating. As it was, Labor got across the line with less than 50 per cent of the overall vote and only with the critical support of Greens' preferences.

Just as Hawke had been helped in 1987 by a serious split within conservative ranks leading up to that election, he was given a leg up again by Liberal discord in the lead-up to 1990. The bitter Peacock–Howard rivalry flared again in 1989, this time with a dramatic coup in May that saw Howard out and Peacock back in.

Howard had stirred dissent in his own ranks in mid-1988 with an immigration policy outline he called 'One Australia'. He flagged an end to multiculturalism and proposed slowing down the rate of Asian immigration in the interests of social cohesion. But if this reignited Peacock's hopes of a comeback, trouble was developing quite separately on another front for Howard. The prominent Victorian businessman and influential Liberal John Elliott, who wasn't even in Parliament, was quietly developing his own elaborate plan to snare a safe Liberal seat in Melbourne, force a by-election, storm into the leadership over Howard's carcass and become Prime Minister at the next election.

It became a story of failure through overconfident arrogance, but in the process Elliott stoked the coals of instability that eventually helped Peacock's comeback. A strong nucleus of Victorian Liberals had by then developed an 'anyone but Howard' mentality. Even so no one, including Howard, saw the well-planned coup coming. It was even more remarkable for the fact that Howard's friend and Coalition partner Ian Sinclair was deposed as Nationals leader at the same time by a fairly obscure newcomer named Charles Blunt. Blunt was to lose his seat at the next election.

The day after the coup I bumped into the Labor Party National Secretary Bob Hogg and the party's pollster Rod Cameron in a Canberra restaurant. They said they were celebrating the Liberal leadership change and told me on background that their private polling had showed Howard had been in a strong position to win the next election; that voters had responded well to his launch of a broad plan for government that he'd called 'Future Directions'. It was less to do with what was in the document than the perception that Howard had a plan for the future and Labor was mired in economic trouble with the added burden of incumbency. They felt that with Peacock the Liberals had handed Labor a 'get out of jail' card.

But after the 1990 election it was a whole new ball game in Canberra. Peacock, the born-to-rule blue-blood Liberal who had inherited Robert Menzies' seat 23 years before, had fired his last shot and gone, but not before using his influence to ensure that Howard wouldn't return to the leadership either. The party embraced a new face in John Hewson, who had entered Parliament from the then safe Sydney Liberal seat of Wentworth only three years before, with a high profile as an academic economist and a banker. He'd also previously served as an adviser to two Liberal Treasurers in the Fraser years, Phillip Lynch and John Howard.

I attended Hewson's first press conference as leader, where he declared he was not a politician, and that he wouldn't be playing by the old cynical rules. I remember thinking at the time that he was either naively arrogant to believe he could somehow elevate himself and his party above the deal-making and compromise that inevitably went with any liberal democracy, that he could be a politician who wasn't a politician, or he was just developing a new marketing line to sell himself as a political cleanskin, somehow above the dirty fray.

I think now that naive arrogance was closer to the mark. It was to cost Hewson dearly three years later, but over 1990 and into 1991 he made serious inroads on Hawke's popularity. As the nation's economic pain progressed, Hewson played to his strength, selling himself as the man who understood economics better than anyone else in Parliament and had the answers.

He wanted to take his party further down the Margaret Thatcher-style free market road than it had previously been prepared to go. The first signs of what was to become his radical 600-page policy manifesto, *Fightback*, started to emerge in his first few months. In August 1990 the Shadow Cabinet gave a tentative nod to a consumption tax.

Keating preyed on Hewson's weakness, which was parliamentary inexperience, particularly as a leader. Where Keating had been living and breathing politics and the parliamentary theatre for decades, Hewson was a confident novice who had more to learn than he thought. Like Keating, Hewson backed himself, but he was a babe in the woods at the rough and tumble.

Keating's cutting responses to Hewson after his ascension to the Liberal leadership, particularly after Keating became Prime Minister, litter the internet, where Keatingisms have a cult following. Day after day Hewson had to sit, trying to look disinterested or with a smile fixed on his face as he absorbed terms like 'feral abacus' and 'a shiver looking for a spine to run up'.

Once in 1992 when, to shouts of encouragement from his backbenchers, Hewson challenged Keating to call an early election, Keating's response brought the house down:

The answer is, mate, because I want to do you slowly. There has to be a bit of sport in this for all of us. In the psychological battle stakes we are stripped down and ready to go. I want to see those ashen-faced performances. I want more of them. I want to be encouraged. I want to see you squirm out of this load of rubbish over a number of months. There will be no easy execution of you.

For the ferocity of his attacks and the language he sometimes used in Parliament, Keating paid a price that we can only guess at, but he was always about dominating his opponents psychologically.

1990 had been a tough year for the government and for the nation. Unemployment was edging close to 9 per cent by November when Keating was finally forced to acknowledge that the recession had arrived. Like every other minister around the Cabinet table, he must have been looking forward to the Christmas break, but in thinking about what 1991 would bring, he must also have wondered when Hawke was going to act on the Kirribilli Agreement and his leadership handover. With each new worsening unemployment figure, Labor's chances of winning the next election were diminishing.

Both men by now would have seen their new year through the prism of the Hewson opposition, and Keating in particular would have been hoping for a year at least, if not eighteen months, in which to bed himself down and have a real chance of beating the newcomer and winning a historic fifth term despite the grim economic backdrop.

This was the landscape in which Keating accepted the invitation to speak at the traditional press gallery end-of-year dinner. This was a strictly off-the-record event where the guest speaker, always a senior politician, was expected to let his or her hair down and speak with at least a little more candour than usual. Politics unplugged. It was Keating's second appearance and he was to say later that, having got through the first one unscathed, he should have quit while he was ahead.

I was at the National Press Club that night. We knew as Keating got up to speak that Chris Higgins, the relatively young head of Treasury, had died from a heart attack on a Canberra running track the night before. We knew the two men were close, but how close became more apparent that night.

There are occasions when you can see a politician is speaking from the heart and not necessarily through a political filter. This was one of them. Keating spoke mostly off the cuff and his comments quickly entered political folklore as the 'Placido Domingo' speech. This was Keating as few people had seen him before.

He has always maintained the speech was not said with the intent of striking at Hawke's leadership, but it is hard to avoid making the connection. Intended or not, it was to shatter what was left of the relationship between the two men at the centre of Labor's success through nearly eight grinding years.

Bear in mind the audience was a roomful of political journalists, bound by Chatham House rules, but always hungry for a story. Given the content, there was always a risk that someone would break the code of silence.

To give proper context to our reflections for the ABC interviews and for this book, here substantially is Keating's speech from that night, as recorded by his then Press Secretary Mark Ryan and not fully published until 1993 in Michael Gordon's book, *Paul Keating: Political Fighter.*

> It's been a low day for me as you know with the death of Chris Higgins. These things come along in your life, and you know somebody well, somebody who is making a serious contribution and making it privately and not going on about it and not getting a great amount of public acknowledgement for it. And when one of those sorts of people go, you feel as if something is happening to you, something moving, the earth is moving on you. Apart from the personal tragedy of it you feel as if you don't quite know where you are.
>
> We've got to be led and politics is about leading people. Now we've got to the stage where everyone thinks politicians are shits and that they're not worth two bob and all the rest of it and everyone kicks the shit out of us every time we get an increase in our salary. But politicians change the world and politics and politicians are about leadership, and our problem is, if you look

at some of the great countries like the United States, we've never had one leader like they've had.

The United States has had three great leaders—Washington, Lincoln and Roosevelt—and at times in their history that leadership pushed them on to become the great country they are.

We've never had one such person. Not one. While the Labor Party is always talking about how great Curtin is and the rest, Curtin was our wartime leader, and a trier, but we've never had that kind of leadership, and it shows. And it's no good people saying, 'Oh, they're two hundred and thirty million'. They weren't two hundred and thirty million when Thomas Jefferson was sitting in a house he'd designed for himself in a paddock in the back end of Virginia, writing the words, 'life, liberty and the pursuit of human happiness'. They weren't two hundred and thirty million then.

They weren't two hundred and thirty million when they were getting the ethos of their country together, when they were getting their great architectural heritage together, when they were rooting their values into the soil. They had leadership, and that's what politics is about. It's about leadership, and that's what politicians are about.

Now we are leading this country, this government is leading this country, and I don't think any of us think we are up to the Lincolns, or the Roosevelts or the Washingtons. There are no soldier statesmen lurking around this city. There might be a few who think they're soldier statesmen. But the fact is we're doing our best.

A decade ago, the national ethos of this country was the thirty-five hour week. You work thirty-five hours, you've got the house you wanted, the Commodore in the drive, the weekender. That was it. Well, it wasn't enough. I don't know why we were in that position. It was probably because of the bounty of our resources and our minerals. But we never laid it down in a constitution—well we did at the turn of the century with the signature of the British parliament on it.

We never said, 'This place is ours and we're going to run it ourselves, and we're going to sit down, we're going to write a constitution which a couple of hundred years later could be as fresh as the day it was written'. These are things we never had.

We have this chance to pull Australia into one of the preferred countries in the 1990s and beyond. And we really do have this opportunity. It's not beyond us. These problems are not irreconcilable or incapable of being defeated. It just requires a national will and a national leadership to go and do it. But basically that leadership will always be about having a conversation with the public.

Leadership is not about being popular. It's about being right and being strong. And it's not about whether you go through some shopping centre tripping over the TV crews' cords. It's about doing what you think the nation requires, making profound judgements about profound issues . . .'

The speech was on a Friday night. On Sunday morning it had been leaked to a journalist, Richard Farmer, who wasn't at the dinner, and published to banner headlines in the Murdoch Sunday tabloids in Sydney and Melbourne.

The conversation with Hawke that ensued wasn't pretty, and he subsequently used the Placido Domingo speech to justify walking away from the Kirribilli Agreement. Five months later Keating launched his first leadership challenge.

Of Hewson, Keating said that night at the Press Club:

You all regard him as a fresh face, and good on him. In political terms, he is. He has only just been on the scene a couple of years, but he will never lift economics and politics to an art form. There is no Placido Domingo working under him ... I walk on that stage, some performances might be better than others, but they will all be up there trying to stream the economics and the politics together. Out there on the stage doing the Placido Domingo. Hewson is doing the hall attendant number back in the theatre, and if you don't think that kind of panache, that kind of experience matters in the transmission of economic ideas—I mean enough of you write me down and good on you, and a few of you have let me down hard—but I'm still around after eight years and I'm still walking all over those bloody people opposite, and I'll keep doing it.

KOB: You'd had a chance to get John Hewson's measure when he became Shadow Treasurer. What was your first impression of him, and how seriously did you take him as an opponent after he'd become Liberal leader?

PJK: I took him seriously because the press gallery would pray for anybody who could challenge us. So good, bad or indifferent, he was always going to get a go, and that meant we were always going to have to deal with him. But I regarded Hewson as fundamentally brittle and politically not up to the task.

KOB: What would you say were Hewson's strengths and weaknesses?

PJK: His strength was an almost manic commitment to his message but the weakness was not being able to deal with the world as it really was, while understanding the progress the country had made with the Accord and inflation, competitiveness, financial deregulation and the rest. His was a view framed by ideology and he couldn't see beyond it.

KOB: We know Hawke had a slow start adapting to Parliament back in 1980, but by the time Hewson came along, Hawke had become a pretty seasoned performer, hadn't he?

PJK: Yes, he had, but he was completely flummoxed by *Fightback*. It's very interesting after all the commentary about my relationship with Bob and the tensions over the leadership, the thing that finally beat Bob was *Fightback*. When Hewson put the *Fightback* manifesto on the table Bob didn't know what to do with it. I had gone as Treasurer by then and he and John Kerin sent *Fightback* off to Treasury to be costed. But what was needed from Labor was a political response to *Fightback* and it never came.

In the end it was Bob's inability to deal with *Fightback* that brought him undone at that critical caucus meeting at the end of December 1991.

KOB: Going back to December 1990 and your National Press Club end-of-year dinner—the Placido Domingo speech—which caused the final big schism between you and Hawke. You've since said you were deeply affected emotionally at the time because Chris Higgins, the man you'd handpicked as your new Treasury Secretary only the year before and for whom you'd developed enormous respect, had dropped dead of a heart attack the night before.

How would you describe what was running through your mind as you got up to speak off the cuff and off the record to that room full of press gallery journalists?

PJK: I was devastated by Chris's death. He'd gone to Melbourne for the day and came to see me when he got back, at five o'clock. It was such a hot day, around 43 degrees, and he came into my Parliament House office and said, 'I'm going for a run before it gets dark.'

I said, 'Oh Chris, you shouldn't be running today, mate. You can't run your way into immortality.'

And he said, 'Maybe not, but it's a habit.'

So we had our meeting, and out he went to have his run. An hour later I got a message that Chris had died on the running track.

When you've been through as many policy battles as I had been through with him, you come to understand that the value of a guy like this is phenomenal, and when I thought of all the charlatans in the system, particularly in the political system, compared to losing a chap of his weight, it really pulled me down, really pulled me down.

Yet I had the Press Club dinner. In the poignancy of the circumstances, what was I going to say? So I thought with Chris's memory in mind, the theme should be about the value of leadership, the quest for leadership and for good public policy, that leadership was everything, more or less in tribute to him.

KOB: But in that context, even the word leadership passing through your brain, sad as you may have been about Chris Higgins' death, surely you'd have also been thinking about the implications of what you were saying and how they might be perceived by gallery journalists.

PJK: Not really, because it was entirely off the record. It is the classic off-the-record, end-of-year deal where the speaker is invited to be relaxed and candid on the very clear understanding that nobody will split. This was the real me speaking, and unguardedly, so I wasn't thinking through any political filter. I just blurted this stuff out. No agenda beyond speaking about the quality of leadership in public life, with Chris Higgins very much in mind. You know broadly what I'd said?

KOB: I was there. And at the heart of your speech was your reflection on what great leadership was and that Australia hadn't yet produced a great leader.

PJK: That's right.

KOB: Wasn't it disingenuous to suggest that you wouldn't have anticipated the offence that Bob Hawke might take from that reference?

PJK: This wasn't about Bob Hawke, not at all about Bob Hawke. I was talking about leadership at critical times in a nation's history, and how Australia had not had that leadership at critical times. When the British were trying to defeat the colonists in the United States the Americans had General Washington. When the Union had come apart in the middle of the nineteenth century, America had Abraham Lincoln. And, when robber baron capitalism which exploded in the late-nineteenth century, collapsed in the 1920s and the country headed into a massive Depression, America had Franklin Roosevelt. I said, 'We have never had that kind of leadership.' And by the way, I think that is self-evidently true.

KOB: I think everyone there was riveted by what you were saying, your comments on the greatness of Washington, Lincoln and Roosevelt, but when you came to the line: 'Leadership is not about being popular. It's about being right and being strong. And it's not about whether you go through some shopping centre tripping over the TV crews' cords. It's about doing what you think the nation requires, making profound judgements about profound issues.' Even if every other line in that speech was carefully crafted to avoid even a hint of insult to Hawke, I would suggest that that line alone would have been enough for everyone listening to assume you were having a shot at his leadership, the great shopping-centre campaigner.

PJK: In fact, I wasn't. It was really a shot at the press gallery for always buying the line that the shopping-centre strolls were the way politics was done. It was to say to the journalists, 'Look, this is the spin, it's not the substance. In truth it's not the shopping centres that matter, it's not the faux populism that matters, it's the real substance that remains the key to it all.'

It was really a message from me to the gallery but I take your point that a journalist could have thought I was referring to Hawke. But it was never intended to wound Hawke. I had no intention on that occasion to do so. He was not on my mind at all.

But even if I had said it, so what? What a criminal thing to say, that truth and substance will always beat shopping-centre visits tripping over TV crews. I mean, even if Bob took it to mean a remark about him, it wasn't such a deadly remark that he was entitled to take such umbrage over it.

KOB: Well, the great offence that Hawke took when someone broke the Chatham House rules and fed what you'd said was that, in his eyes, you had slighted John Curtin as Australia's great wartime leader when he confronted the crisis in the Pacific and the threat of invasion.

PJK: No, no, no! The great offence was that I didn't compare Hawke to Washington, Lincoln and Roosevelt. *That* was the great offence.

KOB: He has written that he said to you that he took offence that you had failed to acknowledge John Curtin as a great Australian leader.

PJK: Yes, he did talk to me about Curtin, but that was only his prop for the greater and real hurt—that I hadn't recognised him as a great leader, that like the Christ child in Joseph's manger, his mother had whispered in his ear at five years of age that he would be the Great One, the great Prime Minister and the great figure of Australia. I hadn't acknowledged this greatness, you see?

KOB: Didn't your own mother and grandmother tell you as a young child that you were special? Are you saying that he was unduly affected by those words and came to believe he was destined for greatness but you were not?

PJK: I always possessed and still possess a core humility. Bob has never had or known this. Bob is not just a narcissist, he's a pathological narcissist. He actually thinks he is, of his essence, a special person.

Bob never possessed the intellectual equipment, the range of interests, the insights to be the person he always thought he was. Whereas I always knew I was a person on the outside looking in; that the party would never volunteer to give me the leadership; that the only way I would get it was by earning it.

Earning it is a different concept to being owed it. I never thought I was ever owed anything, whereas Bob thought he was owed everything. He cheaply seized on the speech as an excuse to repudiate the Kirribilli Agreement and hang onto the prime ministership.

KOB: Why didn't you see that coming, at least as a possibility?

PJK: Because the speech and its contents were not meant for Hawke. Frankly the ideas in it were beyond, way beyond, Hawke's otherwise limited frame of reference.

KOB: But are you seriously saying that there was no point, no moment, when such a supreme politician as yourself, with all the water under the bridge between the two of you, all the ups and downs, didn't see the potential risk of him reading a personal slight in what you'd said?

PJK: Well, you were there. You heard it yourself, what did you think?

KOB: What I thought, and what a lot of other journalists were saying that night, was that Hawke would inevitably hear what you'd said, and take it as directed at him. We were reading those sentiments into what you were saying.

PJK: What, that Hawke was not as great as Washington, Lincoln or Roosevelt? Chris Higgins' death did overtake me, not only the sadness of it, but the value and meaning of his life. And I was sick of the flummery, the nonsense and pettiness that so often pervades politics. That night I gave the gallery credit for supporting me in the big change I sought to bring to public life, and that was to make good policy central to political strategy. This was the end of 1990. We— the press gallery and I—had been together on this journey for nearly eight years. They had been runners in the great building of the new Australia. This is what had happened. And I was urging them to believe in the process. To continue believing in it.

Do you remember I talked about politicians? I said, 'A lot of you think we're not worth two bob, but politicians change the world.' Remember me saying that? 'Politicians make or break the world, and I've offered you a new brand of politics and you have, in the main, run with it. Don't give it up now.' This was the whole point of the remarks.

KOB: What was the intent behind your reference to Placido Domingo?

PJK: That was only because some journalists had been drawing comparisons between me and John Hewson. I was saying, 'Give me a break!'

I said, 'Look, it's like Placido Domingo. A truly great artist. He may be out of sorts one night or another, but he'll always do great singing.'

That's what I was trying to say. I was trying to construct a metaphor on the run. But Bob thought it was in his interest to feign hurt and to take this all personally. He had given a solemn agreement at Kirribilli but then used the speech as a lame excuse to break it. I firmly believe he had never ever intended to relinquish the prime ministership. He thought I was another John Ducker or Charlie Fitzgibbon or another of his trade union supporters who would help him on the way but whom he would walk over if he had to.

Bob always thought he was special, and whenever there has been commentary about it, that was the way his parents treated him. I know most people treat their children as special but I think by 1990 Bob had come to see himself as the great man sweeping through the careers of the rest of us—all in fulfilment of his preordained destiny.

God, give us a break. Give us a break! In brutal intellectual terms Bob could only have got a PhD in ordinariness.

KOB: Just to stay with the night of the press club dinner for a moment. On the one hand you were talking about the great change you were fashioning on Australian politics, and on the other, that Australia hadn't had any great leaders of vision. You didn't see yourself then as potentially a great leader in the wings?

PJK: I knew I had a chance. But Australia is not the United States— what we do doesn't change the world. That's not to invalidate the point that leadership is central and is the key ingredient in public life. Not to invalidate that point, and that at key moments in our history we really need that kind of leadership. That was my point, and Chris Higgins had provided that kind of leadership and he had died the day before. That was the context.

But then Bob's used the speech to tell me formally in January that because of this speech he's withdrawing his commitment to hand over the leadership. Really. The paltriness of it was compelling.

KOB: If it's true that Hawke was at least half-hoping for an excuse to renege on the Kirribilli handover, didn't you give him the perfect excuse? He later said that it just increased his already strong feeling that you weren't ready for leadership.

PJK: He would say that, wouldn't he! As I've said before, I believe he basically never ever intended to give me the job. I believe the Kirribilli Agreement was built on a falsehood. That's the truth of it. In the end I had to execute him, and in the end I did.

KOB: I'm just rapidly casting forward here to a comment that was made by one of your colleagues at the time of the first leadership challenge a few months later, that it was a choice between an egomaniac and a megalomaniac. And I think the finger was pointed at you as the megalo.

PJK: Let's just say I'm a far more humble commodity than Bob ever was or could be.

KOB: Is it true that you subsequently asked Peter Abeles and Bill Kelty to seek to reconvene the Kirribilli group, but Hawke wasn't interested?

PJK: I don't know whether I did say that, because I wasn't so silly as to think it would turn Bob's head after he had said he was staying.

Mind you, at the end of 1990, if the Parliament had gone another four weeks, he would have been in real trouble. The Cabinet and the caucus had had a complete gutful of him. By December there were a lot of stories reflecting that. Go to the record.

Essentially Bob was saved by Saddam Hussein. In January 1991 the Gulf War started and Bob wrapped the flag around himself and went into the command bunker. His decision to commit to the American coalition was the correct one, but Bob used the Gulf War to break the momentum against him in caucus. Clear as day.

KOB: Was it really as clear as day to everyone or was that just your subjective perception?

PJK: It was as clear as day. The last piece of commentary Paul Kelly wrote for the *Australian* on 22 December 1990 was, 'ALP deserting Hawke for Keating.' That was as we got up to end the parliamentary year. 'Keating stalks an old enemy.'

Had Parliament for 1990 not wound up when it did I would have become Prime Minister within the month. Hawke was in diabolical trouble when Parliament rose in December. Yet on 15 January 1991, Saddam Hussein invaded Kuwait. I was holidaying at Surfers Paradise and the moment that happened I knew Bob, the little general, a faux reincarnation of Billy Hughes, would make the patriotic pitch, and so it was.

Every morning in the Cabinet room we would have a military briefing from General John Baker, the head of the Defence Force. There was a certain monotony to these briefings and they had a certain familiar ring. So I asked him one morning, 'John where did this information come from?' and he said, 'We got most of it from CNN this morning, Treasurer.'

When I realised that a lot of our information was just hearsay and the regurgitation of news, I stopped going to the briefings. By the time the war came to an end in May 1991, Saddam Hussein's invasion of Kuwait had completely dislocated me politically. If Bob could have slept in the flag, he would have.

KOB: At some point you had the conversation where Hawke subsequently said you had dropped what he regarded as a great clanger, where he claims you said that Australia was the arse end of the world and you could always go and live in Paris.

PJK: This was a complete lie and a weak apologia for why he decided to break his commitment to an orderly transition of the leadership to me under the Kirribilli Agreement. I had not said this in any of our meetings after my speech at the press gallery dinner. I had said it in Cabinet at least once and maybe a couple of times when someone was arguing against me, and I guess I rounded on this person and I said, 'Look we don't live in the United States of Europe. We have no natural market. There's no great economy next door. We don't live in North America. We're not Canada with the United States at our door.'

I said, 'We're a continent on our own at the arse end of the world. That simply means we have to be better. We have to be open and competitive. We can't rely on the unearned value of size and strength of the market around us. And I made this point a couple of times just to drive home that we were alone on our continent—20 million of us—that no one owed us a living and that the only way we could actually garner one was to be good.'

Bob had taken my phrase, 'the arse end of the earth', and later tried to say, 'Oh, because of that sentiment I decided to not vacate the leadership.' You have to remember that this bloke had always had everything given to him. Everything and always. Yet here was someone trying to take the candy from him.

Keating for Blaxland, 1969. Modelled on JFK's 1960 campaign for President.

The beloved E-type Jaguar that met a tragic end outside a NSW Labor Conference.

Paul Keating sponsors Jack Lang back into the Labor fold after decades of exile, July 1971.

Paul and Annita at their formal wedding party in Oisterwijk, The Netherlands, 17 January 1975. Min Keating (left) and Annie van Iersel look on.

Paul Keating, Gough Whitlam's youngest minister, on the steps of Parliament House about to hand his leader the megaphone to address the crowd on 11 November, 1975. (MICHAEL RAYNER, FAIRFAX SYNDICATION)

The first Hawke ministry on the steps of the old Parliament House, Canberra, March 1983. (Paul Keating is in the second row between Clyde Holding and Kim Beazley Jnr.) (FAIRFAX SYNDICATION)

Australian treasurers don't often get White House access, but Prime Minister Bob Hawke brought Keating along on his first visit to US President Ronald Reagan, June 1983.

The first Keating budget, Canberra, August 1983.

The first big reform. As Treasurer, Paul Keating announces the float of the dollar with Reserve Bank Governor Bob Johnston, Canberra, 9 December 1983.

Paul Keating learned the value of talkback in his early Treasury days. He even arranged a Reserve Bank briefing for John Laws. Circa 1984.

1985. When a wheel fell off the consumption tax cart.

Paul Keating with Bill Kelty. The second most important partnership of the Hawke-Keating years. (GREGG PORTEOUS, NEWSPIX)

Not the way he'd intended to go. Bob Hawke's last day as Labor's longest-serving Prime Minister after losing the caucus vote to Paul Keating in Canberra, 19 December 1991. (TIM CLAYTON, FAIRFAX SYNDICATION)

Not the way he'd intended to become Prime Minister. The victor walks from caucus surrounded by supporters, 19 December 1991. (ANTHONY WEATE, NEWSPIX)

A classic family portrait—Katherine, Annita, Alexandra, Paul, Caroline and Patrick—in their rented home in Forrest, Canberra, 1989.

Eleven days into the prime ministership Paul Keating hosts US President George Bush Snr, New Year's Day 1992.

George Bush Snr recruiting the next generation of allies. The Keating children en route from Sydney to Melbourne on Air Force One, January 1992.

A key first step in a new foreign policy agenda. Paul Keating visits President Suharto in Jakarta, April 1992.

A key ally in getting the APEC leaders concept up, Japanese Prime Minister Kiichi Miazawa with Paul Keating in Tokyo, September 1992.

'The most moving day in his whole political life.' Kissing the ground at Kokoda, Papua-New Guinea, 26 April 1992. (FAIRFAX SYNDICATION)

'We took the traditional lands and smashed the traditional way of life.' Paul Keating's milestone Redfern Park speech signalling his intent to deliver on Mabo, 10 December 1992. (PICKETT, FAIRFAX SYNDICATION)

Nobody had worn a more regular path to the National Press Club. Paul Keating as Prime Minister 1992.

Paul Keating and his first Treasurer John Dawkins. A close political friendship that hit troubled times. Parliament House, 1992.

The sweetest victory of all. Paul Keating wins the unwinnable election. Bankstown Sports Club, Sydney, 13 March 1993. (ANTHONY WEATE, NEWSPIX)

Cementing the first APEC Summit. US President Bill Clinton and Paul Keating at the White House, September 1993.

Clinching a point at the third APEC leaders' summit in Osaka, Japan, November 1995.

Imagine the mixed emotions behind the smiles. The final staff meeting of the Keating prime ministership, March 1996.

Still managing a wry smile as he concedes defeat after four years and three months as Prime Minister at the Bankstown Sports Club, 3 March, 1996. (PHIL CARRICK, FAIRFAX SYNDICATION)

KOB: You absolutely deny saying, 'I'm not going to hang around forever. Australia is the arse of the world. I can always go and live in Paris.'

PJK: Absolutely. It was a complete lie. And what's more I've lived in Sydney for 24 years since. It is true that I had said that I could go to Paris or Britain and lead an interesting life, that I didn't live and breathe politics to the extent that I had no other options in life. But the idea that I would leave Australia because I thought it was an unworthy country is a wicked and sleazy thing for Bob to have said. And, as I've said, the proof in the pudding is that it's twenty-odd years since I left the prime ministership and I'm still here.

I don't believe Bob ever intended to honour his commitment under the Kirribilli Agreement. His wife Blanche says in her updated edition of his biography *Hawke: The Prime Minister* that Bob was very happy about the agreement because he thought it would pacify me and take the leadership monkey off his back through 1989 and 1990. It bought him time—time enough until he seized on the slimiest of reasons to break his word: 'Because Paul said something I didn't like—I decided to walk away from the commitment.'

For anyone who saw the *Australian Story* on Hawke, when confronted with the question, they will notice how weakly Bob gave the answer. I emphasise weakly. Here he has made a solemn commitment to the other leader in the party to move on after nearly nine years in the prime ministership, and he says he is justified in ripping up that commitment because of something I am supposed to have said. But, as he knew, never said.

KOB: What finally led you to declare a formal challenge?

PJK: I decided in the end that I wouldn't let Hawke obfuscate or tread on me any longer. So in May 1991 I decided to challenge him for the

job. I wasn't going to let him off scot-free in breaking his agreement—
in the dishonour of it. I was facing another tough budget process to
which Hawke was showing every sign of contributing little or nothing.
There was a newspaper story from that time, referring to a four-and-
a-half hour Expenditure Review Committee discussion about the
budget strategy in February. At that discussion, Bob did not make
one contribution. Not one.

One reason our relationship had been so successful was because
he was prepared to let me draw down on the popularity, the capital,
to push through the big economic changes. But by 1990 he was no
longer doing that. He had lushed out. He'd backed Kim Beazley,
who was Communications Minister, against me on the reform of
the telecommunications sector. Kim was arguing for the merger
of Telecom and the Overseas Telecommunications Commission to
create mega-com, where I was arguing for an open competitive system.

Beazley was essentially pushing the trade union line. Had I taken
that approach from 1983 we would still have been caught in the
old model, the old Labor orthodoxy. I was utterly consistent in my
approach to telecommunications: get the structure right and trust the
markets. I knew that in an open competitive market Telecom would
be a very effective player.

KOB: Why did you feel the need as Treasurer to buy into the
argument?

PJK: For the same reason I was directly engaged in arguments for
tariff cuts in the manufacturing industry, because it was a critical part
of the government's micro-reform agenda for an open, competitive
economy.

I said to Bob, 'Let's at least get a proper open competitive model in
telecommunications. Let's get away from this idea of a big telecom or
a duopoly.'

What does he do? He goes with Beazley for the duopoly, right?

I believe Bob's support for Beazley in this was influenced by his desire to maintain his base in the industrial movement including the Telecom unions, as well as the Centre Left faction in the Parliament to help shore up his leadership. He knew Bill Kelty and most of the core ACTU leadership I'd been dealing with for years in the Accord process would back me in a leadership contest.

Paul Kelly in an article records Bob saying, yes, he recognised he'd gone for the sub-optimal economic outcome. So I had a Prime Minister who now was not contributing to the debate, who would not go for the best economic outcomes in microeconomic reform. To put it bluntly, he was no longer useful to me.

Then he made another bad decision after a long prevarication not to allow mining at Coronation Hill on the edge of Kakadu. In the end there were a lot of bad structural decisions, and we get to the big Cabinet budget discussion of February 1991 and he fails to make a contribution!

What was the point of keeping the guy? If in the end he was no longer signed up to the economic heavy lifting, then what was the point of his just sitting there? So I decided I was not going to continue to aggrandise Bob by doing another tough budget round and then have him say again at the end, 'Oh by the way, you can leave if you want—there will always be someone to replace you.'

Getting the structural changes for Australia was why I put up with the indignity for so many years: the massive workload and Bob's obvious lack of respect as he came out after the 1988 Budget surplus saying, 'I can do without him.' I then agreed to do 1989 and 1990 on the back of his promise, I set up the 1990 election for him, which he won again, but that still wasn't good enough.

So here I was, lining up for my ninth budget, full of structural changes again, with Bob announcing he was going to have a long trip abroad, leaving muggins to again do the great man's work. While all the time he is hearing voices that he's the great national leader, the one I failed to acknowledge alongside Roosevelt and Lincoln. He's still there and I'm back to the toil. That's my place.

So I decided I wouldn't do the budget, which meant I would either walk as Treasurer or I would challenge him. So I decided to challenge. It was the first bit of cold steel Bob had ever experienced. Simply confronting him made it all worthwhile.

KOB: When you decided that you were going to formally challenge, what were the key steps you took to line up your support base and tell Hawke?

PJK: Graham Richardson was good on that occasion, although he and the other key faction leader Gerry Hand from the Left had wanted to keep the combination of Bob and me going.

KOB: And when you decided to go and see Bob Hawke, what did you say to him?

PJK: I said, 'Bob, I always told you if I was coming after you, you'd be the first to know. Now, I am coming after you and you are the first to know.'

He said, 'Can't we discuss this? What have you got to go on like that for? Can't we discuss this?'

He then went on at length about how he would reconsider the position when he came back from abroad, and that he would think about having another round of conversations about transition arrangements.

KOB: So you had that conversation, then you walked out and announced the challenge?

PJK: I'd arranged for it to be announced. Richardson gave Laurie Oakes on Channel Nine the details of the Kirribilli deal. That was with my agreement.

KOB: Why wouldn't you just be upfront with the public of Australia, walk into a press conference, face the reporters and the cameras and lay it out? Why did that have to be a leak?

PJK: It was a matter of timing, because it was a Thursday and Parliament was going to be up for the week. I had to get to see Bob and there wasn't enough time. In fact, I had only barely walked out of Bob's office when the Channel Nine news went to air.

KOB: Then you must have had the strategy planned before you walked into Hawke's office. You must have had Graham Richardson primed to give Laurie Oakes the document and the detail before you went in to see Bob Hawke.

PJK: That's right.

KOB: So he wasn't the first to know. You had your troops banked behind you all ready to swing into action.

PJK: In the real and absolute political sense, he was the first to know. What I had meant when I had said that to Bob is that I wouldn't be out there for months undermining him, working to get rid of him, before I formally challenged. I made the decision in May and went straight to him and told him.

KOB: Did you think you had a serious chance of winning?

PJK: I thought I'd do all right, but I'd fall substantially short. In the end it was 66 to 44.

KOB: So you went in knowing you would lose, presumably with two possibilities: you would either go to the backbench and wait for a second challenge, or you would walk away.

PJK: That's right.

KOB: Which of those was uppermost in your mind?

PJK: I think walking out and walking away. At the same time Bob always underestimated, failed to appreciate, what I did for him in the House of Representatives. So I thought it would be interesting to see how he fared without me. My bet was that he and John Kerin as Prime Minister and Treasurer would not be able to handle John Hewson as the new Opposition Leader. And not handle *Fightback*.

KOB: It's always puzzled me that if it was so abundantly clear to your colleagues that you were the real leader behind the throne, the real driving force of the government, that Hawke was weary and his time had passed, why did the Labor caucus vote him back?

PJK: Because they always wanted power on the cheap. No hard decisions by them. They liked the double act and wanted to keep it. It was also about how the factional votes were directed. The Queensland AWU Branch split the Right. I'd never had all the Right's votes. Bill Ludwig, who was the AWU Secretary in Queensland, was barracking for Hawke and he put very heavy pressure on MPs from the Queensland Right, so it wasn't actually a clean battle.

But I think Hawke's popularity, as the man who was seen to win four elections was still a strong factor within the caucus and out in his union base. It wasn't the veracity and the integrity of the economic changes or that I had set up the 1987 and 1990 elections that decided the day. It was really what they believed to be Bob's popularity.

KOB: Do you think it was also that a lot of your colleagues actually feared the grenade-thrower aspect of your personality? The two sides to Paul Keating?

PJK: The thrills and spills maybe—but they were always in the name of trying to make another big mark on the national register. To push the country forward.

KOB: But the caucus decision to keep Hawke would have been taken knowing that they were risking losing you, and they were prepared to risk losing you to keep Hawke.

PJK: My bet was that they would collapse, and collapse they did. The caucus had a right to a preference but no innate right to be right. Bob and Kerin didn't know what to do with Hewson. He just ran all over them, and in the end Hewson had put together a grab-bag of Margaret Thatcherite policies and presented them as a blueprint for government and then given it a name—*Fightback*. If Bob had had any real political skill he would have knocked Hewson right over.

Within six months of becoming Prime Minister I had Hewson on the run with *Fightback*, but Bob didn't know how to deal with it. Instead of attacking the big ideological agenda behind *Fightback* you know what they were doing? They were trying to cost his programs. So Bob wasn't responding in Parliament to *Fightback*, he was having it costed.

The first thing I would have said to Bob if I'd still been there was, 'Bob, forget about costing his program! Just gut this guy politically!'

But Bob never had those in-fighting political instincts. He'd always had someone looking after him all his life, carrying him from one thing to another. But when you're alone in the bear pit, that's different. That's the moment of truth.

KOB: But you're saying that your predominant thought was that that you'd probably leave. Yet at the same time you were clearly weighing up the likelihood of Hawke's support collapsing, right through the second half of 1991.

PJK: I thought I'd see what they did, but I began to think about a life outside the place.

KOB: You kept a fairly low profile through that period, but you did make two keynote speeches which were reported pretty closely as one would expect, and still seen by the media and the caucus through the leadership prism.

PJK: I'll tell you my motivation for those two speeches. They were both about policy. One was in response to Bob wanting to return income-taxing powers to the states in what he thought was going to be 'the new federalism'. This was an idea Mike Codd had dreamed up when Secretary of the Prime Minister's Department.

He'd given it to Bob as a kind of make-work program, 'PM, what we need is a far more workable federation, so why not return the income tax powers to the states?'

After all the postwar development of a national economy with uniform taxation, every fibre in my being was opposed to that, so I made a speech at the Press Club attacking it. I would have done that whether I was still a member of the Cabinet or not.

The second speech was to keep a pledge to Bill Kelty and the ACTU. I'd promised the ACTU that I would legislate for compulsory superannuation after the Industrial Relations Commission had knocked back the second 3 per cent superannuation deal and that I would take superannuation to 12 per cent compulsorily.

Bob and Kerin were ratting on my commitment to the ACTU. So I made the speech to the Graduate School of Management at the

University of NSW, arguing superannuation should go to 12 per cent. And that speech was the basis of what is now Australia's superannuation system; that was the keynote speech. The two speeches were about key policy matters.

So when Kerin began talking about not being able to afford the further 3 per cent of wages—mainly because Treasury hated the whole idea of compulsory superannuation—Bill Kelty confronted Hawke and said, 'Bob, what in Christ are you up to? Paul's given us the commitment.'

I said to Bill, 'Don't worry, I'll make a speech about this and get this back on track.'

When I made the speech, Bob collapsed and they agreed to legislate it and announce it in the budget. But they would only go to 9 per cent, not 12.

KOB: What sort of battle was going on inside you as Christmas 1991 approached?

PJK: I had already bought an interest in this debt-laden piggery, which I was going to operate as a business. I had put a joint venture together with the leaders of the Danish pork industry in July or August of that year as a business to pursue when I left Parliament. You have to do something when you leave, and I didn't want to be an ambassador or take some other government position. It was going to be business of one kind or another.

KOB: Why a piggery? It seemed so far removed from anything you'd want to do in a life after Parliament.

PJK: I thought I'd run a business. I had looked at a few different things. This thing was debt-laden but had a ton of possibilities, especially once the Danes became involved, because they were world leaders in that game. So by September, October, November, my mind was right out of the job. The prime ministership had dropped off my radar.

KOB: But looking through the newspaper archive the air was thick with speculation about a second challenge through October, November and into December.

PJK: I know. But that was coming from my supporters in the Cabinet more than it was coming from me. I actually thought Bob would get through to Christmas and then I'd go. But in the end *Fightback* beat him. He'd given John Kerin the Treasury when I resigned and Kerin didn't have a clue how to deal with it politically. You remember that farcical press conference where John didn't know what the Gross Operating Surplus was, an event that forced Hawke to dismiss him and make Ralph Willis Treasurer. Bob then made that fatal mistake of bringing Parliament back for one day—the day his destiny ran out.

KOB: But before Hawke decided to bring Parliament back for that one piece of legislation about political advertising there was a plethora of stories predicting that a second Keating challenge was in the wind.

PJK: I know, that's true, but that was coming from the Right of the party and the Centre Left and in the main it was wishful thinking. Between July and November 1991 I had negotiated a new joint venture agreement with the Danish national pork industry to create a one-million-a-year throughput piggery. That's where my focus was because at that point I no longer expected to be called upon to become Prime Minister. I simply would not have been engaging in that business if I was still seriously planning to take Bob on. I thought the prime ministership had passed for me.

KOB: The media perceptions of Hawke by that stage were that he was going terribly. The air was thick with speculation on both sides of politics. I find it so hard to believe, in that climate, with the political killer instincts you had, and having nursed the leadership ambition for so long, that you weren't by that stage on fire with anticipation of launching a successful second challenge and becoming Prime Minister.

PJK: I wasn't on fire, Kerry. I'd said after the first challenge that I had had my shot at the leadership, that I'd fired it and lost. I'd made clear that I would walk away from the government without further challenging Hawke. I had challenged him, and the party had made a decision to stick with Hawke.

I thought the only chance I would ever have from there on was Hawke's collapse, but I didn't think he was so weak he would just collapse. That only came towards the end of the year after John Hewson's launch of his *Fightback* manifesto. Hawke surprised everyone when he revealed that he simply didn't know what to do with *Fightback*. He didn't surprise me because Bob never had self-generated ideas. There was always a minder to provide them. But, on this occasion, the minder had decamped.

KOB: But wasn't the former senior party strategist Stephen Smith working within the Parliament to organise your numbers?

PJK: No, and once I left Treasury I just had a backbench office with virtually no staff from July through to Christmas. I thought I had done my dash and, notwithstanding the best wishes and well-meaning support from colleagues, I couldn't see how the opportunity would arise through the rest of the year.

It turned out that Bob's collapse was devastating for him and his followers.

KOB: Did Hawke's collapse really take you by surprise?

PJK: Not entirely by surprise. The week I got the leadership, you could check the numbers. Labor's popularity had plummeted to 28 per cent of the primary vote in the Newspoll, and 29 or 30 in the *Bulletin* poll. To all intents and purposes the government was sunk.

I had backbenchers ringing me, saying, 'Bob's doing appallingly in Parliament', and I'd have ministers say, 'Cabinet's become a charade without you there to keep the discipline. Kerin couldn't get a piece of toilet paper through the Cabinet. The place is going to the dogs.'

KOB: But for all that you were still planning to just walk away without another fight against a seriously weakened opponent?

PJK: I had completely emptied my backbench parliamentary office by the time Hawke recalled Parliament for the one-day sitting. When my friends in the caucus came to my backbench office on 19 December to talk with me, every personal effect I had had been taken to Sydney. It was completely empty. The person most startled when he saw how bare the office was, was Leo McLeay. I will never forget his reaction when he walked in.

He said, 'Christ mate, you've gone, haven't you?'

I said, 'Yeah, I've gone.'

I was anticipating that I would formally resign from Parliament early in the new year. But then Bob made that fatal mistake that nobody could have anticipated. He called Parliament back for one day to deal with a bill outlawing political advertising. It was a deadly move for him.

KOB: Now, the sceptical part of my mind is thinking, what a terrific ploy that would be, what a great way to get a message across to caucus. Move all the stuff off your shelves as a clear sign you're going, and they'll be left to sink or swim with Hawke.

PJK: There was no gainsaying on this. Had Parliament not been recalled no one would have known I had already cleared the office. I was going to resign at the end of January 1992. I would not have sat there and ruined their opportunity to win a fifth poll with Bob as leader. I had taken some of my stuff back to my rented house in Canberra and some of it back to Sydney. In my head I was gone.

KOB: What are your reflections now on how that second challenge unfolded?

PJK: In what was originally scheduled for the final week of Parliament in the second week of December, a lot of things happened. Bob decided to sack John Kerin as Treasurer and appoint Ralph Willis. The headlines weren't helpful to Bob and there was a Newspoll that was favourable to me.

Then late in the week five or six senior ministers who had been strong supporters of Bob's—people like Kim Beazley, Robert Ray, Gareth Evans, Michael Duffy and Gerry Hand—went to see him and told him he should pack up and go.

Instead, Bob sent them packing. So the tremors were in the structure. But the rising of the Parliament for the year, more or less gave him a reprieve. But then he recalled the Parliament for a day. Absolutely deadly. I lived in Canberra so it didn't matter to me; I just rolled down the road and turned up to the office, and the next morning I was the Prime Minister. In effect the caucus drafted me.

KOB: Walking into the caucus this time, did you know you were going to win?

PJK: No, but I thought I probably would. Kerry, to get the government out of this particular predicament you had to be able to tell the stories. Hewson had so much support in the gallery with *Fightback* being so uncritically reported and viewed as the new wave of policy. To tackle the ideological fervour of Hewson, you had to have a storyteller in Parliament to do it. And Bob was no storyteller. Bob couldn't tell a real story—a nuanced story, to save his life.

You had the Liberals saying Labor has been in office for four terms, now is the time to bring back the Thatcherite policies, attack the social wage, bring in the consumption tax. So I thought unless you could project a story and take them on in big-picture terms you didn't have a chance, and no one on Labor's frontbench was in a position to do that. For that reason I didn't think the caucus had much choice, if they really thought about it, but caucuses are always moody and unpredictable.

KOB: This had been such a long journey for you. The boy who leaves school at fourteen and joins the Labor Party, whose mother tells the vocational guidance officer you might have your sights on being Prime Minister one day, who starts his working life as a lowly council clerk, a shiny bum, but makes it into Parliament at twenty-five. You're now only 47, but it's been a long and eventful journey. What emotions did you feel as you heard the vote called?

PJK: I felt a big weight fall on me. For all the issues between us, I didn't want to see Bob go on these terms. I was sad to see Bob go down like that. You might think that's strange, but there was a point of affection between Bob and me. You've got to know this. That's why I used to think, 'Do the right thing by yourself, Bob, and stick to the agreement.' When he didn't, he opted to fight it out and lost.

I didn't really want to climb over his body to get the job. I would have much preferred an organised transfer of power for both our sakes and for the party.

I said to him in one conversation, 'Bob, you go on time and I'll write the history for you.' That was a very big offer.

KOB: What did that mean, 'I'll write the history for you'?

PJK: Well, more favourably than he would have otherwise deserved to have it written.

KOB: You've told me how you felt sad for Bob Hawke. What emotions did you feel for yourself to reach the pinnacle after all those years?

PJK: You're sitting in the caucus meeting; the other man is sitting but defeated. This is a man you've worked with for eight-and-a-half, nine years of your life, for whom you've had a lot of personal affection and regard. In a conversation like this it's hard to capture those soft moments in a long career, particularly between two people like Bob and me.

But they were there, and I knew what they meant to me, what they meant for my family, what they meant for the caucus. So there was a very humbling moment. And if you examine my press conference immediately thereafter, it's very obvious that I am not some ebullient person who's just had a great victory.

I felt the moment. People might not have expected me to be overtaken by the moment, but I was.

There was also a moment of thinking, 'What do we do now?'

Because there was a psychological point there. When you take your head out of a job and drop something as massive as Treasury and you're back as a private person and you're letting all the parliamentary hijinks go, you do a mental change. There is a mental sweep away from it. It's very hard to get your head back into it, especially after six months away from it. The hardest thing I found with the prime ministership was putting my head back in the space. It took me months to put my head back, to return to the prior level of intellectual gymnastics—to intellectual speed. Psychologically, I was well out of it.

KOB: Can you remember what you and Annita talked about that night, because this was an event that was to change your lives immensely?

PJK: We did talk about it, and I told her some of how I felt about the way Bob chose to go and my regrets about that. She was much tougher on Bob. She said, 'Bob's fiddled you around for years. There was a justice about all this that just had to be.'

THE
PRIME MINISTERSHIP,
1991–96

'OLD DOGS FOR A HARD ROAD'

To this day Paul Keating regrets the way he came to power, and the timing. No political leader likes to arrive in office with blood on the floor, if not the hands, but in modern politics that's becoming the rule rather than the exception. In the past 50 years, fourteen federal political leaders from Labor and the Coalition have been forced out of office by their own party. Fifteen if you count Alexander Downer falling on his sword under party pressure in 1995 to give John Howard his second chance as Liberal Leader. Four of the fifteen were Prime Ministers.

But timing was a real issue for Keating. Talent was thick on the ground when Bob Hawke put his first Cabinet of fifteen together in 1983. Nearly nine years later, Paul Keating and just four other Cabinet originals—John Button, Gareth Evans, John Dawkins and Ralph Willis—were all who remained when he and his ministry were sworn in on 20 December 1991, by one of the best who had gone, Governor-General Bill Hayden.

The Hawke years had taken their toll. Hawke had created Labor history by leading his party to four successive victories, but Keating now felt he wore Labor's incumbency around his neck like a dead weight. To one of his biographers, Michael Gordon, he described his ministry as 'old dogs for a hard road'.

The other aspect of timing was to do with the economy. The recession Hawke and Keating had inherited in 1983 was a political blessing for them because all of the pain associated with it was easily sheeted back to their predecessors, Fraser and Howard. As the pain largely disappeared within their first year in office, they garnered much of the credit.

But as Paul Keating sat down to his first Cabinet meeting as Prime Minister, there was no such blessing. In the public's eye the political pain of this recession—the most prolonged in Australia since the Great Depression—was his to wear. Its impact was still striking home savagely: unemployment was at 10.6 per cent and rising on a trajectory that suggested no end in sight. The Department of Prime Minister & Cabinet (PM&C) was advising that it might stay above 10 per cent for the next eighteen months, well after the election.

To use Keating's own parlance, the inflation stick might have been snapped as a desirable byproduct of the recession, but that was a virtue that did not get much recognition in opinion polls. The first month of the Keating Government was marked by the lowest inflation rate in 28 years, but in terms of the prevailing political mood, the Tanberg cartoon on the front page of that day's *Sydney Morning Herald* would have struck home. Keating was drawn in classic Tanberg style, champagne bottle in one hand and glass in the other, exhorting a rather glum-looking crowd to 'raise your glasses to a successful inflation rate'. A second figure beside him says, 'The unemployed can't afford champagne glasses.'

The Morgan Gallup poll had Keating at 25 per cent against John Hewson's 62 per cent. Peter Hartcher reported in the *Herald* that the fine print of the Morgan poll claimed that 'The most common comment in support of Hewson was, "I don't like Keating".'

No one knew better than Keating that when he faced his first election as Prime Minister in little over a year, he would be harshly judged if the economy was not clearly in recovery and the sense of fatigue that had gripped the Hawke Government replaced by a fresh energy and vision. And, in the wings, Bob Hawke would be saying to his party, 'I told you so.'

In a television interview before the first challenge in 1991, Keating had promised to bring dash and elan to the prime ministership, and generate change. But after six months on the backbench free of Cabinet preoccupations and the Treasury workload, even he acknowledged it would take time to get his head back into the disciplined space that goes with running a country. After long years of political combat, he would have known that he had to define points of significant difference from the Opposition, not just on the economy, but across the spectrum, to gain an edge when so much was stacked against him. His sense of conviction on issues such as national identity—the flag, the republic, Australia's place in the region—or Mabo and native title when they emerged, certainly helped sharpen the difference between Keating Labor and Hewson Liberal.

By the time Keating was sworn in, Hewson had had nearly two years as Liberal leader to establish his credentials for the prime ministership, and even more than Gough Whitlam and his policy program in 1972, he had an extraordinarily detailed book of policies giving flesh to his vision for Australia. It helped Keating's search for difference that *Fightback!* made Keating's version of market-based economics look positively mild, but Hewson nonetheless was a fresh face driven by conviction and certitude.

On the one hand people were impressed by Hewson; on the other he made them nervous. Fortunately for Labor he was not the kind of personality people easily warmed to, and the sense was evident that the voting public was marking Labor down rather than Hewson and the Liberals up. Three days after Keating deposed Hawke in the caucus vote, the veteran Labor Party pollster Rod Cameron described the election due by early 1993 as a contest between two unpopular leaders: 'the first election in my experience in over 20 years where it really will be about policies.'

But the chink of light for Keating was that the dislike he'd engendered was built on perceptions of an arrogant, one-dimensional character who was only viewed through the prism of remorseless economic change delivered with a swagger and a promise of great prosperity that had seemed to evaporate in recession. If he could be seen to turn the recession around, undo the damage, paint a bigger, broader, deeper canvas beyond just economics—and scare the living daylights out of Australians with *Fightback!*—he might just have a chance.

Hewson had a plan, Keating needed one. His new Social Security Minister, Neal Blewett, noted in his political diaries later that the clear view within Cabinet at its first meeting on 7 January was that the plan Keating was about to generate with his new Treasurer John Dawkins, which he was calling *One Nation*, would be the Keating Government's one big chance to pull the 1993 election out of the fire. Blewett also recalls that at a subsequent Cabinet meeting, as *One Nation* was starting to take shape, Keating was compelled to urge that 'the divisions of the past be put behind us'. The penny must have dropped because by mid-February Blewett and John Dawkins were agreeing over dinner that 'the government is working much better than it had for years' and that Hawke loyalists shared the sentiment.

The climate in which Keating and Dawkins were planning to stimulate the struggling economy was a tricky one. In the same week they briefed Cabinet on the key ingredients *One Nation* would develop, newspapers were recording intense pressure on the Australian dollar. On 11 January, the *Sydney Morning Herald* published two front-page headlines: 'Battered $A facing a bleak future' and 'Teetering on brink of a crisis'. The dollar had dropped 2.5 cents in 36 hours even though it had been heavily supported by the Reserve Bank, with further falls expected, reportedly because foreign investors feared that the government's flagged expansionary plans with billions more in spending would boost inflation again. There was even a suggestion that interest rates might have to rise again. If that happened, the game would be over. The challenge was to come up with a stimulus package big enough to boost confidence without spooking the financial markets. At an annual rate of 1.5 per cent, inflation was now at its lowest level for nearly 30 years, making Keating's case a little easier to argue.

He was soon busy rounding up public support for *One Nation*, even before the statement had been written. After a whirlwind round of consultations with business and union leaders, newspapers were reporting a unanimous endorsement from big business. 'All hands to the fiscal pumps' was the headline over Glenn Milne's story in the *Weekend Australian* of 18–19 January, and 'Unions and business agree on state intervention'. It may not have had the atmospherics of Hawke's economic summit in 1983, but it certainly helped to create the effect that Keating had a plan to get the nation back on track.

At the same time he was trying to tie the recovery into his classic narrative. On the Nine Network's *Sunday* program in early February he told Laurie Oakes, 'Look, this government taught Australia about economic change. It taught the press gallery about change. It encouraged the public into change. I want to keep the change going but we're now in the hardest parts. We're past the big macro changes. We're now into all these areas of the microeconomy— wharves, ports, airlines, telecommunications—where we're dealing with the states, with private companies, so you can't do it quickly. But I'm trying to do things now which induce a recovery, but at the same time provide a long-term plan for Australia. We're trying to beat the clock in a sense. Australia needs it. It needs it now and that's what I'm about.'

While Keating was busy weaving new tales into old, explaining his conversion to Keynes, Hewson was telling Paul Lyneham on the ABC's *7.30 Report*, 'I think he is one of the greatest political manipulators of all time. He will run any argument, run any issue.

He will say and do anything. He will deal with the devil if necessary in order to win the next election.'

But by and large Keating was succeeding in taking the impetus away from Hewson's *Fightback!* in these early months, something Hawke had fundamentally failed to do. For the moment at least, the media were focused on a new Prime Minister and a new plan. He was going to need journalists to stay focused, but he wasn't exactly fawning over them. He told Oakes that journalists who thought he was in the business of 'doing bird calls' every other day to give them stories would have to think again: 'Journos are always looking for a story a week. The answer is they can't have one.' (An amusing reflection considering today's expectation of a story a day—*at least* one a day, even if it's confection.)

Drawing heavily on the old Expenditure Review Committee (ERC) team minus Peter Walsh, Keating produced *One Nation* in a month. Dawkins and Willis were there as the two finance ministers, Brian Howe as Deputy Prime Minister, and Button and Evans as the two Senate leaders. The one newcomer was Blewett, who, as Social Security Minister, would have carriage of a lot of the package's elements.

When the Keating blueprint for recovery was presented to Parliament on 27 February in the first week of the new Parliament it was reported with all the impact of a budget. Along with the *Financial Review*'s headline, 'Labor's clever, risky play—Keating gambles on a push for growth and jobs', was a twelve-page summary of the package. The other papers followed suit. Most editorials broadly supported the plan for recovery. At the heart of the package, apart from the big spend of $1.1 billion on roads, rail and ports, and concessions for business, was a promise of two rounds of tax cuts aimed substantially at middle-class voters. Three-quarters of all workers would have their top rate of income tax cut to 30 per cent.

The political nature of the cuts was clear: they neutralised the tax cuts Hewson had outlined in *Fightback!*, but where his were designed as compensation for his GST, Keating's were there simply as a counter to Hewson's. They couldn't be claimed as part of the stimulus strategy to kickstart the economy because, like Hewson's, the first tranche wouldn't be introduced until July 1994.

As always with economic statements, budgets or otherwise, the foundations for any policy promise are only as solid as the Treasury forecasts they're based on. *One Nation* predicted growth of 4.75 per cent for the following financial year, the start of which was just a few months away. The credibility of the tax cuts was based on that growth forecast and the assumption that it would continue, therefore boosting revenue, which would make the tax cuts affordable and get the budget deficit—forecast to hit $8 billion in the next financial year—back to surplus within four years. Part of that scenario also underestimated the extent to which 'snapping the inflation stick' would rob the government of tax revenue. As Dawkins later acknowledged, lower inflation meant lower revenue.

Market economists questioned both the growth and deficit forecasts, but initially, *One Nation* was accepted as a credible platform from which to attack *Fightback!*. By the August Budget, that credibility was badly shaken. Subsequently a disaffected Dawkins said the key growth assumptions came from the Prime Minister's office, not from his own or Treasury, implying that they might have been driven more by political imperatives than economics. True or not, Keating paid the ultimate price when the tax cut pledge unravelled, but not until the 1996 election. Another *One Nation* forecast, that unemployment would drop to 9.5 per cent by the middle of 1993, also turned out to be heroic.

In *One Nation*, Keating reached back to his old friend and Accord partner Bill Kelty to add an element to the mix that Hewson knew the Liberals couldn't match. The Accord had become almost a forgotten strategy under Hawke and John Kerin the previous year. Keating now produced a new commitment from the ACTU to help lock in low inflation by setting wage claims not to exceed the inflation rates of Australia's major OECD trading partners. The argument was that along with productivity gains delivered by a promised new Keating reform to decentralise wage-bargaining, the real increase in wages for the next few years at least would be no more than around 1 per cent. Keating now had a plan to sell and he sold it. He also had a reinvigorated backbench and ministry.

Blewett's diary entry for 3 March confirmed that Keating's political strategy for the year was to use *One Nation* as evidence he was restoring the economy, use his tax cuts to counter Hewson's, and isolate the GST for a blitzkrieg assault throughout the year. Blewett records Keating telling caucus that with the generally positive acceptance of *One Nation*, the job was to keep hammering the GST 'to strip away all the fig leaves covering it; what will be exposed is a nasty tax collection of $27 billion'.

On Tuesday 11 March, the Bureau of Statistics reported that Australia had recorded its second quarter of growth and therefore the recession was technically over. The *Sydney Morning Herald*'s bold front-page headline read 'Let the recovery begin'. Keating and Dawkins were smart enough not to take a bow.

In the *Sunday Age*, Michael Gordon drew a revealing comparison between the lethargy and depression on Labor's backbench when Hawke made a final, desperate economic statement the previous December to belatedly counter *Fightback!*, and the week just gone, with backbenchers clamouring to get their names on the list of parliamentary speakers in support of One Nation.

The *Australian*'s Newspoll the following Tuesday recorded Keating's personal approval rating rising from 27 to 35 per cent, and the government up six points to 41 per cent in its primary vote. By the end of the month, Morgan Gallup showed Keating's personal approval up from 25 to 39 per cent, and Hewson's down from 62 to 50 per cent. Newspoll on 31 March showed Keating passing Hewson in terms of personal approval and Labor on 43 per cent to the Coalition's 44 per cent in the primary vote: four points better than Labor's primary vote at the 1990 election. Even allowing for the monthly fickleness of polls, Labor was at least back in the game.

KOB: You'd waited a long time for the power that only comes with one job in this country and you finally had it. How clearly did you know what you wanted to do with that power?

PJK: I'd say very clearly. I'd thought about it for a long time, right from the beginning of the government in 1983. The reformation of the Australian economy was conceived radically, not bureaucratically; that is, the opening up of the financial markets and the product markets, and I had flagged my intention to open the labour market. This amounted to the complete dismantling of the whole Deakin structure that emerged post-Federation.

Alfred Deakin put in place the tariff wall and centralised wage-fixing, what's been called the Australian Settlement. The changes from 1983 onwards, those that I superintended, were not designed to alter these things at the margins but to change them wholly, and I always held the view that a change of this scale required a new approach to leadership. I tried to imbue the idea that good policy could become good politics, where we would get away from the lowest common denominator approach.

As Prime Minister I had another set of objectives. I always thought Australia could be a great country, but to be so required it to have a different idea of itself. That is, an efficient, competitive, open, cosmopolitan republic integrating itself with the Asian region. I'd given the country a new economic engine, so what I wanted to do as Prime Minister was to repoint the raft to the area of opportunity and our ultimate security, which was Asia. In other words, we should look to find our prosperity in Asia and our security in Asia, not from Asia.

With the Anglo-style leaders of Australia, the Menzies of this world, strategically we were always looking to secure ourselves from Asia. I knew we could only find our security in Asia.

The end of the Cold War in 1989 created an opportunity for open regionalism and the rise of China, so more than ever I thought the opportunity was there to advance a radically different view of Australia's place in the world.

That is why I thought we had to be a republic, and why, amongst other reasons, we had to come to terms with our Indigenous people. We couldn't approach our neighbours in the region as a European enclave continuing to treat our Indigenous people badly. That was the approach I took and it really governed the whole period of my prime ministership.

KOB: Did you contemplate the extent to which your views were reflected broadly in the Australian community or how much you might have to change opinion?

PJK: I believed in education and teaching. I understood the fundamental importance of education, and I believed I had a role as both Treasurer and Prime Minister in the education of the country, in leading by example and by painting a picture to encourage them to be a part of it.

There is the old measure of leadership in Australia, that is, how many elections you could win, and then there's a measure of leadership based on the quality and pace of reform. I said when John Howard passed ten years as Prime Minister compared to my four that I would much rather have been John the Twenty-third than Pius the Twelfth, meaning you need the rapidity of the changes, the radical sweep of the changes. It's not a matter of how long you're there and how many elections you win. All that matters is whether the necessary decisions were taken, the core changes made. The rest is bunkum.

KOB: Stephen Smith, who was working for you at the time of your second leadership challenge, has since said he would never forget the look on your face when you received the phone call telling you Bob Hawke had called for the leadership ballot that was going to deliver you the prime ministership. He said as you put the phone down he asked you what was up, and you said, 'Mate, I'm carrying such a crushing burden. You know, all this should have happened three years ago.' Do you remember that sense of foreboding?

PJK: Yes. I'd had those years of pulling Bob through all those big economic reforms in his down years when I was at the height of my powers. Those jobs run on energy and momentum, and as a government we'd been implementing dramatic policy change across a very broad front for nearly nine years. We'd won four elections, and within a year I'd be facing a fifth election.

I thought Bob and I had an honourable agreement but in the end I had to push him out, which I would have preferred not to have done. If Bob had gone voluntarily even a year earlier, I might have felt much more buoyant. As it was, I had little more than a year to make up massive political ground, find a response to John Hewson's *Fightback!*, reinvigorate a disheartened government, kickstart an economy coming out of recession and win a fifth poll.

We were down to about 30 per cent in the primary vote in the *Bulletin* poll. That's what I inherited from Bob. Fifteen months later I turned that into a primary vote of 45 per cent for Labor.

To have a chance of pulling that off I had to get out of the box very quickly. The economy was too flat, so we had to put the policies in place to get it going again. But I also wanted to change the whole language of the debate.

KOB: Paul Kelly wrote in the *March of Patriots* that you nursed a secret fear going into the prime ministership, that your best days were behind you.

PJK: I never ever thought my best days were behind me because some of the big jobs remained to be done, namely to peel back the outer cladding of the Anglosphere and to emphatically change the country's orientation towards its future—its future in Asia. That had not been done, and would never be done by a Liberal Government.

KOB: But you've also said in our ABC interviews that after six months on the backbench, by the time you actually became Prime Minister, your head was in a different space after walking away from the Treasury job. You said, 'There is a mental sweep away from doing it. It took me months to put my head back in the same space. Psychologically I was out of it.'

PJK: It's true it took a while to re-ignite the killer instincts, but I knew one thing very clearly after six months looking on from the backbench. The economy was far soggier than anyone believed, and it needed a serious kickstart, which I gave it with *One Nation* early in 1992. That package actually worked because the economy was back to over 4 per cent growth two years later.

KOB: But it wasn't just you who had to fire up again for a whole new ball game. You had to enthuse Cabinet again. They'd been through those long gruelling years too, been stung by the recession, and by the tensions and bitterness that had developed between you and Bob Hawke. Some of the key talent had also gone.

PJK: After years of profound change with all the wear and tear, experienced ministers were dropping out and the game was getting stickier. Those of us who were left had to take more responsibility while new ministers were blooded.

KOB: Peter Walsh has since said, 'The man who had kicked, scratched and gouged to become Prime Minister was a bit like the dog that chased cars, finally caught one and didn't quite know what to do with it.'

PJK: I knew what to do with it all right. Peter just got very jaded and negative in the end.

KOB: John Button, another Cabinet colleague of yours from the start, wrote in his memoir that he thought your best playing days were over, that you 'kicked some brilliant goals and missed some easy ones'. These were people who respected you, who supported you into the prime ministership.

PJK: That's in some respects right, and I know there was a view around that my best days were behind me with regard to economic reform, but I proved that wrong. As Prime Minister I took the heat to see all the tariff cuts into place. In the middle of a recession I still oversaw the tariffs continuing to come down. You can't underestimate how tough it was to stick to those guns. I had all my Cabinet supporters asking me to stop. I had Bill Kelty and the ACTU asking me to stop. I said, 'If we stop we're dead.' The internationalism will dissipate.

Then there was the abolition of centralised wage-fixing. Finally with Bob out of the road I could get on with breaking up the centralised wage-fixing system and move to a system of enterprise bargaining. I put that into place. At the same time I legislated the universal superannuation scheme, locking in compulsory contributions to 9 per cent of wages. In all, three massive economic changes.

Despite these big changes on the economic front, some of my colleagues thought that because we didn't do the same gut-busting work as we did on some of the earlier reforms, these great changes were not as important, but we've never looked back, and nor has Australia since. We embedded these great changes, we embedded low inflation, and low inflationary expectations: we gave the economy the flexibility it now has and could never have had under the old protectionist model.

KOB: Do you remember your mate Bill Kelty giving you a pep talk in those early days? You were down with a cold and complaining that Hawke had left you with the butt end of the political cycle, and Kelty said, 'Well, give up mate, just fuck off. If you don't think you can win, then leave, but you can beat Hewson. Just don't ever give me this speech again about Bob and the political cycle.'

PJK: There's a certain therapy about complaining. You whinge to a friend about something that's bothering you and it makes you feel better. I used to practise on Bill, and he'd get fed up with me, and sometimes I'd get fed up with him.

But I started out as Prime Minister knowing that very few governments get past ten years. The old brain has to keep jumping hurdles, yet I was lifting my own hurdles and jumping even higher.

KOB: You'd always been very careful to try to shield your family from the spotlight as Treasurer, particularly the children, but this was now a very different ball game. I can remember the tabloids going to town on the Sunday after your elevation, with shots of the family and speculation about Annita as First Lady. This was going to be a whole new ball game in personal terms, wasn't it?

PJK: Yes, it was, but they were still little kids. Alexandra was just six. Some were still in primary school, with Patrick just in secondary school. After the rented house in Red Hill, the Lodge was a big change for them but in a way they were too young to absorb it. They've all said to me since they wished they'd been older when we got there because they would have had a better sense of what it all meant.

KOB: Can you remember how you and Annita tried to explain it to them?

PJK: Because they would sometimes come to the big events like the budgets, and had sat in the Speaker's Gallery in both the old and new Parliaments, they were a little in the swim of it. They'd also been to the Lodge with Bob and Hazel and Annita and me on many occasions, swimming in the pool and so on, so they were familiar with the surroundings and what the place meant. They didn't know how it was conducted but they knew the prime ministership was central to the country.

KOB: How did you try to preserve some sense of normality for them?

PJK: I would always try to come home for dinner at seven o'clock. I would see the top of the ABC *News* until about seven ten, when we'd start dinner. If they were hungry they might sometimes eat a little bit earlier but mostly we'd eat together. Usually they would then go to their rooms and we had two young women as nannies who were qualified school teachers. We'd let go of Bob's butler, so that saving in the household expenditure funded the nannies, who would help them with their schoolwork. Sometimes I'd join them because some were more attentive students than others.

Alexandra would always say at about eight o'clock, 'Daddy, will you lie down with me', and sometimes I would. In our rented house my two youngest daughters shared a room, and in the Lodge they had one each so Alexandra at six would sometimes feel lonely going to bed on her own. Sometimes I'd drop off as well, and I'd get a knock on the door to take a phone call, and I'd have to creep out so as not to wake her. At about nine o'clock or quarter-past Jimmy Warner would pick me up and we'd go back to Parliament House.

The kids' routine stayed the same. They still went to ballet classes, they still rode horses. I used to go to the Manuka shops with them every Saturday morning and often we'd give the police the slip because, to be honest, I was never into security. I'd get the kids into the car and we'd be off.

We'd go through Abels Record Shop and they'd pick up pencils and books and other bits and pieces from the newsagency, and sometimes I'd break the rules and they'd pick up a little bag of lollies each. Then we'd do a walk around Manuka and see people we knew. So I tried to give them what you might call a somewhat normal suburban life in an otherwise very un-suburban setting.

Annita was still their sheet anchor as she had been through the earlier years but she now had responsibilities, attending functions, making speeches and so on. She took a particular interest in Australian fashion. I think it's fair to say she was the first Prime Minister's wife truly interested in promoting the early detection of breast cancer, and she had a range of other interests that used to take her around the country. When that happened I would try to be at the house in her place.

KOB: If you didn't like the fuss around security how did you reach an accommodation with your detail because they must have got sick of constantly playing catch up?

PJK: My security detail were great people, but they suffered from my earlier attitudes. I always had instilled in me as a young man, never trust the coppers. And I have permanently been untrusting of police. I didn't want a bunch of them, however well intentioned, driving around, living my life with me. But they did become part of the network and I'm still friendly with each of them years later. The surveillance was something I never quite felt comfortable with, yet they were the epitome of discretion, and showed good judgement in trying not to get in your face.

The first thing I did when I became Prime Minister was to take the flag off the front of the car. Bob used to sit up with the flag flying and I said, 'Bob, getting around in a Holden with a flag on it is one thing laughing at another. It's like a pig with a straw in its bum. Take the flag off', but he wouldn't take it off. He loved that official flutter. As soon as I took the job I said no flags. We all know what the prime ministership is. You don't need to convince yourself by sitting up there with the flag fluttering—particularly this flag.

KOB: You were very decisive in replacing Bob Hawke's Head of Department, Mike Codd, with Michael Keating, whom you knew from Treasury. What drove that? Why was it important to do so early and what were you looking for in Keating?

PJK: I always held Mike Codd in high regard. But he and I had completely divergent views about what was later called new federalism. As Treasurer I had opposed the idea of giving back to the states the pre-war taxing powers, in other words, moving away from centralised taxation. I was strongly opposed to that, and since it was essentially a scheme promoted rather formally by Mike Codd, he volunteered to resign. I didn't have to suggest it. I then appointed him to the Qantas board and I think the Telstra board because he was a capable guy and I was at pains to make the point that his departure wasn't a banishment. He kindly volunteered his resignation and I accepted it.

Michael Keating had been Secretary of the Department of Finance and had a highly developed economic view of the world but with Keynesian resonances, which suited me because I had come to accept during my six months on the backbench that we had to have a big shift up in public demand to offset the fall in private demand and to hasten the recovery from recession. I also had to have someone the public service both knew and respected because the Secretary of Prime Minister & Cabinet is effectively the head of the public service and I thought Michael Keating fitted the bill.

KOB: You had come to see Treasury as the intellectual powerhouse of the public service. How did PM&C compare to that when you walked in the door?

PJK: You've got to do what you say and say what you do. I always believed PM&C could never replicate in its economic division the breadth, depth and quality of Treasury, and as Treasurer I used to say as much. I couldn't now flip my position 180 degrees and try to use PM&C to usurp Treasury. I took the view that the principal economic department of state should remain that and that PM&C should not try to second-guess it. But I still needed PM&C to be alert to all of the issues and able to give me their perspective on the Treasury view, and their views on other departments.

PM&C's relationship with Foreign Affairs is a slightly different matter because in the Westminster system the Prime Minister is, in a sense, the first Foreign Minister. So the shadow role my department played in foreign policy was a legitimately larger role than the department's role in economic policy. I was particularly impressed by two former foreign affairs officers I inherited in PM&C, Allan Gyngell and Michael Thorley. Although they'd spent most of their lives in foreign affairs, they now had a supra-advisory role in my department, which gave them an extra dimension.

For the position of foreign policy adviser in my office, I co-opted Ashton Calvert, who was DFAT through and through, and whose contribution on foreign policy was exceptional.

Since I had to prepare for a visit from US President George Bush Senior only nine days after becoming Prime Minister, and wanted to fashion a whole new set of priorities, these people were pivotal.

KOB: Bob Hawke wasn't the only person who'd walked away scarred from the leadership battle. You were scarred, the whole Cabinet was scarred. They were now looking to you to lead them back to that next election. How heavily did that responsibility weigh on you?

PJK: It weighed heavily because we were dead meat when I took over. It was John Hewson and *Fightback!* that finished Bob and it was incumbent on me to smash *Fightback!* and buckle Hewson. The second thing was to re-engender in Cabinet a sense of optimism and purpose. I began this by embracing Hawke's key supporters, people like Robert Ray, Michael Duffy and Gareth Evans. There was no getting even. I wanted to unify Cabinet and persuade them that we could dig ourselves out of the hole. I'd already said to caucus when I got the job that, 'Hewson is a sort of cold fish washed ashore by the recession and I'll deal with him, but you've got to have the pluck to deal with him too.'

KOB: When you were putting your Cabinet together, Neal Blewett wrote in his diary how you rang him to talk about who should be Treasurer. He said, 'Keating was anguished by the decision on the Treasurer, wanting John Dawkins but recognising the blow to Ralph Willis.' How tough a decision was it and what swayed you other than loyalty to Dawkins who'd been perhaps your bravest supporter in your challenge to Hawke?

PJK: I had a ton of personal regard and affection for Ralph. And he'd finally got the job he'd always wanted, after John Kerin stumbled and

Bob had replaced him with Ralph. Every fibre of goodwill and fair play in me was telling me I shouldn't take it from him.

But Dawkins, with Peter Walsh and one or two others, which included Ralph, had been at the centre of our efforts to internationalise the country. John was a believer. He didn't have to be cajoled. He was a believer, an activist believer, and he'd sat in on all those ERC meetings for long hours and long weeks for years and years. And if the government was to make the big change I thought it had to make, it had to have a true believer at the centre. And besides me John was the most inoculated. Let's say we were co-inoculated. It was one of the hardest decisions I ever made, but then when John resigned I was able to ask Ralph to step up again, which he did.

KOB: Blewett also wrote, 'I pressed for Dawkins even though I thought it was a high risk move. Dawkins and Keating might be as likely to exaggerate each other's weaknesses as augment their strengths given similar temperaments and approaches to politics, but risks have to be taken.' Did you identify risks with Dawkins' appointment? What was the risk side of Dawkins' personality?

PJK: I did take that into account, but the guy was capable of original thought and direct action. Look at the HECS scheme for university students. As Education Minister John had to face the reality that the country could not afford a free tertiary system, and even though HECS had academic forebears in people like Bruce Chapman, John as the minister had the courage and the foresight to take it on. When we came into government in 1983 three children in ten completed Year Twelve. By 1996 we had lifted that to nine in ten. So we trebled the cohort and because we still wanted the same percentage of school-leavers to go to university, we had to treble university places. John's solution was to charge fees and provide student loans, and pour the fees back into funding the extra university places necessary.

As Trade Minister he had also put together the historic Cairns Group of agriculture nations as a very effective bloc of middle-power traders. So I wanted him to step up and do the sorts of things I had done as Treasurer. I knew there was always some risk that he might throw a bomb and blow the rest of us up but given my own propensity to occasionally throw a bomb, I could hardly rule out an associate bomb-thrower.

KOB: I was struck by the fact that apart from you, there were only four of the original Hawke Ministers left in your first Cabinet—Willis, Dawkins, Evans and Button, and there were a few others from the original outer Ministry. An awful lot of talent and experience had gone.

PJK: We had lost a lot of the originals but in the end it is leadership that matters. The spiritual nourishment of the Cabinet matters. Without being bombastic or overbearing, if the leader provides the intellectual framework and the uplift, it's contagious. Properly arraigning the arguments and the authority can get an updraft that lifts the whole Cabinet, and all perform.

KOB: You described the first Keating Cabinet as 'old dogs for a hard road'. What did you mean by that?

PJK: The old dogs were those ministers who'd cut their teeth on the economic reforms and social policy innovations. Some like Duffy and Blewett and Howe might not have been in the first Hawke Cabinet as they were junior ministers in 1983, but they had been very effective Cabinet ministers for years by the time I became Prime Minister.

Ralph Willis was very dedicated with well-calibrated views and a safe pair of hands. We always got on well.

I had a ton of time for Brian Howe even though he was from the Left. He had replaced me as Deputy Prime Minister when I went to the backbench, and I asked him to be Minister for Health, Housing and Community Services. He and I did a lot of things as Treasurer and Social Security Minister. For instance, we set up the Home and Community Care Scheme. We set up the ACAP assessments for aging. We set up the Child Support Agency through the tax system, and, with it the Child Support Scheme. So we had had a good cooperative history. Brian had brought a very conscientious effort and view to the outlays cutting task in the really difficult years, and as a member of the Left that was very difficult for him. So he was a signed up member of the management group if you like.

I also had a ton of time for Neal Blewett. Blewett was a class act from go to woe. He'd been tricky to get savings from as Health Minister, but that was a measure of his competence in protecting his ministry, and his indefatigability. He always kept a clear mind and a sharp eye for the government's best direction.

John Button had been on the long road through all the structural changes and even though we'd miss him on some we'd get him on others. Broadly he was for the template and brought real intelligence to the task.

You could say the same for Gareth Evans, who had held economic portfolios and was by then an exceptional Foreign Minister.

Graham Richardson was really a very competent minister who could speak and write well. You can see even these days in his written articles how well constructed they are, how clear the thought processes are, and being a leader of the Right, he had that authority.

Robert Ray and I sometimes had disputes over things like tele-communications but he was a really conscientious member of Cabinet and a very credible Defence Minister. Defence is such a difficult job. So Robert and I grew to live with each other rather than be bosom pals, but he brought quality to the table.

Michael Duffy I always liked because he was a kind of knockabout black Irishman, so he and I understood each other perfectly. He was also a good and straight thinker.

So I still had the nucleus of a hardworking, wise and ambitious group. They had been foot soldiers for a long time.

No one would dispute that the road we had to travel was going to be hard; we had to turn a disastrous political position around within a year. The big challenge was to make serious inroads on Hewson and *Fightback!* almost immediately and to move quickly with a credible plan for economic recovery and to start creating jobs again.

KOB: You and Dawkins had been very close allies through much of the reform and budget process but this was a very different relationship now. How did that relationship shape up in those early stages?

PJK: It shaped up really very well. When you finally become the first economic officer of the country, what you say and do matters, so I think John felt this was very liberating for him, notwithstanding the fact that the former Treasurer was just down the corridor as Prime Minister. But I was also a member of the nine-year working bee that had made up the core of the ERC, so we were policy affiliates and policy friends.

KOB: You restructured Cabinet to redirect much of the discussion to subcommittees, reduce the size of those committees and the input of junior ministers. Only a handful of Cabinet ministers were across more than a couple of those committees. What was the reason for that, and what was the effect of that?

PJK: I was a high believer in the Cabinet process, in an informed Cabinet with ministers free to express their views across the corporate matters of Cabinet, not just within their own portfolio. It meant the government was stronger. I was for anything that encouraged the better framing of those discussions.

KOB: There were some at the time who cynically saw that as you accruing more power to yourself, that it was a way for you to control Cabinet.

PJK: I think Blewett's diary would tell you otherwise. I wanted a more efficient process. I would always let ministers have their say but as the discussion went on, rather than just watching it fall away weakly I thought it was my job to say, 'Hang on, we're trying to get to a conclusion. We've discussed the elements, there is general agreement around points A, C and D but not B. We can come back to B, but let's think of a package that reflects the elements we're agreed on. If we think that this is an adoptable measure let's try and refine B.'

A good Cabinet process is a bit like a car manufacturer building a car. You get the frame and then you add the doors and put the windows in. Each part has to fit in the overall framework. And in the end you have to be confident the car will do what it promises. Just sitting back and hoping the car will come together mechanically simply because all the craftsmen working on the individual parts are good at their post is not my idea of leading.

There's a bit of scenery that needs setting here. Recovery from the recession notwithstanding, we had broadly accomplished most of the big economic reforms and put the structure in place for a robust new economy. Cabinet had already shifted the Australian national aggregates and the place structurally, but we couldn't sleepwalk our way into the future.

I was on the record saying it was time to think more about the country we'd been given. One of the first things I said to Cabinet was that when they were handing out continents not many people got one but we did. We've got a continent of our own and a land border with no one. It's incumbent upon us now to see that for what it is, to identify the unique opportunity it represents, and seize it.

My message to Cabinet was that under my prime ministership we would be shifting more heavily into foreign policy, more vigorously defining our national identity and coming to terms with Indigenous Australia. It was time to move on the spiritual matters, the things that make a nation glow.

I said these things to Cabinet when we first met, so all of a sudden the Keating Government and the Keating Cabinet had a different focus from the one that Bob Hawke had led just a month or so earlier.

KOB: I want to try to understand the nature of leadership, particularly as it applies to leading a nation. What gave you the confidence to set a course for the nation, to shrug off the knocks and the setbacks, and what about the part ego plays in political leadership?

That you can't have strong leadership without a strong ego is a given. Don Watson had a go at this when he said in *Recollections of a Bleeding Heart*:

> They need something to protect them against both the critics and the flatterers. The paradox might be that, having fewer personal doubts to distract them, leaders with indomitable egos are most able to govern for all. The distant drum they hear above the popular tumult is the signature of leadership. The balance we seek and never find is between the leader we want to look up to and the leader we want to shoot down.

I think there are aspects of truth in that, don't you?

PJK: Yes. Bernie Fraser once said good treasurers are like wise princes and that's pretty right. And that metaphor applies to Prime Ministers as well. A Prime Minister should be a wise prince, using prince in the proper context—a wise leader who's made observations about their country and the possibilities presented by the political moment. Shifting the way the country thinks about itself and the way it functions.

I think there is a great difference between ego and confidence. You've heard me say and it's worth saying again: confidence is not like a can of Popeye's spinach. You've got to earn it through your own tested judgements against difficult circumstances and occasions, but when you have it you have a very new power.

I would like to think that what I had was confidence, but a wary confidence, where I knew I had the vista and the ability to shift the structure but always taking care of the balances and the dangers that inevitably appear.

This is a different question to ego. Ego is a notion that there's some inherent or vested greatness. This is where Bob and I differed. I've said to you that I believe Bob was a narcissist. I believe that sincerely. I was never that. I had to earn everything the hard way, but one of the benefits of doing it the hard way is that it is the thorough way. So when you climb to the top beyond the long and winding road, you have a lot of earned power. But confidence and power and their judicious use are not ego.

I would say that is the central point of my years as both Prime Minister and Treasurer. If you have properly prepared for the task of leadership, and your central interests are truly for the country and its betterment, you invariably do better. If, however, it's more about you personally and your political advancement, then those compromised notions will invariably detract from your capacity to make the seminal changes. People have often said to me since, 'You guys did so many things', and I've said, 'Yes we did, and do you know why? Because we could see what needed to be done and we had the confidence and commitment to do them.'

I wanted to see Australia change. I was prepared to risk my job virtually all the time to bring that about.

You've heard me say that if you manage to do something that is both good and true, then there is a surge, a sense of uprightness, perhaps righteousness that lifts you to do better things. But dreaming is central to the task. If you have the imagination and with it the capacity, you will have a Cabinet or government infused with goodness. And if it's infused with purpose, and the central task is the nation's betterment, then the country will just power along. Power along.

KOB: You had twelve months to restore some economic credibility in the teeth of the recession before facing the electorate. When did you first realise just how deep the recession now was?

PJK: After I left Treasury in mid-1991 I used to go regularly to Sydney where I was restoring a house. I was also getting around Sydney a lot, including putting together a joint venture with the Danish national pork industry after I bought into the Parkville piggery, so I was getting more real-world stories than I might have had in Canberra. I could see the recession was far deeper than we thought it would be, and that both monetary and fiscal policy had to play a larger role in a timely recovery.

KOB: The people who'd lost their jobs weren't just victims of the recession, were they? In his diary Neal Blewett noted Ralph Willis telling your first Cabinet meeting that structural change through the tariff cuts was 'causing a holocaust on the employment front' that would be a killer electorally. This was a double whammy for the unemployed.

PJK: The structural changes we had made through the tariff cuts had impacts in the real economy, but they were gradual. It took thirteen years from 1998 to 2001 for the tariffs to be abolished. It affected Victoria particularly badly because there was so much protected industry there.

But the longer-term story was we had such strong employment growth in the years that followed, and as the service economy grew, we were getting big job uptakes. But people did need retraining and support packages of a kind we tried to provide, particularly in Victoria.

KOB: Bill Kelty and the Accord were still strategically very important to you in terms of both economic policy and the politics in those early months when he agreed to delay a general wage claim that was due in May. But when he came to you with a union delegation asking for a pause in the tariff cuts while unemployment continued to rise you denied his request. Wasn't that a reasonable ask from your friend and Accord partner?

PJK: Bill Kelty and the Accord were important right through the Labor years, whether under Hawke's prime ministership or my own. And it was his members who were particularly affected by the recession. What we were asking of the ACTU and the Accord in 1992 was exactly what we had asked of them to help cement the recovery from John Howard's recession in 1982. In 1992 Bill's support was critical in persuading the strong powerful unions to restrain their wage claims while the government poured its *One Nation* effort into helping unemployed people find jobs.

But I couldn't agree to a pause on tariffs. If I had, that would have been the end of the reform momentum and we would never have completed the critical reform of opening up Australia's product markets. It would be a job half-done. It is in times of real stress that a nation's resolve is tested. Does the country mean to change itself or not? In the end there were not many people who wanted to stick with it. Bill was an intellectual fellow and he understood that shifts in the exchange rate in any one year were often greater than the step down in the tariff that year, but it was his job to run the fight on behalf of his membership.

I had to consider the psychological effects. With a game-changing reform like the tariff cuts, it's a tough process getting Cabinet, caucus and the labour movement to jump the really big hurdles. If we baulk at the next hurdle because of a recession then we're permitting some lingering faith in the old model, the old Australia, the old locked-up model. I wanted to make sure there was no residual faith in that model.

It worried me that if we stopped and looked back we would end up like Lot's wife, turning into a pillar of salt. The moment you rob the reform process of its electricity and energy, its truth, the game falls away.

KOB: Inflation was now flat thanks to the recession, but more than one in ten Australians were unemployed. It was heading for a million people registered for unemployment. No matter how effectively you attacked *Fightback!* you had to have a credible response on jobs.

PJK: Immediately after becoming leader I started work, initially with John Dawkins, on a recovery plan for growth and employment. The *One Nation* package that followed was a classic Keynesian response. Private demand had fallen with the recession and with the high interest rates that had driven it. We had to lift public demand with budgetary expansion: infrastructure projects like the standard gauge railway across Australia through South Australia to Victoria, urgent spending on education support, municipal council projects and direct payments to people to kickstart the place. And it worked—not as quickly as I'd have liked—but by the third quarter of 1994 growth was running at 5 per cent.

KOB: There was an immense irony in this. You had spent years as Treasurer cutting budgets, cutting programs and cutting spending, now you were moving in reverse, so the great cutter became the spender.

PJK: Keynes said, 'When the facts change I change.' Well, I changed too. When Treasury's projections about a soft landing were demonstrably unbelievable and we were left with a much deeper recession than we should ever have had, it was my job as Prime Minister to lift the demand equation. And the demand equation was a classic Keynesian move to take the budget back into deficit. This idea that John Howard and Peter Costello used to proffer that the budget is like some sort of household account and you have to be abstinent and thrifty and keep it permanently in surplus is the sign of untrained and tired minds.

KOB: I can remember one speech of yours where you drew a very similar analogy to the household budget.

PJK: Maybe, but it's a simple proposition. If you need to restart private investment as we did in 1983 you pull public investment back, but if you've achieved surplus and you end up with a significant slowdown for other reasons, you let the budget do some work, you let it go into deficit. This is exactly what Kevin Rudd and Wayne Swan did in 2008 with the global financial crisis, and when the rest of the world plunged into recession, Australia escaped the trap—and it would have been a very costly trap in economic and social terms. I applied the same principle in 1992, which gradually worked, because growth came back strongly.

KOB: Before you gave Treasury to John Dawkins, you did seriously consider becoming Treasurer again as well as Prime Minister. Would that have really been possible?

PJK: Ben Chifley was both Prime Minister and Treasurer and state premiers have often opted to act as Treasurer as well. I had the whole economic structure and all the fiscal and policy changes so sharply in my mind that I didn't need to climb any learning curves, so the management of the Treasury portfolio is something I could have managed with the right support structure.

KOB: While juggling all of the broad responsibilities that come with the top job?

PJK: I'm not understating either job, but when you've been Treasurer for eight years you do get a lot of road feel. Road feel is very important; you turn the wheel slightly, the economy moves slightly. If you're doing it through a surrogate, it's not quite the same. That's not to say it can't be done, but you do not have the certitude that comes with doing it yourself.

KOB: But you've already described how exhausted you were through those long budget processes as Treasurer, and I'm sure there were moments as Prime Minister, particularly when you were grappling with Mabo, when you would have been exhausted too. The combination of the two would have been a huge ask.

PJK: But it's all about the judgements at the turn—judgements.

KOB: Nonetheless Don Russell, your closest adviser, talked you out of keeping the Treasury. What did he say that persuaded you?

PJK: I think he was also tired after all his years working with me on the big changes. In the end I took his advice, but looking back had I been Treasurer and Prime Minister, I would have calibrated things more closely.

As you know I had the big issue of the tax cuts which were part of *One Nation*, and as we subsequently discovered to our cost Treasury had overestimated the revenue on which our calculations were based. When the time came to deliver the tax cuts the revenue base had by then fallen away substantially. Had I been in closer touch with Treasury when we were working on the tax cuts and forward projections, I might have been more alive to the risk.

KOB: But weren't the tax cuts more a political component of *One Nation* than an economic one? Quite apart from your goal to get the economy going again, you urgently needed to at least neutralise John Hewson's promised tax cuts with tax cuts of your own. Didn't your economic adviser John Edwards brief senior officials on your behalf within days of you becoming Prime Minister that with *One Nation* you wanted to match Hewson's middle-income tax cut, to promote recovery from the recession and leave Hewson exposed with his GST?

PJK: What had happened was that the press gallery had decided to give Hewson, the new boy, a free ride. He had promised huge tax cuts as part of *Fightback!* and everyone in the gallery assumed they would be funded by the GST, but they weren't. They were not to be funded by the GST. The *Fightback!* document made that very clear: you had to take the trouble to read it carefully. Hewson was going to fund his massive tax cuts through unspecified cuts in government spending and the normal rise in government revenue—fiscal drag.

I was not going to go to an election with one arm tied behind my back while he was able to run with unfunded tax cuts. At that stage I was the absolute champion cutter of government spending in Australian history—still am—and I'd run four surplus budgets in a row for the first time since Federation. I wasn't going to just hand that inheritance to some blow-in who had never done a budget before, and let him walk away to an election with unfunded tax cuts.

KOB: Hewson was a trained market economist and he had been a senior adviser to Phillip Lynch and John Howard when they were Treasurers.

PJK: Yes, but there was no comparison between that and actually going through the really hard, back-breaking job of seriously cutting outlays. Seven years, five months a year, of ERC and budget meetings. And the courage to take the decisions. Hewson was not in my league, and I was not going to pretend he was.

KOB: But you also were compelled by the politics, weren't you? You had to match his tax cuts.

PJK: Not really. It wasn't so much a political need as it was that I just wouldn't let him slide in on the notion that his tax cuts were funded by the GST when they were not. Notwithstanding that idolent press gallery giving him an uncritical ride.

KOB: But you could have exposed that without having your own tax cuts. Your cuts were there at least as much for the politics as they might have been for the economics.

PJK: I was able to have my own tax cuts because there was enough revenue there. There's a thing called fiscal drag where inflation pushes wage earners into higher tax brackets, which then pushes up the overall tax revenue. Every now and again you have to have a tax cut simply to maintain the real incidence of taxation; in other words, giving taxpayers something back from bracket creep to maintain the real and appropriate rate of tax. So, on Treasury's calculation of compound inflation, there was a tax cut due. There was also the growth. That presented us with a political opportunity to provide a tax cut with no GST against Hewson's tax cut, but with a GST.

KOB: You had *One Nation* ready to go for the first week of Parliament in late February. How hard was that from a standing start—new Prime Minister, new Cabinet, new Treasurer, a total reorientation within the public service?

PJK: It was just a huge undertaking. It was like doing the Tax White Paper in 1985. It was like an instant budget, and it took all hands to the wheel. It covered a lot of ground but it achieved its immediate purpose, which was to stop Hewson's momentum.

It was a four-year plan with an overall goal of 800,000 new jobs in that time without risk to the current account deficit. There was more than $700 million for expanded technical education and a billion dollars for infrastructure projects on railways, roads, bridges and ports. For instance, the Anzac Bridge in Sydney was built from the *One Nation* package.

To give the economy an immediate kickstart we gave cash payments from $125 to $250 to 1.9 million lower-income families. The cheques went out in April.

And then there were the tax cuts. The fact that the package worked in the way we wanted was reflected in the headlines that followed: 'PM's two billion kick start'. 'Keating plays an ace. Can Hewson follow suit?'—that's the *Financial Review*. The story from the *Australian*'s Newspoll: 'ALP turns the corner with Keating riding high'.

KOB: It was presented by you rather than Dawkins, and identified as the Keating Plan. Was that fair?

PJK: It was my job to knock over Hewson and *Fightback!*, and it needed more weight than the Treasurer could provide. Part of the onus on me after replacing Bob was to succeed where he had failed, so I had to identify as the new Prime Minister with the remedial policy. This was my response, leader to leader, and John Dawkins understood that and was happy with it.

KOB: It can't have been easy for him to give up his first moment in the sun as Treasurer, and others picked this up. The cartoonist Moir in the *Sydney Morning Herald* at the time drew a rather haggard-looking Dawkins in his singlet and pyjamas practising a conversation in the mirror while he shaved, saying, 'Look Paul, I'm supposed to be Treasurer, look Paul, I'm the Treasurer of Australia, look Paul, am I Treasurer or not, look Paul ...'

PJK: John was very much on board with the strategy. He helped frame it and politically it did work because in the 27 March opinion poll my rating is 38 per cent and Hewson's is 37, and in two-party preferred terms, Labor is at 43 per cent and the Coalition is on 44 per cent. The Coalition had a 26-point lead over us in December, so to the extent that the *One Nation* package was designed to neutralise and deal with *Fightback!* and for me to deal with John Hewson, the evidence is that it dealt us back in the game.

KOB: Here are a couple of the other headlines from the *One Nation* launch. The *Australian*: 'PM's jobs and votes grab, fixing a recession to buy an election'. The *Age*: 'An unashamedly political pitch for votes'.

PJK: The government was in a shocking position when I took over— 31 per cent in its primary vote. Let me repeat that: 31 per cent. In Bob's 1990 election we had slumped to 39 per cent in the primary vote and needed a larger than usual flow of preferences to win; 31 per cent would have wiped us out. We had to get back into the forties. So some popular things had to be done. A lot of good karma had to happen, and it doesn't happen by magic. It has to be engineered.

FOREIGN POLICY

Paul Keating was born during the preamble to the Cold War, when Britain, America and the Soviet Union were engaged in a deadly race for Berlin, gobbling up as much territorial advantage as they could on the way through. Keating was eighteen months old when America went nuclear against Japan, and five when Mao won his Cultural Revolution and China became communist.

Those three elements then dominated Australia's foreign policy literally up to the moment when Keating became Prime Minister, particularly the Cold War. The Berlin Wall fell in 1989, but it wasn't until 26 December 1991 that the might of the Soviet Union formally came to an end after the breakaway of its various member states, until Russia was all that was left of the Kremlin's fearfully powerful empire.

For Keating this was an enormous opportunity for Australia to deal itself into what would inevitably be a new strategic game in the Asia-Pacific, so he welcomed the serendipitous visit to Australia by US President George Bush Senior just five days after the end of the Soviet Union and six days after the swearing in of the Keating Government.

It had the potential to be an awkward occasion, not just because it was his first foray into foreign affairs as Prime Minister. This was the most important relationship Australia had, and there was a twist. Bob Hawke as Prime Minister had taken pride in the stark contrast between the Whitlam Government's prickly relationship with America and his own. He claimed a personal friendship with Ronald Reagan's Secretary of State George Shultz dating from his ACTU days, which he delighted in demonstrating on the golf course.

Hawke also made a point of establishing a close rapport with Bush, anticipating he would replace Reagan as President in 1988; the two called each other friends. On a trip to America in June that year and five months before the US election, Hawke cemented that relationship: the Labor Prime Minister and Republican President-to-be were throwing horseshoes—Bush's favourite game—for the Australian media cameras. There was considerable kudos for Hawke in Bush's acceptance of his invitation to visit Australia, only the second American President to do so. The first was Lyndon Johnson 25 years earlier. Bush would be the first President to address the Australian Parliament.

None of this appeared to faze the new kid on the foreign affairs block. He could have been forgiven for sticking to a safe and conservative departmental brief in the formal talks and gladhanding his way through the rest of the visit. Instead Keating unveiled his idea to establish an ambitious new leaders' forum for the Asia-Pacific region, expanding on the successful Hawke initiative for a ministerial-level economic forum called APEC. Since the world's most powerful nation tended to like its own ideas best, there was clear risk of a rebuff, particularly since it wasn't even formally on the agenda. But the Americans didn't shut the gate.

In early April 1992 Keating wrote a follow-up letter to Bush, putting his proposition formally on the table, giving it further impact by also writing to Indonesian President Suharto and Japanese Prime Minister Miyazawa, raising for the first time with them the case for APEC to become a leaders' forum rather than ministerial. In his reply

Bush reiterated what he'd told Keating at Kirribilli in January: that Australia should take the lead because if America did it could be counterproductive, in the Asian region particularly.

What followed was a personal quest that took Keating to the doors of every significant Asian leader, negotiating various diplomatic minefields in the process. For instance, China didn't recognise the independent status of Taiwan or Hong Kong, both members of the ministerial APEC, and there was no credible APEC leaders' forum without China.

The stepping stones Keating used make for a compelling tale, particularly in terms of whether the self-confessed grenade thrower of domestic politics was prepared to temper his style on the international stage. The answer is yes, and no.

Certainly the Keating style of diplomacy was not taken from the Foreign Affairs Department playbook. We all remember the guiding hand at the Queen's back during the opening of the new Parliament House and the labelling of Malaysia's Dr Mahathir Mohamad as a recalcitrant on APEC, and the picture also emerges from face-to-face meetings behind closed doors with some of the world's most powerful leaders, of a man who was still prepared to call a spade a spade.

One interesting insight is revealed in the book *The Clinton Tapes*, based on a long series of secret and intimate conversations between Bill Clinton and historian Taylor Branch recorded throughout his presidency. Clinton told Branch of a briefing from Vice President Al Gore who had stood in for him at an APEC meeting in Osaka in 1995. Gore came back with 'a very unpleasant report'. Clinton had chosen to stay home to deal with an emergency government shutdown caused by a hostile Republican Congress. Gore reported that the Japanese were offended and that 'Australian Prime Minister Paul Keating hotly told Gore he had come to Osaka despite a dock strike and paralysed economy back home. Where was Clinton?'

White House National Security Council official Stan Roth told Paul Kelly for *March of Patriots* that:

> What Keating did was offer a vision to President Clinton of what APEC could be . . . Clinton came to office more interested in economic issues than foreign policy and as a free trader . . . It is not an exaggeration to say that Keating inspired Clinton. It's very clear to me having watched this from the White House that this was a special relationship.

But the big international relationship Keating as Prime Minister sought to make his own was that with Indonesia's President Suharto. Relations between the two neighbouring countries were complex and somewhat chequered to say the least. A wartime minister in the Curtin and Chifley Governments, and future Labor leader, Dr Bert Evatt had acted as a mediator while President of the fledgling United Nations General Assembly in 1948–49 to help negotiate Indonesia's independence from its old colonial master, the Netherlands, which would have helped soften Indonesia's view of white Australia's own colonial record in Papua New Guinea and its infamous White Australia policy at home.

But when Indonesia sought also to claim Western New Guinea from the Netherlands in the mid-1950s, the Menzies Government opposed it. Menzies had come to view Indonesia as a potential security threat, a view that strengthened in the period of Konfrontasi from 1963 to 1966 when Indonesia aggressively resisted Malaysia's claims to Northern Borneo and Australia weighed in with other Commonwealth nations to support Malaysia. Australian troops clashed with soldiers from Indonesia in Borneo during the confrontation, which fell away after President Sukarno lost power following a *coup d'état* that led to General Suharto becoming President.

The relationship gradually thawed but another flashpoint came with Indonesia's invasion of East Timor in late 1975, nine days after East Timor declared its independence from Portugal, during which five Australian newsmen—the Balibo Five—were killed by Indonesian soldiers. Although successive Australian Prime Ministers had been tacitly and pragmatically sympathetic to Indonesia's claim to East Timor, the Australian public's view was at best mixed. That ambivalence was compounded by a massacre of pro-independence demonstrators in November 1991 at Santa Cruz cemetery in the East Timor capital of Dili. An estimated 250 activists were killed when Indonesian soldiers fired on what was essentially a peaceful protest. The massacre provoked strong anti-Indonesian sentiment in Australia, which was still fresh in people's minds five months later when Paul Keating decided to elevate the bilateral relationship's strategic and commercial importance for Australia by making Indonesia his first port of call as Prime Minister.

As Paul Keating's vision for Australia's place in the world unfolded, central to it was his view that the way we perceived ourselves at home—from a standpoint of real independence and self-respect—would govern how our regional neighbours would perceive and respect us from abroad.

KOB: Fewer than two weeks into the prime ministership you had to host George Herbert Bush, only the second US President to come to Australia. You could have played it safe, gone through the motions, and seen him off back to America with no risk of a bad press. After eight years as Treasurer and a spell as Deputy Prime Minister you weren't exactly a foreign policy *ingénue* but you wouldn't have wanted anything going wrong either. You didn't play it that way at all though, did you?

PJK: Because I was new to the job I was very careful to listen to the experts—my principal foreign policy adviser, Ashton Calvert, and my own departmental expert, Allan Gyngell. What drove me was my own view that I wasn't going to let a US President visit without doing my best to gain something for Australia.

You've got to remember that the Cold War was well and truly over, and the Soviet Union had been dissolved the week before I became Prime Minister. This was all fresh in everybody's minds, but I could see the Americans paying no heed to the opportunities these events presented in the Pacific.

American policy in the Pacific had essentially been run by the US Navy since 1945, rarely by the President or the State Department, save for Nixon's foray with Mao. What I was seeking was to try to draw the US into a greater engagement in Asia, not through the navy but through direct White House interest.

It was slightly awkward that the President had been invited by Bob but that was easily negotiated. As Ronald Reagan's Vice President, George Bush had hosted me at his house when I went with Bob to meet Reagan in Washington in 1983, and we met again at the funeral of Soviet President Yuri Andropov. I represented Australia because I was in Paris at the time. George and Senator James Baker represented America and we were standing in a small group with Margaret Thatcher and Fidel Castro, watching the parade of soldiers goose-stepping through Red Square. It was minus 23 and Margaret was hopping from one foot to the other in the cold, and I said, 'At that rate you'll be trying out for the Paris Opera Ballet.' She said, 'A more chivalrous person would offer their coat,' and I said, 'I'm not as chivalrous as some members of the British Labour Party.'

By the time we'd got through the long reception line, George Bush was clearly very hungry and invited me back to the US Embassy for hamburgers. So we weren't complete strangers, and when I said on his arrival at Kirribilli House, 'Well, you were meant to be meeting Bob but I'm afraid you've got me, George', he had the grace to laugh.

KOB: What were the dynamics at that meeting with Bush? Ashton Calvert told Paul Kelly for *March of Patriots* that you

were 'shameless and compelling' with Bush and his National Security Adviser Brent Scowcroft, that you basically dominated the meeting.

PJK: I made it an intellectual event rather than a golf game with a bit of formal chat tacked on. There were just four of us around the coffee table. The President had his National Security Adviser Brent Scowcroft and I had Ashton Calvert. It was in the main drawing room at Kirribilli House, which was a pretty inadequate space.

I spun a tale through the strategic history of postwar Europe to the end of the Cold War and the important opportunity that presented to the United States in the Pacific and Asia.

What I particularly wanted to advance was the idea that the APEC forum originating under Hawke as Prime Minister could be seriously upgraded in importance from a meeting of finance and trade ministers to a powerful regional leaders' forum, not just engaged in economics but strategic issues.

I argued that we could stitch together a very pretty piece of foreign policy, with Australia playing a critical part as a middle power with a foot in the American camp and a foot in Asia. Bush was interested, and when he excused himself for a toilet break, Brent Scowcroft said to me, 'Prime Minister, you have articulated a policy for the United States in the Pacific that we haven't articulated for ourselves.' He said, 'That says something about us.'

It was a very honest statement and I thanked him for the compliment.

He said, 'Well, let's see what we can do.'

When the President came back the subject warmed up again and we gave it another go-round. It was left on the basis that it was potentially a good idea, but better pursued by Australia than America because, as Bush said, 'They'll see us coming and they'll run a million miles.' He said if we could get all the doubting Thomases into the basket, then perhaps America would come along.

That was the start of what APEC is now. Bob initiated the original APEC, which was a regional version of the OECD. You show me your statistics and I'll show you mine. It was an important forum, and a necessary stepping stone, but it had no real strategic power. The real power belongs to the heads of government. It belongs to the presidents and the prime ministers and that's where decisions get taken. Once America was committed it would automatically bring a gravitas and strength to the proposal. It would also force the White House to focus on issues in our region in a way it had not done before.

But first we had to see whether the original APEC constituency would come onboard, and China had to embrace it if the whole thing was to have credibility. That was complicated by the fact that Taiwan and Hong Kong were admitted to the original APEC and China wouldn't have a bar of them at a heads of government gathering. I knew I'd always have trouble with Li Peng while ever Hong Kong and Taiwan were there, but it was too late to excise them. So part of my job was to try to drag the Chinese in with Hong Kong and Taiwan. A really hard call.

Within weeks I had written to every regional leader to get the idea going. I wrote again to Bush and he wrote back, asking again that we take the lead rather than America.

'If we lead I don't think we'll prosper,' he said.

KOB: You also singled out Indonesia on your first visit overseas. Why Indonesia?

PJK: Because I always believed Indonesia would in the end be the place of greatest strategic importance to Australia, because of that vast archipelago with a population of 230 million people. It takes eight hours to fly across and spans all the approaches to Australia from the north. So where it goes strategically there is much pressure on Australia to go similarly, or to be as influenced by these events. It is also the biggest Muslim nation in the world.

At the leadership level we'd had virtually no relationship with them. Bob Hawke had visited Indonesia once in eight years. Almost all our dealings with them were viewed through the prism of Timor, particularly after the five Australian journalists were killed in Balibo, which so influenced the debate within Australia.

I always took the view that President Suharto was well disposed towards Australia when he need not have been. Most Australian Prime Ministers made their first overseas visit to the White House. I wanted to break that tradition to make the point that I regarded Indonesia as a supremely important country.

Every strategic briefing an Australian Prime Minister had from the Foreign Affairs Department would begin with this sentence: 'The election of Suharto's new order government was the event of greatest positive strategic significance to Australia in the postwar years.'

And this was true. Had it not been for Suharto managing Indonesia, we would have been spending 5 per cent of GDP on defence, not 2, and we would have had strategic difficulties all the time, but we would never acknowledge this. You would never hear Hawke or Fraser or even Whitlam say it, although Gough did have a reasonable relationship with Suharto. It was true, and I was prepared to say it. I wanted to turn over an entirely new leaf and my instinct about Suharto was right. He had a very benign view of Australia.

KOB: You were subsequently criticised for being too close to President Suharto, even subservient to him. What informed the way you actually presented yourself to him, the way you treated him in your dialogue?

PJK: The conversational protocols in Asia are very polite. This idea that we pride ourselves on speaking frankly often stands in stark contrast to Asian cultures. They usually don't speak frankly in Asia, and are careful to show regard for the person opposite. You can be direct, you can be frank in a well-tailored way, but not in a way that they would consider rude. You give a head of government or a head of state respect for the position they hold and in Suharto's case he was also much older than me. He'd been around a long, long time so I gave him a fair deal of room. I always addressed him as Mr President and he always addressed me as Prime Minister. We never developed a deeply personal relationship but it was a respectful head of government to head of state relationship.

KOB: What was the frankest you got with him?

PJK: I had sharp moments with him over East Timor, one where he excused himself to go to the toilet and his interpreter said to me through my adviser Allan Gyngell, 'I think the President's giving you a signal that this discussion has gone to the point where he can't bear it any longer, within the limits of Javanese politeness. If the conversation is to continue at this tempo, I don't think he'll respond any further to it.'

I took the whole Timor issue right up to him, although we never got any credit from the East Timor lobby. At the same time I was always determined that I would never let the relationship fall hostage to Timor.

KOB: Neal Blewett recalls your comments to caucus on your return from that first visit, that you had told both Suharto and his Foreign Minister, Ali Alatas, that the Santa Cruz massacre was a tragedy, that the Indonesian Government's response was credible. But you warned them that the relationship between the local population and the Indonesian troops was too tough, that they had to establish better relations with the local community and there had to be reconciliation accompanied by real economic development. You also criticised the use of the criminal code against non-violent political protestors. Does that gel with your memory of what you said, and what was Suharto's response?

 He had been President of Indonesia for over a decade before the military intervention into Timor. And in the context of the Cuban missile crisis and the Soviet Union trying to use Cuba as a sort of a staging point in the American western hemisphere, when the Portuguese Communist Party got control of East Timor and they were massacring people, the people around Ramos-Horta for instance, Suharto was encouraged by the United States to do something about it. I think Suharto moved with great reluctance on East Timor, and his wariness turned out to be well placed. There was no profit for Indonesia in ever having occupied East Timor.

KOB: You think he felt that?

 Indonesia about its territorial integrity, worrying that the loss of one part of the archipelago might stir unrest in another.

I raised the idea of setting East Timor up as a special economic zone and giving East Timorese children ready access to Indonesian universities. I told Suharto that we would share the cost but there had to be a different set of political protocols.

And I more or less had him at that point when I finished the prime ministership. I think I could say with all authority that at the time I left office President Suharto was on the cusp of agreeing to special economic status for East Timor in which we would financially participate. Now the East Timor lobby would paint me and Gareth

Evans as lushes who were falling over ourselves to accommodate Indonesia when in fact the opposite was the case.

KOB: How did you go about pitching APEC to Suharto?

PJK: It turned out that as one of the leaders of the non-aligned movement in the Cold War, Suharto had been locked out of the big discussions about the shape of the world. When I started talking to him about being engaged as one of the central figures in a new APEC leaders' forum with the United States, China and Japan, all of a sudden his eyes lit up. He'd been sitting there mostly just managing Indonesian problems for 30 years. All of a sudden he's getting engaged by the next-door neighbour about the state of the world with the promise of an influential role for Indonesia.

Suharto had great intellectual quality. He was well across all the issues. He knew I wanted a fresh chapter in the relationship and recognised that his new order government had had a positive impact on Australia strategically for a very long time.

I warmed him up to the idea. I told him I would also raise it personally with Prime Minister Miyazawa and he was most interested to hear Japan's response. I told Suharto I would have a better chance of picking up Miyazawa's support if I could tell him that, all things being equal, Suharto would come along with me.

KOB: What did you want to walk away with from that meeting?

PJK: Apart from kickstarting APEC, I wanted to walk away with the notion that we could restart the relationship around a broad range of issues, a broader country-to-country relationship. In the course of that discussion I proposed to him that we develop a regular ministerial council meeting so that the next set of meetings wouldn't be just the president and prime minister, but the foreign minister, the trade minister, the treasury minister. He and I set up that ministerial council and, to give Howard and Downer credit, they kept that going after I left, and it still goes to this day. More than twenty years later, the Indonesia/Australia Ministerial Council meets annually. It's a much thicker relationship now than it was when I walked in the door, notwithstanding problems that might flare from time to time.

KOB: After that first meeting with Suharto, you received what the Foreign Affairs Department regarded as a very accurate brief of how he reacted to that meeting.

PJK: Our ambassador was very well connected to Suharto's inner circle. The feedback was that Suharto regarded the meeting with me as similar to the meeting President Sukarno had had years before with President John Kennedy, who was also a much younger man; that Kennedy had given Sukarno regard and respect and Suharto felt I had done the same with him; that I had ideas, that I knew the issues, and that I could move when it was time to move. Suharto also recognised that I was prepared to turn a genuinely new page in the history of relations between Australia and Indonesia and he was very happy with the meeting.

KOB: What view did you take of Australian intelligence gathering in the region when you were Prime Minister?

PJK: I viewed it all with reasonable disdain. You might think that sounds strange, but I never found value in this SIGINT stuff, Signals Intelligence. Let's loosely call it spying. I had little time for intelligence and therefore I wouldn't invest either time or authority in it.

Most things Australia needed to know we were able to know by generally asking ministers around the region what they thought—most would tell you. Most of our open notes from our diplomatic posts would give us an adequate picture. Now the SIGINT, which was basically recovered by the Americans, would occasionally reflect something, and we'd have our ear out for particular things. Through the bases in Australia we shared signals intelligence with the Americans, and sometimes some little nugget of genuine strategic importance would turn up.

Allan Gyngell would very occasionally show me things if he thought they were significant enough but the idea of running through all those cables about what someone had said in the Malaysian Cabinet anteroom or some other piece of gossip, I couldn't be bothered with.

I was much happier on the big policy picture and when I met people like Suharto or Mahathir or Miyazawa I'd make my judgements about them. I didn't need to know what they said in their dressing rooms. So I was the non-SIGINT Prime Minister. On the big panoply of issues can you be bothered spending time on this rats and mice stuff? That's the question. I took the view that if you let yourself become hostage to the spooks it warps your perspective.

KOB: What about your colleagues?

PJK: A lot of them loved it. They loved the idea of access to so-called secret information. Occasionally something would be of some benefit—getting a reaction to an APEC meeting that would give you a steer about what they were thinking—but it's in a different order to bugging someone's telephone or putting bugs in someone's hotel room.

KOB: Were you aware that substantial bugging was going on to a significant degree when you were PM?

PJK: Not really, no.

KOB: What would you have done if you'd found out?

PJK: I don't know. I'm a big boy. I know how the big boys play the game so therefore I would always play a certain game but only because prudence dictated that you played a certain game. But there's a difference between prudence and allowing yourself to be alarmed, or alarming the nation through too much reliance on intelligence.

KOB: I understand the world of realpolitik without ever having been a part of it. But even so, I wonder how easily you were able to dismiss the dark side of President Suharto's history in seeking to establish this relationship, in embracing him so personally. He had a great deal of blood on his hands over the slaughter of more than half a million Indonesians, men, women and children, including many ethnic Chinese in 1965. And not to put too fine a point on it, Suharto was notoriously corrupt at the expense of his people. How easy was it to dismiss those things or put them to one side?

PJK: The thing was, he was unambiguously the President of Indonesia. What were we supposed to do? Just blot Indonesia out for 50 years? We virtually blotted them out for 30 years to our own cost. At what stage do we accept the fact that the Indonesian people had supported this regime and that he was their elected president?

What was I to do? Say, 'Oh well, they're not going to like this at the *National Times* or the *Age* or the *Sydney Morning Herald*, so therefore we're not going to have a proper relationship with Indonesia?'

This is just nonsense and the proof is in the pudding, quite apart from the core of goodwill created with Suharto, which then significantly advanced this pivotal relationship between Australia and Indonesia. Quite frankly, without Suharto I would have had no chance of getting George Bush or Bill Clinton into APEC. Without him I wouldn't have got Miyazawa in Japan. Miyazawa said to me, 'You get Suharto, I will come with you.'

KOB: Outline how those events unfolded on APEC after you began to draw Suharto in. Was Miyazawa the next cab off the rank?

PJK: Miyazawa was the Finance Minister of Japan when I was Treasurer and occasionally I would have dinner with him in Washington after IMF meetings. He was a very cultivated person and we established a good rapport. So when I saw Miyazawa I was able to say, 'If your inclination is to be in it, I can guarantee you Suharto will be in it.'

China was the next step with Li Peng. God, was he a tough guy. He wasn't going to have a bar of it because Hong Kong and Taiwan were already part of the APEC ministerial round. China couldn't stomach the suggestion that this gave Hong Kong and Taiwan formal recognition of their independence from mainland China.

At my dinner with Li Peng he said, 'We won't be there.'

I said, 'Listen, you'll be there. What, the President of the United States is going to be there and the Prime Minister of Japan, but you're not going to be there?' I said, 'You'll be there.'

A Chinese leader is not used to being spoken to like this. His wife said, 'Mr Keating, please have some respect for my husband, he's recuperating from a heart attack.'

So I got a rebuke from the wife. So I had to tone it down.

The next day Allan Gyngell, Ashton Calvert and I decided we had to come up with an alternative title for the forum to accommodate the Chinese. We were originally going to call it the APEC Heads of Government Meeting but after the run-in with Li Peng we proposed a change to the APEC Leaders' Meeting so you could be a leader of an economy without necessarily being a head of government. And the protocol would be with a wink and a nod that the person representing Hong Kong and Taiwan would not be the head of the executive government but maybe a senior minister. Technically

Bill Clinton was there as the leader of an economy, not a head of government.

In any event my great friend Zhu Rongji helped me behind the scenes and the Chinese came on board. It was President Jiang Zemin, whom I'd also seen, who delivered on that, and I had to introduce him to President Clinton in Seattle in November 1993 when we had the first APEC leaders' meeting.

KOB: What about China's relationship with Japan? Did that pose problems?

PJK: I introduced President Jiang Zemin to Prime Minister Morihiro Hosokawa in Seattle. And that was a very embarrassing meeting and handshake. Jiang Zemin knew he had to be there and wanted to be there, but didn't actually want to shake Hosokawa's hand. But he did.

And we had the same kind of difficulty with President Clinton shaking Jiang Zemin's hand. That was something of a stand-off and Bill Clinton would not pose for a photo with smiles. It was interesting to look at the picture gallery when you knew what was going on behind the scenes.

By the second meeting I had Jiang Zemin doing karaoke with Clinton—that's how much it had changed. When the Chinese President's doing karaoke with the American President, things are getting better.

This was a little gift of Australian foreign policy to the rest of the world, certainly to the Asia-Pacific world. But without Suharto I would have had no chance. Suharto had imagination and scale.

KOB: After George Bush lost office at the end of 1992, how hard did you have to work on Clinton to get his support for the whole APEC idea?

PJK: It didn't go well for a while because Clinton initially said that having won the election with his line 'It's the economy, stupid', and having attacked Bush for being too distracted by foreign policy, he couldn't afford also to be seen to be distracted by some new foreign policy exploit in his first year, like a new Asia-Pacific strategic body.

But at the same time the sweep of the idea appealed to his intellectual vanity. Bill had a great brain and he could see the whole template. So he and his foreign policy adviser Tony Lake thought about it for a while and a couple of months later said, 'What about this for an idea: we'll have our first meeting in Seattle, the home of Boeing and Microsoft, and we'll paint the picture that it's about jobs, jobs, jobs and we're looking across the Pacific to trade and we need a body to run the politics of the Pacific for trade and jobs?'

I said, 'Bill, if that's what you need to sell this, we're in business.'

The deal I did with Bill Clinton was that we would make the APEC Leaders' Meeting look like an economic body even though it was of its essence a strategic body. If you've got the President of the US, the President of China, and the Prime Minister of Japan sitting there, it is a strategic body.

KOB: What sort of a rapport did you strike with Clinton in your very first meeting with him?

PJK: I had a very good meeting but in the morning of that day he also had Yitzhak Rabin and Yasser Arafat visiting the White House, so I was the second-order player, albeit with a big strategic idea for them. We got on really well and there were things we had in common but powerful, young successful men—particularly American Presidents— can be very hard to deal with.

But I used the Cabinet technique on him. First I sketched out the opportunity, then teased out the difficulties in making it happen, and then the remedies. I gradually brought it back to a point where we could actually do something very important and well. And it's the old thing, Kerry, there's nothing like the power of a good idea. A good idea properly presented and well argued will always strike a point with a conscientious mind, and this did with Clinton.

By the time I left that meeting I had him in the bag for something. It's very interesting to look at the Australian press and see the reporting of that meeting. It was clear he was genuinely keen, and within a couple of months I'd actually got him to commit to APEC.

KOB: How much continuing contact did you have?

PJK: A lot of phone conversations and letters, which he seemed to enjoy. I'd say to him, 'Look, I think I've got Li Peng in a headlock.'

He understood that sort of language. I'd report on progress with Miyazawa and Suharto, and tell him it just needed a drop of authority.

'A drop of interest and authority from you, and I'll be able to pull all this together.'

KOB: How did Clinton strike you as a political operator at a personal level?

PJK: He was the most accomplished political figure that I have ever known in the way he connected with the public. Charming is not an adjective you apply to most political leaders, but he was so charming, it wouldn't matter if you were the guy on the door. He would grab your hand with both of his and look you directly in the eye. He had a magic about him.

KOB: He was also called Slick Willy—did you see any of the Slick Willy in him?

PJK: Maybe, but it was a terrific brain, and he couldn't quite resist the intellectual opportunity of APEC.

I said, 'Look Bill, we're from fraternal parties. I'm doing all the legwork. I'm gifting this thing to you. All you've got to do is be big enough to take the gift.'

KOB: Did you really speak to him in those terms?

PJK: Absolutely. He loved that sort of political dirty talk. We had a very informal lunch at the second APEC meeting in Bogor in Indonesia three days after he lost the mid-term congressional election to Newt Gingrich through his first term as President. He arrived looking tired, his eyes bloodshot. With all his aides around him he said one of his real points in coming to Indonesia was to hear how we had beaten the Liberal Party, how we'd pushed them to the Right and won. What was the clue? How come the Australian Labor Party had stood on its feet for eleven years against a conservative party similar to their Republican Party? He wanted to know what we were doing right and the Democrats were doing wrong. And so the whole lunch was about how we had split the Liberal Party for years.

KOB: And what was your fundamental advice to him?

PJK: You push them further to the Right and you run up the centre, pulling in your natural constituency on the Left.

KOB: Well, he ended up doing exactly what you'd done, pushing the Republicans to the Right.

PJK: But at that point he hadn't done that although I know they were thinking along those lines. We had a most engaging meeting and Allan Gyngell took a long note, one of those notes that will live in history.

KOB: You referred to talking dirty with Clinton. What does 'talking dirty' mean?

PJK: I'd say power stripped of all the niceties. Clinton had just lost the mid-terms to Newt Gingrich and I talked about how he should rip out the Republicans' throats. Clinton loved it.

When John Howard became Opposition Leader someone in my office remarked that he would be hard to beat.

I said, 'You know what I'm going to do with him? I'm going to put an axe right in his chest and rip his ribs apart.'

That's what I mean by talking dirty. It's power right down to the essence of it. Going for the jugular.

KOB: The day after you introduced the historic Mabo legislation into Parliament towards the end of 1993, you flew off to Seattle for that first tentative APEC leaders' meeting. How did you feel as you watched the summit unfold?

PJK: I felt some substantial sense of accomplishment. As a measure of Australian foreign policy, we had caused the coming together of the leadership of the Pacific nations, most particularly the Asia-Pacific nations as never before; it was a piece of geopolitical architecture in Asia or across the Pacific like never before.

That it was being hosted by the United States President in his own country and celebrated as a way of bringing together the trade and prosperity of the region was a a matter of great satisfaction to me. By now I had a very good personal relationship with President Clinton, which helped, but also a very nice relationship with Jiang Zemin and the Japanese Prime Minister and Suharto, and Goh Chok Tong from Singapore—it was a very nice event. I felt very happy that Australia had dealt itself into one of the top tables in the world where before we'd sat outside looking through the window at these kinds of discussions. Not only were we sitting at the table, but we had actually built the table we were sitting at.

Australia walked away from Seattle with a primary role in foreign policy in the region, and with a sort of bridging role between the United States and East Asia. We certainly walked away with a much thicker relationship with Indonesia and really good bilateral relations with Thailand, Singapore, South Korea and others. We dealt ourselves into the new postwar game, the game of open regionalism, which wasn't possible during the Cold War.

When you look back at Bill Clinton's foreign policy history in the eight years of his presidency, the APEC leaders' forum was really one of the most important things he was associated with. He wrote me a very nice letter about it afterwards, and he really enjoyed the second meeting in Indonesia.

KOB: There was one discordant note with regard to Seattle, and that was between you and Prime Minister Mahathir of Malaysia, which led you to describe him as 'recalcitrant'.

PJK: 'Recalcitrant' meaning he was the odd man out. It wasn't really a rude thing to say, but he decided to take some confected objection to it. He did something similar to Suharto the next year. He wanted his view to be an addendum to the communiqué and Suharto wouldn't have it. He couldn't avoid coming this time because Suharto was the host but he was still playing hard to get. I remember Bill Clinton standing beside me in the urinal on that occasion saying some very tough things about Prime Minister Mahathir.

He said, 'You know what we're gonna do? We're gonna screw this guy. We're gonna screw this guy.'

KOB: Did you enjoy any special place at the APEC leaders' table because even though you'd come up with the idea and driven the whole process, at the end of the day Australia was still dwarfed by the big players?

PJK: True, but as the founder I had secretarial rights, so I virtually ran the agenda. Clinton in Seattle or Suharto in Bogor would say to me, 'What do we do now? What item do you want to bring on next?' Quite often I'd sit next to various heads of government, many of whom were not proficient in English, and although they'd have a brief, it would get overtaken by events and they'd get asked to make a comment and wouldn't quite know what to say. I would write them a note and the meeting would move on, and I would run around all the parties, trying to keep the agenda running.

KOB: Sounds a bit like a Labor Party Conference.

PJK: In a sense yes, because there was a lot of running around with amendments. And to get the Bogor Declaration up, committing the region to free trade in only the second forum, was pretty remarkable. There were many problems between developed and developing countries and a lot of differences to resolve.

It was President Suharto's proposal but the original draft was written personally by Allan Gyngell and me. Suharto then adopted it and it became his draft, but it was my job to defend his draft and to see that amendments to his draft were not ultra vires of its principles.

So I had to run between the competing groups, the Japanese, the Taiwanese, all the pushers and the shovers. They were all trying to get their words in, and I'm saying, 'No, don't try and do this, you'll destroy the thing. We can take that but not this.'

Suharto was very grateful for me pulling off that communiqué. And so were the Japanese, and in the end the Americans. So I was a sort of sherpa.

KOB: And yet in a way it must have been a welcome break from the domestic politics?

PJK: It was a break, and fun in a way. You'd try yourself out against these guys, and we found that mostly they weren't at our level. We were like the Wimbledon players. All the work we'd done in the Cabinet over ten years kicked in, and I found that my kind of executive Cabinet play was way beyond your average APEC leader.

The one big disappointment I had with APEC was that I wanted it to be formally recognised as a strategic as well as economic body. By its very nature, with the people sitting around the table it was strategic, but the formal discussion was broadly limited to trade and economics. Any strategic conversations were conducted as informal one-on-ones away from the floor of the forum.

Bill Clinton missed an opportunity there when he baulked at it, others have also disappointed in that regard. The bravest guy was Suharto, who sponsored the Bogor Declaration. If in the formal sense it was going to be confined to trade and economics then I at least wanted the expression of free trade to be real. So I owed it to Suharto to see his paper get up.

The person who really helped me in that was the then Japanese Prime Minister, Tomiichi Murayama. He was a great bloke. And he then chaired the third meeting in Osaka, which broadly I then ran with him. He was both jolly and good. And he then subsequently protected Australia's position when Mahathir was trying to close us off from attending Asia-centric bodies such as the East Asia Forum. And it was Prime Minister Murayama who pushed further on the Bogor Declaration at Osaka, and then realised what Australia could do in tandem with Japan in foreign policy terms.

Clinton missed the third meeting in Osaka, which was a huge triumph. It cemented the Bogor action plan for free trade in the region. It was important for Clinton to be there but Newt Gingrich had used his Republican majority in the Congress to stop the federal budget payments and freeze the budget, and Clinton didn't think he could go to Japan while the budget was frozen. He sent his Vice President Al Gore along, and I chewed Gore out for Clinton's absence and Gore said to me, 'Well, Prime Minister, you make me feel like a skunk at the party.'

KOB: Did you know that Gore then faithfully reported your comments back to Clinton when he returned to Washington?

PJK: I didn't, no.

KOB: There's a book called *The Clinton Tapes* based on years of secret conversations that Clinton had throughout his Presidency with a respected historian named Taylor Branch, and Branch recounts Gore's 'very unpleasant report from Osaka'. Clinton quoted Gore back to Branch: 'The heads of state were openly hostile to Gore. They said everybody has political problems, Australian Prime Minister Paul Keating hotly told Gore he had come to Osaka despite a dock strike and paralysed economy back home. Where was Clinton?'
  Gore also reported that Murayama was furious because he felt Clinton had insulted all of Japan.

PJK: For the American President not to turn up when the Japanese were hosting it was an affront to them and to Murayama personally. So the fact that we stuck to him when the Americans didn't, meant he stuck to Australia in the Howard years.

KOB: Do you remember Clinton throwing his arms around you at the D-Day fiftieth anniversary in Normandy and declaring his love for you? How real was that? Did you think that your relationship with him transcended the fundamental disparity that exists as a fact of life between the superpower and the middle-ranker?

PJK: Yes. He knew that philosophically I was on his side, although I did say to him I thought he was missing the big post-Cold War opportunity. And I think now he would agree with that. Certainly Hillary Clinton has said that Bill had missed the post-Cold War opportunity. But he was a great guy to be around, the most charming individual you could imagine, and a great conversationalist with a terrific scan of knowledge. And I had some moments with him.

We went across the Channel on the *Britannia*—John Major, Annita and me, and Bill Clinton. We went down two lanes of Allied warships floating beside us like a guard of honour, and as we stood on the deck about halfway there, a Lancaster bomber and two Spitfires went over the ship just above mast height. It was very moving.

And I had a fantastic meeting with Clinton in Paris with Mitterrand. Mitterrand was a crazy guy, so entertaining. And the three of us did a press conference together. Mitterrand knew I had an interest in architecture and showed me around the Élysée Palace.

He showed me the Pompidou Room, which was full of plastic furniture, and Mitterrand said, 'You know the thing about Pompidou?' and I said, 'What, monsieur?' and he said, 'Pompidou was full of shit.'

'We're going to have a little treat,' he said. 'I'm taking you to the Salon d'Argent, the room where Bonaparte abdicated, and we'll have coffee at the table where he signed his abdication papers.'

We were still sitting there when a staff member arrived to tell him Bill Clinton was about to arrive for the press conference, and Monsieur le President hadn't shaved yet. So he asked for an electric razor and shaved in front of a large ancient mirror in the Silver Room, and then we went down to the press conference.

He was a great figure, Mitterrand, but with a zany quality.

KOB: In 1994 you began a very secret process to set up a security agreement between Australia and Indonesia, the likes of which had not been done before. How hard was it to pull that off and what were you trying to secure for Australia?

PJK: We had the ANZUS Treaty with the United States, which has been a fundamental cornerstone of our postwar security, but there was nothing like ANZUS with the other state of great material significance to Australia. We had the five-power defence agreement with Malaysia, Singapore, Britain and New Zealand but nothing with the great state to our north, Indonesia. So I wanted to put in place both a formal structure of consultation between us and a declaration of trust that Indonesia had no territorial designs on us and that we had no territorial designs on Indonesia, and that accordingly we could consider our position somewhat in common in the event we ran into adverse circumstances. I wanted to see that as an agreement with the standing of ANZUS and in the language of ANZUS.

KOB: Even assuming Suharto himself saw the merit of your proposal, how big an ask was it for him to deliver his end of the deal?

PJK: Very difficult for him. He had to deliver the army, which was always a powerful element in the Indonesian equation. He was one of the leaders of the non-aligned movement during the Cold War so every instinct in him would have been not to even entertain the idea. But I had credibility with him because of the benefits he'd enjoyed through the development of the new APEC forum, particularly coming as it did towards the end of his political life.

I said to him, 'Mr President, you're the only Indonesian person who could make this structure happen, for yourself, your country and for

Australia. In your passing, the opportunity may never arise again, so why don't we seize the moment? We have no designs on you nor you on us. So why don't we think about the language of an agreement with a consultative mechanism and a proactive quality so if any adverse circumstances do come by, if you happen to be attacked or we were attacked, we have an active quality in the agreement where we consult one another.'

KOB: Why did those negotiations have to be conducted in secret?

PJK: If it had been known it simply would not have happened. Suharto needed time to get around all the forces in Indonesia to bring on a thing like this. We didn't hear anything for a long time and we thought after a while he'd dropped it altogether. But I caught up with him in Bali in 1995 to prepare for the Osaka APEC meeting in Japan, and he came back to the security idea of his own volition. He said, 'By the way, we've had a year to consider your proposal and I think we can advance it.'

Suharto suggested that we each nominate two people to flesh out the areas to be covered in such an agreement. I nominated General Peter Gration, then Head of the Australian Armed Forces, and Allan Gyngell from my office. The actual work then took place in the few months between the Bali meeting and Osaka. President Suharto and I then agreed substantially at a side meeting of the APEC plenary session that we would enter into a formal treaty arrangement between our two countries.

KOB: How much enthusiasm was there for the idea on your own side, particularly within the defence, foreign affairs and intelligence communities?

PJK: It was my own idea, and it had no real support in either Foreign Affairs or Defence. Not that they thought it was a bad idea, but that we would be rebuffed for even suggesting it. They liked the idea but thought we would be reaching too far, too fast to secure something that was effectively out of reach. It did have real support in the foreign policy division of PM&C and when I told one senior adviser that Suharto had come on board, he virtually burst into tears, overtaken by the sheer scale and import of the thing.

It was quite a moment when we announced it and then Gareth Evans signed for Australia and Ali Alatas the Indonesian foreign minister signed for Indonesia, as President and Suharto and I stood behind them.

KOB: This was in the shadow of the 1996 election with John Howard as Opposition Leader. Do you think the value of that agreement was understood at the time by the Australian people or do you think the electorate's mind was then firmly planted in domestic issues?

PJK: Importantly, it was publicly supported by John Howard and his then foreign policy spokesman, Alexander Downer. I don't think the public might have understood it as I understood it or the government did. The important thing was that it was a great asset for Australia. The great tragedy was that in the subsequent fracas over Timor between Howard as Prime Minister and President Habibie, who followed President Suharto, Habibie abrogated the treaty. For Australia it was like losing the fledgling ANZUS.

KOB: Howard wrote in his autobiography:

> A metaphor for Keating's attitude to Asia and in particular Indonesia had been his febrile excitement when he

concluded secret negotiations for a security treaty with Indonesia just before Christmas 1995. He really believed that this would be seen by the Australian public as a master stroke of diplomacy. I took an excited indeed breathless phone call from Gareth Evans who informed me in utmost secrecy of course that the treaty had been concluded and was about to be announced. The treaty did not shift one vote towards the Labor Party yet one felt the Prime Minister believed it was a real opinion shaper with the Australian people.

Was he right?

PJK: No. It was not procured to shift votes. It was put in place to buttress Australia's fundamental security. It was a major diplomatic achievement. I certainly didn't think it was an opinion shaper but it's the Prime Minister of Australia's task to make the country more secure, to make the country more resilient. And I had this almost unique relationship with Suharto, president of our largest neighbouring state, and through his authority was able to put together a treaty of cooperation using similar language to the ANZUS Treaty.

Why would Howard deprecate that, and why didn't he seek to recover the treaty when he had supported it from Opposition? But against what Howard said years later in his book, his first Defence Minister Ian McLachlan said at the time he regarded the treaty as a key asset for Australia.

That's why Howard supported it in the first instance. To have lost it was a great shame, and it was a great shame that Howard didn't pursue its retention. But to have pursued its retention would have meant him pursuing a measure of mine, and I don't think he was big enough to admit to its scale and importance. Certainly after President Habibie left, he had the opportunity.

KOB: Looking back, do you think that your passion for repositioning Australia in terms of its international linkages gave John Howard the means to paint you as turning your back on old traditions, of going too far in your embrace of Asia?

PJK: That's what he argued. In one of his so-called headland speeches he talked of returning to our European traditions. That's what you would have expected someone who thought in the framework of the 1950s and 1960s to say and to think.

KOB: He was also a smart politician. He wouldn't have said that if he didn't think it was going to resonate with the public.

PJK: He would have said it anyway because that's what he deeply believed. He was the wrong guy for Australia at the time when the panoply of Asia was really opening up to us.

KOB: But did you have to move so far so fast in repointing the raft to Asia, as you've put it? The whole orientation of our foreign policy trend was towards increasingly closer ties with Japan, China and India, and the Southeast Asian countries. That was happening anyway.

PJK: Yes, but not the kind of geopolitical positioning I was undertaking. We had strong trade links with Japan and Bob Hawke had had a first-rate relationship with the then government of China, but Bob had been to Indonesia only once in eight years. The APEC Leaders' Forum was Asia-centric and pan-Pacific. We had never done anything like that, or been in anything like that.

Bob, and Malcolm Fraser before him, had spent their major foreign policy effort in the British Commonwealth fighting apartheid. Now, apartheid was a great issue, and in Malcolm Fraser's case so was Zimbabwe, but Australia's vital interests were never in Africa and could never be.

Australia's vital interests were here, in the region where we live, and I wanted to declare those interests and set up the political machinery for us to participate in those interests. Because of our priorities in government the APEC leaders' meeting, and in Gareth's case the ASEAN regional forum, have Australia's name on the maker's label. The perpetual bilateral ministerial council between Australia and Indonesia has Australia's name on the maker's label. And the security treaty was there, and should still be there, with Australia's name on the maker's label. These are the things conscientious leaders leave behind.

A REPUBLIC

Having signalled to Australia during his first trip to Indonesia in April 1992 that he would be forging a new vision in foreign policy, Paul Keating flew to Papua New Guinea for his first Anzac Day as Prime Minister to mark the fiftieth anniversary of one of Australia's fiercest and most costly military battles in World War II, the Kokoda Track campaign.

This was both political and personal for Keating. Everything about 1992 was inevitably political because this was a battle for survival, and Keating was intent on wrong-footing and unsettling his opponents wherever he could. He had big question marks about Australia's obsession with the disastrous World War I Gallipoli campaign as the birthplace of our national identity and wanted to see a bigger emphasis on Australia's close connection to the Asia-Pacific battles of World War II.

It was personal because his uncle Bill Keating had died at the hands of the Japanese in the notorious Sandakan death marches in Borneo.

With John Hewson looking on, Paul Keating spoke at Bomana Cemetery and acknowledged the things about the Anzac legend that had left an indelible impression on the nation, but said such legends 'should not constrain us when we have to change' nor 'confer on us a duty to see that the world stand still'.

This was no traditional Anzac speech simply lauding the bravery or symbolism of the past. Keating pointedly invoked John Curtin's courage during the war in defying Churchill and demanding that Australian troops in the Middle East come home to defend their own soil from the Japanese. In other words, Curtin put Australia first. The Anzac legend, Keating said, looked back to Britain; Kokoda looked forward to independence.

Keating then flew to the Kokoda Track where Australian troops had stopped the Japanese advance on Port Moresby, and astonished everyone present, including his own close advisers, by kneeling to kiss the ground at the foot of the monument there. This was no copybook Prime Minister.

Shortly after, he was picked up by a boom microphone saying to one of a group of children waving Australian flags, 'Don't worry, sonny, we'll get you a new one of these soon.' Incorrigible. But when he then flew to Lae, he told guests at the official lunch it had been the most moving day in his whole career in public life.

Keating was pushing along one of the initiatives he hoped would define his prime ministership—cutting the formal ties to the British crown and setting up the framework for an Australian republic. The debate had really begun when the Queen visited Australia two months before. Even before she arrived Keating had expressed support for changing the flag, or at least removing the Union Jack from the corner.

Keating stirred up two ants' nest while hosting the Queen on the opening day of Parliament for the year on 24 February. When he dared to put a guiding hand on the Queen's back to direct her towards Dame Pattie Menzies at the official reception, the British tabloids had a field day. Their best effort was to dub him the 'Lizard of Oz'. In his welcoming speech he managed to trigger Opposition anger when he observed that just as Britain some time ago had sought to cement its future security in Europe, Australia was vigorously seeking partnerships in Asia.

'Our outlook is necessarily independent,' he said.

John Hewson said the speech was embarrassing and ungracious. 'It was an occasion to show respect and not to make a political statement.'

Keating's response came in Parliament on 27 February. Picking up on Hewson's comment suggesting Keating had not learned respect at school, he said:

> I learned one thing: I learned about self-respect and self-regard for Australia—not about some cultural cringe to a country which decided not to defend the Malayan Peninsula, not to worry about Singapore and not give us our troops back to keep ourselves free from Japanese domination.
>
> This was the country that you people wedded yourself to, and even as it walked out on you and joined the Common Market, you were still looking for your MBEs and your knighthoods, and all the rest of the regalia that comes with it. You would take Australia right back down the time tunnel to the cultural cringe where you have always come from. These are the same old fogies who doffed their lids and tugged the forelock to the British establishment; they now try to grind down Australian kids by denying them a technical school education and want to put a tax back on the poor.
>
> The same old sterile ideology, the same old fogeyism of the 1950s that produced the Thatcherite policies of the late 1970s is going to produce *Fightback!* You can go back to the 1950s to your nostalgia, your Menzies, the Caseys and the whole lot. They were not aggressively Australia, they were not aggressively proud of our culture, and we will have no bar of you and your sterile ideology. [Hansard, 27 February]

To a Dorothy Dix question from Labor MP Daryl Melham, Keating also seized on comments from John Howard, the Opposition's most senior Anglophile, who in also criticising Keating's speech to the Queen had talked about the 1950s as a golden age. Keating mused that the Old Parliament House down the hill could be converted to a museum of cultural history:

> We thought we could put some of the cultural icons of the 1950s down there. The Morphy Richards toaster, the Qualcast mower, a pair of heavily protected slippers, the Astor TV, the AWA radiogram. And, of course, the honourable member for Wentworth and the honourable member for Bennelong could go there as well. When the kids come and look at them they will say, 'Gee, Mum, is that what it was like then?' And the two Johns can say, 'No, kids. This is the future.' Back down the time tunnel to the future.

It was a performance that incited the Opposition but delighted his own troops, demoralised by the battering they were regularly taking back in their electorates over the effects of the recession, and wearied by the long, debilitating leadership contest between Hawke and Keating. It set the template for what the Opposition, the gallery and the public could expect for the next twelve months, but Keating was also signalling that he was looking for new battlegrounds beyond the economy on which to fight the election.

In March that first year of the prime ministership, Geoff Kitney wrote in the *Financial Review*: 'Mr Keating and his advisers believe that traditional Labor Party supporters ... are very receptive to the case for a new nationalism. They believe it is striking a positive electoral chord like the Labor Party struck in the lead-up to the 1972 election.'

Keating then established a Republican Advisory Committee which included two identifiable Liberals, Nick Greiner and Malcolm Turnbull, tasked to establish a consensus for a republican model, which he believed had to be conservative and minimalist in nature if it was to win bipartisan support. He then travelled to England to inform the

Queen of his intention to carve a path to total independence from the mother country. By April 1994, the Saulwick Poll in the *Sydney Morning Herald* and the *Age* registered 70 per cent support for a republic in the two most populous states, New South Wales and Victoria.

KOB: The Queen's visit coincided with your first week in Parliament as Prime Minister. You had a lot on your plate. You were launching *One Nation* to help pull the country out of recession and get yourself back in the political hunt. As with the Bush visit, you could have played it safe with the Queen, gone through the formalities in the usual way, bid her goodbye and got on with the fray. Instead you chose to use the occasion to open up a new political front.

PJK: It was like the Bush visit in the sense that the Queen's visit was already in the pipeline when I took the job. It was an unexceptional speech but in the context of my broader ambition to reshape Australia's role in the region and to sharpen our sense of ourselves and our independence, I wasn't going to let the moment pass to fall back on the usual platitudes to the monarchy.

I had always believed Australia should break away and leave behind forever what I used to call the Menzies torpor of the 1950s and 1960s, the idea, particularly in the minds of the conservative forces, that we should retain formal links to Whitehall and the monarchy. This was the new post-Cold War world and the opportunity to repackage ourselves for the new century. Yet how could we repackage ourselves with the Queen of Great Britain as our head of state and a flag that was a remnant of all that history?

In welcoming the Queen, I said Australia had to become more independent and now looked to the future: that just as Britain had found its place in the European Union, we too had to find our place in this part of the world. I said in the process, the links between us would change, and the cultural loyalties to the monarchy would change, and that it was worth pondering these things and talking about them. I thought the Queen found this all rather refreshing and that was certainly the kind of indication she gave me personally.

KOB: You provided fodder for the British tabloids when you dared to put your arm on the Queen's back to guide her towards some guests at the lunch. They labelled you the 'Lizard of Oz'.

PJK: I was trying to direct her to people I knew she knew, including Dame Pattie Menzies and some other senior Liberal dignitaries. She said later, 'Take no notice of them', and I said, 'Well, Your Majesty, can I say this. A British tabloid editor is a particularly low form of human life.' And she said, 'Hmm ...'

KOB: If you were looking to provoke a reaction with your speech, Alexander Downer, John Howard and John Hewson all obliged. Downer said your speech was poorly conceived, weakly delivered and downright ungracious. He said you would be remembered as Australia's most petty, mean-minded and ungracious Prime Minister since Federation. Now, I don't imagine you were too displeased or shocked.

PJK: Talk about come in spinner. I used to say about these guys, 'You try to bait these people but you don't really have to. They actually jump on the hook for you.' The Liberal Party were outraged. Those lickspittles Hewson, Howard and all the rest of them were up in arms, saying I didn't know my place. Hewson suggested I hadn't learned respect at school.

I said in Parliament, 'At least I learned respect for one thing, for Australia. You're the same people who went and took your knighthoods from them after they left us with the fall of Singapore and sought to divert our troops to the Middle East. Left us in jeopardy. When did it ever occur to you that we ought to be pursuing our own independence and foreign policy?'

KOB: I'm sure the irony wasn't lost on you that it was Churchill, the person who had inspired you so much coming into your political life, whom you now blamed for the fall of Singapore and for trying to stop John Curtin bringing Australian troops back to defend Australia against the Japanese.

PJK: Churchill's intellectual position was that Britain came first, and Germany had to be defeated before Japan. You can understand that from a British perspective, but you can hardly respect it if you're tasked with defending the Australian nation. And this was Curtin's great insight: to switch camps and get the support of the United States, which led ultimately to the ANZUS Treaty.

And I said, 'Here you were, all you Tories, turning back to Britain after the war, even after Britain had walked out on you and joined the Common Market. You were still going over there for your knighthoods, still clinging to the whole imperial thing.'

I also raised the issue of the flag. I said, here we are, getting around with the flag of another country in the corner of our flag. Who does that? What great nation gets around with the flag of someone else's country in the corner of their flag?

I used to go to schools in my electorate in the 1970s and one of the little rituals we'd have as MPs was to hand the school a new flag. I used to often say, 'Of course it's the wrong flag, with the flag of another country in the corner', which the teachers would duly note as they raised it up the flagpole. As I went through my political life I was more embarrassed by the thing than I'd ever been—we were telling the world we had this deprecating image of ourselves, with the flag of Great Britain posted squarely in ours.

We had the opportunity to do as the Canadians had done with their flag, which says all that needed to be said about Canada as a society. Their challenge was much more complicated than ours, being both a French- and English-speaking country.

KOB: Some of your opponents took your views on the monarchy and the flag as indicative of your Irish Catholic heritage.

PJK: This had nothing really to do with my Irish heritage. I think the whole business about Ireland and the blarney is way overdone in Australia. I don't attend St Patrick's Day events. I never indulged in that nostalgia.

But over 200 years we'd developed into a robust democracy. We were one of the first to recognise suffrage for women, we'd succeeded in remaking the economy and partly integrating with Asia, yet we still had these misleading and discordant symbols.

I remember saying to John Howard at the Sydney Olympics in 2000 when we were watching the swimming, 'Look, John. They're standing up there getting the medals with the flag around their shoulders but they're trying to hide the Union Jack, each one of them.'

And they were: Ian Thorpe and the others were trying to hide the Union Jack to have only the blue and white visible.

And he said, 'Well, Paul, you and I just have different ideas about this.'

I said, 'John, give them a break, give them a new flag.'

KOB: When you went to Papua New Guinea for the fiftieth anniversary of the big battles of World War II, what did you seek to achieve with the visit?

PJK: The Liberals were always soft on the Pacific War. For them it was all about Gallipoli, while our Second World War battles in places closer to home like Papua New Guinea came second. I went to Kokoda to make the point that Gallipoli looked back at Britain, whereas Kokoda looked to our independence, which to me was more relevant to our future.

The Tories hated it because they always wrapped themselves in the flag to claim a monopoly on our patriotism. For them the flag was all about Gallipoli and Britain. Here I was, on the fiftieth anniversary of the Second World War battles, taking the opportunity to remember a more recent past when our own nation was genuinely threatened, and had to look to the future.

KOB: When you kissed the earth at Kokoda was that as spontaneous as we're led to believe?

PJK: It was spontaneous, but I wanted to broaden the Anzac legend, and to highlight the fact that bravery and sacrifice were not the preserve of one time and one place, and to remember the courage of young men, militia, in Kokoda and to show my regard for it as a solemn place, a national shrine.

By doing that I wanted to underline the solemnity and debt we owed them in a very graphic way, rather than simply in a speech that might or might not be reported.

KOB: How strongly did you feel the family connection to the Pacific war through your Uncle Bill?

PJK: He died in March 1945, as the war was ending. The Japanese marched them from Sandakan to Ranau in Borneo, and shot and bayoneted them as they fell along the way, two thousand of them. What I found particularly galling was that the RSL paid them virtually no regard. They wouldn't say this, but the implication was that somehow they had not measured up. They weren't in the big battles, shooting the 303s, so therefore they were sort of second-rate.

This used to drive me nuts. I had the bravery of people on the Burma Railway, Sandakan, Singapore, Changi so strongly in my mind that I thought the fiftieth anniversary was the time to speak the truth, and the truth could perhaps best be demonstrated at that event in Kokoda.

KOB: But when you say you wanted to shift the emphasis away from Gallipoli, I'm not sure you succeeded because, if anything, the myth of Gallipoli has got stronger.

PJK: Howard pushed it very hard as Prime Minister, as you would expect him to do. He's an Anglophile, but Kokoda did speak to our independence as a nation where Gallipoli didn't. I think I shifted the debate. Look at the people who go to Kokoda these days—it has become another national shrine.

KOB: In picking these sorts of emotional symbolic issues so early in your term, was that partly about reinvigorating your own troops, getting a bit of inspiration and passion going in the ranks again?

PJK: No, this stuff was bubbling away in me all my adult life. But, nevertheless, driving the Liberal Party nuts does lift the spirits on your own side. It drove Hewson nuts, and Howard went spare over it. He thought I was attacking everything he'd ever believed in, every Menzian notion. But regardless of what they had to say, what it did do was to shift public attention to a range of wider and more emotional issues.

I think people said, 'Hang on, as Prime Minister Keating is no longer just the guy with the calculator out doing his budget sums with his economic reforms. He seems to have a bigger view of things—another dimension.'

At the time I was fighting *Fightback!*, which I saw as a miserable document trying to desocialise Australia, attacking all the social buttressing we'd had on things like Medicare, minimum award rates of pay, the social security system and so on. But rather than simply tackling *Fightback!* in its own terms, I was intent on sketching out a new agenda that was about moving Australia into the void created by the end of the Cold War. It was about seeing the continent as a raft and turning it directly into the area of economic prosperity and security. Not security relying solely on some strategic guarantor as we relied on the British Navy and then later the American Navy, but security in Asia for ourselves. In other words, conscious and earned security.

KOB: So, in a quite calculated way, you were fashioning a signal to Australia that you were a broader person than simply the guy who'd run the economy for eight years, and caused pain in the process.

PJK: Yes, but no. No, because in this position, the inner me was emerging publicly and yes, because I did wish to distinguish myself against the lickspittles opposite. These things were always going around inside my head, but these were not issues I could make my own while Treasurer.

KOB: You said your visit to Kokoda was the most moving day you'd experienced in public life. That's a big statement.

PJK: I had with me a military historian named David Horner, whose father had served in Papua New Guinea in the war. We flew together in an RAAF Hercules over a lot of the war terrain, around some of the mountains and coastline back to Kokoda, so I had a very graphic idea of where the battles were fought, and how difficult it must have been.

Australians were the first to turn back the Japanese in the Pacific War. The first pushback against Japan and their marines happened at our hands on the Kokoda Track. I was very conscious of that heroism, the singular dedication those young men displayed on behalf of their country and their families, and for everything we'd created here. That's what they were fighting for, and for me it was a very moving thing.

KOB: But at the same time it was as if you couldn't acknowledge Gallipoli at all. You've never visited Gallipoli, is that right?

PJK: No, and I never will, because the Dardanelles was an ill-conceived campaign from the beginning. Churchill wanted to come to the back of the Germans through Turkey. It was a shockingly executed campaign and there was already a big body of opinion in the British Cabinet from Lloyd George and others who were opposed to it. This was a military disaster for us. But the worst of it was the notion that the country required rebirth and that this happened at Gallipoli. The greatest piece of nonsense ever: that the country needed to find its soul there.

In other words, forget the development of Federation, forget that we now had a unified country, the great Australian experiment to 1914. What matters is how we behaved in some poorly executed British campaign in Turkey. Really?

KOB: But couldn't you find it in you to see past that and go there once, simply as an acknowledgement of the Australian effort? The loss of life. The courage of it.

PJK: I acknowledge the courage and the lives sacrificed, I always have, and in Flanders and the Western Front the losses were shocking. But the notion that we had to be reborn and discover ourselves at Gallipoli is such a savage condemnation of all that we had created here and all we stood for as not to be worthy of sustenance. Yet people today still go on with this nonsense.

KOB: You raised the issue of the flag again when you were in Indonesia when you talked about blowing aside the baggage of the past, and in Papua New Guinea you made an amused aside to the kids waving the Australian flag, 'Don't worry, sonny, we'll get you a new one of these soon.'

PJK: I remember that. That was probably an unnecessary remark and it was picked up by one of those boom mikes. To use a more recent American public relations term, I misspoke.

KOB: But did you discern any evidence in the national mood when you became Prime Minister that Australians broadly were fretting about the national flag or that they wanted to cut ties to the constitutional monarchy?

PJK: Well, it's the leader's job to paint the new horizon. That's what a leader does, or should do.

KOB: Neville Wran said once when he was Premier of New South Wales that you could never afford as leader to get too far ahead of the mob.

PJK: I despise those kinds of remarks. They stand for everything I stand against. I've said in the past that when they were handing out continents not many people got one, but we did. And here we are, this massive country with just 23 million of us, now aligned to the fastest growing part of the world. Wouldn't you take every opportunity to capitalise on it? Why would you dumb down your own people?

The biggest issue facing Australia today is a psychological one. Do we want to be in it, in the Asian construct I mean? Do we really want to be in it? Yet we have to be in it both for our prosperity and our security. So somewhere a leader has to tackle the shibboleths. The shibboleths have to be taken on, and the notion that we should just go along with the mob rather than actually lead them is classic New South Wales hustler politics.

KOB: That's the school of politics that bred you.

PJK: They bred me, that's true, but they never had any part of me in an intellectual sense. My instincts about leadership were vastly different. And the opportunity to lead today is even more profound than it was when I was there. Twenty years ago you needed a microscope to find the Chinese economy compared to what it is today, the second largest economy in the world, and soon the largest.

Look at the growth of East Asia. The vast bulk of world growth is coming from our region.

But at what point do we decide we want to be a multicultural cosmopolitan place? At what point do we decide we want to be in it? At what point do we cut the knot with the monarchy? Look at all the recent tomfoolery about the British monarchy and fuss about Prince William as heir. If the poor Brits want to go down that sad road, let them, but let's get out of it while we can. Prince William is probably one of the most congenial royals we've seen, but that is no reason to be fawning over him as our future monarch. It's sick, really sick.

KOB: You used to occasionally drop in on the historian Manning Clark in his Canberra home over the years before his death. What attracted you to Clark?

PJK: He had the big imagination, and tried to tell us where the yardsticks were in our history, putting down markers against a very big landscape in his head. He was a person who was fundamentally interested in truths: sifting through history to reveal them, paint them and prophesise about them.

He also loved music and occasionally I'd take something down to play with him. I remember one Saturday afternoon, it was Yehudi Menuhin at sixteen, playing Elgar's *Violin Concerto*, with Elgar conducting. Elgar was very put out that he had to bring the orchestra together on a Saturday to accommodate a sixteen-year-old boy's itinerary. Menuhin was absolutely in his prime and as he played, Elgar conducted the piece in tears—you can hear it in the music.

Manning and I would put passages back on, you know, turn them back and hear them again. Another thing we played and I liked was Elgar's *Enigma Variations*. He also liked Richard Strauss and his tone poem *Death and Transfiguration*. But he was more at the baroque end of the repertoire himself although he was interested enough in the romantics.

I used to drop in on him not to draw any particular wisdom from him but simply because I liked him and enjoyed sharing the music with him. But we did share a lot of common ground. He despised the notion of the Austral Briton and its domination of the political debate, particularly after the First World War—where they imposed their values on society, never thinking of the Australian way and how Australia was entitled to be a society that gave expression to its own mores and values.

KOB: On 29 April 1992 the *Australian*'s banner headline read, 'Furore over PM's flag move. Keating sets ground for new nationalism'. It was a story that you were promising to take your plan for a new flag to Cabinet within weeks but at the same time you pledged that you wouldn't push it through unless there was clear public support. Nothing concrete ever really eventuated, did it?

PJK: I did test out the Democrats as to whether they would support it in the Senate, because with their support I could have done it. I proposed to Cheryl Kernot that we fly a second flag as well as the existing flag and she said she couldn't get it up. I said as healthy as having a national competition might be, I'm prepared to recommend and legislate in the meantime that we simultaneously fly the Eureka flag with the current flag, and she wouldn't support it.

KOB: In April 1993 you set up the Republican Advisory Committee, chaired by Malcolm Turnbull, and including the former Liberal Premier Nick Greiner, to recommend a framework for a republic. Was this in the best *Yes, Minister* tradition of choosing a committee that would give you the outcome you wanted?

PJK: It was to get a bipartisan examination of the issues with a set of recommendations to produce a model for a republic that the Liberal Party could embrace. Malcolm Turnbull was politically non-aligned at that stage and because of his prominence in the republican debate, was an appropriate person to chair the committee.

It was crazy, thinking for a moment that you could have a viable republican structure that suited you but didn't suit the conservative parties. Because any referendum would fail. So it had to be one that was written and thought about as something the Coalition could adopt and that's what drove me.

By 1994 I had a 63 per cent vote in favour of a republic, according to the polls. And this later rose to 70 per cent. I had taken the risk at the 1993 election of making it a significant piece of the party manifesto.

KOB: Shortly after you presented the committee report on constitutional change to Parliament, you met the Queen in England and briefed her on your plans for a republic. Was she amenable to the idea and were you able to have a natural conversation with her rather than a formal one?

PJK: Yes, it was a good conversation in the drawing room at Balmoral Castle. She told me it had been her grandmother Queen Victoria's favourite room. It still had the original tartan carpets and the faded furniture and looked out over the hills.

I went through the reasons why Australia had reached the point where it had to make a choice about its future as an independent country. I also said I believed that when she visited Australia as the Queen of Great Britain and not as Queen of Australia, there would be even more warmth displayed towards her than the current ambivalence as the Queen of Australia.

While she didn't expressly concur with that, she said, 'Well, my family has always tried to do the right thing by Australia and of course I would take the advice of Australian ministers.' In other words, she was the perfect constitutional head of state in making those remarks.

And I said to her, 'I know that normally after meetings of this kind, the protocol is to say nothing specific about the discussion, but on this occasion I would like to reveal what you have said.'

The Queen discussed this with her private secretary, Sir Robert Fellowes, and they agreed that I should do so. I remember thinking at the time that the Royal Family had already come to the conclusion that Australia would become a republic, and from their point of view almost the faster the better. Prince Charles virtually confirmed that when he came to Sydney in 1994 and said, 'What are you dallying about for?'

When John Howard's eventual referendum was defeated, Prince Phillip is reported to have said to friends, 'Don't those Australians know what's good for them?'

Whether he did say it or not I can't be certain, but I'm as certain as we're sitting here that the British Royal Family believes we'd all be better off with them as friends and former relatives, with us as an Australian republic.

When I did finally announce the government's preferred model in the House of Representatives in 1995, I rang John Howard as Opposition Leader beforehand to give him an outline, and he interrupted me mid-sentence to say, 'I hope you don't have a popular election in there,' and I said, 'No, I have appointment by both houses of Parliament.'

'Oh good, good,' he said. He didn't want to change the fundamental structure of the system of government, and neither did I. In that same call I urged him to take as long as he liked to respond, and said there would be no static from me.

I said, 'I think I've given you a model you can live with.'

He said, 'Very good, we'll have a look at it,' and that was it.

KOB: John Howard says in his autobiography that the president under that model would have effectively been chosen by the government of the day rather than by Parliament. Your model said both houses of Parliament. How would you have ensured a bipartisan approach to the vote?

PJK: I would have been happy for Labor members and Coalition members to have had a free vote in a joint sitting of Parliament, with a shortlist of nominees. The choice could have been a genuine reflection of a free vote of the entire Parliament.

I also said to John Howard in that conversation, 'I have kept the reserve powers in the Constitution. I haven't tried to circumscribe the powers of the Senate to refuse Supply.'

I said, 'John, in a bicameral system where the second chamber is elected by proportional representation, we will always have the potential for deadlocks, and therefore there has to be someone in the system to resolve the deadlocks. Let's just hope it's done more judiciously than Sir John Kerr did in 1975, but the Senate keeps its powers.'

KOB: On 7 June 1995, when you presented the model to Parliament, how important a moment was that for you?

PJK: It was a really important speech for me, and I wrote large slabs of it. I still have my handwritten drafts. That speech was about Australia's coming out. To say that we'd always have a kinship with Britain and that when the Queen visited the Republic of Australia in future she'd more likely get an even warmer welcome than she would as the nominal Queen of Australia.

There was a great emotionalism and a standing ovation in Parliament when I made the speech. Something I had not expected. A large number of members from both sides asked me to sign the speech, nearly all of ours and quite a number from the other side. It was the first and only time an Australian Prime Minister had laid out in Parliament a case for a republic, including outlining a model. It was the full monty, and there was a real possibility of it happening. We just needed a bit of scale and bigness from Howard and the Libs, and it would have got there. But in the end he remained the victim of the picket fence.

The proposition I took to the 1996 election was that if I won I would present a simple question to the people of Australia in a referendum: 'do you believe Australia should become a republic?' The answer to that question already had a 70 per cent approval in the polls. With me pushing, it would have walked in.

But having won the 1996 election Howard lost Australia the opportunity of becoming a republic through events contrived in that referendum of his. He called a convention to decide on a model, which he knew would split the republican movement, and that split was reflected in the referendum vote in 1999. He asked people both to endorse a republic *and* choose a model. Had he put the simple question first, as I had intended, the country would have replied in the affirmative, giving the political community an instruction. It was that 'instruction' Howard contrived to eliminate.

Had he put the single question to voters—'Do you think Australia should become a republic?'—it would have been solidly agreed. Then we could have moved to determine the model. Howard and I were at least agreed on one thing, and still agree: that the moment you go to an elected president, a preponderant power devolves to the president. Much more than the Governor-General now. And with one nationally elected person in the system, the authority of the prime minister and cabinet system will be diminished.

KOB: But without reliving the whole debate again here, isn't it true that while ever the republican movement is split, and a core group remains that will support the monarchy through thick and thin, it will be impossible to get the required majority of states as well as a majority national vote in order to pass a referendum?

PJK: That's why a referendum had to be based on the simple proposition first: do you believe Australia should become a republic?

KOB: And you don't believe that the schism in Howard's republican convention between those wanting your minimalist model and those wanting a popularly elected president would have also emerged in the debate on a referendum sponsored by you?

PJK: No, I don't, because in the post-1996 Parliament, even with a new Liberal leader, or even with Howard still there, both parties would have wanted to see the minimalist model adopted. The one set out by the bi-partisan Turnbull committee.

KOB: It was one thing for you to float the idea of a republic but it was quite another to decide that you were going to firmly place it on the public agenda and make it a real political issue. When I read back through the records, even your own office was divided on this.

PJK: They're called risks. The leader takes risks and burns up the political capital to see the nation properly set for the future. I was prepared to take the risk at the 1993 election when proposing that we go down the pathway towards an Australian republic.

In the same vein I gave the Redfern Park address in December 1992—in the shadow of that same election—where I publicly acknowledged to the Aboriginal community all the factors that had contributed to their dispossession.

This was the election that by all accounts I was supposed to lose, and if I had played it safe as my party friends, the federal secretariat etc., had wanted me to, I wouldn't have made the Redfern Park speech. But the country needed the cleansing, the country required the lift that, on this issue, could only arise from truth.

This gets back to what I saw as a different kind of leadership for the country, not some consensual model or the one made fashionable these days by media advisers and party officials.

KOB: Your critics would say that most particularly you were looking for diversions to draw people's attention away from the economy, which was still feeling the after-effects of the recession very deeply. Unemployment was continuing to climb. How many people do you really think were voting for a future republic or voting for the practical application of Mabo? How many, in contrast, were simply voting against John Hewson's *Fightback!* and, more specifically, against a GST?

PJK: I have no doubt that the people who understood my point about the enlargement of the nation voted for it. Here was John Hewson with his miserable *Fightback!*, massively carving into the social wage while introducing a GST.

In contrast I was talking about our future in Asia as an independent country with an Australian head of state; of building a strong new Asian network including a new piece of political architecture like the APEC leaders; of owning up to our dispossession of the Aboriginal people; and building a new bilateral relationship with our neighbour, Indonesia. This was a completely different approach on fundamental issues. Issues I believed Australia had to address, certainly not some diversion from the prevailing economic realities. I'd been fighting economic arguments for nearly a decade at that point. I didn't require diversions to get my economic message over. I was like the Pied Piper on those issues.

The Liberal Party hated my social and geopolitical program. They hated it. They wanted to stick with the Menzian model, good little Anglophiles waving our little flag with the Union Jack in the corner, bowing to the Queen while paying lip service to our future in Asia.

They hated my stuff, but as Lang said, you stand for little until you attract a reasonable stock of enemies. The enemies define you as they define themselves.

KOB: Here we are, twenty years later, and there's not even a whisper of debate about a republic.

PJK: Yes, I'm surprised by how little progress has been made in taking that next important step in recognising who we are and what we are. We still have the monarchy and now we have all these incantations around Prince William and the new wife.

We've gone nowhere since 1996. You can see that failure perpetuating itself in Tony Abbott's restoration of knighthoods and his recommendation that the Queen knight her own husband as an Australian knight. The shame of it.

MABO

Federal government activism to address the deprivations of Indigenous Australians had been a long time coming. The Holt Government had successfully orchestrated the 1967 referendum, which formally recognised Aboriginal Australians as citizens of the nation, with an undeniable right to vote, 179 years after white settlement. The Whitlam Government introduced land rights legislation and the Fraser Government supported its passage through Parliament, but only to Indigenous residents in the Northern Territory. The Hawke Government established the landmark Royal Commission into Black Deaths in Custody and the Aboriginal and Torres Strait Islander Commission but essentially squibbed a national application of land rights under pressure from the Burke Labor Government and mining interests in Western Australia.

In 1991, Hawke also set up the Council for Aboriginal Reconciliation, chaired by the Western Australian Indigenous leader Pat Dodson, with a goal of achieving national reconciliation by the anniversary of Federation in 2001. Dodson retired from the Council in 1997, a year into the Howard Government, commenting, 'I fear for the spirit of this country.'

There's no record of any passionate interest expressed by a young Paul Keating on Indigenous affairs. But in one of his early speeches as Prime Minister at the Adelaide Writers' Festival in March 1992, he talked of the need for Australia to come to terms with the nation's original inhabitants. If we don't, he said, 'there will always be a feeling among us that we don't quite belong, that we're not serious, that we're just here for the view.' Within days of the Adelaide speech Keating placed himself more explicitly at the centre of debate on Aboriginal affairs. The opportunity came with the revelation by the ABC of a videotape from a party of off-duty NSW police with blackened faces tugging at nooses around their necks three years before, mocking Aboriginal deaths in custody. The story was followed by another, quoting a Northern Territory minister telling an Aboriginal woman at an Alice Springs meeting 'to get off your fat arse and fix your grog problem'.

If Australians needed reminding that racism was alive and well in much of the country, this was it. Expressing outrage was a no-brainer for any serious political leader and Keating wasn't alone in the harshness of his criticism. But the revelations coincided with Cabinet consideration of significant recommendations from the Royal Commission, and Keating signalled that Aboriginal affairs would be high on his personal agenda as Prime Minister; that this was 'probably the last opportunity this decade to do something really substantial' about the problems faced by Indigenous Australians.

In April that year he encapsulated a view of Australia's identity that started with an Aboriginal past, a multicultural present and a future that would be derivative of nowhere else. Asked by James Button of *Time* magazine whether he thought Australia would become a Eurasian country, perhaps the world's first, he replied:

> The fact that our migrants are increasingly going to come from South and North Asia means these people are going to be a

larger component of the Australian population, but it will be a long time before anyone could describe the place as Eurasian.

We've got a unique opportunity. We're the inheritors of a large and old continent. I'm nearly 50. Four of my lifetimes ago there were no Europeans here. It's important for us to come to terms with the country, to come to terms with Aboriginal Australians, and I don't believe we'll ever succeed at feeling at home in the place without doing that, without ensuring they are justly treated, that they have the same opportunities and living standards as the rest of Australia.

Two months later, on 3 June 1992, the Mason High Court essentially threw down the gauntlet to Keating to put his money where his mouth was, with the now famous Mabo judgment. It rejected the notion of *terra nullius*, that the land belonged to no one at the time of white settlement, and found that the concept of native title existed in common law and was validated by a traditional connection to tribal land—not a child of the common law but an ancient title recognised by the common law.

It was a remarkable and historic judgment that included comments describing Indigenous dispossession as 'our nation's legacy of unutterable shame'. This was not a radical High Court: four of the seven judges had been appointed by Liberal governments. Only one dissented from the ruling.

Keating's speechwriter Don Watson wrote in *Bleeding Heart* that 'when Keating owned something he invested it with almost a religious force'. As a chorus of alarm arose from special interest groups, and was given further voice by the states, Keating decided to 'own' it, leading the negotiations with all the stakeholders and wrapping it within a legislative framework that might make practical sense and facilitate one of the High Court's most dramatic rulings. It took eighteen months, a lot of blood, sweat and tears, and a great deal of distraction for a Prime Minister with a wounded economy to tend, and other policy balls to juggle. It dominated his time, which concerned his colleagues.

The strongest signal of the depth of Keating's determination to 'own' Mabo was contained in a speech at Redfern Park in inner Sydney on 10 December 1992 to celebrate the Year of the World's Indigenous People. The speech fell in the shadow of an election he was struggling to win, and probably wouldn't have delivered him a single new vote.

He told a mostly Indigenous audience of 2000, the mood at first subdued and ambivalent, that:

> . . . the starting point might be to recognise that the problem starts with us non-Aboriginal Australians.
>
> It begins, I think, with that of recognition. Recognition that it was we who did the dispossessing. We took the traditional lands and smashed the traditional way of life. We brought the diseases. The alcohol. We committed the murders. We took the children from their mothers. We practised discrimination and exclusion.
>
> It was our ignorance and our prejudice. And our failure to imagine these things being done to us.

The 1967 referendum, introduced by the Holt Liberal Government, had given the Commonwealth scope to legislate on Aboriginal matters and Keating chose to use it.

The implications of the Mabo judgment were exceptionally complicated, potentially affecting farmers, miners and even amateur anglers, making it ripe for an emotive scare campaign. Victorian Premier Jeff Kennett warned at one point that suburban households in Melbourne were under threat.

The mining industry strenuously resisted, as did the states and the farm lobby. Miners warned of a flight of investment capital from big mining developments, while pastoral leases took up 38 per cent of Western Australia's land mass, 54 per cent of Queensland's, 42 per cent of South Australia's, 41 per cent of New South Wales' and 51 per cent of the Northern Territory.

Many of the non-Indigenous players wanted Keating to use Commonwealth powers to remove any perceived native title threat to the status quo. The Commonwealth had that power, but only up to 1975 when the *Racial Discrimination Act* came into law, prohibiting discrimination on racial grounds, including matters of property ownership. After Mabo, that now included native title. So property on which title had been issued after 1975 was especially complex. Meanwhile native title ambit claims were starting to pop up all over the country, in cities and the bush, providing juicy tabloid headlines and easy fodder for the radio shock jocks.

While John Hewson and his Liberal colleagues struggled to formulate a position, the National Party led by Tim Fischer was hostile and at times inflammatory. Fischer attacked the High Court and the whole notion of Indigenous capacity to develop Australia the way white settlers and their descendants had.

'Rightly or wrongly,' he told a 1993 National Party Conference, 'dispossession of Aboriginal civilisation was always going to happen. Those in the guilt industry have to consider that developing cultures and peoples will always overtake relatively stationary cultures. We have to be honest and acknowledge that Aboriginals' sense of nationhood or even infrastructure was not highly developed. At no stage did Aboriginal civilisation develop substantial buildings, roadways or wheeled carts as part of their different priorities.'

Keating chose to lead the negotiations with all the stakeholders personally and found himself plunged into a nightmare of opposing forces, including within his own Cabinet and caucus ranks. At the heart of his problem was the fact that Indigenous leaders didn't trust the states and territories to genuinely accept the spirit of Mabo when under pressure from miners and farmers. The states wanted to retain control of land management in their domains. The hostility wasn't just coming from the conservative-controlled states. The Goss Labor Government in Queensland was one of Paul Keating's biggest ongoing headaches.

The negotiation process was a huge challenge for Aboriginal leaders, in large part because there was no one coherent national Indigenous leadership voice, but many voices representing many communities—rural, regional and urban. No one had the authority to speak for all Indigenous Australians.

Initially, a number of Aboriginal leaders were vociferous in their hostility, and attempts among Indigenous groups to find common cause, and even to sit at the negotiating table, failed. A frustrated Keating, no doubt feeling politically exposed on every front, at one point publicly expressed the doubt that 'Indigenous leaders would ever psychologically make the change to come into a process, to be part of it, and to take the burden of responsibility which went with it—whether they could ever summon the authority of their own community to negotiate for and on their behalf'.

It took Lowitja (Lois) O'Donoghue, backed by several other powerful Aboriginal figures, to break the deadlock. Mustering her authority as chair of the Aboriginal and Torres Strait Islander Commission (ATSIC) she declared that they would join negotiations, and that the leaders of the Indigenous land councils around Australia would be the negotiators.

Keating underscored the seriousness of his intent by inviting them into the Cabinet room, the heart of Australia's executive government, for their first meeting on 27 April 1993. They came to the table with differing constituencies and some differing views. If there was one sentiment that bound them together it was probably suspicion. The eyes of their nations were on them.

As Keating was to say nearly twenty years later when giving the Lowitja O'Donoghue Oration, 'In the 204-year history of the formerly colonised Australia, this had never happened. Never before had the Commonwealth government of Australia and its Cabinet nor any earlier colonial government laid out a basis of consultation and negotiation offering full participation to the country's indigenous representatives.'

Even so, the anti-Keating headlines were coming as much from Indigenous critics as other quarters. If he was seen to yield a point to the states, the farmers or the miners, he copped a chorus of criticism from the Indigenous camp, and vice versa. He had to weather the headlines after stormy meetings of Aboriginal leaders from all over Australia, first at Eva Valley in the Northern Territory in August, then in Canberra in October.

Keating was determined to get his legislation through Parliament before Christmas, and set a frenetic pace, working the phones as well as the meeting rooms to find some kind of credible consensus. From October to December these kinds of headlines were commonplace as draft legislation was massaged and fought over: 'Cabinet accused of moral scurvy in Mabo legislation', 'PM fights to save Mabo deal in marathon talks', 'Black fury over Mabo deal', 'Government to bulldoze Mabo legislation', 'Mabo the big blow-up', 'PJK back from the dead on Mabo', 'Aborigines win in Mabo plan', 'Keating dares Cabinet to sack him over Mabo', 'Farmers, miners reject Mabo deal', 'Keating makes Mabo history', 'Farmers dump Mabo', 'BHP boss blasts PM's Mabo bill', and finally, in the early hours of 22 December 1993, 'At last, a Mabo deal'.

Interestingly, Jeff Kennett, a vociferous opponent of Keating's plans for native title early in the debate, became one of its great supporters, and ended up urging federal Liberal Leader John Hewson to back the legislation.

In the end, the Keating Government relied on a handful of votes in the Senate from the Democrats, two Greens and the Tasmanian independent Brian Harradine to get the native title legislation through, but their support didn't come easily. The Greens had to be dragged to the party even though the legislation was backed by Indigenous leaders.

The bill established a Commonwealth Native Title Tribunal in tandem with mirrored tribunals in the states. Keating won over his own party in the end and most of the newspaper editorial writers, and the Cape York Indigenous leader, Noel Pearson, was to write many years later that it was the one and only time Indigenous Australians were 'invited in from the wood heap'. But it was to be of dubious political benefit to Keating for the rest of his prime ministership.

KOB: You'd been Prime Minister for less than six months when suddenly you were handed one of the biggest challenges I would think any Prime Minister could have—the explosive issue of the High Court ruling in the Mabo land rights case, which had enormous implications both symbolically and legally. How did you read that, and what was your reaction?

PJK: My first step was to put out a statement saying I welcomed the Mabo decision and thought it was a chance to turn a new page in the nation's relationship with its Indigenous population. I then acted to take advantage of the High Court decision but it was always going to be a very complex process with a lot of political risk and not much short-term political gain.

Let me put the Mabo ruling into context. I believed there was always something wrong with the notion of statutory land rights: of the Parliament of Australia seeking to give to Aboriginal people land that was never ours to give. In other words there was a phoniness at the core of statutory land rights.

What the High Court found on 3 June was that a system of traditional Aboriginal titles had survived the declaration of sovereignty by the British Government where previous High Courts had denied native title under the so-called concept of *terra nullius*, the land of no one. According to this view there was no Aboriginal nation, so customary traditions and titles to land simply couldn't exist.

The High Court's ruling in the Eddie Mabo case threw up several options. There was the political possibility of mass extinguishment by the states, which to me was unacceptable. Another was to let a long and complicated process of testing Aboriginal titles by case law, letting it take its course through the courts, which I also thought was undesirable.

The third option, which I chose, was to take up the challenge of putting the essence of the High Court ruling into effect by Commonwealth legislation, in the process removing the risk of mass extinguishment, particularly in Queensland and Western Australia, which I thought would have been a terrible outcome.

It was a massive undertaking, which I took on personally because I believed that if the issue did not have the full weight and authority of the Prime Minister, it would never get through. We delivered the legislation within eighteen months of the High Court ruling, just before Christmas 1993.

KOB: It interests me that of all the things you were passionate about in your early years, and even your years as Treasurer, there was very little evidence that Aboriginal affairs was a big issue for you before you became Prime Minister.

PJK: I always felt it, though. The film *Jedda* had a big impact on me in the 1950s. I remember seeing it when I was about eleven at the Hoyts Civic Theatre in Bankstown. It was a very powerful film set in the Northern Territory, and in a way it mirrored aspects of the stolen generations. It ended in tragedy for two Aboriginal people and left me with the sense that this was their place and we were all interlopers.

I also had very strong memories of going with my father when I was very young to the boxing at the Sydney Stadium before it was knocked down for the eastern suburbs railway. I used to see people like Dave Sands and the Sands Brothers. I also used to go to Jimmy Sharman's fighting tent at the Royal Easter Show.

I also saw the Sharman boxing troupe in Newcastle. They were pretty much all Aboriginal boxers and they'd get belted for tuppence ha'penny. I'll never forget one guy getting into trouble. He had the light behind him and he got punched in the head. I remember the spray of his spit and sweat, and I said to my father, 'This shouldn't happen. This poor guy can't take punches like that.' He was just a bit of meat out there.

And I went away thinking this whole group of Aboriginal boxers in the Jimmy Sharman show was so on the outer, copping the brunt of the game. A respectable white fighter wouldn't take that kind of pounding for next to nothing. Then in the 1970s I knew all about Aboriginal communities in the cities like Redfern in Sydney and I just ended up with a very sympathetic view of them—that's the truth of it.

The person I most took notice of on Aboriginal policy when I first went to the House of Representatives was Kim Beazley Senior. He made a speech one night about Aboriginal malnutrition which was so powerful that Bill Wentworth, Australia's first minister for Aboriginal Affairs in the Gorton Government, moved that the House adjourn for five minutes to recompose itself. You don't see that too often.

Gough Whitlam was the first Labor leader to really step up, with the *Northern Territory Land Rights Act*, as did Malcolm Fraser when he pushed it through Parliament upon becoming Prime Minister. Bob Hawke had the chance to do something at the 1986 Labor Conference by supporting Clyde Holding as Aboriginal Affairs Minister in his proposal for uniform national land rights, using the power conferred by the 1967 referendum.

Graham Richardson and Brian Burke as Western Australian Premier got in Bob's ear opposing it. This was during Bob's long down phase, and I said to him, 'If you and I support this on the conference floor as Prime Minister and Treasurer we'll beat anybody. Don't do a trade with Burke and Richardson.' Bob dropped his support for it and so it sat there in limbo.

Without the Mabo judgment I would have taken land rights on once I had got past the 1993 election but the High Court took the timing out of my hands.

KOB: Don Watson said of you that when you embraced an issue you tended to do so with a passion almost akin to a religious force. Is that what happened here?

PJK: More or less. They're called events, Kerry. It's like Lincoln and slavery. Lincoln's career typically was not built around the issue of slavery but he ended up wearing it in the context of the American Civil War and it became his defining moment.

With the High Court decision I could have been a complete lush and said, 'OK, Mr High Court, you want to make these brave decisions, you live with them. You do all the case law that follows. You decide who's got the title, what the title is, who hasn't got the title. And you stop the states extinguishing it while you sit and think about it.'

I didn't do that. I didn't leave the High Court hanging on the limb of its own decision. I embraced the High Court and built that large body of corporate and cultural law so that we could say what the title was, who had it, who could get it, how you would get it and how it would be protected. Such was the urgency, that I worked on the *Native Title Act* personally in the Cabinet room for seven or eight months of 1993, because it required the authority of a Prime Minister to make all the key decisions as they emerged, and ancilliary ones too: the right to negotiate, rights to exploration, just thousands of issues that had to be dealt with.

I like to think that we could look at this as a case study of a High Court doing something of integrity, matched by a federal government with its own measure of integrity, resulting in something the nation could be proud of. That is, to confront the dispossession while finding a way to give back to Indigenous people the land that had always been theirs.

KOB: But back in December 1992, when you committed yourself to the now famous Redfern speech with an election just around the corner, as a seasoned politician with your prime ministership and the fate of the government on the line over such a potentially inflammatory issue, how did you assess the political risk in making that speech?

PJK: I was the outsider to win the 1993 election but you've got to practise what you preach. I always believed that you should burn the capital as you run to the poll rather than conserving it, being Mr Safe Guy. A seminal issue like this and its remedy provide the uplift that any political personality needs, doing what is right and good. It gives you the surge, and without the surge, what are you? You're just mucking around with tricky press statements and fleeting appearances at doorstops.

The risk for us was in Queensland and Western Australia, where many people didn't want that kind of acknowledgement of Aboriginal dispossession, and there was some apprehension in the cities too. There was always pressure to carry on with the orthodox history on this issue, but you've heard my Road Runner analogy, running so fast you burn up the bitumen behind you so there's no road left for the Liberals. That's why I used to label John Hewson Wile E. Coyote.

The Liberal Party would never have done Mabo. Hewson called it a day of shame when the bill went through Parliament. That dreadful Tim Fischer wrung his hands about it and stirred up negative passions. That's what I was up against, but now with it enshrined, the country's moved forward.

KOB: The Redfern address was the psychological launch pad for the Mabo negotiations. It is now regarded as a landmark moment in Australian history because it was the moment you chose to send a message to the nation, but particularly to Aboriginal leaders, that you were serious about Mabo. Did you have a sense of history as you made that speech?

PJK: We were celebrating the Year of the World's Indigenous People that year, under the auspices of the United Nations, and the Redfern speech was delivered to mark that. I chose to use that speech to make those declaratory remarks and also to acknowledge the opportunity presented by Mabo. I said that by doing away with the bizarre conceit that our continent had no nation and no owners before the settlement of Europeans, Mabo established a fundamental truth and laid the basis for justice.

KOB: Don Watson said in *Bleeding Heart* that it was 'one of those moments when to write for you was an unqualified privilege'.

PJK: It was emotional for me. The words were power-packed. In fact Watson reveals some of the origins of the Redfern speech in his book. He recalls a flight in the RAAF VIP aircraft over desert country in Western Australia, and I looked down at the red plains and observed that we would never do any good in our relationship with Indigenous Australians unless we owned up to it all. This was always my view, that we had done the murders, we had broken the traditional way of life, but in the tricky storytelling of Australia no one had come clean.

I had often told Watson of stories from my grandmother of how relatives had used poisoned dampers to kill Aborigines around the Grafton and Kempsey districts in New South Wales. We just knocked them off, destroyed their way of life, but it was all hush-hush.

The Redfern speech was an opportunity to acknowledge the massive injustice of the dispossession and to point to Mabo as a way forward. I sat through a number of conversations with Watson and my Aboriginal Affairs adviser Simon Balderstone, where we talked about the murders and the grog and the diseases, about the generation of kids taken from their mothers, the whole assimilation policy. The tyranny of it.

When I started speaking in Redfern Park, the crowd was quiet but a bit restless. There were even a few jeers. Then all of a sudden they started to really hear what I was saying.

Sol Bellear, who was a pioneer of Aboriginal activism in Redfern, came up to me at a function in the Sydney Town Hall an hour later, and said, 'Paul, that speech of yours today. You said some very important things. Emotional things. Things no one else has ever said.'

It didn't get very much coverage at the time and there was no political benefit for us other than the truth of it. As I've said, what is right and true carries its own power.

KOB: What exactly did you want from that speech?

PJK: I wanted to acknowledge the original colonial sin, the dispossession, and not to feel guilty. To acknowledge it and all the hurt that attended it; that the nation's soul might be somewhat washed and refreshed by the doing of it. I believed we needed to give ourselves the fortitude and uprightness to approach our regional neighbours with our heads high, not lowered by an incapacity to represent ourselves with integrity.

KOB: Some of your more pragmatic colleagues in Labor must have been urging you to bury Mabo, at least until after the election.

PJK: That was the majority. A lot of people in the party thought this was a vote loser, and a lot of opposition remained through the negotiation process in 1993. There were also some in the party who thought we didn't go far enough in support of the Indigenous case.

We began the consultation process in October 1992 but we were halfway through 1993 before the discussions began in earnest. There was a lot of suspicion, anxiety and even hostility on all sides.

KOB: You'd never really had an experience in politics like this before, had you, negotiating with Aboriginal people on such a substantial and complex proposition, with the added complication that there was no one leadership group for Indigenous Australia? How did you approach that negotiation and how sharp was your learning curve?

PJK: You're right about that—no Australian government had ever negotiated with them. Apart from Gough's Northern Territory *Land Rights Act*, which he had proposed and Malcolm Fraser promulgated, there was no movement under Commonwealth power. So you're right, there was no one leadership group to deal with, but many different leaders. And I am not sure whether the Whitlam and Fraser governments conducted meaningful negotiations with them anyway.

It was Lowitja O'Donoghue who stood up when it counted and used her position as ATSIC Chair as a pulpit, but without any formal power or over-arching authority, to declare that the nation's Aboriginal leadership could and would negotiate. It was an act of substantial leadership on her part. She alone decided that the leaders of the land councils would act as negotiators on behalf of the nation's Indigenous peoples.

Inviting them into the Cabinet room for that first meeting in April 1993 was meant as a very strong statement of intent on my part. It was the very first time Aboriginal people were brought fully and in an equal way to the centre of the national executive—the very first time. And when they came, broadly representing the land councils and ATSIC with their Ten Point Plan I said, 'I will negotiate with you but do you know how to negotiate? What you have are broadly bald claims and if we don't accept all the claims you'll say true to form, either we are negligent or racist.

'You're in the Cabinet room but it's not just the place you're in, you are in a process. You've been invited in. Are you prepared to negotiate. To recognise that your claims are a starting point from which you are prepared to surrender some that are not centrally important to you but hang on to the things which are? In other words, a real negotiation, weighing interests but with a capacity for sensible compromise?'

I said, 'What you lot are good at is making claims and then taking no responsibility as you walk away back to the purity committees, saying we told the government what we really think of them. So have you the courage to negotiate?'

I put that to the Dodson brothers, to Lowitja O'Donoghue, David Ross and Noel Pearson and the others who were there. 'Have you the sense or the courage to negotiate and accept the burden of that responsibility?'

You have to remember people like Mick Dodson had been ratted on hundreds of times before so they had a deep scepticism that any government would really do anything for them. Noel Pearson said later that my remarks had really stung him. He said they walked out knowing I was right; that they couldn't just drop a piece of paper on the table and leave. They had to be prepared to take responsibility as a group to sit down and grind through the principles and in a formal process.

KOB: What did you learn from that experience?

PJK: First, that they had a very clear idea about what they wanted and what the Mabo decision meant to them both culturally and legally.

I grew in confidence that in the intellectualism of it, I could negotiate a satisfactory bill that covered their central concerns and the concerns of everyone else who owned a piece of land in Australia.

People like Lowitja O'Donoghue displayed leadership of a kind that we had never seen before. Finally they decided to negotiate and although they ratted on me halfway through and belted me again in October, in the end they could see that I knew how to run the caucus and parliamentary system. But more than that, that I wanted to see justice done. Those two points won me their regard and without that regard I could not have done it in the end.

They had to deal with a very tough constituency of their own. You may remember the Eva Valley meeting in the Northern Territory in August 1993 representing Indigenous communities from all over Australia, which was charged with emotion. There was another mass meeting at Boomanulla Oval in Canberra in October where they burned the draft legislation as a gesture of repudiation.

In the great weight of the Mabo judgment and all the ups and downs of that high-pressure year, the Indigenous leader with the greatest weight on all the technical and cultural issues was David Ross, the Chairman of the Central Land Council. The courage to drive the organisation came from Lowitja O'Donoghue, and the legal round up was driven principally by Noel Pearson. They were a formidable group.

One of the legal challenges was to achieve an outcome; to validate post-1975 titles without suspending the *Racial Discrimination Act*. And that was technically very hard to do. Every land title issued after the *Racial Discrimination Act* in 1975 was now invalid, so a lot of major mining titles were invalid. The question was how to validate them without doing so in a discriminatory way. It took time, but we worked a way through it.

KOB: You also argued up hill and down dale with the state premiers. They walked out on you at the first substantive

meeting in June 1993 just days after your first tough set of
negotiations with Lowitja O'Donoghue and the others.

PJK: I've still got my handwritten notes from that meeting. I told
them we should view the Mabo judgment as a national issue requiring a national response. That we were taking a cooperative approach
but the Commonwealth would not resile from its responsibilities.
That the existence of native title in Australia had been confirmed by
the High Court and it was our job to give effect to that recognition
and deal with it in Australia's land management system.

I made plain from the outset that we would not be attempting to
suspend or tamper with the *Racial Discrimination Act* to validate
titles issued after 1975.

I stressed that the single most important objective as far as
Indigenous leaders were concerned was that the basic framework for
native title should be established in Commonwealth legislation even
though there should be complementary state/territory legislation
as well.

I said the native title tribunals could be in the states but they would
be subject to a uniform Commonwealth approach, with the federal
government retaining the right to take action to avoid having the
policy being hostage to a protracted native title negotiation process.

I took them through all the key points and emphasised that none
of the principles represented any radical or extreme policy. I said I had
not uncritically accepted the Aboriginal peace plan, for example. But
in the end they walked away without agreeing to anything.

KOB: Can you remember the scare tactics that Jeff Kennett
used not long after that, talking about the threat to suburban
backyards? Did that surprise you because I know you came to
have regard for Kennett?

PJK: I never quite understood what Jeff Kennett's motivations were at that first meeting. He always had the ability to be the stand-out guy among the premiers, and I don't believe there's a racist bone in him.

I said, 'Jeff, you've got to remember the part of Australia where Aboriginal society was completely atomised was in Victoria, right? You don't have groups of Aboriginal people with representative strength like you see in Queensland and Western Australia because they were wiped out, atomised in Victoria like they were in the country around Sydney. They were the first ones knocked out. In a sense then you have a greater responsibility.'

When they walked away from that meeting with nothing agreed I wrote to them, offering to talk separately with each of them over the next fortnight, but it would depend on them accepting two fundamental premises: that native title was a reality that must be recognised, identified and dealt with justly, and that there must be a national approach.

Richard Court, the Western Australian Premier, claimed I was trampling over state rights and said he'd persist with state legislation to extinguish native title. And he did. That failed eventually in the High Court. Jeff Kennett said my handling of Mabo would become Labor's GST. In other words it would be my Waterloo as the GST had been John Hewson's in the 1993 election.

KOB: Geoff Kitney later wrote in the *Sydney Morning Herald* that 'Jeff Kennett, who had publicly been quite inflammatory in his criticism, emerged from a private meeting with you deeply impressed by both the passion and the grasp of detail in your explanation to him as to why Mabo was important.' Do you remember that meeting?

PJK: I do, vaguely. You cannot afford to take on an issue as complex as this one without understanding the many principles at source, which

I did. I had said to the states that the Mabo decision had three parts to it: the white part, the black part and the grey part.

The white part was where the High Court said that following sovereignty and claims by imperial Britain on Australia, any grants of interest in land by a state land manager extinguished native title. So all existing landholders were protected by that extinguishment.

The black part of Mabo was where land had not been alienated from the Crown or been subject to a freehold grant of interest, and where Aboriginal people could demonstrate a continuing association with the land and maintenance of their traditional culture. They could apply, and in the appropriate circumstances be given title to the land.

So, to take the formality out of it, the High Court is saying, 'Look, all you whities who've got your blocks of land in the cities, don't worry, because in our judgment those grants of interest will extinguish any claims by Aboriginal people.'

To the Aboriginal and Torres Strait Islander community the Court was saying, 'To the extent that the Commonwealth or the States have never alienated land from the Crown, you can apply for it and you can get it providing you've maintained an association and traditional connection with it.'

The difficult part was the pastoral leases. This was the grey part. The pastoral leases broadly covered half the country. The High Court judgment was silent about pastoral leases but the Attorney-General's Department had told me and the Cabinet that, in its view, the High Court judgment implied that the native title was extinguished under pastoral leases by the granting of the lease.

Now, I never accepted that advice and said at the time that I couldn't see why the Court wouldn't, upon reflection, take the view that there could be coexistence of title; that there was no point of conflict in a cow grazing over hundreds or thousands of acres of land, and Aboriginal people at the same time maintaining a traditional way of life across the same land. I accepted the argument that if there was a point of conflict, the grazing imperative would predominate, but if the grazing ceased I could see no reason why the High Court wouldn't take the view that there could be revival of title; that is, that the underlying native title would reassert itself once the pastoral activity had ceased and the lease had been terminated.

So I was saying to the premiers, including Jeff Kennett, don't make a mountain out of a molehill. There'll be problems here and probably quite a lot of them, but it won't be a problem in terms of the great body of titles across the states.

I also had meetings with people like John Laws, and I give John a lot of marks for this. I said, 'Alan Jones and other commentators may attack Mabo and make friends in the process, but the important thing for you John, is not to be wrong, and if you say that blocks of land are threatened or people's property entitlement to them are threatened, it'll be proven to be wrong. So how can you advance yourself or the program actually being wrong?'

I gave John some documentation and briefings and told him the story about the black, the white and the grey parts of Mabo, and I give him credit for dealing with the issue responsibly. Remember his program went all over rural New South Wales and Queensland. You can imagine the kinds of people who would ring him to complain that Aboriginal people were going to take their land.

These were the points I'd run through, and when I had a reasonable premier in front of me I could shift them. I think I did shift Jeff Kennett and John Fahey and, to an extent, Wayne Goss, but Western Australia continued to try to extinguish native title rights until the High Court quashed their legislation.

Here's a story by Paul Chamberlin in the *Sydney Morning Herald* on 6 October, 'Kennett ready to sign deal over Mabo'. It says, 'If there is agreement with Victoria, a similar pact is likely to be made with NSW, Queensland, South Australia, the Northern Territory and the ACT.'

But each time I made a concession with one party, it was likely to set someone else off, but that was how the whole process was conducted. It's called negotiating. Mega-negotiating.

Here's another story in the *Sydney Morning Herald* on 10 August: 'Goss attacks the PM on Mabo':

> The relationship between the nation's two most senior Labor leaders went close to breaking point over Mabo yesterday with the Queensland Premier resorting to personal attacks on the Prime Minister. Mr Goss said Mr Keating had been misled by bad advice and did not appear to understand the seriousness of the threat to investment. The row between Mr Keating and Mr Goss reflects a significant widening of the Aboriginal land rights debate beyond the specifics of the High Court decision. It also highlights the deteriorating relationship between Mr Keating and Mr Goss.

KOB: So did your relationship with Wayne Goss deteriorate through that process?

PJK: Yes, it did. I had a very thin relationship with him. It never really recovered.

KOB: You'd set yourself an October deadline to get the legislation into Parliament, and every time you got past a hurdle with one party, another one would scream. You must have been moving around them in a constant cycle. When were the breakthroughs?

PJK: When the Indigenous leaders accepted my assurances that I wouldn't allow the states to extinguish their rights. When they indicated that they were prepared to work with the notion that they agree to validation of past grants with the Commonwealth paying compensation if it was in the framework of national legislation. With the principles of native title enshrined.

Mick Dodson was obviously struck by the clarity I brought to each of the points. He told friends, 'Prime Ministers just don't do stuff to this level. They don't understand this sort of detail so if this guy understands all the detail and he's promising to see it through, then we're going to get something from this.'

Here's a headline from August that year: 'Keating's vow is to stand by Mabo'. That referred to a meeting with the Council for Aboriginal Reconciliation where I said if anyone tried to force the government into unacceptable compromise on the basic principles I would get out the blowtorch. I acknowledged it was going to be difficult but told them my government would not be a government of shame.

But even if the Aboriginal leadership were prepared to be in it we still had to handle validations of land grants after 1975 that satisfied the *Racial Discrimination Act*. Noel Pearson was pivotal in clarifying the ability to implement special measures for the enhancement of Aboriginal people under the *Act*, which we subsequently provided in a social justice package including the Aboriginal land fund that has now built to nearly $2 billion. A fund to buy back pastoral leases.

Once we began to find a way to implement the validations without suspending the *Racial Discrimination Act* the rest became somewhat easier.

KOB: In the Geoff Kitney piece I mentioned earlier, he said it was a pity you hadn't spent more time selling the Mabo story to the electorate, that your failure to do so was good reason to question the political sense of your post-election decision to keep your distance from the media. He was referring to the widely held perception that you were still punishing the press gallery for having failed to, in your terms, properly question and expose *Fightback!* before the 1993 election.

PJK: I did a lot of explaining on radio. There's a piece *Four Corners* ran on the twentieth anniversary of the *Native Title Act*, showing me arguing the case against racist remarks on the John Laws program. I was out doing a lot of that kind of stuff.

KOB: But you were bypassing the press gallery, quite possibly to your cost.

PJK: I was dealing with the principals, with the Indigenous leaders, with the Mining Industry Council, with the National Farmers Federation and with the state premiers, and we were running up against a deadline to get it all resolved. We'd adjourn from meetings at 6 p.m. while Sandy Hollway, the Deputy Secretary of PM&C, worked up a note on the current sticking point and we'd be back into it at 8.15 and wouldn't finish until 10 or later. And the same would happen the next day. It just went on and on.

There was always the possibility of going up to the press gallery and telling them what we were doing but then they would inevitably ask, 'What have you got to report to us?' and I would have nothing to say other than the fact that we were grappling with a set of complexities you wouldn't believe, which is at this point unresolved.

In any event I'd lost respect for the gallery. A couple of important things happened in the 1993 election campaign. One, that down to almost one or two of them they had all written me off. But secondly, when Michelle Grattan wrote that it was smart of John Hewson not to come to the National Press Club and account to the media in the ritual of the leaders' Press Club appearances in the final week of a campaign, I thought that was indefensible and also indicative of the gallery's attitude generally.

And here I was, muggins, who'd been doing hour-long press conferences for nearly a decade and who had gone again to the Press Club, for the eighteenth time since becoming Treasurer, told by an important person in the gallery it was quite smart to ignore the gallery, that it was a smart, political thing to do. Whereas that dumb Prime Minister had turned up, yet again, to account for all the measures.

KOB: But how smart politically was it for you to ignore them through 1993? It had been a deliberate act on your part to make yourself much less accessible.

PJK: Yes, but honour demanded that response. The fact that they were complete rats to the big reform project meant that I could never deal with them conscientiously again. They simply weren't good enough.

KOB: Many of them had reported on your work as Treasurer quite conscientiously.

PJK: Look, they reverted to type. When I picked them up they only talked about three things: tax cuts, election speculation and leadership changes. I educated the whole body of them on the panoply of issues that required reform. The first time they were tempted even by an inexperienced and rigid person like Hewson, they embraced him without question. Even after the whole of *Fightback!* had been exposed for the fraud it was and the public had rejected it, they were still hopping into me. And while I was continuing to run probably the largest reform program in the Western world. Not just Australia, the West generally.

The veracity of that claim is that because of Australia's economic flexibility, induced by our policy changes at the time, Australia has had 24 consecutive years of economic growth since. Unprecedented in the postwar years anywhere.

But more than that, Australia had the big social graft going on at the same time—superannuation for everybody, native title, the republic and so on. In press and media terms, it was a jamboree. The gallery had never seen anything like it, and haven't since.

KOB: Through all those Treasury years you had made the investment, you'd spent more time in dialogue with the gallery than any other politician, and you reaped the dividend, not in their slavish worship of you, but in the extent to which they covered the broad storyline. Now you were basically telling them to get stuffed.

PJK: I gave them the clue in the Placido Domingo gallery speech in 1990. I encouraged them to remain participants and not become voyeurs. To remain integral in the great reformation. But their feckless, tinsel instincts got the better of them.

I won't be extravagant or rude in saying I was feeding caviar to pigs, because some, a minority of them, remained true to the big undertaking. But I can say I was working with a very weak side.

KOB: But you couldn't look beyond that?

PJK: I thought, in the broad, they had dealt themselves out of the game, and that it was doffing my lid too much to deal conscientiously with them again. I still did press conferences but nothing on the scale I used to do. Because in the end you knew you were appealing to a bunch that was populist, tabloid and jaundiced.

KOB: Coming back to Mabo, Kitney touches on the seemingly endless nature of the negotiations in another piece in mid-October titled 'PJK back from the dead on Mabo'. He talked about how:

Keating had sat in the middle of all the competing interests and set out to build a consensus layer by layer ... Keating has probably never worked so hard on any policy issue. Certainly no issue since he became prime minister has so tested his political skill and stamina or involves such political risk, but by last night the possibility of a national Mabo solution which all the key parties could live with was emerging. If it does and Keating can get it through the Senate, it'll be a personal political triumph.

It was such a battle to get Mabo through the Senate. How close did you and your Cabinet colleagues come to giving up in those final weeks?

PJK: I had Gareth Evans, Robert Ray and Bob McMullan who was the Leader of Government Business in the Senate come and see me to say that they couldn't get it through and I'd have to give it away. Gareth's words were, 'Good try cobber, but we're not going to make it.' I told them we would sit right through Christmas, including Christmas Day if we had to. And that I would flog the Greens who were jamming it. Once they knew I was immovable, then the core decision is kind of made. The rest of it is then facilitation, which Gareth did magnificently and so did Robert Ray. They all did.

KOB: I've seen Evans' performance in the Senate described as Herculean. At one point from a Friday to a Monday he was on his feet for something like 48 hours dealing with a Coalition filibuster. Geoffrey Barker wrote in the *Age* it was a *tour de force* and possibly his finest moment in politics.

PJK: Gareth had fought a long and distinguished fight in the Senate, particularly against the two Greens from Western Australia and the Opposition, and there were desperate moments in the passage of it, but if you want to crunch the big policies through you've got to hold your nerve and squeeze the system.

KOB: How did you persuade the Greens?

PJK: I certainly threatened them, and badly. Bruisingly threatened them. I said I would come to Western Australia and campaign against them over their scant regard for Aboriginal justice and for their uppity view that they knew better than Aboriginal people what was best for them.

I said, 'This is a classic whities' view. We know better. Here are the senior Aboriginal people in the nation working with the government to see a bill into place but you know better.'

One of the spin-offs from the *Native Title Act*, as part of the social justice package and apart from the Indigenous land fund, was to recognise and place on the record the whole process of assimilation where Aboriginal children were taken from their mothers and brought to the towns and cities for what was essentially a white education and white way of life. So that over a long period of time the Aboriginal nation would have disappeared. As I said in the Redfern speech, 'We took the children from their mothers.' Horrendous.

I agreed to set up an inquiry into this, and I asked Ronald Wilson, who was a very decent man on these issues while on the High Court, to take on the job. I knew it would be a big can of worms, a big set of emotional issues.

KOB: It was John Howard who received the 700-page report, *Bringing Them Home*, in 1997, a report concluding that Indigenous families and communities had endured gross violations of their human rights, and that they were acts of genocide aimed at wiping out Indigenous families, communities and cultures vital to the precious and inalienable heritage of Australia. Did you agree with those substantial findings?

PJK: Yes, this was the report I had commissioned and I agreed absolutely with its findings. The country needed the cleansing, it needed to recognise that this had happened and to apologise for it.

KOB: It would be nearly eleven years before the Rudd Government formally apologised to the victims identified in the report and you attended Parliament that day. How will you remember it?

PJK: What sticks in my mind is the Aboriginal women who sat in the galleries in tears as Kevin made the speech. The nation apologises. It was a very, very important day. The injustice can never be overturned because it happened, but at least there is recognition and contrition.

I like to think that the *Native Title Act* went some way in settling the fundamental grievance of Indigenous Australia, the brutal dispossession of their land and the smashing of their way of life at the hands of an alien imperial power. And Gough said something very nice about this. He said the development of the *Act* was—and I'll quote him—'a shining example of promptitude in a century-old story of procrastination'.

I spent more than half my political life either as Treasurer or Prime Minister and I got a lot done, but I was especially pleased with native title. Noel Pearson later said in the *Griffith Review* that:

> never before and likely never again would indigenes be invited in from the woodheap to sit at the main table as they did during those Keating years. This just confirmed the opinion that Aborigines are electoral poison. No more bleeding hearts, no more prime ministerial insistence that the black fellas come in from the cold.

Well, I did insist and they did come in from the cold and they'll own something like 40 per cent of the continent thanks to the *Native Title Act*. And I hope that through that inheritance and that wealth they'll dig themselves out of the hole and move off the woodheap.

KOB: Noel Pearson emerged from the whole Mabo process as a very dynamic and articulate young Aboriginal leader and his profile grew enormously from the Mabo negotiation process. I've read that you actually had him to the Lodge one day for quite an extensive conversation over lunch about whether he should go into politics or not. He was asking your advice, is that right?

PJK: Yes, that happened. He is an amazing wordsmith and a truly intellectual fellow, and he had leadership qualities that I had rarely seen. But Noel had to make commitments and perhaps one of the flaws in Noel's political character is that he was never quite able to make the kind of commitment which the party system demands. He has a tremendous mind, a very original legal mind and was a great storyteller and spinner of words. These are rare skills.

KOB: He subsequently said that the message he took from that discussion was that you were dissuading him from politics, that he would spend a lot of time waiting around in politics, and that he might be better thinking of a career in law.

PJK: He could have won preselection for the very safe Melbourne seat of Lalor when Barry Jones retired but in the end he didn't think the time opportune to take it. He then accepted a spot with a law firm in Melbourne and three years later he flirted with the idea of a federal seat in New South Wales. But then he came to a very determinist view that without conservative Australia being part of the compact, the Aboriginal people wouldn't get anything sustainable. I think he was wrong about that, but it seems to have governed his active political life ever since. I think the country has missed the services of someone who, in the broad, had the capacity to be a great leader.

THE NEW MARCH OF REFORM

As Paul Keating was still absorbing the Mabo ruling, he was also dealing himself into two other complex and risky policy areas that had been long-term distractions for the caucus and Cabinet.

One was the privatisation of the publicly owned Australian Airlines and Qantas: one domestic, the other international, both iconic. The other was shaping the framework for the introduction of pay television. Keating's approach to both was classically high-wire. While his primary focus was on breaching John Hewson's confident march to the next election, he couldn't afford to be seen to drop the ball on policy reform, and these two issues had kicked around without resolution for years.

In its early days the Hawke Government was aggressively anti-privatisation. Public institutions such as Qantas, the Commonwealth Bank and Telecom with their large, highly unionised workforces were not only icons for the Labor faithful and the federal parliamentary caucus, but a potent weapon to use against the Liberal Opposition, particularly since privatisation was associated with the tough social face of Thatcherism in Britain.

In September 1985, at the inaugural Ben Chifley Memorial Lecture in Bathurst, Bob Hawke had thundered, 'What in the name of reason is the justification for breaking up and selling off the great and efficient national assets, like the Commonwealth Bank, Telecom, TAA and Qantas? The fact is that this recipe for disaster represents the height of economic irrationality.'

This wasn't a random observation but preparing the ground to damage the new Liberal leader John Howard, who had just taken over from Andrew Peacock and for whom privatisation had appeal. Hawke, Keating and others had then sought to damage Howard further via a vociferous attack on South Australian Liberal leader John Olsen who had declared that the state election campaign would be a national test for privatisation. Olsen wanted to sell off state assets and lost the election.

Immediately after the 1987 election in which Hawke defeated Howard, who was still pushing asset sales, Hawke put privatisation squarely on Labor's agenda. With Gareth Evans as minister for the new super ministry of Transport and Communication, Cabinet was heading towards a policy of selling off 49 per cent of both Qantas and TAA, which had by now been rebranded as Australian Airlines, but the party was not for turning. Evans instead developed his so-called 'open skies' policy, flagging that the long-standing two-airlines agreement would end within three years and greater competition would prevail. It was a policy area in which Keating was always involved. It wasn't until 1990 that a special national party conference changed the policy platform to allow a 49 per cent sell-off of both airlines. It had rattled around the government corridors through Hawke's last year without resolution.

The pay-television issue had also languished for years, only coming back into focus with the government's sale of the Aussat domestic satellite to Optus in 1991. Pay television was also risky business within the caucus because media policy was always sensitive, particularly if the big players such as Packer and Murdoch stood to gain. In this case, Murdoch appeared to have no interest at first, but Packer certainly did and made his ambitions plain.

After the 1990 election Environment Minister Graham Richardson asked Bob Hawke for the Communication portfolio. Hawke has remained coy as to why he knocked Richardson back, and offended him by giving him Social Security instead. The widespread assumption is that even Hawke thought Richardson was too close to Kerry Packer, despite Hawke's own professed friendship with the media mogul.

When he became Prime Minister, Paul Keating didn't have any such concerns, although when he appointed Richardson as Transport and Communications Minister, John Hewson commented that it was like giving Goldfinger the keys to Fort Knox. Conservative governments had almost always had comfortably close relationships with media proprietors, and few were closer than that of Sir Robert Menzies with Sir Frank Packer, Kerry's father, but many in the Labor caucus hadn't yet become comfortable with the access people like Kerry Packer and Rupert Murdoch now had with Labor governments.

But just as Graham Richardson was trying to persuade some deeply wary caucus colleagues to embrace a pay-television policy that happened to suit his friend KP, he was forced to resign from Cabinet over an ill-judged business reference for a family member on ministerial letterhead that became known as the Marshall Islands affair.

Richardson resigned from the ministry on 18 May, and Senator Bob Collins was elevated from the outer ministry to replace him. But Packer's interests were still represented by his lobbyist and Bob Hawke's former advisor, Peter Barron, who also remained quite close to Paul Keating.

Then Keating went on the Nine Network's *Sunday* program with Laurie Oakes on 31 May, and without consulting either Cabinet or caucus, essentially launched a new pay-television policy, interpreted by some as even more friendly to Packer than Richardson's, which was bound to put caucus' teeth on edge. He also announced that the government was going to sell Australian Airlines to Qantas and privatise two-thirds of the merged company.

His intent, as Neal Blewett wrote in his diaries, was 'to galvanise the party and electorate by a flurry of policy proposals' to get the government's earlier momentum going again after losing Richardson. Keating's intervention certainly had a galvanising effect on every front but he now had to somehow bypass the party platform with the merger and sale of the airlines, and get support for his pay-television proposals through a stubbornly resistant caucus. To lose on either policy would be destructive.

The justification for the airline sales was that both airlines were struggling, that it made no sense to sell each separately and, according to Finance Minister Ralph Willis, a merger would increase the overall value by $300 million. It had taken a big effort to change the party platform to allow the sale of 49 per cent of Qantas, but what emerged from a late-night Cabinet meeting was a proposal to sell 100 per cent of the combined airline, with a 'golden share' left in the government's hands with a power of veto in the national interest, which Cabinet endorsed around midnight. It passed through caucus the next morning, according to Blewett, after 'a superb political display' by Keating.

Pay television was another matter. Every time the issue had come up in the past, the free-to-air commercial networks had argued against it, happy with their protected patch and aware of the inroads cable television had made into mainstream commercial television audiences in America since the 1970s.

In 1986, the Hawke Government had frozen any move for pay television until 1990, and the ban was extended for at least another year, according to Paul Barry in *The Rise and Rise of Kerry Packer*, because the government believed 'the financial position of the networks was too precarious to compete with pay'.

In 1991, Kim Beazley as Communications Minister was charged with the sale of the domestic satellite Aussat, and argued that it would bring a much higher price if it could be designated as the exclusive carrier of a new pay-television service. This time the Hawke Cabinet went against the commercial networks' lobbying efforts and announced in October 1991 that licences would be made available for six pay channels to be delivered by Aussat. But the government banned advertising on the new medium for the first five years of operation in response to screams from the commercial proprietors that advertising on pay television would be catastrophic for them.

Policy confusion took hold once Keating came to office as first Richardson, then Keating himself, sought to change the pay-television formula, each time favouring the three commercial networks, the strongest of which was Packer's Nine Network because the others were struggling to survive. Each time, the caucus communications committee held out for greater media ownership diversity.

There was relief all round when Keating finally threw up a proposal that excluded the existing networks from the first pay licence with four channels, and gave the new licensee a year's head start before releasing a second two-channel licence that Packer and the other proprietors could bid for. Caucus endorsement avoided a loss of authority by Keating, although the policy was to go through various confusing permutations for more than two years before the final outcome.

When the dust finally settled in 1995, Rupert Murdoch, who had earlier expressed no interest, emerged in the pay-television box seat, establishing Foxtel in a 50–50 partnership with Telstra using Telstra's cables in the cities for distribution. Packer ended up with no stake in pay television at all—his last throw of the dice, a partnership with Optus sharing the market with Murdoch and Telstra. His failure to clinch the deal was a major contributor to the complete breakdown of his relationship with Paul Keating.

KOB: When you became Prime Minister, you inherited two tricky policy areas that had been developed in the dying days of the Hawke years. One was the sale of Qantas and Australian Airlines as two separate assets. The other was the introduction of pay television.

Both decisions would raise significant money for the budget bottom line, which was important to you in trying to contain the deficit. But both were stalled in caucus when you lost the minister responsible for both, Graham Richardson. Why did you choose to break the impasse so dramatically by announcing new policies on Channel Nine rather than through the Cabinet process?

PJK: When I became Prime Minister our stocks were very low. We introduced *One Nation*, put some life back into the government's performance in Parliament, started to make inroads into John Hewson's leadership and *Fightback!*, and built some impetus around a more visionary foreign policy and a national debate about who and what we are. By April–May I'd made up about 10 points in the primary vote.

I'd given Graham Richardson Transport and Communications in the new ministry. He was a very able and clever fellow and his street sense was an asset for the party. I'd spent a large part of my life working with him in one way or another and he'd played a part in my accession. He'd made a success of two Cabinet portfolios, and I thought I'd take him on trust and give him the job he really wanted.

He had made early progress on the privatisation of Qantas and Australian Airlines and in reshaping the policy on pay television but then struck trouble over the so-called Marshall Islands affair. He'd recommended a relative on his office letterhead to the Marshall Islands Government, the relative had done the wrong thing, and Graham was compromised.

To his credit Richardson resigned, but not before a fair bit of damage was done to the government. So I lost some of the speed and altitude I had gained with *One Nation*. I was trying to get the plane up to cruising altitude and was maybe 70 per cent of the way there when this happened.

I wanted to get the public's attention back on the fact that this was a policy-driven government so I went on *Sunday* with Laurie Oakes and kicked the process along on three big issues: the future of pay television, the future of the airlines, and the future of technical and further education.

Let me deal with the last one first. From the 1950s onwards about 40 per cent of Year Twelve kids went to university, but many were leaving school before then. We had trebled the number of children completing Year Twelve, so we had to treble the number of university places to keep up the 40 per cent run rate, and we did that by extra funding and through the Dawkins HECS reforms. But the training for the other 60 per cent of school-leavers was woefully inadequate, with kids cascading from school into nothing. It was catch as catch can out there in the state-run TAFE systems. There were no real private training bodies in those days and the states were pulling back on the oars in the TAFE system.

I always had in my mind that the states should have responsibility for primary and secondary education and the Commonwealth should do tertiary education and TAFE. Dawkins had started the TAFE reform process the previous year, and with Kim Beazley as the new Education Minister, we'd put another $720 million into the system for the next three years through *One Nation*. But the talks with the states were dragging on, and some of them were being obstructionist over our proposal to take over the funding, and I didn't want them welching on their commitments to growth in TAFE spending.

On *Sunday* I threatened to phase out TAFE funding to the states and build a whole new Commonwealth system of vocational education with a national training authority and much closer focus on the labour market, in some cases in tandem with industries. That got their attention.

KOB: In your *Sunday* interview you threw up a completely different proposition on the privatisation plan for the two government-owned airlines to what Cabinet and caucus had been considering. It changed from selling 100 per cent of Australian Airlines and 49 per cent of Qantas as two separate sales to merging them and selling at least two-thirds of the lot. It sent a rather defiant message to caucus—back me or we all go down.

PJK: It wasn't as cavalier as it might have seemed. I never did anything outside Cabinet without talking to the appropriate ministers privately. I always consulted ministers, always. We hadn't yet run this through the full Cabinet but I'd discussed it all with Dawkins and Willis as the two money ministers and Bob Collins as the new Transport and Communications Minister, and we were all in lock step. Not only was the logic right but it would also deliver a much more substantial return to the government through the sale.

KOB: You'd always had a hand in any discussions about aviation policy going back to your relatively early days as Treasurer, including the open skies policy. Why the interest?

PJK: That's true. I was very keen in terms of the microeconomic reform agenda I picked up after the 1987 election, but even before that I was keen for us to terminate the two-airline policy that was enshrined in legislation. Airfares were agreed to by an independent commission but invariably it was at the request of the parties. There was no element of competition about it at all. This meant that the travelling public never got a break, and if you were a traveller through Sydney, Melbourne or Canberra airports as I was every week, you saw that the people travelling were mostly businesspeople. There were very few people of lower and middle means travelling as tourists or for other personal reasons. In other words, the airlines were really for those people who were well off, at least partly because of the structure. I wanted to get some sort of competition, so we set about removing the two-airline policy.

KOB: What part did you play in that and how hard was it to push through?

PJK: It took a bit of doing because Peter Abeles was Ansett CEO, and he was Bob Hawke's best friend so the idea of actually terminating the guaranteed gold seam of aviation and chopping it off legislatively was not something Peter welcomed. He thought he could compete in a competitive sense, but as far as he was concerned, when you're on a good thing stick to it. So not surprisingly, he was arguing for the maintenance of the two-airline policy. There were a lot of meetings with Bob, me and Peter Abeles before the two-airline policy actually went down.

KOB: How did you find him to deal with?

PJK: Charming and reasonable. He had his own objective, namely the absence of as much competition as possible, but if the government insisted on competition and he could also see the sort of civic virtue, he was not a crude businessperson who would try to hang on to it forever. He was in many respects a pleasure to deal with, but only if you knew what you wanted, otherwise his combination of charm and resistance were pretty formidable. At a certain point, I can't quite remember when, he could see the writing on the wall and agreed to let it go.

But when it got down to Qantas and Australian there were a number of things going on. Qantas was an international carrier at the end of the global line. It built its brand on the kangaroo route to London via Singapore and Bangkok, and then across the Pacific to San Francisco and Los Angeles. But because it was excluded from carrying domestic passengers, often it was flying almost empty aircraft around Australia, between Melbourne and Perth and so on. Yet in the same government ownership was TAA before it changed its name to Australian Airlines, which operated in duopoly with Ansett.

The proposition now before Cabinet was to sell 100 per cent of Australian and 49 per cent of Qantas, but sell them separately. I figured this would not do anything structurally for either Australian or Qantas, and wouldn't do much for the budget either in terms of dividends or proceeds of sale. So I thought the right answer was to roll them together and privatise them as a much stronger entity. This way Qantas had domestic carriage, particularly on the profitable Brisbane–Sydney–Melbourne routes, and it would rationalise Qantas carriage around Australia for its often empty 747s. This made sense to me.

By the time we got to caucus with the airline proposal two days after the Oakes interview, Cabinet had already agreed to sell off 100 per cent of the merged airline with the government retaining a golden share that allowed a right to veto in the national interest. It was endorsed by caucus with very little argument.

The challenge was to extract a strong result from an initial partial sell-off but at the same time make Qantas better. The question then was how to lift the quality of the management group inside Qantas and on the board. It will be no news to anybody that Qantas was one of the boards governments used to put friends on, and while some of these friends were quite competent people, most of them weren't chosen for their commercial or airline experience.

So I decided that one way to do this was to pick up some of the efficiencies that might come with a partner airline with a strong commercial culture. The two obvious airlines to consider were British Airways and Singapore Airlines with the synergies they might bring with their routes through the Middle East and East Asia, so we ran a kind of Dutch auction between those two for 25 per cent of Qantas.

When Don Russell and I visited Singapore Airlines and their executive group in Singapore, my judgement was that in putting their bid together, they overestimated the influence our developing orientation towards Asia would have on our decision.

British Airways, on the other hand, had a very good reason to bid more than Singapore Airlines and if you look at the route carriage that existed between Qantas and BA, we flew to Johannesburg and Harare in southern Africa and they had routes that went from Johannesburg and Harare to London. Singapore Airlines had synergies too, but British Airways was the more earnest bidder.

I actually sold the 25 per cent of Qantas from my prime ministerial office in Parliament House to Sir Colin Marshall, the British Airways CEO. It was a very funny morning. The Department of Finance had an assets taskforce but I thought you had to be more an investment banker to run this sort of an auction rather than simply 'give us your prices in an envelope'.

On the day Sir Colin Marshall was due to come to my office I said to Don Russell, 'I'm going to sell this airline to this guy today, but I'm going to make him pay for it.'

I told Guy, the prime ministerial office butler, 'There may be a moment, Guy, when I press the button but instead of tea, I'll want you to bring in champagne.'

In the discussion I said, 'Colin, I want you to think of Qantas as the last full free-standing house in Belgrave Square. There's not going to be another one. This is a supra-quality asset.'

And he said, 'And Prime Minister, I expect you want me to pay a supra-quality price?'

I said, 'Well, yes, I do.'

He mentioned a number and I said, 'No, that won't make it.'

He then had to get Lord King, his chairman, on the telephone. They had a big discussion and finally he came back to meet my price, which I think from memory was well over $600 million for 25 per cent of Qantas.

He said to me, 'Prime Minister, Lord King and I will meet you on the price but there's one condition, and that is, that if and when you float Qantas you guarantee us you won't sell the stock at a price lower than what we're paying.'

I said, 'Sir Colin, we won't make you look silly. We think we can make the synergies work and get the value of the airline up.'

I pressed the button and Guy came in with the two champagne glasses. I knew it was a big moment when Sir Colin couldn't quite keep his champagne in the glass. His hand was shaking so much that the champagne was running into the cuff of his shirt.

It was a very big deal for them, and it gave Qantas a huge injection of intelligence. The merger of Qantas and Australian lifted Qantas right up. We then injected some of the capital from the British Airways sale back into the business. Before that Qantas had no discretionary capital. With that and some fresh intellectual oomph on the board we started building Qantas into a superior carrier, which was then subsequently floated.

KOB: Why couldn't Qantas have survived and prospered as a government-owned airline like Singapore Airlines or Emirates, with the advantages they're perceived to have in a cut-throat industry, if you assume the nation should always have its own iconic airline?

PJK: Before it was freed up commercially, Qantas simply lived on government guarantees. It was perpetually short of capital. As Treasurer I would sign off on the guarantee attached to the leasing of each aircraft but Qantas had no capital to invest in its future, and on a day-to-day basis had only modest working capital.

In the end you can't run a competitive business on a guarantee. You've got to have capital, and it was struggling. It would only have survived as a government-owned airline with very large funding from Australian taxpayers. Look at the competition for funding within the Abbott Government's budgets. How is the treasurer of the day going to find the money for a large capital injection into the government-owned airline when it's struggling against tough international competition? It's just not going to happen, and it never should happen. Government priorities should not include providing airline seats when myriad carriers are offering loads of them, and at discount prices.

KOB: Going back to the *Sunday* interview, where you were trying to get traction for the government again after the Richardson scandal, what was the imperative for your dramatic intervention on pay-television policy? Why couldn't that be left to the new minister, Bob Collins, to handle?

PJK: For years, I had resisted Australia going down the path of a pay-television service built on analogue platforms because I knew the analogue platforms would be superseded before long by superior technology and I thought it was foolish for us to rush into it.

There we were in the 1980s, trying to get over a big current account imbalance. Why on earth would we have invested in a redundant technology for a service we had so far lived without? So for a number of years in Cabinet I thwarted the movement to pay television for that reason. When it was clear to me that we had a lot of these structural reforms behind us, we had the budget well and truly back into surplus, and the structural outlays under control, and our international profile was better, I thought, well, the country could afford a pay-television service, but the question is what sort of service and who should own and operate it?

It wasn't a high-order priority and Neal Blewett in his diary records me telling Cabinet in the discussion after *Sunday* that pay television was 'simply a video shop on a bloody wire', but I wanted the policy resolved, and bringing it on the way I did simply emphasised that our mind was on the job and we had a framework for government. There were two available routes for national distribution—satellite, with rooftop dishes getting smaller, and cable, which would carry much more capacity. We just had to determine the best way to introduce new players into the market.

My thinking was affected by the fact that the Hawke Government had adopted the wrong policy in telecommunications by giving the country a duopoly between Telstra and Optus rather than a competitive model. I wanted competition in the delivery of television services as well as competition in the telecommunications industry, and I did not want to see Optus have the de facto rights to the alternative television network by virtue of the satellite. It had the monopoly with the satellite and at that stage satellite was the only analogue modality. You would receive it via a dish on your roof in the same way as people in the country still do today.

Because I knew digital technology was going to make the satellite delivery redundant in the cities, we had to have a policy that did not allow this to fall to Optus by default. The question was how we would inject competition in television services on the ground.

Caucus was very wary of the networks—and with good reason. Not that the caucus was always a great champion of competition. Nevertheless the call to have a greater diversity of ownership running the new pay networks was in my view desirable.

I thought: we've got a new minister, a real discussion going with caucus, inhibitions within caucus about the existing networks, so I looked for a different approach. That is, we end up with four licences available on pay and those licences would go to any competitor outside the three existing commercial networks. That is what we adopted, with the rider that the existing networks could have a share in two additional licences one year later; in other words, giving the new entrants a year's head start. The networks were limited to a total of 35 per cent among the three, and no individual network could own more than 15 per cent.

KOB: We've talked about Bob Hawke's relationship with Kerry Packer earlier, but did you have a personal relationship too?

PJK: Yes, I did. I got on reasonably well with him, but Packer had two views that he put to me often, sometimes in jest, sometimes more as a boast. He would say, 'I believe in monopolies at best, and duopolies at worst.'

And the second thing he would say is, 'it's not what you can do for governments, it's what they can do for you.'

Of its essence he was speaking of interests by way of licences and of governments being responsive to him whenever licences were being discussed or opened up. To protect the existing oligopoly of Seven, Ten and Nine, but particularly Nine, he wanted to delay the introduction of pay television until the latest possible moment. And if it was on, he wanted a significant part of it. That was his position and I understood that. I didn't need to be too friendly with him to understand that, but I was friendly enough to have these sorts of conversations.

KOB: When the dust finally settled and Murdoch and Telstra emerged as the dominant force in pay television with Foxtel, did that bother you one way or the other? It wasn't exactly adding to the diversity of media ownership.

PJK: Because I believed that cable and digital technology gave us the capacity to bring much greater bandwidth to homes than we could ever have done via satellite, I gave what is now Telstra something like

$100 million a year in dividend remission to provide an incentive for them to lay cable around the capital cities. That was in effect a big capital boost.

Telstra under the American businessman Frank Blount made the most of the extra $100 million a year, and he and his Telstra executives then chose their content partner from a beauty contest that included Rupert Murdoch's News Corp. They went for News because of its Twentieth Century Fox production facilities and programs, which provided the core programming for the Fox network in America.

There were claims around at the time that the government had assisted Murdoch into the deal to gain political favour in News Ltd's coverage. That was untrue. I still have the file with the Telstra submission in it. I did not even know Telstra was in discussion with Murdoch until it was revealed to me by Frank Blount. Cabinet gave Telstra the go-ahead on the merits of its submission, but I don't think Packer ever believed that. He went barmy about it.

KOB: By the same token, you had always put yourself at the centre of media policy reform, and Packer and Murdoch had both done well in the Labor years. But what was left of your relationship with Packer finally evaporated over the ownership and control of Fairfax. Packer had originally tried and failed to find a way into Fairfax in a consortium called Tourang with the Canadian newspaper man, Conrad Black. Black emerged with management control of Fairfax, but with only 20 per cent of the stock, and he wanted more.

PJK: What happened was this. After Warwick Fairfax Junior's takeover of Fairfax ended in disaster because he'd borrowed to the hilt at high interest rates and couldn't run the business, the ownership ended up in a sort of no man's land. Conrad Black ended up running Fairfax with the American businessman Dan Colson but, as you say, his shareholding under the foreign ownership restrictions was limited to 20 per cent.

He came to the government and said, 'Look, everyone at Fairfax thinks I'm just a truant owner and a bit of a joke. The Fairfax management and the managing editors see me as some sort of truancy through the place. If I had a more substantial shareholding I would have authority and without that authority Fairfax can't re-establish its equilibrium.'

Essentially Ralph Willis and I bought that argument and we allowed Black to go to 25 per cent of the stock.

KOB: Black wrote in his book *A Life in Progress* that you had intimated to him that you might actually consider going to 35 per cent after the 1993 election, but that you hoped the Fairfax coverage of the election would be balanced.

PJK: No wise government asks for favourable treatment but you can ask for objectivity, and I believed Fairfax became a tyranny run by the journalists, particularly in the hands of John Alexander as editor. I wanted some sort of guarantee from the putative owner or controller that it would return to being a newspaper of record rather than what the *Herald* had become, a kind of pamphlet, under John Alexander. Black assured me the paper would be objective and, as near as a modern paper could be, a paper of record. On that basis Willis and I agreed that he should be able to raise his ownership to 25 per cent and stabilise Fairfax's ownership.

Meanwhile, having bought the Nine Network back from Alan Bond, Kerry Packer had hung onto his prescribed 14.9 per cent of the shares, and everyone assumed he'd given up his interest in controlling Fairfax. But the assumption proved to be wrong.

Conrad Black came to see me one day and I can give you the conversation verbatim. He came in, well dressed with that silk handkerchief in his pocket, and said, 'Prime Minister, I want to ask you a question. This is an OECD country, isn't it?'

I said, 'Last time I looked it was, yes.'

'And the rule of law is paramount in such a society?' he asked.

I said, 'Yes, that's how we normally conduct our affairs.'

'How then can interests associated with Mr Packer have 23.5 per cent of Fairfax when his prescribed limit as a television proprietor is 14.9?' he said.

I said, 'I wasn't aware that he had 23.5 per cent of Fairfax.'

He said, 'Well, I can assure you he does. Everyone in Fairfax knows he has, which makes me look like a very uncertain proprietor who will soon be eclipsed by the main man. I'm looking for both your guidance and your undertaking on this.'

I told Black if what he said was correct we would insist on the maintenance of the law.

He said, 'I can ask for no more', and that was the extent of the conversation.

When I checked, Black was correct. Packer's organisation had taken advice from some barrister specialising in media law who found what they thought was a loophole. From memory, Packer was in Argentina playing polo, so I spoke to one of his representatives and said, 'Conrad Black's been to see me and I understand Consolidated Press has 23.5 per cent of Fairfax.'

The answer came back immediately. 'That's right.'

I said, 'You understand what the law says? The prescribed limit is 14.9.'

He said, 'Everything we are doing is legal.'

I said, 'You may think so but I made the law so I have a particular interest in its maintenance, which means your interest in Fairfax must return to 14.9 per cent.'

He replied, 'Well, as long as you understand that will mean war, I'll relay the message.'

KOB: Was it your old friend Peter Barron you were talking to, who was now working for Packer?

PJK: I can't say who it was. But the message was conveyed to Packer, who sent back the return message: 'It's war.'

I said, 'Well, conflict is what I do.'

KOB: That was actually reported at the time in the *Sydney Morning Herald*. 'I told Packer yesterday I was in the conflict business. I don't take the troubles, I give them to people like that.'

PJK: Yes, I said 'conflict is what I do'. I then asked Michael Lee, who had become Communications Minister, to get an amendment together and I saw Cheryl Kernot and the Democrats and pushed it very quickly through both Houses, which meant the loophole Packer was using was shut off.

I came to understand that Kerry wanted to control Fairfax to get square with the journalists he believed had gone after him maliciously over the references to him in the *National Times* under a code name in the Costigan Royal Commission. I understood his anger but we had a media diversity policy that he was not entitled to break.

From that point on we were on either side of a kind of World War One no man's land. The whole Channel Nine system turned against me, and early in 1995 after John Howard took over from Alexander Downer as Opposition Leader, Kerry Packer took himself onto *A Current Affair* with Ray Martin to say he thought Howard would make a good Prime Minister.

So notwithstanding that a rational and good media policy restricting cross-media ownership had delivered a great bounty to his company and to him personally, Packer still reserved the right to go king-making with the conservative leader, all on the basis that I wouldn't let him suborn the Fairfax group.

KOB: What about your threat to hand out a fourth television licence for a network devoted to family viewing, rubbing salt into the wound by announcing it on Packer's own network, with Laurie Oakes again? Were you having a bit of fun at Packer's expense or did you actually mean that?

PJK: I genuinely felt that there wasn't enough family quality programming on the commercial networks, and in that same period I changed the film classification rules because the networks were showing material at 7.30 and 8 o'clock at night that was becoming increasingly less child-friendly, so the case for a family-friendly network was genuine.

KOB: But it didn't bother you that even floating the idea might give Kerry Packer more heartburn along the way.

PJK: Yes, and I thought it might just put some ginger into the argument about the viability of the three existing networks. At any rate the fourth network didn't eventuate.

KOB: Your friction with Packer continued through the last year of your prime ministership and after he endorsed Howard, you then accused them of doing a secret deal in which Howard would remove the cross-media restrictions on ownership, which would remove any impediment Packer had to buying Fairfax without having to sell his television network.

PJK: And Howard did try to overturn the cross-media rule when he got into government.

KOB: Don Watson records in *Bleeding Heart* that Peter Barron had told you the Liberals were 'in the bag' about changing the cross-media rules in Packer's favour, and Graham Richardson had said to you, 'Don't drive us to Howard.' But as Howard himself pointed out when you first made the accusation, he'd already made no secret of his desire to change the policy and do away with the cross-media restrictions well before then.

PJK: John Howard was too cute and experienced an individual, and Kerry Packer was way too worldly for them ever to have had any formal agreement about any such matter. But I was completely certain that a Howard Government would try to overturn the cross-media rules to the benefit, among others, of Consolidated Press, and I had heard on the grapevine that there had been discussions, and a wink and a nod.

KOB: As Watson tells it, you were in Germany. You had a great story to tell of a very successful meeting with Helmut Kohl, Europe's chief statesman, who was clearly impressed. There was kudos to be garnered, but instead you used a media conference to come out punching on Kerry Packer and John Howard.

PJK: In truth it was off-message, and I would have been better keeping the punch until we got home, but there we are.

KOB: But even if you'd waited until you got home to take Packer on, what would you have gained? Howard says in his autobiography:

> It was foolish of Keating to pursue a personal vendetta against the owner of the most powerful TV network and also courtesy of his knockabout style, quite a popular figure with many Australians. Keating's obsession with Packer reached absurd proportions when he devoted a large chunk of a news conference in Germany to attacking

Packer and alleging some secret deal he'd made with me with regard to the repeal of the cross media prohibitions. This was a ludicrous charge. I had been publicly opposed as far back as 1987.

PJK: I'm the only person in public life who ever took Packer on. Ever. This was a person who wielded great influence over a succession of governments, and not one single individual in the polity ever crossed swords with him. I not only crossed swords with him, I gave him a number of beltings. I wanted to make it clear to Packer, you may think we are a bunch of toadies there to do your bidding, but not me.

But Packer came after me after I'd left politics. If you read Niki Savva's account in her book of how Paul Lyneham volunteered to do Packer's bidding on the piggery claims against me, aided and abetted by the former Liberal Party President Tony Staley, you'll see this was all payback for stopping his attempts to control Fairfax. Now out of office because I wanted to be effective against Packer at the time and not to engage in a public slanging match, after the disgraceful Channel Nine documentary on *60 Minutes*, I then lobbied Brian Harradine and a number of other senators to stop the cross-media rule change in the Senate.

A journalist said to me at the time, 'Mr Keating, are you going to take a defamation action against Channel Nine and Mr Packer?'

I said, 'No, I have much more expensive remedies in mind for him.'

The remedy I had in mind was to beat the cross-rule amendments in the Senate, which I succeeded in doing.

KOB: Would you have done that anyway to protect what you regarded as a good policy, or were you spurred particularly by that?

PJK: I was spurred particularly by that, and I lobbied Harradine, who was the swing player. I convinced Harradine to vote against the proposals when they came into the Senate, so after the attempts to change the policy were beaten, Packer sold out of Fairfax.

All those *Sydney Morning Herald* journalists who went on and on about my delinquency as far as the *Herald*'s interests were concerned forget the fact that I stopped two major proprietors getting hold of Fairfax. One was Rupert Murdoch, who sought my support in 1995 to take control of the *Sydney Morning Herald*, the *Age* and the *Financial Review*, and the second was Packer's creeping ownership with a view to controlling the whole organisation, at which point I have no doubt he would have wrought vengeance on some of those same journalists.

KOB: What would you have been required to do to assist Murdoch into his plan to own Fairfax?

PJK: His proposal was that he would bid for John Fairfax & Sons on the basis he disposed of the News Ltd mastheads but his proposal was to put them into a trust headed by someone friendly to him. I just said to him I couldn't even think about such a proposal. This occurred at a meeting I had with him when I accompanied Tony Blair to a News Corp executive meeting at Hayman Island.

KOB: When you knocked Murdoch back, how did he react?

PJK: Like all newspaper proprietors Rupert thought if he had half an adoptable proposition then the government of the day might go along with it to keep him happy, but Ken Cowley, the head of his Australian operation, had told Rupert the chance of me accepting this proposition was zero.

His proposition was for the News Ltd papers to be put into a trust that would be chaired by Ken Cowley.

I said, 'Rupert, the thing is, you own the current stable of newspapers. No one else is going to buy them from you, and while ever you own them, whether they're in trust or not, we can never think of you owning any of the other mastheads.'

KOB: Did he accept that with equanimity?

PJK: He didn't remonstrate about it at the time but I think Ken Cowley had conditioned him that that was the answer he would likely get.

KOB: Was there a difference between Murdoch and Packer in that regard, as personalities? There was always that bullying side to Packer that he was notorious for. He could be charming one minute and verbally ripping your head off the next.

PJK: Rupert was always polite and, in the main, charming, even when you said no. You may pay a price later, but he was always polite.

THE POLITICIAN & THE PROFESSOR

If 1991 was the year John Hewson got the better of Labor's longest serving Prime Minister, 1992 was the year the same John Hewson became Paul Keating's best chance of winning Labor's fifth straight term in office and his first as Prime Minister.

Hewson had two great strengths: he was a fresh face and a clean break for a weary electorate from the old familiar faces of the 1980s—Hawke and Keating, Peacock and Howard. Secondly, he had a big new plan to go with the fresh face. He was also a professor AND a doctor of economics, with an air that suggested he knew more than any of those tired old pollies about how to run an economy.

The political downside of *Fightback!*, which Keating identified and set out systematically to exploit as the year progressed, was that it was the most radical plan for change ever presented to Australian voters. No portfolio, economic or social, was left untouched. Not only was its centrepiece a 15 per cent goods and services tax on almost everything including food, but the old industrial relations model was to be dismantled; the biggest public asset of all, Telecom, sold lock, stock and barrel; remaining tariffs slashed to zero across the board; and the welfare system given a serious shake-up.

Fightback! was too big in detail and sweep for even discerning voters to properly get their heads around, but they could grasp that it represented more big changes after nearly a decade of Labor reform, and Keating made sure they understood the reach of the new Hewson tax. He had no shortage of lines, but a favourite was to plunge his hand in his pocket as he said, 'You put your hand in your pocket to get some money and you find John Hewson has already been there.'

But to suggest that Keating's progress through 1992 was free and easy would be a gross overstatement. Polls seesawed through the year, and the economy refused to follow the Keating–Dawkins script. GDP growth at no stage came even close to the heroic *One Nation* forecast of 4.75 per cent. The same was true of its projection on jobs growth.

Only inflation represented genuinely good news, but even inflation had its downside because it, along with all the other key economic indicators, affected the credibility of Keating's promised tax cuts, and the pledge to return to surplus within four years. Without growth boosting revenue into the government's coffers, with the fiscal burden of unemployment benefits going up rather than coming down, and without inflation feeding bracket creep, the tax cuts arguably were irresponsible and the surplus unattainable.

By the time Dawkins' first budget was delivered in August there wasn't an independent economist in the country who regarded the tax cuts as credible. The evidence that Dawkins was feeling the load was his admission that there might be a need for tax increases after the election—a gift to the Opposition.

Hewson's main attack on Keating was that *One Nation* was based on fraudulent figures; Keating's on Hewson was yes, Hewson had a plan, but it was the wrong plan to help Australia out of a recession. It would slow recovery rather than speed it up.

Keating's audacity in seeking to make the recession a negative for Hewson was breathtaking. He was saying, 'Yes, we caused the recession but we can get you out of it. Hewson will make it worse.'

Hewson seemed oblivious to the rich potential he was offering Labor through *Fightback!*. You might get away with a minimalist policy outline as Howard did in the 1996 election, but not only did Hewson go so far as to provide a detailed blueprint for radical change, he took pride in filling in the gaps.

One of the benefits of Keating's massive newspaper archive is the story it tells from the brace of headlines even before you get into the detail. It's uncanny to look back at the 1992 headlines and see the pattern throughout the year of a bad Keating headline followed by a bad Hewson headline, or vice versa. In the *Financial Review* of 6 July, for instance—'Lib plan to slash youth wages up to 40 per cent'— followed by the *Age* on 10 July: 'Jobs: a national disaster'.

There were similarly contrasting headlines right through the rest of the year. Most of Keating's negative headlines—dominated by unemployment figures that came inexorably closer and closer to the politically devastating one million mark, particularly when they were supposed to be going the other way—reflected the simple fact the economy was far slower recovering from the dead hand of recession than Keating had promised.

Most of Hewson's negatives came from the way he kept finding new ways to alienate more and more blocs of voters. He insulted renters by saying you could identify them as the ones with the untidy front yards as you drove through suburban streets. He risked offending childless couples by attacking NSW Labor Opposition Leader Bob Carr as 'a guy who doesn't drive and doesn't like kids'. He catalysed hostility from carmakers with his scorched earth tariff policy reflected in headlines such as '60,000 jobs could go under Libs: Ford'. He earned the wrath of the churches with the toughness of his welfare policies.

Even so, regardless of Keating's competitive position in the opinion polls through most of the year, Hewson was almost always the front-runner. It became clear to Keating as he moved closer and closer to the electorate's judgement that he had to create a climate of anxiety around the GST. He was successful to the extent that more and more pressure built on Hewson from within his own ranks, if not to abandon the GST, at least to soften its impact.

In early November, Keating upped the ante. He took everyone by surprise, including his own caucus, by announcing that in the event of a Liberal Government, Labor would support the GST through the Senate. The message to voters? Don't think you can get rid of me and avoid the GST. It was the kind of brinkmanship he revelled in.

As that reality sank in, Liberal anxiety was reflected in headlines through the rest of November: 'Hewson battles unrest on GST' in the *Age* and 'I'LL RESIGN: Hewson's GST threat' in the *Telegraph-Mirror*.

By mid-December, Hewson had dumped the GST on food, but Keating's negative headlines on unemployment—'Jobless worst in 60 years'—remained, and the polls flipped back to Hewson. What must have been a personal embarrassment for the Liberal leader with his GST u-turn was nonetheless acknowledgement of a political reality that paid him a dividend.

On 13 December, a story in the Sydney *Sun-Herald* detailed a phone conversation between Keating and Graham Richardson weeks before in which Keating asked what Richardson thought of having a 19 December election. According to the journalist Bruce Jones, Richardson said, 'When you wanted to become leader I said to you, "your job is to bring us out of the wilderness. We can't win but what you can do is make sure we don't get slaughtered." If you have an election on December 19 you'll achieve that. We'll lose by a few—two, four, six—but not many. We'll go real close and everyone will say nice things about you.'

According to Jones, Keating's reply was, 'Fuck that. I want to win!'

Late in the year Keating had also fanned anxiety over *Fightback!*'s industrial relations reforms, exploiting a massive backlash among workers in Victoria to newly elected Liberal Premier Jeff Kennett's assault on workplace practice in his own state. What Kennett was doing in Victoria, said Keating, Hewson would inflict on the nation.

On the day after Labor lost power in Western Australia, Keating announced an election for 13 March 1993, wrongfooting the press gallery in the process, which delighted him. It had been a very long year for the fledgling Prime Minister, and it was now to be an all-or-nothing campaign. He'd successfully changed the landscape and evened up the race, he'd won the psychological battle in Parliament, but almost all the journalists still predicted he would lose, something he would never forget.

There's no doubt Keating's experience as a campaigner and his well-honed political instincts gave him an edge over the new boy, but perhaps the biggest single blow for Hewson in the campaign was an own goal. The infamous birthday cake interview with Mike Willesee on *A Current Affair* was devastating. When the architect of a new tax can't answer a simple question of how much GST you'd pay on a cake, where does that leave his credibility on the other 600 pages of *Fightback!*?

As Keating recaptured momentum in the second half of the campaign, Hewson's inexperience told again as he put his faith on some rather messy and increasingly desperate-looking public rallies, culminating in him losing his voice. It wasn't a good look.

Even so, as Keating sat down with his closest staff in a Sydney Chinese restaurant the night before the election for what looked to be his last supper, no one was confident, including him. His words were quite revealing:

> They are contemplating taking us back. Not with any relish whatsoever. It's Hobson's choice. We want their votes, not their appreciation. We have been able to spin a giant tale, an interesting tale, and they'd like to dispense with us but they're not sure. It's a bit like a mouse trap—you put your finger in and bang.
>
> Their hearts are going to be beating away in the ballot boxes tomorrow when they put their pencil on the paper. As to whether they strike us down or not, it's quite a thing, striking a government down. You don't do it easily. That's what we're relying on.

We are the entrepreneurs of political life and are the people who dream the big dreams and do the big things. There are no bigger dreamers than in our office. It's a mixture of econocrats and bleeding hearts. But together we make a pretty powerful combination. If we win it will be the win of the century, and I have a sneaking suspicion that we might.

But according to Don Watson in *Bleeding Heart*, Keating told adviser Mark Ryan the next morning on his way to vote in Bankstown that the combination of high unemployment and ten years in office would 'probably bring us undone'.

KOB: Politically, your first big shot against Hewson and *Fightback!* was *One Nation*, but it was also important, as a new Prime Minister, to re-establish your dominance in Parliament over John Hewson and be seen to do so.

PJK: I had to take him very seriously as an opponent because he was way ahead of us in the polls when I took the leadership, and people were impressed with the fact that he had a plan. For better or for worse, he had a plan. But my impression of him was that he was rigid and brittle. He lacked what I call stagecraft; the malleability to move a bit and in a pretty way, when necessary, and also to know when to respond to an argument and when not to. You knew what he'd be asking you and why at Question Time.

I'd seen these investment-banking jokers turn up before. Very few businesspeople do well when they come to public life. Public life has a sophistication about it that's very different from anything they would have encountered in their former career. They don't understand it, and even if they have some sort of a clue, they haven't the skills to capitalise on them.

Here was Hewson with his grab-bag of nasties, trying to market those old reactionary policies as the new way forward. Here we'd led the country out of the old closed economy of the past 80 years, the blue sky was on the other side of the recession, we had broken inflation, and secured strong productivity on the way, had an orderly process of tariff cuts in train, and he was going to hit the country and push it into a kind of ideological Armageddon.

Essentially he was about pulling the Commonwealth budget more rapidly back towards surplus, when the need in the economy was to have the natural stabilisers cushioning the recession. So he was on the wrong tram for the moment, on the wrong foot. But as well as having the wrong economic policy response, politically he also had to carry the bad political and social embroidery of Thatcherism through *Fightback!*.

To understand why Hewson felt compelled to produce that 600-page document that ultimately became a millstone around his neck, I think you have to look at how I had changed the ground rules for the Australian economic debate as Treasurer.

When I came to the job the budget documents only included one year's forward estimates of outlays. I made the whole Commonwealth budget system much more accountable, and after being burnt as Howard was in the 1987 election campaign with his unfunded tax cuts and accounting black hole, I think the Libs were forced to measure up to a new accounting standard.

We had also pushed the Liberals further to the right, and the combination of these things with Hewson's natural zealotry brought them to *Fightback!*. That was good for us because it gave me some ammunition to fight with. Not only were the economics wrong, but *Fightback!* was essentially an attack on the social wage of Australia, on all the things that had come to shape the way we saw ourselves as a society—Medicare and the fairness it brought to the health system, the general social security system and the safety net it provided, superannuation, rent assistance and all the other things he was criticising. Essentially he wanted to unwind a large part of the welfare side of the budget.

I thought Hewson was brittle and inflexible and that I would simply outbox him. A rumble, but not in the jungle.

KOB: Don Watson revealed in his book that although you were well served with various specialised advisers you insisted on keeping your own Question Time files—that was very much your own thing. Four or five well thumbed files that even accompanied you on election campaigns. What went into them?

PJK: I have one here. The last one I used is still here in the office. I used to read the papers early in the mornings and I'd just tear any noteworthy story out of the paper, or I'd ring someone in the office and ask them to prepare a note on an issue. I'd make a note of anything Hewson or his senior frontbenchers had said overnight. I'd construct a political framework as opposed to a policy framework, and I would conduct that day's Question Time within that template.

It's about the mental gymnastics. You're reading so much and mentally processing more and more material; the more you read, the more you comprehend. You just keep on feeding, feeding it so you get to a tremendous level of intellectual speed. After nine years of Cabinet government I had a huge base of residual knowledge. Having sat through all those years of ERC rounds, social security, foreign policy, defence, the infrastructure of knowledge I'd built up was so profound that I could find an answer to most things, even if they hadn't been flagged by the day's events.

I had the field more or less covered. I'd also keep articles in the Question Time file from prominent commentators or economists, or the various business and non-government organisations. I mightn't use them for months, but they'd always come in handy at some point.

I took the view that I could never afford to be caught out. I assumed the responsibility as Prime Minister that I had in the Parliament as Treasurer. I had to be hitting balls into the stand all the time, and if there was a perception that I'd had a bad day in Question Time, I'd redouble my efforts the next day. While laborious, the sport of it always kept me on a high.

KOB: Neal Blewett writes in *A Cabinet Diary* about the pep talk you gave to caucus one day about taking the fight up to the other side in the Parliamentary chamber: 'It's the task of Labor to attack the conservatives constantly. Indeed, we all have to become villains in the cause.' Blewett says you noted a piece of advice from Rex Connor when you first came into Parliament: 'Your job here, sonny, is to bash the Liberals and keep on bashing them all the time.'

PJK: He used to say, 'Bash the Libs, bash the Libs.'

KOB: Blewett writes: 'Keating urged a volume of sound every time Hewson attempts a monologue before asking his questions. McLeay looked distinctly uncomfortable at this, and Beazley, as a scatological aside, noted a need to wipe down McLeay's seat after Keating had declared his remarks!' Does that bring back memories?

PJK: Yes, it does. I used to say to them, 'Our job is never to be passive, never sit there as some sort of passive player in the scenery.' You've got to keep the psychological edge in Parliament, and that means playing all the psychological games.

I used to call Tim Fischer Daisy, as in Daisy the cow, and when he'd get up to ask a question I used to turn to the Labor members and go 'ding-ding, ding-ding' like a cow bell. Everyone on our side would laugh, so he was put off-balance before he'd even reached the despatch box to ask the question. I had stock lines for various of their frontbenchers and our side would react, which always unnerved them.

KOB: And did you instruct the caucus to disrupt the other side with noise?

PJK: Maybe, modulated, studied noise. It was a tough school and Hewson was a brittle guy who did not go well under pressure. So if you lifted the bar on him, he would invariably fold.

KOB: On the other hand your old foot soldier Leo McLeay was a pretty hapless Speaker at times. He knew the rules but he wasn't exactly quick on his feet, and the claims that his independence was compromised wasn't without foundation. When it all boiled down, McLeay the tribal warrior was as much in evidence as McLeay the Speaker.

PJK: I would say that was a tribute to him, rather than a demerit. He was smart enough to run the place with intelligence. He looks like the prince now compared to Bronwyn Bishop, who was just so partisan, and so unable to construct any notion of equilibrium, that Leo McLeay looks like Solomon in comparison. And I was pushing the limits in Parliament. I always did, both as Treasurer and Prime Minister. I did make it tougher for the Speaker. But never too tough.

I thought McLeay had great political instincts, and he generally knew when to hit the accelerator and when to hit the brake. There may have been more sophisticated occupants of the chair, but he knew when to let a matter go over his shoulder, when to intervene, when to direct a minister to sit down or wind up his answer or speak to the question. Put it this way, Leo McLeay turned out to be a more competent Speaker than perhaps many in the caucus thought he would be.

KOB: But you don't accept that the Speaker in the Australian parliamentary culture is ever going to be truly independent?

PJK: No, I don't.

KOB: You think if it's a Labor Government there will be a Labor Speaker in every sense of the word?

PJK: More or less. But you hope you are not appointing a dummy. One who is smart enough to keep the balance. I'm not so naive as to think either party would produce a truly independent Speaker.

KOB: So part of your job as the leader was to exploit the fact that you had a Labor Speaker?

PJK: Yes, but only to a point. Not burn the Speaker, not to embarrass the Speaker and not make his or her position untenable. In the end, the chamber has to work. Because the Speaker is the keeper. All of us have to respect that—party loyalties notwithstanding.

KOB: At one point the Liberals composed a list of Keatingisms to try to undercut your effectiveness in Parliament. I'll read a few: perfumed gigolos, harlots, pansies, scumbags, clowns, pissants, gutless spivs, half-baked crims, nongs, dummies, dimwits, many more. This wasn't just letting off steam or paying out on your enemies, this was psychological warfare.

PJK: It was psychological warfare, but a lot of those lines are made up. I've never used a word like 'pissant' in a public place, certainly not in Parliament. I never use expletives in the public domain, ever. I mean ever. And you see those little joke books about me and they've got certain words in, but more often than not, they're not true. But I would have fun with some of the personalities on the other side.

I remember one episode where Peacock was interjecting all the time as Opposition Leader, and I was Treasurer. The Speaker was Harry Jenkins and he chastised Peacock a few times and when Peacock kept it up Jenkins warned that he'd suspend him if he continued.

I then got up and said, 'Mr Speaker, can I say something on the point of order?' I said, 'Can I ask you to exercise some understanding about the Leader of the Opposition? He's been here a long time— I knew him when he had grey hair.'

So a lot of my interjections are not on the Liberal Party list. Only the ones they thought they might be able to use against me, but they verballed me on a number I never, ever used. I did say some were perfumed gigolos, and I did call Andrew the sunlamp kid. And how could you resist having fun with that killer line from Shirley MacLaine when she said, 'He's the only guy I know with a Gucci toothbrush!'

I've said before you can't win in the country unless you win in the House of Representatives. You can't be persistently behind in the House of Representatives and be winning in the country. You must have the psychological hegemony in the House of Representatives and whatever people say about me, Kerry, I always maintained the psychological hegemony in the House of Representatives. I used to throw these guys around like rag dolls and that's as it should be if you want to stay on top and in charge.

KOB: But this also came at a cost for you because while you might have had the psychological advantage in Parliament, there were a lot of voters out there who fundamentally had your fate in their hands every three years—and a lot of those people were not liking the vision of you throwing these people around like rag dolls, as you put it.

PJK: But the point was, I got the changes done, didn't I? I got the big ones through. I remodelled the whole economy, and massively increased its wealth. People might say, 'Well, we didn't quite like the way you did that', but I didn't play the public as mugs. I always gave them value.

But when I had the psychological edge it wasn't simply that I had shaken them up with a few jibes, and this is what's never understood about that side of the parliamentary game. It's a combination of two things. You have to be copperplate good on the text of the answers, technically, copperplate good. And I invite anybody to read the *Hansard*s of my time. They'll find my answers were always tightly constructed. I always believed a minister should answer the question, and on television or radio or at a general press conference I would take the same approach.

In Parliament I would always seek to conscientiously answer the question, but do it so tightly it would defeat the political point of the question. But then I would put the political sting in the tail in order to drive the nail into the wall. You've got their hand up on the wall and you drive the nail through it. That was the bit that would get reported, not the tight, technical answer that gave you the authority to drive in the nail in the first place.

The sting in the tail would only work in the bearpit of Parliament if the answer had a basis in reason and authority. If there is a legitimate reply, and it is competent, knowledgeable and well delivered, then it gives the minister a kind of moral upper hand to make a political jibe at the end.

That was why I resisted the introduction of television to parliamentary coverage. Before television the press gallery was more inclined to assess the whole picture rather than just the lively bits. It was the funny or the feisty bits that most lent themselves to short grabs on the television news. But I always thought that to stay on your feet in the House of Representatives, to stay psychologically on top, you had to be reasonably fearless in the answers, and be prepared to take no prisoners. If some people marked me down for it, that's the price I was prepared to pay.

KOB: Do you remember the long budget session in that first year as Prime Minister, where your economic adviser John Edwards says you were wearing Hewson down, and he wrote:

> Concluding a gruelling Question Time on Tuesday, September 8, Keating leant over to Hewson.
>
> 'You're white,' he said, 'your face is white, you can't take it.'
>
> 'I can take care of you,' Hewson said.
>
> 'No, you can't,' Keating replied, 'your face is white.'
>
> Edward says Hewson used to whisper at Question Time, 'you're a loser, Keating.'

PJK: Yes, he used to say it across the table. It had a rather juvenile quality to it. 'Tell us what you're doing on the weekend, loser! What did you do on the weekend, loser? You're just a loser!' This was the stuff Hewson said across the table. There was no particular cleverness to it.

I did say, 'I love to see these ashen faces; those ashen-faced performances.'

I said, 'That's where I want you and that's where I have you.'

KOB: Someone asked Hewson once how he intended to neutralise your attacks on him, and he said he thought about what he could call you and he thought the worst thing he could actually call you was Paul Keating—the biggest weapon he could muster against you was yourself.

PJK: It didn't work though, did it? He came second in 1993, as I recall. One thing I would never do, I would never attack them in a personal way about their finances or their family lives or anything like that.

KOB: But you did often target their personalities in a very personal way.

PJK: Not in a hurtful, personal way. I might refer to the hillbillies on the other side, I might have the odd joke at their expense and play on their insecurities, but I never went after them at a really personal level, which they did with me. They claimed my house in Sydney had been built by Multiplex. The piggery I bought into when I was on the backbench became another focal point for them. Liberal and National Party members owned piggeries or other farms everywhere but when I owned one that was somehow a matter of national moment. They would hop right into me personally using every bit of innuendo they could throw at me. They had a target centred on my back for years and years and years. I resisted the temptation to do that to them but I never let them get on top of me in a broad political sense.

KOB: Had you come to accept that by now, while there was a solid minority of people who loved you and were passionate about you, there was also an equally solid minority of people who hated your guts, with a lot of people in the middle who were really quite ambivalent about you?

PJK: This is pretty much true of all political leaders. For instance, Labor people hated John Howard. But I think of all those who did like me, who still approach me in the streets these days. The whole notion of contempt for me was broadly a piece of Liberal propaganda which the press gallery swallowed. The actual poll ratings give the lie to this claim. Besides, I lived in sweet equanimity about all that, Kerry. It never worried me a bit. Didn't then, doesn't today.

KOB: But just in the purely pragmatic terms of politics, shouldn't it worry a political leader to have such polarisation in the community about you?

PJK: A lot of people might have thought, 'We could put a cross against this guy but he does get the place changed.' I was more interested in their appreciation and respect than their love. I didn't need their love. I had enough of that going around me personally but I needed their respect and their appreciation and, in the end, their support.

KOB: Who did you respect on the other side as a parliamentary performer in the Hewson years?

PJK: Howard was the best, the most politically competent and most mercurial. I think Costello sometimes harmed us by rote, repeating things outside the door of Parliament House every afternoon until they kind of stuck. But in Opposition I didn't think Costello had great political dexterity in the chamber. You remember me saying he was all tip and no iceberg.

Howard's strength was the ability to articulate an issue we may have raised or which was being debated, but then frame it in the Coalition's terms of reference. He was good on his feet and he also knew the value of repetition. If you say something and then you say it twice, and you say it with intonation and you say it with gesture, it's like hammering that nail into the wall. Howard understood the value of the political synonym, he understood the value of repetition and he understood the value of coordinating words with physical gestures.

KOB: So repetition was a very conscious part of your performance, very deliberate?

PJK: Yes, I'd say such and such, Mr Speaker and I'd repeat it, and when the exclamation point is made further with your hands and your arms as the idea reaches its crescendo, then in a way Question Time is a bit like a dance.

I wasn't conscious of every gesture. But, for example, if you say, 'This is going to make a huge difference', and you move your hands wider and wider apart, you are painting a picture of something growing in scale. You're linking the physical gesture with the idea. Or you're saying, 'Under Howard interest rates were 21 per cent at their peak', and you've got your finger up pointing to the ceiling, you're tying the two ideas together.

KOB: How important was physical appearance for you in politics?

PJK: I think it is very important. I like to think I re-dressed the House of Representatives. After Ming, I brought back the double-breasted suit. I think in public life you should look like you are in charge. Blewett made a point, it may be in the book, that in a really difficult meeting Keating would do two things—he'd wear his power-dressing suits, which were always dark navy with silver or dark blue ties, and he would have the nonchalant game going of having the Christie's or Sotheby's sale catalogues beside him. This was intended to convey the impression that he wasn't as focused as you would think he would be on the argument, but rather distracted by his side interests. But he would then come back to the point, said Blewett, and strike like a black widow spider, making all the authority in his dress count.

KOB: And was that right?

PJK: Yes, it was right. On days that I thought demanded it I would dress more sharply. I regarded greys as casual, navies as formal, and then the tie combination added or subtracted from the formality.

But my long suit in the Cabinet had nothing to do with dress. This was why I started using ink pens, which I still do to this day, because you can write so much more quickly with ink. When colleagues were engaged in debate in Cabinet they would often say things unguardedly, and if you got their points down you could use that to effect later in reply. So I would sit there and would be like the black widow spider: I'd wait until they came across the web and I'd then go and snap them, using their own words. Blewett said whenever I turned up in a dark suit, he took that as a sign that authority was going to be vested in certain issues.

KOB: In talking about the importance of physical appearance, what about things like height and voice?

PJK: I was never blessed with a great voice. If I'd had Barry Jones's voice I could've done miracles in public life, being able to be heard across any chamber with clarity. Like a lot of Australians, I speak from the throat rather than the antrums of the sinus, and it's the nasal resonances that carry. I always spoke from my throat, which was wrong, and my voice wasn't strong. So in many respects I had to play a game of higher content and reason than I might have had to play if I'd had a strong, cut-through voice.

But I understood early in my career that I would always have to lift my performance and be listened to to make up for the voice.

KOB: Outside Parliament the economy was pursuing a course that was defying your *One Nation* predictions, although inflation was now at its lowest point since the 1960s. In July unemployment hit 11.1 per cent: 963,000 people were registered for work but couldn't get a job. I'm sure you'll remember the headlines. The *Herald*: 'Australia hits the wall'. The *Age*: 'Jobs—a national disaster'. The *Weekend Australian*: 'Don't panic over jobs, Keating'. You must have had the sweats when you saw those figures.

PJK: I did think sometimes our days were numbered. But in the end I did sell the public on the central point: in the cause of a better economy and lower endemic inflation and the maintenance of a decent wages system, we have induced a recession that has brought particular pain to the economy and to people. But as true as that is, it is also true that it is this government that has the capacity to get the country out of this particular hole.

Broadly, I think the public bought that argument that the government had found itself in this recession, not wishing to be there, but having got there, was determined to get out, and in the end was more believable on economic policy than the Coalition.

KOB: But having been seen to produce the highest level of unemployment since the 1930s, there was no way at that point that you could possibly win the election just on the government's record. You had to hope for a big vote against Hewson and the GST and the total sweep of *Fightback!*, didn't you, and try to exploit the Opposition accordingly?

PJK: Yes, there was a tremendous amount of ideology in *Fightback!*, and the breadth of it was reflected in the number of groups in the community Hewson managed to alienate.

KOB: So my general point is right, isn't it, that you had to rely on turning *Fightback!* and Hewson himself into the big political negative?

PJK: That was the ace in the pack.

KOB: In the same week as the unemployment figures jumped, the *One Nation* forecast for the deficit blew out from $10.5 billion to $13.5 billion in the space of four months— which must have made it even harder for you to spruik your economic credentials. In fact the *Financial Review* not so kindly pointed out that your $8 billion surplus in the 1989–90 Budget had blown out by $21.5 billion in three years.

PJK: Yes, but bear in mind that through the early to mid-1980s, the Labor Party had completely thrown off the post-Whitlam perceptions that Labor was not a good economic manager. We had reversed the figures and were regarded as better economic managers than the Opposition, by almost two to one. And, of course, we were.

We maintained that advantage right through the 1980s, and although our reputation took a bruising through the recession, we still maintained the economic reform edge. Remember, we ran the first four consecutive budget surpluses ever and they were as large as 2.5 per cent of GDP. Outlays had been structurally cut, inflation had been defeated after two decades, the tax system had been renovated, the top income tax and company tax rates had been slashed, and we introduced a full dividend imputation system. There were still categories of people who thought this government was pretty good.

KOB: But in the first few months of 1992 you'd built a big set of expectations around the *One Nation* forecasts, one of which was getting back to surplus in four years, but after that first surge back in the polls, the figures kept going against you. The deficit kept getting bigger, the growth wasn't happening as quickly as you'd forecast, the new jobs weren't kicking in as you'd said they would.

PJK: It was a great grind but again you can see from the headlines that as we moved through the year I was beating Hewson.

KOB: There have been claims since that you essentially manipulated the key economic forecast for *One Nation* from your office.

PJK: That was untrue. Paul Kelly in his book, *March of Patriots*, spoke to all the key players, including Ric Simes, who was the former senior Treasury econometrician back then in my office, and Kelly was convinced as I think any reasonable person would be that the *One Nation* forecast was simply a Treasury forecast.

KOB: An adviser to John Dawkins at the time, Tony Harris told Kelly in *March of Patriots* there was 'a big tussle between your office and Treasury with regard to those *One Nation* forecasts, that Treasury was very opposed to them and relented only reluctantly'. Now that's a pretty specific recall from a respected official who was in the thick of it.

PJK: That is completely untrue. Paul Kelly also quotes Tony Harris, saying that in the end Ric Simes was more accurate with the forecasts than Treasury. The point is that Treasury will always resist tax cuts. They're never going to give away revenue without a fight. There was no way that either my office or I confected the level of receipts in prospect. We could have an internal argument about what should happen to those receipts, and whether we should bring the budget back into surplus earlier, but it was Treasury's role to provide the forecasts, and Cabinet's role to decide what to do with the revenue.

KOB: After the election John Dawkins said *One Nation* was your baby, the forecasts were exaggerated and he had to live with the consequences.

PJK: The forecasts were never exaggerated. Treasury was trying to have John bring the budget back to surplus more quickly. We all have to live with the consequences of budget forecasts. Budget forecasts can be out of whack six months or even three months after they are presented. The *One Nation* package was delivered in complete good faith but it did present problems when the revenue slowed as economic activity slowed down.

KOB: The respected journalist and author George Mega-logenis, has written that as winter 1992 approached you 'first confessed to Cabinet colleagues that the economy might not be generating enough growth and the revenues to pay for *One Nation* tax cuts'.

PJK: I don't know whether I said that explicitly. I can't recall, but it's possible the economy at that stage was not creating enough growth to validate the revenue estimates. Treasury estimates of economic growth have had periods when growth and revenue have been underestimated for years and then overestimated for years. Somewhere in the national income forecasting model it doesn't pick the turn in the economic trend.

KOB: John Edwards, your hand-picked economic adviser and subsequent biographer has also written that by mid-June the rapidly increasing deficit suggested that 'the second round of tax cuts would have to be withdrawn'. That was June 1992, nine months before the election.

PJK: That's not right. Neither Ric Simes or Don Russell said or believed that in the middle of 1992. I certainly didn't. We would never have gone to the election leaving tax cuts in place knowing that far out we could no longer afford them. We wouldn't have left them all there. It's hard to know where all these conversations go and what people's recollections of them are years later. The key thing is when the government took the decision on the tax cuts in 1992 it was on the basis of Treasury's then estimates of growth in the economy.

KOB: The drastic revision of the *One Nation* forecasts in the budget put further heat on the credibility of your promised tax cuts. The growth forecast was cut by nearly 30 per cent, your deficit went up by nearly 30 per cent, tax revenue was in trouble because inflation was lower than forecast. Peter Hartcher wrote in the *Herald* that the tax cuts were unaffordable, fiscal madness. Alan Ramsey, in a column that was largely supportive of your budget, said, 'You'd have to believe in Father Christmas if you think the tax cuts Paul Keating talked so enthusiastically about last February remain a viable promise in two years.' Ramsey was right, as it turned out.

PJK: He was right, but I don't think it's because Alan is an econometrician. Look, as I have said, we had periods where the Treasury overestimated revenue for years and years and years, and then underestimated it for years and years and years. They underestimated it during the Howard/Costello years, particularly the boom years and as a result, Costello was producing rabbit-out-of-the-hat surpluses year after year. And in my period from 1992 to 1994, Treasury was overestimating the revenues. These are errors in econometrics, but we simply have to live with the outcome. What can a government do if in fact the principal economic department says the revenue is going to decline? All the government can do is adjust its policy to the forecast decline.

KOB: As those *One Nation* figures looked more and more shaky, there were other headlines reflecting that John Hewson wasn't travelling all that well either. He was becoming your best hope. His announcement that a Coalition Government would halve the minimum youth wage to $3 an hour for under eighteen-year-olds, and $3.50 an hour for eighteen to twenty-year-olds, sparked a lot of negative headlines for the Liberals, which must have been manna from heaven for you.

PJK: It was, and combined with his series of attacks on renters, churches, teachers and so on, people had just a hint he might attack the whole social fabric. People thought the idea of taking ordinary kids back to $3 an hour was red-hot in an economy where there'd been lots of growth and wealth, notwithstanding a recession that would pass, leaving the economy in very good shape.

With the whole blueprint of *Fightback!* spelt out so specifically across so many areas touching people's lives and with a GST on top, it was beginning to dawn on people that Hewson was about to unleash the whole conservative orthodoxy on the country. But even if you weren't perturbed by the ideology, it was the wrong medicine for an economy struggling to come out of recession. Going to zero tariffs across the whole of industry was a classic example. He even had business leaders speaking out against him.

But I knew I had to do regular handstands to keep the impetus going and through 1992 and up to 1993 I really did a trick a week. You can see that in the press coverage. Here's Glenn Milne writing in August 1992:

> Keating declares psychological war on Hewson. Paul Keating's savaging yesterday of the Opposition's tariff policies as the primitive capitalist abandonment of Australia's industrial base marks the beginning of Labor's attempt to make John Hewson the issue at the heart of the next election. Keating's attack poses fundamental questions for Hewson about the suitability of policies to a recessed economy and seeks to put pressures on one of the Hewson's key weaknesses, his shaky relationship with business.
>
> As well as sharply lifting the level of political rhetoric Keating yesterday viciously personalised the Coalition's policies as a symptom of Hewson's flawed psyche and extended the increasingly recurrent theme of Labor's compassion.

This is where Hewson left himself completely open as a target because he seemed determined to prove he was more hairy-chested than we were. He said he'd slash tariffs on motor vehicles to zero. By that stage, with pain and suffering, I'd taken the 90-year-old tariff wall down very substantially. I'd taken cars down from effective protection of 80 per cent to, I think 15 per cent. I don't want to get sharp about this, but I had this jerk telling me, 'I can do better than you. You might have busted the tariff wall, taking it down layer by layer, but I'll kick the last brick out and that'll prove that I'm a more hairy-chested market person than you are.'

Hence the headline, 'Hewson's car plan stalls': 'The Opposition's plan to cut protection for the car industry has become a major problem for the Opposition Leader Dr Hewson with criticism yesterday from the Prime Minister, some car companies and his own party. And in the *Age*: 'The Federal Opposition was last night under pressure on two key policy fronts after a new embarrassment on car tariffs and concern from big business over the plan to open coastal shipping.'

I have that whole saga in a file here in the office. That was my first real break on Hewson and *Fightback!*. I'd made gains on and off through the year, but that was the first time I think the press gallery began to catch on as to how vulnerable he was. The smarter journalists in the gallery knew I had taken years to get the tariff cuts through and stuck with them in a recession against all opposition. He comes along and says, 'I'll top you mate', so I thought, I'll just paint this bloke as an uncompromising fool who doesn't understand what he is dealing with in the car industry, and big business will say we have to watch this fellow. That was my first real break on him.

KOB: Two weeks after he announced he was going to halve the youth wage, you had a youth summit where you promoted your new deal with the states to reduce youth unemployment, with a $770 million federal package to shift the 132,000 unemployed teenagers into training courses and subsidised jobs. You and Hewson were both attacking the same problem but with markedly different solutions. He wanted to impose a market solution, whereas you, the old rationalist market supporter, were throwing public money at the problem. I assume the contrast you were drawing was deliberate. You were looking for policies that defined a difference.

PJK: Yes, he was revelling in being the hard man, into the old punishing and straightening routine, and by comparison I presented us as inventive, expansionary, kindly. Do you remember he said, coming up to the 1993 election, 'When the Prime Minister says he'll lean back and pull those deserving up behind him, what he's really meaning is he'll pull the rest of us down.' I nailed him on those remarks, and I think that sentiment about him being ratty got around.

KOB: By September you were obviously under pressure to shore up the credibility of your tax cuts. It wasn't just that economists were calling them into question because the forecasts used to justify them had changed for the worse, but that the cuts were so far into the future—1994 and 1996—made it easier for the Opposition to claim they would never happen. So you felt compelled to write them into legislation, get it passed through the House of Representatives and the Senate. That was when they became the L–A–W tax cuts.

PJK: The thing is, when governments portend tax cuts, the public take virtually no notice of them. I felt if I enshrined those tax cuts in legislation that had passed through the House of Representatives and the Senate people would have to take them seriously. Because without a remedial legislative change they would automatically be paid.

KOB: Wasn't it the case by then that virtually no one believed they'd happen?

PJK: Not virtually no one, but they were called into question by some, and I said the tax cuts had been made for good and proper reasons, and more than that, they've been legislated, they were now L–A–W law. But even in the election campaign the L–A–W tax cuts didn't get any traction. I couldn't get any interest in them. When I said in the election campaign the tax cuts may not be paid and could perhaps only be paid if growth could be maintained, even that didn't attract much attention.

Here's the story on 23 February. 'Tax cuts could be ditched', says PM: 'The Prime Minister, Mr Keating, has conceded for the first time that Labor's planned $6.94 billion in income tax cuts could be ditched if the economy deteriorated.'

Here's another bit: 'The Minister for Finance, Mr Willis, said yesterday that the cuts would be re-examined if the economy performed much worse than expected.' So, before the election both Ralph Willis and I made clear the tax cuts or part of them may be off if economic growth and revenue was insufficient.

KOB: I don't understand why that admission didn't threaten to become a very damaging issue for Labor in the campaign.

PJK: I can tell you—because the tax cuts never mattered in the electorate. I could never get any traction for them. I couldn't get a line for them.

Now, in the post-election budget in August 1993, we didn't ditch the tax cuts—we in fact brought the first tranche forward—but we did put the second tranche back, and changed them to be paid as superannuation. When that happened we were roundly criticised for a broken promise. We were never as a government given any credit for the honesty of saying before the election that we might ditch the tax cuts if growth wasn't sufficient.

KOB: In the second half of 1992 you complained to Cabinet, with some vitriol apparently, about the media coverage, that the government was constantly doing new things but the media saw you all as exhausted. You said you were sick to death of being hounded to jump through hoops, that a great part of the press gallery had known nothing but a Labor government for ten years and had developed a negative mentality against the government out of boredom.

Are you sure they weren't just reflecting a valid scepticism about a Treasurer who had led the country into its deepest recession for 60 years, and who had produced an economic statement with deeply flawed forecasts? Was caucus hearing a bit of siege mentality creeping in?

PJK: In the speech I gave to the press gallery at Christmas dinner in 1990 I'd said that the gallery had come along with us in the great reform of Australia and had proselytised in favour of the big structural changes. And I said, don't give us up now because a new player comes along who may seem attractive and distracting—that's Hewson—because he'll never do what we're doing, spinning the economics together and making the structural changes.

This was a government of a kind Australia had never had in the postwar years. We were sticking to the big shifts in structural policy like the tariff cuts in the face of a recession and in a year when a less committed government might have thrown it out the window to chase votes. Yet the press gallery decided to peel away and go to the queen bee on the other side of the street.

I came to the conclusion that they were no longer interested in reporting the reform task and had been seduced by the idea of a political contest that they in a very large measure had themselves engineered. When Bob Hawke and John Kerin then failed so comprehensively to explode *Fightback!*, I think the gallery came to believe it was dent-proof.

By the time I became Prime Minister the journalists had all gone across to the other side. They decamped. The real reform government was still in office doing the big reform work, but I found it very hard to interest them in the continuing adaptation of the framework. For instance, a year later, after the election I abolished centralised wage-fixing after 100 years and legislated compulsory superannuation.

My complaint against the press gallery was not one of bias. It was a complaint of being feckless.

KOB: Even so, when I look back through 1992 there were a lot of headlines that would have made Hewson wince. '60,000 jobs could go under Libs, Ford Australia'. 'Church defends right to strike'. 'Church attack on Fightback grows'. 'GST support stumbles'. By the end of 1992 he was under enormous pressure within his party to change *Fightback!*, partly because of your attacks on him, but also because of the media coverage. So even by your standards they weren't completely feckless.

PJK: Well, they still had to report events. To report news. I didn't have to thank them for that. But these stories occurred only when I started to undo him and we started to shift back to a position of primacy in the polls. Having all faith in the polls the gallery then said, 'Oh, maybe the government is not out of this. We thought it was all over, but maybe it's not all over.'

I had to make a fair bit of our own luck. As I chipped away at *Fightback!* and it gradually dawned on the gallery that maybe *Fightback!* was not supreme, was not necessarily a well put together new model for the economy and society, but rather a piece of political ideology put together by a very brittle character, the journalists started to say, maybe we should still take some of the government stuff more seriously. I think that's what happened. We dented their judgement.

KOB: We touched on the piggery in talking about your brief period on the backbench. You'd invested in it with an eye to a post-parliamentary future after losing the first challenge against Hawke's leadership. That came back to haunt you as Prime Minister, particularly in the second half of 1992, as the Liberals tried to catch you out in some way. When you became Prime Minister did you sit down and take a hard look at any potential conflict of interest with the piggery and take action to head it off at the pass? Did you call in any expert on that issue and take advice?

PJK: Not really, among other things, for the reason that Doug Anthony had had a piggery at his home in his electorate around Tweed Heads when he was Deputy Prime Minister and Minister for Trade, and a number of important Coalition ministers, including Malcolm Fraser, had grazing properties, and were able to conduct their parliamentary life and have agricultural businesses. So I didn't see any conflict of interest arising.

The Liberals tried to make this phoney argument about Commonwealth Bank loans to the piggery I'd invested in. I remember a question in Parliament to Doug Anthony referring to a claim that one of the largest ever agricultural loans written by a bank was provided by the Commonwealth Bank to Doug Anthony. Now, I would never for a moment say that Doug Anthony had used any influence as a minister to secure that funding. But in my case, the funds had been lent three years before I bought into the business. I never, ever asked the Commonwealth Bank for the funds; they were applied for three years before I bought into the piggery. This occurred when Goodman Fielder sold the piggery to cash up to make a bid for the Rank Hovis bread business in London. So it sold the piggery among a group of other assets rather quickly, and the new proprietors borrowed from the Commonwealth Bank before the high interest rates hit. At that stage, I had absolutely no association with the business. In fact, I had never heard of it.

I did deal with the Commonwealth Bank, but on the loans that were outstanding at the time I became a shareholder. And the security for those loans were the piggeries as well as the properties of the former owners, so I was effectively a shareholder in remedy, a shareholder in a sort of financial reconstruction of the business. By bringing the Danish pork industry into it, it meant that all of a sudden what was just a dead loss on the CBA balance sheet for loans earlier advanced by it imprudently, became a complete return funding position for them by virtue of my entrepreneurship.

KOB: How distracting was that for you through 1992? This is a year when every ounce of your energy really needed to be poured into the effort of returning the economy to health and winning that election.

PJK: It was a bit distracting. But only a bit. They would ask questions in the Senate and John Button or Gareth Evans would promise to check the claim in the question and provide an answer the following day. They'd then come and ask me, and I'd then give them the detail to shoot down each phoney claim. Nothing ever stuck. There was never any basis for their claims. It was just a tactic of political annoyance.

Seven years later, long after I'd left public life when Channel Nine and *60 Minutes* attacked me, urged by Tony Staley, as federal president of the Liberal Party, John Howard's Attorney-General Daryl Williams asked his department to investigate the facts to establish if there was a genuine basis for an inquiry into my dealings in the piggery. Williams then announced late one Friday so it wasn't reported widely, that there was nothing to investigate. So all of the Liberal Party claims had been voided by their own Attorney-General. But that was cold comfort for me three years after I'd left public life.

KOB: So it was a serious distraction to you in office?

PJK: It became a distraction, and in the end that's why I sold it.

KOB: What about the conflict of interest claim, that the person who ultimately bought your share in the piggery was one of Indonesia's wealthiest businessmen, who was also a close friend of Suharto's?

PJK: That was the point—he wasn't. See, the person who ultimately bought the piggery was the one really wealthy Indonesian who stood against Suharto and the cronies, the Soeryadjaya family, the one who had built the great industrial business in Indonesia. The Indonesian equivalent of BHP.

So while ever the Liberal Party tried to make the claim that the ultimate owner of the business was someone connected with Suharto, everybody who knew anything about Indonesia knew that the Soeryadjayas, particularly old William Soeryadjaya, had been an opponent of Suharto's all those years. They couldn't make that stick. In the end it all fell over, but it was a distraction.

The Libs always fight dirty. You can see it lately with Tony Abbott's royal commission into Kevin Rudd and the pink batts, and Julia Gillard and the alleged union slush fund. These are attacks on people after they have left public life. That's what they did to me also.

KOB: In October, Labor was rocked by Jeff Kennett's landslide victory for the Liberals in Victoria, but it wasn't all bad news for you, was it? The unions came out in force over Kennett's tough new industrial laws and public service retrenchments, including a rally of 100,000 people swamping Melbourne in the biggest protest since the Vietnam moratoriums. You sought to connect Kennett's take-no-prisoners approach to industrial relations to Hewson, John Howard as the Industrial Relations spokesman, and *Fightback!*.

PJK: Kennett's victory gave us the opportunity to paint the story that Kennett, Howard and Hewson were all IR ideologues with draconian industrial relations policies that would come at a cost to the ordinary working person. It was a simple message: what Kennett has for you in Victoria, Hewson and Howard have for you right around the country. We tried to give our government response to Kennett's plans a higher purpose. You'll see in the *Financial Review* on 3 December:

> Keating's IR master plan. The federal government has opted for a momentous expansion of the federal arbitration system to stymie the radical labour market deregulation being pursued by the Coalition parties in Victoria. The expansion is also designed to head off major industrial changes made by the Kennett government by bringing state workers under the federal system. The federal government will venture into new constitutional territory for industrial relations to protect workers reluctant to shift to a deregulated system of individual job contracts.

Kennett was moving down the road of individual job contracts, which was exactly the Howard/Hewson policy. I was not identifying with recalcitrant unions, but rather trying to extend the federal government's coverage and expansion of the federal arbitration system to include the state awards.

I argued that Kennett's attempts to cancel the state award system represented a threat to social cohesion, and would put the national economy recovery at risk. That had an immediate effect.

Here's another story: 'Keating takes on Kennett. The ACTU is likely to abandon its international industrial campaign after the federal government announced yesterday it would legislate for workers to escape Kennett's industrial relations reforms by moving to federal awards'.

KOB: So Kelty was in there working with you against Kennett, and therefore against Hewson and Howard.

PJK: He would have had a role in it, yes. He would definitely have had a role in it.

KOB: I take it Howard's announcement at around that time that a Hewson government would abolish penalty rates for workers wouldn't have hurt you either?

PJK: No. And Howard's general support for individual wage contracts was a reflection of the Kennett policy, so I was able to glue the Kennett label onto Hewson and Howard.

KOB: Your biggest single attack on *Fightback!* across the year was directed at Hewson's GST. Did you have the grace to feel embarrassed as the man who had promoted the Option C consumption tax as Treasurer in 1985 with every fibre of your being, and who was now virulently opposed to the Opposition's tax on consumption?

PJK: No, and I'll tell you why. Back in 1985, after the explosion in government outlays under Whitlam and Fraser, with John Howard as his Treasurer, Treasury simply couldn't believe that any government was capable of seriously cutting government spending to deal with the current account deficit crisis. They didn't think a Cabinet could do it, so the only way to redress the fiscal profligacy of the previous ten or twelve years was to introduce a new tax on consumption.

It's now history that when I lost the fight to introduce a consumption tax back in 1985, Peter Walsh, John Dawkins and I did what Treasury thought no politician was capable of doing. Over five years of budget purgatory we cut government outlays back from 30 per cent of GDP to 24 per cent. Six per cent of GDP in today's dollars is $90 billion. That achievement voided the need for a consumption tax. It was no longer necessary. Why would I then support a regressive tax on consumption when it wasn't necessary? And their GST was a much more regressive tax than the one I proposed.

KOB: On 5 November, you dropped a bombshell on your own troops. You announced in Parliament that if John Hewson won the election you would not oppose the GST in the Senate. In other words, if a Hewson government was elected the GST would be guaranteed to get through. The *Herald* reported that it surprised your mob and delighted the Opposition. The *Financial Review* said you'd stunned your Cabinet. Hewson described it as the single most important statement that has been made in many a long time and even celebrated that night with a party in Parliament House. How big a gamble was that? How much confidence did you have that you were right?

PJK: I'd thought about it a bit, but on the spur of the moment in Question Time I decided to put a clear proposition to the public. I did not want them to go to the election thinking they could have it both ways: that they could have a change after ten years of Labor but they wouldn't have to suffer the GST because they could safely assume Labor would vote it down in the Senate.

In effect I said, 'Just in case you are wondering, let me tell you what will happen. If you elect Hewson, you will also get the GST because in the Senate we will vote for it as part of his mandate.'

My people were horrified—they thought I'd thrown the election away. And for a moment after Question Time I even doubted my own judgement owing to the Liberals' elation!

KOB: That's a rare moment of doubt. How much thought had you put it into it before you did it?

PJK: Not a lot. People used to say to me, what are you going to say in Question Time today? And sometimes I'd have to say, truthfully, I've got no idea. It would just depend what had happened and what would turn up. But there was Hewson going on endlessly about the GST, and I think I said to my staff, who were undecided about it all, 'You know what, the public think they can have him and not have the GST, and we should say to them, if you take him you get the GST.'

I remember Stephen Smith saying, 'Oh god, Paul, don't say that, don't mention that!'

So, I'd been thinking about it, but hadn't decided what to do. All of a sudden something happened in Question Time and out it all came. These are the big calls.

KOB: And then you thought, Oh.

PJK: I thought, oh! The reaction to my remarks was debilitating because of the sheer euphoria on the Opposition side and the resignation and depression on my side. But notwithstanding I believed it was right, I wasn't sure I would convince both parties of the force of my position.

I felt I had to strike again very quickly before the moment was lost, so I arranged an interview on the *7.30 Report* with Paul Lyneham to articulate the reason for my remarks and the consequences. Having made that decision I needed a period of calm to prepare for the interview. So I went back to the Lodge for dinner and to think through my lines.

I'll let you in on a little secret. Every Friday night in Canberra I used to have acupuncture, and if you have someone who's a really good acupuncturist they can make you very relaxed. What acupuncture does is make you relaxed but brighter. A drug like Valium will make you relaxed but dull. What acupuncture does is make you relaxed but brighter, confident, so I called my acupuncturist friend around to the Lodge to give me half an hour of acupuncture.

It worked a miracle. He put me to sleep in ten minutes. I went down like a sack of potatoes. When I woke up I was so relaxed and so bright, so confident, I could've gone in and knocked the studio door down. When I sat there in front of Lyneham, I must have been like a Cheshire cat, whereas when I arrived at the Lodge from Parliament House I was in a different frame of mind.

I walked into that studio with no hint of doubt, and the brightness of optimism. As a result I just hit the ball right into the stand. The Liberals realised I'd stuck them with the GST to wear like a hairshirt, and my people watching *7.30 Report* said, 'God, mate, it might just turn out to be a masterstroke!'

Then Kim Beazley made the opposite judgement on John Howard's promise of a GST in 1998 by saying that he would oppose it, and he lost the election even though he won more than 50 per cent of the vote. You've got to live with the calls you make.

KOB: Looking back, the way you describe it sounds like your decision might have gone either way, particularly if close advisers thought it was a bad idea. Who were your political confidantes through that period?

PJK: I had a very talented staff and some smart political thinkers in the Cabinet but I talked a lot to the caucus members so I'd pick stuff up. If I was walking between offices and bumped into backbenchers in the corridor I'd stop for a chat. I always made myself available after

Question Time in the corridors, and I always had a good feel for the thoughts running through caucus. But on this occasion I came to the conclusion that the community believed they could have Hewson and not have the GST and I wasn't prepared in the end to go the election with that thought in their mind.

KOB: You were almost too successful really at that point, with an election not far into the new year, because the more unpopular the GST became in the polls, the more Hewson felt the pressure to change it, despite his threats to resign if the party tried to force him to soften it. You hit the front in the polls again, but suddenly he announced he was going to significantly change the GST. He was a proud man, so he would have been embarrassed, but it worked because suddenly the polls surged back to him. It did change the ball game for you, didn't it?

PJK: It did, because he exempted food, which he originally intended to tax, and he also made a remedial change to his so-called dole reforms. He tried to make himself look a little more acceptable, which worked for the moment.

KOB: The reaction did underscore that a significant number of voters were looking for reasons not to vote for Labor and Keating. The recession was officially over but the economy still wasn't behaving as you said it would. I interviewed you for *Lateline* on 19 November, the detail of which showed how fragile the government's own credibility had become, because nine months after its introduction, your growth forecast had been cut from 4.75 per cent to 4 to 3 per cent, and it was about to drop again. You had promised 800,000 new jobs within four years and 150 to 200,000 in the first year, but at that point two jobs were disappearing for every new job created. Even with his changes, Hewson and his program were still your only real hope of winning, weren't they?

PJK: They presented a distinguishing alternative. And that suited me. But isn't it true that it's always going to be the Opposition and the nature of the Opposition that decides whether you're going to win or not? We were still the big reforming government, the recession notwithstanding.

KOB: Don't they say governments lose elections, oppositions don't win them?

PJK: That's true, but here's the *Australian* on 26 December: 'ALP lifts prospects with Western Australia, South Australia'. That's immediately after Christmas as the media are starting to anticipate an election. 'The Keating government has staged a comeback amongst South Australian and Western Australian voters that would save Labor if repeated at the next election, according to the latest Newspoll.'

So we were doing something right. I think what was happening was that the community had a look at Hewson and his program and they fundamentally didn't like it.

KOB: You needed only to suffer a swing of less than 1 per cent in five seats to lose government. Looking back at it now, that's a very tenuous hold against all the frustration and the hurt and the anger out there. How many others in caucus can you remember who still believed at that point that you could win?

PJK: I've got to say of the caucus, they were fighters. They were never going to lie down. They never said, 'Look, we're done, we'll not try anymore.' They were fighters.

A fighting Prime Minister, rather than simply Bob doing his version of the royal wave, an intellectual fighting Prime Minister, is a big encouragement for the caucus to join the fight. So I think our caucus thought we could steal the show if we showed the grit.

KOB: I was interested to see, reading Neal Blewett's diary, that you were still pushing policy through Cabinet in late November and into December, policy that had little electoral appeal at the time. There was one issue on which Blewett wrote: 'Rarely had Cabinet been faced with so stark a division between ministerial heavyweights, each with a powerful case.'

Michael Duffy as Attorney-General wanted to revoke a 1986 directive banning gays in the military and Robert Ray as Defence Minister strongly opposed it, despite acknowledging that it was discriminatory. Can you remember your intervention, which swung the debate? I want to know whether it was a totally pragmatic issue for you, or whether you were swayed by a point of principle.

PJK: No, no. I had, through my interest in the arts, quite a number of friends who were gay. When I first discovered news of the AIDS virus when first I became Treasurer, I had such concern for homosexual men particularly that when Blewett brought the funding proposals in for the first AIDS campaign, part of his success in getting it was my willingness to fund them. You remember the original one, the grim reaper?

KOB: Yes, I do.

PJK: I always had a position of non-discrimination in my head about gay people and the gay community. I've never been to a Mardi Gras, I don't go for the razzamatazz, but when the question came up about gays in the military, I felt the case opposing it was prejudicial. The Americans had a policy with the military of 'no see, no tell', which

I thought was weak and wrong. It made sense to me to actually support the right of gay people to be part of the armed services, to be who they were and to say who they were. So I came down on that side of the debate.

And you're right, there were no votes in it, just like there were no votes in the Redfern speech on Mabo the same month. It was another one of those issues where you have to ask yourself: do you do the political weak-kneed thing or do you do the right thing? I always felt that in a testing moment I wanted to pass the test. That's all. I thought it was right.

You see, the government was a champion government. Notwithstanding that some senior ministers had retired, it still possessed vigour, scale and substance. But the leader and the Cabinet process have to induce it. Keep the big canvas on the wall, and good ministers will keep adding brush strokes.

KOB: On 6 February 1993 Labor was soundly beaten in the Western Australian election, though not as badly as some had expected after the years of WA Inc. and the taint of corruption in the Burke Government. The following day, when most sane people in your position would have been feeling somewhat defensive and wondering how long you could delay your election, you climbed into the family car and drove out to Government House and announced your own election for 13 March, which I thought took chutzpah.

PJK: There were some nerves around the office about the timing but when I did decide on the date I did get some fun out of taking the gallery by complete surprise. There was a view that I would go in late March but I opted for 13 March instead.

I drove out to see Bill Hayden at Government House in Annita's red Magna with my three daughters. It was a Sunday morning. I recommended to Bill that we have an election and we had a cup of tea and a scone and a bit of a walk around. And the proverbial good time was had by all. There was not a soul at Government House from the media to record it, much to their chagrin when I called a press conference that afternoon to announce it.

I had a very relaxed view about it all. I was either going to win or I wasn't, but I reckoned I could beat this guy. I had what I hoped would be the political and economic framework more or less set, but whatever happened, I would do my best. Rather than thinking I'm under pressure here, I was very relaxed about it. I was in a lethal mood.

By the end of the year, even though Hewson had watered down the GST, he'd declared war on so many target groups: nurses, teachers, renters, churches and welfare groups, even business, and I said, 'He is going to have a go at the whole fabric of our country and give you a GST into the bargain.'

I said, 'Under the Labor Party we have developed a really genuine and good social democracy with strong economic growth bonded to a good social wage.'

On the recession I said, 'We were responsible for the recession being deeper than it needed to be, but we will also get you out of it. No one else will.'

KOB: Your timing meant that you were stuck with two new sets of unemployment figures over the course of the campaign. There was one at the start and one at the end, and as luck would have it, in the first one unemployment passed that million mark. That would be a first in Australian history, I would imagine, a Prime Minister calling a poll just as unemployment is about to hit the million mark.

PJK: Yes, but I was always a momentum player. You're always better to crash through. If you regard these—let's call them the portents of bad news coming—they're like waves at a beach. Technique allows

KEATING

you to handle waves. You find the point where there's less disturbance and where the potential damage to you is minimised. So I would have made judgements about those two sets of figures.

KOB: When it comes to the speech for a campaign centrepiece, the policy launch, I know a huge amount of focus from many people goes into what key points should be highlighted and how. It's probably the least spontaneous, most straightjacketed thing a political leader has to do. Informed by polls and focus groups, party strategists and, somewhere in there, the leader and the speechwriter.

Don Watson has described the last night at Kirribilli House before your 24 February policy launch at Bankstown, where you, Watson, Mark Ryan and Don Russell were working on the final draft deep into the night. And there was a big difference of opinion about whether there should be a reference to the republic in there, whether it was a positive in the electorate or not.

PJK: In the end, I am a punter. You don't make social changes of this scale and type without a commitment. The problem about the republic was that the political commitment to it in the party had not cut deeply enough, and without political commitment it just languishes. But the moment a Prime Minister is committed to it and its essence becomes clear, it starts to rise in popularity again.

I thought, I have half a chance of winning this election, and if I'm going to win, I'd rather win with some big changes. If I lose, at least I've put the big issues on the table. So in the end I was convinced that without political patronage at prime ministership level the republic had no chance, and if I wouldn't take it on, who would?

Bob Hawke used to say *ad nauseum* we can't touch the republic until the Queen dies. I never accepted the premise. I thought this is the time to make a move, this is the right moment to establish the framework coming up to the centenary of our federation.

KOB: Just to indulge the personal for a moment, even allowing for the tight discipline imposed on that speech, there must've been some room in there for emotion. It was at Bankstown where your politics had been spawned. Your father Matt wasn't there, but your mum Min was there with your brother and sister. Annita, who'd carried much of the family load through the parliamentary years, was there, who had seen all the ups and downs from the inside, with the kids. It had been a long ride. When you stood in front of that crowd as the Prime Minister of Australia, did you feel the moment?

PJK: It was in the Bankstown Town Hall, which had featured so much in my life over the years. I stood there as the kid from the fibro house at Number 3 Marshall Street, Bankstown, putting out the big nation-building framework speech. There was a poignancy about that.

Baz Luhrmann and Catherine Martin did the set, which gave it a different kind of look, and had a simplicity about it, which pleased me. And you're right, Dad missed seeing me become Prime Minister but Mum was there with the siblings along with Annita and the kids. So it was the culmination of a long, long political innings.

KOB: Hewson's GST was always a significant part of your strategy but it wasn't until midway through the campaign and you clearly were not making headway—you'd hit a flat spot—that you demonstrably upped the ante on the GST. You went on *A Current Affair* with John Hewson and Mike Willesee and pursued Hewson quite aggressively. Not pretty, but effective.

PJK: It was one of the things that turned the tide. The Liberals were kidding everybody that they had this GST but they didn't want to talk about the detail of it, and they'd been getting a free ride from the Canberra press gallery on *Fightback!* for much of the past eighteen months. In the end it was up to me to really make it clear that the GST was an actual threat, that people had a real prospect of getting it. And yes, Hewson didn't come out of that melee well.

That got me back a bit more momentum, but I also think Hewson called it very badly in his general prosecution of the campaign. He kept having these silly rallies, chanting 'Labor's got to go, Labor's got to go'.

I don't think the public like that kind of street campaigning, with people throwing bottles and scuffles and the rest. He had a very bad last week as a consequence of that while I kept talking about the future. I kept talking about Asia and about our growth opportunities, I kept talking about the social equity of our policies, reminding everyone not to trade all this now for this glib ideological manifesto, *Fightback!*.

KOB: There was a telling moment on the night before the 13 March election, when you addressed your last supper with staff and spoke very candidly. The speech was recorded and subsequently came out.

PJK: It shouldn't have, but it did.

KOB: People listening to you that night were convinced that you didn't think you were going to win.

PJK: That may be what they did think, but I said at the end of the speech, we just might sneak in. I could feel the momentum shifting to us. I thought Hewson's last three days were disastrous with the big public rallies and the scuffles in the streets, the anti-Labor chants, and Hewson losing his voice. I thought, 'Well, I hope you keep it up', because I could feel the thing building. You're always better in a big race to be one out and one back, able to power to the front in the last yards.

I thought we might just slide over the line. I couldn't say it with a ton of confidence that night because I didn't have that, but I did think we might just get there.

KOB: You described yourself that night as half-economic rationalist and half-bleeding heart.

PJK: Yes, I said we had changed Australia for the better as no government before had; that we'd walked away from the industrial museum, we'd remodelled the economy, we'd given the country a new engine and a good social wage, that this was social democracy at its best and that I didn't believe the Australian people would turn their backs on that kind of society as the Liberals were enjoining them to do.

KOB: In the end were people voting for Paul Keating or against John Hewson?

PJK: Probably both. Probably both. I had my rusted on supporters and many didn't like what the Tories had on offer, Thatcherism Mark II.

KOB: But without the GST for you to pin on them, they would have won that election surely.

PJK: I cannot say. My critics would say no, the Liberal Party would say no, that I wouldn't have won without the GST, but I was pretty good at counter-punching on the big topics. I counter-punched this bloke almost senseless.

KOB: When did you start thinking, gee, maybe I've got to start thinking about a victory speech?

PJK: During the Saturday on 13 March I went with Annita to Bankstown to vote. I thought then, what am I going to say if we win? The mood in the polling booths was good. There was a sense that things had moved our way. I did have a few words worked out, but the line that night about the true believers was spontaneous.

I don't know whether you recall Bob Hawke standing up in 1983 saying we're going to govern for every one, including those who supported Fraser and all he stood for. After Fraser had divided the country by bringing about the dismissal of the Whitlam Government causing bitter hatred among Labor's followers, Bob got up on the night and said, 'We've won this election not just for our supporters but for everybody including those who opposed us.'

And many people in the Labor ranks groaned, thinking, give us a break. The implication of Bob's remarks was that maybe sometimes we might not govern for everybody, but this time we would. Nevertheless I felt a commitment to people who had stuck with the Labor Party in belief of its model, so that's why I said, 'For those who in difficult times have kept the faith, this is the sweetest victory of all.'

John Howard and others later talked about my hubris that night but they misread the driving words. I didn't want to accept victory with restraint. I wanted to celebrate it. That's the fact of it. I wanted to give Labor people the sense of victory they'd so desperately wanted and had earned.

KOB: You and Hewson had some pretty bruising things to say about each other in that year of campaigning. Here's what John Hewson told Andrew Denton about you on *Enough Rope* in 2006:

I do respect him and I think he had a view for Australia and he fought for it. But I had a very interesting experience as we went back for the resumption of Parliament after the 1993 election. He called me over behind one of the columns and said, 'How are you?'

I said, 'I'm fine.'

He said, 'No, I mean seriously, how are you? I called you a lot of terrible names in that campaign, a lot of terrible names, and I want you to understand that I didn't mean any of them. I quite like you and I quite respect you, but you've got to understand, mate, that politics to me is a game and I'll say or do whatever I have to, to win.'

This is him saying that sort of bastard factor, if I could use that expression, is essential to be a good leader in politics, it's something I didn't have.

Is that a fair description of what happened?

PJK: Some of it, but not the essence of it. We were walking to the Senate chamber for the Governor-General's speech in the new Parliament.

I had always remembered a story told in the 1970s by a champion Australian boxer named Tony Madigan who lost to Cassius Clay in the gold medal heavyweight bout at the 1964 Olympic Games. Madigan said, 'Clay was so good I couldn't put a glove on him. But he was also kindly, and after he'd obviously spared me a hiding I said to him, "Thanks for looking after me, Cassius."' Madigan said Clay put his arm around him and said with a deep measure of understanding, 'That's alright, Tony.'

The polls had gone up and down through the year but I was well on top of this fellow politically. I didn't need to scratch him, bite him, hate him. I only had to beat his policies. To paraphrase the essence of what I said to him, I said 'I hope I didn't beat you too much. Beating up people politically is what I do and I had to beat you up enough to win, but I hope I didn't beat you up too much. In the end I have a view about how the country should advance itself and it's very different from yours—that's what I'm fighting about, not you'. That's what I said to him.

KOB: Just differentiate for me about what you regard as acceptable battle and unacceptable battle. Why was it acceptable to get in his face with comments like, 'I love to see you ashen-faced', clearly implying that you've got him scared?

PJK: That's what I call the battle inside the place—the battle for the balance of the psychological power inside the chamber.

KOB: So if he went away really shaken up by that kind of verbal assault, that wouldn't have bothered you?

PJK: Not in the least. But it would bother me if I had said something really personal, hurtful or mean that he was hurt and affected by. Like a reference to his personal finances or family. I never, ever touched that stuff.

This was the election Hewson's party believed he should have won. This was the chap who thought he had it in the bag, and a short time later there he was, like a sort of squashed tomato in Parliament House, having to listen to the Governor-General's speech, which was written broadly by me. So I just wanted to say to him, 'Look, be assured the battle was about the issues, mate, not about you. Don't take it personally.'

IN HIS OWN RIGHT

It's hard to imagine a more treasured moment in the career of Paul John Keating than waking on Sunday morning, 14 March 1993, in Kirribilli House, looking out on a glistening Sydney Harbour and hearing the echos of his true believers' speech the night before.

He'd have had the Sydney *Sun-Herald* and the *Sunday Telegraph* waiting on the coffee table downstairs. At a guess I'd say the *Sun-Herald* would be on top; 'KEATING MIRACLE' would have been hard to avoid. The election had been so close that Melbourne's *Sunday Herald-Sun* had prepared for both eventualities: 'Hewson in photo finish', 'Keating in photo finish', both of which made way for 'KEATING BACK'. He has all three covers.

But Keating barely had time to savour the victory before Treasurer John Dawkins was on his doorstep with a message delivered with great intent—and, as it turned out, portent. In the past year, all Dawkins' efforts including his public support for the shaky forecasts of *One Nation* had been dictated by one goal—setting up the new Prime Minister to win an election. That goal achieved, Dawkins said he intended as Treasurer to be much more his own man. There was a further hint of what that might mean when on his return to

Canberra he was met by his namesake, Michael Keating, the head of his department, with confirmation of what everyone really knew by now—that the economy's failure to follow the government's optimistic predictions meant that the promised tax cuts were no longer affordable.

Paul Keating had to wait to see what all that would mean by the time the August Budget was shaped and presented, but in the meantime he'd just secured a fifth term for Labor, won legitimacy for his overthrow of Australia's most successful Labor Prime Minister and, as he saw it, a fresh impetus for his agenda to remodel Australia.

While pushing on with Mabo, the republic and a greater reorientation towards Asia in foreign policy, Keating also had other reform fronts to open up. His authority within caucus and Cabinet had been well and truly strengthened. A swing of nearly 2 per cent to the party and a swag of new seats in an election he was supposed to lose will do that for you.

The ongoing misery of John Hewson did nothing to prick Labor's balloon either. Before the month was out, Hewson was forced by his party room to dump his GST from the Liberal platform, just hours after he said it should stay pending a two-year policy review. For the moment his leadership was safe, but mostly because of an ongoing stand-off between Peacock and Howard forces. Behind the scenes Peacock was doing all he could to ensure that John Howard would never lead the Liberal Party again.

All of this was a bonus for Paul Keating as he embarked on his next big reform. Trade unions had preceded the Australian Labor Party by more than 50 years. Their first significant industrial campaigns in Sydney and Melbourne in the 1850s saw the introduction of the eight-hour day or 48-hour week, putting Australia in the vanguard of workers' rights around the world. This was an era when a worker could be jailed for leaving work to go to the pub. The Labor Party as the political arm of the labour movement was spawned in the wake of the shearers' strike.

Within three years of Federation, the template for what was to frame industrial relations in Australia for almost a century was established—the Conciliation and Arbitration Commission. Initially sponsored by the country's second Prime Minister, Alfred Deakin, we were already onto the fourth, George Reid, by the time the act to establish it was passed. It was a system of compulsory arbitration of industrial disputes based on the premise that it would balance the scales between workers and bosses.

Ninety years later, informed by a system that had become extremely inflexible in its one-size-fits-all formula, and in which myriad awards had grown like topsy with workplace demarcation disputes commonplace, Keating wanted to turn the system on its head. An award simplification process with union amalgamations was already happening, driven by the ACTU, but Keating wanted industrial negotiations largely taken out of the Commission and put in the hands of unions and employers as a collective bargaining process within an enterprise framework.

On 21 April, Keating told a luncheon of 800 company directors he intended to deregulate the labour market to allow individual firms to negotiate wages based on productivity improvements, and entrench collective bargaining as the principal form of wage negotiation. The goal underpinning the new enterprise bargaining system was to foster greater flexibility within the wage system, including a greater recognition of individual merit among workers, with productivity gains at the heart of the negotiation process. From the moment the Hawke Government walked down the road of financial market and tariff reforms, labour market reform was just a matter of time, but the inevitability of that didn't make it easy.

Once again this all came under the umbrella of the Accord with its usual co-sponsor, Bill Kelty, albeit a more fractious sponsor than in the past. Kelty told Paul Kelly for *March of Patriots* that 'By 1991 Australia was going into an open economy . . . The productivity growth of some industries was going to be 6 per cent, and of others, minus 2 per cent. You can't sustain a centralised system in an open economy like that, even with all the goodwill in the world'. The Arbitration Commission's role would primarily be retained to guarantee a wages safety net for the lowest paid workers.

The friction between the government and the unions largely came from Keating's decision to appoint a fellow New South Wales factional scrapper, Laurie Brereton, as his new Industrial Relations Minister, which really signalled Keating's intent to keep the unions honest. While there was a core of support among senior trade union leaders, there was also a great deal of unrest and suspicion. This was a serious shakeup of the only system the members had ever known. Most of the big employers were broadly on side.

So while deep in his negotiations on Mabo, staying in some sort of contact with John Dawkins over what was shaping as a nightmare budget, and trying to convince world leaders to embrace APEC, Keating was periodically called in to play a kind of good cop to Brereton's bad cop, in order to keep Kelty and the rest of the ACTU leadership in the reform camp.

By September, the government was in deadlock with Indigenous leaders over the Mabo negotiations, in deadlock with the Senate over the budget, and in deadlock with the ACTU over Laurie Brereton's determination to get union agreement for a package of legislation that included a right for non-unionised workers' groups to be able to make enterprise agreements. At one point the Accord itself seemed under threat.

Looking back, Keating acknowledges that he stretched himself too thinly over his second term as Prime Minister. If you're an intervention-ist leader by nature and also a reformer, the moral of the story is to be careful that you're not fighting on too many fronts at the one time.

The man who at one point at least half-seriously considered being both Prime Minister and Treasurer had become so preoccupied with his new policies—Mabo in particular—that he hadn't seen the political danger signs building around the 1993 Budget, nor fully registered what John Dawkins had meant when he said post-election he intended to be his own man.

On 27 April, the *Financial Review* scored a front-page headline from a long interview with the Treasurer, 'Liberated Dawkins: I'll do it my way': 'Mr Dawkins tells the Australian *Financial Review* why he wants to be an activist economic manager and outlines his plans to reshape the national agenda away from the Keating shadow.' Fair enough in one sense, because Keating as Treasurer hadn't spent much time in Bob Hawke's shadow, but the difference this time, which both Dawkins and Keating now acknowledge, was that much of the old discipline of the all-important Expenditure Review Committee developed in the Hawke–Keating years, had fallen somewhat fallow.

I got the sense from my conversations with Paul Keating for this book that more than a few of his pre-budget conversations with Dawkins were threaded through some intense stages of his various Mabo negotiations. If so, they and the government paid a big price politically for the budget that emerged.

By now Keating's reform horizons had further expanded to encompass competition policy—the sort of issue that might cause a journalist's eyes to glaze over, like most things to do with premiers' conferences, but this was another reform with far-reaching consequences and difficult to orchestrate. Dealing with the premiers on reform at any time was worse than herding cats, but introducing competition to public monopolies that tended to be revenue gravy trains for governments, and setting up something like a national electricity grid were not conducive to easy overnight policy solutions, and Keating was in the thick of it. A Sydney academic and former McKinsey consultant, Fred Hilmer, had handed the federal government a set of ambitious recommendations riddled with political implications almost immediately after the 1993 election.

The Australian Competition and Consumer Council was just one important outcome of the competition reforms, and they all took time and energy. Keating was conducting that process at the same time as Mabo, the republic, APEC and the budget. As the year progressed, the front pages of Australia's newspapers reflected as much. There'd be good news on one front and bad on the other, or bad on two fronts at once. Rarely was a front page universally good news. Take these three headlines on the *Age*'s front page on 22 July: 'Keating wavers on tax', 'No simple route to republic, says Turnbull' and 'Canberra may shield CRA on Mabo claim'.

In tandem with this Keating was also making far less effort to bring the press gallery along with him, so how much the public was following with any real interest or comprehension is left to guesswork. The only clues at the time really revolved around the regular sampling of voter sentiment in the opinion polls, which mostly favoured Labor through the first few months of 1993, but plummeted disastrously in the budget aftermath.

Why was the budget so damaging? Because Keating was seen to renege on half of his LAW tax cut package, and secondly, because in the public's eyes he was hitting them with billions of dollars in indirect tax increases to pay for the other half—in other words, giving with one hand, and taking with the other. The message to voters now was that not only had they been shortchanged on the tax cuts, but what tax cuts they were getting, they'd be paying for themselves. What they didn't know at the time was that John Dawkins had originally proposed hitting them even harder.

Having had to defend in 1992 the *One Nation* forecasts that were refusing to follow the script, and the heavily criticised tax cuts to deeply sceptical economists and journalists—and, as he saw it, sacrificing his own credibility in his first year as Treasurer to help build Keating's platform for victory in 1993—Dawkins was determined to restore his professional pride through a budget of much greater fiscal purity.

In the shadow of the budget, Keating felt compelled to prune back some of what he saw as the harsher measures. Hence his off-the-cuff comment to his speechwriter, Don Watson, on his way to the Press Club for a speech acknowledging the tax retreat in late July, that if Dawkins didn't comply with his wishes, he might have to 'knock his block off'.

The end result was still a political time bomb. Where Keating had said late in 1992, 'The tax cuts have been legislated—they are not a promise, they are LAW law,' John Hewson could now say in July 1993, 'No one should ever again believe anything the Prime Minister says.'

Somehow, by year's end, Keating chalked up a triumph at his first APEC conference in Seattle, delivered on Mabo and enterprise bargaining, the Accord was back on track, competition policy was in train, the economy was finally starting to gallop along, he was back in front in the polls, and Hewson was on borrowed time. John Dawkins, on the other hand, one of Keating's great stalwarts, had gone, resigning in the shadow of Christmas, giving Keating no opportunity to dissuade him. Looking back now, Keating says the government never recovered from the 1993 Budget, an extremely sore point with Dawkins.

KOB: What authority do you think was delivered to you by winning the unwinnable election in 1993, and what difference did it make to what you wanted to do in your first full term? Graham Richardson said it made you the most powerful Labor Prime Minister in history.

PJK: It made a huge difference to me. Remember the story about Churchill's driver taking him to Buckingham Palace the night Hitler's armies moved into Calais and Dunkirk? The Dutch queen flees from Holland to London, and that day Churchill is sworn in as Prime Minister.

Leaving Buckingham Palace without any fanfare in the dead of night his driver says, 'Mr Churchill, I'm sorry that you've had to take the prime ministership in such circumstances.'

And Churchill says, 'Ah yes, Fred, but you understand now I'm in full command of the field.'

That is the point. When I won that election I was in command of the field, and it meant I was able to take on some more of the sacred cows within the party, like industrial relations.

I had a clear view of my priorities. Apart from Mabo, the republic and APEC, which I continued to develop, the other big economic reform still to be done was to open up the labour market.

In the early 1980s I'd opened the financial markets. In the late 1980s I'd opened the product markets with the tariff cuts, with the third large remaining field being the labour market. What we had succeeded in getting under the Accord was aggregate wage flexibility, where on a national basis, wages would move up or move down according to economic and political judgements. But flexibility within industry sectors meant the really productive employee, who deserved better remuneration than the average couldn't secure higher pay from so rigid a system. Nor could you get multiskilling in the workplace where workers were prevented from crossing restrictive demarcation lines. These inflexibilities were holding productivity back—productivity that was otherwise to everyone's benefit; the nation's benefit.

That was largely because we still had a centralised wage-fixing system, with a lack of flexibility within sectors and within individual enterprises putting a crimp on productivity. Having got the share of national income going to wages and to profits back in reasonable proportions, and having again refired investment, what we really needed was a more flexible labour market, and I regarded that as a primary objective for the second term.

Because Bob Hawke had been a very effective choirmaster of the centralised system as ACTU President, he would never consider removing the central role played by the Conciliation and Arbitration Commission when he was Prime Minister. You might remember his great relationship with James Kirby, who was President of the Commission and Bob's whole love affair with the Commission.

The idea of turning his back on the Commission as the primary arbiter of wages in Australia was anathema to him. And, I might add, to Ross Garnaut, his alter ego. But I knew that unless we could get the efficiency that would flow from workplace agreements between employees and employers replacing the big national award cases, we wouldn't realise the full productivity benefits and full potential of an open and flexible market.

KOB: In April 1993 you laid out your ambitions for what the *Australian* described as 'a historic deregulation of the labour market', effectively terminating a century of centralised wage-fixing. How tough did you anticipate that would be?

PJK: I knew it would be tough, and would cause Bill Kelty some pain and put strain on the Accord, but it had to happen. Bill wanted me to appoint Bob McMullan as Minister for Industrial Relations, and he didn't like it when I told him I was giving the job to Laurie Brereton. Laurie was from the New South Wales Right and Bill didn't trust them.

I said, 'Yes, Bill, but although I have a ton of time for McMullan, you will simply treat him as one of your foot soldiers and roll him into your position, whereas Brereton will unambiguously be mine.'

So I appointed Brereton, which Bill didn't like but in the end accepted, notwithstanding the fact that he never had a comfortable relationship with Laurie.

Bill and I had long discussed reducing the number of awards, making the labour market more flexible coming up to the 1993 election, and he and I had thought about a shift from centralised wage fixation. Bill knew the open economy would put stresses on the rigidity of the centralised system and had said as much. But there had to be a catalyst, so I announced a major overhaul of the whole industrial relations system to entrench workplace or collecting bargaining as the principal form of wage negotiation. That signalled a major reform for the Industrial Relations Commission, which had been re-established, with an adversarial system at its heart.

I believed this adversarial structure needed to be changed. And changed to a culture where employees and employers were able to negotiate in good faith. I said Brereton would consult with industry and unions over the period but this would mean that the Accord would broadly be left only to maintain the safety net of the award system and the steady accumulation of occupational superannuation. I said I wanted to see close to 100 per cent of all workers on federal awards brought under the workplace agreements, and indicated also that I wanted workers under state awards and those without unions to be brought under the new system.

KOB: In terms of that national safety net, the national wage case and establishing minimum award rates, that was it as far as the Accord was concerned?

PJK: Yes, but Bill Kelty and I shared many unity tickets, as you know. One we definitely shared was the need of a set of minimum award rates for people who could not access the bargaining system, like women and kids in retail, cleaners, people covered by miscellaneous workers' union awards. These people had no power with which to bargain for fair wages and conditions. I didn't want to go down the road of the United States where people on the bottom level were on miserable rates of $5 and $6 an hour, living in penury. I thought as a democratic, industrial society we had to do better than that, and that was always Bill Kelty's view. He was a champion on minimum rates.

KOB: In terms of the future of the Accord structure beyond 1993, theoretically the government and the ACTU would still sit down and broadly agree on what wage case would be taken to the Industrial Commission?

PJK: Indeed, and that's why in the heady days of growth in 1988 and 1989, when industrial companies were offering employees 12 and 14 per cent wage increases, and Bill Kelty was trying to keep them to 6 and 7 per cent and we were trying to bridge the difference with tax cuts, it was a great battle. But once we succeeded in getting into the period of low inflation, in fact zero inflation in 1993, it became much easier to run an industrial system without the attendant pressure of keeping a perpetual tight rein on wages. Running any industrial relations policy is always tougher in the context of high inflation. In future the wage claims of the wider workforce would be driven by and related to productivity.

Once we got inflation back to zero and 2 per cent it was much easier, because by then, we had productivity running at 3 per cent. All the structural economic changes were kicking in to double trend productivity. Two percentage points of productivity we were giving to labour, by way of real wages and one percentage point to profits. If you've got three percentage points of productivity to play with and the inflation is only 2 per cent, it's a much easier system to run.

Therefore it was good to get the Commonwealth out of the award system and into enterprise agreements. But at the same time to not turn Australia into some sort of industrial refuse where the least powerful people end up with derisory increases. It is true today, as a result of that policy, notwithstanding John Howard's vicious attempt to smash the safety net with *WorkChoices*, that Australia still has the strongest set of minimum award rates in the world.

KOB: What were your biggest sticking points in terms of getting the changes through?

PJK: A lot of members of the Labor Council in New South Wales never agreed with my views. A lot certainly didn't agree with moving away from the Industrial Relations Commission. They loved the old system. And what's more, many expected to be commissioners at some time as well. I'm not saying their positions were driven by self-interest, but they were very caught up in the extended Industrial Relations family.

This was a really important top-end-of-town club where former employer representatives rubbed shoulders with former trade union representatives and they were shown a lot of deference. It wasn't just the practical tensions of trying to get wage flexibility and better agreements and more productivity, which should've been what they were really about. They were obsessed with the deity of the IRC.

KOB: It was a reasonable concern of business, wasn't it, that in some instances a formidable set of powerful unions representing a particular industry could hold that industry to ransom with the threat of industrial action during a negotiation period?

PJK: That was true in part but with the right framework, it did give both sides the prospect of writing new agreements, with larger increases in real wages but with greater flexibility built in for employers, and with fewer, simpler awards.

In the first twenty or so years after the changes to enterprise bargaining in 1993, real wages in Australia grew on average by 1.85 per cent a year. That's around a 40 per cent real increase; the highest rate of increase and one beyond anything in the twentieth century. If you look at the comparable workforce in America, their real wage increases have been around 2 to 3 per cent over the same period: 2 to 3 per cent versus 40 per cent in Australia. That is why Australian cities are full of restaurants, why consumerism is high, that's why people have choices in motor vehicles and services—because they are now wealthier; they now have the money.

I used to say to some of my less enthusiastic supporters, 'This will deliver real wages of a kind you're never going to get from the Industrial Relations Commission. Your remit is to get people increases in the real living standard, not to be part of some process club you might find comfortable.'

In the Beazley Opposition when there was a debate about going back to centralised wage-fixing, I remember saying behind the scenes, 'Can't you explain how much benefit has accrued to workers from enterprise bargaining?'

And one of Kim's frontbenchers said to me, 'Well, that's absolutely true, the gains have been dramatic, but we're not sure ordinary people understand it came from enterprise bargaining, and they feel safer with the IRC.'

KOB: Through the year you had headlines like 'Brereton grabs IR powers' with a story describing 'an unprecedented expansion of the Commonwealth's industrial powers'. There was another one: 'Kelty slams Brereton reforms', which carried a very real threat that if you didn't meet Kelty halfway on what you were proposing you'd be humiliated when you addressed the 800 union delegates at the looming ACTU conference. Do you remember that?

PJK: Skirmishes went on between Brereton and Kelty around some of these things, and I was using Brereton as a kind of front-row forward to push the changes. Bill knew it was broadly me, so he could attack Brereton rather than attack me. He was first and foremost a tactician. And Brereton was tough in counter-punching.

In the end there was a very strong intellectual pull towards the bargaining system, and I think my commitment to the award minimums, to the safety net, was so strong that Bill was prepared to take the package. The intellectual weight came from people like Kelty and Laurie Carmichael at the ACTU and Tas Bull of the Waterside Workers. They understood the new framework better than my colleagues at the Labor Council of NSW.

At any rate, the country got this enormous shift up in flexibility. You have to remember, Kerry, we had a flexible exchange rate, interest rates set in the market and then broadly by the Reserve Bank, not around the Cabinet table. There were rapidly declining levels of protection, so imports were keeping manufacturers honest in terms of prices. Against that we had this rigidity in the labour market. It just didn't compute. The brighter guys in the ACTU knew this, Bill particularly, but around the edges they pushed and shoved to get the structure they wanted. That was okay, by the way. Pushing and shoving is what we all did.

KOB: The union movement today is a pale shadow of what it once was. What part did your reforms play in that quite dramatic decline over the past twenty years? And where does that leave the labour movement and the workforce today? In other words, by shifting the system in the way you did, were you ultimately weakening union power, and with it the Labor Party's base?

PJK: The truth is, many of the unions have lost their edge. With the great growth in hospitality in Australia for instance, the Liquor Trades Union should have signed up thousands and thousands of people, those who worked in the new jobs in restaurants and bars and so on—but it just didn't happen. The same in tourism—it just didn't happen. The organisational guts fell out of the trade union movement, and instead of responding to the great opening up of the economy and its flexibility, they failed to rise to the new challenges in a changing workforce.

Obviously the decline of manufacturing and the disappearance of so many of those traditional blue-collar jobs played a part, but the digital age has changed and is changing the shape of the workforce.

Public sector unions and unions in areas like oil-refining, shipping and the wharves retained a base, but the middle declined. Now, to what extent were our changes central to that decline? Perhaps to the extent that real wages growth was so strong, the whole imperative of sharp industrial organisation fell away.

In some unions the quality of leadership had declined. Some of these people had sat for years broadly doing nothing. They sat waiting for the national wage case. All of a sudden they had to go out to enterprises and organise the workforce and negotiate smart agreements. All of a sudden they were being asked to go to this factory, that factory, this retail business, that retail business, and some of them were not intellectually equipped to do it. It didn't suit them.

But then again, it's also true to say the movement away from a rigid system of award demarcations and central adjustments would probably inevitably have meant that the natural platforms on which union membership had otherwise sat would have been degraded by the flexibility coming into the labour market. But in the end, what's the whole point of an industrial movement? It is to secure increases in real wages and conditions. The new model gave increases in real wages and conditions greater than in any period of the twentieth century, but unions weren't able to adapt to the new landscape while continuing to maintain their significance. In some ways that's problematic because the modern workforce is still open to exploitation. But the worst thing was the unions failed absolutely to take credit for the 40 per cent increase in real wages growth since 1991. They walked away from a world-beating performance.

KOB: Competition policy was another of your early reform challenges in 1993—the inefficiencies and protection from

competition for some big public enterprises like energy generation and distribution, the heavily regulated ways much of
Australian agriculture was run. You'd commissioned the Hilmer
Report in October the previous year and Hilmer dropped his
recommendations in your lap almost immediately after the
election. How important was this in the reform landscape and
how tough were the politics it threw up?

PJK: The more disposable income people have, the more money they
spread through the economy. People get increases in their disposable
income in two ways: through growth in real wage, and from falling
prices. If people's wages are rising and the price of motorcars and
goods is falling, the amount of disposable income available for them
to spend or save rises.

The great problem Australia has always had is that it had a
monopolist or an oligopolist view of how the country should operate.
This was true in the big industrial sectors, it was true in banking, it's
true in retail. The country too easily falls into duopolies or oligopolies,
and yet we know prices will only come down through competition.

Inflation in the traded goods sector of the economy was then
running at zero or near zero because our tariff cuts had promoted
real competition between imported goods and locally manufactured
goods. By comparison, in the non-traded goods economy—ports,
electricity, hospitals etc.—where there was no import competitor,
inflation was running at 4.5 per cent or thereabouts. The two sectors
came to around 2.5 per cent overall.

The question then was, how do we introduce competition to
those industries that cannot be competed against, like gas, water
and electricity? Clearly Australia had to shake up its closed and
monopolised sectors, but that wouldn't happen without a lot of
agitation by at least some of the state governments. And the workforce
in the state-owned enterprises also had a big stake in the game.

I used to say to caucus, 'competition' is our word and we should own it. It has never been part of the Liberals' culture. The Tories don't believe in competition, they believe in business, in the old-boy network, they believe in the boardrooms, the industry cabals, the cosy commercial oligopolies. That's their stock in trade.

Whereas if you represent the great body of men and women as we do, then you want to give them goods and services at lower prices and you want the economy working for them, which means it will fall to the Labor Party, not the Coalition parties, to raise the whole notion of competition. And, in our terms, to make it a Labor value. In other words, we put our faith in the markets, we don't put our faith in business. And there's a great difference between markets and business. Particularly well regulated and competitive markets.

Genuine markets perform in a socially good way whereas business will often be as uncompetitive in any environment as it can get away with. So the whole competition reference that I gave to Fred Hilmer was really in many respects nothing to do with Fred Hilmer, but everything to do with my view and, I might say, Bill Kelty's view, that we had to get prices down in many of these sectors, including in the state sectors, the non-traded good sectors like gas, electricity and water.

The states had monopoly rents from their enterprises which they then fed into their budgets, so the dividends out of the Elcom of New South Wales or SECV in Victoria or their water bodies were subsidising their recurrent budgets at the cost of consumers. Business was paying too much for these services and also passing that cost on to consumers. Ordinary workers were paying too much for their gas and electricity. It was like an invisible form of regressive taxation.

So I sought to bring competition policy within a single construct-ive national framework built around the Hilmer recommendations, with the cooperation of the states through the Council of Australian Governments (COAG).

KOB: You had at least one activist premier in Jeff Kennett from Victoria, who was right behind this agenda. Did that help?

PJK: It was also true in New South Wales before Nick Greiner resigned. His successor John Fahey wanted to do very little—he wouldn't even agree to an accounting separation of electricity generation and distribution, much less do anything structural. He thought it was all a state preserve.

When Jeff Kennett was elected he came to see me on the Monday after his election, and he said, 'You know, we're in trouble, with the debts.'

I said to him, 'Premier, the only way you are going to get Victoria out of this hole is to sell assets, and the group of assets most saleable for you are the electricity generators, particularly the old brown coal ones, But to get good prices for these assets you'll have to be able to sell electricity beyond the borders of Victoria.'

'You can have access to that market if we set up a national electricity grid down the east coast of Australia, so where there's a contract, say, for Visyboard in Albury setting up a new newsprint mill, they would invite tenders for their electricity and that might be provided by a Victorian producer, a New South Wales state generator or a Queensland state generator.

'So to be able to get decent prices for your power stations in Victoria, you will have to help me change both John Fahey's and Wayne Goss's minds about the necessity of a national electricity market—with the full separation of generation from distribution.'

As it turned out, Jeff Kennett did help me do that, he was great, and gradually I turned John Fahey around to the point where we did establish the national electricity market, the NEM, and as a consequence Jeff Kennett was able to sell his power stations at very high prices into that new market. But we had to have a framework for that, and this framework turned up at the Council of Australian Governments around the Hilmer principles.

It required an injection of capital to physically join the grids together, and eventually I got the states' agreement for the national grid to run from Brisbane to Adelaide, so South Australia came into the grid as well. It took two years but from that day since we've had a national electricity market.

KOB: How big a reform do you regard that as now, looking back?

PJK: It was gigantic. George Megalogenis wrote in the *Australian* in December 1994 that consumers would receive $9 billion a year if protection was removed from key sectors, including electricity, water, gas, transport and the legal profession. He was quoting from a major report from the Industries Assistance Commission. The Commission also said federal and state governments would collect another $8.9 billion in revenue. Although more than 80 per cent of the reforms would have to be delivered by the states, the federal government would collect 66 per cent of the revenue windfall flowing from a more efficient economy. My proposition was to give some of that back to the states.

In April 1995 we signed the intergovernmental agreement supporting a comprehensive national competition policy reform package, and signed agreements implementing the reforms. The reforms involved extending trade practices legislation to state and local government business enterprises and unincorporated businesses, encouraging competition in the business activity of governments.

All members signed the two intergovernmental agreements, reaffirming their commitment to continuing microeconomic reforms in key industries, and this was reflected in a third agreement which also provided for financial arrangements, including a series of competition payments. We also established the Australian Competition and Consumer Commission (ACCC). We folded the Trade Practices Commission and the Prices Surveillance Authority under the one umbrella.

This whole process was about establishing principles for the structural reform of public monopolies, and competitive neutrality between the public and private sectors, with price surveillance for institutions with significant monopoly power, and a regime to provide access to essential facilities like pipelines, with a program of reviewing legislation that might be restricting competition.

The Keating Government promised to maintain real per capita guarantees of financial assistance to the states and local government on a three-year rolling basis plus further financial assistance in the form of competition payments. In other words, if a state did something that promoted competition and the Competition Council agreed, they would be eligible for an incentive payment. We promised to provide a total of $200 million to be shared among the states in the first year, then $400 million in the second, $600 million in the third. By 2000 it would have reached $1.2 billion, but in their first budget Howard and Costello pulled the competition payments out. They didn't think state sector reforms were worth supporting.

KOB: What was the make-up of the Competition Council?

PJK: The make-up was all about the voting rights and we worked on a formula of two votes and a casting vote for the Commonwealth with a single vote for each state. A lot of good things started to happen.

KOB: As Prime Minister, when you're pushing an agenda like this and looking for support, looking to enthuse and convince, how did you treat these guys around the table? Different states, different political dynamics, different personalities.

Was it all a set piece, each of you following your script, or was there room for spontaneity?

PJK: I always sought to treat them courteously. Charm is a very effective lubricant. Secondly, I didn't discriminate between Labor and Coalition premiers and treasurers because some of the better ones were on the Coalition side. In other words, I took them as I found them and tried to treat them all fairly and reasonably. By and large we developed a cooperative framework.

It's worth saying that this agenda was not an obvious vote winner. I think journalists and the public often found this dry and boring so you had to want to do it. If you don't have a Prime Minister or a Treasurer interested in promoting competition, then there will never be any, because the system is set up not to provide it. The way oligopolies and monopolies operate—Australia is not set up for competition. So unless you are trying to shape markets, which we do these days with the ACCC and competition policy, and unless you have a federal Treasurer or a Prime Minister trying to pull competition from the pores of the skin of the economy, it doesn't happen. It's a peculiar thing about the conservative parties, they fundamentally don't believe in competition. I'm not overdoing this—they believe in cabals, they believe in easy business accommodations.

KOB: And yet under John Howard particularly they were quite determined to break up what they saw as the industrial relations club of employer and union advocates.

PJK: That was their anti-union phobia; nothing to do with oligopolies or anti-competitive arrangements. But in terms of market power and pricing power by the big Australian companies and their businesses, certainly in my years, it was only the Labor Party that was interested in competition, never the Coalition.

KOB: You and Jeff Kennett were both instinctive political warriors, and of all the state premiers he was certainly public enemy number one for the labour movement at that time. In the latter part of 1992 you'd had a big public fight with him on industrial relations and in the early stages of Mabo you were also in dispute. Yet you two forged a kind of friendship. What was it based on?

PJK: He would do things! In the end, if you could get him to agree to things or if he wished to do things, he would actually go and do them. He was a man who made decisions and put them into effect, so I had that point of identification with him. And once he found some common cause between us—for instance, selling the power stations in Victoria, creating the national electricity market—being smarter than average, he would try to reposition himself and bring the other conservative premiers on board. He was somebody.

The South Australian Premier, Dean Brown, was another Liberal who was also open to this. He and Kennett were, in the end, cooperative with me, which was not the case with John Fahey or Wayne Goss. But ultimately they all tucked in and we got this done. But I found when a Premiers' conference ended, the guy you'd like to have a drink with was Kennett more than the others.

KOB: Was there a certain rascal element to him that you liked, a bit of extra spark?

PJK: Yes. He was a bit of a rascal, and being one myself, it takes one to know one.

KOB: Your biggest political problem in 1993, perhaps of your whole prime ministership, was brewing from the election in March to the budget in August. John Dawkins was obviously smarting from what he felt was the damage to his credibility as the price he had to pay in signing off on those *One Nation* forecasts and the tax cuts you promised.

It was a combination of things—an economy that was still not giving you the growth you needed to justify your promised tax cuts and keep a rapidly expanding deficit in check, coupled with a Treasurer who signalled that he intended to be much more his own man in this term. The *Financial Review* headline read: 'Liberated Dawkins, I'll do it my way. From now on Paul will be much less involved'. How did you interpret that at the time?

PJK: Well, it was a bit of a worrying message from him because I'd never at any stage sat on John or circumscribed his action. But it is very difficult being Treasurer to a Prime Minister who had been Labor's longest-serving Treasurer and an active one. John came to Kirribilli after the election. He was delighted we'd won, but said I'm going to be much more assertive in this Parliament.

I said, 'Well, that's fine John. I don't want some mouse in the job. I want someone to have command of the portfolio.'

I said to him, 'John, I've always regarded you as being an independent and wilder spirit, otherwise I would have left Ralph in the job. The mere endorsement by me of you as Treasurer means that your remit is there.'

But I said to him, 'By the same token you have to always be politically smart. The one thing Bob could always rely upon with me if I took a series of big budget measures through a May Statement or a budget, he would know that politically they would work.'

John said, 'Don't you think I've done that?'

I said, 'You have, so I don't think we're debating much.'

I would have liked to think that John's sense of achievement, substantial as it was, and sense of inner confidence, was such that he did not have to make such declarations, and that any issues he had in policy were ones he was able to cope with in the Cabinet context. Ministers go through these phases. People get very tired by the process and they get cranky and despondent and then they get irascible. You have to roll with the punches in the Cabinet room, either as Treasurer or Prime Minister. It happens to a lot of people.

KOB: But what he was saying broadly was that he felt he had to go along with your strategy on *One Nation*, including the promise of tax cuts in that first year to win the election even though he was uncomfortable about them and wasn't sure they could be afforded. But he was signalling to you that he was going to stand up more this time, he was going to be his own man.

PJK: It was news to me John was in any way uncomfortable with the *One Nation* tax cuts or the forecasts at the time. He had been very much my partner through all the really bad ERC years. Peter Walsh too, but it broke Peter and he got out. John also backed me against Hawke and went to see Bob of his own accord in 1988 and told him it was time for him to leave. He'd been very loyal to me and I loved John. I had great feelings towards him. You live in that pressure-cooker environment with these people for a decade or more and you end up with quite deep relationships with them. That's why it hurt me deeply to take Treasury away from Ralph Willis but I made an honest call. Ralph was a very good Treasurer but I honestly thought John would do it better at that time, and I felt I owed it to him.

I didn't think we'd had any dispute over *One Nation*, over putting the budget back into deficit to pull the economy out of the hole after the recession. But when we got into 1993 Treasury were pushing hard to get back to surplus earlier than they needed to. Well, Treasurers are meant to be alert to what their department is up to. That's what Labor governments expect of their Treasurer, to stop the bureaucrats in Treasury pulling the show down around your ears. It requires some smartness.

KOB: Yes, but the deficit kept rising through 1992 and into 1993, and it wasn't supposed to. It was up to $16 billion.

PJK: But this was not some budget emergency. As the economy picked up the natural stabilisers would change, unemployment benefits would come down, tax receipts would rise, and gradually the surplus would come back out, finding its equilibrium again. Because the underlying level of structural outlays had been cut so much by John Dawkins and Peter Walsh with me.

KOB: It became increasingly clear that the tax cuts were becoming less and less affordable. In April the Reserve Bank governor, Bernie Fraser, was warning of another balance of payments crisis without a medium-term plan to reign in the deficit because growth wasn't doing the job. Markets were getting skittish and so was Dawkins. He was still upset over the way he felt the LAW tax cuts had undermined his credibility as Treasurer. As you got closer to the 1993 Budget he wanted to walk away from them.

PJK: He did. He threatened to resign, and it wasn't just a private threat, it was actually reported in the newspapers. He said, 'You can either take my changes in the budget, or I'll go. They'll say you're not up to the changes anymore, and I'll walk away and you'll be left with a smouldering heap.'

Through this long run-up period of budget deliberations, which usually started around March–April, I was sitting in the Cabinet room working on the native title legislation. I chaired the native title committee of Cabinet, working with the responsible ministers and the

Aboriginal community, the mining community, the farm communities. I'd had a big row with the states, who weren't cooperating. So I wasn't quite on the job through the budget process as I'd been in all the other budgets. That's how importantly I valued native title.

KOB: Bear in mind that you'd started your time as Prime Minister thinking you could handle being Treasurer as well.

PJK: But the reason I said to you I would have preferred to remain Treasurer is I would have seen Treasury coming. They are like the gang who can't shoot straight. They only shoot straight when guided. When Treasury put on a song and dance about pulling the budget back into equilibrium earlier than the natural stabilisers permitted, I would have just told them, from my own experience, to go away. I would have said, 'Don't give me that line please. I don't want to be pulling economic activity back now, when the economy most needs it.'

KOB: Nonetheless you did come round to the view that the tax cut formula would have to be changed.

PJK: Of course I did. When the facts change, when the aggregates change, I change. As the revenue collections became clearer, prudence kicked in and we started talking about how we should reshape the tax cuts. We eventually decided to bring the first cut forward by two months, but put the second cut back from 1996 to 1998. A pretty sensible thing to do—a right thing to do—and certainly no policy crime.

John was determined to be a conscientious Treasurer and what he wanted to do was a good thing in theory—consolidating the budget and doing it earlier. As a former Treasurer I can't criticise him for that in one sense.

But you've got to be politically sharp too. You've got to stay on your feet in this game, you've got to keep on punching. If you shoot a big part of your own strategy away you're in trouble.

I was quite happy to acknowledge publicly that revenue had been overestimated, that we could no longer do the two tax cuts to the promised timetable—which I had already hinted at during the election campaign. Actually, not hinted at, said. If you're the Treasurer that's what you want the Prime Minister to say, and I was prepared to say it. But John wanted to introduce some other horror elements into the budget as well, like indirect tax increases. That is, bring the overall budget balance back earlier. I did not think, in the prevailing economic circumstances, that this was good policy.

In the end I intervened and knocked a lot of things out, but the horror stuff that did stay still gave me the biggest caucus problem I'd had, either as Treasurer or Prime Minister. The caucus reaction to that budget was very bad for me and for the government, and that fed a big reaction from the state labour councils and the ACTU. The Democrats played around with it in the Senate and the Liberal Party opposed everything, and it took from August to November to have the budget passed.

KOB: Let's take this in stages. John Dawkins told Paul Kelly in *March of Patriots* that the old ERC gang had broken up: 'Paul was not as attentive as he should have been. Peter Walsh was gone. I wanted to cut Defence, but Paul wouldn't take on Robert Ray . . . The essential discipline of the Hawke era had gone.'

PJK: I don't think the ERC in this period did have the discipline that John and I had brought to it with Peter Walsh in the years when we were doing the big reductions in the budget balance. But I didn't think that our problems were insurmountable either. We just had to accept that with the economy, the budget would not come back into balance as early as Treasury would have liked or had forecast.

The Treasury was not a politically smart outfit. I had come along as Treasurer and reformed the whole economic structure of the country and given Treasury relevance of a kind it had never had. Not even in the salad days of postwar growth had Treasury had such a pre-eminent place in policy, or presided over such an enormous program of structural change. Yet within a month of the 1993 election they're trying to tear the budget back into surplus as quickly as possible. I mean dumb, dumb, dumb.

They should instead have been saying, the natural stabilisers are working here in an economy that is still relatively weak. We don't want to be taking too much cash from it, we don't want to be unsupportive of those who need support, and so the best thing is not to panic about this, just give it a bit of time because growth will restore the budget equilibrium. The underlying level of the outlays was so tight, around 24 per cent of GDP, it was only the cyclical outlays, like unemployment benefits, which were the problem. But instead of saying let's give the country, the economy and the government a break, Treasury were riding John into the ground.

If I had taken too much notice of the department through all my years as Treasurer, we would never have had a national superannuation scheme, or dividend imputation the way it is now, or the massive cuts to the company tax rate which I presided over. If you blindly follow Treasury you'll be out on the street very quickly. What you've got to do is see where the right balance for the economy lies. That's the job of ministers. If I have any criticism of John, it was not his motives, but the methodology. He took Treasury's interest to heart to such a degree it derailed the government's ability to manage the debate.

KOB: But you'd also have to agree with Dawkins when he said that the old disciplines in the ERC of the Hawke era had gone.

His implication is that you weren't as attentive as you should have been.

PJK: That's not accurate for this reason. The economy was then coming out of recession. The job of policy was to lift Commonwealth activity, not to cut it. The thing is, in terms of the aggregates, we didn't have the same concentration program for program, but why would we continue doing that after doing it for a decade? We didn't need to. But by the same token, there was no spendthrift behaviour. And you can never underestimate the cost of the native title legislation through 1993, and the toll it took on my time. I was caught up with it for at least three days a week through much of the year. That's the sacrifice one has to make to put in place a social change on that scale.

KOB: As you drove to the National Press Club to make your speech on 22 July announcing the tax changes, you told Don Watson in the car that if Dawkins didn't calm down you'd have to knock his block off. I assume you meant that figuratively, not literally.

PJK: Basically what Treasury had sold John was that we would have to pay for the tax cuts with a whole lot of increases in indirect taxation. That was a gift to the Opposition, giving the tax cut on one hand and taking it back with the other. They sold him the zeal package and John bought it.

John's motives were always good. He tried to do a good thing fundamentally, an earnest thing, to bring the budget more rapidly towards surplus. But in the end what it did was lose the government such altitude, and you can see that in the polls. Our position deteriorated so rapidly that it was economically counterproductive. The Treasury view would have been, oh well, bring on a new Treasurer.

KOB: When you announced the changes to the tax cuts in July, the journalists had no inkling of the plans to raise indirect taxes in the budget, but even so you suffered political damage. Geoff Kitney asked whether LAW law had become T–R–I–C–K trick.

John Hewson said, 'No one should ever again believe anything the Prime Minister says.' How hard is it to take such political embarrassment on the chin?

PJK: I did say quite honestly in the election campaign, if the economy slows down and revenue slows down, we may not pay the full tax cuts but nobody, certainly not the gallery, gave me the benefit of flagging that before the election. But then I couldn't get a line for the tax cuts themselves from the press gallery during the election campaign. Absolutely no help in pointing to the tax cuts, but all detriment in pointing to their alteration.

I said to Don Russell a number of times in the campaign, 'I don't know what I've got to do or say to get anyone to focus on these tax cuts.'

I couldn't get a line for the tax cuts! Not a line. That's why I got barely a line for the warning that I may not pay them. Yet the gallery tried to pretend later I'd won the election, in part, because of the tax cuts. They were terrible.

KOB: Where were the other ERC ministers in terms of their political antennae on all these sales tax increases that they would have signed off on?

PJK: I can't remember now precisely because of my absences in the Mabo discussions, but I don't think the body of ministers liked the political framework.

Part of the success I had as Treasurer was not just getting the big changes, but selling them, and doing so in a way that the Prime

Minister was happy with and could live with. This is the great bond that Bob and I had through those years. He would know that if he gave me a job it would be all politically done and dusted. John was now threatening to upset that for me, and he could only go to a certain point, and I would have had to knock his block off, meaning I'd have to put him in his place.

John yielded in the end. We did reach a compromise, but the compromise was most unsatisfactorily portrayed publicly, and after the 1993 Budget I don't think I had any great prospect of winning the 1996 election, so great was the damage.

The question that should have prevailed in any consideration between John and Treasury was, 'Why is the budget in deficit anyway?'

It's in deficit because the economy is too weak to push up the revenue, and there are too many people still unemployed, relying on the transfer payments of unemployment benefits. The budget should be there to support them, not ripping the carpet from underneath them.

KOB: But even with the indirect tax increases that survived, the budget was still projecting a deficit of $16 billion.

PJK: Not a worrying proportion of GDP.

KOB: Paul Kelly in *March of Patriots* asserts that budget was your political death warrant.

PJK: That's probably a bit dramatic, but the underlying sense of it is right.

KOB: John Howard wrote in his autobiography that it was an outrageous repudiation of your campaign against Hewson in 1993—not only a mangled tax cuts promise, but big indirect tax hikes after attacking Hewson's GST.

PJK: Well, it was not smart in the sense that we'd had a good win at the election, we'd won the campaign, but after the budget it seemed the government felt comfortable in repudiating its mandate. Newspoll in the *Australian* after the budget showed a drop in Labor's primary vote from 41 per cent to 31 per cent. We'd dropped ten percentage points in two weeks. As preferred Prime Minister, I led Hewson 38 per cent to 31 per cent two weeks before the budget. My rating dropped to 27 per cent.

KOB: Your old mate Bill Kelty rather succinctly summed it up: 'Paul had said don't vote for a GST, vote for me, and then we increase all these taxes. The budget was a catastrophe.'

PJK: The ACTU hated it, as did the labour councils, and so did the public.

I had huge affection for John. He was such a conscientious guy and he'd been through the torment of all the years of the ERC, and I thought, if I can't rely on his judgement, whose can I rely upon? But in the end those important, balanced judgements, I would have been better taking as Prime Minister and Treasurer rather than simply as Prime Minister.

KOB: Except that that would have taken a huge and probably unworkable toll on your time.

PJK: I know, but then I wouldn't have had the budget outcome that John's budget delivered. That's the point.

KOB: John Dawkins was to say later, 'The truth is that Hawke gave Keating as Treasurer more support in Cabinet than Paul gave me.'

PJK: That's true only to the extent that John wanted me to support in Cabinet his otherwise broadly unsaleable proposals. My inclination was to back John in all things out of my huge regard for him. But in the end you've got the corporate responsibility of the government and its welfare to think of, which has to come first. When you refer to Hawke's support for me, my retort would be yes, but I didn't give Bob the unadulterated Treasury religion. I gave Bob practical, doable, digestible, saleable measures.

Instead, the whole of Labor's base was in revolt. Here's the *Sydney Morning Herald* on 31 August:

> Caucus forces budget retreat: the government's humiliation increased yesterday with a hostile caucus demanding and getting further concessions to repair the political damage. Participants described the mood as 'mutinous' although the admission by Mr Keating that changes were needed appeared to have headed off any large-scale revolt.

KOB: Do you also remember the press conference around that time where the question was asked about the caucus members who'd taken you on and you described them as wounded soldiers who were peeved either because they'd been dropped from the ministry or hadn't been picked for the ministry? Alan Ramsey translated that as you telling them 'up yours', implying it would be 'business as usual from the emperor'. I know you've talked of keeping up a close relationship with caucus, but there were complaints by then that you had become isolated, too caught up in the big policy areas like Mabo and APEC.

PJK: There were a number of people spouting that line. I can't remember exactly, but there were a few disappointed ministerial aspirants who were in that group, people who had never made the ministry. And I remember Michael Easson, who was the Secretary of the NSW Labour Council, a member of the Right, calling the budget 'an act of bastardry'. This sort of stuff really fanned the flames.

KOB: By this time Labor's primary vote had plunged to 26 per cent against 49 per cent for the Coalition. Hewson had a twenty-point lead as preferred Prime Minister. After the excitement, the euphoria of the true believers' victory, it was gone in less than six months.

PJK: The great pity of it was that the government was an exemplary social democratic outfit with all the right balances between reform, consolidation and care. One indifferently constructed budget blew that away.

KOB: How do you recover from that? How do you pull the troops back from that?

PJK: I did, because by November we were back up to 41 per cent in the polls. By that time the economy was flying along with investment growth at 6 per cent. The headline is 'Keating declares economic victory'. Normal investment growth annually was around 2 per cent. Six per cent was phenomenal, so by the end of 1993 we were back in front, in polling terms.

KOB: Even so, John Dawkins had had enough. He'd threatened to quit at a press conference on 21 September over what he saw as lack of support within government ranks as he unveiled his third version of the budget. As Christmas approached he resigned. He walked with you out of the last Cabinet meeting of the year, and in the five-minute walk to your office he told you he was leaving.

PJK: It was the last hour on the last day he could practically do it before Christmas. He gave me no inkling. I would have preferred to have seen him weather this particular period and come back out into the sunlight on the other side, which he had more than enough capacity to do, but he decided for reasons best known to himself and without any notice to me, to resign.

I said to him, 'John, don't. Come into the office, let's talk about it.'

'No,' he said, 'that's why I've given you no notice. I don't want to be turned around, because I know if I listen to you long enough I will be.'

So he'd made his mind up. I received his resignation with great regret and much sadness because by then we'd got the budget through and I thought we faced a much better period going into 1994. I was sorry he was leaving but I then had to make the decision to replace him, and I had no hesitation in giving the job to Ralph Willis.

KOB: Even though you were back in front in the polls by the end of the year, voters never forgot the fractured promise of the LAW law tax cuts, did they?

PJK: And what was the outcome? The first round was paid in full and paid early. The second round we were forced to postpone, as I'd hinted in the election campaign, and they're the ones Peter Costello and John Howard cancelled when they came into government in 1996. This was the second round of the LAW tax cuts that we decided to convert to a 3 per cent superannuation contribution for every wage earner. We decided to pay them as savings, not as cash, to take their super from 9 to 12 per cent. The people who broke the LAW promise in the end were Peter Costello and John Howard. That is a matter of record.

KOB: You can't say they broke a promise they'd never made. It was your promise, not theirs.

PJK: But they were the ones who were attacking us for changing the LAW tax cuts. Had they done nothing but simply inherit Ralph Willis's 1995 Budget, everyone's superannuation contribution today would be at 12 per cent as those tax cuts were perpetually paid into people's accounts. So, having made such a song and dance about us reneging on the LAW tax cuts, Howard and Costello then knocked out the 3 per cent super contribution in their first budget. They killed the second LAW tax cut.

A NEW FOE—BUT REFORM GOES ON

No one's bulletproof in politics, but for a time in 1994 Paul Keating gave a good impression of it. The headlines through January alternated between great news for the economy and Hewson's ongoing struggles within his own party.

The stockmarket was at its highest levels since the 1987 crash, and the message was starting to sink in that Australia was going to have a strong recovery without an outbreak of inflation, the magic combination that had evaded governments after the previous two recessions. On 21 January, the *Australian* reported the Reserve Bank's view that 'the Australian economy has moved up a gear into a strong and sustainable recovery that will bring higher economic growth, more jobs and lower inflation'. For Ralph Willis, the nicest guy in any Cabinet, having previously been robbed of Treasury twice, the stars were finally aligning. One of his first jobs as John Dawkins' replacement was to upgrade the budget forecasts—growth up from 2.75 to 3.5 per cent, inflation down from 3.5 to 2 per cent.

More bad news for John Hewson came from the tough, ambitious Bronwyn Bishop, who'd set her sights on becoming Australia's Margaret Thatcher, and moving from the Senate to the House of

Representatives, Hewson firmly in her sights. As it turned out her ambition wasn't matched by ability and her run fizzled, but not before damage was done. More ominously, John Howard, the self-described Lazarus with a triple bypass, was peeking around the party-room door, allowing himself to dream again.

The *Australian*'s front page on 2 February neatly summed up Hewson's misery: 'Bishop leaves way open for Hewson challenge' and 'Economic signs the best for 30 years'.

Even when Keating lost one of his more promising ministers, Alan Griffiths, over allegations that he'd used ALP funds to help support a sandwich shop in which he was a partner, the polls didn't waver. The first Newspoll for the year had Labor's primary vote back in the forties, with Keating leading Hewson by a comfortable ten-point margin as preferred Prime Minister.

Then Prince Charles dropped in for a visit and made it plain he and his mum wouldn't be fussed if Australia became a republic: 'I'm not going to run around in small circles, tear my hair out, boo-hoo and throw a fit on the floor as if somehow, like a spoilt child, your toy's been taken away.' Keating didn't mind that at all.

Even when he lost a second minister, Ros Kelly, within weeks, less for the sin of pork-barrelling marginal Labor electorates than for the politically incompetent way in which she dealt with the ruckus, the Liberals obliged Keating with another internal distraction. From the *Australian*: 'Howard fuels Liberal tension. Rift with Hewson over policies widens'. Without the Liberal shenanigans, Keating's ruthless use of Parliament in defending Kelly could have cost him quite dearly. When Hewson moved a censure motion over Keating's failure to sack her, Keating orchestrated a wall of noise from his own backbench to seriously disrupt Hewson's speech. When Howard got up to complain about the strategy and Speaker Steve Martin failed to rein it in, he was supported by spontaneous applause in the public gallery. It was a reminder of what many people didn't like about Keating.

Alan Ramsey was characteristically blunt in the *Sydney Morning Herald*:

> We often think he's Mandrake or Houdini. He thinks he's Julius Caesar, Alexander the Great, Marco Polo and Genghis Khan all wrapped in one sleek feline package. Since last March the power of the emperor is complete, and he now administers it, often effectively, just as often wilfully, with all the overtones of the street thug that Keating, beneath all that style and clever language and personal brilliance, cannot stop himself from being.

Keating kept flying high with his reform agenda, with headlines again trumpeting his latest breakthrough with the states—by now all but one had conservative governments—on competition policy. In the *Australian*, 'PM, States in deal to carve up monopolies', and the *Financial Review*, 'Competition revolution. Canberra to fast track its reforms'.

Then came another headache for Hewson. The former Western Australian Labor Premier, Carmen Lawrence, actually recorded a swing to Labor in the by-election for Dawkins' seat of Fremantle, almost unheard of in mid-term by-elections.

This was the period in which Keating felt impregnable enough to announce he intended to cut back his Question Time appearances to two a week during parliamentary sessions, the first Prime Minister to do so. In the process, not only was he playing to the Opposition's mantra that he was arrogant, but he was blunting one of his party's most lethal weapons. For all the ups and downs in Keating's political career, there was one constant you could never take from him: his ascendancy in Parliament. But the misgivings of colleagues and advisers fell on deaf ears. The wind was in his sails.

And still the momentum kept running Labor's way. Growth surged to 4 per cent, leading the western world, and the OECD declared

Australia was in its best shape for a decade. In the mid-March Newspoll, Labor's primary vote jumped to a commanding 45 per cent and Keating had opened up a 21-point gap on Hewson in personal approval, 46 to 25. After four years, the Opposition Leader was on borrowed time.

Perhaps this would have been a good time for Keating to revise his hostility to the press gallery. He had further reforms in mind, somewhat more inclusive ones like tackling long-term unemployment, and a supportive media was a damn sight better than a resentful one.

As Don Watson observed in *Bleeding Heart*, 'Paul Keating would always be Paul Keating, which meant extended smooth sailing was out of the question.' But the gallery had comprehensively written him off in the 1993 election and as Watson also wrote, 'Nothing in his nature would allow him to forgive; even when it was clear that his contempt only made their spite and revenge more certain.'

In May 1994, Hewson finally tumbled—not to Bishop or Howard— but to the cherry-cheeked son of the Adelaide Liberal establishment, Alexander Downer. He'd stayed out of trouble as Hewson's new Shadow Treasurer, but there's nothing more exposed in politics than leadership.

The cartoonist Bill Leak summed it up in the *Sydney Morning Herald* that week. He drew Keating as a dentist in his surgery doorway with bloodied white coat, calling 'Next!' Hewson's head is in a rubbish bin by the door, and Downer looks on as an unsuspecting and cheery Billy Bunter schoolboy.

But that's not quite the way it ran in the early weeks of Downer's leadership. Teaming up with another relatively untried young Turk Peter Costello, Downer soon rocketed to the top of the polls, taking his party with him. The public reaction had little to do with the so-called Liberal Dream Team, and everything to do with the fact that Downer was neither Keating nor Hewson.

It was now close to mid-term in the electoral cycle and once again Keating had slipped down the mountain. The biggest question would be whether he retained the interest to make yet another effort to claw his way back up to the top. On the one hand he'd always treated Downer with amused disdain and found him easy sport in Parliament; on the other hand the economy was now throwing up a rather ominous new hurdle. Growth was galloping along so strongly that, although inflation remained low, the Reserve Bank Governor, Bernie Fraser, was threatening to put interest rates up again to nail inflation down for the future.

It was against this backdrop that Keating considered giving the game away, becoming only the second postwar Prime Minister to leave on his own terms.

KOB: You must have felt real relief going into 1994 as the good economic figures started to flow. And after all the anger from the 1993 Budget you had the calm and under-rated Ralph Willis as your new Treasurer, although no sooner was growth up than you had to start worrying about containing it. The *Herald*'s headline at the time: 'Rates fear as growth soars'.

PJK: The economy started to come good with a vengeance in 1994. The *Financial Review* carried a headline on 6 January: 'Investors scramble for shares'. The Reserve Bank in January had hailed a strong recovery and inflation came out at 1.9 per cent for the year. In February the stockmarket hit a record high. Here's another *Fin Review* headline: 'Economy runs hot, inflation falls flat' and the 1993–94 growth forecast was now revised up to 4 per cent.

In political terms we were back on top. On 1 February, the *Age* reported Labor's primary vote up to 43 per cent, which put us well in front in two-party preferred terms and I led Hewson as preferred Prime Minister by 38 per cent to 28 per cent.

KOB: I guess it's always good to be in front but once again this reflected enormous volatility in the electorate, didn't it?

PJK: Volatile, that's true. But whether I was up or down in the polls I was still relentlessly pressing on with reform. Unemployment had finally started coming down but long-term unemployment was a black mark on the nation. In the labour market, unemployment is like a pool of water. As people fall in, if they're adaptable enough or lucky enough, they swim across it and get to the other side and back into employment. But other people get stuck in the pool and have to be helped to the other side. You can't do that just by wishing them well. You've actually got to make the effort to help them manage their life back to employment.

A lot of traditional blue-collar jobs were disappearing. I could see that we would have a pool of long-term unemployed people as a consequence of structural reform and the recession. No matter how much we were seeking to lift employment growth and people were finding jobs, it wasn't a neat equation. The long-term unemployed were left out, and I regarded this as a social tragedy. I wanted to do something about it, so I asked Michael Keating and the department to produce a policy paper to come up with some answers.

I was disappointed with the departmental drafts; something got lost in the movement between departments. It seemed to have developed into a story of defeat rather than hope. The drafts didn't have the flavour and essence of what I was after. In the end, in large part, I constructed the Cabinet submission myself and broadly wrote a lot of the explanatory memorandum from the Lodge. This was to be Australia's first substantial statement on employment in 50 years.

When the Prime Minister has to construct Cabinet submissions and personally write the public presentation, it says something about the bureaucracy.

I had Don Watson sitting by the fax machine in his Parliament House office as I fed material through from my office at the Lodge where I could have peace and quiet. Because I had the carriage of the whole idea in Cabinet, I had in my head the whole sense of the

Cabinet discussion and the whole development of the policy, which no speechwriter could ever have. So I told Watson I would write the public service memoranda myself and that that could inform the speech. It took me about three or four days to do it.

KOB: What does that say about your style of leadership? You seem to have been very much an interventionist within portfolios. Bob Hawke had an extremely talented ministry, but he also gave them the room to run their own portfolios. Here you were personally negotiating Mabo, personally shepherding the world's most powerful leaders into a new regional forum and, as you say, effectively writing a new national employment policy blueprint.

PJK: As Prime Minister, Bob was a delegator, and that's okay, but he also had me to superintend the whole policy framework and identify the broad philosophical directions. Being a delegator is great if you have someone to delegate to. I still had a very strong team of ministers but I didn't have someone fulfilling the role I had done for Bob. I was a different sort of Prime Minister from Bob, but in a sense, in the circumstances, I was obliged to be.

We brought out the *Working Nation* white paper, we took some comments from the community, refined the policy and then I announced a four-year $6.5 billion package targeting unemployment, $4.8 billion of which was for the long-term unemployed. They were the centrepiece, but it was a package addressed to the whole complex challenge of unemployment. I said in a speech to the Press Club the next day that where the 1945 white paper on unemployment sought to help a million service people to demobilise, *Working Nation* would seek to remobilise a million unemployed.

The essence of *Working Nation* was a kind of contract that we would offer the long-term unemployed a job place and a job subsidy providing they took the work. They couldn't turn their nose up at it. This was a new activist model, and I think we had one case manager for every 24 people. A case manager would get to know each person in their pool, and would stay in close touch with their progress, including talking with their employer. Remarkably, around 70 per cent of those people maintained their jobs at the end of the subsidy period.

KOB: One of your very early mentors, the political and economic journalist Max Walsh, described *Working Nation* as 'Field of dreams management, a dangerous road paved with good intentions'. He was recognising the irony that Keating the budget cutter, the rationalist reformer, was now Keating the Keynesian spender, Keating the deficit man.

PJK: More than that: Keating with a heart, with a Labor heart. You could never expect the *Financial Review* editor to proselytise with a Labor heart. You can expect them to talk about all sorts of things about economic reform and the budget balance but not the very real social cost of these kinds of changes. Newspapers like the *Financial Review* would always proselytise in favour of economic change and structural adjustment, but not similarly in favour of policies to support the people hurt through the adjustment process, the real people at the end of the queue. We took the view that if we were to inflict those kinds of changes on the economy, and desirably we were, we then had to pick up those people who had taken the butt end of the change.

KOB: I can remember asking at the time you announced the policy how you could guarantee employers wouldn't just cynically let the person go after the subsidy ran out and replace them with a new person and a new subsidy.

PJK: We anticipated that by offering employers a $500 payment to keep the job compact employee on for at least three months after the subsidy had ended and in its first two years it ran very successfully. For 70 per cent of people to stay in the job was hugely successful, a ground-breaking answer to a worldwide problem.

Working Nation was a world first. The Blair Government picked up the essence of it in Britain in 1997 and ran with it. That wouldn't have happened if it had not been seen to have worked. It's a tremendous statement when the country says to people who've been out of work for six to twelve months, 'We are interested in you, and we will assign someone to you who will take a personal interest in your retraining and recommend a job subsidy go with you.'

It remains one of the things I was most proud of and I think it behoves a country to do things of this kind in the circumstances. The *Working Nation* program was one of the first casualties of the first Costello budget. The Howard Government walked away from *Working Nation*, which was a great pity because rarely has a government done anything as kindly or as conscientious as this.

KOB: It was also in May that John Hewson finally toppled from what was left of his leadership pedestal. The rumblings had been building through the year. There was a sense of the inevitable. Alexander Downer was the surprise replacement, but only because Andrew Peacock had worked very hard to keep John Howard out. Were you surprised to see the sudden elevation of Alexander Downer? It was inexplicable to many in the gallery.

PJK: Yes. Although it was obvious that the Coalition had to replace Hewson, I was surprised that they would choose Downer, of all people. I'd always treated him as a figure of fun so when he got the job, I thought I would very quickly get on top of him. I thought, well, the most dangerous guy for me has actually gone, things will get easier.

KOB: Peter Costello had accepted the deputy's job, but probably could have had the leadership if he'd chosen to go for it. Could you understand his judgement?

PJK: No, I couldn't understand it, because I thought he was the person I would most likely face in the end. In a way I felt sorry for Peter Costello on that occasion because I thought he'd either knocked himself out of the ring or he'd been advised not to have a go. He had the chance but he didn't step up to the plate. Perhaps it was symptomatic of what came later when Howard stayed on but Costello wouldn't seize his moment.

KOB: Instead they were marketed as the Dream Team, making a virtue of the team combination rather than Downer standing alone as a strong leader. But even allowing for the fact that he did not have a big public profile or leadership recognition in the polls, public opinion swung very strongly behind him— arguably a message of anyone but Keating.

PJK: I think after you've been on your feet making the kind of changes I'd been making for eleven years, and after the horror budget of the previous year, you had an inkling that they would consider anybody else if they thought they could get away with it. So Downer appeared and straightaway his vote went up and ours went down. It was another comment on the state of the Coalition, by the way, that Hewson only lost by 43 to 36, a matter of only four votes.

KOB: By now it's mid-year. Some of your colleagues and the journalists are starting to speculate that you seem bored. Paul Kelly in *March of Patriots* quotes your foreign policy adviser, Allan Gyngell, as saying:

The longer he went, the more tedious Paul found politics and the more focused he became on policy—whether it was Mabo or APEC, Indonesia or 'super'. The political staffers would get furious because they wanted him at the Dubbo RSL, but Paul's fascination, more and more, became policy ideas.

Would you agree broadly with that?

PJK: Yes, I think that's right. In the end I was only about the changes. It's hard to tell people this today, but the whole point of a public life is public change. It's about the policy shifts. If you allow the tedium of the daily political rituals to overtake you, then the whole impetus for the policy changes begins to wane. If you look at the years I was Prime Minister, from 1991 to 1996, I never lost a moment in terms of the changes. Not a moment. Even coming up to the end, I locked away the big security treaty with President Suharto just before the election. I never lost a moment in policy terms, so the criticism about my prime ministership substantially is that I should have been more political. I used to remind people I did win the fifth election.

KOB: And yet you were such a political animal and you had earlier devoted so much time to getting the politics right. On a trip to Europe in June 1994, Tony Wright wrote in the *Sydney Morning Herald* about the conversation you had with the travelling journalists over drinks at the ambassador's residence in Paris:

At one point Keating was asked about his apparent lack of interest in politics in recent times. He had arranged it so he spent less time in Question Time, and when he was there he sometimes looked distant, peering off into space.

'Oh, that,' said Keating, 'that's my Jack Benny look.'

What was your Jack Benny look?

PJK: Jack Benny had a particular look. He'd be talking with somebody and he'd look away, almost to say, 'Look what I've got here.' That was my look of confected disdain. It wasn't really disdain. I'd like to say I'd sometimes have this look, a bit like a rattlesnake dozing, with an eye on some piece of prey. But I was always ready to strike.

I remember President Mitterrand had an answer to a similar question once which I much admired. A journalist said, 'Monsieur le President, you seem more relaxed these days, less on your game.'

Mitterand said, 'Yes, I'm like a cat, but I still have my claws.'

Well, I was a bit like a cat, and I definitely had my claws.

But the reason I reduced my presence in Question Times was only to do with policy, because Question Time is such a chronic disruption to the daily tasks. If you've got a big reform program running it's just so hard to keep doing the kabuki show.

KOB: By the same token, you were your party's best weapon in that Parliament and you were reducing the capacity of that weapon. You've always talked about the importance of having the psychological edge in the Parliament. Wasn't that an irritation you should have been prepared to bear?

PJK: As it turned out, I think I made the wrong judgement. If I had my time over again, I wouldn't have done that. I shouldn't have given them the free kick, just grinned and borne it, but every time I went into Parliament it was a distraction from the main game. On non-Question Time days, I used to get so much done.

KOB: Tony Wright continued in that piece in the *Herald*: 'Pressed on his alleged boredom, Keating declared, "Look, I'm sick of day-to-day politics, I'm sick of the Opposition, I'm sick of you lot. What I'm about is kicking the big goals." Here he pretended to kick a football. "And the important thing to remember is I don't give up."'

I assume that was an accurate reflection of how you felt, sick of day-to-day politics?

PJK: I'd won the election I was not supposed to win, and some of the advice I was getting was to slow the pace and give more time to the politics. My judgement always was that you had a limited time in public life and that you didn't have a second to lose. These very important changes like *Working Nation*, the republic, the foreign policy initiatives all demanded time through 1994. The idea that I should become a Neville Wran figure living off the front page of the *Daily Telegraph* with a 24-hour spin cycle—I just couldn't do it.

No matter how cleverly I played it, I was up against the odds of winning a sixth election—sixteen straight years of Labor—so the risk was always there. Why compromise my commitment to policy to make token appearances in shopping malls or at vacuous doorstops?

KOB: Don Watson says around this time you also discussed giving it all away with a handful of close confidantes. The Kerry Packer lobbyist, Peter Barron, urged you to do a Wran and leave at the top of your game. Geoff Walsh, who had been Bob Hawke's media adviser and was now on your team, thought you should go, that you'd struggle to win the next election. How close did you come to taking their advice?

PJK: Not at all close, but they did advise that and I took their advice both carefully and kindly. They meant well.

KOB: But hadn't you canvassed their views? Wasn't this playing on your mind?

PJK: No, this just happens in the course of friendships. I think both Peter Barron and Geoff Walsh suggested to me that I should go at the end of November that year. Kim Beazley was Deputy Prime Minister and I don't want to diminish Kim in saying this because he was a very capable minister, but there was nobody in Labor at that time with quite the fighting spirit or the arraignment of power against the Coalition that I had. So without wanting to sound like Bob, saying that he's the only one who could win an election ever, I still thought I was a better chance of winning in 1996 than anyone else.

KOB: Very few political leaders in this country over more than a century have chosen the timing of their own departure. Menzies was one of a tiny handful. Did wanting to choose your own timing rather than having it decided for you feature in your thinking at all?

PJK: I don't think it matters. What matters is what you do with the time given to you. You've got to be a fighting unit to the end. That's my belief.

KOB: It was through this period that Bob Hawke released his autobiography—in August 1994—and he didn't really try to hide his feelings towards you, did he? Did that get through your defences?

PJK: No, but it did damage and the party disowned him as a consequence. It was a dreadful, sleazy attack on me. He showed no judgement, no decency and no loyalty to the party. And every bit of jealousy that Bob ever held, and there was much of that, he blurted out in that poorly written book.

KOB: You don't think he would have felt he didn't owe you loyalty anymore, that you'd knocked him over?

PJK: I had covered for Bob for six years. Who does that for any Prime Minister? Tony Wright covered Bob's book launch in the *Herald* on 17 August and quoted Hawke saying that I was in poor physical and mental condition and buckled under pressure. On the top of the newspaper on the day in question, which is now in the National Archive, I wrote, 'The truth is that from the moment Hawke learned that Rosslyn had been injecting herself with drugs, he mentally collapsed. He went politically comatose. It was the same semi-comatose state that led him to commit us to an ill-conceived tax summit on a radio station in Perth during the 1984 election campaign. I carried him on my back for years; Hogg and Garnaut *et al.* simply smothered for him.'

Now, that's very uncomplimentary to Bob, but it's completely true.

KOB: In his book he was critical of your response when he asked your advice on whether Australia should contribute to the coalition America was putting together for the first Gulf War after Iraq invaded Kuwait in early 1991. He said you responded, 'What's America ever done for us?'

PJK: As I said a day or two later in 1994, this was a complete lie, and it's easy to illustrate why. There are two contradictory accounts on the public record as to what I was supposed to have said at that meeting, both of which could be attributed to Bob, and both wrong.

The first account was written in the *Sydney Morning Herald* a little while after the meeting saying that I had supported immediate and strong action against Saddam Hussein. That was wrong, but it was a leak that must have come from Hawke's office, and it subsequently came back to me that he had told people on the Left of the party that I was a warmonger. I was all about supporting the UN and going after Saddam Hussein.

Three years later in his book he had a completely different account of the same meeting in early 1991. That I didn't support the United

States, that I queried what America had ever done for us, and that John Button and I had to be dragged to the decision to make a commitment to America. Button shot that down when he volunteered that it was he who had asked what America had ever done for Australia, not me.

What actually happened was this: I was Deputy Prime Minister by then and Bob called me to a meeting about the flashpoint in the Middle East. Michael Duffy was there as acting Foreign Minister and I think Hugh White was there as Bob's defence adviser.

Bob as usual was slumped behind his desk and said in those sort of half-finished sentences that characterised his conversations: 'Paul, we might get a call from the President overnight, and we probably have to make a decision about whether we will participate in this military exercise in Iraq.'

I said, 'Well, this is my view: I don't really believe in supranational bodies like the UN, where sovereignty is passed across to an international body. It rarely works, and the vetoes in the Security Council of the United Nations have more or less rendered it impotent on the big issues.'

I said, 'If you were really brutal about the UN you would say it's a lemon. But the Cold War has just finished and here is Saddam Hussein marching across borders into Kuwait, a smaller state, and the United Nations for the first time in the postwar years without the Soviet veto, is putting its hand up to say, "Let's organise a force and let's deal with this incursion." If the United States under the leadership of George Herbert Bush is prepared to lead a coalition of forces which carry a mandate from the United Nations, I can't see why we wouldn't support them.'

He said, 'So you would support them, is that what you're saying?'

I said, 'Yes, Bob, I would support them, but let me ask you some questions—what about your mate, Mulroney in Canada, where is he?'

'Oh well,' he said, 'I had a conversation with Mulroney and he's thinking about it.'

I said, 'What about John Major?'

He said, 'Oh, I think he's in the same boat.'

I said, 'So the natural allies, the larger countries, they're not going to do much, right? What I think we should do is to say we'll support the United States and the Coalition, but if we get in early and quickly our entry price will be low. They'll want the moral support rather than the material support or the equipment.'

So I said, 'I understand from the briefing we've got a frigate in Aden and a tanker in the Middle East somewhere. Why don't we put the tanker and the frigate up the top of the Gulf and call it quits?'

Bob then asked whether I thought we should commit planes.

I said, 'No, Bob, no planes. I've told you what I think the terms should be: two ships up the top of the Gulf. We put our hand up early, no troops, no planes.'

That is an accurate recount of what I said at the Gulf War meeting with Hawke. I wrote on the *Sydney Morning Herald* story when it came out: 'This story was leaked from Hawke's office'. Hawke then called a second, wider meeting, and it was at that meeting that John Button asked what America had done for us.

When the full bitchiness of the book became evident, even Bob's erstwhile supporters in the party rounded on him. Here are some of the published comments. Howe said, 'Frankly in the 1990s he's not there; Paul Keating is there.' Bob Collins commented that autobiographies were a personal arrogance. Barry Jones said there's a feeling of disappointment and regret. The headline in the *Age*: 'The ALP rounds on Hawke'.

Then Creighton Burns in the *Age* writes a piece called 'Hawke's bitter fruit', and the *Telegraph Mirror* in Sydney on 16 August has a front-page headline with pictures of Jones, Richardson, Bob McMullan, Howe, Collins and Con Sciacca saying, 'Hawke cast adrift, deserted by old allies.'

So he did himself enormous harm by showing not a shred of loyalty to the party that had given him the prime ministership.

KOB: Distracting though that might have been, you had bigger problems looming on the economic front. Growth was galloping now; in fact, growth for the September quarter pushed the annual rate to 6.4 per cent, the highest growth since 1985. That should have been great news but it carried implications for inflation. Bernie Fraser put interest rates up in August, October and December of 1994 by a total of 2.75 percentage points, all of which you were forced to defend. It was the first rise in rates since the height of the recession, and must have brought back bad memories for a lot of people.

PJK: There were two things about that. I was central to the development of an independent Reserve Bank, and both Bernie Fraser and I did not want to see inflationary expectations rise again. So it was right for the newly independent Governor of the Reserve Bank to put his hand up to say, 'Sorry, but we've got to put a ceiling on inflation. We can't let the genie out of the bottle again after ten years of pain and effort.'

I could have squeezed Bernie, rung him and argued the case to minimise our political pain, but in the end I wanted to break inflationary expectations, as did he, and while it was absolutely bad for me, it was completely right for the country.

I was prepared to live with that decision, but it was the Keating economic policy that had broken the back of inflation along with the Reserve Bank—the Accord, the tax cuts in lieu of wage increases, the high interest rates through 1988–89, which I encouraged and had to bear and took responsibility for. More than any other public figure, in partnership with Bill Kelty, I had the breaking of inflation notched on to my belt. I was happy to join Bernie Fraser in nailing inflationary expectations.

KOB: But didn't you have a meeting with Bernie Fraser at the Lodge where you argued for less than the 1 per cent rise he intended in August, which persuaded him to ease that first increase back to 0.75 percentage points?

PJK: One per cent was a big hit. Bernie accepted the argument for moderating that first rise slightly. I couldn't have forced that decision on him but I did have the right to make the argument.

KOB: You must still have winced when it happened.

PJK: Those three rises hurt me because John Howard seized on them to talk about five minutes of economic sunlight when he replaced Alexander Downer as Coalition leader in 1995. But what really cost me in the end was that Bernie and the Reserve Bank didn't lower the rates before the 1996 election. By then it was clear that short-term influences on the CPI had gone, and that underlying inflation remained modest with wage claims well and truly in check, so the right thing to have done in economic terms—never mind the politics—would have been to start cutting the rate in 1995.

Kelty and I smashed inflation. I had the Reserve Bank put the rates up and I took responsibility for the recession. That's what broke inflation. By the end of 1995, the Keating Government had earned the right to see interest rates coming down. Certainly, in early 1996. But Bernie and the bank thought it would be 'political' to touch them before the poll. As a consequence, the bank left the rates untouched through the 1996 election, giving no indication as to their direction.

The 'reward' of lower rates was delivered by the bank, to of all people, Peter Costello on 1 August 1996. Imagine Costello or the Liberal Party being able to break Australian inflation. They could barely spell it, much less understand it. Yet the Reserve Bank put the low interest rate crown on Peter Costello's head twenty weeks after he took the job. Institutions like the Reserve Bank and the Treasury treat their masters with a mix of inappreciation and indifference, including those who have done things beyond their wildest dreams.

The end result of that sustained effort over the life of the Hawke and Keating Governments, Kerry, is 24 years of low inflationary growth. That represents a big lift to the Australian economy over a very long period of time. In 1994 we did crack the inflationary expectation nut. We might have used a sledgehammer to crack the nut, and I fear that Bernie might have cracked my nut too.

KOB: He has said since 'The notion that it betrayed Keating is one that I found hurtful. Paul has had no more staunch defender than me.' All three interest rate increases were supported by the government.

PJK: Bernie Fraser had a very positive view about the Accord and the government I led and served as Treasurer and he was an extremely conscientious public servant. There's no doubt about that, but I believe he was too slow bringing the rates down in 1990 and the same in 1995.

CREATIVE NATION

It took Alexander Downer fewer than three months of very ordinary leadership to squander his substantial lead over Paul Keating in the polls. In August 1994, after one of the briefest political honeymoons in Australian history, particularly after an error-strewn trip through the Northern Territory's Indigenous communities, Downer's approval rating slumped seventeen points. For the first time Paul Keating moved ahead of him as preferred Prime Minister.

Downer's stocks sank even lower a few weeks later when he suggested that the recently released party policy on domestic violence—under the banner of a broader policy manifesto called the 'Things That Matter'— could alternatively be called the 'Things That Batter'. He managed to send up his own party policy—never a good idea if you want to be taken seriously as a fledgling leader—and outraged everyone in the country who cared about domestic violence. The leader of the Dream Team had become the Liberal Party's worst nightmare.

At that point Keating could be forgiven for feeling pretty good about his position. Not only had he won the unwinnable election, he'd now seen John Hewson off, and must have been looking on Alexander Downer as an unexpected gift from the Gods.

It was in this climate that Keating added the arts to his policy ambitions. Given the number of pies he had his finger in as Treasurer it was hardly surprising that he would be an interventionist Prime Minister across the policy spectrum, and almost nowhere was he more opinionated or more passionate than on the arts. In putting *Creative Nation* together with his Arts Minister, Michael Lee, a process that had begun early in the year with Lee's predecessor Bob McMullan, he again sought to prod Australians to reflect on the kind of country Australia was or should aspire to be.

'It is very much an attempt,' Keating said, launching the document on 30 October 1994, 'to lay the foundations of a new era, to pull the threads of our national life together to ride the waves of global change and create our own. I hope this will be the day we said goodbye to our postcolonial era, to the dark days of our cultural cringe.'

As well as a $250 million boost to funding for cultural institutions, the report also linked the policy to economic goals. It defined culture as 'that which gives us a sense of ourselves' and sought to break down some of the elitism attached to the traditional arts, stressing its commitment to funding projects reflecting cultural diversity. It argued that culture created wealth, employed 336,000 Australians, generated $13 billion a year and made an essential contribution to innovation, marketing and design. One-third of the $250 million went to support information and multimedia entertainment services. This was the first government recognition of the information superhighway—the internet age.

The seeds for the digital and multimedia aspects of the arts package were sown in February that year in conversation with Bill Gates and Microsoft's Australian director of advanced technology, Daniel Petre. Microsoft was then the unchallenged giant of the digital age. Petre subsequently told Mike Gordon for the *Weekend Australian* that Gates had remarked to Petre as they walked away from the meeting that Keating was one of the smartest leaders he had met, 'and Bill meets them all and he doesn't give compliments lightly'. Keating apparently had impressed them both with his 'big vision' and conviction that the new multimedia could serve two goals if handled properly: 'It could place Australia at the leading edge of the information revolution, and protect and promote the nation's cultural identity.' Hence Keating's determination to marry the artistic with the economic.

Creative Nation had Keating's fingerprints all over it. As Treasurer he had been inspired to create generous creative fellowships to support talented mid-career artists, writers and performers who were struggling to fund their own work, after discovering the brilliant pianist Geoffrey Tozer supported himself on $9000 a year as a piano teacher. Tozer was one of the first recipients.

As Prime Minister he was no different. On 8 October Anne Davies wrote in the *Sydney Morning Herald* that Keating had set the cat among the pigeons at a Sydney Symphony Orchestra concert when he remarked that Australia's orchestras would be forever trapped in mediocrity while ever they were run by the ABC. Released from those bonds, they might have a chance to become world class. Eighteen days later that's exactly what happened, as part of *Creative Nation*. The Sydney Symphony Orchestra was untethered from the ABC and given $7 million in new funding to increase the number of players to the international standard of 110, increase salaries, provide more for world-renowned guests and allow for more touring and recording activities.

If this was a political document, as some inevitably claimed, its merit in that regard was dubious because the post-1996 critics in his own party argued that his 'obsession' with policies such as Mabo, the republic and the arts delivered few votes and may have even lost some, while diverting Keating from issues far closer to the hip pocket of the electorate rather than appealing to the heart or the imagination. But to this day Keating continues to argue it is the job of the leader to paint the nation on a big canvas, with all the parts coming together to tell a complete story.

He told me on *Lateline* on the night he released *Creative Nation* that 'these are strands of our national life that one looks at, whether it is fidelity to the unemployed, whether it is a focus on our creativity and our culture, whether it is on the truth of Mabo, whether it is on the shift to Asia with APEC, it's plaiting the strands into a whole. So, I see this as an important strand in the rope of Australia'.

But the *Sydney Morning Herald*'s front page the next day reflected the two sides of Keating's political coin at that point: the main headline read 'Keating's $252 million big picture', and immediately below, 'Spending surge signals 1% interest rate rise'.

The vision, and the reality.

Paul Kelly subsequently wrote in *March of Patriots* that 'Keating's dilemma can be precisely stated—he wanted his prime ministership to be defined by a transformed national identity but this quest lacked grass-roots electoral backing. He was unable to resolve this conundrum.'

KOB: Michael Lee was the Minister for Communication and the Arts when *Creative Nation* was launched, but how much of that document came from you?

PJK: Well, a large part of it was me because I always believed the arts were central to a society like ours and that a good society is able to look at itself in the mirror, know what it is and who it is. I think the arts provide this kind of reflection and, more than that, the fantasy of creativity and imagination. These acts are purely creative and not derivative.

You can say science is a derived art, in that we are adding to an existing bank of knowledge by further exploration. But a Mahler symphony never existed before Mahler created it. It began and ended with Mahler. It's purely an artistic creation, purely an act of creativity. So the creativity of the arts and also the performance within the arts, where we try to get near the sublime, were things I always thought the country needed and was entitled to.

I could also see the digital economy coming. And even though the internet was not a name that existed in the *Macquarie Dictionary* at that time, you could see the facilitation of digital technology and microprocessing. These were the two things that drove *Creative Nation*, and in Michael Lee I had a good and willing minister.

KOB: The website the *Conversation* wrote in a feature on *Creative Nation*'s twentieth anniversary last year that it was 'the first Commonwealth cultural policy document in Australia's history'. What does that say about how we, as a nation, up to that point, valued our arts and culture? I know Gough had had a crack at it, and Gorton too, but what does that say, if this was the first broad cultural policy document in our history?

PJK: It says there's something wrong with us, that's what it says. You need to have emotional experiences with the arts to engender the kind of commitment I had to them. But once you have it, once you put your foot on the gold seam, it pulls you along with such fantasy and reward that you want to share it with the country. These are not pleasures or secrets one should keep, but rather disseminate. And it didn't matter for me what it was.

I remember being invited to a dance performance for Graeme Murphy's fortieth birthday at the Sydney Dance Company. He had choreographed a ballet to the music of Shimanovsky. It was phenomenal: the mind-boggling cleverness of the choreography, not just the quality of the dancing.

I asked Graeme if the event was recorded and he said no.

I said, 'That is really tragic.'

So I rang Nick Shehadie, the SBS Chairman, because you couldn't get the ABC to do anything quickly, and I said, 'Nick, I want you to do me a bit of a favour.'

He said, 'What's that, PM?'

I explained what would be lost to the arts if the ballet went unrecorded and said, 'I wonder whether you guys could take two or three cameras down and record it for posterity.'

He called me back a few days later and said it could be done but not within the existing SBS budget.

I said, 'What are the staff estimating it might cost?'

He said, 'About $30,000.'

So I said to Don Russell, send SBS the $30,000 and we'll have this recorded, and it was. This is the fascination with the sublime, or getting close to it, that only the arts really deliver. And I always wanted the whole country to have the chance to experience those feelings.

KOB: John Howard said in his memoir that, 'To be a successful political leader you've got to identify with a certain strand or current in Australian life.'

He could never work out which strand to identify you with. He was talking about the kind of cultural nerve that political leaders tap into. Hawke loved his horse-racing, for instance. Howard loved his cricket. You seemed to have absolutely no passion for sport. Do you think any of that really mattered?

PJK: I don't think it mattered, no. I actually had some passion for sport but it was not particularly publicised. I wasn't engaged by rugby or rugby league although I had some interest in Australian rules. I used to sit through all the main heavyweight boxing title matches and always watched Wimbledon from beginning to end.

As a young man I was a competitive swimmer in the shallow end of the Olympic hopefuls, let me put it that way, so I always had a natural interest in sport. But Patrick White struck a chord with me when he said that sport had addled the Australian consciousness. I felt there was a real risk that sport was addling the consciousness at the expense of other things of real value in our culture. I found myself gravitating to the spiritual uplift of things like music, dance and theatre and writing, areas of Australia that I thought were too often forgotten, certainly not preferred by government. And I tried to lift those things up rather than being simply another cricket tragic or another rugby league tragic.

I wanted to do and say some important things about the arts, particularly in the context of the coming digital age, and I offered, I think, $250 million of extra funding. For the arts that was a lot of money for the major companies who operated on very tight budgets, maybe the equivalent today of $500 to $600 million.

KOB: Don Watson describes how, right on the deadline to finish the *Creative Nation* statement, it was sent to you at the Lodge late at night. This is the old fax machine again, I guess.

Watson wrote: 'At 1.30 in the morning he phoned me back and read out to me a long section on the new media, which he had just written. "With the information highway," it said, "we have crossed the technological Rubicon."'

Watson wrote, 'No one in any office or department could've written the section better.'

Can you remember that?

PJK: Yes, I can vaguely remember it because I wrote a lot of these statements myself and with Watson. At that stage, Kerry, the internet was in its infancy but people were just starting to find their way gingerly around it and this was a revolutionary development in the digital age. So a large part of the *Creative Nation* spending was actually targeted to steer the artistic institutions in the direction of those digital formats. Seems trite to say today. We tried to encourage by particular funding initiatives, particular companies to do particular things.

These days the internet is simply part of life, like the oxygen we breathe. I thought then we could reach a point where the digital technology would underwrite a new creativity, and if we were early and quick about it, we would be in there at the beginning. That's what encouraged me into it. If you look at George Miller's film *Happy Feet* or no doubt at his current production, *Fury Road*, all this microprocessing expands the horizons of all creativity.

Creative Nation had two strands. One was a focus on new prospects in the digital age. The other was financial support for and refurbishment of the traditional artistic institutions.

One of the things I personally did was to take the Sydney Symphony Orchestra out of the ABC. Australia, like a lot of countries, had radio orchestras in each of the states, but in Australia they'd become the happy hunting ground of the ABC musicians' club. It meant a kind of equalisation of standards had developed across the country, whereas what we needed to do was reach up and produce an international standard that the old model wouldn't allow.

The end result is that we've since seen the Sydney Symphony Orchestra develop to a point where it's as good as any orchestra in the world. Not long after, it was followed by Melbourne. It was achieved with a funding boost of about 25 per cent. Without that kind of initiative from the government with direct patronage from the Prime Minister I don't think these things would have happened.

KOB: A bit Medici-like, don't you think? The sort of old-style patronage of the arts like Renaissance Florence, but on a national landscape. Was that good policy for the nation or personal indulgence?

PJK: This is a country that will never be able to fully support a flourishing arts community on a purely commercial model. We just don't have the scale, the critical mass. The state of the arts in a country goes to the heart of what a nation is. There's a great talent bank out there but only a small percentage will rise to the top without well-funded support from government, and you would never know what we'd deprive ourselves of as a nation in the process.

KOB: Can I get a sense of how much influence you had on arts policy through all those Labor years, even when you were Treasurer? Were you always a part of that discussion?

PJK: I was always a part of that discussion and I'd always kick it along. Donald McDonald came to me a couple of times wearing his Opera Australia hat before he went to the ABC, and he said, 'Treasurer, the Australian Opera is still losing money on the orchestra, which is in Melbourne. We've cut back and cut back, and we're still losing.'

Here was an arts administrator, trying to do the right thing, trying to give the country a lift in the productions of the Australian opera. And yet the accounting imperative is on him, trying to make the numbers work with the costs of the orchestra for the whole thing for the year.

I said to him one year, 'OK, Donald, give me the bad news, what do you need?' I think he said $250,000. So I just gave him the $250,000.

The same happened with Graeme Murphy and the Sydney Dance Company. One year he was about $130,000 short; I gave him the $130,000. Why wouldn't you?

KOB: The way you describe it, doling out a bit here to record Graeme Murphy's dance and a bit there to Donald McDonald to top up the opera, sounds like you personally were making very subjective judgements on behalf of the government and the public.

PJK: There was some subjectivity about it, but in my own defence, although I preferred going to performances of the symphony orchestras than to the opera, I would listen just as intently to a plea from the Australian Opera as I would the Sydney Symphony Orchestra. I would do the same if we were talking about one of the smaller companies or one of the dance or artistic companies. But why wouldn't I? The money was critical to the companies; it was never wasted. They had no chance of getting big financial sponsorship like the sports codes—in a pinch, they only had the Commonwealth to help them.

Then there were the Australian Artists Creative Fellowships, which I set up in the 1988 Budget to reward and give economic support to artists of accomplishment in mid-career, people who really had enormous ability but had peaked in their artistic attainments and yet couldn't commercialise them. Were we to just lose them, or try to hang on to them?

Frank Moorhouse wrote his trilogy on the League of Nations, the first of which was *Grand Days*, from the first awarded grants. That trilogy could never have been written without the creative fellowships. Garth Welch, the dancer, had one. There were all manner of people like my friend Geoffrey Tozer, who was the greatest pianist Australia had ever produced.

Some were for three years and some for five years, at around $75,000 a year. They were designed so the recipients could concentrate full time on their creative effort and didn't have to run around doing other work. These were highly gifted artists who, through no lack of effort on their part, might not be able to live on their artistic earnings.

KOB: What of the criticism that with *Creative Nation* you were paying the arts community back for support at the 1993 election?

PJK: That was low-rent political comment. I would have done *Creative Nation* even if they had barracked for John Hewson, but even the arts had to draw the line somewhere.

KOB: When your friend Geoffrey Tozer won his second Keating award, as the Creative Fellowships had become known, that attracted criticism. Did you have a hand in his selection for that award or, for that matter, the first one?

PJK: The inspiration for the Australian Artist Creative Fellowships came from Geoffrey's poverty. I thought it was a national shame that a genius who was playing with Sir Colin Davis and the London Symphony Orchestra in the Albert Hall in London at fifteen years of age and winning awards across Europe would return to Australia and end up teaching kids at my son's high school for $9000 a year to pay the rent—and have to get there on a pushbike.

Because he was the inspiration for the awards I encouraged him to put an application into the Australia Council. The second time around Geoffrey had to take his chances. He put his application in and the panel awarded him again.

KOB: He was in the end a tragic figure, not the first musical prodigy to be so, not particularly worldly. Were you drawn to that sense of vulnerability in him, because you helped him in all kinds of ways at a personal level as well?

PJK: Not really. I was simply drawn to the magic of the playing. He was in a class of his own. I first heard him play at my son's high school concert. Geoffrey carried too much weight and he walked onto the stage with a bad gait, looking like a blob in an ill-fitting suit, and I thought 'Who is this guy', and then he just exploded. I was completely hooked on the magic of his playing. This is someone playing like Gilels, one of the great twentieth-century pianists.

I thought, never in my lifetime would I ever have the pleasure of such proximity to such greatness.

On one occasion when I was in London as Treasurer, I rang a man named Brian Couzens, Managing Director of Chandos Records, which was the greatest recording company in Europe at the time, and he agreed to see me. His office was at Colchester to the west of London.

When we sat down he said, 'Why on earth would the Treasurer of Australia want to see me?'

I said, 'Because I want to tell you about an Australian pianist who I think plays like someone in the late nineteenth or early twentieth century, like Gilels, or Busoni, or people of that ilk.'

I gave Couzens two tapes of Geoffrey's work but he wasn't interested because he said he'd had doctored tapes from artists in the past to try to get through the door. But he agreed to see Tozer if he came to England.

I said to Couzens, 'In the period of his two fellowships, Geoffrey has worked up three very important works. They are the three piano concertos of Nikolai Medtner, never recorded before.' Medtner was Rachmaninoff's master, and the music is so complex very few people can play it.

He said, 'No one can play Medtner.'

I said, 'Well, he'll play it and he'll play it for you, and what I'd like you to do is to record the three.'

He said, 'Well, that's a very big cost to us, he'd have to be really unbelievably good to do it.'

So I went back to the embassy and paid for the cost of the hire car because I didn't want anyone saying I was indulging myself at the Commonwealth's expense. I then personally paid Geoffrey's fare to London and went through some repertoire with him.

Couzens subsequently sent me a note saying, 'He is absolutely fantastic. It's like music from another age. But more than that,' he said, 'he gets the orchestra ready, and by the time the conductor arrives there's no work left for him to do. Tozer has already taken them through the music.'

He said, 'This man can do anything. If he's playing Purcell, he plays like an Englishman. If he's playing Medtner he sounds like a Russian. If he's doing Liszt, he sounds like a Hungarian.'

In the end Geoffrey did 33 recordings with Chandos, and the first one, the three piano concertos of Nikolai Medtner, won the French Gold Prize, the Diapason d'Or, and missed winning the American Classic Grammys by one place to Yo-Yo Ma. That was the first time round. He was phenomenal.

KOB: You helped him renovate his house, didn't you, or helped him paint it?

PJK: I encouraged him to buy the old convent in Queanbeyan, which was a very large building on the hill, because the Catholic Church always had the best locations. It was large; not derelict, but empty. I suggested he make one wing a music studio and a mini concert hall, live there himself, have artists in residence and make it a music centre.

I said, 'You would always find work in Canberra as the best pianist in the country, and you would have your own place.'

The last thing I did on the day before I became Prime Minister was rollerpaint Geoffrey's bedroom. Mark Ryan and I were there in overalls on ladders and planks, painting Geoffrey's bedroom.

The next morning in the shower I had to remove the dried paint off my face to front up to the caucus. So it was all ready for him to move in. But then his manager, Reuben Fineberg, talked him into selling it. Fineberg convinced Geoffrey he wouldn't be able to rely on the fellowships to continue to pay the mortgage.

I said, 'Look, Geoffrey, this is nonsense because you still have something like another $150,000 of fellowship money, so you'd wind up with a mortgage of virtually nothing.'

He said, 'Oh, we've already exchanged contracts.'

So he went ahead with the sale, which was a great pity because he would have lived a more anchored existence there, and I don't believe he would have got into the social trouble he got into in Melbourne later, being left alone after his mother died and after Reuben died.

Geoffrey himself died in a very sad way. He'd had hepatitis earlier in his life, which affected him when he drank, and his health deteriorated rapidly. In the end he lived and played in some sort of squalor in a rented house in Melbourne.

KOB: When he died in 2009 still a relatively young man, you were a pallbearer at his funeral and you didn't hold back in the eulogy. Stuart Rintoul wrote in the *Australian* that you let loose the reins on your anger, lacerating the nation's musical establishment for treating Tozer with indifference, contempt and malevolence.

PJK: I think those were Rintoul's words. I didn't say contempt and malevolence, but he was reflecting my anger. What happened was that the Sydney Symphony Orchestra and the Melbourne Symphony Orchestra failed to give Geoffrey any work in the last decade of his life.

KOB: Why do you think that was?

PJK: Because they felt we have the local genius under our nose so we're obliged to take him, are we? Whereas what used to happen in these orchestras is that they'd pick up a great violinist or a great tenor from Europe, and the agency would say, 'You can have this cellist or this violinist but we also want you to take so and so pianist to play a particular thing.'

I don't know whether you'd call it snobbery on the part of the program managers of these orchestras to take Europeans over Australians, but there was no pianist in the world playing in a higher form than Geoffrey.

One of their complaints was that he would improvise, a bit like Liszt did. Liszt was a great improviser. I remember Geoffrey doing one of the big Liszt works, the *Mephisto Waltz*, I think it was, which is a huge piece. There's a lilt at the end and you could just hear 'Once a jolly swagman camped by a billabong'. It just drifted in for a second and then drifted out again, and everyone laughed. But that was frowned upon. He had this huge Chopin-like ability and they'd say, 'too clever, too clever!'

KOB: You said Tozer deserved to be remembered alongside Nellie Melba, Percy Grainger and Joan Sutherland, but for the last fifteen years of his life he was left to moulder away, largely playing to himself in a rented suburban Melbourne house.

PJK: Yes, that's the thing. I said in the speech, we all thought he had enough resources to sort of hang on, but it turned out he didn't. So he's one of the tragic losses of my lifetime. I have his picture here in the office.

I always thought it was an indication of our relative cultural poverty that we don't put a premium on true greatness in the arts. If Tozer had been a soccer star, he'd have been getting millions of dollars a year and being acclaimed in every newspaper every other week. Here was someone of world standing living in poverty at the gate of the national capital, and the nation was oblivious to his prodigious talent and energy.

KEATING VS HOWARD

John Howard records in his autobiography that when Alexander Downer and Peter Costello were elected to the Liberal leadership midway through 1994 he felt a completely new era had arrived, and for him, it had an air of finality about it. He says he wrote in his diary at the time: 'On Friday 20 May 1994 I was given my last chance ever to reclaim the leadership of the Liberal Party and again seek the prime ministership of my country.' Interesting insight into the uncertainties and surprises of politics from a man who went on to serve as PM for twelve years.

How quickly things can change in politics, not unlike the dynamics of a cricket test. Within three months, as Downer began sinking into the mire of his own ineptitude, Howard was starting to take calls, and began to hope again, particularly when his *bête noir*, Andrew Peacock, announced his retirement from politics in September, breaking the cycle of their enmity. By October, Howard now says, there was a strongly held view in the Liberal Party that if Downer hadn't noticeably recovered by Christmas, Howard would be drafted to replace him. In December, Howard was made aware of internal party research that suggested the Opposition could lose 30 seats under Downer.

The dilemma Downer presented to Paul Keating was exquisite. As 1995, the final year of the electoral cycle, approached and Downer's position worsened, what was Keating to do? Even with three big interest rate hikes to help him, Downer was simply not skilled enough to recover from his lapses. Keating could either coddle Downer and try to keep him there—a pretty unlikely option in the bearpit of Australian politics—or he could help see him off as quickly as possible and hope he had enough time to do it all again, probably with Howard, before the next election.

The other proposition, running to an early election against Downer after less than two years, was never seriously considered by Keating, not least because of the risk that the Liberals might do what Labor had done in 1983, and change leaders as an election campaign began. It had certainly worked for Hawke.

Howard also revealed in his book that Tony Abbott, one of his close supporters who had arrived in Parliament via a by-election earlier in the year, was pressing him to undo the damage done to him by his own remarks back in 1988 urging caution on Asian immigration. Abbott arranged an interview for Howard with his friend Greg Sheridan for the *Australian*, which duly ran in January 1995 with the headline 'I was wrong on Asians, says Howard'.

While Downer wallowed and Howard built his support backstage, Keating continued his journey of ups and downs—garnering what credit he could for what was a major foreign policy triumph at the second APEC Leaders' Summit in Bogor, Indonesia, working closely with President Suharto to cajole the powerful and the paranoid around the table into signing a free trade manifesto for the region— but then returning to another round of interest rate hikes from the Reserve Bank.

Two of his ministers, David Beddall in Resources and John Faulkner in Environment, were in dispute over the future of wood-chip and logging licences. Beddall, a junior minister and a right-wing factional hack who didn't bring much political skill to the table, wanted to issue more licences to log in old-growth forests. Faulkner, who was in Cabinet, was intractably opposed.

Keating tried and failed to resolve the deadlock before Christmas with the Greens, whose preferences would be vital at the next election, growling at the edges. So as the negative woodchip headlines continued to build for Keating and the loggers threatened mayhem, Howard quietly stitched up a leadership transition deal with Alexander Downer.

On Australia Day 1995, Australians woke up to 'Howard's day of triumph'. Lazarus was back, and Keating had a year to claim his third and toughest Liberal scalp within one parliamentary term. One of Keating's worst memories in a very long career would have been to look on helplessly as Howard made his way through a blockade of logging trucks to get into Parliament House. Howard didn't have to say much to exploit the sense of a government in chaos.

The Howard honeymoon was further assisted by the kind of Jekyll and Hyde economy that had developed. The magic combination of healthy growth, projected at 5.5 per cent, and low inflation continued but Keating had to suffer headlines through the weeks leading up to the May budget such as 'Willis sounds the alarm—Fears of BoP blow-out force fiscal tightening' in the *Financial Review*. It was based on revised budget forecasts showing the current account deficit jumping by $8 billion to $26 billion for the year and expectations of spending cuts and tax increases in the budget grew—all grist for Howard's mill, which he skilfully exploited in his first week in Parliament.

On 14 February, a *Herald*-McNair poll gave the Liberals a 47 per cent primary vote to Labor's 37 per cent—a potential Howard landslide. It was the same pattern as happened early in Downer's leadership, but John Howard was far less likely to squander it.

It was in this period that Keating chose to take on Kerry Packer very publicly after the media giant's attempt to thwart the cross-media rules and buy control of the Fairfax newspaper group. Keating accused Packer and Howard of stitching up a 'wink and a nod' deal in which a Howard Government would dump the cross-media rules in return for Packer's support.

At the same time Keating had become convinced that John Alexander, the editor of the *Herald*, a Fairfax paper, and subsequently hired by Packer, was also running a hostile campaign against him. He wrote across one *Herald* front page on the fight with Packer, 'Only a fool would think Howard hasn't come to terms with Packer. Barron told me he has. But Alexander is Packer's man at the *Herald*'. Keating collected a long run of *Herald* headlines that were critical of the government, many of which he argued were inaccurate and unjustifiable. It was another distraction the government didn't need.

In late March there was a further gift to Howard, this one from Keating himself. He allowed Ros Kelly, having lost her ministry in the 'sports rorts' scandal, to resign from Parliament, triggering a by-election for her normally safe Labor seat in Canberra. It was a debacle. On the same weekend that voters in New South Wales rejected the Liberal Government and narrowly embraced a new Labor Government led by Bob Carr, voters in Canberra dumped massively on federal Labor in an 18 per cent swing, bigger even than the disastrous rejection for Labor in the Bass by-election of 1975, which had signalled the beginning of the end for the Whitlam Government.

One fringe benefit for Howard in coming to the leadership in the final year of the electoral cycle was that his mere presence as a new and more credible leader than his two predecessors guaranteed that virtually everything Keating did that year would be seen through the political prism, therefore with heightened cynicism, certainly by the media.

That was true for the May Budget. Keating's budget announcement that the rest of the Commonwealth Bank would be sold, netting $3 billion, was reported as a ploy to allow the Treasurer, Ralph Willis, to boast a small surplus for the next financial year, and 'a surplus run not seen since the 1980s'. The budget ultimately delivered the Howard Government a $10 billion deficit, and Peter Costello would later claim credit for the long run of surpluses.

The politically tricky part in this budget for Keating was that he backed away again from the second tranche of the tax cut he'd originally promised in 1992–93, converting it instead to a 3 per cent government contribution to workers' superannuation, which would be delivered in full by 2001–02. That would have sounded a long way off in May 1995, with as many as two elections in between, but it attracted largely positive headlines, although the *Sydney Morning Herald*'s 'Keating abandons tax cuts' wouldn't have helped.

Nicholson in the *Australian* depicted Keating behind the wheel of a large American convertible in a workshop. Ralph Willis, as the mechanic, had the engine out, and sitting on Keating's lap was the voter depicted as a young woman. With his arm around her Keating is saying, 'Ralph's working on a long-term project and I'm working on a short-term project.' That was about as easy as it got through 1995.

As the budget was about to be presented, the Court Liberal Government in Western Australia announced the terms of reference for a Royal Commission to scrutinise Carmen Lawrence's role as Premier in the tabling of a petition in the State Parliament that was subsequently seen to contribute to the suicide of a woman named Penny Easton. Like many other royal commissions, this one had political overtones.

Lawrence by now was one of Keating's most senior and high-profile ministers running the Health portfolio, and Keating decided from the outset that he would defend her to the hilt. He vigorously pursued the Commission through the Parliament as only Keating could, no doubt damaging it in the process, but that too became a big distraction for him and took much of the oxygen away from his primary battle, which was to gain the upper hand over Howard.

Howard was very consciously a policy-free zone throughout the year in stark contrast to John Hewson and his cherished *Fightback!*. Instead he gave a series of what he called headland speeches to sketch outlines of his policy directions with not much detail. When Keating tried to goad him into releasing his policies, Howard simply said he wouldn't capitulate to psychological warfare. His shadow cabinet endorsed his determination not to release policy detail until the election campaign. A Tanberg cartoon showed reporters saying to Howard at a doorstop, 'You're not telling us anything,' and Howard replying, 'That's the policy.'

Keating continued to have occasional policy wins, such as his breakthrough agreement with the states on competition policy in which the states would garner billions for delivering a breakup of various public monopolies and promote greater efficiencies and drive productivity—but this was hardly a sexy issue for rank-and-file voters around the country.

In June, Keating released his blueprint for a republic with a referendum before the turn of the century, with a simple line, 'We are all Australians. We share a past, a present and a future. Our Head of State should be one of us.' The largely positive coverage the next day was accompanied on the front page of the *Financial Review* by a warning from the Reserve Bank Governor, Bernie Fraser, that speculation that interest rates might have peaked was premature. In other words, not only were they staying high for now, they might yet go higher. Once again the economy's strength was a two-edged sword for Labor.

The polls were slightly kinder for Keating in June and July. After the release of his blueprint for a republic, a poll commissioned by Melbourne's *Sunday Herald Sun* registered 59 per cent support for a republic by 2001, with 62 per cent support in Victoria. Howard moved soon after to say that a Howard Government would have a referendum on a republic, and would even campaign for a republic if a constitutional convention set up by his government identified which model it supported.

This was a pattern through the year. If a policy difference between Labor and Liberal threatened to cost him, Howard would soften the difference. On tariffs, where Hewson had threatened a scorched earth zero tariffs approach, Howard's shadow minister for Industry, John Moore, flagged the possibility that even the rate of Keating's tariff cuts might be slowed.

The other poll that gave Keating momentary hope was the *Herald-McNair* poll in early July, which showed that a fourteen-point gap in favour of the Liberals had closed to four points, the closest margin since Howard's ascension to leadership. The broadly positive economic news continued, but always with a political sting. On 14 July, the *Financial Review* headline read, 'Markets soar as bulls roar', but while ever there was a hint that the economy might overheat, Bernie Fraser was always going to keep interest rates up. Although inflation remained remarkably low, Fraser was keeping a critical eye on wages growth.

Keating's antipathy to John Alexander's editorship of the *Sydney Morning Herald* continued. In the second half of July the *Herald* ran a front-page lead headed, 'Howard plan for growth and unions'. Written by political correspondent Tony Wright, the story said Howard had a plan he said would provide higher growth but also solve what he called a current account deficit crisis. Wright added that Howard had failed to spell out the details. Keating noted at the top of the page: 'Wright says Howard failed to release policies but Alexander gives him the front page for what otherwise should be a page five report.'

Having upset expectations and won the New South Wales election, Bob Carr reneged on a clear promise to lift road tolls from two freeways in Western Sydney. It was a nasty double bunger for voters who might still have been harbouring resentment against federal Labor for playing around with its tax cuts. Keating wrote on that story, 'This will really hurt us', and there's no doubt it did.

Ralph Willis was at least winning headlines hailing 'Labor's economic fightback' and reporting that the worst of the current account deficit problems were over.

The *Australian's* Newspoll in mid-August seemed to confirm the trend to Labor, with both parties now neck and neck, each with 43 per cent of the primary vote, and both leaders level-pegging on 40 per cent as preferred Prime Minister. It was such a dramatic improvement from the previous poll that Keating wrote beside it 'Cannot be right'.

At the end of August the *Age* flagged that the perceived current account crisis was over, with the headline 'Exports lift, $A soars', but Bernie Fraser was still in the wings warning that if interest rates were going to move at all, it would be up.

In February, Howard had mocked Labor's recovery from recession, pointing to the big interest rate rises in 1994 with the claim that Australians had had little more than five minutes of economic sunlight. This must have resonated with the public through the year because in September, Labor took the unusual step of taking out full-page newspaper advertisements saying that Australia had now enjoyed sixteen consecutive quarters of growth, 3.7 per cent for the past year, overall the best result for 24 years. The idea had been pushed on a reluctant ALP National Office by Keating himself and strongly resisted by ALP National Secretary Gary Gray. Keating won out, but according to Don Watson in *Bleeding Heart*, Keating's dislike and mistrust of Gray grew from that point on, ending in deep friction through the election campaign.

Against this, Labor was suffering distracting headlines about Carmen Lawrence and the Western Australian Royal Commission. Howard has subsequently argued that Keating should have cut Lawrence adrift. Through September Keating ripped into the Royal Commission in federal Parliament, and had moments when he morphed into a rampant barrister. But it was all to no avail. The distractions proved too costly, and Lawrence fell on her sword. The Commission ultimately recommended charges of perjury against Lawrence, which she eventually faced in court and was found not guilty—but not until 1999.

As the year neared its end, Keating attended his third APEC leaders' meeting in Osaka, where he and Indonesian President Suharto met on the side and clinched their historic security treaty. He also racked up further credit on the regional free-trade agreement.

But back in Australia, industrial bedlam reigned. The unions were locked in battle with the mining giant CRA (now Rio Tinto) over its determination to push through individual contracts for its workers. Two days before Keating was due to fly out to Osaka, 3000 coal miners walked off the job at Weipa, and the ACTU warned that a five-day waterfront strike would follow.

Keating intervened, thought he'd resolved the dispute and said so publicly as he flew off to Japan. By the time he got off the plane, the dispute had blown up again. What happened next threw Keating completely. His great mate Bill Kelty decided to call on the old Labor hero, Bob Hawke, who'd become such a public Keating critic, to argue the ACTU case against CRA in the Industrial Relations Commission.

Next to the *Sun-Herald* headline, 'HAWKE THE PEACEMAKER' Keating had written 'this is Bill at his silliest'. It was followed in the next day's *Financial Review* with 'Hawke splits Labor mates'. The case was eventually resolved, but it wasn't Paul Keating kicking goals in Osaka that attracted the most news coverage over the next few days.

One interesting contradiction emerged in the opinion polls and continued into the campaign. Before and after the election it was accepted as a given that Paul Keating was on the nose with the electorate, an assumption that went all the way back to the 1993 election. And yet Keating's approval rating as Prime Minister was often equal to Howard's and sometimes better. For instance, an *Australian* Newspoll on 30 November asserted that Keating was seen as more capable of managing the economy by 43 per cent of voters, compared to Howard's 35 per cent. His leadership approval rating actually improved further over Howard's through the campaign.

As the election loomed closer, Keating's poor regard for the press gallery was more than matched by his frustration with his own mob. He had walked away from his 1993 victory angry at what he saw as the defeatist attitude of the party machine through the election campaign and his belief that veteran Party Secretary Bob Hogg had told at least one journalist he expected Labor to lose.

That anger was nothing compared to the contempt he developed for Gary Gray, Hogg's replacement. On 9 October, the *Herald* ran a story detailing how Keating had attacked the veracity of Labor's own internal polling, which suggested the government was in serious trouble. Keating particularly went after the 'nervous nellies' who had leaked the polling to newspapers, describing them as childish. Next to that quote, Keating had written in the margin, 'Gray'. The relationship was poisonous by the end of the campaign.

On 27 January 1996, Paul Keating made his second trip to Government House as Prime Minister to seek approval for an election on 2 March, this time to Sir Bill Deane rather than Bill Hayden. But there was also a new Liberal Leader, a much more elusive one, an extremely jaded electorate and Keating stood at the foot of a very steep hill. Only four days earlier *The Australian*'s headline, taken from Newspoll, was: 'Libs leap to 10-point lead over Labor.'

He may have been capable of contemplating defeat, but he was biologically incapable of surrender and ran his campaign accordingly. Where the Howard campaign had one script, Labor's campaign had two: Gary Gray's and Paul Keating's. Nonetheless, on 20 February, with nine days to go, Newspoll showed Labor had halved the Coalition's lead to 4 per cent. It was simply a bridge too far.

Howard said at the time, 'If you think he's smug and arrogant now, just imagine what he would be like if he wins again. Just imagine'—a premise that sat neatly with one of their more effective negative ads against Keating.

In the final days two events killed off whatever chance Labor had left. One was when Bill Kelty promised an industrial war against a Howard Government. At a union rally in Melbourne with Keating in attendance, Kelty raged, 'If they want a fight, want a war, then we will have the full symphony with all the pieces, all the clashes and all the music.'

John Howard noted later in his autobiography, 'this may have pleased the assembled throng, and the Prime Minister, but it was poison to the Australian public.'

Actually, it didn't please Keating at all. He hadn't even wanted to be there.

The other event that went savagely against Labor was a bizarre episode involving anonymous documents sent to Labor and the Democrats purporting to reveal confidential correspondence from the Liberals as evidence that a Howard Government planned to heavily cut state grants. The Democrats chose to ignore them, but while Keating was in the air between Cairns and Adelaide, Ralph Willis's office and Gary Gray at Labor's campaign headquarters decided to release them as evidence of Liberal chicanery, with disastrous results. The documents were fakes.

Election day was the day John Howard silenced the true believers and ended Paul Keating's long political career in a landslide.

KOB: Alexander Downer managed to get himself into all sorts of trouble through the second half of 1994. I imagine all your instincts were to keep going after him, but I would have thought the last thing you would have wanted as you got closer to an election was to see the Liberals come up with yet another leader and have to start all over again. Did you consider the possibility of going somewhat soft on Downer for a time at least, to try to keep him in the job until the election, although I'm not quite sure how you'd go about doing that.

PJK: You can't ever play that game. There is a difference between trying to preserve an opponent and not running one over, but this guy was so denuded of confidence so quickly that he was making his own mistakes and would have gone, with or without my further efforts.

The press gallery were desperate for someone to put up against me, and this gave Howard an easy run. There was his great apologia interview in the *Australian* from Greg Sheridan under the editorship of Paul Kelly to say that Howard wasn't really a little suburban racist, as he had formerly been painted by his own utterances, that he had seen the light and was a fit and proper person to be the next Prime Minister. So the first real support for Howard occurred in the *Australian*. This was in January 1995 while Downer was still technically the leader.

KOB: The first time you faced Downer in Parliament after he became leader was 26 August 1994. By that time he'd already done himself a lot of damage with voters in only three months. Christine Wallace wrote in the *Financial Review*: 'If Paul Keating were any more relaxed he would stop breathing.'

You quipped, 'All by himself, single-handedly he took himself from the top of the poll to the bottom of the poll.'

You didn't seem to have to do much at all.

PJK: I used to say he was a sook. Here's a front page in the *Age*: 'Downer a policy sook'. Sook is a very Australian word, and if you can actually attach it to somebody it's very bad for them. He made enough mistakes for me to use it. I said, 'The one thing the Australian people will never tolerate is a sook.' This idea got around, then when I'd bait him he would actually jump on the hook for me.

KOB: Once you felt you'd got his measure in the polls, did you give serious thought to an early election? Surely some of your strategists would have favoured that, you were so far in front.

PJK: A lot of people did encourage me to do that and I did give it some thought but the public doesn't like opportunistic behaviour. These three-year Parliaments are too short and they're hard to win and hard to earn. In a five-year term like in Britain, maybe you could justify going to an election after four-and-a-half years, but the Australian electorate doesn't like its government serving only two-and-a-half years of a three-year term. They think it's a bit tricky.

KOB: When Howard did become leader in late January his first gift came courtesy of your Cabinet. In December you'd become embroiled in a war between loggers and environmentalists, reflecting policy differences within the government over woodchip policy. David Beddall as Resources Minister wanted more logging in old-growth forests. Environment Minister John Faulkner was opposed.

PJK: They did the government no good in their management of this and gave us a large problem.

I was particularly angry with David Beddall because, without proper Cabinet consideration, he had increased the woodchip quota, which meant increased logging of old-growth forests. I had been building a bridge to the environment movement and had, only a month or so before, made a personal commitment to environmental protection. But both Beddall and Faulkner handled it badly. Notwithstanding my efforts to resolve the issue in a sensible way, by January Parliament House had been ring-fenced by a blockade of logging trucks instigated by the forestry union, the CFMEU.

It was a completely unnecessary act by the CFMEU and an absolute gift to Howard, and his arrival at Parliament House as the new Liberal leader was through the cordon of timber trucks. It did the government and me enormous harm. It was a dream run into the leadership for Howard because Downer had just buckled and at the same time it looked as though a government of order and discipline was actually a government in chaos.

Bob Collins, who was the Transport Minister, persuaded me to meet the loggers in his office, coming into the second week of their blockade. Bob introduced me to one of the union organisers, a guy with a gold neck chain, and Bob said, 'I don't think you two have met before,' and I said, 'Yes, we've met. I've been meeting spivs like you all my life. Of course I know you.' I said to them, 'You know the two trucks at the front ramp blocking the cars, the iridescent red one with the chrome horns and the iridescent blue one? I want you to think what they're going to look like when I put a tank tow vehicle across the top of them.'

They said, 'You've got to be joking', and I said, 'I've got two tank tow vehicles on standby at Puckapunyal waiting to be loaded onto a railway flatbed car. If this continues I'll get them up here and run over the top of your shiny trucks, and what's more, I'll push the rest of them into the lower ring road, regardless of the consequences.'

Bob Collins said, 'I think you mean this,' and I said, 'Absolutely I mean it.' They were gone the next day, but the damage was done, including to a lot of green preferences at the election. Looking back I really regret not clearing their trucks.

KOB: You were also at war with the Editor of the *Sydney Morning Herald*, John Alexander, at that time. How did that help you?

PJK: He was an avowed enemy of mine. I always thought he had the worst case of small man's syndrome I'd ever known. Late 1995, going into 1996, it was almost laughable, the daily headlines against the government in the *Herald*. I wrote across one headline, after ten consecutive negative ones, 'The *Sydney Morning Herald*'s royal flush of bile.'

At one point I did discuss with my staff putting up a display of the *Herald*'s headlines in A3 format in the gallery and personally pointing out all the distortions and explaining why they represented a corruption of the news, but they talked me out of it. I should have followed my own instincts.

KOB: You'd seen two leaders off, but John Howard was the danger man, wasn't he?

PJK: Yes. I had to then beat a third leader in three years, and that was a tough call, particularly when I knew Howard was going to get an absolutely free ride from the the press gallery. And he was getting a completely free ride from his major promoter, the *Australian*.

When Howard came in, I wasn't worried about my capacity to knock him over, but I was worried about whether I'd have enough time to do it. If he'd got the job a year or eighteen months earlier, that would have suited me just fine. The fact is, Kerry, I beat two Opposition leaders in two years. I couldn't quite beat three in three years.

I'd landed the killer blow on Howard in 1987 and if there'd been a four-year Parliament this time, instead of three, there was every chance I'd have beaten three Liberal leaders in four years, but the odds were against me. When you are in your fifth term looking for number six, that's sixteen consecutive years, or four American presidential terms in a row—you are stretching the friendship with the electorate.

KOB: But I don't think Howard was ever again going to give you the opening he gave you in 1987, nor did he make a policy target of himself the way John Hewson did.

PJK: I was now dealing with a much more wily character and I took Howard completely seriously. I knew he was the ultimate conservative.

He said himself he was the most conservative leader the Liberal Party had ever had, and he was. But he got an enormous lift in support, particularly from the craven press gallery.

KOB: The same press gallery you once prided yourself on having in your thrall.

PJK: But I was truly in the nation-building business. Who else was? Yet it behoved them to be seduced by Howard's flimsy headland speeches bereft of any policy detail. They bought the Kelly/Sheridan line that he was no longer the old John Howard, the white-picket-fence John Howard with the conservative views.

KOB: But who says the press gallery should be in one camp or the other?

PJK: No one. But they were giving a free and easy ride to an Opposition absolutely without a framework, when the government had frameworks everywhere. Their so-called policy releases, when they had them, were glib one-page summaries.

You know what? The journalists were bored with a then twelve-year-old government and wanted something new. There was one rule for me and another rule for Howard. I remember saying in a press conference that if I produced rubbish like Howard, they would down me the next day.

And Laurie Oakes piped up and said, 'Yeah, but you're too good, Prime Minister. We have you on a high handicap.' In one sense a compliment, but that's how blatant it was.

As a result Howard sailed through 1995 on a wing without even needing a prayer.

KOB: But you're overlooking the things that had gone wrong for you that the electorate was not going to forget, like the

1993 horror budget and the big interest rate hikes of 1994, all the inevitable accumulated baggage of the recession years and the high unemployment.

PJK; No, I'm not overlooking those things and of course, a lot of that was real. But it was to some extent offset by headlines about the stockmarket reaching a record high—it doubled that year—about the economy hitting top gear, about the May 1995 Budget showing an average of 4 per cent growth over the next four years. The economy was really solid. Even Howard admitted after he won the election, 'I couldn't possibly say I wasn't given a good economy.'

KOB: In his first week in Parliament as leader John Howard made clear what his strategy was going to be and it was what he saw as your Achilles heel: that same economy. His first two questions were on interest rates and tax increases, followed by a rowdy censure motion on the economy.

He said Australia under you had enjoyed 'a bare five minutes of economic sunlight'. Now, you love the great political metaphor. You'd have to acknowledge that wasn't a bad one.

PJK: It was clever but it wasn't true. We'd had at that stage four straight years of economic growth. It was a piece of high cynicism by Howard. Bernie Fraser came out and corrected him and then the Liberal Party attacked Fraser for being partisan. We then ran ads showing the official figures for sixteen consecutive quarters of growth. But that piece of cynicism, the five minutes of sunshine, our friends in the press gallery gave that a run everywhere. So it was a clever metaphor but it had more impact than it deserved to have.

KOB: You've previously talked about your favourite front-page headline from politics, which came from the 1987 election campaign: 'Howard: My sums wrong'. Well, the headline John Howard had framed came from that first parliamentary week in 1995 after he'd become leader and it said, 'Round One, the day Keating met his match'.

PJK: The bottom line was that we had come out of the recession strongly, we were enjoying consistently strong growth, and interest rates had had to go up briefly because we were growing too strongly. That's not five minutes of economic sunlight, that's protecting a rapidly growing economy from inflationary expectations, and it's paid a big dividend to Australia ever since. Twenty-four years of dividends. In the end if you want to change Australia inexorably and for the better and ambitiously, you'll lose skin doing it.

KOB: When did you realise that you were in trouble with John Howard?

PJK: I knew that when Downer inevitably went and John Howard got the job, we would fall back again in the polls. This is more or less true today as well: whenever a leader gets into a poor situation and loses the job, the new leader gets a lift. I also knew I would have no more than a year to get on top of him. That in itself didn't trouble me because I had always been on top of him—in the house, out in the electorate at large and at critical moments like the 1987 campaign. Psychologically, I well and truly had Howard's measure. But the timing was tight.

KOB: Everything you say about John Howard suggests that you dislike him with a passion. If that was so, do you think you were able to analyse him dispassionately in order to work out a strategy to beat him?

PJK: Actually, I don't dislike Howard. Let me be clear about that.

KOB: That would surprise a lot of people.

PJK: I don't dislike him. But he represented all that I stood against. He represented a return to the mediocrity of the past, a return to the old value system. The fact that we were a multicultural country engaging much more with Asia and needed the uplift of things like a republic and that independence of thought—were things he was never going to provide, and that's what I stood against. Not John Howard personally, because I would have preferred John Howard to a lot of Coalition leaders. What I stood against was his policies.

KOB: So who did you prefer Howard to?

PJK: I preferred him to Peacock because he was a more serious guy. I'd prefer him to the likes of Doug Anthony and Peter Nixon because they were political savages who had joined with Malcolm Fraser in blowing the system up in 1975. I don't believe John Howard would have done that. I preferred him to Hewson for the fact that he was a foot soldier making his way through the infantry like I had done over a 30-year period, rather than coming in late and pretending somehow to be above politics.

I absolutely accepted the genuineness of John Howard's commitment to public service.

KOB: Yet it always sounded very intense with you.

PJK: Yes, because it needed to be. Howard was a combatant. He was a combatant. And that was the business we were in. I always respected that in him, and I would like to believe he respected that in me.

KOB: We talked much earlier about the parallels between you and John Howard in your early lives. You both came from working-class backgrounds in western Sydney, raised not far from each other. Both touched by family loss in world wars. Both from a young age admiring Winston Churchill. Both of you strongly influenced by your fathers' politics and therefore ending up in diametrically different places politically. But I guess the starkest difference is personality.

PJK: It's interesting how these things happen but you do get a choice in public life. You can be on the side of the angels, that's the great body of working people, or you can be on the side of the people with capital and position. The Liberal Party barracks for the people with capital and position. The Labor Party barracks for the people who've got nothing to sell but their time.

KOB: But here's the irony. When John Howard did become Prime Minister he stayed there for twelve years and one of the biggest reasons he stayed there for so long was that he was seen to have the support of the people who became known as Howard's battlers, who had formerly been Labor's constituency, the working people.

PJK: In part that's true. But Howard opposed every wage increase to my knowledge from 1983 to the time he became Opposition Leader for the second time, opposed every one for the people who battled most. I knew he would attack the safety net I'd set up with enterprise bargaining. That's the thing that protects low-paid women and kids in jobs, and he attacked that with *Fightback!* as John Hewson's Industrial Relations spokesman, and then ultimately as Prime Minister with *WorkChoices*. He claimed to be the battlers' friend but his industrial relations policies were the most vicious ever on the battlers. The true party of the battlers, of the ordinary people, was and only is the Labor Party.

You get a choice in these things and in my early life I wanted to lift 95 per cent of the people up, not 5 per cent. I didn't want to lift up Vaucluse and Bellevue Hill in Sydney or Toorak in Melbourne. I wanted to lift the whole society.

KOB: Here's another irony: you *did* lift up Vaucluse and Toorak. A lot of rich people became a lot richer through your reform agenda.

PJK: In a growth economy that happens. But the hard thing is to lift the 95 per cent, and give them support like access and equity in health with Medicare; access and equity in education by boosting retention rates in high school and entry to university; a universal superannuation scheme and strong employment. These were reforms for the national economy but also for the vast bulk of Australians. Howard ended up on the side of preference and capital. I ended up on the side of the mass of working people.

KOB: He ended up with significantly better support from middle-class Australia and battler Australia through his time as Prime Minister.

PJK: That is immaterial to the main point. Without the reforms of the Hawke and Keating Governments this could never have happened. Those changes doubled the economy's capacity to grow. Doubled it, and doubled trend productivity from 1.5 per cent to 3. Of those three percentage points, 2 per cent went to working people, and 1 per cent went to profits. Two per cent a year for the twelve years Howard was in office gave people a 20-odd per cent increase in real wages. No thanks to John Howard, but thanks to the changes Hawke and I and the Labor Party presided over.

A new government can't just lift things like real wages overnight. It takes a decade to achieve something like that. So he was a lucky guy, Howard. We gifted him thirteen years of major economic reform by virtue of him winning the 1996 election. No Australian political leader has ever had such a gift as John Howard had when he won in 1996. As I've said colloquially, hit in the backside by a rainbow.

KOB: Why do you think you polarised people so much?

PJK: I'm not sure I did polarise people. The recoded approval ratings I enjoyed don't support this.

KOB: Do you really not think you had a capacity to polarise? There was one poll in 1989, for instance, which featured in Michael Gordon's biography on you. One-third of the people surveyed thought you were the bees' knees. Some even found you sexy. One-third hated your guts, and the third in the middle still didn't like you but rather admired what you did and thought you knew what you were doing. I would call that polarisation. One-third love you, one-third hate you.

PJK: But I think that would be pretty much true of John Howard too. I think it's more or less true of all of us at the top of the game. One-third loves you, one-third hates you and one-third are swingers. But you can't pursue a program of the kind I pursued with these enormous changes for nearly one-and-a-half decades and walk away smelling like a rose to everyone. Either you are conscientiously in there to give people a better country, a richer society and a better way of life or you're not. And you're going to lose skin along the way. That's just what it's about

KOB: Your last year of office was clearly a struggle politically. The economy was performing strongly again but the polls weren't reflecting that. The Labor historian and former politician, Rod

Cavalier, has said that your broad vision agenda based on the republic, native title, engagement with Asia, multiculturalism and the arts cut no ice with the electorate at large, especially core Labor voters. John Howard has acknowledged that this is precisely the kind of sentiment he set out to exploit.

PJK: I don't accept Rodney Cavalier's characterisation. I thought Cavalier lived a very trivial political life and is in no position or vantage point to comment whatsoever on the scale or depth of the things I was doing. They were light years beyond the Macquarie Street frame of reference.

An Australian republic will be as important to Australia in the future as it was then. Building political architecture in the Pacific will be as important to Australia in the future as it was then. The changes to a more efficient wages system and the lifting of real wages will be important to Australia in the future as they were then, and native title, of which Cavalier was a critic, will be important to the Aboriginal community and to all of us in the future as it was then. I think there's a great risk, Kerry, of taking notice of armchair critics who have an ephemeral commitment to the broader community and who don't understand risking political capital in lifting the country up.

KOB: But they weren't all armchair critics. Paul Kelly wrote in *March of Patriots* that late in 1995 your speechwriter Don Watson sent a distress signal to your old right-hand Don Russell, who was by then Australia's Ambassador in Washington, to come back and 'help get the ship back on the road', as Watson put it.

He said Russell 'found Keating hemmed in and isolated. He was absorbed in the issues close to his heart, the republic, Mabo, the arts and foreign affairs. The government got little credit for growth in the economy or for its array of social welfare programs'.

Did Russell say those things to you at the time?

PJK: Some he did. Don Russell famously was my most effective private secretary and to have him back coming into an election was a great godsend for us. He thought like I did. You could put us in two separate rooms and give us three problems and the answers would be more or less the same. Russell's ability was to coordinate the office and all the various policy responses, and at that stage, I was up against it. Of course I was.

KOB: But Kelly also said of this man who thought like you:

> In Russell's view, Keating had dressed as a Labor traditionalist to beat Hewson in 1993 and forgot to reposition after the victory ... Russell was adamant— Keating 'should have come back to the Right but he didn't'. In terms of the 'econocrats and bleeding hearts model' it was too much 'bleeding hearts'. This was no way to beat John Howard.

PJK: But you get one chance to do something about native title. You get perhaps once chance in your life to do something about a republic. You get one chance to build a significant piece of political architecture in the Pacific. You get one chance to embed superannuation. I wasn't going to give those up.

KOB: But wasn't the evidence there that while you were preoccupied with these things, other elements of what you regarded as good economic news weren't getting through to the grassroots and to swinging voters, with private polling showing your economic credentials not resonating anymore with the Australian people?

PJK: This was just focus group hype put around at the time by people like Gary Gray. The 1995 Budget was full of good economic news. We were projecting 3.75 per cent growth for three years, an extra 3 per cent in superannuation contributions, the doubling of maternity allowances with inflation at 2 per cent. And a further $12 a week in wage increases. What else should we have been doing?

KOB: But the contention was that because you had your other preoccupations as Prime Minister that weren't grassroots issues, you weren't adequately selling the real grassroots issues to the people who were going to determine the government's fate at the next election.

PJK: You'll also find Don Watson saying in his book that it wouldn't have mattered what we did, we couldn't get a line for it with the Canberra press gallery. He makes this point over and over. And if you got a line you got it for only one day. They were all about changing the government. It was very difficult.

Watson asked in his book, 'What have we got to do, send up smoke signals? What do people want us to do?'

I'd do the television interviews, I'd do one big statement after another. We persuaded the ACTU to adopt the Reserve Bank medium-term inflation target of 2 to 3 per cent across the cycle, which had to be a world first. Imagine signing up organised labour to the central bank's inflation target. Yet the gallery would only go through the motions of reporting seminal events of that kind.

KOB: Do you accept that those things weren't getting through to the people who ultimately voted you out of office? Is it possible that journalists were losing interest because people had stopped reading or listening?

PJK: Some of it got through, of course it did. But the point is that when the trends start running against you it's very hard to reverse them. Meanwhile John Howard was doing those hollow headland speeches. That's around the time Laurie Oakes acknowledged in the press conference that the gallery had me on a handicap. In other words Howard by comparison was given a soft ride. It's very hard to beat that.

KOB: But you can see from our conversations how engaged you had become in your policy agenda, of which Mabo was the outstanding example. You buried yourself in a lot of big policy areas, even virtually writing or rewriting some policy statements yourself. The balance between your attention to policy and your attention to the politics had changed. Is that a reasonable observation?

PJK: In a sense, but, of course, not absolutely. You can't be in the game I was in and not be accountable and not be out there on the television shows and on the radio. I was still doing that. I still did a lot of media and to an extent I bypassed the gallery and went to John Laws and others. I went on shows like *60 Minutes*, on *7.30 Report* and on your *Lateline*. It's not as if I'd gone home.

I'll acknowledge that the recession damaged me to some extent within the gallery, but substantially it was the mere appearance of John Hewson as a viable alternative for the Liberals to the decade of bickering between Peacock and Howard. And when Hewson fell they hailed Downer and Costello as the Dream Team. Downer was so awful as leader they couldn't keep that up, so they then latched on to the born-again Howard, even though he was a mobile policy vacuum.

It was the boredom factor, the feckless factor. When journalists go to restaurants around Canberra with ministers or go to social events and get closer to Cabinet ministers and gain greater access to informed discussion, they like the connection to power, they like getting glimpses of the view from the inside. But by 1993 they were in the tenth year of this, and journalists had had their umpteenth lunches and dinners with their favourite Labor politicians and there was little more to discover.

I said to them when I came to the prime ministership that the broad economic reforms had been done and that in the 1990s we would see the biggest economic boost to Australia you could imagine—low inflation, high growth, high productivity and high wages growth. And they thought I was just mouthing politically attractive stuff to help my case. What's more, their response was, oh, this bloke's lost it, but the predictions were true, and proved to be true. And I said, no, I haven't given up, I'm now on another big project that is also fundamental to the future of the country, but they'd stopped cooperating.

When I became Prime Minister I did so from a position of complete fidelity to the interests of the broad community. I always wanted people to see and understand the value I saw and my deep interest in them rather than me doing phoney things in shopping centres and the like where I was joining in the game of trivialising their attention.

That's not to say one should not be humorous, witty or engaging. I believed in all of those things, but I could never make myself believe in these hollow appeals to the vacuous centre, because I always felt once I went there I would become just like many of the others before me.

KOB: What do you mean by the vacuous centre?

PJK: Where people are amused by silly trivial things, or where you've convinced yourself that people are so easily flattered by a televised handshake in a fruit shop or on a factory assembly line they will reward you for it in the opinion polls. Really?

KOB: You famously said as Treasurer that when you had to pull the switch to vaudeville you would, but in a way you never really did.

PJK: What do you mean I never really did? I entertained the country for nearly a decade and a half. My parliamentary performances still remain a daily hit on YouTube. They get hundreds of thousands of hits. I gave them a lot of theatre in the Parliament but it was high brow. I always wanted to talk up to the public. The idea that the people out there were a bunch of nincompoops who couldn't recognise a cheap line or a cheap trick in a shopping mall was an insult to them and offensive to me. Once you succumb to those strategies you deny yourself the bigger pulpit.

KOB: Do you think a price you paid for that attitude was that it made it easier for your political enemies to paint you as elite and aloof?

PJK: They were going to paint me that way in any event. Look who I was competing against. I could have used the 1993–96 Parliament to bend the curve against the odds for a sixth parliamentary term. I could have devoted most of my time to doing vaudeville. But I had got the prime ministership after eight hard years as Treasurer, and after winning in 1993, I knew it might be no more than a four-year prime ministership and my whole focus was on using those years to promote big changes, the big beliefs.

I thought the public's discernment in seeing value and understanding what I was doing would in the end pay off. The problem I had was that the value of the economic work was only becoming apparent as I left. Even though we'd had four-and-a-half years of growth by that time, it was coming out of a recession off a low base and it only became apparent in the following Parliament how completely powerful my changes were. Had I won the 1996 election there was a big political dividend waiting. The deficit would have disappeared, interest rates would have come down, and the prosperity would have been undeniably linked to the Labor reforms.

KOB: Had you won, you would have walked away sometime in that term, wouldn't you?

PJK: The likelihood is I would have turned the government over to Kim Beazley early enough not to handicap his chances of winning a seventh term for Labor. I would not have done to Kim what Bob Hawke did to me.

KOB: Don Watson said the perception was that Keating operated alone. Regardless of how much collegiality you felt you participated in through those Labor years, are you at heart pretty much a loner?

PJK: I was a loner perhaps, in the way I set my goals, but I was very much not a loner in the Cabinet context. I always believed in the Cabinet process and treated the Cabinet with great seriousness. You can't make changes on this scale without the Cabinet and caucus coming with you. And despite how some of the cartoons may have depicted me, you can't rule the Labor Party like some sort of emperor.

KOB: That's an intellectual commitment you're talking about, working through the Cabinet or caucus, but what about your natural instinct, the kind of person you are by nature?

PJK: I might have been somewhat alone on the mission at times but certainly not alone in the doing of it.

KOB: The Scottish poet Robbie Burns is famous for his line, 'Oh to see ourselves as others see us'. Do you think you were good at seeing yourself as others saw you or didn't you spend any time thinking about it?

PJK: Probably not enough, but you've got to remember this. Even in 1996, after thirteen years, I ended up with 38.75 per cent of the primary vote. Bob Hawke won in 1990 with 39.2 per cent. In 1993 I won 45 per cent of the primary vote. The difference in Labor's primary vote between Bob's win in 1990 and my loss in 1996 is less than half of one per cent.

KOB: But it was a very different story after preferences were counted, and you lost a lot of seats. It was a landslide for Howard.

PJK: That's because Democrats and Greens support fell away. But it's not true that the message wasn't getting through because for a while there in 1995 Labor's primary count in the polls was back up to 41 per cent. I was actually a show of getting up against Howard but the Labor Party absolutely failed to support me in the election campaign.

KOB: In August you appointed the respected High Court Judge Sir William Deane as the Governor-General. Can you take me through the process of choosing Deane? Just what exercised your mind?

PJK: The head of my department, Michael Keating, had given me lists of potential nominees for Governor-General, which had a lot of names you might recognise, but Bill Deane wasn't one of them. I didn't think any of them necessarily had the breadth, depth, technical understanding or compassion that I thought Deane would bring to the job. I'd also heard on the grapevine that Deane had become somewhat tired of writing judgments and there was some talk of him retiring.

One day Michael Keating said to me, 'PM, I keep sending you these notes about the governor-generalship but I don't hear from you!'

And I said, 'Well, you're hearing now, Michael. I have decided on somebody: Sir William Deane.'

Michael didn't immediately recognise his name because he wasn't on any of the lists.

Quite apart from Bill Deane's obvious virtues, I felt confident with a head of state who understood all the constitutional issues around the governor-generalship, the prime ministership and the Cabinet. Unlike Sir John Kerr in 1975, this was a man who was without caprice but who had the values I thought a Governor-General at this point in our history should have. It's probably true to say that Bill Deane believed Australia should be a republic but I did never inquire of him, nor did he give me an indication. I thought he was not just stable, but miles better than stable.

KOB: Through much of the second half of the year you were dogged by coverage of the Western Australia inquiry set up by the Court Liberal Government, which became known as the Easton Royal Commission. It involved Carmen Lawrence as the former WA Premier in a case related to a woman called Penny Easton and the tabling of a petition that was claimed to trigger her suicide three days later.

Lawrence was an important addition to your Cabinet team—highly articulate and credible. The Royal Commission threatened her career. You stuck by her and painted the inquiry as a kangaroo court. How distracting was that for you and the government as a running sore?

PJK: It was very distracting, but if you believe and understand someone to be innocent of a claim of this kind, made against them in a royal commission, one which had been structured by a government of the opposing party and where the commissioner seemed to be doing that government's bidding, then I felt I was in no moral position to stand Carmen Lawrence down. Commissioner Marks accepted the West Australian government's political terms and its limited terms of reference.

If Carmen had insisted she should stand down, I probably would have accepted her resignation, but she wanted to fight on and I fought on with her. Subsequently I made a mockery of Marks in the Parliament. I visited ridicule and contempt upon him after shredding his utterances daily.

Every day in Question Time, I went through the transcript of the Commission hearings from the previous day, and Roger Giles QC, the barrister representing Carmen Lawrence, said he would have been pleased to have done as well himself in any courtroom in the country. I took that as a reasonable compliment.

Here's a story on 9 September:

Easton Inquiry in disarray. The Easton Royal Commission is verging on chaos after Commissioner Marks conceded yesterday his inquiry was almost impossible to control. Mr Keating leapt on Commissioner Marks' comments that he'd been placed in an irrecoverable position because of the inquiry's restrictive terms of reference. Mr Keating said the admissions by Mr Marks were a sad testimony to the jaundiced political task he'd been given. Mr Marks acknowledged his findings would be open to doubt.

KOB: But politically you lost.

PJK: I think in a broadly political sense, we lost.

KOB: In mid-November the Royal Commission found that Lawrence had lied and acted improperly to promote her own personal political interest. You responded by declaring complete confidence in her. Isn't there a point where your responsibility to the credibility of the government outweighs loyalty to the individual?

PJK: Arguably yes, but it had all the appearance of a kangaroo court and I just wasn't able to say, 'Look, I'm going to forever indelibly mark in history our implicit belief that you, Carmen, were party to this and as a consequence I'm standing you down.' Incidentally, she eventually went to jury trial on three counts of perjury and the charges were dismissed.

KOB: John Howard said of the Carmen Lawrence matter in his autobiography that in keeping Lawrence on you violated an important principle of the Westminster system, that a minister should resign or stand aside when his or her continued membership of the Cabinet is damaging the government. Howard said that if you had applied that principle to Lawrence a great deal of prime ministerial energy over 1995 would have been conserved for other pursuits.

PJK: No humbug please. He would say that. In his first term he either stood down or saw off five ministers, three parliamentary secretaries and his own chief of staff through scandal or perceived conflict of interest. I never believed any guilt attached to Lawrence and that she was indeed the victim of a political show trial. That's the difference.

What did hurt me though, was the by-election for Ros Kelly's seat of Canberra, after she resigned from her ministry and then Parliament. In hindsight, I should have asked Ros to stay on in Parliament for the twelve months until the election. And I'm sure she would have agreed. There was a savage swing against us in the by-election, but Labor was still back up to 41 per cent in the primary vote in Newspoll on 19 December 1995. From that by-election hole I had fought my way back—again. And my personal apporoval was at 42 per cent to Howard's 34 per cent.

This was not much different from the same period in the 1993 election cycle, so I strongly believe a great campaign in 1996 could still have made a great difference. A 41 per cent primary vote for Labor in an election would almost always be enough to give us victory on Democrat and Green preferences. But the federal organisation of the party went missing in action. In Flanders, the Federal Secretariat had taken the train to Paris.

KOB: In November–December you had two setbacks on the industrial front. There was the threat of a five-day waterfront dispute and a potentially more damaging blue over individual work contracts between unions and the mining giant CRA in Weipa in North Queensland in November, which threatened to develop into a crippling national strike. You took off for the APEC summit in Osaka after announcing that the Weipa dispute had been resolved, but before you'd landed in Osaka the deal had come apart from the ACTU end. Bill Kelty then offended you mightily by inviting Bob Hawke to represent the unions before the Industrial Relations Commission. That must have tested the friendship.

PJK: I had more or less settled the CRA dispute with Tim Pallas from the ACTU, but as I flew out for Osaka, Bill Kelty decided he wouldn't accept the terms I had agreed with Pallas. I don't know why Bill decided to be unhelpful at this stage, but I took great umbrage and exception to Bill and the ACTU President Jennie George inviting Bob in on the act. Clarence Darrow, perhaps; Gary Glitter, no.

Only the year before Bob had attacked me up hill and down dale with his paltry book and great lie that I had said Australia was the arse end of the earth, among other petty things. He said he thought Downer would beat me at the next election. Bob was completely disloyal, and I was up against it with Howard. And suddenly here he was, limping back on the stage, invited there by Bill. That saga took all the oxygen from what was a very important story for us with APEC.

KOB: How badly did that affect the friendship? The way I've read it, it sounds like it knocked you for six.

PJK: It put a big dent in the friendship for quite a while, but Bill and I were great friends before that incident and we have remained great friends ever since.

KOB: On 27 January you announced the election for 2 March. Only four days before, the *Australian*'s Newspoll had recorded a ten-point lead to the Coalition with you and John Howard on the same 39 per cent approval rating as preferred Prime Minister. The *Sun-Herald* predicted the campaign would be 'one of the most bitterly fought and personal campaigns in history'. Was that right?

PJK: I wouldn't say bitter, but it was important for each of us to beat the other, and with Howard's history I thought we could use his own record to down him. This is a guy I had very low regard for in policy terms.

Going into 1996 they had no policies and were trying to pretend they were us, the Labor Party. In other words they were trying to say as their radio ads had said, 'won't it be nice on polling day because where both parties will have the same policies on industrial relations, both parties will have the same policies on Medicare'. In other words, you can change leaders without losing the policies that are important to you.

As Pamela Williams noted in her book *The Victory* on the 1996 campaign, page 149: 'While the debate raged [about when to release policies] around Howard, his Chief of Staff Nicole Feeley had some concerns of her own because if Howard did decide to release the policies early she knew there was little to offer.'

I'll repeat, 'little to offer'. This was his Chief of Staff speaking.

She said, 'The policy was just simply not ready.' Now, this was the true position of the Liberal Party. They had no policies ready up to January 1996.

KOB: Also according to Pamela Williams' book, many of your caucus and Cabinet colleagues were becoming frustrated with the sense of disorganisation in your office, that you were coming to meetings late, going home early, sometimes still in your pyjamas at the Lodge at midday.

PJK: That is just nonsense. No one in the Prime Ministership had ever worked at my level. That was all stuff given to Williams by Gary Gray, who had taken over from Bob Hogg as the National Secretary, running the party machine. Gary Gray and I ended up with no relationship after the 1996 election. I believe he was incompetent and lacking fortitude. I went to the election with no support from the party office, and then he made an opportunistic speech at the National Press Club disavowing responsibility for the loss, and compounded it by giving Williams material against me for her book. In the book he proudly boasts that he had persuaded the campaign committee not to run the very strong anti-Howard ads John Singleton had prepared and not to inform me of their decision. That is, to lie to me, the leader. This, he says, explicitly in Williams' book. At a critical point in the campaign I wanted a boost to the advertising budget to run the negative ads against Howard and Williams records on page 301 Gray telling Robert Ray, who was on the campaign committee: 'We'll keep him happy and tell him we'll deliver it. But we can't, it's a complete waste of money.'

Williams also has the Liberal Party campaign director, Andrew Robb, revealing the cynical way they planned their negative personal ads against me right through the campaign. While at the same time Gary Gray is rejecting some very telling ads by Singleton against John Howard —ads that would have laid Howard bare. One was on Medicare and another was on industrial relations, using Howard's own words.

So I fought the 1996 election without effective advertising support and the first clue I got was a call from John Singleton himself, whose advertising agency was making the ads for Labor.

He rang me while I was on the north coast of New South Wales, 'Paul, I think you should know you might have a problem. I've done these ads which are deadly to Howard, using Howard's own words against him. We've got him on the John Laws program in 1987 when he said Medicare was a disaster and he'd rip it up, and then he rips a piece of paper. It was all captured on film and I've really got him in the frame. I think they're killer ads and I showed them to Gary Gray.' But Singleton told me Gray said, 'John, you book them, you pay for them.' That's the first inkling I had that Gray and that seditious campaign committee were ratting on me.

By 1996 Howard was telling the press gallery he'd had a change of heart and that he was actually adopting the Labor policy on Medicare and industrial relations, and the gallery accepted it like lambs. I said to the journalists at one point, 'If John Howard told you he was actually a wombat would he be a wombat or would he be John Howard?' They just looked at me. Howard had opposed these policies all his life.

But the Labor Party's own strategists were worse. The message from Singleton was that they were not going to support me. To this day I believe Howard was completely vulnerable, but Gray decided not to fight, not to run the ads.

KOB: And why do you think they wouldn't support your ideas?

PJK: They were saying words to the effect of 'That silly Prime Minister thinks he can actually win. We know he can't win, the numbers are against him, and we're not going to destroy our coffers spending for a lost cause. What we should do is preserve the money now, try to minimise the losses, and give ourselves the chance to come back next time around'.

I used to call Gary Mr Two Step. He was always going to win in two elections. He could never think of winning in one go, making the big effort to snatch victory like I did in 1993.

KOB: On the other hand he reportedly called you Captain Wacky.

PJK: I had run a really exemplary campaign, including easily winning the last televised debate against John Howard. He was not in my league. I was relying on the rats and mice. I had seen the Howard advertisements that Singleton had put together. They would have been deadly to Howard. Ten or eleven days before the election I wrote a letter to Gray essentially saying, 'Gary, where are the ads?'

I got no reply. No reply to the Prime Minister from the campaign director and Federal Secretary. He boasted later through Pamela Williams that he had told Singleton only he and John Della Bosca from the campaign committee could approve the ALP ads and without that endorsement Gray would refuse to pay the bill. Here's a direct quote from the book that obviously came from Gray, 'If Keating phoned with any ideas he was to be given a hearing but then ignored.'

KOB: Williams also says in the book that Gary Gray believed polling had shown that all your negative attacks on Howard through the year had not shifted the polling to Labor.

PJK: Newspoll had me as preferred Prime Minister to Howard all through February, 42 to 38, 43 to 37 and in the last week of the election,

45 to 40, but through that whole period Gary Gray was arguing I was on the nose. If you were the party office, wouldn't you at least support your incumbent Prime Minister, who's got you to within shooting distance of a victory?

The Labor Party's archaic structure was such that all the smarts a political leader could bring to the table every hour of every day in the House of Representatives over a three-year period could then be undermined by the fools running the party organisation for the last four weeks of a three-year political cycle. It was a hopeless situation and when the federal office of the party offered me life membership a decade later I refused it. I didn't want their accolade. I hold the Federal office of the Labor Party in complete contempt.

KOB: What was your mood going into the 1996 election?

PJK: I knew I was up against it but I always liked fighting one out and one back, sitting off the front runner, but the question this time was whether, in the final lap, I could bridge the gap. I was asking Australians to elect a Labor Government for the sixth time in a row. But I felt by then at least the Australian people knew I would always have a go. People had a clear choice between the vibrant new model of Australia I had provided and the old fossilised one championed by Howard.

By comparison Howard told voters he thought we should all be relaxed and comfortable, which was a line for those who were feeling tired of the long march of reform, and enough of them said, 'Yes, John, that's probably right, we're tired of that Mr Keating pushing us around.'

KOB: I think it might have been stronger than 'that Mr Keating'.

PJK: Maybe, but they are damn lucky Mr Keating had been pushing them around for a decade and a half. Damn lucky.

KOB: Why do you think Gary Gray came to see you as Captain Wacky?

PJK That was post-election rationalisation by him to muddy the waters in an attempt to exonerate himself. There was nothing 'wacky' about my performance in the campaign. Malcolm McGregor, writing a campaign diary for the *Financial Review* as a former Labor strategist, said on 1 March 1996: 'Keating has been very disciplined and maintained his focus without much to sustain him in the published polls.' He went on to add, in the same piece, 'Labor needed more from its paid media.'

KOB: Gray and other campaign workers talked about your personal involvement in some of the campaign minutiae when you were supposed to be out there leading the big fight against John Howard, that you allowed yourself to get caught up in things like arranging the seating for the launch, or the time you put into selecting the music for your walk to the stage at the launch.

PJK: The leader is always asked about these things. They would have drawn my attention to what they had in mind for particular elements of the launch, like they would in any campaign. I'm quite certain in the same circumstances the federal director of the Liberal Party would have shown these sorts of things to John Howard. He would have said, 'Yeah that's all right, that's not all right.' That would have been no distraction for me.

KOB: But doesn't this fit the picture of the sometimes idiosyncratic guy who always insisted on running his own race, doing things his way, not always a team player?

PJK: A team player? What, with the incompetents in the party office? Team? Look at the party's federal office. It consisted of an executive director and a handful of others. The demands of political life in the House of Representatives mean that every day you are with sophistication tailoring the questions or the answers. You're making sophisticated political judgements minute by minute and being judged in turn by your colleagues, your opponents, the press gallery and the electorate. My judgements were honed over decades. You're making calls on election timing, on the language of policy and announcements. All of that reflected smartness is supposed to stop four weeks before an election, and these clodhoppers from the party office are supposed to take over and tell you how you should be conducting the public election campaign. They were oafs. Mugs not up the the sophistication of the task.

KOB: But there have been Labor campaigns where significant credit has fallen to the strategists in the party machine. Can you really credibly claim that people in the party machine automatically were clodhoppers?

PJK: Mostly clodhoppers, but not all, no. Certainly in my two election campaigns as Prime Minister I did not have the active and unqualified support of the party office. And that's simply a matter of record now, on Gary Gray's own admission.

KOB: Bob Hogg ran the campaign in 1993 and he came to that job with a great deal of political experience. He'd been credited as the architect of John Cain's rare win for Labor in Victoria in 1980, had been involved in many state and federal campaigns, and served as Bob Hawke's political adviser through his most successful years as Prime Minister. He'd earned a lot of respect in the party.

PJK: The difference between Gary Gray and Bob Hogg is that Bob had some real talent and a wider view of the world. I didn't believe that

Gary was up to the job. I ended up with a relatively polite relationship with Bob Hogg, as he had supported me against Bob Hawke, but in the end I had no relationship with Gary.

Bob Hogg is on the record during the 1993 campaign saying he didn't think we would win, and told journalists as much. My complaint is that the party office should have been a fighting unit with victory as its goal, particularly when the parliamentary leader is prepared to put up a strong fight. I didn't need the party secretary to be the oracle. You don't find people like Tony Nutt in the Liberal Party behaving like this. The problem the Labor Party has is that a long run of federal secretaries regarded their real constituency, their key one, as the Canberra parliamentary press gallery. They defined themselves by their media image, relevance and influence on the gallery. Somehow we breed these media-centric people. The Liberals never seem to do that. Their federal officers remain much more anonymous.

I used to say to them, 'Hang on, I'm the one who's going to lose skin here, what have you got to lose? All you've got to do is back me in.'

KOB: They certainly had skin in the game to the extent they, too, were dedicated to seeing a Labor Government running the country.

PJK: In 1996 we had this incompetent, lazy show wanting, in their own halting way, to reshape the smartest and most effective political language of the past decade. To recut my words and phrases, my instincts.

KOB: Eleven days out from the election Newspoll showed that you'd closed the gap to 4 per cent on the primary vote; you'd cut the Liberal lead in half, but it would still take a huge surge from there. You couldn't afford a single error.

What an irony that three days later your old mate and fellow warrior Bill Kelty tried to come to your rescue with a declaration of war on John Howard and his industrial relations policies and it backfired. He threatened wage demands of up to 30 per cent. Don Watson wrote Kelty had responded to Howard's comfortable and relaxed line by calling him Captain Snooze. Unfortunately, said Watson, he didn't leave it there.

PJK: I was campaigning in the central west and the Blue Mountains in a bus and Don Watson was insisting I turn up for this union rally in Melbourne with Bill. I wasn't convinced about turning up for a big jamboree of trade unionists in the middle of an election campaign but, under pressure, I went.

Bill was devastated the next day when he saw the impact of his speech. He was trying to draw an unmistakable line of difference between Howard's take no prisoners industrial relations approach and ours. The Liberals interpreted it as industrial blackmail. They made the most of the fact that I was at the rally, and I started then travelling back down in the polls.

KOB: At what point did you know for sure you had lost?

PJK: In the last week when Ralph Willis as Treasurer decided to publish letters which had been sent to Willis anonymously, supposedly from within the Liberal Party, allegedly between Costello and Kennett to say that a federal Liberal Government would cut state grants after the election. It was three days before the election where every single thing we did was amplified and critical.

I was flying from Cairns to Adelaide and without any consultation with me, Gary Gray, the campaign director, with David Epstein, the head of the national media liaison office, and Ralph's private secretary, David Cox, gave the tick to Ralph to make a fallacious statement that a Liberal Government would make savage cuts to state grants, and he had letters to prove it.

By the time I landed in Adelaide three hours later the damage had been done. My instincts after decades of political life would have told me it was a set-up. They should have waited to consult with me. I would have said don't bother with it. Don't even touch it. If I had seen these letters there's no way I would ever have fallen for it. But Gary, Mr Process, did not even observe the process of consulting the leader on so critical a matter, three days before the poll.

KOB: That may have been the killer blow but do you really think the election hadn't already been lost by then?

PJK: The *Sydney Morning Herald* said I lost six percentage points in their McNair poll in that final week. Six percentage points from the beginning of the final week up to election day. In other words, I had lost all momentum. My speech to the National Press Club that week was probably the best political speech I had given as Prime Minister, but the lunch was dominated by questions about Ralph Willis and the letters. I got no coverage for the content of the speech.

And Howard had had a very ordinary week. He'd had a bad interview with John Laws and then he fell off a stage, which could have become a sort of totem for the fact that things were starting to get ragged for him. And they were. I felt I had the momentum rolling the previous weekend to come home strongly. Let me remind you of some polls and headlines that weekend.

The *Australian* front page, Tuesday 20 February 1996: 'Strong swing back to ALP—Newspoll', 'Labor has more than halved the Coalition's lead in the past week and now trails by just four points.' That is, requiring two points to change.

The *Financial Review*, 22 February 1996: 'Howard suffers through a third day of stumbles—cracks are emerging in Howard's campaign for the Lodge.' The *Weekend Australian*, 24–25 February 1996: 'Keating closes in on Howard—the momentum of the election campaign changed this week.'

The Sydney *Sunday Telegraph* front page 25 February 1996: 'Labor surge', 'A national poll conducted for the *Sunday Telegraph* shows Labor and the Coalition with 50 per cent of the vote each after distribution of preferences.' 'The Prime Minister, Paul Keating's rating as preferred Prime Minister has risen from 47 per cent in January to 50 per cent last Thursday and Friday.'

The Melbourne *Herald Sun* front page, 25 February 1996: 'Neck and neck—Keating closes the gap on Howard', referring to the same *Quadrant* poll.

And, the *Daily Telegraph* front page, Monday 29 February 1996: 'Keating's night—Prime Minister outpoints "aggressive" Howard in final debate.' The report said Howard failed to derail Paul Keating's election momentum.

I had momentum but the problem was, after Willis and the letters, we just sank.

You have to have every gun blazing in that last week. You need all the advertisements running your way. You need all the psychology running for you. In the end I didn't have them.

I turned up on the tarmac in Adelaide and Mike Rann, who was Labor Opposition Leader in South Australia at the time, came up to me and said, 'Paul, while you were in the air Ralph Willis has made this press statement about the Liberal Party intending to introduce state income taxes but now he's had to come back to the media and admit the letters are fakes.'

As I walked off the tarmac I said to Watson and Russell, 'That's the end of it. We'll never pick up after this', and we never did. It was obvious to me and others that the letters were planted by somebody from the Liberal Party. But this was another Gray masterstroke.

KOB: Election night 1996 was such a contrast in mood to your true believers' speech three years before. How did you feel on that Saturday night as you prepared your statement of concession?

PJK: It was a very different mood that night and I knew I would be facing a defeat. I had been in public life for 27 years. I'd been either Treasurer or Prime Minister for half of that time so I couldn't say I had been robbed. In a healthy democracy countries make changes and I always thought winning a sixth election was going to be a tough mountain to climb. Annita and I were at the Bankstown Sports Club in Sydney with my staff and there was an obvious sense of foreboding about the place. We knew we would have to face the crowd and say the things that needed to be said with all the stoicism we could muster.

I said that the Liberal Party had been forced to adopt our policy on industrial relations, on health, on education and on superannuation to be able to win. It had to say all those things to win the election, so I said that at least the Labor Party had made a new marker in social democracy in Australia. That's what a political party's supposed to do: to put the new building blocks into place. I wished John Howard and his government well, which I meant—said and meant—and made what I hope was a generous speech both to my own party and to the Opposition, and left.

KOB: This was the end of a very long road for you, one that began all those decades ago helping your father to letterbox for Labor as a kid. This night was a moment that would be enshrined in history. If you had to distil it down, what was the essence you wanted to capture in that moment as you were seen to face the music, to face the judgement of the Australian people?

PJK: While acknowledging we had lost, I wanted to make it clear that Labor had created a new standard, a newly made economy with a strong social framework, one having a premium on fairness and equity, with a new orientation in the region. While there was now a new government, these key reforms of Labor would be broadly maintained. And by the time the country had come back to Labor twelve years later, broadly they had been.

KOB: How do you feel that in the end it was John Howard, the man you'd once dismissed as the bowser boy from Earlwood, who brought you down?

PJK: We all get carried out in the end, Kerry, even John Howard was carried out by Kevin Rudd. He even lost his seat of Bennelong. We all get carried out in modern political life. In the end they catch up with you. The big question is, what sort of a trail can you blaze, and with what sort of elan.

KOB: You've spoken throughout these conversations about the legacies of the Hawke and Keating years, including your prime ministership. How do you feel about the way the Labor leaders who succeeded you, Kim Beazley and then Simon Crean, became very defensive about the Keating legacy, about the recession, and about the deficit you left for the Howard–Costello Government, which of course they exploited as you had exploited Fraser's and Howard's in 1983.

PJK: Kim and the others were too defensive, to their own detriment. There was a great deal to be proud of, of Labor's legacy under Bob and me, which more than offset any negative sentiment left from the recession. And while Howard and Costello were busily claiming credit for turning a Labor deficit into a surplus—which would have come back anyway as the economy grew—people should not have been allowed to forget that it was a Labor Government under Hawke and Keating that converted a big Liberal deficit in 1983 under John Howard into four surpluses in a row, which was unheard of at the time.

Labor had presided over the biggest and most intense transformation of the economy in Australian history. And we're still reaping the benefits today. What did Beazley need to be defensive about?

The joke about Howard and Costello claiming what an achievement it was to struggle back into surplus is that all they had to do was simply wait two years for growth to do its job and the budget would have naturally whirred back into surplus anyway. The reason that was possible was because of all the structural outlays—work we had done in all those years in the Expenditure Review Committee.

The difference between achieving a surplus when I was Treasurer and when Costello was Treasurer was that we started with the neglected inefficient economy and had to fashion a new model, while they had the new efficient framework to work within. We had to work ceaselessly with years of real cuts—reducing spending from 30 per cent of GDP to 24 per cent—to produce our four years of surplus, while their surplus would have been delivered by the revenue from the economic growth they inherited from Labor, even if they had made no cuts at all. Subsequently their surpluses were sustained by the massive budget dividend from the mining boom, much of which John Howard squandered on middle-class welfare and tax cuts to buy votes.

In other words, the big bogey of the Keating deficit was only a bogey because the Labor Opposition was unable or unwilling to explain that as the deficit was a direct result of the recession with reduced revenue and higher unemployment payouts, it would disappear as the economy came back, significantly assisted by the structural reforms we had put in place.

KOB: I want to move to more personal things now. Politics has many ironies, one of which is that in the altruistic sense the politician is giving him or herself to the public, while at the personal level it's a very self-absorbing pursuit that can come at great cost to the people around them, the people they love and care about the most.

PJK: It is first and foremost a vocation. You can't do this for a quarter of a century without a guiding light. And what is the guiding light that keeps this enormous effort running? It is the wellbeing of the community at large, the wellbeing of the Australian people at large. The people close to you become part of the compromise.

People say about public life, 'Well, everyone knows what they're getting into', but they don't, really. I think both the politician and the family get into this not knowing just how long it will take, nor how scarifying the demands on family life are going to be, and on individual time and the impact on children and the rest. It's an enormously challenging thing to do and it's mystifying to me why the public don't have a higher regard for people in public life, because most are certainly not going there for the money. It's really only to advance the national interest but you do it at great cost to yourself and your family.

KOB: I understand that sentiment but you also have to recognise the other side of the coin, which is that so often politicians let themselves down, whether it's being seen to be giving themselves overly generous superannuation schemes or pay rises while asking workers to moderate theirs, or abusing the privileges.

PJK: I don't think there are two sides to this coin, Kerry. It's a very modestly paid profession for the enormous demands it makes on people's time, their privacy, their whole personal life. If you're doing what you were elected to do it might be high on the psychic income, the intellectual income, but it is certainly low on the monetary income compared to many other occupations. It is also very high in the stress on families and on people's personalities and private lives.

KOB: When it was over, all over, the dust had settled, you did hit something of a hole. You wouldn't have been human if you hadn't: 27 years of parliamentary life, thirteen years of Cabinet government, four-plus years at the apex suddenly all comes to a screeching halt, rejected by the nation you felt you'd done so much for. How deeply did it affect you?

PJK: My wife and I separated at the end of 1998. That's had a much greater impact on me than losing the election. Some people may have assumed that I was kind of disoriented or something similar but it wasn't really about losing the election. I never liked losing, but you couldn't expect to go on winning forever

KOB: Did the demands of politics come at the cost of your marriage?

PJK: It was a contributing factor, particularly those last three years as Treasurer and the fact that Bob pulled the wool over my eyes with the Kirribilli Agreement. That period put a very big strain on me and on my family. That shocking workload over such a long period of time.

We lived in three rented houses in Canberra while I was Treasurer. I know this comment will be jumped on by some; the way the Commonwealth treats its most senior ministers in this country, with the policy load they carry, is pretty shocking. Having decided to bring the family to Canberra and put the kids in school there so we could have some semblance of a normal life, we had to scramble around every couple of years looking for another place to rent because the owners would come back from a diplomatic post or somewhere else and you'd be punted out.

The alternative for me as Treasurer would have been even worse: continuing to live in Sydney but being hostage to the job in Canberra and playing almost no part in the family's life. In Britain the Chancellor of the Exchequer is housed in Downing Street next to the Prime Minister's residence and office. In Australia, the demands on a Treasurer trying to do the job conscientiously are hard on you and very hard on the family.

KOB: In terms of leaving politics, what about the seduction of power, having it and using it? Did you miss that?

PJK: You should only ever want power to use it. Some people in public life want it because they're attracted to the trappings, to power for its own sake. I have never had any regard for those sorts of people, and in the end they are found out. I believe the only thing that can sustain you through the hellfire of it all is the holy grail of national improvement. I was always driven by national improvement. I'd go after each reform as best I could and for the highest quality each time. And if that's not driving you, I don't know how you would keep going.

I understood power and I certainly used it. You don't get to use it unless you understand it and are comfortable with it. Someone said grabbing the naked flame and hanging on—you've got to grab the naked flame and hang on. And I think if you are afraid of power and don't know how to use it, then you can't hope to achieve the changes the country really needs.

KOB: Still in the personal vein, you've said Bob Hawke came to be pathologically narcissistic. You don't think there was anything of the narcissist in you?

PJK: I'm a complete shrinking violet compared to Bob. An absolute shrinking violet!

KOB: But you saw nothing of the narcissist in you?

PJK: I was always proud of my work, but I don't think I was ever narcissistic in the way I understand the term. I never needed to bask in the reflected glory of those around me, to feel self-worth. I don't think even my enemies would throw that charge at me.

KOB: But there had to be a very strong ego driving you for you to have such self-belief, such self-faith and confidence.

PJK: I've got a healthy ego and I've got a lot of earned confidence. You know my saying that in politics and in life you don't just take in your confidence as something like a can of Popeye's spinach. Confidence has to be earned. But once you have it, it gives you the power to make the big judgement calls.

KOB: Sometimes confidence can breed arrogance.

PJK: It can, but mostly it gives you strength to make tough calls and the ability to craft things that people without the same degree of experience and confidence wouldn't comprehend doing or be able to do. To be an effective political leader, you need a large measure of confidence and judgement.

KOB: You were there 27 years in the end. You were barely an adult at 25 when you came into Parliament. You must have learned some lessons, not just about politics, but about human nature, about yourself, about life. What are the lessons that stand out to you, the lessons that really resonate?

PJK: Lang was right in one thing: you really don't have a second to lose. History flicks by very quickly. So if you want to be in the business I was in you've got to take every opportunity you can to gain political power, and then use it wisely and effectively, for the right reasons, having a sense of the dynamism of the society and the country, rather than some static model; an idea of how it's changing or should be changing in the times you are living in and the part you can play in that.

KOB: Can you see how you grew decade by decade?

PJK: I can see how I got better at the job. If you're any good, you do get better at it.

KOB: You told a German newspaper in an interview a few years ago that you would have made a better Prime Minister now than you were then. In what way?

PJK: Being older and wiser; getting around the world for another twenty years, looking at developments in the international economy, particularly in this rapidly growing part of the world, looking at the way the domestic economy has further developed, industry by industry, and with it the financial markets.

Through most of my life I had a kind of public rounding on one side, but I've now had twenty years of another rounding in the private economy. So today I would be smarter in the job but I wouldn't quite have the energy I had for those reams of paper that came with the Expenditure Review Committee rounds of the 1980s. I don't think I'd fancy sitting through all that again.

KOB: That almost suggests an argument for taking a slightly longer route into politics, experiencing life out in the wider world first, coming into politics later, so that you might have ultimately been a smarter Prime Minister.

PJK: That could conceivably be true, Kerry. But it's the hit-and-miss game of Australian public life. If one does not have a House of Representatives seat that is relatively safe, you cannot get the consistency. And if you don't have it relatively early, you cannot build the position in the party.

You might also have noticed how many people who have been successful in business or some other pursuit and have moved into public life and failed. Some of them have made the mistake of assuming that the political game is not as skilful as the world they had succeeded in. But it is skilled and it is super-sophisticated. Some arrived as shooting stars, as skyrockets, but many dead sticks fell to earth. I'd like to think you could go and have a private life and then drift into Parliament in one's late forties or fifties and make a big contribution in public life. But I don't think that necessarily gives you a public head.

One thing John Howard and I do have in common is that we both had and have a public head. We think in public terms. We are not industry people with a latent longing for public service. We are first and foremost people with public heads. And I think it's very hard to develop instincts for that culture out of the game, out of the structure of public life.

KOB: In your Placido Domingo speech in 1990 you said that up to that point there'd been no great leader in Australia. You were drawing a comparison with a handful of the great American leaders who faced great crises and rose to greatness through them. How close do you think you came to being a great leader?

PJK: That will be for someone else to judge. But my focus was this: I always wanted to see Australia become a great country, but I believed then and believe now it can only be a great country with a new idea of itself. And that new idea has to require, of its essence, a new approach to leadership. It cannot be accelerated incrementalism, it can't be a sort of suboptimal consensus. It has to be the rather more radical, holistic approach.

I tried in my way to affect such a change, admittedly, a lot of it at the back end of my time in government, but I tried in all those bigger areas—foreign policy, social policy and economic policy—to affect such a change. But Australia has still to make a further jump, and it won't make it without that kind of leadership.

KOB: You've said the sum of the parts of Cabinet were greater than the individual efforts of any of you. Do you think that might also have been true of your partnership with Bob Hawke, that together you were a greater force than either of you would have been apart?

PJK: I would agree that was true in the policy framework of the Hawke Government. That is, Bob had a bank of political goodwill and an ability to use that goodwill in the Cabinet process. I had a new economic framework for the country, and broadly he supported me in that framework. We saw eye to eye on many things, and I was prepared for nearly nine years to hold a subordinate position, to draw that power down to make secure those changes.

KOB: You've also said in the past that he envied you. That may or may not be true, but don't you think that you might also have envied him his popularity, his charisma, that phenomenal connection he had to the people?

PJK: I never envied Bob. I just wanted him to keep spending the political capital. I was never for preserving it. I wanted to burn it up to get the changes. I just wish he had had the judgement and the discipline not to hang around so long. It would have been in his interests and my own, but particularly in his interests, to have gone when he said he would, rather than to be dragged out of the job, which was bad for him and bad for me.

We were both interested in doing big things and in the thrill of the chase, and that's where we found common cause. There was the tension in 1988 leading up to the Kirribilli Agreement, but then for most of the next three years we continued that great partnership. Finally it ended in tears, but how many partnerships of that kind last eight-and-a-half years? Not many. But the Keating Government is an entirely different matter. There there was no Bob, no compromises. An entirely new canvas and loads of paint. Its program of national identity and orientation has no equivalence in Australia's federal history. It was Jackson Pollock and Picasso all mixed into one potent policy pot.

KOB: You're talking about two brilliant artists, at least one with a touch of genius, who made up their own rules as they went along. They could indulge their passions and their eccentricities, and dance to their own tune. What is the comparison you're drawing?

PJK: These people looked at the world and saw the possibilities and expressed what they saw in a very different way. In broad political terms, our program was a lot like that. A new way of looking at our opportunities, our symbols and sense of ourselves; the resonances of Australia. Occasionally, paint was splashed with a Pollock-like flourish, while in other ways, the deconstruction of the old order had Picasso-like overtones.

KOB: There is one policy initiative in your government that we haven't discussed but would be remiss to leave out because it has since become one of the most divisive issues in Australian politics, and that's the question of asylum-seekers trying to reach Australia by boat. Yours was the first to walk down the road of mandatory detention in remote Australia, when Gerry Hand was Immigration Minister in 1992 at a time when there weren't a lot of boats coming to Australia. Was that your only alternative?

PJK: To be honest, it was not a great human rights issue for Cabinet at the time because Gerry was the leader of the Left faction from Victoria as well as the minister. And the Left had the most libertarian views in the party about migration and settlement. In very large measure for me and the Cabinet in the broad, if Hand was advising the Cabinet to set up detention centres for the orderly processing of asylum-seekers, always within the framework of the philosophical Left, then he would have the human rights issues covered.

His point was that Immigration was losing track of people before they were able to properly test their bona fides as refugees, to assess their health and keep in touch for subsequent processing. He wanted a temporary holding point. From memory the proposition went through Cabinet virtually without debate. When the Immigration Minister tells you his Department is losing control of the process, and this was the remedy coming from the leader of the Left, we accepted it. There was no political heat at the time that I can recall, so our antennae were not up.

The difference between having a temporary processing point under us and the quasi-penal settlement it became under John Howard, and even more so now, is really quite stark.

KOB: What do you think of the course Australia has taken since?

PJK: I think I would have come at the problem differently had we been presented with a problem of high-volume boat arrivals. The issue is that the people coming in boats to Australia don't leave the Middle East by boat. They fly to Malaysia first.

They take the boat for the final part of the journey. Therefore I think relationships with Malaysia and Indonesia were always crucial in preventing the traffic from happening. My view would have been that if the people who were genuine refugees were able to make their way here, they should be settled in Australia. If they were economic refugees who were not fleeing for their lives, but simply seeking a better life, using criminal smugglers in the process, that was a different question.

Any government I ran would have tackled the problem in its totality, not just in our own waters. The problem is that Howard corrupted the debate with *Tampa*, trying to wedge the Labor Party. If the Labor Party had forcefully resisted him at the time, the issue would not have the atmospherics it has today. That accommodation of Howard's jingoism set off a virus in the bloodstream of the Australian polity that has never abated.

KOB: Twenty years after leaving Parliament, how do you reflect on the state of politics in Australia? In truth there's no evident inspiration, no real passion, no real leadership on either side. It's become just another profession, hasn't it, as opposed to a calling in which nobility sometimes flourished?

PJK: It has become too much of a profession which obliterates the instincts for national ambition, the commitment to do what is both good and right, as I've said before. There's no substitute for leadership, so when the big ideas are put together and a leader pushes them, it generates a flux that draws in other comment and support. But when those big ideas are not in evidence and the momentum isn't there, the flux never materialises. Then the static takes over and the static is now writ large by social media and the vacuous news cycle. I still believe that the power of the big idea or the power of a guiding light will always take precedence over the static of the Twittersphere or anything like it. It's more the pity that enough people in public life don't believe that.

KOB: What is left of the Labor Party you joined as a kid?

PJK: I think the Labor Party is still faithful to the true and best interests of the great majority of Australians, that is, the great body of working people. I think it retains that sentiment. And I believe it tries to look for the societal turns or the big trends in picking the right pathway for its well-placed sentiment.

KOB: Many of the people who gave the Labor Party its heart, people like Clyde Cameron, Mick Young and their like, came not just from the trade union movement, but from the shop floor—in the case of those two, from the shearing shed. And they brought a lot of those down-to-earth, real-life experiences with them, and that's where their passion came from. They came up through the Labor ranks side by side with its educated class, people with white-collar jobs and professions. There was a diversity in the ranks that doesn't exist anymore.

The unions are rapidly losing relevance as evidenced by the steep decline in membership, and their failure to sign up young Australians entering the workforce. Even the party's name has become a *non sequitur*, and I wonder how Labor stops itself from becoming the blurred other party to the conservatives like the Democratic Party in America now seems to be. The traditional channels from the party back to working people are largely gone.

PJK: It is true the party has become a professional party, there are too many 'professional' politicians these days, there isn't enough openness to the broad community and to the growth of that community. The bank of talent making its way from across the whole workforce culture has withered and the party is no longer open enough to the modern workforce. Some of the best seats in the House of Representatives go to people who are not going to add value. The party is not open to the new professional and business classes, which carry a share of people with good Labor values.

Not too long ago a traditional tradesman might have been a plumber with a ute, a dog and his tools. That person today might employ twelve or thirteen people and run a little business. That person should be a Labor person but we've let them go. We've lost them. As the nature of the workforce has changed we haven't changed with it. The influence of unions within the party is now too great, and I'm speaking as a person who was an active trade unionist in the workplace and then a union organiser. The union presence has, in the broad, become a corrupting influence, and I don't mean that in a money sense but in a policy sense. In the sense that the union influence is denying access to the Parliament for a wider bank of thought and talent.

Any party that so confines itself to one area of talent must suffer on its shortsightedness, and the Labor Party is suffering as a consequence of this. It's got to open up, but you'll notice that notwithstanding debates about the organisation of the party over at least a decade, there have not yet been the shifts in the openness of the system at a federal or state level.

KOB: How have you filled your time since leaving Parliament? Public life seems to have ended for you the day you walked out of Parliament. How have you enriched your life to fill the void after 27 years of public purpose?

PJK: I have a formal position in investment banking, a very clever business providing investment advice to corporations. You get to see all the various elements of the economy at work against an international backdrop, so it keeps me across what's really going on in the economy. That's very uplifting. I have continued to lobby governments with some success, to lift superannuation from 9 to 12 per cent and to retain dividend imputation.

I spent nine years trying to frame the reconstruction of the western side of Sydney's central business district with the so-called Barangaroo Project, dealing with four premiers, a number of treasurers and umpteen departments. That's now coming to fruition. The CBD of Sydney resides on a spur that is three kilometres long and one kilometre wide, and you get just one chance every century to get something like this done. I gave that all the executive ability I could muster for eight-and-a-half years, and I think it will change the way Sydney works into the twenty-first century.

I'm chairman of the International Advisory Board of China Development Bank, which has a balance sheet three times the World Bank. It is the most important policy bank in China, so I get an insight into the domestic Chinese economy and the bigger, strategic conversation among the leadership. I've enjoyed that. I occasionally turn up in the United States, I occasionally go to Japan, I occasionally go to Indonesia, and so I generally keep a region-wide feel.

KOB: Is there a loose network of wise old heads among the leaders of the world from the past?

PJK: Henry Kissinger sits on my board, as did Paul Volcker until recently. What you find with accomplished people is that they remain accomplished. They continue to think in original terms. They don't allow themselves to be embedded in the orthodoxy.

It's another version of what I said earlier—if you want a quick meal, go to a busy restaurant. If you want ideas, go to a head that's been turning them over. I've got to say by the same token, I don't think old leaders' clubs have much going for them; those sodalities of old leaders. I think they're all old hat.

But if you have a particular focus and you're on a board doing a particular thing with people who have done important things as leaders in the past, invariably you find their mind is modernising all the time; turning all the time to the contemporary problem. It's a pleasure to be in the company of these sorts of people.

KOB: You've told me one regret you have is that you didn't study music at university when you left Parliament, that you'd have liked to give yourself the chance to build the skills to conduct an orchestra.

PJK: Yes. I should have taken on the discipline of walking through the front door of music, rather than coming to it from the back. I have a great memory for symphonic music. I can sit and, in my terms, conduct most of the large symphonic works, certainly in the romantic period at the end of the nineteenth century into the early twentieth century. But that is not like being note perfect, and to be note perfect you have to be on the score. And I'm not on the score. And I should have been. It was something I should have done.

KOB: How big a regret is that?

PJK: A big regret. I picked up the problem with tinnitus back in 1988 during the 1988 Budget, and that doesn't take kindly to being belted at a symphony concert. I could have done without that, but to be able to pick up a major manuscript and be able to read it competently would have been a great pleasure, something new to accomplish.

KOB: You told me early in our conversations that you still visit your grandmother's grave. You two obviously had a very strong bond. What did you think when you went out there recently?

PJK: I am very conscious that it was my grandmother and my mother who invested such a bank of love in me. One of my biographers said, 'I think it led Paul Keating to the point of view he didn't therefore need the love of anyone else.' That's not true. But it is true to think that you need at least one person in the world who thinks you're special.

KOB: So when you go out to her grave, what do you reflect on?

PJK: Just to think, I'm near you. I'm still here, you're still my grandmother. I still love you.

KOB And since we're talking in this vein, what's the spiritual side to Paul Keating? Some people might say the soul, the core? Do you see yourself as a spiritual person now?

PJK: If you mean spiritual in a deeply religious sense, no, but I am spiritual. I think the tension between passion and reason is the pathway to an enlarged life. If it's all about reason, all just about a process of deduction or about scientific discovery, and if it's not informed by passion and intuition, then I think the outcomes for your life personally and for public life are much more limited.

This is why I think the music, architecture, decoration, neo-classicism, all of these things give me a sense of a perfection, a nirvana, which you need to balance the reasoning part of your life, where passion and reason vie with each other, and move you onto a larger plane. That's how I've found it. I would feel barren without the romantic dimension and the sustenance these things bring you, living instead in a purely rational world.

KOB: In these later years, you must have had moments where you've reflected on the personal cost in your life, the emotional cost to you and to those around you of taking on such an all-consuming pursuit.

PJK: Those who loved me paid a price being around me. There's no doubt about that. They all pay a price being around us in public life. But in the end, in the crucible, in the furnace, what is it all about?

I always shied away from the phoney, what I thought were phoney inclinations towards the public, to say things to give people a sugar moment, where in fact, the earnest soul does the really important thing. In the end, after a long public life, I look around cities like Sydney and Melbourne, and I see how much richer, wealthier, how much more prosperous they are today than the relative poverty I found at the end of the 1970s. It's a world of difference. I look around and I feel good about it.

KOB: What epitaph would you like?

PJK: That he did his best. And his best may not have been good enough, but it was the best he could do. I never shortchanged the public ever. I'm sure there were other Prime Ministers as conscientiously committed to the Australian public as me but none more.

I was only interested in outcomes for them. I took them into my confidence on radio, on television, in the long press conferences. I tried to involve them in the same debates we were having around the Cabinet table. This might sound like a statement of the obvious but these days particularly, I'm not sure it is.

The greatest compliment you can pay to the Australian public as a politician is to conscientiously include them in the conversation, and I was prepared to go through the tortures of the damned to lift the place up. And lift it up I think we did.

ACKNOWLEDGEMENTS

There are of course, people to acknowledge and thank for their part in the production of this book, first and foremost Paul Keating. He had a big stake in the game but even so he was more generous with his time than he needed to be, and when necessary he brought the same focus and flourish to it that he did to any of his big policy passions all those years ago.

I had no idea what I was getting into with this book, so I am particularly grateful for the skill and insight the Allen & Unwin team brought to the project, particularly Sue Hines, Foong Ling Kong and Rebecca Kaiser. Their support was warm and consistent.

The original Keating project, the four part ABC TV interview series, was also supported by a small but excellent team of craftsmen led by Ben Hawke and Justin Stevens, and their efforts too are reflected in the book. It was also a big call for Mark Scott and Kate Tawney to so vigorously endorse four hours of unadulterated talking head television. I don't think that's ever happened on Australian television before.

Sue Javes, my partner and trusted sounding board for 36 years, has been as sharp as a tack in her advice—although she did muse at one point that she now had some understanding of what Princess Dianna meant when she said it felt at times as if there were three people in the marriage.

NOTES

BLEAK TIMES FOR LABOR
Pages 14–15: 'I will never forget the scene when Eddie Ward ...', Fred Daly, *From Curtin to Kerr*, p. 28

THE HAYDEN YEARS
Pages 106–07: 'I knew only too well my shortcomings for the task ...', Bill Hayden, *Hayden*, p. 311

REINS OF POWER
Page 130: 'All of us must have been reminded of Dr Johnson's famous remark ...', Geoff Kitney, *National Times*, 13–19 March 1983

THE FLOAT
Pages 149–153: 'I was completely open with him ...', John Edwards, *Keating*, p. 543

TAXING THE RELATIONSHIP
Page 215: 'The result was a dramatic omen ...', Paul Kelly, *The End of Certainty*, p. 162

Page 218: 'Is it true, as Paul Kelly wrote, that you called Bob Hawke "jellyback"?', Paul Kelly, *The End of Certainty*, p. 162

Page 223: 'Tax go-slow rebounds on PM ...', *Sunday Telegraph*, 22 September 1985

Page 224: 'It snapped the collegial bond of trust ...', John Edwards, *Keating*, p. 278

THE MEDIA: POLICY AND PAYBACK

Page 267: 'Hawke had a courageous and capable minister ...', John Button, *As It Happened*, p. 227

Page 276: 'It became apparent that neither the Hawke nor the Duffy positions ...', Gareth Evans, *Inside the Hawke-Keating Government*, p. 238

Page 279: 'The Treasuer is a product of the NSW right wing ...', Colleen Ryan, *Corporate Cannibals*, p. 173

THE 1987 ELECTION

Pages 290–91: 'Hawke continued to govern indecisively ...', John Howard, *Lazarus Rising*, p. 164

INDUSTRY: A NEW WORLD FOR SURE

Pages 311–12: 'In Melbourne a young GMH executive came to see me ...', John Button, *As It Happened*

OF BUDGETS AND BACON

Page: 364: 'Bob was happy about the Kirribilli Agreement', Blanch d'Alpuget, *Hawke*

Pages 367–68: 'Macfarlane observed that the more entrepreneurial borrowers had ...', Ian Macfarlane, 'The Search for Stability', Boyer Lectures

Pages 369–70: 'The issue of how monetary policy ...', Ian Macfarlane, Boyer Lectures

Page 370: 'Macfarlane was 'the most prescient of ...', John Edwards, *Keating*

Page 371: 'Button wrote that ...', John Button, *As It Happened*

THE WINDS OF RECESSION

Page 387: 'This was the point ...', John Edward, *Keating*

OLD DOGS FOR A HARD ROAD

Page 442: 'the first election in my experience ...', *Sun-Herald*, 22 December 1991

Page 442: 'the divisions of the past ...', Neal Blewett, *A Cabinet Diary*, p. 32

Page 442: 'The government is working much better ...', Neal Blewett, *A Cabinet Diary*, p. 51

Page 463: 'They needed something to protect them ...', *Recollections of a Bleeding Heart*, p. 189

Page 446: 'to strip away all fig leaves', Neal Blewett, *A Cabinet Diary*, p. 66

Page 449: 'Mate, I'm carrying such a crushing burden ...', Paul Kelly, *The March of Patriots*, p. 34

Page 451: 'The man who had kicked ...', Peter Walsh, *Confessions of a Failed Finance Minister*, p. 251

Page 451: 'kicked some brilliant goals ...', John Button, *As It Happened*, p. 402

Page 452: 'Well, give up mate ...', Paul Kelly, *The March of Patriots*, p. 54

Page 457: 'Keating was anguished', Neal Blewett, *A Cabinet Diary*, p. 17

Page 463: 'They need something to protect themselves against ...', Don Watson, *Recollections of a Bleeding Heart*, p. 189

Page 465: 'causing a holocaust ...', Neal Blewett, *A Cabinet Diary*, p. 24

Page 470: 'Didn't your economic adviser John Edwards brief ...', John Edwards, *Keating*, p. 456

FOREIGN POLICY

Page 476: 'a very unpleasant report' and 'Australian Prime Minister Paul Keating hotly ...', Taylor Branch, *The Clinton Tapes*, p. 316

Page 477: 'What Keating did was offer a vision ...', Paul Kelly, *March of the Patriots*, pp. 171–2

Page 480: 'Shameless and compelling', Paul Kelly, *March of the Patriots*, p. 162

Page 483: 'Neil Blewett recalls ...', Neal Blewett, *A Cabinet Diary*, p. 101

Pages 502–03: 'A metaphor for Keating's attitude ...', John Howard, *Lazarus Rising*, p. 227

A REPUBLIC

Page 508: 'I learned one thing ...', Paul Keating, *Hansard, House of Representatives*, 27 February

Page 523: 'John Howard says ...', John Howard, *Lazarus Rising*, p. 217

MABO

Pages 529–30: 'The fact that our migrants ...', James Button, *Time Magazine*, 6 April 1992, p. 17

Pages 533–4: 'In the 204-year history of the formerly colonised Australia...', Paul Keating 'The Lowitja O'Donoghue Oration', Adelaide, 31 May 2011

Page 540: 'one of those moments ...', Don Watson, *Recollections of a Bleeding Heart*, p. 291

Page 556: 'never before and likely never again ...', Noel Pearson, 'White Guilt, victimhood and the quest for the radical centre', *The Griffith Review, 'Unintended Consequences'*, vol. 16, 2007. Also published in *The Age*, 19 May 2007.

THE NEW MARCH OF REFORM

Page 561: 'the financial position of the networks ...', Paul Barry, *The Rise and Rise of Kerry Packer*, p. 471

Pages 577–8: 'in the bag' and 'Don't drive us to Howard', Don Watson, *Recollections of a Bleeding Heart*, pp. 555–6

Pages 578–9: 'It was foolish of Keating ...', John Howard, *Lazarus Rising*, p. 216

THE POLITICIAN & THE PROFESSOR

Page 590: 'It's the task of Labor ...' and 'Keating urged a volume of sound ...', Neal Blewett, *A Cabinet Diary*, p. 139

Page 595: 'Concluding a gruelling question time ...', Michael Gordon, *A Question of Leadership*, p. 211

Page 603: 'first confessed to Cabinet ...', George Megalogenis, *The Longest Decade*, p. 68

Page 603: 'the second round of tax cuts ...', John Edwards, *Keating*

Page 621: 'Rarely had Cabinet been faced ...', Neal Blewett, *A Cabinet Diary*, pp. 267–8

Page 624: Difference of opinion on policy launch, Don Watson, *Recollections of a Bleeding Heart*, p. 331

Page 629: 'I do respect him ...', interview with Andrew Denton, *Enough Rope*, ABC-TV, 7 August 2006

IN HIS OWN RIGHT

Pages 633–4: 'By 1991 Australia was going …', Paul Kelly, *The March of Patriots*, p. 136

Page 657: 'Paul was not as attentive as he should have been', Paul Kelly, *The March of Patriots*, p. 217

Page 659: If Dawkins didn't calm down, Paul Kelly, *The March of Patriots*, p. 217

Page 661: mangled tax cuts promise, John Howard, *Lazarus Rising*, p. 201

Page 662: 'Paul had said don't vote for a GST', Paul Kelly, *The March of Patriots*, p. 220

Page 662: 'The truth is …', Paul Kelly, *The March of Patriots*, p. 221

A NEW FOE—BUT REFORM GOES ON

Page 677: 'The longer he went …', Paul Kelly, *The March of Patriots*, p. 92

Page 668: 'I'm not going to run around …', interview with Paul Kelly, *The Australian*, 7 February 1994

Page 669: 'We often think …', Alan Ramsey, *Sydney Morning Herald*, 23 February 1994

Page 676: 'The longer we went …', Paul Kelly, *The March of Patriots*, p. 92

Page 679: 'Peter Barron urged you …', Don Watson, *Recollections of a Bleeding Heart*, p. 501

Page 686: 'The notion that it betrayed …', Paul Kelly, *The March of Patriots*, p. 119

Page 692: 'to be a successful …', George Megalogenis, *The Longest Decade*, p. 310

Page 693: 'Don Watson describes …', Don Watson, *Recollections of a Bleeding Heart*, p. 517

KEATING VS HOWARD

Page 703: 'Tony Abbott, one of …', John Howard, *Lazarus Rising*, p. 207

Page 712: 'This may have pleased …', John Howard, *Lazarus Rising*, p. 224

Page 723: 'There was one poll …', Michael Gordon, *A Question of Leadership*, p. 192

Page 725: 'In Russell's view …', Paul Kelly, *The March of Patriots*, p. 241

Page 734: 'in keeping Lawrence on …', John Howard, *Lazarus Rising*, p. 216

Page 737: 'that is, to lie to me …', Pamela Williams, *The Victory*, pp. 226, 301

BIBLIOGRAPHY

BOOKS

Barry, Paul *The Rise and Rise of Kerry Packer*, Bantam, Australia, 1993

Black, Conrad *A Life in Progress*, Random House, Sydney, 1993

Blewett, Neal *A Cabinet Diary*, Wakefield Press, Adelaide, 1999

Branch, Taylor *The Clinton Tapes*, Simon & Schuster, New York, 2009

Button, John *As It Happened*, Text Publishing, Melbourne, 1998

Carew, Edna *Paul Keating Prime Minister*, Allen & Unwin, Sydney, 1992

Daley, Fred *From Curtin to Kerr*, Macmillan, South Melbourne, 1977

D'Alpuget, Blanche *Hawke: The Prime Minister*, Melbourne University Press, Melbourne, 2010

Edwards, John *Keating: The Inside Story*, Penguin Books, Melbourne, 1996

Evans, Gareth *Inside the Hawke Keating Government: A Cabinet Diary*, Melbourne University Press, Melbourne, 2014

Fraser, Malcolm & Margaret Simons *Malcolm Fraser: The Political Memoirs*, Melbourne University Press, Melbourne, 2010

Gordon, Michael *A Question of Leadership: Paul Keating Political Fighter*, University of Queensland Press, St Lucia, 1993

Hawke, Bob *The Hawke Memoirs*, William Heinemann Australia, Melbourne, 1993

Hayden, Bill *Hayden: An Autobiography*, Angus & Robertson, Sydney, 1996

Howard, John *Lazarus Rising: A Personal and Political Autobiography*, HarperCollins, Sydney, 2010

Hocking, Jenny *Gough Whitlam: His Time*, The Miegunyah Press, Melbourne, 2012

Jones, Barry *A Thinking Reed*, Allen & Unwin, Sydney, 2006

Kelly, Paul *The End of Certainty*, Allen & Unwin, Sydney, 1992

Kelly, Paul *The March of Patriots*, Melbourne University Press, Melbourne, 2009

Megalogenis, George *The Longest Decade*, Scribe Publications, Melbourne, 2006

Megalogenis, George *The Australian Moment*, Penguin Group, Melbourne, 2012

Keating, PJ *After Words: The Post-Prime Ministerial Speeches*, Allen & Unwin, Sydney, 2011

Ryan, Colleen *Fairfax: The Rise and Fall*, The Miegunyah Press, Melbourne, 2013

Ryan, Colleen & Glen Burge *Corporate Cannibals: The Taking of Fairfax*, William Heinemann, Melbourne, 1992

Walsh, Peter *Confessions of a Failed Finance Minister*, Random House, Sydney, 1995

Watson, Don *Recollections of a Bleeding Heart: A Portrait of Paul Keating PM*, Random House, Sydney, 2002

Whitlam, Gough *The Whitlam Government, 1972–1975*, Viking/Penguin Books Australia, Melbourne, 1985

Wilkinson, Marian *The Fixer: The Untold Story of Graham Richardson*, William Heinemann, Melbourne, 1996

Williams, Pamela *The Victory*, Allen & Unwin, Sydney, 1997

Uren, Tom *Straight Left*, Random House, Sydney, 1994

OTHER SOURCES

Labor in Power, ABC-TV series, 1993

The Keating Archive

Macfarlane, *Search for Stability*, 2006 Boyer Lectures, ABC Radio

INDEX